Revolution and Politics in Russia

ESSAYS IN MEMORY OF B. I. NICOLAEVSKY

RUSSIAN AND EAST EUROPEAN SERIES

VOLUME 41

BORIS IVANOVICH NICOLAEVSKY, 1965

REVOLUTION *and* POLITICS *in* RUSSIA

Essays in Memory of B. I. Nicolaevsky

EDITED BY

Alexander and Janet Rabinowitch
with Ladis K. D. Kristof

INDIANA UNIVERSITY PRESS • BLOOMINGTON • LONDON
for the International Affairs Center

RUSSIAN AND EAST EUROPEAN SERIES, VOL. 41
RUSSIAN AND EAST EUROPEAN INSTITUTE
INDIANA UNIVERSITY

Library of Congress catalog card number: 79-183608

ISBN 0-253-39041-9

Manufactured in the United States of America

Frontispiece photo courtesy of Praeger Publishers, Inc.

Contents

Illustrations

Foreword

"We have all sat at his feet." So wrote the late Louis Fischer in the *New York Times* (November 21, 1965), referring to the several generations of Western scholars and students of Russian history and politics who were privileged to use materials from Boris Nicolaevsky's renowned library and archive of the Russian revolution and with whom Nicolaevsky shared his encyclopedic knowledge and unique understanding of developments in Russia. Most of the participants in this collective tribute have vivid memories of long, extraordinarily rewarding conversations with Nicolaevsky, in Europe, New York, or California, and of elusive bits of information or documents, memoirs, or the like, which only he could supply and which instantly clarified a heretofore hopeless historical puzzle. All of the contributors have benefited from Nicolaevsky's pathbreaking historical studies and analyses of Soviet politics. In a very practical sense, then, this memorial volume is an acknowledgment of each author's profound debt to Nicolaevsky.

Boris Ivanovich Nicolaevsky was born October 20, 1887, in the Ural town of Belebei, the son of an eighth-generation Russian Orthodox priest. Growing to maturity in a surprisingly enlightened and progressive home, and exposed firsthand to the political, social, and economic injustices of provincial life in late tsarist Russia, Nicolaevsky was stirred by the literary ferment and caught up in the swirl of popular unrest and rebellion that was to culminate in 1905; he was wholly committed to the Social Democratic movement while still in his teens. By the time of the February Revolution he had paid the inevitable price of revolutionary activism; all told, he had spent some thirty-one months in tsarist jails and another seven years in four terms of exile, three in the frozen Arctic and one in eastern Siberia. These crucial early chapters in Nicolaevsky's life are described by Professor Ladis Kristof in the carefully researched biographical study, "B. I. Nicolaevsky: The Formative Years," with which this volume begins.

Nicolaevsky first became interested in history and journalism as a *gymnasium* student in Samara. It was in Petrograd in 1917, however, that his lifelong passion for what Kristof aptly calls "the making *and* study of Russia's socio-political history" was first demonstrated most clearly. On the one hand, Nicolaevsky was on the editorial board of *Rabochaia gazeta* and, affiliated with the Martov "Internationalist" wing of the Menshevik organization, was a member of the Central Executive Committee of the All-Russian Soviet of Workers' and Soldiers' Deputies. On the other hand, he was the Soviet's representative on a commission headed by the well-known historian P. E. Shchegolev, created to investigate the tsarist *okhrana* archives. Many years later, recalling the long days spent poring over old documents, letters, and police reports for the Shchegolev commission, Nicolaevsky was to write that "my systematic work on questions relating to the Russian and international revolutionary movements dates precisely from that time."

Nicolaevsky continued his historical investigations for the Shchegolev commission even after the October Revolution. Moreover, in the earliest months of Soviet rule he played a leading role in the organization of official Soviet archives. Thus he was closely associated with the main Soviet archival administration in the beginning of 1918 and later, from 1919 to 1921, he was director of the Historical Revolutionary Archive in Moscow. During this period Nicolaevsky remained active in the leadership of the Menshevik Party. On behalf of the party's Central Committee he traveled throughout Russia, crossing and recrossing the battle zones of the Civil War. In the autumn of 1918 he was an observer at the Ufa Conference of Constituent Assembly representatives. While traveling in Siberia, in 1919, Nicolaevsky's sensibilities were shocked by the plight of peasants under the Kolchak regime; upon his return to Moscow he appealed for a united revolutionary front against Kolchak. However, when the Soviet regime tightened political controls after the Civil War and the Kronstadt uprising Nicolaevsky was among a group of fifty Mensheviks arrested at the central Menshevik club in Moscow. Detained for a year in the Butyrki prison, he was released and exiled abroad in February, 1922.

Nicolaevsky's affiliation with the Soviet archival administration did not come to a halt with his forced departure from Soviet Russia. In 1924 he accepted an invitation from D. B. Riazanov, director of the newly established Marx-Engels Institute, to become the institute's Berlin representative, a position which he held until Riazanov's arrest and the merger of the Marx-Engels Institute with the Lenin Institute in 1931. For the Marx-Engels Institute, Nicolaevsky hunted through central and western Europe tracking down and collecting unique source materials on the international workers' and socialist movements, particularly on the periods of the 1848 revolutions and the First International, and on the activities of Russian revolutionaries abroad. He also worked with Riazanov in preparing for publication the complete works of Marx and Engels, a project interrupted by Riazanov's arrest. During this time Nicolaevsky remained involved in the Menshevik leadership. Thus in 1922 he began to write for the *Sotsialisticheskii vestnik* (Socialist Courier), which had been founded by Martov and Rafael Abramovich a year earlier. From its inception until it ceased publication in 1965, the *Sotsialisticheskii vestnik* was the focal point of all Menshevik activity abroad; for much of this period Nicolaevsky was one of the journal's main supports.

At the time of the Nazis' triumph in Germany, Nicolaevsky was associated with the archive of the German Social Democratic Party in Berlin. When the German Social Democratic leadership was forced to flee Germany, Nicolaevsky was left with the dangerous task of somehow transferring the party's file to safety. Ultimately he superintended the shipment from Berlin of two full boxcars of invaluable archival materials. Included were manuscripts of Marx, Engels, Bebel, and Liebknecht and the archive of the First International. Many of these documents were put into the hands of the International Institute of Social History just then being organized in Amsterdam. In the years immediately preceding the Second World War, the Amsterdam institute became a storehouse for historical documents smuggled out of German hands from all over eastern and central Europe. Nicolaevsky became director of the institute's important Paris branch.

Of course, any hope that socialist archives in Amsterdam and Paris would be safe from the Nazis was dashed with the German occupation of Holland and the capitulation of the French in 1940. The rich holdings of the Institute of Social History in Amsterdam were successfully spirited away to England just before the institute was taken over by the Germans. The quick collapse of the French resistance was so unexpected that transfer of materials from the institute's Paris section was much more difficult. Moreover, in 1934-35, as a specialist in Russian history, Nicolaevsky had figured prominently in the exposure as a crude forgery of the "Protocols of the Elders of Zion," a major document in the Nazi campaign against the Jews. Thus the Nazis in Paris were looking for Nicolaevsky, as well as for the archives under his control. Ultimately, a substantial portion of Nicolaevsky's library did fall into German hands; however, many of the most valuable items both from his personal collection and from the Paris archive of the Institute of Social History were saved. Part of this material was taken to the provinces and kept in the cellars of farmers on the Loire until after the war. A vital part was entrusted to the American Ambassador to France, William Bullitt, just before the fall of France. Bullitt brought these materials to the United States as personal baggage. Nicolaevsky himself successfully evaded the Nazis, departing France for the United States in November, 1940.

Nicolaevsky was to live in this country for over twenty-five years, first in New York and from 1964, in California. He died in Menlo Park, California, on February 21, 1966, at the age of 78. This last full chapter in Nicolaevsky's life provides the focus for the essay by the late distinguished Professor Philip E. Mosely, "Boris Nicolaevsky: The American Years." In a memorial service held in New York after Nicolaevsky's death George Kennan paid tribute to him and acknowledged America's debt to Nicolaevsky in these words: "I know of no one . . . whose personality better reflected the merits and ideals of the spiritual and political world to which he belonged than Boris Ivanovich. . . . If today the interest in Russia and the study of Russia in this country, and particularly among our youth, are incomparably deeper and more serious than was the case thirty years ago, we owe this in no small measure to Boris Ivanovich, to his inexhaustible interest in everything that was taking place in his homeland, to his long and sustained literary endeavor."

Nicolaevsky's death interrupted a number of ambitious projects upon which he was at work. Among the most notable of these were several volumes of largely unknown documents, with detailed commentaries, relating to the history of the Russian Social Democratic movement from 1908 to 1912. Initiated under the sponsorship of the Research Program on the History of the CPSU, this project is now being completed by Nicolaevsky's widow and long-time associate, Anna M. Bourguina. During his lifetime, Nicolaevsky had published three major historical studies, several hundred essays, and some half-dozen important document collections. His works have appeared in ten languages. The laborious, often frustrating task of tracking down and identifying these writings was undertaken for this volume by Anna Bourguina (see pages 322-41). Suffice it to note here that Nicolaevsky's published works include a now-classic book on the notorious double agent Evno Azef; a pioneering biographical study of Marx done in collaboration with O. Maenchen-Helfen; a penetrating investigation of forced labor under Stalin (co-authored with David Dallin); and important essays on such varied subjects as Chernyshevsky in Siberia, secret societies and the First International, and the murder of Sergei Kirov.

In the mid-thirties, Nicolaevsky began analyzing contemporary developments in Stalin's Russia for the *Sotsialisticheskii vestnik* on a more or less regular basis. Appalled by the human impact of collectivization and repelled by the purges and terror, Nicolaevsky now devoted increasing attention to the study of Soviet politics. The best known of his periodic political reports, which continued over some thirty years, is "The Letter of an Old Bolshevik," an inside account of developments in the Soviet Union on the eve of the purges, based on private conversations between Nicolaevsky and Bukharin in Paris in the spring of 1936. "The Letter of an Old Bolshevik," termed by George Kennan "the most authoritative and important bit of source material on the background of the purges," was republished in 1965 in *Power and the Soviet Elite,* a collection of Nicolaevsky's essays edited by Janet D. Zagoria. Reviewing *Power and the Soviet Elite* in the *Russian Review* (July, 1966), Professor Robert C. Tucker observed: "For many in the present generation of Anglo-American scholars in Russian studies, Nicolaevsky has been and remains in the fullest sense a mentor. Over many years his articles on current Soviet developments . . . have been a never failing source of information and stimulation. They have taught us how to analyze leadership politics in the Soviet one-party system. And his assiduous researches into the Russian revolutionary past and contributions to the history of the Soviet Communist Party have given us models in the writing of political history." Emphasizing the importance of documents collected and edited by Nicolaevsky for an understanding of the early history of the Bolshevik Party, Professor Leonard Schapiro observed in the *New York Review of Books*

(September 22, 1966), "It is no exaggeration to say that anyone who ignores this material in writing about the period will write nonsense." Recalling the feverish energy and remarkable resourcefulness with which Nicolaevsky instinctively unearthed, collected, and interpreted historically valuable documents, publications, and memoirs, Alexander Dallin wrote in *Problems of Communism* (May-June, 1966), "Only he could find them, decipher them, and make sense of them; but what treasures they held!"

A few words should be said about the genesis of this volume. The idea of organizing a *festschrift* honoring Nicolaevsky to be presented on October 20, 1967, his eightieth birthday, was Professor Kristof's. In the fall of 1965 Kristof made plans for such a volume and invited associates and admirers of Nicolaevsky, most of them well-known specialists in the Russian field, to participate in the project. At the time of Nicolaevsky's death a few essays had been received and a number of others were in preparation. Consequently, it was agreed not to halt work on the project; what had been started as a *festschrift* would become a memorial volume. Subsequently, for one reason or another, some prospective contributors withdrew; other scholars formerly associated with Nicolaevsky were invited to take their place. During this time, Kristof's work in connection with the book was handicapped by health problems and even more by the pressure of other obligations. Consequently, the practical task of reorganizing and editing the volume has devolved for the most part upon myself and my wife, Janet.

The editors wish to thank the numerous people who helped make publication of this memorial collection of essays possible. Our greatest debt is, of course, to our distinguished authors, many of whom submitted their contributions what has seemed ages ago and have remained loyal to the project despite endless delays. I should add that the essays of two American scholars who wished to honor Nicolaevsky, Professor Terence Emmons of Stanford University and the late Louis Fischer, do not appear in this volume. Their contributions, excerpts from larger works in preparation at the time they were submitted, have long since been published elsewhere in full. Thanks are due Frederick A. Praeger for permission to use the photograph of Nicolaevsky which first appeared in *Power and the Soviet Elite* as the frontispiece to this volume, and to Jane Kristof who prepared the index. Most important, the editors are deeply indebted to the Russian and East European Institute, Indiana University, for providing the generous subsidy which made publication of this volume possible; to Edith G. Albee, Editor of the Indiana University Press International Affairs Center Publications; and to Sally Neylon of the Indiana University Press who had the unenviable task of readying the manuscript for publication and also to Linda Bippen who saw it through the press.

Wardsboro, Vermont
August, 1971

Alexander Rabinowitch

NOTE ON DATES AND TRANSLITERATION

Unless otherwise indicated, dates of events in Russia prior to 1918 are given according to the Julian calendar, used until February, 1918, when the Gregorian calendar was officially adopted. In the nineteenth and twentieth centuries, the Julian calendar was twelve and thirteen days, respectively, behind the Gregorian calendar of the West. Transliteration is according to the system used by the Library of Congress with some minor modifications. Thus proper names are in some cases spelled in their more familiar English forms.

Revolution and Politics in Russia

ESSAYS IN MEMORY OF B. I. NICOLAEVSKY

B. I. NICOLAEVSKY (BERLIN, 1923)

LADIS K. D. KRISTOF

B. I. Nicolaevsky: The Formative Years

The lives of some people are marked by turning points—sudden emotional or intellectual experiences which generate the driving impetus for the next stretch of life until some new idea or event redirects the heart and mind. On the other hand, there are people whose lives seem to be guided by a constant, an *a priori* commitment to, or at least a strong inclination for, a certain path, practical and moral. Nicolaevsky undoubtedly belonged to the second category. His life, although turbulent, filled with diverse activities and marked by periodic migrations which took him further and further from his homeland, was nevertheless a logical unfolding of certain tendencies which crystallized while he was still in his teens. It was then and there, in the beloved country between the Volga and the Urals—in Belebei, Ufa, and Samara—that his lifelong political and scholarly inclinations took root.

FAMILY BACKGROUND

Boris Ivanovich Nicolaevsky[1] was born on October 8/20, 1887, in the foothills of the Urals, in the little town of Belebei in Ufa *guberniia.* Although the town is located in what is now the Autonomous Bashkir Republic, about two thirds of the population of Belebei were Russians with the balance composed mostly of Tatars, some Chuvash (descendants of the ancient Bulgars), and a few Jews. Boris Ivanovich remembered a common town joke that the population numbered 3,333 of which 3,000 were Russians, 300 Tatars, 30 Chuvash, and 3 Jews. He remembered also that as a group the Russians were the best off, with the Tatars closely following. The Chuvash, on the other hand, were very much at the bottom of the ladder, socially, economically, and culturally. The better lands had been taken from the native Chuvash and Bashkir population by the Russian colonists who moved in steadily throughout the eighteenth and nineteenth centuries. Both in town and in the surrounding countryside some well known noble families had settled. S. T. Aksakov's autobiographical sketch, *Detskie gody Bagrova vnuka,* immortalized in Russian literature places located only a few miles from Belebei.

Boris Ivanovich's father, Ivan Mikhailovich Nicolaevsky, born about 1860 in Orel *guberniia,* was a priest who had followed, albeit reluctantly, a long family tradition when choosing his vocation. Seven of his direct ancestors were priests, as were his two brothers. His mother, Evdokiia Pavlovna Krasnoborov, from the city of Orel, was the daughter of a merchant of peasant origin. It was apparently through her that some non-Slav, Mongol blood was inherited. Settled in Belebei in the mid-1880s, the Nicolaevskys had seven children, five boys and two girls, of whom Boris was the second oldest. In time five of the children became involved in the revolutionary movement with Boris being the first to join and politically the most active.[2] The atmosphere at home was nonpolitical but enlightened (within the limits of the milieu of a small, literally backwoods provincial town of nineteenth century Russia) and forward looking in social and educational matters. Even in questions of faith the father seems to have been unusually liberal in his thinking. He strongly emphasized education, and specifically secular education, and had a definite preference for his children not to follow religious careers. In a sense, the outlook which prevailed in the Nicolaevsky home reflected the progressive spirit of the era of the Great Reforms except that, given the humble origins of the family–socially only one step, and on the mother's side only one generation, removed from the peasantry–it was populist rather than liberal, and more Russian than Western. There was nothing contrived, self-conscious, or even conscious about the Nicolaevskys' relation to the peasant masses. They did not need to "go to the people"; they *were* close to the people.

Of course, the parish priest of Belebei, even if only the junior one, with but a small church located in the cemetery, was both culturally and economically a cut or more above the average dweller of the town, not to speak of the peasants in the countryside. The additional income from teaching religion in the local school, a sizeable plot of land, an orchard, a fairly large two-story home (part of which was rented out), a few horses, servants–all of these provided a relatively secure if not comfortable existence. Nevertheless, Boris Ivanovich always recalled that he imbibed in the home atmosphere a compassion for the downtrodden, a certain sense of elementary social justice. The lowly were seen for what they primarily were–people suffering from poverty and, more often than not, from the consequences of some kind of injustice or arbitrariness. Not even the generally despised ethnic minorities, like the Chuvash, were mocked or treated with contempt in the Nicolaevsky home, though a true understanding of the causes of their plight may have been lacking.[3] One of Boris Ivanovich's earliest recollections was the hunger of 1891-92 when peasants were streaming into town to beg for food and he would run into the kitchen for bread whenever one of them knocked at the porch.

Another source of intellectual influence in those early years was the reading material available at home. Among the periodical press there was *Svet,* a conservative newspaper, very patriotic, even imperialistic and, above all, virulently anti-English in sentiment. There was also *Niva,* a general-interest, illustrated weekly oriented towards the provincial intelligentsia, and *Russkaia mysl'*, a serious "thick" *(tolstyi)* journal with a semi-populist orientation. Years later Boris Ivanovich sometimes wondered why his father chose to read a right-wing, monarchist paper. But in those days it may not have been so incongruous as it may seem now to subscribe to *Svet* and *Russkaia mysl'* at the same time. Dostoevsky for one combined views quite close to those expounded on the pages of these two periodicals: a *narodnik*-type concern for the suffering and downtrodden on the one hand and a Pan-Slavist, Anglophobe and imperialistic patriotism on the other.

Whatever the elder Nicolaevsky's reasons for subscribing to *Svet,* the discussion of its contents in the family circle awakened in Boris Ivanovich an interest in foreign policy. Grand strategy on the Asian continent and Russia's role in it, the geopolitics of Central Asia and of the Indo-Russian and Sino-Russian border lands, the problem of Afghanistan and of the straits—all these questions were first brought to his attention by *Svet* and remained an on-and-off preoccupation throughout his life. The study of geopolitics, for instance, became something of a hobby to him. He became well versed in the geopolitical ideas of Karl Haushofer and closely followed their impact within the Soviet Union. In 1942 and 1943 he published a series of articles in *Novyi zhurnal* on Soviet foreign policy elucidated from a geopolitical perspective and with special reference to Asia. In 1949 he returned to this theme in an article in the *Far Eastern Quarterly* in which he analyzed Soviet foreign policy towards Japan and the Pan-Asiatic movement.

In this early adolescent period, however, the natural sciences and not politics or history were his primary interests. Flammarion's *Pictorial Astronomy* particularly impressed him. While later it was historical documents and manuscripts which became his treasures, in those years he collected minerals, insects, and plants; but the streak of scholarly investigator and collector was unmistakably manifesting itself.

SAMARA AND UFA: FROM REBELLIOUS MOOD TO REVOLUTIONARY COMMITMENT

In 1898 Boris Ivanovich was sent to high school *(gymnasium)* in Samara (now Kuibyshev) where he was to spend the next five years. For four of these he lived in a dormitory; the last year, because his family's material situation had grown more and more precarious, he stayed at the home of his closest school friend, Levka.[4] His father died in 1899 and soon afterward his family moved to Ufa. Thus ended the Belebei era. Though Boris Ivanovich was to return there only once, emotionally he remained forever attached to it.

Physically, what made the greatest and most indelible impression on Boris Ivanovich in Samara was the Volga. If there was anything he liked in the dreary students' *pansion* (dormitory), with its stifling atmosphere and meager meals—reduced virtually to starvation level by dishonest supervisors—it was the panorama of the great river which extended in front of it. "I would just open a window, or the door, and there she was right before me, the real Volga," he reminisced.

Intellectually, Samara awakened in him a mood of rebelliousness. In the immediate sense it was a rebellion against the school and the spirit which pervaded it; against outdated curricula and old-fashioned pedagogical methods; against incompetent and often morally corrupt educators, ready to crawl before any official who might influence the course of their careers. With some rare exceptions, Boris Ivanovich was simply unable to feel any respect for his Samara teachers.

It was different in Ufa where the *gymnasium* was on a much higher level. In the few months he studied there he did develop a genuine esteem for some of his teachers, both as pedagogues and as human beings. But by that time he had already crossed the Rubicon between the mere rebelliousness of a frustrated schoolboy and the conscious commitment of a social revolutionary, and the sequence of events that followed—illegal activity, arrest, and the *volchii bilet* (exclusion from all schools in Imperial Russia)—was a foregone conclusion.

In general, the defiant spirit of the youth of Samara was stimulated by stories circulating in the town about Gorkii, who in the eyes of the establishment was a *buntar'* (rebel) in every way—by birth, by deed, and by appearance. Considered something of a local-boy-made-good (or bad, depending on the viewpoint), Gorkii had grown up on the Volga and had lived in Samara just a few years earlier (1895-96). Under the pseudonym Iegudiil Khlamida he had written reviews of the regional press and satirical essays on the local scene for the *Samarskii vestnik* which became, in 1896, the first Marxist newspaper in Russia. His long hair and the long cane—intended as a weapon in rougher neighborhoods—with which he strolled through the streets had become a fashion which every schoolboy wanted to imitate. Boris Ivanovich, too, wore long hair until ordered by the school authorities to cut it, which he did. "I would not have become another Khlamida anyway," he consoled himself.

During the first three Samara years the *buntarstvo* (rebelliousness) of Boris Ivanovich remained understandably quite boyish in character and was at most potentially political. His two main interests, the natural sciences and poetry, earned him the nicknames of astronomer and scholar. His great passion was geology, which he had developed a taste for earlier, in Belebei. Given the proximity of the Urals with their numerous mines, which were just then being expanded and modernized, it was a natural interest. What was characteristic of Boris Ivanovich was that he went about it so seriously in a systematic, scholarly way. He was not satisfied to read about minerals in the library but went to the local museum for further study and finally attracted the attention of a young professor, Preobrazhenskii, later to become an Academician, who was heading a geological expedition in the environs of Samara. The expedition had a laboratory at its disposal and Preobrazhenskii opened it to Boris Ivanovich for various experiments.

His interest in poetry was directed above all to Nekrasov, the poet of the Volga and of the *bunty* (rebellions) along it. Boris Ivanovich made a concerted effort to collect poems permeated by the populist spirit and had various friends, including some at the girls' *gymnasium* attended by his older sister, copy this type of poetry from library books for him. Many of these poems he knew by heart and could recite with feeling more than sixty years later. These literary interests led, in 1902, to the formation of an informal reading circle composed of some eight boys of more or less similar background–sons of merchants, declassé nobility, functionaries, and other *raznochintsy*[5]–sharing a certain mood of restlessness. They gathered in the apartment of his friend Levka and read Pisarev, Dobroliubov, Pomialovskii, Gorkii, Nekrasov, Pushkin, and others. Specifically under the prodding of Boris Ivanovich they also studied K. A. Timiriazev's *Life of Plants* and made some scientific experiments. On his own, and as a result of his frequent visits to the museum, Boris Ivanovich began in this period to be interested in history, and when their group decided, early in 1903, to publish a little journal, *Podsnezhnik,* he startled everybody by contributing to the first issue a study "On the History of the [Ancient] Bulgars."[6] His friends laughed at so much learnedness for they were satisfied with the authorship of lighter essays and poetry.

At this point, Boris Ivanovich and his group of friends were not yet acquainted with the revolutionary movement. Although the Decembrists did attract their attention, they had only the vaguest notions about the more recent "to the people" and People's Will movements and were not even aware of the contemporary polemics between the populists and the Marxists. Boris Ivanovich distinctly remembered that he read Chernyshevskii's *Chto delat'* only much later.[7]

Nevertheless, bits and pieces of revolutionary propaganda began to drift into his hands quite early. In 1900, he had the great excitement of seeing, and actually laying hands on, a clandestine leaflet, a mimeographed sheet of paper which he and a friend found in some bushes along the street. The leaflet was antireligious in character and ridiculed the custom of kissing icons–"kissing the behind of a saint" as it was described. It had been written in connection with the arrival in Samara of an allegedly miraculous icon which was ceremonially kissed by all the school children and teachers of the town.[8]

The chances of a Samara school boy coming into direct contact with an active revolutionary were quite slim, at least until the influx of exiled students in the wake of the major disturbances which took place at several universities in the course of 1901.[9] There was in the town a small contingent of old-time exiles, activists from the heyday of populism, surrounded by an aura of fame; but they had to be very circumspect in their contacts. Boris Ivanovich made his first acquaintance among these old timers quite accidentally (in December, 1902), at a public commemoration of the twenty-fifth anniversary of Nekrasov's death. There he met Vasilii P. Artsybushev, an old revolutionary of the 1870s who had spent many years in Siberian exile and in time become a convert to Marxism. It was from him that Boris Ivanovich received his first piece of illegal Marxist literature—Plekhanov's pamphlet on Nekrasov.[10]

Boris Ivanovich was to recall, however, that the "revolutionary instinct" was awakened in him not by some underground political tract, but by an ably written piece of critical reporting published in 1901 in *Permskii krai,* a small provincial paper shut down by the censor later that same year.[11] He did not know at the time who had written that fateful article and it was not until four decades later, in New York, that he was to meet its author, a fellow Menshevik, Ia. M. Lupolov.[12]

The pace of Boris Ivanovich's conversion to the revolutionary movement quickened considerably in the course of 1903. For one thing, it was a year in which the ferment within Russian society began to manifest itself more frequently and more violently. The explosion that was to erupt in 1905 was already stirring close beneath the surface, even in the provinces. Samara experienced a bakers' strike; the lack of bread for several days had a serious impact. In Zlatoust, near Ufa, there was a major strike resulting in a number of fatalities and with a number of workers subsequently condemned to death. The governor of Ufa was assassinated. At the same time, news from other parts of Russia, for instance about the Kishinev pogrom, added to the tensions on the local scene.

Another factor was that Boris Ivanovich now began systematically to familiarize himself with the ideological and historical foundations of the revolutionary movement. Instinctively, drawing on the atmosphere within which he lived, he considered himself a Social Democrat by the end of 1902;[13] yet his acquaintance with Marxism was still limited to what little he could derive from Gorkii's articles in *Zhizn'.* It was only in the spring of 1903, in a circle organized by a Social Democrat, Pavel V. Bekenskii, that he first heard a more or less coherent exposition of Marx's teachings.

Meanwhile, the authorities throughout Russia were deciding on measures to check the spread of subversive ideas. The director of the Samara *gymnasium* thought that an appropriate step in that direction would be to get rid of the young Nicolaevsky and some of his closest friends, and this he did. Thus, in June, 1903, Boris Ivanovich moved to Ufa to join his family. Two of his younger brothers were attending the local *gymnasium* where he was accepted. But he arrived from Samara armed with a secret address *(iavka)* of Sergei F. Gordenin, a member of the local Social Democratic group,[14] and immediately plunged into studies and activities more serious and more political in character than those in Samara. He gained access to a good private library, that of "Nadezhda" Kozlov, a Socialist Revolutionary and veteran revolutionary of the 1870s, where he read extensively in the literature of the populist and the People's Will movements. He also gained access to various Marxist brochures and to the legal Marxist journals *Novoe slovo* and *Nachalo.* Thus his instinctive revolutionary ardor began, for the first time, to acquire some theoretical grounding.

At the *gymnasium* he directed his energies toward the organization of a circle with a definitely revolutionary-political profile. The success of his efforts can be judged from the fact that in the 1905-1906 period virtually all the members of this circle then present in the town joined the "fighting *(boevaia)* organization" of the Ufa Social Democrats.[15] In the fall of 1903, however, the members of the circle were still relatively peaceful, quietly reading and spreading revolutionary propaganda and organizing for the future. Not all of them professed to be Social Democrats. Some leaned towards the Socialist Revolutionaries; others were still uncommitted. Their reading list included such items as Lavrov's *Historical Letters* and current issues of *Iskra.* Their organizing efforts were directed towards the creation of a Society of Students for all Ufa. Boris Ivanovich insisted also on the need to publish a journal. The first issue of the mimeographed *Rassvet,* of which he was editor and to which he contributed a long essay on Novikov as the precursor of the Decembrists, came out in the second half of January, 1904. Simultaneously, the circle issued a proclamation authored by Boris Ivanovich in which the publication of the journal as well as the formation of a Center for the Society of Students were announced. A young Socialist Revolutionary, an ex-student at Moscow University, Mikhail Kozlov, was caught carrying a copy of this proclamation, and his indiscretion led to the arrest of Boris Ivanovich on January 24/February 6, 1904.[16]

REVOLUTIONARY ACTIVIST

With this first arrest, at the age of sixteen, Boris Ivanovich's formal education came to an end, and he entered the adult world. From this point on his days were to be wholly devoted to the making and the study of Russia's socio-political history. This was particularly true of the years up to the February, 1917 Revolution during which his career literally oscillated between periods of frantic revolutionary activity at large and quiet reading in jail cells. The latter periods, which he called his university years, totaled thirty-one months (in eight "installments"). There were also four terms of exile, three in the Russian Arctic and one in Northern Siberia, which added up to seven years. While in exile he divided his time between political and scholarly activities.

The five-and-one-half months in the Ufa jail were especially conducive to study because he was kept throughout in isolation. For the first few days he had access to a window through which he observed with admiration how Zlatoust workers, the strikers from the previous year, organized a demonstration in the prison courtyard while being taken in groups to the court house. Later, except for a few furtive direct contacts, and some communication by knocking on the walls, he was entirely cut off from his fellow

А. 21758. **Борисъ Ивановъ НИКОЛАЕВСКІИ.**

а) сп. свящ., 24 л., газет. коррект. **б)** мт. Евдокія Павлова—г. Уфа. **в)** бр. Викторъ, Михаилъ—при мат., Владиміръ—г. Уфа, сс. Александра—змж., Наталія. **г)** р. выс., л. шрк., в. чер. **д)** фт. пр. **е)** скр. г. Кеми, 26 Іюня 11 г., апрх. ком. **з)** всл. идз. Архангельск. г. 3 г. съ 18 Авг 10 г. **і)** ар. об. прир. расп. Арханг. Г-ра. **к)** VIII—10857 и 11161.

А. 21758. **Борисъ Ивановъ НИКОЛАЕВСКІИ.**

from the archives of the tsarist police, 1911

B. I. NICOLAEVSKY

prisoners. Nevertheless, he remained in high spirits, for he had been psychologically ready to accept the inevitable fate of every revolutionary. He had also been coached on how to behave in case of arrest and had refused to testify. In fact, he was unnecessarily cocky at the hearing and paid dearly for it by being deprived of the privilege of receiving packages, tantamount to being cut off from any outside reading material. Only two months later, after he threatened a hunger strike, was this privilege restored to him.

At first, then, Boris Ivanovich's readings were limited to what was available in the prison library, and he ploughed through the Bible from cover to cover, something he had never before attempted. After the ban on outside packages was lifted, his sister Alexandra began to supply him with literature, both Marxist and populist, particularly the latter because her sympathies and connections were with the Socialist Revolutionaries. It was then that he systematically read the six volumes of the writings of Pisarev, whose primitive rationalism and utilitarianism greatly appealed to him. He also read all of Dobroliubov, various populist writers like Koronin, Lipkin, F. M. Reshetnikov, G. I. Uspenskii, and Zlatovratskii, and back issues of the Marxist and populist journals *Novyi mir, Nachalo, Novoe slovo,* and *Russkoe bogatstvo*—of the latter, complete sets for several years. Among the works by Marxist authors which he read were P. B. Struve's *Critical Observations on the Question of the Economic Development of Russia,* and Kautsky's *The Agrarian Question.* He also read Plekhanov but clearly remembered being put off by the polemical tone of his writings. On the other hand, he recalled that he was very favorably impressed by some articles of V. M. Chernov published in *Russkoe bogatstvo* and *Zhizn'* on the question of the capitalist and agrarian type of evolution and in defense of the labor theory of value.[17]

This reading reinforced Boris Ivanovich's inclinations towards Social Democracy. Thus when he was freed in mid-July, 1904, in the care of his mother—a trial was still pending—and was approached by a representative of the Socialist Revolutionaries urging him to join their group, his answer was that he was already definitely committed. Formally he did not join the Social Democrats until a few months later, after moving to Samara. He remained in Ufa until late September, 1904, spending his time making contacts with various adult groups of revolutionaries. Among his new acquaintances was A. F. Ogorelov, a young but already prominent party member, with whom he was to be bound by a lasting bond of friendship.[18] The decision to become a journalist prompted his move to Samara. Ufa was a much smaller center and had no newspaper while Samara had two.

In Samara, at the age of seventeen, a new chapter began in Boris Ivanovich's life. He was now entirely on his own, embarking on a career of professional journalist *and* professional revolutionary—more the latter than the former—and at the same time embracing a highly bohemian style of life, at least for a time. When he arrived in town he at once settled down to live in a miniature "commune" of six youths more or less his own age.

There were then in Samara quite a few such "communes" of intelligentsia, or rather semi-intelligentsia, usually unemployed and mostly composed of students expelled from local schools. Many of these youths were of peasant, worker, or small-town origin who had attended either the technical or the agricultural schools situated on the outskirts of the town. Frustrated yet cheerful and carefree; iconoclastic, roughish, sometimes lawless, yet essentially idealistic; dead serious in their half-serious undertakings, these were natural rebels who needed only some leadership and discipline to become dedicated professional revolutionaries, fearless members of fighting squads if need be.

Penniless, constantly hungry, their own earnings sporadic to say the least, they depended for survival on Boris Ivanovich's meager honoraria as a budding reporter. Even then it sometimes took considerable feats of imagination to find ways of filling their empty stomachs. Once, Boris Ivanovich recalled, one of the lads had "a brilliant idea." From their window overlooking the yard of the neighboring house they could "fish" for chickens. This they did, and successfully too. Then the reporter sat down and wrote an item for the paper about chicken stealing having taken place at such-and-such an address; he then pocketed what was due for the story. Soon after it was printed the neighbor came running. He was a friend of theirs, and had no suspicions, but he wanted to tell them how "incredibly clever" that newspaper was. He, the owner of the chickens, had not even noticed that any were missing, and here it was already reported in the paper. Amazing!

This tough and unorthodox school of life produced some of the keenest activists of the 1905 upheaval. One member of Boris Ivanovich's "commune," Razumnik Nikolaevich Dmitriev, was to become a leading figure of the revolution in Samara. A native of Syzran', son of a former railwayman, he had for a time attended the Technical School of Samara.

At the time his sympathies were with the Bolsheviks, although later he was to die in a Soviet prison. His specialty in 1905 was making contacts with the peasants coming to market. He authored and produced leaflets addressed to the peasantry and soon began to tour the villages himself. By late summer, 1905, a formal Social Democratic Village Organization was already functioning, and when a joint Bolshevik-Menshevik conference on rural problems was held in September, he attended it as the delegate of Samara.[19]

Boris Ivanovich himself also played a leading role in Samara during the 1905 Revolution. When he arrived in October, 1904, he took a job as a reporter for the *Samarskii kur'er,* a newly-established paper, whose editor, N. N. Skrydlov, was leaning towards the Socialist Revolutionaries.[20] His first article to appear in print concerned the public library in Ufa and its reading room. Then, in November, wishing to switch to historical themes, he wrote a long article, well researched and based on original material, about the writer N. V. Shelgunov, whose eightieth anniversary was then being celebrated. The quickening pace of events, however, and the atmosphere they generated, inexorably deflected his writings and his attention from historical themes and towards contemporary, political issues.

In October he formally became a member of one of the two cells of the Samara Social Democratic organization. Like practically all future Mensheviks who joined the party in this period, he sided at first with the Bolsheviks. In fact, he did not remember ever having met any Menshevik until the middle of 1905. His initial preference for Bolshevism, shared by virtually all his comrades, was not, however, due to a firm espousal of the programmatic and ideological bent of Leninism as opposed to that of Menshevism. There was in general little knowledge of the causes that had brought about the break within the party and even less understanding of the underlying differences in outlook. The issue was seen as simply that of a minority refusing to subordinate itself to the majority. The Mensheviks were universally blamed for the split and were consequently out of favor, for there was an overwhelming desire for unity, not merely among the Social Democrats but also across party lines, among all the revolutionaries, among all the enemies of autocracy. An upshot of this urge for unity was that the sentiments of the party rank-and-file ran counter not only to Menshevism but also to Lenin's directives, even if the latter were still not generally known. While declaring themselves for the Bolsheviks, the great majority of Social Democrats insisted on a conciliatory attitude towards the Mensheviks, precisely what Lenin did not want.[21]

The most important party member then in Samara, I. F. Dubrovinskii (known under the pseudonyms of Leo and Innokentii), a Bolshevik, a professional revolutionary, and a member of the Central Committee, was also a "conciliator" *(primirenets),* unwilling to follow Lenin's tough policies towards the Mensheviks. When Boris Ivanovich arrived in Samara with the underground address *(iavka)* of the Eastern Bureau of the Central Committee, Dubrovinskii was just planning to launch a paper. This was contrary to the directives of Lenin who did not favor locally initiated party organs which he well knew would be virtually impossible to control effectively and which would thus inevitably disseminate various heretical ideas. Nevertheless, Boris Ivanovich was recruited for the task of gathering documentation for a review of the domestic scene. The whole plan fell through only when Dubrovinskii, together with eight other members of the Central Committee, was arrested in Moscow on February 9/22, 1905, in the apartment of the writer Leonid Andreev. Boris Ivanovich considered that it was this arrest which, by wiping out almost the entire membership of the Central Committee active within Russia, and with it its "conciliatory" faction, finally permitted Lenin to push through his plans for the Third Party Congress from which he excluded the Mensheviks.[22] If Lenin did not at this time achieve his aim of a final, irremediable split within the party, it was because the Third Congress coincided with the outbreak of the 1905 Revolution which brought to the fore an irresistible pressure to conciliate and forget factional quarrels. By September, 1905, reconciliation of the two factions was a fact of daily revolutionary practice everywhere in Russia and the emigre leaders and theoreticians, including Lenin, had to accept it. Only after the revolution was crushed was Lenin able to resume his plans, and not until the Prague Conference of 1912 did he succeed in bringing about the final split within the party, the aim of the Third Congress seven years earlier.

However, Boris Ivanovich was not ready to put all the blame for the Bolshevik-Menshevik split on Lenin alone. He considered that there was a time in 1904 when, after losing Plekhanov and *Iskra,* and under growing pressure from his "conciliatory" Central Committee, Lenin probably had doubts about the wisdom of his intransigent policy vis-à-vis the Mensheviks and would have been amenable to some kind of reconciliation. But at this point the Menshevik leaders in exile made the mistake of "bending the twig too far" *(peregnuli palku)* and continued to breathe righteous indignation and attack Lenin without seriously exploring every possible avenue for bridging the gap. Thus, Boris Ivanovich believed that "a chance at reuniting the party was lost"; by the same token the chance of going into, and coming out of, the 1905 revolution as a better defined social force, more appealing to broad strata of the society, and ultimately stronger both numerically and politically, was lessened. Reconciliation would have facilitated the open, mass movement approach in politics favored by the Mensheviks as opposed to the conspiratorial and undemocratic approach favored by Lenin. Of course, at some point Lenin might have split the party anyway, but his strategies and policies would have had to be different, too, had the Social Democratic movement meanwhile grown broader and more mature.

The Samara Social Democratic Committee embraced the conciliatory attitude.[23] There was also considerable cooperation and interpenetration across party lines. For instance, in November, 1904, while in jail for a week after participating in a street demonstration,[24] Boris Ivanovich struck up a friendship with Petr Voevodin.[25] They roomed together after coming out of prison and jointly engaged in various revolutionary activities. Yet Voevodin was at that time still hesitating between the Socialist Revolutionaries and the Social Democrats, though he was leaning towards the latter. Since there were many others in the same position there even existed a Union of Socialist Revolutionaries which embraced both populists and Marxists, and to which Voevodin had belonged shortly before. Another friend of Boris Ivanovich, Professor Preobrazhenskii, the geologist who had befriended him a few years earlier, became active in the Union of Liberation; but he also had connections in Menshevik circles and copies of *Iskra* were sent to his address. He then passed them on to Boris Ivanovich. A close collatorator of Preobrazhenskii, V. M. Pototskii, a chemist in the laboratory in which Boris Ivanovich had been permitted to experiment while still in high school, was a member of Samara's Social Democratic Committee. Each knew of the other's activities but that did not matter. The immediate common goal—the overthrow of the autocracy—which bound them was much more important than what divided them; the ultimate goal and the ideological justification of their actions.

While still in high school, Boris Ivanovich and his friends were well aware of the distinction between the minimum and the maximum program of the socialists. The former was directed against direct oppression and aimed at political freedom—democratic self-government, civil rights, and what is broadly known as negative freedoms, the freedoms *from*—while the latter was directed against all forms of indirect oppression and exploitation and aimed at social justice: the freedom to live in a just society. Both the Socialist Revolutionaries and the Social Democrats were at the time aiming only at the minimum program. The former, Boris Ivanovich felt, justified their position by subjective factors, the latter by reference to objective conditions of life, and this was one of the major reasons why Social Democracy held greater appeal for him. The fact that the liberals did not look beyond a political revolution (i.e., the minimum program of the revolutionaries), and were in fact opposed to a social revolution, exposed them to criticism on the part of the socialists. Psychologically the socialists also felt a need to put a distance between themselves and the liberals, to emphasize that the latter belonged to the privileged—the "ins," the social establishment—while they, the socialists, were the underprivileged outsiders.[26] This was the main thrust of their argument at public meetings. At a big public banquet organized by the liberals in Samara early in January, 1905, Boris Ivanovich recalled that Petr Voevodin spoke in this vein about "we the workers," and "I who have just come out of jail," and "you who are only talking while we are preparing ourselves in all seriousness," etc.

Nevertheless, what was decisive was the general mood within the country. Boris Ivanovich emphasized that even prior to 1905, when he was still in the *gymnasium* and engaging with his friends in illegal political activities, he was never really afraid that some classmate might give him away. Though some of his colleagues, sons of noblemen, were obviously not sympathetic with his political views, he did not remember a single case of deliberate denunciation. In 1905, in Samara, there were moments when one could, according to Boris Ivanovich, almost speak of something akin to a "popular front." It so happened that only a minority of the top town officials were hard core reactionaries. The chief of police was not interested in arresting every revolutionary in sight. His main concern was to keep things as quiet and nonviolent as possible. A Colonel von Galin, second in command of the local military garrison and who, as Boris Ivanovich was to find out only in 1917 when the police archives were opened, had as a youth been a member of a Social Democratic circle in the 1880s, openly collaborated with the revolutionaries in order to frustrate the plans of the reactionaries. This was in the early fall of 1905 when the counterrevolutionary Black Hundreds hit upon the idea of stirring up the rabble *(Lumpenproletariat)* and with their help organizing a pogrom against the Jews and intelligentsia whom they identified as the chief villains.[27] The revolutionaries, of whatever shade, were determined to prevent this and Boris Ivanovich and his young friends were charged with the organization of a self-defense corps. Local business leaders, most anxious to avoid a situation in which an irresponsible and leaderless mob would rampage through the streets destroying life and property, encouraged them and helped to mediate an agreement between them on the one hand and the police and the military on the other. The self-defense corps, of which Boris Ivanovich was the unofficial chief, took it upon itself to supervise the streets and keep order, and the police and army agreed to stay in the background. If any trouble developed an emissary of the self-defense corps would come to them with a password and ask for help.[28]

This did not mean, however, that the revolutionaries in general, or the Social Democrats in particular, were in any way more restrained in Samara than elsewhere. Boris Ivanovich emphasized that of all the political parties active in 1905 on the Samara scene the Social Democrats were the most successful in expanding the circle of their supporters. This was particularly true among the younger generation. The Social Democrats, who in this period developed a special pride in the party (Boris Ivanovich called it "party patriotism") vigorously vied with the Socialist Revolutionaries and Anarchists for the allegiance of the underprivileged and of the youth, regardless of social origin. In all the schools the Social Democrats had the strongest organization except for the Theological Seminary where the Socialist Revolutionaries prevailed. Least successful among the students were the liberals. There were also at this time no tensions between the intelligentsia and the workers. These developed only later, with the crushing of the revolution and the disillusionment that followed, and it was only then, beginning in 1907, that the Social Democrats lost quite a few followers to the Socialist Revolutionaries and Anarchists.

A special Social Democratic Committee, of which Boris Ivanovich was a member, was formed in the spring of 1905 for the organization of the strike movement which was fairly successful given the limited number of industrial plants–mostly flour mills–in Samara. The newspapers were also shut down for a time. The main task of the Committee members was to give expression to and formulate into concrete demands the amorphous grievances of the workers. Boris Ivanovich recalled that workers were seeking them out asking to put down on paper specifics with which they could confront the employers. Some of the demands were economic, some were of a more general, political character. There was great confusion as to what could or should be demanded and from whom. At the peak of the revolutionary tide everybody thought he should demand something. Boris Ivanovich recalled getting word from a rather exclusive girls' school that the students needed advice because they, too, wanted to present some demands. He went but it was only after long deliberations that the girls could think of any grievance. Suddenly one remembered that their old Russian stoves always smoked because the dampers were defective. They wanted also, however, to demand something more general, for everybody—something political. So it was agreed and set down on paper: new dampers for the stoves *and* a Constituent Assembly.

Boris Ivanovich admitted that not all that he and his fellow Social Democrats were doing at the time was very serious or significant. But it reflected their mood, aspirations, and hopes, and what *was* significant was that so large a segment of the population looked towards them as the leading element or at least sympathized with them. In fact, except for the narrow, ultraconservative circles, everybody was ready to help in one way or another. Boris Ivanovich recalled that at one point he was asked to find a good hiding place for the archives of the Eastern Bureau of the Central Committee of the party, and after thinking it over, went to a friend of his sister who was the granddaughter of the chief archpriest of the local Orthodox cathedral. He was introduced to the archpriest and found a sympathetic ear. Soon the party archives were safely stored in the attic of the archpriest's house.

The sympathetic public response to the revolutionaries was also helpful in making employers conciliatory. The workers did in the course of 1905 win many significant concessions, of which the right to collective bargaining was perhaps the most important. The organization of trade unions became the task on which the Social Democrats concentrated after the October 17, 1905, Manifesto granted the freedoms of speech, press, and assembly. Boris Ivanovich organized unions of typographers, of clerks, and of "ordinary employees," the latter term being interpreted broadly enough to include a local of prostitutes.

His organizational activities however were not to last very long, for the tide began to turn against the revolution. A new governor and a new military commander were appointed in Samara and they reneged on the informal arrangements made or at least tolerated by their predecessors. In December a house where Boris Ivanovich and other revolutionaries were meeting was surrounded by troops. It was quickly decided that the most valuable revolutionary activists should go into hiding and he was among those who escaped through a back door.

From this point on the emphasis was on propaganda among the soldiers and subversion of the army. While in 1905 the instrument for bringing the government to its knees was the general strike—essentially an economic, indirect weapon—now it was a question of disarming the government, robbing it of its coercive arm, rendering it literally powerless. Boris Ivanovich had for some time looked with envy at the military organization of the Socialist Revolutionaries. This was one area where they were much stronger than the Social Democrats. Now he set out to correct this deficiency and concentrated on the establishment of a Social Democratic military revolutionary organization. Boris Ivanovich and his several collaborators were making good progress when in May, 1906, he was arrested while carrying leaflets which they had prepared for distribution among soldiers. He was tried five months later and would have received two years in a fortress had it not been for the fact that he was still under twenty-one. Still, he did not leave the Samara jail until July, 1907. He spent his time reading and his greatest regret was that he missed the period of the first two Dumas.

When he walked out of the Samara jail Boris Ivanovich was more than ever determined to devote himself in all earnestness to party work. He went to Omsk and there did some propaganda work among the soldiers but without much success. After less than two months he decided to move on because Omsk was too dead and too provincial for him and the revolutionary movement there was on the downgrade. He took the train and, stopping from time to time, began to move towards St. Petersburg, which he had never seen before. He arrived in the capital late in August, 1907, during the period of elections to the Third Duma. The Bolsheviks were in control of the St. Petersburg Social Democratic organization and what struck him immediately was that nowhere before had he seen the lines between the two factions so sharply drawn. He sided with the Mensheviks. Once he even participated in a kind of verbal duel with Lenin when at a meeting he argued for the Menshevik point of view while Lenin spoke for that of the Bolsheviks. "My speech was rather poor," Boris Ivanovich conceded but he was not given a chance of bettering the score for he was arrested very soon afterwards at a meeting of a council of the unemployed in which he participated in his capacity of party secretary of the local borough. After four months in jail he was exiled for two years in the White Sea region.

FROM BOLSHEVISM TO MENSHEVISM

The transition from Bolshevism to Menshevism was a slow, gradual process. It was for Boris Ivanovich as much, perhaps even more, a question of becoming acquainted with the issues, of grasping the deeper meaning of the differences in outlook, as of changing his own views. He had sided originally with the Bolsheviks because he favored strong party discipline and, above all, unity within the party. He had regarded the Mensheviks as "splitters," an undisciplined minority defying the majority. In the course of 1905 there were in Samara no real tactical differences between the Bolsheviks and Mensheviks. The former were somewhat harsher in their attacks on the liberals, denouncing them as traitors, while the latter criticized the liberals mainly with the idea, and hope, of pushing them further to the left. The issues most frequently discussed between the Bolsheviks and Mensheviks were those of the Party Statute—who should be considered a party member. On this Boris Ivanovich tended at the time to side with the Bolsheviks, not because he opposed a large, mass party—he definitely favored it—but because, reacting to the split which he blamed on wayward behavior, he was for tight discipline and because he favored activism. He and his friends were determined to be full-time revolutionaries, and, in his youthful enthusiasm, he wanted every Social Democrat to come as close as possible to this ideal. In this he reflected the prevailing mood of 1905 which was that of impatient activism; direct revolutionary activity, not reflection and long range tactics and policies, was what seemed to be paying off in 1905, at least until the fall.[29]

To orthodoxy in ideology, on the other hand, he and his group of young friends, as well as the overwhelming majority of the Social Democrats active within Russia, attached only secondary importance. Briefly, the emphasis was not on ideological unity but on unity in action: unity of the forces struggling with the common enemy and complete, if possible, full-time, devotion to the pursuit of the immediate goal, the minimum program of overthrowing the tsarist regime. Boris Ivanovich recalled how unpopular any independent initiative on the part of either the Bolsheviks or the Mensheviks was among his friends. Factional publications—newspapers, manifestos, leaflets, etc.—were frowned upon. Ideological disagreements among Social Democrats were readily admitted and taken in stride, considered tolerable; not so organizational separatism or going one's own path, however revolutionary. If the mood of the Samara Social Democrats was representative of the Social Democratic organizations within Russia, which it probably was, Lenin's Third Party Congress was a tactical mistake. While previously the onus for splitting the party had been laid at the door of the "insubordinate minority," the Mensheviks, now it was Lenin who, with his attempt at creating an entirely separate party organization, was earning the odious name of "splitter." The Samara Social Democratic Committee had no Mensheviks within its ranks;[30] yet it did harbor two factions: the regular Bolsheviks (better called simply "majority Social Democrats") who were "conciliatory" *(primirentsy)* and opposed the Third Party Congress, and the factional Bolsheviks, that is, the Leninists who favored the Third Party Congress. The latter were in the minority.

The margin of tolerance of ideological (and, to some extent, programmatic) diversity was wide enough among many Social Democrats to make them wish the Socialist Revolutionaries, too, would simply join, thus consummating the much sought revolutionary unity. Boris Ivanovich was well aware that this was not quite possible even though he considered that the outlook of a Socialist Revolutionary leader like V. M. Chernov was in fact a mixture of populism and Marxism. He was also, as were his friends, in favor of vigorous competition with the Socialist Revolutionaries for the allegiance of the peasantry. Like every good Marxist, he considered that his party had the best, the most rational and scientific understanding of sociohistorical developments, and consequently he wanted to unite under its banner all the revolutionary forces, the great masses of both town and country. But he could never bring himself to condemn and denounce the Socialist Revolutionaries wholesale and with vituperation as was often done by his comrades. More, he readily admitted that he saw nothing essentially wrong in a situation in which one revolutionary party, the Social Democrats, emphasized the proletariat while another, the Socialist Revolutionaries, put more emphasis on the peasantry.

Underlying this reasoning was Boris Ivanovich's conviction that given the fact that the Social Democrats had both in theory and in fact concentrated on the proletariat—on the task of revolutionizing the worker and championing his interests—it was natural, and to some extent even desirable, at least temporarily, to have another party which was, so to speak, redressing the balance by concentrating its attention primarily on the peasantry.

The peasant issue, it must be said, was a sore point in Boris Ivanovich's relation to Menshevism, and to Marxism in general. It was a point on which he felt strongly and was never quite in harmony with the great majority of his party colleagues. Through the years he openly reproached the Mensheviks for consistently displaying a certain aversion towards the peasants which often bordered on outright "peasantophobia." This was, he said, "the tragedy of Menshevism," both morally and politically.

Boris Ivanovich's position towards the Bolsheviks as well as within Menshevism was repeatedly and decisively influenced by the peasant issue. In 1919, after a journey to Siberia convinced him of the plight of the peasants under the Kolchak regime, he veered sharply to the left. In a public speech which Lenin was to quote,[31] he described at length the sufferings of the peasants in Siberia and called for a united revolutionary front with the Bolsheviks against Kolchak. Eleven years later, in Berlin, reports of the terror and famine accompanying the forcible collectivization of the peasantry again stirred him to take a political position after nearly a decade devoted almost exclusively to strictly scholarly, non-partisan work in the course of which he had collaborated closely with the Marx-Engels Institute of Moscow. His political conscience—his old "revolutionary instinct" as he called it—was aroused and he turned to political writings and began to attack the Soviet regime, all the more so because F. I. Dan was then promoting a Menshevik policy which he considered a *de facto* acquiescence to the Bolshevik collectivization program. In his last political speech, given in New York in January, 1964, two years before his death, Boris Ivanovich once more blamed the Mensheviks' woes principally on their persistent anti-peasant attitude.

It should be mentioned here that there was another issue on which Boris Ivanovich was not quite in harmony with his fellow Mensheviks. This was the question of national minorities for which the Mensheviks, the majority of whom were themselves members of some national minority, showed very little understanding. They were impatient Marxists, rigidly orthodox internationalists when faced with the demands of the various minorities. In contrast to Lenin, they did not understand the enormous historical and emotional force represented by nationalism. They believed, like Marx and Engels when writing the *Communist Manifesto,* that nationalism was waning on the socio-historical scene. Hence they were not willing to make any serious concessions to it and (although making an exception for Poland) took the desirability, and political expediency, of maintaining the unity of the multinational Russian Empire so much for granted that their pronouncements sounded dangerously similar to those of the right wing Russian nationalists who insisted on the "one and indivisible" *(edinaia i nedelimaia)* Russia.

Boris Ivanovich, while emotionally and ideologically favoring the maintenance of Russian unity under some form or other, however loose, showed a deep understanding for the historical roots and actual and potential strength of the national movements. In emigration, he alone among all the Mensheviks maintained some contacts with nationalist, independence-seeking groups (for instance, the Ukrainians) and was willing to participate in their public meetings to debate the issue of Russia and its national minorities.

It was in fact part of his general political strategy, which in contrast to many of his fellow Social Democrats he did not abandon after 1905, always to seek an understanding and to cooperate with various groups—to aim at a united front of the broad masses regardless of certain ideological disagreements. Characteristic in this respect was his effort in 1947, "to unite all the forces of the Russian democratic, socialist and non-socialist, emigration (both old and new)." This initiative resulted in the formation of a League for Struggle for the People's Freedom *(Liga Borby za Narodnuiu Svobodu,* also known as *Liga Svobodnoi Rossii)* which was headed, among others, by V. M. Chernov, formerly Chairman of the All-Russian Constituent Assembly, and A. F. Kerenskii, formerly prime minister of the All-Russian Provisional Government.[32]

From his very earliest days as a Social Democrat, Boris Ivanovich believed that the emphasis of the revolutionary movement had to be on mobilizing the broadest masses; that only a genuine mass movement could give it the strength it needed. The professional revolutionary was not a substitute for but a means of generating the mass movement. The tactic had to be two-pronged. On the one hand, the revolutionary movement had to be broadened through coalitions into a united front of all the democratic forces opposed to the tsarist regime and, on the other hand, the mass base of Social Democracy had to be broadened. This was, of course, not an original idea. Lenin subscribed to it to a considerable extent. The question was, however, how consistent one was in pursuing it. Ideological purity and strict centralization of leadership had in Lenin's eyes higher priority. Boris Ivanovich, on the other hand, opposed sectarianism, factionalism, and elitism as well as "partisan actions," etc., precisely because he considered them to be incompatible with grassroots work among the masses, with the so-called "organic work" in the broadest sense.[33]

Boris Ivanovich was a great admirer of German Social Democracy. He had begun to study it in 1904, in the Ufa jail. He was awed by its organization, press, systematic activity and, above all, its steady growth in numbers, influence, and power. The party had done its spadework conscientiously, rationally, and it seemed ready to reap the harvest. Here, he thought, was a real mass movement advancing irresistibly, forcing the old order to retreat. It was Marx's prediction coming true, the logic of history unfolding. However, in the heat of the 1905 Revolution and the continued struggle in 1906 the German model was somewhat forgotten, Boris Ivanovich admitted that he had been quite hotheaded in those days. Reflection came with defeat and the new study period in the Samara jail. It was then that he made the decision to devote himself to systematic, long range, "organic" party work; it was this decision which led him to the Mensheviks on his release. The same decision took him on a path which signified the final break with Bolshevism. What really tipped the scales was that the Bolsheviks turned to "partisan actions." "That was the end," Boris Ivanovich recalled. He had always been against terror not because he opposed it on moral grounds but because he considered it futile, if not directly counterproductive. He admired the heroism of the revolutionaries of the People's Will days but not their wisdom. Still, those were different times and one could understand them. But to turn to terrorism at a time when a mass revolutionary movement was already a reality, when a revolution had just shown the power of the organized masses to shake and weaken, though not yet overthrow, the autocratic regime, was tantamount to an immense step backward. It was, in Boris Ivanovich's opinion, turning to meaningless exploits instead of concentrating where potentially the real power lay; it was fighting the organized state machinery with isolated pistol shots instead of mobilizing the weight of millions against it. More, it meant missing the opportunity of rationally and systematically preparing the masses as well as the party for the Revolution *and* for the day after the Revolution.[34]

MEETING STALIN

From late 1908 until February, 1910, Boris Ivanovich was in exile in northern European Russia, in the White Sea area. He lodged with peasant families and paid his way from the thirteen-and-a-half ruble monthly allocation which the government paid every exile and which was quite adequate for maintenance. Rustic life, even in the far north, with its harsh climate and isolation from populated centers, never bothered Boris Ivanovich. On the contrary, he retained very pleasant memories from this as well as later Siberian exiles. He loved nature, liked and felt at ease with the peasants, and appreciated the freedom and free time to roam and do what he liked. He studied the peasants and their culture and beliefs and explored the area and its economic potential. With the authorities' approval, Boris Ivanovich and several other exiles journeyed to the very edge of Arctic Siberia, and explored with his friends the Vorkuta coal fields which were to be opened for exploitation only later, when the Soviets established infamous concentration camps there.

When his term of exile ended in February, 1910, Boris Ivanovich received a passport to Ufa. He was now of military age and, reluctantly, presented himself to the draft board for a physical examination. Seeing a tall, healthy young man, the board at first wanted to send him to the Imperial Guard. Luckily, a secretary who knew about his unreliable political background spotted him at the last minute. After a whispered conference and "a good examination," the doctor heard some "heart noises" which were deemed serious enough to grant an exemption from military service. However, other troubles were soon awaiting Boris Ivanovich. In Ufa, in the summer of 1910 he was jailed for two months for associating with revolutionaries. Released, he went to Samara to work for the local paper but was again arrested and sent back to the now familiar tundra region, this time for a three year term. He spent the winter of 1910-11 on the shores of the White Sea, where he studied local history and authored a series of articles on the development of Russian schooners. A shipbuilders' society became interested in these writings and they were collected in a separate volume, his first book.

Still, no matter how much he enjoyed roaming the Northern expanses and studying local history, he could not forget the broader problems—the ills of Russia and the duty he felt to do something about them. In the spring of 1911 he fled, smuggling himself on board a small steamer dressed as a local fisherman. He landed at Arkhangelsk, took a train to the Ukraine and thence to Baku where he knew police control was weak.

From August, 1911, to June, 1912, Boris Ivanovich stayed in Baku, working as a journalist, and was not bothered by the police. One evening shortly after his arrival, a Bolshevik, Avel' Enukidze, took him to a little Georgian winery. Just off a main street, in a half basement, it was a hangout of the Georgian Social Democrats, many of them veterans of the uprising in Guriia now living under false identities. Boris Ivanovich remembered that first evening as a memorable event—his introduction to the Georgians to whom he was thereafter bound by lasting sympathy and close ties.[35]

During the evening Enukidze warned him that "we Georgians are very different from you Russians," for a friend a Georgian will "give his last shirt," but with an enemy he is tough; he may kill him. Then Enukidze asked: "Do you know our Peter the Caucasian—Tiflisian (i.e. Stalin)?" Boris Ivanovich answered that he had only heard about him. "If you don't know him you'd better learn about him and remember," said Enukidze, and he went on to characterize Stalin as one who had a long memory—"very vengeful, doesn't forget anything, so be careful."

In fact Enukidze's main purpose was to test Boris Ivanovich's reactions to see whether he should be let into the local party organization. Despite the fact that, in response to close questioning, Boris Ivanovich identified himself as a Menshevik, the memorable evening in the winery ended on a friendly note and he was welcomed to work with the Baku Social Democrats.

He soon became a member of the local Social Democratic Committee and found himself struggling with the Bolsheviks who controlled the organization.

In the fall of 1911 when many party members, mostly Bolsheviks, were arrested, Boris Ivanovich rose to a leading position[36] and as a result was to meet Stalin.

The occasion was a party investigation of a Bolshevik, a member of the old Baku group, who had escaped arrest and attended a regional Social Democratic conference in Baku on the basis of a document to which a two-year-old party seal had been affixed. That seal, a round one, had been discarded when the police gained knowledge of it; since then the party was using a new seal of a different shape. When, in April, 1912, Stalin arrived in Baku as a representative of the Bolshevik Central Committee (newly elected at the recent Prague Conference), Boris Ivanovich was empowered to talk to him about the matter.

The encounter took place at the home of the Bolshevik Sosnovskii, who later became a prominent journalist. When Boris Ivanovich arrived Stalin was already there, sitting in a dark corner, his face hidden. He began by talking about the Prague Conference and the Bolshevik organization and plans. Boris Ivanovich pressed for a clarification of the circumstances under which an old seal, already known to the police, was used and made it clear that he suspected infiltration by police agents. Stalin could not give any explanation, claiming that he did not know because he had been away in exile and would first have to investigate. Thus a second meeting was arranged at which Stalin gave an involved story about two unions of oil workers, one of which had issued the seal. Boris Ivanovich was not satisfied and asked for further clarification, and Stalin again said that he would investigate but refused to meet for a third time.

The paths of Boris Ivanovich and Stalin were to cross directly only once more, this time in jail. It was about three months after their last meeting. Boris Ivanovich had been arrested on May 28, when his false identity was discovered (he had been living under the name of Golosov), and he was being transported back to his place of exile in the White Sea region.[37] Meanwhile Stalin, who had gone to St. Petersburg to work on *Pravda,* had also been arrested and was on his way to exile in Narym in Siberia. They met in the transit jail of Vologda and had a friendly chat. Stalin even asked Boris Ivanovich to give him his kettle *(chainik)* as he had none and was scheduled to be shipped out the same day, without companions, while Boris Ivanovich was in a party, several of whom had kettles. Boris Ivanovich gave him his kettle—"a good, blue enamel kettle," he remembered—and that was the last time they ever talked.[38]

Indirectly, however, the paths of Boris Ivanovich and Stalin crossed in more significant ways than their three face-to-face meetings would suggest. The shadow of Stalin's operations profoundly affected Boris Ivanovich's nine month Baku period, and ultimately his whole attitude toward Bolshevism and later toward the Soviet Union in general. His attitude towards Bolshevism, it should be emphasized, was not something which crystallized overnight, or even within the few months of 1906-1907 when he made the switch to Menshevism. On the contrary, it was the product of a slow process marked by many ambiguities and for a long time devoid of exclusive, clear-cut loyalties. After all, this was the era following the Stockholm Unity Congress when the overwhelming majority of Social Democrats believed that the two factions represented merely nuances which could and should be able to cooperate within one party organization. Only slowly, first among the emigres and the *politiki* (party politicians), did a more aggressive stance, stressing the irreconciliability of the factions, gain in strength. Among the *praktiki* (practical party workers), and in Russia generally, the idea of an actual split within the party organization was resisted much longer, even by centers otherwise dominated by Lenin's ideas. Baku was somewhat of an exception in that the local party organization had already split in February, 1908 (undoubtedly a reflection of Stalin's influence); but as Boris Ivanovich's experience proved, even in Baku there were many Bolsheviks quite ready to welcome a confessed Menshevik into their organization.

When he came to Baku Boris Ivanovich was an outspoken *primirenets* (conciliator),[39] who had no compunction about working with Bolsheviks, even within their organization, or about cultivating old or striking up new friendships with individual Bolsheviks. On his arrival he had expressed readiness to work within the framework of the local Bolshevik controlled organization and said that he neither had, nor intended to seek, an introduction to the parallel Plekhanovite-Menshevik organization.[40] Of course, Boris Ivanovich felt at ease primarily with those Bolsheviks who, like Enukidze, were *primirentsy,* and like himself sought to minimize the conflict between the two Social Democratic factions, while he found it more difficult (but not impossible) to collaborate with irreconcilable Leninists some of whom (for instance Stepan Shaumian) nevertheless commanded his respect.

It was in the course of rebuilding, and then leading, the Baku Social Democratic Committee following the mass Bolshevik arrests of September, 1911, that Boris Ivanovich encountered for the first time a brand of Bolshevism with which he could not cooperate on either political or moral grounds. Bolshevism in Baku was a product, on the one hand, of the mores of the local milieu which generated mafia type ties and interrelationships and, on the other, of the mode of operation of Stalin, who was himself the product of a similar milieu. According to Boris Ivanovich, it was in 1905-1906 that Stalin had created for himself a personal power base in Baku. At that time a Tatar millionaire named Tagiev, owner of the newspaper *Kaspii* and head of a Muslim sect, tightly controlled the whole Baku Tatar population. Conforming to the local custom, he had a squad of body guards called *kochi,* who also served as an enforcement arm. During the 1905 Revolution Stalin was able to infiltrate, win over, and organize Tagiev's *kochi* and thereafter used them as his own body guards and executive arm. In 1906-1907 some suburbs and areas of Baku became dangerous territory for the Mensheviks because of frequent roughing ups by these minions of Stalin.[41]

Politically, Stalin's success in organizing Tagiev's *kochi* was of considerable significance for it was apparently the first time that the Social Democratic movement had penetrated and created a base in the Muslim population of Transcaucasia. The reputation which Stalin acquired among the Bolsheviks as an expert in dealing with minority nationalities may well have originated with this success. It also gave the Bolsheviks an incontestable advantage over the Mensheviks whose base remained very narrow in places like Baku. Characteristically, when Boris Ivanovich began his drive to re-establish a Baku Social Democratic Committee after the September, 1911, arrests, his core of organizational strength was a union of mechanical workers and a much smaller union of draftsmen, both of which were composed of skilled, ethnically Russian workers. Bolshevik, and in particular Stalin's personal strength, on the other hand, rested with a union of oil workers, the great majority of whom were unskilled Tatar laborers. Seregin, the secretary and seal holder of this union for over a decade, a follower of Stalin and his trusted man, was discovered in 1917 to have been a police agent all along. Boris Ivanovich was convinced that Seregin informed the police selectively, denouncing some revolutionaries while protecting Stalin's followers.

Stalin's mode of operation in Baku left an unfavorable impression on Boris Ivanovich. Later, while in exile in Siberia, he was to hear unconfirmed rumors further questioning the reliability of Stalin himself. Then, in 1918, Martov openly charged that Stalin had at one point been expelled from the party for organizing so-called "partisan actions" which had been expressly forbidden by the Central Committee. Stalin countered with a suit for defamation and Boris Ivanovich was sent to the Caucasus to bring back documents concerning the episode.[42] Still, it wasn't until Stalin emerged as undisputed ruler of the Soviet Union and Stalinism showed its true face as a political doctrine that Boris Ivanovich took a militant anti-Stalinist stance and began to write prolifically on the evils of Stalinism. In 1933 Boris Ivanovich published in *Sotsialisticheskii vestnik* a series of "Letters from Moscow"[43] about the G.P.U., Stalin, and the men around him. These "Letters," based mainly on information supplied by the writer Isaac Babel[44] but supplemented from other Bolshevik sources, are to this day a valuable source for any student of Stalin and his era. In 1937 Boris Ivanovich published the now famous "Letter of an Old Bolshevik," an analysis of Stalinism based on a conversation with Bukharin who visited Boris Ivanovich and F. I. Dan, while on an official trip to Paris. Still later came a series of articles in *Novyi zhurnal* analyzing the evolution of Stalin's foreign policy in the late 1920s and early 1930s. Finally, in 1947, Boris Ivanovich co-authored (with a fellow Menshevik, D. Dallin) a book on forced labor in the Soviet Union. This work caused an international stir and was the object of a blistering attack by Andrei Vyshinskii, the Soviet representative at the United Nations.

From the 1940s on, various people turned to Boris Ivanovich for confirmation of their suspicions that Stalin was at one time a police agent, but he consistently refused to admit this even though his own investigations had at times strongly tempted him to accept some variant of these suspicions as truth. All that Boris Ivanovich was willing to say was that he considered Stalin so devoid of any moral scruples as to be certainly *capable* of stooping to collaboration with the police. The degree to which he considered Stalin a virtual embodiment of evil and a menace to the whole world can be seen from a letter he wrote in August, 1948, to a boyhood friend in which he said that Stalin was "worse than Hitler" and consequently another war, "more terrible than the last one," was inevitable.

What undoubtedly restrained Boris Ivanovich from ever mentioning in public or in print any suspicions concerning Stalin's past was the tradition strongly rooted in him that the basest of all crimes a revolutionary could commit was collaboration with the police. Hence to accuse a revolutionary of such a crime was so damning that it was permissible only when incontrovertible proof was at hand; Boris Ivanovich always emphasized that in the case of Stalin such proof was not available.

CROSSING PATHS WITH LENIN

Boris Ivanovich met Lenin only twice. Their second meeting was the episode described above, during the electoral campaign in the fall of 1907 when Boris Ivanovich attempted rather unsuccessfully to compete with Lenin from the speakers' tribune. The first encounter also took place in St. Petersburg, somewhat earlier that same fall.[45] At the urging of I. N. Konovalov, Boris Ivanovich published in the Bolshevik *Vpered* an account of his talks with soldiers returning from the Far East and Lenin, having read the article, expressed through Konovalov a desire to meet its author.

The meeting took place at the University of St. Petersburg and Lenin asked many questions about the mood of the soldiers and requested Boris Ivanovich to write more on this subject for *Vpered.* Boris Ivanovich considered this suggestion quite characteristic of the conciliatory atmosphere within the party during this period, for he made it clear during the conversation that he was a Menshevik and the secretary of a Menshevik district *(raion).* Otherwise Lenin's personality made no particular impression on him, and he later wondered why others reminisced again and again about Lenin's striking, especially penetrating eyes, while he had noticed nothing extraordinary.

A frontal clash between Lenin and Boris Ivanovich occurred in October, 1913. Boris Ivanovich had been released from his exile in the Arkhangelsk region in June, 1913, and had settled, after a visit to Ufa, in St. Petersburg where he worked as assistant to M. I. Skobelev, a Menshevik deputy and secretary of the Social Democratic fraction in the Fourth Duma, and as secretary of the Menshevik paper *Luch.* As a collaborator and old friend of Skobelev, he was closely involved in the work of all Menshevik deputies and wrote speeches or reports on meetings with constituents for some of them.[46]

The dispute opened when Boris Ivanovich published an article in *Luch* protesting an attack by Lenin on N. S. Chkheidze's loyalty to the party. Lenin came lashing back with a redoubled attack on Chkheidze aimed at undermining the latter's prestige and authority among Social Democratic deputies in order to facilitate his plan of splitting the Bolsheviks from the Mensheviks within the Duma fraction. Boris Ivanovich wanted to answer Lenin again but F. I. Dan, unwilling to start a great debate with the Bolsheviks for the sake of a Chkheidze whom he did not consider a real party man, firmly opposed the move.

The polemic around Chkheidze left a bitter taste in Boris Ivanovich's mouth for it showed Lenin's ruthless readiness to attack party members and question their loyalties and political integrity if that suited his partisan politics. The episode occurred after Boris Ivanovich's experiences with Stalin and Seregin and on top of mounting suspicions of the police connections of Malinovskii[47] and other Bolsheviks in St. Petersburg. Finally there was the question of censorship which the Mensheviks felt was hitting their paper harder than the Bolshevik *Pravda.* A highly provocative article, virtually a call for an armed uprising, passed the censorship in *Pravda* while *Luch* was confiscated for far milder statements.[48] Possibly, even probably, the Bolsheviks were simply bribing the censor. The business manager of *Luch*, Liubov N. Radchenko, did not have the money and furthermore, as Boris Ivanovich put it, she had never been capable of taking or giving a bribe. Profoundly alien to the Mensheviks was the shadowy world in which one had to wheel and deal with corrupt government officials, not to speak of Okhrana agents, and in which money obtained abroad or at home from undisclosed sources–perhaps by extortion, marriage of convenience, or "expropriation" with murder–was used to further the revolutionary cause. The fact was that the Mensheviks neither knew nor wanted to learn how to operate in such a world. There was, however, a growing feeling among them, shared at the time by Boris Ivanovich, that in one way or another the Okhrana was favoring the Bolsheviks.[49]

It should be stressed, however, that Boris Ivanovich by no means equated Lenin with Stalin. Of course, he disagreed with Lenin politically, condemned his tactics, and disliked many of the people with whom he allied himself. In 1917 he advocated a hard line against Lenin and even had a sharp disagreement with Martov on this issue.[50] However, Lenin possessed qualities which Boris Ivanovich appreciated and admired and which he would have liked to see in Menshevik leaders. One such quality was total devotion to the cause of revolution. It should be remembered that from his late teens until the age of thirty Boris Ivanovich was a full time professional revolutionary, and though he was not as demanding or inflexible as Lenin in requiring every party member to live only for the revolution, it pained him to see how in the post-1905 era the ranks of the professional revolutionaries began to thin rapidly, especially among the Mensheviks. Everyone was preoccupied with his own affairs he recalled; revolutionaries were talking about such things as planning marriage and a family, about getting out of the revolutionary movement–temporarily, they claimed–in order to finish school and find a job. Even among the more educated and intelligent workers, precisely those who were most needed in the movement, there was a tendency to desert the ranks of the proletariat, to take up teaching or some other white-collar job in order to achieve a more promising personal career and life. The intellectuals within the party, too, often turned to more lucrative types of writing and other intellectual pursuits not directly related to the revolutionary movement.[51]

Boris Ivanovich also admired Lenin as a good *khoziain* or party manager. With the exception of V. N. Krokhmal, Boris Ivanovich felt that among the Mensheviks there was no good *Iskra* type of organizer. The Mensheviks were more in the tradition of *Rabochee delo,* that is, they knew how to start a movement but not how to weld together the kind of organization that gave the party strength in underground conditions. Boris Ivanovich often wistfully reminisced about how skillfully Lenin generated loyalties by showing, in little things, that he cared for and remembered the services of party activists. For instance, Krupskaia would write a letter to an exile to which Lenin would add a short note, thus forging a lasting bond between the exile and the party leader who remembered him. Nobody ever received such notes from Martov or Dan.[52]

Finally, Boris Ivanovich contrasted Lenin's skill and perseverance in wooing the masses with the Mensheviks' poor record on this score. Talented and sophisticated as the Menshevik writers were, they often failed in the narrower publicistic sense because of a tendency to broaden and generalize issues when a narrower and more specific focus would have been more easily understood by the masses.

The Mensheviks were no better at oral propaganda, at least not in 1917. Boris Ivanovich cited the example of Tsereteli who soon after the February Revolution commanded enormous prestige among the masses, but did not succeed in putting it to use or maintaining it, to a large extent because during the long and decisive spring and summer months he went no more than two or three times into the workers' neighborhoods to explain his policies and seek support for them. The same was true of other Menshevik leaders, but, as Boris Ivanovich explained, it was not simply because of lack of time or, as in the case of Tsereteli, ill health. The underlying reason was that the masses were beginning to move spontaneously in a direction which the Mensheviks considered catastrophic. To flatter them demagogically in order to win their support and thus gain power, but then to turn against them, was unthinkable to the Mensheviks. To oppose the masses (openly and frontally), and thus perhaps keep company with all kinds of non-socialists or even anti-socialists, was, however, an equally unpalatable alternative. So the field for propagandizing the masses was left, by default, largely to the Bolsheviks.

THE REVOLUTION AND NICOLAEVSKY'S EXPULSION FROM RUSSIA

When war came in 1914 Boris Ivanovich was promptly arrested and exiled to Siberia to a distant village on the Angara. He settled fairly comfortably in a peasant's house with one room serving as a bedroom and another as a study. He was soon able to supplement his government allowance by writing historical articles on the basis of materials he had gathered during his previous exile in Arkhangelsk *guberniia* which had been lying around unused while he was actively engaged in revolutionary activities. Subscriptions to all the important legal party periodicals and newspapers, ample correspondence, and occasional trips for talks with other exiles were enough to keep him abreast of political developments, so that when he emerged a free man on the first news of the overthrow of the tsarist government he was well versed in the political trends of the day and counted himself among the so-called Irkutsk Zimmerwaldists led by Tsereteli and Dan.

Boris Ivanovich believed that his group's position was based on a genuine Marxist analysis of the concrete historical situation and the choice of the lesser evil. Thus while Martov's Internationalists considered all the western powers equally imperialistic, the Irkutsk Zimmerwaldists saw France and England as essentially democratic countries, even though deviating from democratic positions in many respects, and Germany as an essentially imperialistic power. Accordingly, the group dispatched a telegram to Martov (Boris Ivanovich was one of its signers) urging him not to travel to Russia from Switzerland by way of Germany, which greatly irritated Martov.

Boris Ivanovich settled in Petrograd in an apartment with Dan and his wife Lidia Osipovna (Martov's sister), and Martov himself. Thus he had the opportunity of hearing the top Menshevik leaders discuss the issues of the day and of participating in these discussions himself. His main job was serving as a member of *Rabochaia gazeta's* editorial board. Politically he wished to see the Mensheviks act much more energetically. He wanted a strong and well advertised move for peace—not a separate peace but a general settlement—and was dismayed to see that when Tsereteli finally did make the unspectacular move of sending Aksel'rod abroad on a peace mission it hardly received any notice in the papers. On the question of government, he favored full participation by the Mensheviks.

Of course, Boris Ivanovich was in many ways as disoriented and at a loss about what to do throughout 1917 as most people both within and outside of the Menshevik ranks. However, he did recall with some bitterness his disappointment at the lack of leadership, the mood of drift and disorganization, which characterized the Menshevik party during those days. "Martov had no line" he was to repeat. When it came to criticizing his opponents, or giving a sophisticated analysis of their behavior, Martov excelled; but when pressed for an alternative, a clear and precise statement of what should be done, he faltered. "Martov was not a man for big decisions," especially under pressure, Boris Ivanovich emphasized. The tragedy of Menshevism in 1917, Boris Ivanovich believed, lay in its refusal to take power because of the fear that it might be necessary to use that power against the workers. Since the proletariat was wrong—it was heading down the road towards *pugachevshchina*—the Mensheviks could not ally with it, but neither could they desert it.

Boris Ivanovich's last great hope was the Constituent Assembly. He believed it to be vested with such prestige and self-evident authority that the masses would naturally rally to it and the Bolsheviks would not dare touch it. This hope faded quickly but by that time Boris Ivanovich had already become less involved in politics. During the August Party Congress, he became so disgusted with the inability of his fellow Mensheviks to set forth a clear new policy and put some energy behind it that he turned his primary attention to organizing archives;[53] this led to a collaboration with Riazanov which was to last almost fourteen years. During the next two years Boris Ivanovich traveled widely through Russia—twice to the Caucasus and once as far as Vladivostok—gathering archives for the Academy and performing also various missions for the party.

On February 21, 1921, he was arrested by the Cheka. His political and scholarly career on Russian soil came to an end when after a difficult year in jail marked by a hunger strike, he was expelled from Russia early in 1922. Ten years later he was deprived by decree of his Soviet citizenship. Still, until 1931 he continued to work and write from Berlin for the Marx-Engels Institute in Moscow. With Riazanov's arrest this last official tie with the Soviet Union was broken.

However, all Boris Ivanovich's activities as well as his writings during his thirty-five years in emigration—in Germany, France, and the United States—cannot be understood unless we remember that he never became a *former* Menshevik—never simply an immigrant, never even an American citizen—but always remained a *political* emigre conscious of the responsibility he bore towards his native country.[54]

The Austrian Marxist Friedrich Adler believed that "everybody has an *a priori* of his political consciousness" and that it is essential to realize "which convictions are so deeply rooted in us that they are no longer subject to discussion."

> These deepest convictions can be strengthened by experience and scientific understanding, but they spring from a pre-scientific understanding. They are, in the words of the psychologist Jung, a religious experience—religion being here understood in its broadest sense of faith in contrast to scientific understanding. . . . In my life, socialism was such a *religious experience* long before I came to know and understand its scientific doctrine.[55]

Speaking of his early home influence Boris Ivanovich emphasized that it consisted of a certain elemental humanitarianism—a sympathy for the broad masses *(narodoliubie)* and a love of freedom *(svobodoliubie)*. Whether innate or imbued at home prior to the awakening of the real capacity to understand and judge, these two sentiments, *narodoliubie* and *svobodoliubie*, were undoubtedly the *a priori* of Boris Ivanovich's political consciousness. If he later turned to Marxism it was because he found in it a rational explanation, an intellectual foundation for what he instinctively already knew—for what he believed in before he knew. And when he switched from Bolshevism to Menshevism it was not so much because he discovered new truths as because he found himself in conflict with the original, *a priori* truths. Menshevism, too, was not to him a house of truths. If the house did not fit his truths he unceremoniously shaped and reshaped it until it did.

In emotional moments, Boris Ivanovich could sometimes so startle his friends with a gesture that they would wonder whether what they thought was really he was not merely a shell under which some original, pre-political self, going back to the Belebei days, still persisted. Indeed, perhaps all political life and theory was to him merely an outward scaffolding, a crutch practical or intellectual, beyond and above which loomed the essence, his pre-political commitment to the elemental humanitarianism of *narodoliubie* and *svobodoliubie.*

PHILIP E. MOSELY

Boris Nicolaevsky: The American Years

The year 1940 marked a new turning point in the turbulent life of Boris Nicolaevsky, as it did in the lives of millions of people and entire nations. While other democratic leaders were beginning their first or second exile, many Russian political exiles, among them Boris Ivanovich, sought a new refuge for the third time. As Hitler's still advancing power overwhelmed the defenses of France and flooded onward to the Pyrenees, it swept along in its undertow the wreckage of many hopes; it also threatened the lives of numerous devoted democrats and socialists from many European countries, including Russia. Through its prompt action, and through its political influence and financial support, the American labor movement literally rescued from annihilation hundreds of political and intellectual exiles and helped many of them find their footing once more, this time in America. An adequate description of this rescue action still awaits the pen of an historian.

The actions of Boris Ivanovich in 1940, like so many before and after, expressed values that lay deep within him. Repeatedly he postponed leaving France while he worked day and night, using his early training in conspiratorial methods and moving from one hide-out to another, both to promote the exodus of other political refugees and to place in safekeeping the tremendous and unique collections that he had accumulated in the previous three decades. Many Russian, German, Czech and Austrian socialists were persuaded by Nicolaevsky to escape from Hitler's Europe via Marseilles or Lisbon; many others refused to heed his warnings, and among these many perished.

Nicolaevsky's other aim was to place in secret safekeeping the vast collections he had assembled on the Russian revolutionary movements, the European socialist parties, and the Second and Third Internationals. Major sections of them were concealed in attics, one part even in a chicken coop. Characteristically, Anna Mikhailovna Bourguina, later Mrs. Nicolaevsky, risked her own life by remaining behind in occupied France in order to safeguard the collections. Unfortunately, the major part of Nicolaevsky's library was discovered by agents of the Alfred Rosenberg Office and transferred to the notorious Institute on Judaism and Bolshevism, at Frankfurt-on-Main. There, in the confusion at the end of the war, this treasure-house was again uncovered, this time by Soviet agents who ranged throughout occupied

Germany in search of captured Soviet "booty." Because most of the materials were in Russian, a major part of the collection was reportedly turned over to Soviet officers by an American lieutenant and removed promptly to the Soviet Union.

Once in New York, Boris Ivanovich again resumed, with his youthful hope and unflagging energy, the task of systematic accumulation of historical materials, and was also able, once the war was over, to retrieve and transfer to New York nearly all the remaining collections he had been forced to leave behind in 1940.

It is impossible to think of Boris Ivanovich, in Berlin, Paris, or New York, except surrounded by his enormous collection of books, journals, newspapers, pamphlets, diaries, letters, handwritten memoirs, and manuscripts. The setting has been described vividly by the late Louis Fischer.

> One would sit in his two-room [actually four-room] apartment near Columbia University, the walls covered, floor to ceiling, with tightly packed shelves of ancient and new Soviet publications. The overflow was stacked on chairs and desks or on the floor. Suddenly he would mention an event, hoist his heavy frame and insert an arm behind a row of volumes, rummage for a moment, and bring out, for instance, a pamphlet, yellow with age, published in Russian in Geneva in 1887, the work of Lenin's executed brother, Alexander, or some equally antiquarian treasure elsewhere unobtainable.[1]

One of the strongest memories of many dozens of American and other scholars, who either met or worked with Boris Ivanovich, is his unstinted sharing of his experiences, his deep and intricate knowledge of people and events, and his wide-ranging and unique collections. Out of habit Boris Ivanovich was reserved toward each newcomer, but once he placed his trust in him, he gave generously of his time and knowledge.

The work of collecting never ceased, right to his sudden demise on February 2, 1966. Writing at high speed on his Russian typewriter, Nicolaevsky maintained an extensive correspondence with survivors of the many parties and groups of the Russian revolutionary movement. With the devoted assistance of Anna Mikhailovna, he developed a system of identifying and locating materials that was clear to them, if to no one else. A large and valuable part of the books and pamphlets, comprising between 10,000 and 12,000 titles, was acquired in 1955 by the Indiana University Library. The Indiana Nicolaevsky Collection includes many periodicals published before 1917 by revolutionary groups outside Russia, clandestine revolutionary journals published in Russia, legal but scarce left-wing publications, and a large number of Russian publications of the post-1917 emigration. Individual items of special interest include two supplements to the famous *Kolokol* of Alexander Herzen, rare issues of *Chernyi peredel,* and a wealth of materials relating to the pre-1914 International Socialist Congresses and Conferences.[2]

The remaining and far more extensive Nicolaevsky collection was acquired in 1964 by the Hoover Institution on War, Revolution and Peace, at Stanford University, which thus further strengthened the position it had achieved in the 1920s as the leading archives of Russian history outside Russia (and, since World War II, as a major library and research and publications center on the history and politics of all nations). At that time Boris Ivanovich, now installed as curator of the Nicolaevsky Collection, established a new home, not far from the Hoover Institution, and, with Anna Mikhailovna's assistance, continued his work of collecting, systematizing, annotating and, in too small measure, making use of these rich materials for his own research projects. Since his death Anna Mikhailovna has continued the work of indexing and annotating the Nicolaevsky Collection and has also performed a similar service for Nicolaevsky's personal archives, which include his voluminous correspondence and memoranda.

By instinct a man of action as well as the leading historian of the Russian revolutionary movement, after 1940 Boris Ivanovich continued both interests from his new base in New York. During the war years, when his new host-country, the United States, relied on Soviet military cooperation to defeat Hitler and hoped that the victorious powers could work together to build a peaceful and cooperative postwar order, a guest and a refugee such as Nicolaevsky could only speak in quiet tones to remind people of some of the essential features of Soviet totalitarianism; the depth of his knowledge was impressive even to people who preferred to listen to their own wishful thinking.

With the refounding of the *Sotsialisticheskii vestnik (Socialist Courier)* in New York (1940), Nicolaevsky and other recently arrived socialist refugees regained and enlarged a small but select audience, and Boris Ivanovich began with increasing frequency to publish his articles and reviews in English translation as well. His first book in English, *Aseff; the Spy, Russian Terrorist and Police Stool,* published in 1934, had created for him, in advance of his arrival in America, a reputation as an historian of the Russian Revolution, and now his interpretations of Soviet events and prospects also came gradually to be received with great respect.

The year 1947 saw a major contribution by Nicolaevsky to the study of one of the grimmest aspects of Soviet life. The publication of *Forced Labor in Soviet Russia,* by David J. Dallin and Boris I. Nicolaevsky, as Brooks Atkinson wrote (*New York Times Book Review,* Aug. 31, 1947), ". . . reconstructed a somber and ominous portrait of daily life inside a police state." Careful collecting and checking of Soviet sources, many previously overlooked or ignored by analysts, was supplemented by the first-hand accounts of a growing number of new Soviet non-returners and refugees, many of whom had barely survived their experiences in Soviet prisons and concentration camps. Much of what Dallin and Nicolaevsky brought together in 1947 in systematic analysis was dramatically confirmed in Khrushchev's secret speech of February, 1956, and since then, in a wide range of Soviet autobiographies and novels.

In the postwar years Nicolaevsky resumed his efforts to define democratic socialism as an alternative to Bolshevism in Russian political life. He remained in active consultation with the principal groups among the much-divided Mensheviks, whose center had been moved to New York in 1940. His active sympathy and intellectual support went to those party leaders who emphasized the democratic goals within democratic socialism, and he had scant patience for those who sought a reconciliation with the Communists, and, in some cases, advocated a return to Russia.

In the late 1940s Nicolaevsky's political "action" seems to have followed three main channels. One of them was the familiar one of uniting the Mensheviks and the Socialist Revolutionaries in exile into a single democratic force. True to his village origins, and deeply sympathetic to the long-suffering peasantry, Boris Ivanovich had long regarded the antagonism between Socialist Revolutionaries (SRs) and Mensheviks as damaging to both. In exile he worked constantly to heal the partisan wounds of past battles and promoted good personal and intellectual relations among the various groups of exiled revolutionaries in their latter years.

A second line of action arose from the postwar influx of new Soviet refugees into the West, and from Nicolaevsky's keen interest in and sympathy for them. After the end of World War II, and especially after the Allied military authorities had finally abandoned their policy of promoting and even compelling the return of ex-Soviet "displaced persons" to the Soviet Union, a large number of ex-Soviet citizens sought and found refuge in the West. Nicolaevsky was keenly interested in understanding this new generation of Russians, and especially of younger Russian intellectuals. After all, these were part of "the people" for whose sake several generations of revolutionaries had fought and suffered. But who and what manner of men were these ex-Soviet "sons," and would they even acknowledge aging exile democrats and socialists as "kin" in any meaningful degree? To Boris Ivanovich, the new arrivals also brought reinforcements–first-hand knowledge of Stalinist Russia, and a deep repugnance for some aspects of Soviet life blended with an unconscious set of assumptions and attitudes deeply ingrained in their lives. Who knew what new talents they might bring to replenish the thinning ranks of Russians in exile? And would they, being from ten to thirty years younger than the post-1917 exiles, take up the political struggle against Stalinism outside Russia?

Many, perhaps most, of the exiled intellectuals of the post-1917 emigration found it difficult to enter into intellectual and human communication with the wave of new arrivals. The new refugees' experiences in growing up under Soviet rule had made them very different people, often untutored in intellectual matters, often greedy for a material security they had never known, often uncouth in language and manner. Unlike most exiles of his generation, Boris Ivanovich had kept a "feel" for the "new Soviet man," and he was able, far more than most of his own generation, to understand and help many talented individuals find a new footing in a strange country.

If he was disappointed or disillusioned in his hopes for recruiting new political forces in exile, somehow combining the idealism and deep historical memory of the older exiles with the practical energy of the new arrivals, he had too much sense of the varieties of human experience to bemoan this failure.

Finally, as part of the reaction, after 1948, to the mounting alarms of East-West tension, Nicolaevsky threw his energies into the creation of a coalition of Russian political forces in exile, League for the Struggle for the People's Freedom, which he hoped would form a common front embracing liberals to socialists, in opposition to Soviet totalitarianism. Again, the fissiparous effects of exile politics led to early disillusionment, and Boris Ivanovich again vowed to himself and his friends that he would give up squandering his time on "politics" and would devote his principal efforts to completing several of his projects of historical research.

One of Nicolaevsky's favorite projects was a documentary and analytical history of the First International. In one of his expansive moods he would draw from the shelf any one of several enormous folders, pointing lovingly to previously unknown and still unpublished letters, diaries, draft memoranda and resolutions, and would explain how this and that of his materials would turn upside down many of the accepted notions of historians. Yet, there were always a few more sources that must be brought to light, perhaps copied from obscure party newspapers or extracted from some family archive, before he could be sure of his ground with respect to this or that detail. It was useless to argue with Boris Ivanovich that, even as they stood, slightly short of perfection, it would be a great service to historians, and a monument to two decades of his labors, to publish this monumental study in its present state.

In 1955 Boris Ivanovich, assisted by Anna Mikhailovna, undertook another of his monumental documentary histories, this time with support from the Research Program on the History of the CPSU. He had earlier undertaken a minute restudy of the evolution of Bolshevism from the revolutionary ebb of 1907-1908 to the second founding, this time definitive, of Lenin's "party of a new type." To him, the final schism of Russian Social Democracy, in 1912, was far more significant for the history of Russia and the world than the much-studied split in 1903 between Bolsheviks and Mensheviks. Building on his own collection of original and largely unpublished sources, and supplementing them with a truly youthful zeal in searching out still other materials and questioning the few survivors in minute detail, Nicolaevsky brought together six manuscript volumes of documents on the development of the Leninist party, 1907-12, and provided them with extensive commentaries. Scholars who have had the privilege of making use of this collection and discussing its findings with Boris Ivanovich have given it the highest praise and urged strongly that it be published, even though its compiler insisted that he needed still more time and more materials before he could let it out of his hands. Hopefully, it will some day see the light of day through the devoted ministrations of Anna Mikhailovna.

A third project to which Nicolaevsky made innumerable and invaluable contributions was the Research Program on the History of Menshevism, under the direction of Professor Leopold Haimson. Through his personal encouragement to present and former Mensheviks to make their political and personal records available and to write their memoirs in detail, and through his thoughtful advice and criticism to the research workers, Boris Ivanovich made a very large investment in the success of the entire project. Anna Bourguina, with assistance from him, prepared an authoritative bibliography of Menshevism, published by the Hoover Institution.[3]

These are only three examples of the historical enterprises to which Boris Ivanovich devoted many years and much of his intellectual energy. Torn between history and political action; responding with youthful zest and a warm heart to new events, especially if they affected his beloved Russia and its prospects; delighting in long and deeply informative discussions of both historical and current events; responding to new books and constantly writing reviews and articles; answering the queries of scholars, both established and novice, sometimes in greater detail than they could fully assimilate; sustained by a few intimate and lifelong friendships, Boris Ivanovich enjoyed all his manifold activities, even though he was the first to say that he must learn to shun distractions and get on with completing one or several of his documentary histories.

In the end, despairing of badgering Boris Ivanovich to bring his own major studies to completion, a group of friends did persuade him to allow them to select, with his approval, a number of his most important essays. Thus, his *Power and the Soviet Elite*[4] saw the light of day in November, 1965, in English, just three months before his unexpected death. Obviously, this final collection of essays need not be described here, in a volume dedicated to the memory of Boris Ivanovich, for *Power and the Soviet Elite* provides its own recommendation and its own commemoration of the author. It illustrates the importance, in attempting to interpret and even predict the unfolding of Soviet policy and the struggle for power, of turning the spotlight of analysis alternatively to the fundamental factors that shape the political, social and psychological environment and to outwardly minor changes in personnel, assignments and policies, which may indicate whither the all-powerful party elite is turning the massive and cumbersome machine through which it rules.

The gifts Boris Ivanovich left his friends and even to many who did not know him were those of character and integrity, of love of freedom, even more than the studies he completed. Through his active concern for the strength of the democratic tradition in the world and through his generous sharing of his wealth of historic experiences and insights, Boris Ivanovich repaid the country of his final quarter-century many times over for the haven it had provided him in a time of mortal danger to freedom and humane values.

MARC RAEFF

Russian Youth on the Eve of Romanticism: Andrei I. Turgenev and His Circle

> Ibo ne redko v izobrazheniiakh umershago naidesh cherty v zhivykh eshche sushchago. [For often you will find in the representation of a dead person the traits of the living.] A. Radishchev, *Zhitie Fedora Vasilevicha Ushakova.*

The accession of Alexander I not only overlapped very nearly with the beginning of a new century, it also coincided with the coming of age of a new generation in Russia's intellectual life. The new youth differed more sharply than is usually the case from the ways and traditions of their parents. Within the closed framework of seminal and dynamic small groups (or secret organizations), they gave currency and first rank importance to those cultural and ideological elements which, as a rule, are contrasted to the rationalism of the Enlightenment and associated with Romanticism. In the following pages we shall try to come to grips with this phenomenon with the help of the evidence provided by the activities and ideas of Andrei Ivanovich Turgenev and the circle of his close friends in the *Druzheskoe literaturnoe obshchestvo* (Friendly Literary Society).[1]

Andrei Turgenev's life was extremely short–he died suddenly from a chill and fever at the age of twenty-two–and in fact quite unremarkable, its outward events differing little from the existence of other young members of the Russian nobility. He was exceptional, however, in his discerning literary taste, his genuine (albeit minor) poetic talent, and the intensity of his friendships. For these reasons his brief existence throws much light on the social and cultural dimensions of the emotional and intellectual development of educated Russians at the dawn of the nineteenth century.[2]

The research for this article was carried out under the auspices of the USSR Academy of Sciences–American Council of Learned Societies scholarly exchange program, and with the additional support of the American Philosophical Society. I wish to thank the staff and officers of these organizations, as well as the librarians of the Institute for the History of Russian Literature *(Pushkinskii Dom),* for their kind and efficient help. Because of the delay in publication, a somewhat different version of this study has appeared in French in *Cahiers du Monde russe et soviétique,* 8, No. 4 (1967), pp. 560-86.

Turgenev was born in 1781 to Ivan Petrovich Turgenev, a friend and associate of N. Novikov, V. Lopukhin, and other prominent freemasons and mystics in the reign of Catherine II. The elder Turgenev had had an ordinary, lustreless career in the military and civil services.[3] In 1792, in connection with Catherine's closing of the masonic lodges and persecution of their leaders, he was exiled to his estate. In 1796 Paul I allowed him to return to Moscow where he became Director of the University. Thus, part of Andrei Turgenev's formative years was spent on the family estate near Simbirsk, in close contact with and under the supervision of his father, a situation that was far from typical of the eighteenth century pattern of noble upbringing. He later entered the University of Moscow (1799), where he found himself close to such major figures of Russia's cultural life as the writers Karamzin, Dmitriev, and Izmailov. After a few years' study at the University Andrei entered state service in the College of Foreign Affairs, and "worked" first at the College's archives in Moscow. In 1801 he became a translator and junior secretary at the College's chancellery in St. Petersburg. He served as courier to Vienna where he spent several months in the winter of 1802-1803. He died in St. Petersburg in early spring, 1803, soon after returning from his Viennese mission. Even if allowance is made for the earlier maturation of young people a century and a half ago, the short life of Andrei Turgenev could hardly have been more than a token of what he might have done and become. To his friends and contemporaries his short existence seemed exemplary of their own aspirations and dreams, and thus for young Muscovites he became both symbol and legend of the unfulfilled promise of the first decade of the nineteenth century. Hence, it is important to consider the details of his emotional and intellectual development. Fortunately we are in a position to do this, since his papers—diaries, drafts, letters—have been largely preserved.[4]

In fashion characteristic of a member of the educated nobility, Andrei Turgenev was raised with the conviction that he had a task to perform on earth. To this end he received a careful and well-supervised western education, first at home, then at the Noblemen's Pension, and later at the University of Moscow. More important still was his own feeling that his life had to be meaningful, by assisting others to rise to a higher moral and cultural level. This consciousness of a duty to lead a socially useful active life went hand in hand with an equally strong sense of personal accomplishment. Realizing that his interests and ability lay in the realm of literature, he wanted to make his contribution as writer, critic, and poet.[5] This striving, the ambition to leave a mark on contemporaries and posterity, was perhaps the paramount avowed concern of all the young men around him.[6]

What were the driving forces behind this attitude? The old-fashioned orientation toward state service helped create the psychological and mental climate in which the educated and progressive nobility grew up in the eighteenth century. The Turgenev family stressed, as did families of nobility, social utility as the goal of education.[7] The children's readings and first writing exercises were full of didactic tirades on duty and work, on the obligation to devote one's life to the service of others,[8] and particularly on the ethical values implicit in these precepts. Injustice, misery, and evil caused by man to man were not only to be condemned completely but also to be redressed through charity and philanthropy. Horror seized Andrei Turgenev at the sight of brutality and abuse of authority. How much he would have liked to have helped remedy the evil, console the afflicted and the wronged! But awareness of moral and physical evil seemed to paralyze his energies and he could only express sympathy in the form of literary reminiscences.[9]

At the same time Andrei Turgenev's philanthropic attitude and moral concern involved a curious paradox; his commitment to serve was not only an end of the *vita activa,* it was also an instrument of the *vita contemplativa.* Indeed, like the freemasons of his father's generation, Andrei believed that it was his duty to give maximum development to his inner moral sense. Thus, the improvement of each individual's mind and soul demanded constant dedicated effort. Such purpose, however, implies quite a strong streak of selfishness. At the least clash with an outer barrier, the cultivation of the "inner garden" could easily turn into the cultivation of one's own garden *tout court,* an escape from personal sacrifice and a withdrawal into the private sphere. Andrei Turgenev and his friends asserted that to be merely a good *pater familias* also meant to be a good citizen and a worthy individual.[10] To be sure, the warm family atmosphere prevailing in the Turgenev household was an inspiration. But withdrawal into private family happiness meant giving up striving and accepting oneself and one's present condition. But could one? Did one even know oneself? Fulfillment of the ideal set forth by Andrei's educated young friends meant finding the person whom one was sure of and with whom one could contentedly share one's condition. This required a decision to cease the pursuit of unfulfilled expectations and to accept the daily drudgery of "small deeds" and responsibility. For such an act of will Andrei Turgenev lacked courage.[11] He feared that present actuality was but a mirage of what was possible; would not the realization of the possible be foreclosed if the present were seriously and fully accepted? He was not unaware of the weakness of character that this hesitation implied, but his complaints and regrets about it were self-pitying and not devoid of a touch of narcissism. In a sense Turgenev was escaping the finality of the present and fleeing into the safety of the "open" future. This was quite an understandable reaction, since his moral premise was the selfish enhancement of his own spiritual and moral being, without recourse to any transcendental values or hierarchies. Hence his hesitations, the alternations of desires and expectations, and the fear of fulfillment.[12] The result was a romantic stance of unremitting grief about lost possibilities, the regret of past time, and the ever recurring accent on future hope.[13]

The history of Andrei Turgenev's one love, Catherine Sokovnin, is characteristically revealing in this respect. It was a rather banal story of infatuation and sentimental correspondence, ending in his withdrawal. It would not deserve particular mention were it not for the insight it provides into his character. The romantic involvement, quite short lived, may be told in a few words:[14] Andrei Turgenev met the sisters Sokovnin at a theater party in the Noblemen's Pension. His younger brother Alexander was in love with one of the sisters, Anna Mikhailovna, and at first Andrei fell in love with her too. In the beginning he felt a little guilty vis-à-vis his brother, but then consoled himself with the hope for a kind of *ménage à trois.* But finally, after some hesitation, he turned his attention to another sister, Catherine. The involvement grew deeper, although it always was hesitant and filled with much sentimental daydreaming and regret, spiced with appropriate reminiscences of *La Nouvelle Héloise* and *Werther.* When Andrei left for St. Petersburg the connection continued by mail. At this point Catherine openly declared her love for Andrei and pledged to be his alone. Catherine's avowal frightened him; he trembled for his liberty and for the future of his literary hopes and career. He withdrew, albeit hesitatingly and without breaking the relationship; but when he left for Vienna, his letters became rare and finally stopped altogether.

In letters to his brother Alexander and his friend Andrei S. Kaisarov, both in Goettingen, he was full of regrets, sentimental *épanchements,* and self-justificatory tirades.[15] The next time we hear of his amours, it is a passing affair in Vienna, but this was a purely physical involvement which left his emotions free and unaffected.[16]

In view of Turgenev's pretensions at moral elevation and purity, the selfishness of the rationalizations that he proffers to justify his shying away from genuine personal commitment is revealing. He makes two points which deserve brief mention. He says that he is not worthy of Catherine Sokovnin's pure, devoted, self-abnegating love. Objectively, of course, he was not; but the point is that it was not only an excuse for escaping but an expression of his genuine conviction that he was spiritually and intellectually still incomplete, that he had achieved nothing to give him a sense of genuine identity; this was the course of the malaise experienced by Andrei Turgenev and his generation. The other point emphasized by Turgenev in the letters to his friends is the fear of losing his liberty. To be sure, it is a fear common among men, especially those still close to adolescence, when faced with the finality that the marriage commitment (church sanctioned, of course) entails. But it is also the fear of jeopardizing one's ability to strike out in new directions, to be creative, and actively to pursue the ideal of the *vita contemplativa.* In this sense the fear of losing one's liberty is but another aspect of the feeling of not yet having found one's identity. The struggle for identity was hard on Andrei Turgenev's generation and personal emotions were made to pay the price.

Why was this search for identity, especially in the intellectual and spiritual realms, so difficult? Why did it present special problems to the young men in Moscow around 1800? This question leads us to ask also why did Andrei Turgenev and his friends feel so different or "alienated" from their elders. In view of the fact that Andrei Turgenev and his circle shared the characteristic traits of the early *Sturm und Drang* forms of Romanticism, we may further ask why the acute sense of a break with the older generation and the search for identity were such powerful forces in this Russian generation (as they had been in its German prototypes personified by Schiller's dramatic heroes)?

It seems to us that the answer is to be sought in a fundamental contradiction in the system of values and ideas of the generation of Andrei Turgenev's parents.[17] By the last quarter of the eighteenth century, educated Russians had fully assimilated the basic notions of Enlightenment thought. They had acquired a secular view of progress, especially with respect to the economic, social, and cultural welfare of the nation. They had accepted and internalized the Petrine belief that the goals and norms of the state took precedence over all, and that, by virtue of their leadership function, the monarch and the government brought glory and modernity to Russia. They had also developed a virtually "Protestant" bourgeois sense of duty and service to society. In other words, the transcendental values and goals of medieval society had given way to secular and rational interests and concerns. The Russian Church, captive of the state since the establishment of the Holy Synod, had declined as a source of moral authority, inspiration, and spiritual guidance and had shriveled to the mere policing of ritual conformity. It is true that these aspects of secularism were accompanied by a revival of personal religious life and a genuine concern for the moral and spiritual welfare of the people. It was "philanthropy" (but not Christian charity!) in the best meaning of the word that was associated with the activities of Novikov. But the interesting thing about philanthropy, whatever its spiritual and religious fount, is that it aims at the improvement of the condition of man in *this* world, not at preparing his salvation in the hereafter. In short, the emphasis is on the material and intellectual progress of the individual, in terms of rational judgment, rather than on a transcendental system of values justified *sub specie aeternitatis* with reference to the historical drama of salvation. It was this orientation that found repeated expression in the didactic and juvenile literature which Andrei Turgenev and his friends read and absorbed in their childhood.[18]

At the same time, and in conflict with this secular, rational and individualistic outlook, the traditional insistence on complete submission and obedience to authority—the monarch and parents—was not abandoned. Both the ruler and the family-head were endowed with a God-given aura of authority, borrowed heavily from Lutheran precepts and behavior, that made their orders and directives the object of unquestionable obedience.[19] What had been easy to accept in a traditional society became a source of unresolved conflicts in values in a rationalistic and welfare-oriented civilization. If the goals of human activity were to be based on nothing but rational and utilitarian considerations, why then insist on unquestioned obedience not even justified by a transcendental view of history and society? As long as the ruler (or parent) fulfilled a visible function of leadership in the country's (or family's) cultural progress and modernization, his authority could be accepted. But by the end of the eighteenth century this ceased to be the case.[20]

Particularly striking to Andrei Turgenev's generation was the fact that most of their elders served only *pro forma* and did little, if anything, to justify the obedience that they demanded.[21] It is little wonder that Turgenev and his friends felt that they were being asked to act contrary to the social and intellectual values of their culture when unquestioned submission to authority was demanded of them.

The value conflict helped to shape the young generation's relationship to their parents and to their service obligations. Andrei Turgenev, like all young nobles of his day, entered state service as a matter of course. But it did not take much experience to realize how insignificant his service obligations were. It is clear from many remarks scattered throughout his papers that his official work was neither absorbing nor meaningful. The young men's knowledge and talents, in languages for example, were not put to good use. It was merely a way to pass time; obviously the important tasks were performed either by experienced clerks or a very few high dignitaries. In some ways the offices to which they were attached served as a kind of "post-graduate" educational institution.[22]

In the literature on Andrei Turgenev and his brothers much stress is laid on the warm and genuinely good atmosphere that prevailed in their family. Credit for this is usually given to the mildness and kindness of their father, Ivan Petrovich, to his genuinely humane interest in his children as well as to his religious and philanthropic concerns. From all the evidence, Ivan Petrovich was indeed a benevolent, kind, affectionate man whose sincere love for his children (and for mankind in general) cannot be doubted. Yet this same man was a serf owner, who apparently allowed his wife and stewards to treat the domestics harshly, and who also constantly preached complete submission and obedience, even to evil. In part this reflected his timidity, for he was not a courageous or forceful individual and did all he could to avoid clashes with authority. When he did get into trouble with Catherine II for his masonic activities, he not only submitted to his fate but plaintively tried to deny any responsibility for his actions.[23] As Director of the University he was a gentle and understanding but not forceful supervisor; one has the impression that he performed his duties conscientiously, but without much energy or display of initiative.

Not surprisingly, therefore, his son's attitude to him was somewhat mixed. He had learned to obey him and there is little doubt of the genuine feeling he had for his father. Ivan Petrovich returned Andrei's affection in full. Yet Andrei's does not seem to have been an affection based on genuine respect. Andrei felt sorry for his father, he loved him, but he did not identify with him.[24] It is very reminiscent of the relationship which Karl Moor, in Schiller's *Die Räuber,* had to his own father, and not the least reason for the enthusiasm of Andrei Turgenev's generation for Schiller's early works. Perhaps Andrei also saw a good illustration of this unfulfilled yearning for identification with his father in Goethe's poem *Mahomets Gesang* which he tried to translate.[25] We note manifestations of this ambivalence when, in his middle teens, Andrei was faced with the choice of obeying his father or following his inclination to be with his good friend A. S. Kaisarov. He obeyed, but his obedience did not come from within, it was not derived from a felt sense of right or a recognition of his father's moral or intellectual superiority.[26] We see similar instances of ambivalence later in connection with his service and questions of his health and personal future.[27]

Naturally, the mother's personality, too, played an important role in the relationship between a son and his family. As was true in the case of A. Kaisarov (and there are many more examples to be found in this period) the mother was stronger and more domineering than the father. Yet she was barely literate and did not share her husband's and children's cultural interests. She was concerned only about her sons' prospects in service, and the management of the family estate, and she was not easy to please. She was also a person of great temper, strong willed and irascible, which in the context of serfdom easily led to capricious and cruel treatment of servants and serfs. Obedience to such a woman was hard to justify on rational or moral grounds; it could only be a matter of injunction and outward submission.[28] Characteristically, Andrei's letters home sound contrived and formal in their expressions of obedience and respect; they reveal little of the interests which he willingly shared with his friends.

The young men of Andrei's generation, as has been noted earlier, were educated to obey, but not told why; they were also taught to rely on reason, to think in terms of social utility, and to promote their own spiritual growth and intellectual independence. Submission or revolt seemed the only alternatives, the former implying the acceptance of a vegetating life. This was an impossible choice, if only because their service-oriented upbringing had been directed at a constructively active life and career. But for this Russian reality offered little scope; activity in service seemed artificial, useless, unrewarding, and ill-directed. They were forced to escape into literature and intellectualism. All this created an all-pervading feeling of discontent and a sense of futility.[29] They were dreaming of what they could and should accomplish, of what might happen in the future or could have occurred in the past. Hope and regret were the leitmotifs of their existence—and they were forever failing to cope with the present. But identification in terms of a distorted past or a future hoped for meant an identification forever incomplete; they remained perpetual adolescents.

The first overt goal of the friendship that linked Andrei Turgenev and the members of his circle was to help them to further their individual development and become useful to society. Clearly the bonds of friendship were much stronger and tighter than those resting merely on personal sympathy; each partner expected to gain in spiritual stature from the friendship. We also note the extremely heightened emotional tone of these friendships. A friend exists and is chosen, they felt, to make one better, to help in one's moral growth and spiritual development. Quite naturally the friendship, or association, was formed to study together, to discover new mental horizons, to become acquainted with new books and writers, to help each other in drawing out the full meaning of these discoveries.[30]

The emotional quality of their friendship was so strong that it is best described by the French phrase, *amitié amoureuse.* It is unlikely that it had overt homosexual aspects, but we may not be quite certain in view of that generation's great reticence about matters sexual.[31] Naturally, there is an element of unfulfillment—sexually speaking—in this kind of relationship. As we shall have occasion to observe, this feature fits in with the major intellectual and spiritual characteristics of this generation. It was a passionate involvement that required constant presence, or at least daily epistolary contact; it also had to be confirmed and strengthened by tangible evidences which we associate with sentimental girlish crushes.[32] It is also very noteworthy that this kind of friendship imposed an obligation on both partners to be better, to improve morally so as to prove worthy of the affection of the friend. It was a stroke of luck to gain a friend, it created a moral and spiritual debt that could not easily be paid.[33] As a result, the relationship was fraught with tensions, with constant questioning of one's own worthiness. It was in a sense a substitute for the lack of an older object of identification as well as a manifestation of an inadequate sense of identity, of a lack of certitude with respect to one's own worth and role in life.[34] We also detect an urge to remain pure vis-à-vis one's friends, a purity that was interpreted not only in spiritual and moral, but in physical and sexual terms as well, underlining the amorous element and latent homosexuality of the bond. Sexual promiscuity and emotional experiences that lacked purity and ethereal idealism were seen as a betrayal and a sullying of one's friends.[35]

A friend was either someone to look up to, to identify with, or someone for whose sake one had to be particularly good and worthy. This might also explain why goodness, a good heart *(dobryi, dobroe serdtse),* was the most valued trait.[36] It implied the ability to feel for the friend, to be understanding and, what is more, to be forgiving. Hence the interest in small instances of benefaction and charity, the happiness produced by cases of simple and heartfelt piety.[37] It was not so much sentimental admiration for the alleged simple virtues of the people, as had been the case with Karamzin and his imitators, but rather a genuine personal involvement in the fate of specific individuals. To be sure, some amount of sentimental idealization was not lacking, but instead of leading to lachrymose moralizing it provoked an urge to do something about redressing the wrong. Literary models for their standards of judgment were readily available. Schiller's dramas gave their feelings the additional dimension of universality and also supplied the young men with a comprehensive ethical and psychological outlook.[38]

We have seen that the older generation did not provide adequate objects for identification or models for emulation. It was, therefore, the friend and the circle of friends that had to serve as the framework for the process of identification. There was no possibility of breaking away, since it was this youthful generation that had "created" the identity of its members for the remainder of their lives; it is little wonder that there was always a touch of adolescence in the Russian intelligentsia. One left this group and its ethos only at the price of suicide or surrender to the Establishment. The lesson had been made clear by their great literary hero, Karl Moor. In order to be himself, he had to identify with his brigand friends and sacrifice to them his personal love and happiness. As they had "made" him (and he them) he could not turn from them except through death. Sacrifice to friends and friendship became a binding cement, and it is quite easy to see how the fate of those who had left the circle early and young could be interpreted in sacrificial terms. It was not an accident that the source of inspiration and the model to be emulated should have been those who had been torn away from the circle, either through early death, like Andrei Turgenev or N. Stankevich, or through arrest and imprisonment, as was to be the case of later generations.

Not only did friendship play a major part in the personal lives of Russian youth in the 1800s, it was the setting for their literary and cultural activities as well.[39]

In 1801, Andrei Turgenev and his friends A. F. Merzliakov and A. S. Kaisarov, along with Andrei's younger brother Alexander and V. Zhukovskii, who were still pupils at the Noblemen's Pension, decided to organize their own literary circle. Unlike the associations founded by their fathers' generation, their society–*Druzheskoe literaturnoe obshchestvo*–did not have a public purpose. It was a friendly society for the promotion of the literary culture and taste of its members. True, literature was defined broadly and, as we shall see, was considered in its relation to other general topics. Essentially, it was as a study group, based on a cult of friendship, whose members wanted to be better individuals and more worthwhile citizens. To be useful to the fatherland and to be friends, such was their purpose.[40]

The society proved to be shortlived. It met for only about half a year, in the course of which twenty-three papers were read at its sessions.[41] The public impact of its activities at the time was practically nil. But memory of it was profound in the minds of its surviving members and this secured it a seminal place in the intellectual history of nineteenth century Russia. Scholars have tried in recent years to situate the group with reference to the literary factions of the time and to draw ideological implications for its role in the pre-history of the Decembrist movement. But it seems to us that this is stretching the evidence. The speeches read at the society's meetings are rather formalized statements of general ideas for purposes of discussion. Let us examine some of these ideas and their implications for the members of the group, so as to obtain a clearer picture of the mental and emotional climate in which this generation came to maturity.

Quite naturally, the theme of friendship occurred repeatedly in the speeches addressed to the group. In an early speech which he delivered in January, 1801, A. F. Merzliakov (the society's main organizational figure) stressed the role of the bonds of friendship for the moral and intellectual development of each member; he also remarked that thanks to these bonds they could cope with the harsh cold world outside.[42] But, Merzliakov maintained, friendship had a still higher function, namely that of endowing the sciences and arts with an emotional quality, making them reflect the life of the heart. Under the impact of friendship and the emotional side of life, science would no longer be cold pseudo-knowledge but a truth relevant to man. That was also the reason that the friendly society was a good preparation for its members' future public role as true sons of the fatherland. This basic point was repeated by V. Zhukovskii in a later speech.[43] But Zhukovskii also stressed the importance of those qualities of the heart that made a friend more worthwhile to others and to himself. In short, what we noted earlier in Andrei Turgenev's correspondence is now repeated in the group more comprehensively and within a broader context. The primary historical contribution of the friendly society was to have emphasized the intimate connection between the emotional bonds uniting several individuals and their potential public utility. No wonder that Schiller's *An die Freude* was their ever recurring source of inspiration!

The role assigned to emotional involvement and friendship in an individual's progress was closely related to the views of psychology and epistemology held by Turgenev's circle. Mikhail Kaisarov postulated the innate quality of basic moral reactions and values[44] although he admitted that they might become conscious only through man's ability to make comparative and analogical judgments. Thus he departed from eighteenth century Lockean empiricism, even though he accepted the utilitarian teleology of the Enlightenment. This could be further proven, argued his brother Andrei Kaisarov,[45] by recognizing that even misanthropy had at its origin the innate good heart of man. Finally, Alexander Turgenev insisted that the world is the way we look at it.[46] Our predisposition and will, he maintained, form our perception and experiences, Zhukovskii echoed these beliefs by saying that our happiness and unhappiness are exclusively within us. In typical rejection of eighteenth century optimism, he added that both are necessary if we want to experience happiness, for we know it only by contrast.[47] All in all, we have here the elements of the "romantic" view of man and of his relation to the outside world. This was not a novel discovery, to be sure—Pascal's writings alone testify to the prior existence of the "romantic" outlook. But this insight had been pushed into the background in the eighteenth century, especially in Russia, where there had been much stress on the rationality and uniformity of human cognition and behavior in order to bridge the gap that still separated the Russians from their Western European models.

We find again an affirmation of the individual aspect of dignity and liberty in the curious encomium to Peter III pronounced by A. F. Voeikov.[48] In praising Peter III for freeing the nobles from compulsory state service, Voeikov gives an unexpected twist to the most fundamental belief held by his entire generation, that the educated individual must be free spiritually and allowed to do his duty voluntarily. Peter III is further praised for freeing millions of serfs from the darkness of Church rule (more precisely from the monasteries), by transferring them to the status of state peasants. Besides the obvious political implications (which, however, Voeikov's subsequent life and career would belie), one may note the emphasis on the necessity for individual enlightenment and culture.

It was not only the desire to keep up with and imitate the most recent developments in Western Europe that accounted for the circle's enthusiasm for German literature.[49] In the writers of the *Sturm und Drang* (later also in early English romanticism and in Shakespeare) they found expressions of personal liberation, of the ambivalent relationship to their elders, of the human emotions, basically simple, yet complicated in their manifestations, which corresponded best to their own needs and moods. Although they had been nurtured on sentimental literature—and they went on reading and even translating it—they were not carried away by it in the way their fathers had been. Their own preference went to the moralizing dramas and stories of writers like August von Kotzebue. In them they found nourishment for their sense of outrage at the sight of moral wrongs and of pity for the poor and downtrodden. Of course, the subject matter of some of these works reminded them directly of Russian social reality (and of their ambiguous position in it), for example Kotzebue's *Die Negersclaven,* which Andrei Turgenev and A. S. Kaisarov set out to translate.[50] *Werther,* naturally, was a *livre de chevet;* the hero's hopeless and unfulfilled love seemed to them an accurate image of genuine love, which existed only as a remote ideal. In the long run this highly charged emotional diet proved to be unsatisfying, and our young critics and *littérateurs* perceived the need for greater formal discipline and tougher intellectual fare. They turned again to the French classics, especially Racine, whom they rediscovered as a truly great master. Here again, however, it was the poet of individual experience and of the fatal consequences of emotion which appealed to them.[51]

This is not the place to analyze in detail Andrei Turgenev's literary criticism. But a few words should be said about two of his speeches to the society in which he dealt with the state and task of Russian literature.[52] In essence he made two major points. He attacked the misuse of literature and he deplored the absence of a truly national literature in Russia. The work of Karamzin had become the main focus of literary debate in the early nineteenth century and, not surprisingly, Andrei Turgenev turned his argument to Karamzin's role in Russian literature. He had, we know, liked and respected Karamzin mainly as editor of the children's readings on which he had been raised, and also as a friend of his family. In his speech, he further acknowledged Karamzin's contribution in introducing Western sentimentalism; this had helped to turn the Russian reader's attention to the inner life, to the moral and spiritual qualities of the common people. Karamzin thus widened the horizon of Russian spiritual experience. But this positive contribution had to be balanced against one important negative consequence of Karamzin's writings. Sentimentalism, especially in the hands of Karamzin's many imitators, had resulted in shallowness of feeling, the drowning of genuine psychological and emotional traits beneath an accumulation of vapid sentimentality. Thus the moral and emotional value of literature had been debased. It was, of course, taken for granted by Andrei Turgenev and his friends that literature had a moral function, that it served to improve man, society, and culture. By lowering the demand he made on his readers, Karamzin had diverted Russian literature into the by-ways of mere entertainment for the semieducated. Quite consistent with his elevated view of literature, Turgenev leveled a similar criticism at Lomonosov. Besides his incontestable merits as the founder of modern Russian literature, this "Peter the Great" of the modern Russian language had also done much to debase literature by writing verse on command for every imperial anniversary, birthday, and court occasion. To laud great men of the past, and on occasion even the living ruler, was perfectly consonant with the high calling of the poet. But to lavish indiscriminate and extravagant praise on sundry members of the imperial house was to betray the high calling of literature. In the eyes of Andrei Turgenev and his generation, literature no longer had the didactic cultural function it had had for eighteenth century writers; a high moral and national role had been conferred on it.[53]

His ideas on the exalted function of literature were related to Turgenev's second point, namely that Russian literature was not as yet a truly national one. This was because it did not portray real Russian characters and heroes, but only foreigners with Russian names or costumes. Even those works that claimed to follow the Russian popular and epic tradition were nothing more than imitations of Western European prototypes with pseudo-national trappings. This criticism was quite valid, as a perusal of contemporary journals and popular literature will readily show. The demand for a truly national, folk-inspired literature was not merely a parroting of western romanticism and historicism; it had Russian roots going back at least to the second half of the eighteenth century. But the generation we are describing had been raised in the ideas of cosmopolitanism. Their early ideal had been not only to become Russians but to merge in a broader family of nations, become truly European, cosmopolitan citizens.[54] Of course, this had also been their fathers' aim. Now, however, in the first decade of the nineteenth century, educated youth felt that cosmopolitanism was a mere construct of the mind, that it had no emotional, historical, or social reality.

To the young men of the 1800s, to be consciously Russian meant to acquire an identity of their own, different from that of their parents and related to their nation. They did not feel that they were complete individuals as long as they were floating in mid-air, outside the human context of Russia. This was their way of overcoming the sense of alienation from land and people that had been characteristic of the Russian educated nobility in the previous century. Their fathers and grandfathers had tried to overcome their alienation by identifying with the West, something outside themselves, and by attempting to create a new type of Russian man who was an European.

But already Radishchev and Novikov had shown this way to be sterile, leading only to further oppression of the serfs and a drawing away from the people. It was natural, therefore, to return to a reassertion of the national element. It was less a feeling, or even a consciousness (to borrow Hans Rogger's term), of nationalism than a genuine and fully conscious patriotism. It was love of the fatherland, *otechestvo,* in the direct physical sense of love of one's land, as Karamzin had understood it; but it was also a means of self-fulfillment in the service of a wider community, of dedication to the welfare of one's country and nation.[55] This was the kind of patriotism that found its fullest expression during the Napoleonic wars: "we are ourselves, we are Russians and we need not be ashamed of it, on the contrary! " This is what Alexander Turgenev noted in Goettingen upon hearing Schloezer's praise of Russian history and comparing his own national consciousness to the bored indifference of his German fellow students.[56] This was how Andrei Turgenev felt when, on his trip to Vienna, he attended a play about Peter the Great and visited a Czech scholar (whose efforts to promote national literature he approved with quite a touch of patronizing superiority and condescension).[57] It was this very sentiment that made A. S. Kaisarov volunteer for military service and meet his early death in battle near Görlitz in May, 1813. Love of country and sacrifice for the common good was the legacy of the Turgenev circle which inspired the Decembrists as well.

It is not only the personalities and ideas of Andrei Turgenev and his friends that are of interest to us. Equally important is the historical memory of the circle and of its young hero and *spiritus rector,* for this memory provides a link to the first generation of the Russian intelligentsia, *sensu stricto,* and foreshadows some features of its subsequent "organization" in circles.

The Friendly Literary Society existed for only a few months; Andrei Turgenev died barely twenty-two years old. Other members of the circle not only survived but participated actively in the cultural life of the two capitals. A. F. Merzliakov moved to St. Petersburg and became a known *littérateur* and professor of rhetoric; he also joined another important literary-cultural society, *Vol'noe obshchestvo liubitelei slovesnosti, nauk i khudozhestv,* where the new "romantic" mood combined with enlightenment traditions. Many members of this society were later closely associated with the Decembrists.[58] A. F. Voeikov, too, became associated with this society. A. S. Kaisarov made a name for himself in scholarship and became professor of Russian literature and language at the University of Dorpat. During the campaign of 1812-13, he organized and directed the publication of proclamations and political pamphlets in Kutuzov's headquarters, thus helping to give an ideological and intellectual dimension to the war against Napoleon. His personal contacts in the army and his brother Paisii's (also a friend of Andrei Turgenev) command of partisan units point to connections with the future Decembrists.[59]

Historically and literarily, the most influential member of the group turned out to be V. A. Zhukovskii. He was the mainstay of the prominent literary society *Arzamas* (where young Pushkin was a shining light). Even though he was close to the imperial court, Zhukovskii kept up a friendship with the Decembrists, as well as with all prominent personalities in mid-century intellectual and literary life for whom he often acted as petitioner. Finally, Alexander Turgenev (also a member of *Arzamas*) kept in close touch with all things cultural despite his own literary and scholarly sterility, official position, and lengthy absences from Russia. He was the *colporteur* of literary and philosophical news, a collector of books and documents pertaining to Russian history, and a petitioner for his fellow *littérateurs.* All these men kept alive the memory and interests of the Friendly Literary Society with which they had been associated in their youth.

But these are only tenuous personal links. More significant is the fact that the *kruzhok* (circle) became and remained the framework for the development and education of every generation of the intelligentsia and, later, revolutionary youth. Indeed, only the *kruzhok* provided the means to still the craving for the kind of vital "existential" knowledge not to be obtained either at home or in the universities. The young people thus turned to each other for guidance in their reading and discussion of the ideas discovered. The Friendly Literary Society and Turgenev's circle of friends were prototypes whose example was followed throughout the nineteenth century.

The psychological and intellectual success of the *kruzhok* depended very much on its members' finding a figure to follow and emulate, someone who would inspire and guide them, someone with whom to identify. Under the conditions prevailing in nineteenth century Russia, the older generation was excluded from this role; nor could the object of identification be men of recognized accomplishment. Indeed, the very fact of a successful career (or public reputation) meant acceptance of the Establishment and, by implication, betrayal of the hopes, ideals, and aspirations of their youth. The hero of the circle had to be someone whose promise had remained unfulfilled—be it because of early death or political persecution. It also had to be someone capable of inspiring enthusiasm and worship by his character and example. Finally, the hero had to be a "whole" *(tsel'nyi)* personality, that is, someone whose identity was perceived strongly enough to be the source of unquestionable moral authority. In other words, it had to be someone who was convinced of possessing the moral truth, yet kind enough to overlook the weaknesses of his friends and to help them obtain the same insight. Such was the light in which N. Stankevich was seen by the intelligentsia of the 1830s and 1840s, and he is often cited as the model hero of the *kruzhok;*[60] no doubt he best personified these traits. But he was far from being first or alone in this role in the history of the Russian intelligentsia. We may mention D. Venevitinov, N. Ogarev, and M. Butashevich-Petrashevskii. This is the role in which Andrei Turgenev was cast by his friends.

The "canonization" of Andrei Turgenev started immediately upon his unexpected death—here was a classical case of unfulfilled promise. His brother Alexander Turgenev and his close friends A. Kaisarov and V. Zhukovskii were most active in creating the "myth" of his life and role.[61] Like everyone who holds the memory of someone dear, they overlooked the blemishes and remembered only the good. Andrei, as we have seen, was far from perfect and far from truly having found his identity at the time of his death. His friends turned his expectation of identification into actuality, and thus the promise of his existence became the myth of his life.

Another element in the process of mythologizing the inspirational leader of a *kruzhok* was the glorification of his role in introducing new ideas, styles, and philosophical interests. In this respect Andrei Turgenev's contribution was quite characteristic and very significant. He played a major part in introducing the literature and ideas of the German *Sturm und Drang* and in paving the way for the powerful impact of Schiller on Russian intellectual history. He thus helped lay the ground for the reception of German philosophic idealism. It is not altogether accidental that the "heroes" of later *kruzhki* also were carriers of new philosophic and aesthetic revelations: Venevitinov propagandized Schelling's *Naturphilosophie,* Stankevich, Hegel's metaphysics; Ogarev, Christian socialism; Petrashevskii, Fourierism. It is important to repeat that mere literary and philosophical contributions—such as they were—were not enough to confer the aura of spiritual leadership in the *kruzhok.* What was needed was an emotional and moral commitment that could serve as inspiration. This is what Andrei Turgenev offered his friends, and what Odoevskii or Khomiakov or Herzen did not.

Were there no antecedents for this phenomenon of the *kruzhok* hero? What about the "circle" of Radishchev and his fellow students in Leipzig and the "myth" about their friend Fedor Ushakov? In reading Radishchev's life of Ushakov (characteristically called *zhitie,* i.e., life of a saint), we are struck first of all by the fact that Ushakov was actually the senior, energetic, practical leader of a group whose members had come together accidentally, at imperial command, and who found themselves disoriented in a foreign environment, at the mercy of their supervisor. In the second place, Radishchev and his friends seem to have had no problem about identification. They clearly belonged to Russian society, they had a concrete task to perform, and their future existence was both clearly mapped out and accepted by them. Radishchev's subsequent writing of the *Journey from St. Petersburg to Moscow* was occasioned by a *crise de conscience,* not a crisis of identity. I would suggest that Radishchev's generation had no more than the universal adolescent problem of identity; consequently the societies and associations that they founded had quite a different character and function from those of the early 1800s.

The features we have noted in Turgenev's circle stemmed from a feeling of disorientation, largely motivated by a sense of uselessness, futility, and alienation from a social and political world that was spiritually and morally unacceptable, and by the strong urge to discover new truths for themselves. The fateful thing was that the basic condition which engendered this feeling among Russia's youth did not change materially to the end of the nineteenth century, and even to the eve of the 1917 Revolution.[62] That is why the *kruzhok*—with its blend of intellectual and psychological traits, emotional needs, and moral demands—remained the institutional framework for the intellectual, moral, and ideological development of every generation of the Russian intelligentsia. For similar reasons, the *kruzhok* also played a seminal role in the history of the revolutionary movement. It is not surprising that the revolutionary study and propaganda circles owed many of their basic traits to the experience and tradition which had originated in the circle of Andrei I. Turgenev.

Boris Nicolaevsky, whose memory we honor in the present volume, was in many ways—albeit under the special conditions of his time and life—a representative of this tradition, a tradition which has contributed so much to the glories, as well as the sorrows, of modern Russia's cultural and political history.

JONATHAN FRANKEL

Voluntarism, Maximalism, and the Group for the Emancipation of Labor (1883-1892)

Until recently Marxism was described by most Western historians as a doctrine radically opposed to Russian revolutionary populism. It was argued that in adopting Marx's doctrine of economic determinism, Plekhanov and his Group for the Emancipation of Labor were bound to reject point by point the ideology of *Zemlia i volia* and *Narodnaia volia.*

For the populists—so runs this widely-held thesis—capitalism in Russia was a feeble growth of uncertain future, but the Marxists saw it as deeply and securely rooted. The peasant commune, depicted by the populists as the sure basis of the future socialist society, was described by the Marxists as disintegrating and hopelessly fragmented between rich and poor. For the populists, Russia was unique, destined to move directly from feudalism to socialism; for the Marxists, Russia was simply one more latecomer to the capitalist stage of European history. The proletariat, secondary in populist thought, was represented as the only true revolutionary class by the Marxists. A tightly-knit band of conspirators, the populists saw terror as the main revolutionary weapon while the Marxists, believing that the proletariat had to make its own revolution, rejected terror and demanded the patient preparation of organized conscious action by the masses. The populists dreamed of a socialist coup in the immediate future; the Marxists argued vehemently that it would be suicidal for the socialists to seize power prematurely, at the bourgeois stage of socio-economic development. A prolonged stage of parliamentary democracy had to separate the bourgeois from the socialist revolution.

In short, the populists were voluntarists and maximalists: they believed that history could be dominated by the human will and that the coming revolution would therefore be socialist. But Marxist doctrine exalted the objective laws of socio-economic development, confident that they worked surely, albeit sometimes slowly. As a forceful example of the way in which Western authors have tended to present this clear-cut dichotomy, we can take the analysis made by Isaac Deutscher in his *Stalin: A Political Biography.* "Plekhanov," he wrote,

This article, which was written specifically for the present volume, has meanwhile appeared in somewhat different form in *Cahiers du Monde russe et soviétique,* No. 9, 1968.

> made the confident forecast that capitalist industrialism was about to invade Russia and destroy its patriarchal feudal structure and the primitive rural communes on which the *Narodniks* wanted to base their socialism. An urban industrial working class, he argued, was about to grow up in Russia and would fight for industrial socialism very much on the western European pattern. The vision of a peculiarly Slavonic rural socialism springing straight from pure feudalism was Utopian. . . . The fundamental dispute was widened by a controversy over tactics. . . . The Marxists would have nothing to do with terroristic methods. . . . They set their hopes on the industrial proletariat that would act against autocracy *en masse;* but since the proletariat was still numerically far too weak to act, they had no choice but to wait until the growth of industry produced the big battalions of workers. Meanwhile, they could only make propaganda, enlist converts to socialism, and set up loose groups of like-minded people.[1]

Here, then, all is sharp and clear. But qualifications and reservations suggested over the last few years have tended to blur such hard-and-fast dividing lines. The process of revision began, perhaps, when Solomon Schwarz and Richard Pipes each published studies highlighting the fact that Marx and Engels had on occasion conceded to the populists that Russia could pass directly from feudalism to a communist social order; that the peasant commune could serve as the fulcrum of this radical transformation; that the socialist intelligentsia could well overthrow Tsarism single-handedly and that it might even seize power without any ill effects.[2] In itself, of course, awareness of the negative attitude shared by Marx and Engels towards the Russian Marxism of the 1880s did not call for any radical revision of the basic idea that in Russia the Marxists and populists held diametrically opposed ideologies. If Marx encouraged *Narodnaia volia* and if Engels reacted critically to Plekhanov's major Marxist treatise, *Our Disagreements,* this could mean simply that, interested in the overthrow of Tsarism at any price, they had chosen to remain neutral in the dispute between the two Russian camps or even to side with the more effective populist wing against their own bookish disciples. "It is quite impossible," concluded Pipes, "to determine whether in Russian matters, Marx himself was a 'Marxist' or a 'populist.'"[3] And Schwarz goes even further: "We cannot avoid the conclusion that Marx took his stand on the populist concept—basically on the version which Chernyshevskii had developed."[4]

But the revisions did not stop here. John Keep and Samuel Baron pointed out that in its early publications, at least, Plekhanov's Group for the Emancipation of Labor had itself advocated many of the theses traditionally regarded as characteristically "populist."[5] Leadership by the revolutionary intelligentsia, conspiratorial methods of party organization, the advocacy of Jacobin methods, and the idea that in Russia the coming bourgeois regime would be overthrown before it could consolidate itself—all these planks had somehow been fitted into the platform of the Group side by side with its more familiar "Marxist" theses.

The relationship between populism and Marxism in Russia thus emerges as far more complex than is generally assumed. And an examination of the studies on early Russian Marxism published in the USSR in the 1920s does little to dispel the confusion. One school, represented by Bystrykh and Rakhmetov, for instance, followed the same line of thought as most Western and emigre historians seeing the Group as the obvious forerunners of Menshevism. The Group, after all, had regarded "popular representation and universal suffrage as the most reliable road to socialism" and Aksel'rod, in particular, was clearly dedicated to the "Menshevik" view of democracy as an end in itself.[6] Vaganian, on the other hand, devoted much of his lengthy biography of Plekhanov to proving by constant reference to his writings that he had anticipated all the "maximalist" and "Jacobin" elements in Lenin's thought.[7] In short, if Marx in Russian affairs was not a "Marxist" then the Plekhanov described by Vaganian and, to a lesser extent, by Baron and Keep, was certainly no "Plekhanovite" in the normal sense of that term.

However, should we in reality accept this paradox at its face value? Can we attribute the Group's deviations from "Plekhanovism" to inconsistency? Or, rather, do we have to fundamentally revise our conception of what Plekhanov and his comrades actually meant? No doubt, they did not always display that power of logical and incisive thought on which they prided themselves. "Plekhanov," writes John Keep, "was caught in a conflict between his head and his heart."[8] Or as Baron puts it: "It is apparent that Plekhanov's system embraced elements both of voluntarism and determinism which he did not succeed in reconciling."[9]

No doubt, too, it is possible to write off the populism of the Group as the natural weakness of that transitional period when *Narodnaia volia* was still a force and the Marxists had yet to find their feet. The leading Soviet historian of the party in the 1920s, V. I. Nevskii, concentrated on this point, explaining that it took some years for the ex-populist members of the Group to free themselves from their former prejudices. "The Group," he wrote, "did not perfect its program at one fell swoop."[10] This same thesis was developed—albeit with a different gloss—by Plekhanov himself, writing some thirty years after the formation of the Group. In the years 1883-84, he explained, the Group had outwardly accepted various populist theses only in order to convert the rank-and-file following of *Narodnaia volia* to Marxism. "In order to propagandize our own ideas," he wrote in 1910, "we took our stand on their point of view."[11]

But, granted that there were elements of compromise and inconsistency, it is surely misleading not to give at least equal weight to the factor of conscious ideological commitment. In 1903 David Riazanov argued that the seemingly extraneous or contradictory "populist" elements in the first works of the Group should be regarded, rather, as an integral part of Russian

Marxist thought at its most powerful.[12] In its first decade, he suggested, the Group had made its greatest efforts to apply Marxist categories to the peculiarities of Russian life and, as a result, their analysis had been at its most realistic and effective. Later attempts to "universalize" Russian Marxism had weakened the movement, blinding it to its surroundings.

Clearly, a number of questions have to be faced before deciding to what extent the Group's dualism was merely contingent, superfluous to its Marxism, and to what extent it was essential. What were the voluntarist and maximalist elements in the program of the Group? How, if at all, did it reconcile these, its "populist" ideas, with its evolutionary and determinist philosophy? Which of these ideas were dropped, which retained or developed even further?

Of all the "voluntaristic" doctrines which found their way into the Group's ideological arsenal, the support of terrorism is perhaps the most curious and also the most transient. Plekhanov had, after all, parted company with *Zemlia i volia* in 1879 as a result of his opposition to terror. The sensational successes of *Narodnaia volia* and the abject failure of his own *Chernyi peredel* subsequently led him to modify his earlier stand, but he could never work up any enthusiasm for assassination as a political weapon. Even so, the first program of the Group produced in 1884 declared that with regard to the assassination campaign as such it had no quarrel with *Narodnaia volia,* that it "recognizes as essential the terrorist war against the absolutist government."[13] This laconic statement hardly signified enthusiasm, but even so it conceded far more to *Narodnaia volia* than did the program prepared in St. Petersburg late in 1884 by the Blagoev group, or Party of Russian Social Democrats, which dismissed political assassination as strictly of marginal value. "Of political terror as a system designed to force concessions from the government," read the Blagoev program, "we have to say that it cannot be regarded as effective under given conditions where there is no strong labor organization to force home its attacks."[14]

It must have come as a welcome surprise to the Group to discover active revolutionary circles in Russia which gave such priority to the creation of a powerful workers' movement that they rejected terrorism. And this fact probably encouraged Plekhanov, when composing a new program in 1885, to solve the problem by simply ignoring the assassination campaign. The program of 1885 stated unequivocably that the primary weapon of the revolutionaries was "agitation among the working class," and "terror" was now mentioned only as a possible by-product of the revolution itself.[15] In later years, Plekhanov was to explain that assassination was a perfectly legitimate weapon in the hands of the revolutionaries but one which under normal conditions should not be used for fear of diverting attention from the central goal–the organization of the proletariat into a revolutionary force. In effect, the "terrorist" phase of the Group was over by 1885.

The problem of what role to assign the intelligentsia in preparing the future revolutions was more complex. The Group believed that the intelligentsia had to fulfill an essential and major function in the movement because it could grasp with more ease than any other social group the principles of scientific socialism. By its very nature, it was ideally suited to guide the workers in the direction demanded by the laws of history. In the first program of the Group this belief was boldly stated: "On the socialist intelligentsia falls the obligation to organize the workers and to *prepare* them actively for the struggle. . . . The Group for the Emancipation of Labor is convinced that not only the success but the very possibility of a purposeful movement of the Russian working class is dependent on the efforts of the intelligentsia in its midst." At the same time, however, the Group could not evade the fact that the socialist intelligentsia as yet showed little inclination to adopt its Marxist approach, and the program therefore added a cautionary note: "The intelligentsia must first adopt the viewpoint of contemporary scientific socialism."[16]

Here, of course, was the crucial issue. An intelligentsia prepared to apply Marxist principles could accelerate Russia's progress towards its two coming revolutions; an intelligentsia that rejected those principles would only confuse the workers and so delay the natural advance guaranteed by objective socio-economic developments. Thus there was a built-in ambivalence in the attitude of the Group towards the revolutionary youth, a potential force for—but also a major threat to—historical advance. The Group was often sorely tempted to dispense with the services of the intelligentsia and to rely solely on the forces of the urban proletariat. In its program of 1885, it side-stepped the problem, omitting all mention of the intelligentsia, not specifying who would form the party leadership. And here, again, the views of the Blagoev circle probably influenced Plekhanov's trend of thought, for the program of the *Blagoevtsy* clearly stated that the spontaneous "movement of the people" would be decisive and would act largely in independence of any revolutionary high command.[17]

Yet even though the Group on this occasion evaded the issue, the problem of who was to organize and head the revolutionary movement would constantly recur. More and more disappointed by the apathy of the student youth, the Group in the late 1880s frequently turned to the "worker intelligentsia" hoping to find and win over a new generation of Khalturins and Obnorskiis. Their writings of the years 1885-92 were often marked by a distinctly hostile tone towards the intelligentsia. "Among the revolutionaries drawn from the 'youthful intelligentsia,'" Plekhanov explained to the workers in 1889, "there are many gentlemen who even . . . assert that [the working class] simply does not exist. Others admit its existence but add that all the workers are very stupid and uneducated and that therefore it is not worth paying attention to them."[18] Would it not be more sensible to rely on the workers who, after all, were the chosen instruments of history? "The

Russian worker," wrote Plekhanov in 1892, "cannot but be a westerner just as the Russian *intelligent* could not be anything but an 'isolationist' *[samobytnik]*—at least hitherto."[19]

In contrast to the repudiation of terror, this change-over foreshadowed by the program of 1885 was neither complete nor permanent. With the new influx from the revolutionary intelligentsia into the revolutionary movement in the 1890s, the Group began to swing back, if not exactly to its original position of 1883-84, then at least to a policy centered largely on the intelligentsia. The campaign of the late 1890s against mounting "economism" and "revisionism" could hardly be won without the active participation of the "orthodox" intelligentsia. Thus Plekhanov could now write that the intelligentsia, "the revolutionary bacillus, is duty-bound to develop the class consciousness of the working class."[20] For his part, Aksel'rod declared that the Russian proletariat "taken *en masse* is sunk too deep in general barbarism and ignorance to be able, while still in the clutches of absolutism, to rise to the heights of a conscious revolutionary force absolutely independently and without some outside help." And deliberately enough, Aksel'rod now recalled the fact that for the Group in its early years "the idea of organizing a labor party in Russia was most closely linked for the Group with those political and social ideas and goals which then—as now—stirred all the democratic elements of our intelligentsia."[21]

In organizational terms the idea of the intelligentsia as guide of the proletariat tended to imply a highly centralized party, custodian of long-term proletarian interests, while the idea of history as the direct driving force of the proletariat tended to imply a loose-knit party sensitive to immediate proletarian demands. Thus, the Blagoev circle was careful in its program to emphasize that the party was to be organized along decentralized lines. As the *Blagoevtsy* wrote in a letter to Plekhanov's Group: "We are indeed socialist revolutionaries but we take our stand only on the basis of the real and actual demands of the workers themselves. . . . Another characteristic of the organization itself is that we strive for the greatest possible reduction of centralization . . . and that we grant as much independence as possible to the various groups and individuals."[22] In fact, we have here something close to those "loose groups of like-minded people" which Deutscher described as typical of Plekhanov's political outlook. However, Plekhanov himself never accepted the logic of the argument that Marxist doctrine by its very nature demanded broadly-based decentralization.

On the contrary, the Group's program of 1884 called on the intelligentsia to "*undertake at once the organization* of the workers of our industrial centers . . . in secret circles linked together by one well-defined socio-political program,"[23] while the 1885 program explained that the secret circles had to be "tightly bound together as one unit."[24] In essence, Plekhanov never changed this view of party organization. Even when he had repudiated terror and temporarily despaired of leadership by the intelligentsia, he remained firmly wedded to the idea of maximal centralization. "What we want," he wrote in 1893, "is to found a mobile and militant organization on the model of *Zemlia i volia* or *Narodnaia volia*—an organization which acts anywhere and everywhere it can deal a blow at the government."[25]

Plekhanov's centralism was largely a product of his belief that the Russian Marxists could have only one immediate political goal—the overthrow of the autocracy. But how, in fact, did the Social Democrats of the 1880s envision the coming anti-tsarist revolution? The *Blagoevtsy* made it clear that they expected the revolution to develop from a series of more or less spontaneous conflagrations spreading almost unaided from village to village and town to town. According to this scheme of things, the role of the party was to be strictly auxiliary. "It is impossible to say," they stated in their program, "what form this people's movement will take, but it is our task to regulate as far as possible the course of the revolution, to guide its forces . . . by coordinating the peasant revolution with the political movement of the workers and intelligentsia in the [urban] centers . . . ; the initiative must be with the population itself."[26] Anticipating waves of popular unrest and violence as the prelude to a total revolution, the *Blagoevtsy* considered it within the realm of possibility that at the last moment the tsarist regime would liberalize itself. In contrast, Plekhanov evidently believed that it was the duty of the party to plan and initiate the revolution. Thus the 1885 program states that

> the struggle against absolutism is obligatory even for those workers' circles which constitute the embryo of the future Russian labor party. The overthrow of absolutism must be their first political task. . . . Tightly knit together, these organizations, not satisfied with random clashes against the regime, will rapidly go over at the right moment to a general and decisive assault against it. And they will not hesitate to use even so-called terrorist acts if these seem necessary in the interests of the struggle.[27]

The workers' section of *Narodnaia volia* had developed this same line of thought in its program of 1880 which declared that "only the social revolutionary party in its entirety can fall upon its enemies with a hope of victory."[28]

The image of revolution as a well-prepared action to be organized from above recurs elsewhere in the Group's statements. Combined with the concept of leadership by the intelligentsia, it is to be found in Plekhanov's famous speech to the Paris Congress of the International in 1889: "Our revolutionary intelligentsia must adopt the views of present-day scientific socialism, spread them among the workers and, with the aid of the workers, must take the bastion of the autocracy by assault."[29] This military-like approach which pictures the intelligentsia as officers, the workers as soldiers, and the revolution as a well-planned battle should be seen as an integral part of Plekhanov's thought in the 1880s just as the more famous statement which followed in his Paris speech—"the revolutionary movement in Russia can triumph only as the revolutionary movement of the workers."

That the underground party could both prepare and direct the revolution was an idea suggested not only by Plekhanov but also, at times, by Aksel'rod. Thus, in 1884 Aksel'rod could write of the "power which a group of three or four hundred people with an advanced socio-political standpoint can represent in a moment of free-moving social upheaval."[30] Again, in an article of 1889, he dwelt on the great strategic significance of the fact that the industrial workers were centered in the major cities: "It is in the capital where the Tsar and his ministers live and in the towns where the main governmental offices are to be found that the final defeat of tsarist power can be executed. . . . It is here that the forces for the assault against it can be concentrated."[31] In 1892, comparing the revolutionary possibilities in Germany and Russia, he pointed out that while the Hohenzollern regime stood firmly on a broad base of active middle-class support, Tsarism rested "primarily on the inertia, lack of organization, and backwardness of the population. Therefore," he concluded, "if Russia had a well-run organization of energetic revolutionaries (such as that of *Narodnaia volia* or *Zemlia i volia*) which could gain popularity among only a few thousand Petersburg workers, it would have greater chances of victory in a military clash with the government than would the Social Democrats in Germany."[32] Looking back on the 1880s from a post-1905 vantage point, Plekhanov was to recall that, debating against the *narodovol'tsy,* he had frequently summed up the Marxist case in a nutshell: "Give us 500,000 politically conscious workers and nothing will remain of absolutism."[33] Clearly, however, the publications of the time suggest that the Group would have opted for a figure infinitely lower than half a million.

It seems probable that the failure of the socialists to unleash revolution even at the time of the great famine had a sobering effect on the Group. After 1892, at least, no more was heard of revolution to be planned or manipulated from above. And in later years Plekhanov could write scornfully that "anybody who can ask himself seriously, as Lenin does, in which month we must begin the armed uprising is, of course, much closer in tactical matters to Mr. Tikhomirov or to Tkachev than to the Group for the Emancipation of Labor."[34] If all had gone smoothly, therefore, the earlier speculations of the Group might well have sunk gradually into oblivion only to be unearthed by post-revolutionary historians. But this was not to be. In 1897 Aksel'rod republished the 1885 program, implying that it was still in force as the platform of the Group and that it was to be regarded as the official credo of the Russian Marxist movement. At its inception in 1895, the Union of Russian Social Democrats Abroad had formally recognized the ideological authority of the Group. Thus, the new generation of Social Democrats was brought face to face with the earliest concepts of the Group, and the resulting clash, in which Prokopovich bluntly repudiated the 1885 program, became the immediate cause of the economist schism. A decade later, the first publications of the Group again became the center of public controversy when their purpose was disputed in a vituperative debate between Kamenev, Martynov, and Plekhanov.

Both Prokopovich in 1898 and Martynov in 1909 argued that, strictly speaking, the Group in the 1880s had held views on party organization and on the coming revolution which were alien to Marxism. Two aspects of the Group's early writings struck them as being particularly anachronistic. The Group, they wrote, had exaggerated both the importance of the intelligentsia and the power of a tiny conspiratorial party to bring down the tsarist regime. "A program suited to intellectuals seeking out the workers," declared Prokopovich in 1898, "is not suitable for the workers themselves defending their own 'self-chosen interests.' " And of the Group's hopes for the overthrow of Tsarism, he wrote: "It is always possible 'to fall' on the autocracy even without taking account of the forces and means at hand. But what will such an 'assault' produce?"[35]

Ten years later, but following the same line of thought, Martynov was to ask how Kamenev could read into the Group's early writings the concept of "the hegemony of the proletariat" in the bourgeois revolution. The Group, he pointed out, had believed that the workers could not organize an effective mass or class party under tsarist conditions and that at most the intelligentsia could set up a network of workers' cells "to take the bastion of the autocracy by storm." In short, the Group could not conceive of a really *"independent* role for the proletariat *prior to the revolution"* and, in this sense, Plekhanov's speech of 1889 represented a concept of revolution little different from that of Blanqui.[36]

It is, of course, striking that on both these controversial points, the *Blagoevtsy* had followed a line far more acceptable to these latter-day critics than that of the Group. Commenting on this fact, the Soviet historian N. L. Sergievskii suggested that in the 1880s the Group was out of tune not only with the *Blagoevtsy* but with nearly all the Social Democrats at work within Russia.[37] The explanation would seem to be that while the Marxists inside Russia took the German Social Democratic Party as their natural prototype, Plekhanov was influenced equally by the *Communist Manifesto,* by Zheliabov (the martyred leader of *Narodnaia volia*) and Guèsde (the dominant French Marxist whose revolutionary temperament he admired).

Called upon to defend the Group, Plekhanov developed one line of argument against Prokopovich in 1900 and another against Martynov in 1910. In his *Vademecum* he declared that there could be no clash of interests between the party of scientific socialism and the real interests of the working class. True, the Group had demonstrated that the intelligentsia could destroy the tsarist regime only with proletarian help—and hence had taken the intelligentsia as its starting point—"but in our eyes the worker was never a simple weapon for the attainment of aims foreign to him. . . . Our program was written in the spirit of Marx. But a program written in the spirit of *that* man *cannot be a program of political exploiters."*[38] Clearly, Plekhanov had in mind the passage in the *Communist Manifesto* which states that the communists "always and everywhere represent the interests of the movement as a whole," that they are "the most advanced and resolute section of the working class parties, . . . that section which pushed forward all other . . . and [has] the advantage of clearly understanding the line of the march."[39] It was highly characteristic of Plekhanov to feel that a successful reference to Marx decided the argument in his favor. Furthermore, countered Plekhanov, the idea that the Group had advocated "a military assault on Tsarism" was based on nothing more than a false interpretation of one stray quotation from Aksel'rod.

But what was at issue was, as noted above, not one out-of-the-way reference, but a number of statements in well-publicized sources which pictured the coming revolution in terms of an armed assault led by the party on the tsarist governmental machine. This point, made by Martynov in his article of 1909, provoked Plekhanov to formulate the full-scale reply earlier denied to Prokopovich. All references to the apparently Blanquist declarations made by the Group in the 1880s were, Plekhanov now argued, irrelevant to an understanding of what the Group actually thought in those years. The fact was, he explained, that "at that time *we did not count on the revolution* as something for the near future." The revolution would come only after "a more or less prolonged process of the economic development of Russia."[40] Therefore, the historian should simply write off all those passages which spoke of leadership by the intelligentsia, of armed assault on the regime, of the imminent overthrow of Tsarism. "This," he concluded, "answers the entire question. . . . What you encounter there are not my own views but the revolutionary conceptions of *those times long ago* which I took into account *in order to bring the reader over to my own way of thinking.*"[41]

This approach was astonishing (as Martynov and Riazanov were quick enough to point out on various occasions). Plekhanov, famous in the history of the revolutionary movement for his devoted defense of orthodoxy, now claimed that important passages in some of his best-known Marxist works did not represent the Group's ideology but that of their populist opponents. It was hard not to see in this argument simply a polemical maneuver neatly designed to put an end to all further discussion. As to the specific issue—did the Group really consider a revolution possible in the immediate future?—it can only be said that they often wrote as if they did and that it seems more logical to accept at face value what they said at the time than what Plekhanov said in his disavowals twenty and thirty years later. In an article of December, 1881—when he was already largely converted to Marxism—Aksel'rod actually declared that "we are now evidently living through the eve of a major revolution." Three years later he repeated this statement almost word for word.[42] And in an article of 1885 written for the Blagoev circle Plekhanov expressed the same idea in only slightly veiled terms: "We are living on the eve of important events and the Russian working class must appear as an active participant in these events and not as a sorry mass of slaves."[43] In sum, Riazanov certainly had adequate grounds for his judgment of 1903 that "the first Social Democrats were distinguished by no less naivete than the revolutionaries of the '70s. They did not see the revolution as something far distant and, just like the *narodovol'tsy,* they were in a hurry to create the force on which to pin their hopes."[44]

It was in fact partly because the Group regarded imminent revolution as possible that it found itself attracted to elitist concepts of organization—leadership by the intelligentsia, an ideologically monolithic and closed party, a revolution at least partially planned in advance. In the 1880s there was as yet no autonomous labor movement and it was logical to regard *Zemlia i volia* and *Narodnaia volia* as the most effective models for an underground organization preparing revolution. Broader perspectives only appeared with the emergence of an embryonic "trade-union" movement in the mid-1890s, and eventually both Aksel'rod and Vera Zasulich were to decide that the new realities demanded new—less centralized and more open—forms of organization. Plekhanov, too, became increasingly hostile to the thought of planned revolution, but he clung to the idea of a tightly-knit, highly selective party, thus placing himself on Lenin's side at the Second Party Congress of 1903 and again during the so-called liquidationist crisis of 1909-11.

The belief that the autocracy was toppling encouraged the Group to toy not only with voluntaristic ideas of organization but also with maximalist visions of revolution: the notion that although Russia was still barely industrialized, the socialist revolution could follow hard on the heels of, or even merge with, the constitutionalist and bourgeois anti-tsarist revolution. Clearly, if the overthrow of Tsarism were regarded as far distant, there could be no point in worrying about the nature or timing of the subsequent socialist revolution. In her famous letter of February, 1881, to Marx, Vera Zasulich said that if Russia had to follow exactly the same path as the West, then

> it only remains for the socialist as such to busy himself making more or less speculative estimates of how many decades it will take for the land of the Russian peasant to pass into the hands of the bourgeoisie and of how many centuries it will perhaps take for capitalism to attain the same stage in Russia that it has in Western Europe.[45]

Conversely, if the Russian socialists could regard the unique peasant commune *(obshchina)* as the ready made cornerstone of the future communist society, then they would not have to wait for economic evolution, but could throw themselves on the tsarist regime, confident that victory was attainable, socialist society an immediate possibility.

In 1881, Vera Zasulich was still a populist. But, contrary to what is often thought, the adoption of Marxism by Zasulich, Aksel'rod, and Plekhanov in the years 1882-83 did not make this dilemma any less real for them. If Tsarism were to be overthrown in the near future, the Social Democrats too would have to decide whether or not to exploit the weakness of the Russian bourgeoisie and press ahead with a socialist—or at least a social—revolution. In fact, both Plekhanov and Vera Zasulich made it clear enough in their writings of 1883-85 that they expected the socialist revolution to follow shortly after the establishment of the bourgeois regime. Thus, in *Socialism and the Political Struggle,* Plekhanov explained that even though the two revolutions could not actually coincide, "it depends on us to bring [them] close together."[46] In 1884 Vera Zasulich wrote: "The immediate future in Russia belongs to the growth of capitalism, but only the immediate future."[47] And in *Our Disagreements,* Plekhanov again developed this theme: "Our [populist] intelligentsia argues that it is possible to dispense totally with one phase of social development . . . because it does not appreciate the fact that *the duration* of that phase *can be shortened.* . . . Our capitalism will fade without having fully flowered."[48]

Plekhanov and Zasulich advanced a number of arguments to buttress their maximalist or quasi-maximalist prognosis. Doctrinally, the idea of the rapid transition from a backward or feudal economy to a society organized on socialist lines had ample backing from Marx himself. And in *Socialism and the Political Struggle* Plekhanov quoted approvingly the opinion formulated by Marx and Engels in 1882 that "if the Russian revolution were to serve as the signal for a workers' revolution in the West in such a way that the two revolutions were to complement each other, then the existing form of Russian land ownership could serve as the starting point for communist development."[49] Could it "enter the head of any populist," asked Plekhanov, to deny the validity of this judgment? And he concluded that "the stupid prejudice about his [Marx's] extreme 'Westernism' is thus shown to lack all semblance of truth."[50]

But even more important than Marx's brief comments on the prospects of Russian socialism was Plekhanov's reading of the *Communist Manifesto.* There seems to be no doubt that Plekhanov was immensely influenced by the *Communist Manifesto* because the Russia of the 1880s could then be regarded as having reached the stage of economic and political development attained by Germany in the 1840s. In both cases, the "feudal" landowners and the autocratic monarchy constituted the enemy common to the bourgeoisie and to the nascent proletariat alike. Therefore, argued Plekhanov, "we must follow the wonderful example of the German communists who, in the words of the *Manifesto,* went 'together with the bourgeoisie in so far as it was revolutionary'," but never ceased to develop the class consciousness of the proletariat. "In this way," he pointed out, "the communists hoped [as stated in the *Manifesto*] that 'the German bourgeois revolution would serve only as the direct prologue to the workers' revolution.'"[51]

The *Manifesto* not only gave the stamp of ideological orthodoxy to the more messianic tendencies of the Group, but also suggested how its maximalism could be reconciled with belief in the primacy of economic causation. In the *Manifesto* we read that the "communists turn their attention chiefly to Germany" because "that country is on the eve of a bourgeois revolution that is bound to be carried out under more advanced conditions of European civilization and with a more developed proletariat" than existed at the time of the English and French bourgeois revolutions of the seventeenth and eighteenth centuries.[52]

Pursuing this line of thought, Plekhanov and Zasulich stressed the crucial idea that in Russia at the time of the anti-tsarist revolution, the proletariat would be relatively strong and the bourgeoisie politically ineffectual. The proletariat would therefore be able to seize the initiative in a way barred to it in the French Revolution, for instance, but foreseen by Marx in his analysis of the German situation in the 1840s. "The development of capitalism in Germany," wrote Plekhanov in 1884, "found the working class at a higher level of development than had been the case in England or France and so the resistance to capitalist exploitation was swifter and more decisive. The German communists did not even consider the possibility of their having to wait upon capitalism."[53] Or as he put it in *Socialism and the Political Struggle:* "If the German bourgeoisie *'came too late,'* then the Russian came later still and its reign cannot last long."[54]

This same theme was taken up by Vera Zasulich who explained that as Russia benefited from the latest industrial techniques developed by the West, its capitalism progressed incomparably faster and its life-span would therefore be much shorter. "These borrowings, this constantly growing influence of Western Europe on the trend of our development . . . exclude the possibility of our going through those same consecutive stages of development characteristic of England or France." To recognize that "economic factors are basic in history" does not mean to ignore the fundamental differences between various countries for, in reality, the sum of factors influencing the character of a country's development is "infinitely varied."[55]

Vera Zasulich and Plekhanov also gave full play to the other factor which, according to the *Communist Manifesto,* could open the door to socialist revolution in a semi-feudal country—the "advanced conditions of European civilization." The Europe of the 1880s was, after all, even riper for an international proletarian revolution—that is, far more industrially developed—than that of the 1840s. In Western Europe, wrote Zasulich, "the days of capitalism are already numbered. The socialist revolution in the West will put an end to capitalism in Eastern Europe too."[56] And in the previous year, 1883, Plekhanov had already advanced this same idea: "The influence of international relations on the development of society in every civilized country gives us the right to hope that the social liberation of the Russian working class will follow very quickly on the fall of absolutism."[57]

Given so wide a measure of consensus between the Group and *Narodnaia volia* in the years 1883-85, it is only natural to ask what nonetheless divided them. The Group's 1884 program narrowed the area of disagreement to two points: "the so-called seizure of power by the revolutionary party" and "immediate activity by the socialists among the working class."[58] That as

Marxists the Group should lay major stress on work among the industrial proletariat was only to be expected, although it should not be forgotten that in their heyday (1880-81) the *narodovol'tsy* devoted considerable effort to recruiting support from the working class. The area of disagreement here was, in reality, narrow enough.

The Group's opposition to "the so-called seizure of power" requires more comment. As we have seen, the Group frequently supported the idea of a socialist revolution following hard on the heels of the bourgeois revolution. Nevertheless, Plekhanov was adamant in his opposition to proposals that these revolutions could coincide or merge. The revolutions had to be separate, the one acting as "the prologue" to the other. Plekhanov apparently had two considerations in mind here. First, it would take a period of freedom, however short, for the underground skeleton organization to form into a truly proletarian party capable of establishing a class dictatorship. Second, if the revolutionaries were eager for an alliance with the liberals against the autocracy, they had to distinguish between their minimal program, a democratic republic (acceptable to the liberals), and their maximal program, the proletarian dictatorship and socialist revolution (abhorrent to these same liberals). Thus, Plekhanov was free to unleash his barbs at Tikhomirov, the major spokesman of *Narodnaia volia* in the years 1883-85, who specifically advocated that the revolutionaries seize power in the initial stages of the anti-tsarist revolution and begin at once to reconstruct the socio-economic life of Russia. "The dictatorship of a class," wrote Plekhanov in 1883, "is as different from the dictatorship of a group of revolutionary *raznochintsy* as heaven from earth."[59]

Here, then, we seem to have a truly clear-cut difference between Plekhanov and *Narodnaia volia,* but even so two reservations have to be made. Plekhanov's attacks on Tikhomirov hardly applied to all the leaders of *Narodnaia volia.* Zheliabov had come out specifically in favor of the idea that the revolutionaries distinguish sharply between their immediate aim—political freedom—and their final goal, socialism. In short, Plekhanov's quarrel was more with Tikhomirov's wing of *Narodnaia volia* than with the party as a whole. Again, in addition to the idea that only the proletariat as a fully conscious and well-organized class could attempt to initiate socialism, Plekhanov, as we have seen, also defended the apparently contradictory idea that, given luck, the interval of bourgeois rule would be extremely short. However, as Tikhomirov asked, if "a worker fit for class dictatorship hardly exists" in contemporary Russia[60] how was an entire class fit for this task to emerge almost overnight?

Plekhanov's reply to Tikhomirov provides us with the key to his mode of thought when making political predictions. "Mr. Tikhomirov," he wrote in 1884, "does not understand that a worker incapable of class dictatorship can yearly and daily become more and more capable of it."[61] This statement foreshadowed his rebuff to Martynov in 1910 in which he declared that the Group had expected the revolution to result from a "more or less prolonged process of economic development." Such a process, he then pointed out, was more than nil and less than infinity.[62] In both cases, Plekhanov presented an argument which was watertight both logically and doctrinally but which was almost meaningless politically. Between nil and infinity, after all, stretches the entire range of political choice. Plekhanov, however, preferred to leave all the options open. It is thus hardly surprising that, from the first, Plekhanov's attitude to the coming revolutions has been interpreted in such radically different ways.

Despite all that has been said hitherto, however, there was undoubtedly one major point of disagreement between the Group and the populists. They held opposing views of what socialism actually meant. When Tikhomirov said that the first task of the revolutionary regime would be "to begin the socialist organization of Russia," he apparently envisaged above all the distribution of the landed estates among the peasant communes. In populist thinking, following the Proudhonist tradition, this was a rudimentary form of socialism. But for Plekhanov, socialism meant not only equality and nationalization, but the administration by the community—that is, by the state—of the means of production and distribution. "The question of *expropriation*," wrote Plekhanov, "leads to the question of the *exploitation* of the confiscated estates." The fact that the commune would now be responsible for the partition and repartition of all the land in its area did not lessen the capitalist nature of the village economy, for each peasant would still be responsible for his own share and would pocket his own profits. "It is unfortunate," explained Plekhanov (echoing Marx's attack on Proudhon), "that Russian socialism as presented by Mr. Tikhomirov thus stands much closer to the socialism of the petty bourgeoisie than to that of the workers."[63]

Given this emphasis on a strictly Marxist definition of socialism, the statements of the Group that the socialist revolution was close at hand were all the more surprising. As Plekhanov himself put it: "Will the majority of our peasantry vote for communism? Even Mr. Tikhomirov does not expect this. At its level today and in the near future, the people could not and would not know how to build a communist society."[64] Yet scattered across the Group's publications of 1883-85, we find reaffirmations of the idea that if the political revolution were not too long delayed then the peasant commune could be saved from disintegration and thus be "of the greatest service to Russia," as Zasulich wrote, in the building of socialism. She herself clearly felt that the peculiarly Russian traditions of land-holding would enable a socialist regime to coax the reluctant peasant to accept collective production and egalitarian distribution. "Given broad preparatory propaganda," she concluded, "the government could win the sympathy and understanding of the mass of the peasant population, rely in the practical sphere on the remnants of the communal institutions, and so immediately adopt the broadest measures of the most decisive character."[65]

But Plekhanov—here anticipating Lenin by twenty years—had little faith at this stage in persuasion alone:

> When the time comes for the final victory of the labor party over the upper classes, then it and it alone will take the initiative in the socialist organization of national production. Under its influence—and on occasion under its pressure—the village communes, still preserved, will really go over to a higher communist form. But, protest the populists *[samobytniki]*, the small-holders will put up powerful resistance to the labor party. Very probably this is true, but there will be somebody to fight this resistance. The emergence of the class of small-holders will be matched by the growth in number and in power of our revolutionary proletariat which will of course give life and movement to our cumbersome state machine. There is nothing terrible about opposition when there is a historical force capable of defeating it.[66]

In this passage, we see signs of voluntarism and maximalism actually outdistancing that of *Narodnaia volia* which, after all, was peasant-oriented and, in the last resort, willing to adjust its dreams to those of the peasants, the vast majority of the population.

The years 1883-85 represented the high point of the maximalist tendency in the thinking of Plekhanov and Vera Zasulich. Even in that period, the third member of the Group, Pavel Aksel'rod, apparently did not share the idea that Russia could radically shorten the transition to socialism. Strongly influenced by the development of the German Social Democratic movement, he clearly hoped that after the overthrow of Tsarism, Russia would enter an open-ended period of parliamentary politics and capitalist economics in which the Russian Social Democrats could build up a powerful and representative labor party.

This same position was adopted by Vera Zasulich in the late 1880s. In an article published in 1890 she explained why she had abandoned her earlier hopes that Russia could avoid a lengthy period of capitalist development. At one point, she admitted, she had believed that "in its struggle against the autocracy our revolutionary movement . . . would adopt the point of view of the Communists fighting for political freedom in 1848 not as an ultimate goal, but as the first step in that social revolution which they had made their objective." But the failure of the revolutionary youth to adopt scientific socialism and build up a powerful underground movement among the proletariat had put an end to these dreams. Now, she concluded, even after the fall of the autocracy the socialist revolution would be far distant:

> The [communist] revolution is not carried through at one stroke, with one rising, but is an entire more or less prolonged process during which the proletariat grows, educates and organizes itself, taking part in every struggle . . . but remaining an opposition and not a governing party because, for the socialists, the premature seizure of power at a time when a major part of the proletariat itself remains unorganized would mean not victory but a delay in the ultimate triumph.[67]

In this passage, Vera Zasulich presented the essentials of the "minimalist" approach which was later to characterize the mainstream of Menshevism.

Plekhanov was more reluctant to abandon his maximalist positions *in toto,* although he frequently modified them. Even in *Our Differences* he had toned down one of the themes presented a year earlier in *Socialism and the Political Struggle*—the idea that the Russian revolution would be guaranteed a socialist character by the outbreak of a proletarian revolution in Europe. This idea had been eagerly exploited by Tikhomirov to show that the attainment of socialism in Russia was not dependent on the development of capitalism. If the socialists could rely on aid from abroad why did they have to wait until the Russian proletariat was ready for revolution and then for power? Clearly irritated by the boomerang effect of his own—and Marx's—argument, Plekhanov took pains in his second book to explain that a European socialist revolution would exert little positive impact on Russia unless she already possessed a well-organized proletarian party which could join forces with the international movement. The French revolution of February, 1848, he wrote, "met with a positive response in almost all the countries which were similar to France in their social structure. But the wave it raised broke against the barriers of peasant Europe. Watch out that this same thing does not happen with the future revolution of the proletariat."[68]

Of itself, this qualification did not indicate a repudiation of the "maximalist" option, but towards the end of the 1880s Plekhanov, like Vera Zasulich, was clearly coming to the conclusion that the direct road to socialism no longer had any place in Russian Marxist thought. Indicative of this decision was his approach to the peasant commune. The Group in its first years had repeatedly referred to the fact that the commune could be preserved by state intervention and that it could serve as a basis for socialism. But at the end of the decade Plekhanov made it plain that in his view there was only one route to socialism: the disintegration of the commune, the formation of a rural bourgeoisie, the emergence of a large rural and urban proletariat.[69] This viewpoint, of course, had always been implicit in Plekhanov's Marxist writings, but earlier he had taken care to keep in reserve an alternative prognosis.

Even now, however, it would be erroneous to think that Plekhanov, following Vera Zasulich, had come to share Aksel'rod's belief in parliamentary constitutionalism as the natural form of government for the post-tsarist "bourgeois" period. In contrast to his two comrades, Plekhanov still wanted to be able to choose between two alternative blueprints for the coming revolution, one moderate and political, the other all-embracing and social. Although he now regarded rapid transition to socialism as utopian, this did not exclude the possibility of some kind of radical dictatorship. Thus, in his first booklet on the famine of 1892, Plekhanov had held out the possibility of an alliance with liberals, with a parliament and a constitution as their common goal. But in his second booklet, *On the Tasks of the Socialists in the Struggle Against the Famine,* he toyed with the idea of the Social Democrats putting themselves at the head of a rising of the land-hungry peasantry. They would not be content with the calling of a national assembly *[Zemskii sobor]* but if necessary would immediately undertake to drive out its more conservative members, "to purge" the assembly "with a new revolutionary sweep of the hand." The Marxists would at once demand *"the full expropriation of the large landowners* and the conversion of the land into *national property."* In the years 1883-85, too, the Group had mentioned the possibility of "nationalizing" the land but at that stage they apparently had had in mind primarily its conversion into farms to be run by the state. Plekhanov now made it clear that he was thinking in terms of land distribution either among the peasants individually or via the communes. "A mighty revolutionary movement will emerge," he wrote, "which we could not desert without betraying the principles of socialism."[70] Land distribution, he explained, would not delay the development of capitalism in Russia; the rapid disintegration of the commune would continue unabated, but the socialists would have established themselves, sure of peasant gratitude, in an impregnable political position.

In developing this radical alternative to constitutionalism, Plekhanov had in mind first and foremost the course of the French Revolution moving inexorably from constitutional monarchy to Jacobin dictatorship. "What," he asked, "would the calling of a *Zemskii sobor* mean? It would mean the same as the calling of the Estates General at the end of the last century in France–a recognition by the government of its lack of viability, a concession torn from it by the irreversable march of historical events, the *prologue* of revolution."[71]

In addition to the model of the French Revolution, another influence may well have been at work. At least one Soviet historian[72] has pointed to the similarities in tone between Plekhanov's second booklet on the famine and the *Address* sent by Marx and Engels to the Communist League in 1850, but only published by Engels in 1885. It seems almost beyond doubt that Plekhanov was attracted to the idea stated there that "above all things, the workers must counteract . . . the bourgeois endeavors to allay the storm and must compel the democrats to carry out their present terrorist phrases. . . . Far from opposing so-called excesses, instances of popular revenge against hated individuals or public buildings . . . must not only be tolerated, but the leadership of them taken in hand."[73] It should be remembered that the Group's program of 1885 had declared that at the time of the revolution the Social Democrats "would not hesitate to use even so-called terrorist acts if these seemed necessary in the interests of the struggle."[74] Plekhanov frequently returned to this idea, explaining that "the terror of 1793" was far more effective and justified than that of 1881 or as he sometimes put it: "Against Russian despotism dynamite is not a bad method but the guillotine is better still."[75]

It is clear that these "Jacobin" tendencies of Plekhanov were utterly out of tune with the entire attitude of Vera Zasulich and Pavel Aksel'rod as it had developed in the late 1880s. In a letter of 1893 Plekhanov said specifically that Aksel'rod had the right "to restrain" his [Plekhanov's] "Jacobin leanings" whenever these seemed to be getting out of hand.[76] But they remained a persistent element in Plekhanov's way of thought at least until his breach with Lenin at the end of 1903.

In sum, then, Plekhanov and Vera Zasulich, at least, did not assume that their conversion to Marxism called logically for a radical revision of populist thinking on the forms of revolutionary organization, strategy and tactics or even of populist thinking on the transition to socialism. For them, Marxism implied a new approach to philosophy—and, in particular, to the philosophy of history, to economics, and to sociology. They were now firmly committed "Westerners" in opposition to the more extravagant "Slavophile" leanings of many populists; they played down the power of the individual to alter fundamental historical processes; they gave clear priority to the proletariat over the peasantry as the class which would ensure revolutionary victory and build socialism; above all, they welcomed the growth of capitalism where the populists had feared it. It was logical to draw the conclusion (as the Group did) that, for the revolutionaries, the city had priority over the village and work among the proletariat over terrorism. But the first of these ideas had been upheld in practice by *Narodnaia volia* and the second by *Chernyi peredel.* In fact, while Plekhanov, the populist of 1879, had split *Zemlia i volia* rather than adopt a policy centered on assassination, Plekhanov, the Marxist of 1884, specifically stated that his new Group accepted assassination as a weapon in the fight against Tsarism.

In reality, the organizational model adopted by the Group was that of *Narodnaia volia* and *Zemlia i volia:* a tightly-knit, strictly selective, highly centralized party led by the intelligentsia. Hopefully, the revolution would be sparked off and directed by the revolutionaries, and the post-tsarist bourgeois regime would be overthrown by the socialists before it had time to consolidate itself. In other words, their Westernism, their proletarian-centeredness, and their belief in the inevitability of capitalism by no means implied for the Group that Russia was bound to follow the path of Germany, France, or England, but simply that no country was exempt from the working of universal economic laws. The revolutionaries had to understand how these general laws interacted with the specific conditions of Russian life and exploit their understanding in order to ensure a socialist revolution in the near future. Logically, of course, it was possible to draw far more "revisionist" conclusions from Marxist doctrine, and those who took the German Social Democratic movement as their model were inclined to go much further than Vera Zasulich and Plekhanov in rejecting populist modes of organization and thought. Thus, the Blagoev group in their program of 1885 openly opposed terror, advocated a decentralized movement, argued that the revolution would be almost entirely spontaneous and that, given Russian conditions, the transition to socialism would be long and drawn out. But in the Plekhanov and Vera Zasulich of 1883-85 it is reasonable, as Sergievskii has pointed out, to see not only the pioneers of Russian Marxism but also the heirs of the *narodovolets,* Zheliabov. Like him, they saw socialism not as a far-distant dream, but as a practical program; yet like him, too, they did not think it wise for the socialists to attempt to seize power in the early stages of the coming revolution.

It is true that the maximalism of Zasulich and Plekhanov was short-lived and that the influence of Social Democratic thinking in Germany came to have a greater and greater hold over the emergent Marxist movement in Russia. But it should be remembered that it was in the "maximalist" years, 1883-85, that Plekhanov produced his two most influential Marxist studies of the revolutionary situation and his two draft programs for the Group. Furthermore, Plekhanov himself clung doggedly to two tenets from these early years: one, the party organization, he believed, had to remain highly centralized, doctrinally homogeneous, the avant-garde, supported by the labor movement but not under its control. Second, even when Plekhanov came to regard the peasant commune as hopelessly doomed to disintegration and socialism as therefore far distant, he did not reconcile himself to bourgeois parliamentarianism as the only possibility but advanced his "Jacobin" alternative: a social revolution of the peasants under socialist leadership, and the overthrow of constitutionalism.

In the last resort, it did not fall to Plekhanov to develop the voluntarist, maximalist, and "Jacobin" strands of his thought. His arguments were usually double-edged and in both revolutions (1905 and 1917) he employed the anti-Blanquist blade of his sword. But he was not allowed to forget the existence of the other side. Thus, writing in 1903, Riazanov argued that the Social Democrats would have to subject the post-autocratic Constituent Assembly to militant demonstrations and street violence. Even if the revolution were confined to Russia, there was no reason why the socialists should be satisfied with constitutional government. Here was Plekhanov's "Jacobin" alternative. "Our motto," wrote Riazanov, "is revolution *in permanentia,* not order in place of revolution but revolution in place of order." But it was reasonable to hope for more than this. "If the revolution of the Russian proletariat will serve as the signal for the European proletariat then our revolution will only be the direct prologue for the social[ist] revolution."[77] Basing himself explicitly on the early writings of the Group, Riazanov had thus anticipated by more than two years Trotsky's ideas on permanent revolution.

Until 1914, of course, Lenin was more cautious and was careful never to go beyond the "Jacobin" alternative. Socialism, he wrote in 1894, could not be the immediate aim of the Social Democrats, but a thorough-going economic revolution was possible. "Land nationalization," based on "the complete expropriation of the nobles' estates," had its place in the minimal Social Democratic program.[78] The immediate goal had to be the maximal economic transformation possible given Russia's semi-feudal stage of development—an approach hardly designed to win liberal support in the struggle against Tsarism, and therefore increasingly shelved by the Group during the 1890s. But with his booklet of 1894, Lenin made it clear that he was a natural heir to the "Jacobin"—and ultimately to the maximalist—elements in the Group's program.

ALLAN K. WILDMAN

Russian and Jewish Social Democracy

Much can be learned about the development and character of early Russian Social Democracy by observing its striking parallels with the Polish and Jewish Social Democratic movements. As the populist-type groups of these nationalities drifted toward middle-class national liberalism in the late 1880s, the more radical segments of their intelligentsias were attracted to Marxism and Social Democracy, which by contrast represented a more cosmopolitan, and at the same time more intransigent, revolutionary faith. Polish and Jewish Social Democrats viewed the tsarist autocracy as the oppressor of all workers and the patron of all capitalist exploiters, regardless of nationality. Their cognizance of the founding of the Second International (1889) and the dramatic gains of socialist parties in Germany and Belgium widened the context of their emotional identification, overcoming their particularistic concerns as members of repressed minorities.

In the latter half of the 1880s, Marxist study groups and worker propaganda circles spread throughout the Polish and Western border provinces of Russia, stealing the march on the Russian movement by perhaps three or four years. In 1888 floods in Poland stimulated nationwide political awareness and illicit political activity; their catalytic effect was indeed much like the famine of 1891 in Russia. The revival of revolutionary hopes spurred the Polish Marxists to address themselves directly to the masses, which was effected by the "Union of Polish Workers" *(Zwiazek Robotnikov Polskich)* in opposition to the older purely propagandist organization *Proletarjat.* Mounting strike campaigns reached a peak in the general strike at Lodz in 1892.

Mass agitation in the Jewish movement was undertaken by Vilna Social Democrats in 1894, unleashing a strike wave which spread through the predominantly Jewish regions of the Western provinces. The rapid development of the Jewish movement was soon followed by the Russian; a major textile strike in Belostok by both Jewish and Russian workers was followed by the stupendous strike of the St. Petersburg textile workers in 1896. Except for the shift toward national particularism, the Russian movement proceeded along the lines laid out by its predecessors; it lagged a year or so behind the Jewish, and several years behind the Polish movement.

In spite of the similarity in patterns, the relationships of the Polish and Jewish movements to the Russian were two entirely different orders. Whereas news of the Polish movement reached the Russian Social Democrats only as distant echoes, the influence of the Jewish movement was from the very start direct, personal, and intimate. Indeed, one could say that until the founding of the Bund in 1897, there was no fixed demarcation between the two movements: Jewish Social Democrats worked simultaneously in both without sensing the slightest conflict in loyalty. Even after the founding of the Bund there was much moving back and forth, while the Bund itself functioned as a constituent part of the Russian Social Democratic Workers' Party, which it helped establish in 1898. The Russian movement matured more rapidly and moved with greater awareness into the era of mass organization precisely because of its close relationship to the Jewish movement.

The purpose of this brief study is to take a close look at the motive forces in the Jewish movement which produced this remarkable phenomenon and to assess its role in shaping Russian Social Democracy. It does not presume to give a total picture of either movement, but rather to focus on the character of their interrelationship.[1]

In the south of Russia, an area which fell within the Pale of Settlement, many of the first generation Marxist intellectuals were of Jewish origin–D. B. Gol'dendakh (Riazanov) and Iurii Nakhamkes (Steklov) in Odessa, O. A. Kogan (Ermanskii) in Tiflis, M. A. Zaslavskii, E. G. Mundblit, and Teitel'baum in Ekaterinoslav, E. Abramovich, B. L. Eidel'man in Kiev, and F. A. Lipkin (Cherevanin) in Kharkov. Although several (Abramovich, Zaslavskii) had formerly been associated with Jewish groups in the western sector of the Pale, in the south they worked side-by-side with non-Jews in organizations that were exclusively Russian-oriented. With few exceptions they remained in the Russian movement. In addition, there were a number of Jewish students from the Pale attending universities and institutions in central Russia; not infrequently they became Social Democrats and were fully assimilated Russian intellectuals, unmoved by the problem of ethnic identity. If Jewish Social Democrats came into contact with Jewish workers (as happened in Odessa, Kiev, and Ekaterinoslav), they felt their background rather as an embarrassment, and often sought to shift their sphere of activity to Russian factories and large-scale industry (the Jewish "proletariat" consisted mostly of craft workers–tailors, locksmiths, printers, cabinet makers). North of Kiev the nationality problem seldom came within their field of vision.

Because of their variegated population–Jews, White Russians, Poles, Lithuanians, and Germans–the situation was substantially different in the western border provinces. Here Russianized Jewish intellectuals of Marxist persuasion had no choice but to turn to the Jewish workers, since they did not know the language of the other ethnic groups. Although Marxist circles sprang up simultaneously in Vilna and Minsk, the Minsk circle dissolved by the end of the 1890s as a result of arrests, emigration to America, and the distracting enthusiasm of some of its members for establishing artels (in essence, a defection to populism). Vilna, with its larger factory and artisan population, became the fountainhead of Marxism in the western regions of the Pale. Around 1888, L. A. Aksel'rod (later an *Iskra* collaborator and devoted philosophical disciple of Plekhanov, but no relation to Pavel Aksel'rod), in her salon for the local radical intelligentsia, sponsored a group of Marxist pupils, among them Timofei Kopel'zon, Leo Iogikhes (the famous "Tyshko," lifelong collaborator and companion of Rosa Luxemburg), John Mill, and I. A. Aizenshtat (Iudin).[2] With this group providing the nucleus, a cohesive, enterprising Social Democratic organization sprang up in the next six to seven years, concerned principally with spreading the Marxist faith. Through propaganda circles, the Vilna Social Democrats provided Jewish and Polish workers with a complete "university education" in socialism (the Polish circles later broke away under the leadership of Iogikhes). They were often obliged to prepare their pupils in the Russian language before proceeding to substantive matters, as instructional literature in socialism was available only in Russian. To the Polish Social Democrats active in the same area, they were obnoxious "Russifiers," beguiling future Polish citizens.[3]

Of more significance for this investigation was the systematic indoctrination the Vilna Social Democrats gave to large numbers of radically disposed youth, which the *numerus clausus* for Jews in Russian educational institutions (introduced in 1887) produced in abundance. A few of these young Jews managed to squeeze through and enter the Russian world of learning and culture, first in *gymnasia* (secondary schools) and later in the universities. The overwhelming majority, however, were turned back upon the ghetto, seething with resentment. A pitifully large number, having been refused admittance into *gymnasia,* continued to prepare themselves through private tutors for the diploma exams provided by Russian law, hoping subsequently to surmount the hurdle of university percentage norms. These so-called *eksternaty* were ripe material for indoctrination by older Social Democrats, though, conditioned by the ghetto milieu, their appropriation of Marxism was more primitive and more explosive. Unlike their tutors, they spoke fluent Yiddish, but their command of Russian was poor. Precisely because of their imperfect assimilation, they were better equipped than the older Vilna Social Democrats to appreciate the distinctive needs and traditions of the artisan classes, and thus became a potential source of nationalism in the movement. These *eksternaty* and kindred groups such as pedagogical and rabbinical students were known as *poluintelligenty,* regarded as second-class members in that enviable fraternity, the intelligentsia. Although this junior order of intellectuals was more effectively mobilized in Vilna than elsewhere, it became the model for groups on the periphery of Social Democratic organizations throughout the Pale for the following decade.

That this large-scale work in an exclusively Jewish environment did not sooner issue into a national movement was due to the strongly assimilationist outlook of the Vilna Social Democrats, who, unlike their Polish counterparts, thoroughly identified themselves with the Russian revolutionary tradition. Their Marxism was actually a latter-day expression of a cultural trend originating in the 1860s, when the Jewish bourgeois youth, admitted for the first time to Russian educational institutions in significant numbers, developed an enthusiasm for the classics of Russian literature and followed the idols of the radical intelligentsia from Herzen to the People's Will.[4] Whereas this first generation of educated Jews, not ceasing to be Russianized in habit and thought, reacted to the pogroms and senseless repressions of the 1880s by emigrating or by turning toward a "national" solution, the disaffected youth found the same catharsis in embracing the most radical creed of the dominant culture. To them "Palestinianism" or "Jewish Enlightenment" meant still to be imprisoned within the confines of Jewish particularism, whereas they sought a mode of identification with the general march of European civilization. To them Russian culture was an avenue to European culture, and Russian Marxism as expounded in the writings of Plekhanov happily combined their assimilationist and cosmopolitan yearnings. One of their number, Timofei Kopel'zon, thus reflected on their outlook of that time (1888-90):

> We were assimilationists who did not even dream of a separate Jewish mass movement. . . . We saw our task as preparing cadres for the Russian revolutionary movement, and acclimatizing them to Russian culture.[5]

Not only did the Vilna Social Democrats regard their own organization as a constituent part of a future Russian movement; many of them saw their sojourn in Vilna as temporary and looked forward to transferring their sphere of activity to Russian industrial centers. After all, the Jewish "workers" whom they were indoctrinating were primarily craft workers in scattered storefront workshops, whereas in Russia proper there was a genuine "proletariat" in the giant textile and metallurgical plants of St. Petersburg, Moscow, Ekaterinoslav, and Ivanovo-Voznesensk.

The Vilna Social Democrats were, in point of fact, in active communication with Russian groups from the very beginning. Most of them had attended Russian schools at least for a brief time and had been sent back to Vilna because of illegal political activities. This meant they had friends and acquaintances in central Russia who shared their convictions. Soon gymnasium students indoctrinated by them moved on to Russian institutions of higher education—Ia. A. Liakhovskii to Kiev, Aaron Lur'e, L. B. Fainberg, and E. A. Levin to Kharkov, and B. I. Gol'dman (Gorev) to St. Petersburg. These Vilna graduates invariably joined Russian Social Democratic groups and brought back news on semester vacations. Relations with St. Petersburg circles were considerably strengthened in 1893 by the arrival of Iulii Tsederbaum (Martov), an active Social Democrat expelled from the capital; he chose Vilna as a place of exile precisely because of its reputation as a thriving Social Democratic center. Firm connections with Moscow were established through a gentile, E. I. Sponti, one of the founders of the Moscow Workers' Union in 1893. At one time, Sponti had spent a term of military service in Vilna, and while there had actively participated first in Polish, then in Jewish Social Democratic work.[6]

Very early (by 1892), the Vilna organization performed two very special services for the Russian Social Democratic groups with which it was in contact: first, it helped fugitives who desired to go abroad to cross the border illegally; second, it served as an entrepôt for propaganda literature smuggled in from abroad, particularly from Plekhanov's Liberation of Labor Group. Since envoys from Russian organizations came to Vilna to pick up this literature, Vilna became a natural coordinating center for the Russian movement long before the latter was in a position to perform this function for itself. In fact, in early 1894 the Vilna Social Democrats took careful soundings of other Russian groups to see whether some sort of association or joint enterprise might be feasible. To their disappointment they found that the other Russian organizations were for the most part still in the embryonic stage and feared that ambitious undertakings would detract from the modest beginnings of their propaganda work. Vilna had no alternative but to turn toward its own internal affairs and wait for the Russian movement to catch up.[7]

At this point, a variety of considerations forced the Vilna Social Democrats to rethink their approach to practical activities. Quite independently of their activities, unrest among the artisan masses was growing. The miserably exploited journeymen, losing the possibility of becoming independent masters as the crafts became concentrated in larger shops, came to approximate a wage-earning proletariat and fought for their interests through strikes and mutual aid funds. The younger artisans, eager to settle accounts with the proprietors of their shops, felt little attraction to the intellectual rigors of the propaganda circles. The older workers, products of the "Russified" socialist education, disdained the crude protests of their ghetto-bound fellows, sometimes even actively sabotaging them. Moreover, many carefully trained worker-socialists escaped the frustrations of their milieu either by emigrating to America or by employing their cultural attainments (particularly their facility in Russian) to establish themselves as proprietors of their own shops. In the latter case they unhesitantly proceeded to hire and "exploit" apprentices and journeymen. Caught in an impossible dilemma, the Vilna Social Democrats made the momentous decision to abandon their painstaking former mode of work and adopted the cause of the masses as their own. The experience of the class struggle itself, it was felt, would prove a far better instructor in socialism than organized propaganda.

The theoretical justification of this revolution in tactics was worked out by Arkadii Kremer and Martov in the famous pamphlet *Ob agitatsii* (1894). The remarkable feature of this work was that, although designed to meet the crisis arising out of the specific conditions of the ghetto sweatshops, the theoretical arguments and practical guidelines were cast purely in general terms of Marxist theory, capable of universal application. Starting from the premise that the chief aim of Social Democracy should be to mold the consciousness of the working class as a whole, and that masses are moved "not by intellectual considerations, but by the objective course of events," the pamphlet proposed activating the class struggle through strike agitation, which should concentrate at the outset on "everyday needs and demands." This purely "economic" struggle would give the worker "confidence in his own strength and consciousness of the need for solidarity," thus placing before him "more important tasks demanding resolution." This more conscious form of struggle would "create the soil for political agitation, the goal of which is to change the existing political conditions to the advantage of the working class."[8] Since a relatively small ethnic group could scarcely hope by itself to change "existing political conditions," it was clear the authors felt they were formulating the goals, not of the Jewish minority, but of the workers' movement of Russia as a whole.[9]

Given its intention, the appearance of *Ob agitatsii* was quite timely, since the Russian movement itself was approaching a turning point. While Marxist instruction in propaganda circles was spreading at a steady pace, a series of industrial disorders broke out early in 1895 in Iaroslavl, Ivanovo-Voznesensk, and in both capitals. Taken by surprise, the Social Democrats looked for practical guidance, some favoring active intervention in the disorders, others opposing it. When news of the Vilna technique reached Russian organizations, it was a foregone conclusion that it would become the focus of the debate. Two Moscow Social Democrats, E. I. Sponti and S. I. Mitskevich, becoming familiar with Vilna methods through extended visits, brought news of it along with the precious manuscript to their own organization.[10] Martov brought a copy to St. Petersburg in the fall of 1894, and it promptly evoked lively discussion among several Social Democratic circles, including the group known as the *stariki* ("old hands"), of which Lenin was a member. When Martov resettled in St. Petersburg in the fall of 1895 and joined forces with the *stariki,* the new program was introduced with determination and success. Although most of the *stariki,* including Martov and Lenin, were soon arrested, the idea took firm hold; new converts were drawn in from the student intelligentsia, who carried the efforts forward.

News of the Vilna technique soon spread to Kiev, Ekaterinoslav, Odessa, Nizhni-Novgorod, and Ivanovo-Voznesensk, and the issue was settled once and for all by the enormous impact of the St. Petersburg textile strike in 1896. For the next half decade, *Ob agitatsii* was the bible of the rank-and-file underground workers in Russia. Undeterred by never-ending waves of arrests and exile, local groups instigated one strike after the other, educating thousands of Russian workers in the essentials of socialism. That an entire epoch in the history of Russian Social Democracy owed its inspiration to the Vilna experience is eloquently attested by P. A. Garvi, who entered the Odessa Committee of the Party in late 1900.

> Emerging from the narrow confines of the secret propaganda circles, the basic tactical problem of Social Democracy was to break through to the masses and embark on the path of leading the struggle of the working class by means of agitation. The well-known brochure *Ob agitatsii* clearly reflected the critical moment of the Social Democratic movement of

> Russia. It exercised on all of us, the party workers of that time, a tremendous influence. The experience of the St. Petersburg strikes, the strike movement in Poland, and particularly in the Jewish movement . . . was the best illustration of the correctness of the new tactical position of *Ob agitatsii*, which essentially did not "discover" the new strategy, but simply formulated and expressed an empirical change in local Social Democratic work.[11]

The unanticipated success of the Vilna Social Democrats in launching a mass Jewish workers' movement led to a rapid restructuring of its own organization. Trained agitators from Vilna were transferred to other Jewish communities where strike fever was spreading. Vilna thus became the natural coordinating center of the burgeoning Jewish movement. This sudden expansion in the scope of Vilna's underground operations created a strong demand for the promotion of new organizational cadres from the ranks. Since agitation, in contrast to propaganda, had to be conducted in Yiddish, the new functions could most easily be performed by the large fringe of *poluintelligenty*, whose theoretical talents may have been weak, but who craved action and were thoroughly attuned to the plight of the artisan class. Day-to-day leadership and all technical functions in the Jewish movement soon passed into the hands of representatives of this stratum, assisted by the more energetic of the artisan workers. A few of their more cultured seniors, including Arkadii Kremer, M. D. Srednitskaia, and V. Levinson (Kossovskii), formed a special collegium for matters of high policy, such as communications with outside groups. Other Russian-educated leaders, finding their services no longer at a premium, looked beyond the Pale for more suitable application of their energies. When his term of exile ended, Martov returned to St. Petersburg, where he was joined by his Vilna acquaintance Liakhovskii; Aizenshtat settled in Odessa to revive a Social Democratic organization broken up recently by the police; Timofei Kopel'zon resettled in Warsaw, and later in Berlin, to facilitate the flow of agitational and propaganda literature into Russia.[12]

Although it was felt most keenly by the older generation of Social Democrats, the urge to "emigrate" to the Russian movement filtered down to the *poluintelligenty* and gifted artisans who had "graduated" from the propaganda circles. A group of locksmith apprentices tutored by Martov, having obtained certificates of proficiency in their craft entitling them to the coveted "right of residence," debated whether they ought not to resettle in central Russia to plant the seeds of "agitation." On Martov's advice, one of their number, M. Frankfurt, moved to the Volga region, while his comrades joined the *intelligent* Gozhanskii in "colonizing" Belostok, where the Jewish and Russian textile workers had just displayed their solidarity in the strikes of 1895. P. O. Gordon, a product of the Vilna pedagogical institute, accompanied Aizenshtat to Odessa. Moisei Dushkan, a bookbinder and pupil of Martov, settled in Ekaterinoslav with a dedicated group of tailors and locksmiths, to bring the gospel of agitation to that untouched locality.[13]

Some, like Kremer and Mutnikovich, chose to remain with the Vilna organization and make their career in the Bund, while others, like Dushkan and A. Gel'fand (Litvak), after a period of "wandering" in the Russian movement returned to become prominent in the Jewish movement. A considerable number of those who crossed over to bolster up the budding Russian organizations remained there permanently and never felt themselves to be anything but "Russian" Social Democrats. In Vilna, the schooling of *intelligenty, poluintelligenty,* and workers alike had been oriented toward the Russian revolutionary movement, of which the Jewish contingent was viewed as a constituent part. If the Russian movement was lagging behind, then it seemed natural to offer one's services.

Although the dispersion of Jewish practitioners of the faith to other parts of Russia originated in Vilna, the concurrent flowering of the Jewish movement soon set up secondary centers of the missionary impulse.

Vitebsk was one such prominent center of dispersion.[14] Its founder and preceptor, Kh. Usyshkin, was later exiled to Poltava, where he provided a few services to Russian organizations and later became a Bolshevik. His pupils, a cohesive group of *eksternaty* and artisans, systematically scouted the south for a suitable locale in which to implement their carefully nurtured Marxist convictions; they finally settled on Ekaterinoslav, where they ran into the Vilna group brought by Dushkan. The Vitebsk group, being slightly more Russianized, decided to concentrate its efforts on the growing factory population, whereas the Vilna-ites continued their efforts among the Jewish artisan population. I. Vilenskii from Vitebsk and Dushkan from Vilna set up a secret printing press for *Rabochaia gazeta,* an organ sponsored by the Kievan Social Democrats to further unity in the Social Democratic movement and pronounced the official organ of the party at the First Congress of the RSDRP, in 1898. Later (1899) they performed the same service for *Iuzhnyi rabochii,* an exceptionally popular underground journal, which competed with *Iskra* in the south until it was disbanded by the Second Congress in 1903.

A second wave of emigration from Vitebsk soon followed the first. In 1898 a *poluintelligent,* A. M. Ginzburg, departed first for Kharkov, then Minsk, and finally Ekaterinoslav, making his contribution to local Social Democratic work in each of these centers. He eventually joined Vilenskii in the founding of *Iuzhnyi rabochii* and the two for a time (until their arrest) were the soul of the enterprise. A cabinetmaker from Vitebsk, Iosif Ioffe, migrated with Ginzburg to Kharkov, where police reports marked him as the most able and dangerous of the worker-agitators. Two years later he was a key member of the Odessa Committee of the party whom Garvi accounted an outstanding worker-revolutionary.[15] Ginzburg expressed the sentiments of many of these fugitives from the Jewish movement.

> I chose Ekaterinoslav out of definite party considerations. I decided to devote myself to agitational work among the Russian factory and indus-

> trial workers, which in my eyes had incomparably more interest and prospects for success than work among the artisan [i.e. Jewish] masses.[16]

Another center of infection was Gomel, of which General Novitskii, the chief of police of Kiev, exclaimed when arrests were made in 1901: "Not another from Gomel! What a rats' nest! No matter where arrests take place in Russia, there's always a *gomelchanin.*"[17] The prominent Menshevik Grigorii Aronson, a participant in Gomel circles, best captured the climate which spawned this remarkable phenomenon. A group of Social Democratic *gymnasium* students (of which he was a member in 1902-1903) systematically organized and indoctrinated the numerous *eksternaty* who flowed into Gomel from surrounding localities in quest of education and culture:

> They forsook their traditional-religious families and turned up with no means of livelihood, often no nook to live in. At times they were almost adults, in any event 18-20 years of age [i.e., older than their tutors]. The eagerness with which they threw themselves into Russian grammar, devoured Gogol, and Turgenev, was a wonder to behold. Popular works on science went from hand to hand. The majority of the *eksternaty* spoke Russian poorly, were ignorant of grammar, and understood little of what they read. . . . Many of them later became pharmacists, grammar school teachers, and Talmud scholars, but a chosen few passed their diploma exams and went on to the university, for the most part abroad.[18]

Although Aronson's group initiated a goodly number into the Social Democratic faith, this was apparently the last generation to feel the cosmopolitan attraction of Marxism. The Kishinev and Gomel pogroms of 1903, with their police-inspired horrors, permanently shattered the lure of assimilation, and the privileged Jewish youth ceased to transmit Russian culture and ideology to their less fortunate peers, who in large numbers now turned to terrorism, Zionism, and the several varieties of Zionist socialism.

Odessa is another interesting case in point. In the ethnic potpourri of this port metropolis, the Great Russian element was minimal and the Jewish exceptionally large. The Social Democratic organizations of the 1890s in Odessa had always been predominantly Jewish and had carried on their activities primarily among the Jewish artisan and factory population.

Yet the Social Democrats of Odessa were thoroughly assimilationist and adhered exclusively to the Russian movement rather than to the Bund. P. A. Garvi, a product of the Odessa movement and the typical offspring of the impoverished Jewish middle classes (his father, unlike his prosperous uncles, had no talent for business and remained a miserably paid clerk), vividly portrays his beginnings.[19] He and a group of fellow *eksternaty,* while preparing for diploma exams, put great zeal into working out a "world-view" which might promise deliverance from surrounding injustices. Though often going to bed with an empty stomach, he claimed he sensed his "debt to people" like a "repentant nobleman" (it goes without saying that he revered the heroes of the People's Will and knew its legends by heart). His tutor and mentor, Evsei Kogan, who obviously had connections with some sort of conspiratorial organization, occasionally entrusted him with secretive errands such as delivering messages or hiding illicit materials.

After what seemed like an incredibly long apprenticeship, Kogan sponsored Garvi's entrance into the Odessa Committee. Though he passed his diploma exams, he was denied entry into the university by the percentage norms for Jews. His only alternative was to continue his underground committee work, supporting himself by tutoring the sons of other impoverished Jewish families who hoped to force the narrow entrance to social advancement. Thus, Garvi and his companions were channeled into the career of professional revolutionaries before they reached the years of maturity. After completing the usual cycle of arrest, prison, and exile, Garvi fled abroad just after the party split, where he declared himself an adherent of the minority faction, thus beginning his long career in the service of Menshevism.[20]

Though less so than in Odessa, most of the southern party committees (Kharkov, Ekaterinoslav, Kiev, Rostov, and Kremenchug) were predominantly Jewish in composition, due in no small measure to "emigration" from the western Pale. Their orientation, however, was entirely toward the Russian movement and remained so long after the founding of the Bund. They made use of Bundist practical experience, but their actions were directed solely toward the construction and solidification of a Russian Social Democratic party. It is remarkable that in almost all the ambitious undertakings in the Russian movement during these years (the operation of underground printing presses and the calling of regional and nation-wide congresses, for example) the drive and practical talent were supplied by offshoots from the Jewish movement. A numerical calculation of the Jewish contingent in Russian Social Democratic organizations would be a rather complex task; suffice it to say that it ranged from substantial to preponderant in the southern committees and was noticeably present elsewhere.[21] Throughout the 1890s and well into the following century, Jewish Social Democracy continued to supply the thirsting Russian organizations with an abundant supply of talented, energetic committeemen and revolutionary entrepreneurs.

The emergence of a separate Jewish Social Democratic movement and the founding of the Bund in 1897 did not of itself signify a break with the former sympathies. Although the conversion to agitation in 1894 necessarily imparted a certain national coloration to the Jewish movement due to the use of Yiddish as the operating tongue and the involvement of the unassimilated artisan masses, genuine "nationalism" in theory and emotion made little headway in the Bund until the turn of the century. Tsive Gurvich, a well-schooled worker-socialist who was active in the Bund during these years, asserts that "we envied those who left for work among the Russian proletariat" and disclaims any signs of nationalism in the Bund except the use of Yiddish, to which he and other Russianized workers were originally opposed. He states that he heard the notion that the Jews constituted a "nation" and deserved political autonomy for the first time at the Third Congress of the

Bund in late 1899, where its only defender was the emigre Bundist John Mill.[22] Another comrade, Damskii (also apparently a worker), states that the "only thing that kept us from settling in Moscow or on the Volga was the difficulty in securing the right of residence."[23] The only recorded expression of nationalism in this period was a speech by Martov at a May First gathering in Vilna in 1895, a lapse which Martov later sincerely regretted. He called for the formation of a Jewish Social Democratic party separate from the Russian on the grounds that Jewish workers, suffering from legal disabilities, could not depend upon their Russian comrades to fight for the particular interest of Jewish civil equality. This was a rather mild form of nationalism to be sure, but as a result Martov was reproached by his well-taught pupils, and this approach was quickly dropped.[24]

Even after the Jewish movement had progressed far beyond the Russian groups in the scope of their endeavors, the Vilna center still aspired to found an All-Russian rather than a specifically Jewish Social Democratic party. Several times in the years 1895-97 the Vilna organization broached the question of coordinating efforts toward common goals. They carried on negotiations among others with Lenin's *stariki* in 1895 and with Moscow, St. Petersburg, and Kiev in 1897.

It is quite certain, therefore, that the founding of the Bund in the fall of 1897 was not consciously conceived as a break-away from the Russian movement; rather, its founding was intimately connected with the forthcoming First Congress of the Russian party, in the arrangements for which the Vilna Social Democrats were apparently already involved.[25] Tsoglin ("David Kats"), a participant in both affairs, insists that the major considerations were of a practical, not an ideological, character: first, it was felt that the Russian Central Committee should not be burdened with the problem of supplying literature (a major function of the projected Central Committee) in Yiddish; secondly, there was a feeling that the Russian Social Democrats were too lax in the rules of conspiracy, and therefore it was considered safer for the Jewish organizations to be related to the party indirectly through their own leadership rather than each one separately.[26] Probably the particularism of the Bund went a step or two further than this in the realm of sub-surface feelings: Vilna already enjoyed a practical, functioning hegemony in the Jewish movement and was undoubtedly reluctant to surrender this position to the uncertain vicissitudes of a wider party organization ("regionalism" on such grounds was not unknown in the Russian movement).

Shortly after the founding of the Bund, the Kievan and Bund leaders coordinated their efforts in planning the First Congress of the Russian party, and any rivalry between them seemed to disappear. It is significant that the Bund handled the physical arrangements (which demanded complete secrecy) and that the Congress took place in Minsk, the new seat of the Bund Central Committee. The Russians did not seem to be disturbed that three of the nine delegates were from the Bund, nor did they offer any objection to the Bund's request to enter the party as "an autonomous organization, independent only in questions especially concerning the Jewish proletariat" (in all other matters presumably they were bound by general party decisions).[27] The phrase was designed primarily to allow the Bund to handle its own literature and to conduct its own campaigns in behalf of civil equality for Jews, to which the Russian comrades might devote insufficient attention. At the Bund's request the party was designated as *Rossiiskaia* rather than *russkaia* to underscore its territorial, rather than its national, basis. It was felt that Poles, Lithuanians, Latvians, Georgians, and Jews could all feel at home in such a party. (The Bund did not come to regard the party as a federation of national units until its Fourth Congress in 1901, and then only after a bitter fight within its own ranks.) Kremer was one of the three elected to the Central Committee of the party and the only one to carry on his duties after the devastating arrests which followed the First Congress. He saw to it that the Manifesto of the party was printed by the Bund's secret press, though he disagreed with its contents (for reasons unknown). He also made plans to revive the party organ *Rabochaia gazeta* and in a coded letter requested Lenin and Martov in Siberia to be collaborators.[28]

As a matter of course the Bund continued to play its role as the chief purveyor of literature from abroad and operator of the underground railroad, even though the high point of its association with the Russian movement was past. Still, old traditions lived on. Aaron Ginzburg, now representing Ekaterinoslav, approached the Bund in the summer of 1900 to discuss the possibility of reviving the Russian party. Lenin and Martov, whose plans to establish *Iskra* were known, were to be invited to edit the party organ. The effort was thwarted by crippling arrests and the unwillingness of the *Iskra* group to participate except on its own terms.[29] In 1902 Timofei Kopel'zon, now representing the Union of Russian Social Democrats Abroad, contacted the Bund and suggested that it arrange for a new party congress, its object being to offset the growing influence of *Iskra.* Although the congress duly met in March, 1902, in Belostok, the unexpected arrival of an *Iskra* emissary, Fedor Dan, obliged those present to declare the meeting an unofficial "conference" and to appoint an organizing committee for a congress on which *Iskra,* the Bund, *Iuzhnyi rabochii,* and the St. Petersburg Committee would be represented.[30] Although the Bund representative was the only one to survive the arrests which followed, his conscientious effort to get in touch with *Iskra* gave Lenin his opportunity to organize the Congress under *Iskra's* auspices. To his agents in Russia Lenin wrote:

> I just gave the Bund your contact address. This concerns the congress. . . . Act with authority, but *with care.* Take upon yourself the responsibility for as much territory as possible in making preparations for the congress, . . . and let the Bund for now limit itself to its own bailiwick. . . . The make-up of the committee must be as favorable as possible for us (perhaps you could say the committee has already been organized and you would be happy to have the Bund take part). . . . In short make yourself master of this undertaking.[31]

Although Lenin had already laid his plans for a showdown with the Bund over the nationality question, he was anxious that formal relations with it be proper in order to keep up the pretense of carrying on the work of the Belostok Conference and not to appear ungrateful to the Bund's historical services. Lenin's agents followed his instructions to the letter. One of them notes that at a planning conference the Bund "somehow didn't show up" and that "it was therefore all the easier to make certain decisions and to draw in more of our own people."[32] The Bund was scrupulously notified of the proceedings and requested to accede to the decisions. A protest by the Bund in its emigre organ *Posledniia izvestiia* received a conciliatory reply in *Iskra,* expressing regrets for the misunderstanding and hope for the Bund's full participation in the near future.[33] Just as hypocrisy is the tribute paid by vice to virtue, so Lenin's cunning was his own peculiar way of acknowledging the unchallengeable contribution of the Bund and the Jewish movement to Russian Social Democracy.

ISRAEL GETZLER

Marxist Revolutionaries and the Dilemma of Power

This paper seeks to investigate the dilemma of power which Marxist revolutionaries seem to have faced when active in "backward" societies like that of Germany in 1848 and Russia in 1905 and 1917. I became interested in the subject in the course of my study of Martov and through conversations with the late Boris Nicolaevsky and N. V. Vol'sky-Valentinov. My examination of the Marxist foundations to which the Russian debates of 1905 and 1917 were related benefited greatly from a reading of *Karl Marx, Man and Fighter.*[1] Though it may be doubtful whether Boris Nicolaevsky would have agreed with my conclusions, I am certain that he was passionately interested in the questions I propose to raise.

My starting point is the failure of the Mensheviks in the 1917 revolution. The most current explanation of the failure is that the Mensheviks, a party of great talents and considerable political experience, saw their Russian world with Marxist blinkers and were in the end "ruined by their pedantic Marxism."[2] That is to say, they were in the straitjacket of a doctrine according to which the Russian revolution of their day could be none other than a "bourgeois" revolution and would put the liberal middle classes into power.

The Menshevik concept of bourgeois revolution postulated that, in a backward, absolutist, and semi-feudal country like Russia, it made no sense for socialists and the party of the proletariat to seize power and plunge Russia into socialism. Capitalist development under bourgeois-democratic auspices was not only the order of the day: it was also desirable. Abstention from power, a socialist version of the self-denying ordinance, even when power lay within easy reach and the temptation to seize it was great, was the *basic practical commitment* inherent in the concept of bourgeois revolution.

In 1917 the Mensheviks did abstain from supreme power only until the April crisis, after which they joined the first coalition government (formed on May 5) as junior partners to a bourgeois majority. They repeated the performance by entering the second coalition government (formed July 24), but on even worse terms. Was Menshevik political thinking as developed in the 1905 debate on power and as practiced in 1917—first abstention from and then acceptance of a minor share in power—grounded in Marxist theory, prescription, or precedent?

Marx and Engels were extremely wary about offering advice on revolutionary strategy in Russia, and it would be futile therefore to search in their works for an unambiguous revolutionary recipe for Russia. Still, Marx and Engels, between 1846 and 1850, were practical revolutionaries in pre-bourgeois and pre-industrial Germany, a situation in many ways comparable to that of pre-1917 Russia. Like their Russian disciples they too faced a dilemma of power. What revolutionary strategy did they advocate and pursue, and above all, what was their attitude to the question of power?

Before 1848, Marx and Engels hoped and prophesied that the German revolution would be a *bourgeois revolution.* Marx, in his famous row with Wilhelm Weitling in Brussels on March 30, 1846, did more than ridicule Weitling's Utopian *Handwerkerkommunismus* as "sentimental drivel"; he insisted that in Germany a bourgeois revolution was on the agenda. This, he stated, meant that "there could be no talk of the immediate realization of communism—first the bourgeoisie must come to the helm."[3] Yet Weitling had no time for the moderate counsel of scientific socialism which told impatient maximalists like himself to wait. To him "mankind was always or never ripe [for communism]" and Marx's patient writing-desk analyses were developed "in aloofness from the suffering world and the tribulations of the people."[4]

One reason why Moses Hess fell foul of Marx and Engels in 1847 was his insistence that in Germany, because of the cowardice and weakness of its bourgeoisie, a proletarian and not a bourgeois revolution was on the agenda. However, thanks to the German *Misère,* that proletarian revolution would have to rely on an "external stimulus," the "approaching storm" of a French revolution.[5]

Karl Heinzen, who campaigned in 1847 for an immediate insurrection in Germany, was thus lectured by Engels and Marx: in a country like Germany, which "industrially was so dependent and enslaved," the only possible change in property relations would be "in the interest of the bourgeoisie and of free competition."[6] To try to do more in a situation where the political rule of the bourgeoisie corresponded to the stage reached in the development of productive relations was futile.

> Even were the proletariat to overthrow the political domination of the bourgeoisie, its victory could only be transient, nothing but a passing moment in the service of the *bourgeois revolution* as in Anno 1794.[7]

Against this general principle of social evolution "no powerful effort of the mind or of the will" could be of much avail. The "definitive fall of the political bourgeois domination" would come only when the material conditions had been created which necessitated "the abolition of the bourgeois mode of production."[8] However, a patient acceptance of bourgeois revolution and bourgeois rule did not mean that socialists ought to wash their hands of the revolutionary movement; they must support the bourgeoisie when it was making its bourgeois revolution, knowing that their "own struggle against the bourgeoisie can begin only on the day, when the bourgeoisie has been victorious."

While bourgeois revolution may have been a handy stick with which to beat maximalist rivals such as Weitling, Hess, Heinzen, and all the Straubingers, in a nascent German labor movement, to Marx and Engels it was far more than a mere polemical concept. It was the rationale of a minimalist revolutionary strategy. In backward, absolutist Germany, state-power was conceded to the bourgeoisie at a time when the working class was still an insignificant political force, on the grounds that bourgeois rule was a necessary precondition for eventual proletarian rule. Engels thus explained why even in the "ancient-Germanic" democracies of Switzerland and Norway, "*modern* democracy" (i.e. socialism) was not yet on the agenda:

> In all civilized countries the democratic movement aims in the last resort at the political domination of the proletariat. It presupposes then that a proletariat exists, that a ruling bourgeoisie exists, that an industry exists which creates the proletariat and which has brought the bourgeoisie to power.[9]

Thus, in spite of all their democratism, what Switzerland and Norway still needed was a bourgeois revolution and bourgeois rule. Likewise, Engels' "Basic Principles of Communism" of October-November, 1847, postulated that in Germany it was in the interest of the communists to help the bourgeoisie come to power as soon as possible, so that they could overthrow it again as soon as possible.[10] What he expected from bourgeois rule by the "lords of capital" and its fatally transient nature Engels spelled out in a memorable passage in his review of the year 1847:

> We need you for the time being; we even need your domination here and there. You must remove for us the relics of the Middle Ages and the absolute monarchy; you must destroy patriarchalism, you must centralize; you must transform all more or less property-less classes into real proletarians, into recruits for us by means of your factories and trade connections; you must supply the basis for these material means which the proletariat requires for its emancipation. As your wage for this you may for a short time rule. You may dictate laws and bask in the majestic splendor which you have created; you may feast in the royal hall and wed the beautiful princess; but do not forget—"The executioner stands at the door."[11]

Both points, the necessity of a bourgeois revolution and bourgeois rule in Germany *and* its transient nature, are reiterated in the *Communist Manifesto*. It diagnosed Germany to be on the eve of a bourgeois revolution and prescribed a revolutionary strategy of full support for the bourgeoisie "whenever it acts in a revolutionary way against the absolute monarchy, the feudal squirearchy, and the petty bourgeoisie." Such support must not gloss over the fundamental antagonism between bourgeoisie and proletariat which must burst into the open immediately upon the overthrow of the reactionary classes. Then the proletariat will embark on its struggle against the bourgeoisie. Thus the German bourgeois revolution (by contrast with those of England in the seventeenth century and of France in the eighteenth) would not usher in a long historical phase of bourgeois domination. The question then was how long. Was it to be measured in decades or in years? If only in years, how could the bourgeoisie manage to do all that Marx and Engels expected it to do and prepare the ground for the proletariat? While Marx and Engels may have seen the brevity of bourgeois rule as a function of its belatedness, the fact that they expected the bourgeoisie to come to the helm, whether for a brief period or for an entire historical phase, exempted them for some time from the responsibility of making ready for government. Moreover, it gave them theoretical justification for restraining their more maximalist followers without robbing them of the hope of seeing socialism realized in their time.

In the early phase of the 1848 revolution Marx reiterated the minimalist view that the Germans in 1848 were now where the French had been in 1789.[12] Marx and his followers in the Communist League merged with the general democratic movement.[13] But by June, 1848, he and Engels began to strike a more maximalist note, reminiscent of the "heresy" of Moses Hess.

The big bourgeoisie, they now discovered, was already *revolutionsmüde* and had cheated the revolution of its democratic fruits, aiming at establishing its domination by way of compromise with the old police and feudal state. This compromise was effected at the expense of its most natural allies, the peasantry, whose feudal burdens had not been seriously relieved. This, more than anything, proved that the German revolution of 1848 was no more than "a parody of the French revolution of 1789" which within three weeks of the fall of the Bastille had made a clean sweep of all feudal burdens.[14]

History knew no more despicable wretchedness than that of the German bourgeoisie, an *Allerweltsknecht,* especially the Prussian bourgeoisie:[15]

> Without initiative, without faith in itself or in the people, without historical vocation, . . . thus the *Prussian bourgeoisie* found itself at the helm of the Prussian state after the March revolution.[16]

The German bourgeoisie was at the helm but had failed in its historical task of completing the bourgeois revolution. Marx and Engels now pinned their hopes on another revolution in Paris which would issue in revolutionary war and then, *Vae Victis!,* democrats in Germany would get their revenge.

> The cannibalism of the counterrevolution will have convinced the nations that there is only one means to *abbreviate,* to simplify, to concentrate the murderous agonies of the old society and the bloody birthpangs of the new, only one means–*revolutionary terrorism.*[17]

The whole course of the 1848 revolution in Germany proved that in Germany a "pure *bourgeois revolution*" was impossible; the alternative was either "feudal absolutist counterrevolution or the social-republican revolution."[18]

For some time then Marx and Engels in the *Neue Rheinische Zeitung* spoke of a new victorious revolution, of a people's revolution,[19] a democratic revolution which would come in the wake of a new French revolution—a "February in higher potency."[20] "Bourgeois revolution" had disappeared from their revolutionary vocabulary.

Marx's and Engels' left-turn in the *Neue Rheinische Zeitung* was paralleled in the tactical sphere by their renewed interest in the *Arbeiterverein* and their exodus from the Democratic Association and the attempt to create a "purely social party" upholding the "principles of social democracy."[21] From their early role as radical left-wing democrats they now began to assume the role of leaders of a socialist class-party of the proletariat.

In review then, Marx and Engels reacted to the shattering experience of the failure of the 1848 revolution in Germany by modifying, if not abandoning, their deterministic scheme and above all by lifting their taboo on power. Surely a revolution which aimed at the establishment of a social republic would put socialists at the helm of government. But the flirtation with the notions of a "social-republican" revolution and of revolutionary terror never matured into hard policy; it merely reflected a passing mood of despair when the revolution was crushed in Berlin and Vienna.

Early in 1850 Marx and Engels expected a new revolutionary upheaval in Germany which would be sparked by an uprising of the French working class or by a counterrevolutionary military invasion of France. In the March, 1850, *Address of the Central Bureau to the Communist League,* they prescribed a minimalist-maximalist revolutionary strategy for Germany's second revolution. The "revolutionary workers' party" which they hoped to create and lead should give its support to the petty-bourgeois democratic party in its struggle against the reactionary government and even allow it to seize power. Yet it must prevent the democrats in government from consolidating their power and freezing the revolution since "our interest and our task is to make the revolution permanent, until . . . the proletariat had conquered state power." Therefore it must take an attitude of "unconcealed mistrust in the new government," harass it, and "dictate such conditions to them that the rule of the bourgeois democrats will from the outset bear within it the seeds of their downfall and that their subsequent extrusion by the rule of the proletariat will be considerably facilitated." This could best be done by keeping up the "revolutionary excitement" and by "establishing simultaneously and alongside the new official government their own revolutionary workers' governments whether in the form of municipal committees and municipal councils, or by way of workers' clubs or workers' committees." In other words, the new revolutionary strategy aimed at *dual government:* while the "momentary, inevitable dominance of bourgeois democracy"[22] was grudgingly accepted, the proletariat was to entrench itself in "revolutionary workers' governments" and assume the role of irreconcilable revolutionary opposition which would push the official government into realizing, in spite of itself, as many radical and social objectives as possible and thus prepare for its own advent to power.

While it was true that German workers could not as yet "attain power and realize their own class interests without completely going through a lengthy revolutionary development," their advent to power lay at the end of that permanent revolution which was about to begin and which would possibly coincide with and be accelerated by the victory of the proletariat in France.[23]

While the ambiguity of the *Address* on the cardinal question of power may be partly a concession to maximalist followers like Willich and Schapper, partly a realistic appraisal of the immaturity and impotence of the "workers' party" and of the working class in Germany as an aspirant to governmental power, it certainly illustrates a reluctance to take power and govern. Dual government and permanent revolution were the answers with which Marx and Engels resolved their dilemma of power when the classical answer of bourgeois revolution and abstention from power proved impracticable and unattractive. This represented a more radical resolution of the tension that existed between the maximalist, subjective will of the revolutionary socialist and the objectivity of the social scientist, a tension which defies resolution in a backward situation where the objective prerequisites are missing. In other words, the "scientific socialism"[24] of Marx and Engels gave no satisfactory answer to the dilemma of power in the backward, pre-bourgeois, and pre-industrial situation in which they found themselves as active revolutionaries in Germany in the period 1848-50.

Marx's and Engels' hopes for a new revolutionary upsurge in Germany (and France) in which the working class and the *Arbeiterpartei* would play an independent role soon proved a delusion. Europe was settling down in a counterrevolutionary mold, while their Blanquist allies in the Communist League, all stranded in the frustrating atmosphere of London emigration, proved as impatient and maximalist as ever.

It was in conflict and debate with Karl Schapper and August Willich and in the course of the split which Marx and Engels provoked in the Communist League, that they returned to and reiterated the concept of bourgeois revolution as an inevitable and necessary historical stage during which socialists must abstain from power. By the autumn of 1850 Marx and Engels assumed that the first phase of the revolutionary period had ended and would be renewed only by a new world-wide economic crisis.[25] Efforts at playing with revolution by Blanquist elements in the Communist League made no sense in these circumstances and could not be tolerated. It was necessary for Marx and Engels to part company with them, as they were in complete disagreement on the vital question of "the position of the German proletariat in the next revolution,"[26] i.e., on the question of power. While Marx and Engels told workers, "You have fifteen or twenty or fifty years of civil and national wars to go through, not just to change conditions but to change yourselves to become fit for political rule,"[27] the maximalists in the

Communist League, who "stressed the *will* as the main thing in the revolution instead of the real conditions," insisted they "must *immediately* come to power or . . . [they] might as well go to sleep"[28] and trusted that in a new German revolution "the final goal of the movement could be realized."[29] Schapper reduced the whole debate to the brutal

> question [of] whether in the beginning we shall chop heads or our heads will be chopped. In France the workers will come to power and with them *we* in Germany. Were this not the case, I could indeed go to sleep and would then have a very different material position. Should we come to power we could put through measures which would secure domination to the proletariat. I am a fanatical enthusiast in this matter.[30]

Marx did not think it required much "enthusiasm to belong to a party which one thought would soon be in government"[31] and thus the cardinal principle of Marx's revolutionary strategy in Germany was that communists must not form "the *governmental* but the *opposition party of the future*":

> We devote ourselves to a party which in its own best interest cannot as yet take power. Were the proletariat to come to power [now], it would be able to realize only petty-bourgeois, but not directly proletarian measures. Our party can take over the government only when conditions permit it to realize *its* ideas.[32]

Even were the proletariat to come to power in France, it would have to share that power with the peasants and the petty-bourgeoisie and pursue *their* policies rather than its own. Louis Blanc's performance in the Provisional Government of 1848 was a warning of what happened "when one comes prematurely to power."[33]

It fell to Engels to set out in detail the danger of coming to power prematurely. In his *Peasant War in Germany* (written in the summer of 1850), referring to Thomas Münzer's failure as president of the Council of Mühlhausen and to the failure of Louis Blanc and Alexandre Martin in the French Provisional Government of 1848, he sounded this warning:

> The worst that can happen to the leader of an extreme party is that he is compelled to take over the government in a period when the movement is not sufficiently mature for the dominance of the class which he represents and for the realization of those measures required by the dominance of that class. . . . inevitably he finds himself in an insoluble dilemma: what he *can* do contradicts his entire previous performance *(Auftreten),* his principles, and the immediate interests of his party; and what he *ought* to do is not realizable. In a word, he is forced to represent the class for whose domination conditions are ripe, and not his own party and class. In the interest of the movement he must realize the interests of a class which is alien to him, while feeding his own class with phrases and promises and with the assurance that the interests of another class are its own. Whoever falls into such a false position is irretrievably lost.[34]

In a letter to Filippo Turati (January, 1894), Engels analyzed the dilemma of power which the Italian socialists faced, a situation in which the bourgeoisie had "been neither able nor willing to complete its victory" and destroy feudalism. There was no question, Engels urged, that in Italy, for both objective and subjective reasons, a socialist revolution was not on the agenda and that all one could hope to gain from a successful revolution was a "bourgeois republic."[35] Faced with this prospect, socialists, as an "independent party," ought to cooperate with the radicals in a "positive way" when making a revolution which was to be "genuinely national" and not just another irresponsible conspiracy. After the achievement of such a victory, "our ways will part," and socialists "shall constitute the *new opposition* to the new government" and press on to "new conquests." However, the new opposition, Engels insisted, must not enter the government.

> After the common victory, we might be offered some seats in the new government, but always in a *minority*. THAT IS THE GREATEST DANGER. After February, 1848, the French socialist democrats (of the *Réforme*, Ledru-Rollin, Louis Blanc, Flocon, etc.) made the mistake of accepting such posts. Constituting a minority in the government, they voluntarily shared the responsibility for all the infamies and treachery which the majority, composed of pure republicans, committed against the working class, while their presence in the government completely paralyzed the revolutionary action of the working class which they claimed they represented.[36]

Engels had no doubt that the general tactics which he and Marx had advocated in similar situations in the past had proved correct. "As regards their application to present conditions in Italy," he added, "that is another matter; that must be decided on the spot, by those who are in the thick of events."[37]

During the years 1873-75 and in the course of the debate with their Bakuninist opponents, Engels and Marx had occasion to reiterate their views on the position of socialists in the bourgeois revolution with regard to such backward countries as Russia and Spain. Commenting on Peter Tkachev's impatient call for a *social* revolution Engels observed:

> The revolution aimed at by modern socialism is, to put it briefly, the victory of the proletariat over the bourgeoisie and the reorganization of society by the destruction of all class distinctions. To accomplish this revolution not only a proletariat is needed, but also a bourgeoisie in whose hands the productive forces of society have developed to such a stage to allow the final destruction of class distinctions. . . . The bourgeoisie is consequently . . . as equally necessary a precondition for a socialist revolution as the proletariat.[38]

Therefore a Tkachev who believed that socialism could easily be realized in Russia because it had no bourgeoisie, even though it had no proletariat, had still "to learn the ABC of socialism."[39] In a similar vein Marx censured Bakunin's *schülerhafte Eselei,* his reliance on "the *will*" to make a "European social revolution, which is founded on the economic basis of capitalist development, at the level of the Russian or Slavic agricultural and pastoral peoples."[40]

Engels took the Spanish Bakuninists to task for having bungled the 1873 revolution in Spain by their maximalist boycottism and subsequent *volte face* on the question of power:

> Spain is industrially so backward a country that as yet there can be no talk whatever of an *immediate,* complete emancipation of the working class. Before it gets there, Spain must go through various preliminary steps of development and must clear the road of a whole series of obstacles. The republic [which the Bakuninists initially boycotted] offered the opportunity to contract the course of these preliminary steps into the shortest possible period of time. This opportunity, however, could have been utilized only by the active *political* intervention of the Spanish working class.[41]

After their maximalist principle proved unrealistic, i.e., that "workers should not take part in a revolution which does not aim at the complete emancipation of the proletariat," the Bakuninists did an about face and even went so far as to join the various provisional governments which cropped up in the cities, "almost everywhere as an impotent minority which [was] outvoted by the bourgeoisie and politically exploited by it." Thus the Spanish Bakuninists set an "unsurpassed example" of how "one ought *not* to make a revolution."[42]

There can be little doubt that when Marx and Engels were active revolutionaries (during the period 1848-50) or when they were concerned with the prospects of revolution and socialism in Germany, they showed little enthusiasm for immediate power. They seemed to have been happy to see the bourgeoisie (and after it had disappointed them, the radical petty-bourgeois democrats) form the government on the morrow of a successful revolution in Germany. Even as late as the 1880s, after Germany had gone through an unprecedented spurt of industrialization and had already acquired a substantial industrial proletariat with Social Democratic allegiances, Engels thought a bourgeois republic was still on the agenda and counseled German Social Democratic leaders not to strive for *immediate* power. As he put it in a letter to Eduard Bernstein:

> In our country the first immediate result of revolution can and *must* be nothing but a *bourgeois* republic. But here [i.e. in Germany] this will be only a brief transitory moment as fortunately we have no republican bourgeois party. The bourgeois republic, headed perhaps by the progressive party, will serve us in the first place *(zunächst) to conquer the vast workers' mass for revolutionary* socialism; this will be done within one or two years—and to allow for the thorough exhaustion and self-destruction of the middle parties that are still possible, apart from us. Only then will our turn come and we will succeed.[43]

In other words, Engels still recommended the revolutionary strategy of the *Address to the Communist League,* which, as he wrote in 1885, was "still of interest today, because petty-bourgeois democracy is even now that party which during the next European upheaval soon due, must certainly be the first to come to the helm in Germany."[44]

It appears then that Marx and Engels, as practical revolutionaries in a backward, pre-industrial, and pre-bourgeois situation, faced a dilemma of power to which they provided a number of solutions. None of these solutions (with the exception of their irate ephemeral toying with a "social republic" and "revolutionary terrorism") advocated or envisaged an immediate accession to power; rather, they accepted a long-term or short-term role of "oppositional party" vis-à-vis the new post-revolutionary government. While *generally* recommending modified forms of the revolutionary strategy of the *Address to the Communist League* to socialists in backward countries (to be adapted to the local situation by those who were in "the thick of events"), Marx and Engels' hard and fast rule was never to repeat the performance of Louis Blanc and join a post-revolutionary coalition government "in a minority."

As for their later comments on the prospects of a socialist revolution in Russia without a preceding bourgeois revolution,[45] Marx and Engels, while understanding the populists' aversion to seeing Russia "plunge into capitalism," refused to commit themselves either way. In the end, they offered no more specific guidance than Engels' statement of 1894 that "the coming disintegration of capitalist society in the West will also place Russia in a position in which it can shorten its now inevitable transition through the capitalist system"[46] – a statement which could be interpreted to mean both "bourgeois" and/or "permanent" revolution. Neither Marx nor Engels presumed to offer advice on the general revolutionary strategy which ought to be pursued in Russia or on the question of power.

Marx, in his notes on Bakunin's *Staatlichkeit and Anarchie,* seems to have envisaged the possibility of a seizure of power and victory by an industrial proletariat which (thanks to "capitalist production") "occupied at least an important position among the mass of the people," provided it "were at least capable of doing directly for the peasants what the French bourgeoisie in its revolution did at the time for the peasants."[47] Thus with no hard and fast guidance from the founders of Marxism, it fell to George V. Plekhanov to work out Marxist revolutionary strategy in Russia.[48]

Plekhanov came to grips with the question of power in his earliest Marxist work, *Socialism and the Political Struggle* (1883). This work took issue with *Narodnaia volia* and its scheme of "seizure of power by a provisional revolutionary government" as the instrument by which socialism could be realized. Marxists, Plekhanov urged, were not opposed in principle to the seizure of power as such but to its seizure by a revolutionary minority which, establishing itself as some sort of "socialist caste," presumed to engage in "social experiments" from above. Russia being what it was, "we do not believe in the near possibility of a socialist government in Russia." In Russia a bourgeois revolution, i.e., the overthrow of tsarism, the establishment of free political institutions, and the formation of a workers' socialist party, was on the agenda, no more. Warned Plekhanov:

> To fuse into one, two such essentially distinct phenomena as the overthrow of absolutism and the socialist revolution, to wage the revolutionary struggle on the supposition that these two phenomena will *coincide* in the history of our fatherland—*means to delay the occurrence of one and of the other.*[49]

Since seizure of power in Russia by a socialist minority was foredoomed, even agitation for it was harmful, for it would frighten and alienate such potential allies as Russian liberals and bourgeois Europe from the Russian liberation movement.[50] Similarly, in his "Letter to P. L. Lavrov" (1884), Plekhanov denounced, from the standpoint of "scientific socialism," the impatient will to power of *Narodnaia volia* and its obsession with conspiracy.[51]

In his essay *Our Differences,* Plekhanov recommended the revolutionary tactics which had been pursued by the Communist League in Germany, approved of Marx's action against the maximalist faction of Willich and Schapper, and quoted from Engels' polemics with Tkachev and from his *Peasant War* to warn against the danger of a premature accession to power by a socialist party in Russia. The most likely result would be a "shameful fiasco."[52] True, because capitalism had come so late in Russia, "it was bound to wither away before it had fully blossomed," so that the historical phase of bourgeois rule and capitalist development would be greatly abbreviated. Still, the coming revolution in Russia could bring only "the victory of the bourgeoisie and the beginning of the political and economic emancipation of the working class."[53]

It was not surprising that, in his first draft of the program for the Marxist Group for the Emancipation of Labor of 1884, Plekhanov (while still conceding the need for "a terrorist struggle against the absolutist government") should single out the question of "the seizure of power by a revolutionary party" as the major point of disagreement with *Narodnaia volia.*[54] Russian Marxism, therefore, began by fencing itself off from those populist maximalists who saw in the seizure of power an integral part of revolution making.

When Plekhanov concluded his speech at the Paris congress of the Socialist International in 1889 with the emphatic words: "The revolutionary movement in Russia will be victorious only as a workers' movement, or it will never be victorious!"[55] he unwittingly posed a new problem which his teachers Marx and Engels had not known in their revolutionary days in Germany: that of a backward situation where the bourgeoisie was relatively weak and meek, while the working class was relatively strong, alienated, and rebellious. The *Manifesto* of Russian Social Democracy of 1898, drafted by Peter Struve, while ignoring the question of power, spelled out the problem of a bourgeois revolution in a backward society:

> The further east one goes in Europe, the more feeble, cowardly, and mean the bourgeoisie becomes in the political sense and the greater the cultural and political tasks which fall to the lot of the proletariat. On its strong shoulders the Russian working class must carry and is carrying the burden of conquering political freedom.[56]

The conquest of "political freedom" was only the "first step" in the realization of the "historical mission" of the proletariat. The struggle for socialism would begin after the proletariat had thrown off the "yoke of autocracy."

The program of the RSDRP, which was adopted at its Second Congress in 1903, "resolved" the dilemma of power simply by dividing itself into minimum and maximum programs: the specifically Russian *minimum* program, i.e., "the immediate political task being the overthrow of the tsarist autocracy and its replacement by a democratic republic" in which the liberal bourgeoisie was expected to rule, and the *maximum* program, i.e., the realization of the "final goal" which Russian Social Democrats shared with Social Democrats of all countries, and which would begin with the establishment of the dictatorship of the proletariat. However, this matter-of-fact division of the program into "immediate aims" (minimum program) and "final goal" (maximum program) without theoretical props, was already the product of Lenin's war of attrition against Plekhanov's original two drafts of the program of January, 1902, in which Plekhanov had spelled out the reasons for minimalism in terms of the necessity of bourgeois revolution *and* abstention from power:

> Russian Social Democrats can still secure only those legal institutions which constitute the natural, legal complement to capitalist relations of production which exist already in the advanced capitalist countries and which are a prerequisite *for the full and all-sided* class-struggle of wage labor against capital.[57]

There can be no doubt then that "bourgeois revolution" and acceptance of a liberal bourgeois government to issue from it were by 1903 part of Social Democratic revolutionary strategy in Russia, while the division into minimal and maximal programs resolved, or rather shelved, its dilemma of power *and* absolved Social Democrats from the responsibility of government on the morrow of a successful revolution. We might as well note in passing that it was very likely owing to the insistence of Lenin[58] that the *rationale* of the minimalist self-limitation of Russian Social Democracy was not advertised in its program.

There is no evidence that in the Menshevik-Bolshevik feud in the aftermath of the split the dilemma of power played any divisive or polemical role. Even Aksel'rod's famous essays in *Iskra* did no more than taunt Lenin with turning the party into a "Jacobin club."[59] Ironically, it was Trotsky who, in his vitriolic tract *Nashi politicheskie zadachi* of August, 1904, attacked Lenin and especially his Ural supporters for their Jacobinism *and*

Blanquism.[60] Neither Lenin nor Trotsky are on record as having disagreed with the doctrine of bourgeois revolution and its self-denying ordinance before Bloody Sunday. Trotsky, as late as August, 1904, expected the "period of the liquidation of autocracy" to usher in "honeyed years of a liberated bourgeois Russia" and feared that "Russian capitalism, intoxicated by the new sources of development which had opened up for it" after the fall of Tsarism, might divert the working class from its political struggle into economist and trade-unionist channels.[61]

True, in the debate on the organizational question some of Lenin's die-hard supporters in the Urals seem to have made light of the self-denying ordinance. In their manifesto in support of Lenin's centralism, the representatives of the committees of Ufa, Sredne-Uralsk and Perm urged that "not only Russia but also the international proletariat" create a highly centralized, homogeneous, "strong and authoritative" organization, led by a "good commander" and training "dictators" to enable it to "administer" and "utilize for its ends that power which—ere long—would fall under its control." Were the proletariat, so the argument ran, "not to have state-power, it could not only not realize its maximal goal but not even all its minimal desires," indeed, its "immediate task coincided with the final task"; consequently, to prepare the proletariat "for the dictatorship is such an important organizational task that all others should be subordinated to it."[62] In the same vein, another Bolshevik activist described the seizure of power as the "immediate task" of Social Democracy, even if its tenure were "only temporary."[63]

There is no evidence that Lenin inspired the letters. In fact, the words "commander" and "dictator" which the Ural Bolsheviks used, as well as their maximalist argument, suggest that he did not. But Lenin did not disown them and remained "eloquently silent." Martynov and Trotsky interpreted this to mean that Lenin had prudently refrained from coming out into the open with his heterodox views.[64]

Whatever the significance one may attribute to the maximalist manifesto of the Ural Bolsheviks (to the Mensheviks it was no more than a handy stick to beat Lenin with[65]) the momentous debate over power within Russian Social Democracy began in earnest during the 1905 Revolution. The debate over power became part of the perennial Menshevik-Bolshevik feud, reaching its climax in the 1917 Revolution and ending only when silenced by the *force majeure* of the Soviet state.

The opening shot in this debate was fired by Alexander Martynov's *Dve diktatury,*[66] a frontal attack on Lenin and Leninism. Mocking Lenin's organizational principles as simple Jacobinism and trying to discredit as Blanquism Lenin's campaign for a planned and well-timed armed insurrection, Martynov painted a nightmarish picture of a premature seizure of power by a Leninist party:

> Imagine a party whose membership has been narrowed down to include only professional revolutionaries, which has managed to "prepare, schedule, and carry through a popular armed insurrection." Is it not obvious that on the morrow of the revolution the popular will would appoint this very party the provisional government?[67]

Yet this party, which had come to power in a backward country "thanks to the blind play of elemental revolutionary forces," would be unable to fulfill its role as the dictatorship of the proletariat because all objective conditions would be lacking. Its fate could be none other than that of a "fraudulent bankrupt." Martynov cited Engels to support his gloomy prediction, quoting the warning from the *German Peasant War*—a work destined to become the *locus classicus* for the Mensheviks' self-denying ordinance. In the dogmatic formulation of Martynov:

> The proletariat cannot accept all or part of the political power in the state, as long as it does not make a socialist revolution. This is that incontestable proposition which divides us from opportunist Jaurèsism.[68]

What "opportunist Jaurèsism" was, Martynov, Martov, and Plekhanov took pains to spell out in a number of lengthy articles published in *Iskra* in March, April, and June, 1905.[69] It meant above all the assumption of power by socialists in petty-bourgeois Russia and thus their inevitable acceptance of its "bourgeois limitations." This would commit them to an abstention from their "many-sided struggle against the bourgeois order in all its manifestations," to the sanctioning of and responsibility for all the shady and oppressive aspects of a bourgeois regime, with its army, police, jail wardens, magistrates, and bureaucracy. This would bring socialists into "sharp conflict" with the workers they represented who would not cease to suffer from "all the immanent laws of the bourgeois order whose name is poverty, unemployment, inequality and lack of liberty." The Social Democratic duty was not to accept the "bourgeois limitations" of a bourgeois order, but to fight them, and this could best be done from "without," from the position of "principled, irreconcilable opposition" to the existing order.[70]

True, Martynov did not exclude the possibility that the "internal dialectics of the revolution" would carry Social Democrats "regardless of their will" to power at a time when "the national conditions for the realization of socialism have not yet matured."[71] Martov, more specifically, envisaged a situation in which Social Democrats might have no right to "turn their back on political power," e.g. if "those strong bourgeois revolutionary parties" on whom so much depended in the Menshevik scheme of things were not serious aspirants for power but had "withered away without ever blossoming," then Social Democrats must throw overboard their "anti-Jacobin" scruples and save the revolution by assuming power.[72] Once in power, they could not help bursting the "framework of the bourgeois revolution" and heading for collision with the whole of bourgeois society and the fate of the

Paris Commune, unless they succeeded in spreading the revolution to the West. But a situation in which the proletariat proved to be the only serious aspirant for power was hardly likely to arise: a hundred million peasants, ten million craftsmen and professionals contained "ample fuel for revolution" and constituted a "sufficiently broad social basis" for a petty-bourgeois "Jacobin" movement and pretension to power.[73]

Plekhanov's main, if not sole, contribution to the debate was an attempt to shore up the Menshevik self-denying ordinance with the authority of Marx and Engels, by way of a detailed analysis and (legitimate) interpretation of Marx's *Address of the Central Bureau to the Communist League* and a (less legitimate) paraphrase of Engels' letter to Filippo Turati of January 26, 1894.[74]

Yet even the authority of Marx and Engels could not do away with the basic contradiction in the Mensheviks' revolutionary strategy: casting the working class in the heroic role of "vanguard in the national liberation struggle" and assigning it a position of "hegemony" in the Russian revolution, the Mensheviks then expected it to accept the modest task of gadfly to *"exert revolutionary pressure on the will of the liberal and radical bourgeoisie."* Further, such a strategy compelled the bourgeoisie, who would by then hold state-power, to "carry the revolution to its logical conclusion," i.e., to those extreme republican and democratic limits which would serve as the best starting-point for a socialist revolution.

Whatever the flaws in the Mensheviks' revolutionary scheme, their resolution of the dilemma of power—abstention from power—was dictated by their understanding of backward, peasant Russia, their Marxist theory of the state, *and* their democratic commitments. While they believed that Russia's vast millions of peasants, craftsmen, and urban poor contained "ample fuel for revolution," they were even more convinced that these "petty bourgeois" masses did not want socialism. Had socialists then the right, asked Martynov in an article called "In Struggle with the Marxist Conscience," to seize power and "use the authority of state-power to neutralize the resistance of the petty bourgeoisie to the socialist pretensions of the proletariat?"[75]

It was thus in a struggle with their Marxist conscience that the Mensheviks came to rule out the assumption of power by Social Democrats in the coming Russian revolution, except as a tragic necessity. Unable to see past the blinkers of their narrow Marxist "executive committee" theory of the state, they could discern no better choice than abstention from power or a premature and suicidal plunge into socialism.

Abstention from power in the bourgeois revolution became official Menshevik doctrine when the Menshevik conference of April-May, 1905, in Geneva reaffirmed the bourgeois nature of the revolution, enjoined the party not to capture or share power in a provisional government, and defined its relation to whatever governments the revolution might create as that of "a party of extreme revolutionary opposition." It allowed the seizure of power for the purpose of building socialism in one situation only—if the revolution should "leap over into the advanced countries of western Europe."[76]

While, or because, supreme power was taboo and the Mensheviks saw their role as that of militant *opposition* to the official government which would issue from the revolution, they adopted and developed, in the second half of 1905, the concept of revolutionary self-government. That concept, rather than their justification of the taboo on power, was their positive and significant contribution to the Marxist debate on power and to Social Democratic revolutionary tactics and practice in Russia.

The Mensheviks' concept of revolutionary self-government may have been modeled on the revolutionary strategy of Marx's *Address of the Central Bureau to the Communist League* (1850)[77] and on the historical precedent of the Paris Commune;[78] it certainly was stimulated by the municipal revolution in Georgia and Latvia, where early in 1905 tsarist police and officials were ousted from entire areas and replaced by revolutionary authorities, and in particular by the heroic example of the military republic which the sailors of the *Prince Potemkin of Taurus* set up on their battleship in June, 1905.[79] Whatever its origins, the watchword revolutionary self-government and the organizational projects and forms it fathered stood in the center of Menshevik political thinking and agitation in the second half of 1905. The Menshevik campaign for the creation of trade unions, so-called "non-affiliated workers' organizations" in which workers were to be united on the basis of social-economic and political needs common to the entire working class, regardless of their trade and industry,[80] as well as Aksel'rod's plan for a workers' congress,[81] expressed the Mensheviks' educational concern with the organization and activation of the vast and amorphous working mass which had remained outside the party.

The Mensheviks' call for the creation of an ever-growing "network of organs of revolutionary self-government" in towns and villages expanding "gradually all over the country with the perspective of a last assault on the center of government" was the means by which they hoped to unleash from below a "people's revolution" against Tsarism.[82] They envisaged the revolutionary process taking the form of conflict between aggressive organs of revolutionary self-government and a defensive central government.

Finally, the Mensheviks provided the theoretical basis and the initiative for the Soviets of Workers' Deputies which sprang up in St. Petersburg and in a number of provincial towns in the latter part of 1905: they urged workers and peasants to "cover the country with a network of organs of revolutionary government," and to form "workers' agitational committees" which would elect an illegal "National Duma" representing the *pays réel* to confront and possibly oust the State Duma of the *pays légal;*[83] above all, they called for the creation of "non-affiliated workers' organizations." These were intended initially to serve as "the point of departure for the political rallying of the working class" and then to become "the permanent revolutionary organizations of the proletariat (revolutionary workers' clubs) aiming at constant intervention in state and public affairs in the interests of the working class."[84] It is small wonder that Martov, upon his arrival in Petersburg at the end of October, 1905, recognized in the Soviets "the embodiment of our idea of revolutionary self-government."[85] One may perhaps go further and recognize in the Menshevik project of a rival "National" Duma confronting the "State" Duma–a scheme of "dual parliament," and in the "nonaffiliated workers' organizations" and Soviets aiming at "constant intervention into state and public affairs in the interests of the working class" and thus confronting and challenging the official government–a system of "dual government." Generally, the Mensheviks' projected network of "organs of revolutionary self-government," when combined with the role of irreconcilable revolutionary opposition to the new government which they proposed to assume upon the fall of Tsarism, shows a political thinking to some extent akin to that of Marx in 1850 and foreshadows the "dual power" of the Provisional Government period in 1917.

Martynov's prediction that Lenin was bound to advocate the seizure of power proved correct when in March, 1905, Lenin began to agitate for a "revolutionary-democratic dictatorship of the proletariat and the peasantry," i.e., a revolutionary coalition government of Social Democrats and various agrarian socialists and radicals. Yet the more radical revision of the doctrine of bourgeois revolution came sooner and from within the Menshevik camp, from Parvus (who stood close to the Mensheviks) and from Trotsky.

In his preface to Trotsky's pamphlet *Do deviatogo ianvaria,* and writing soon after Bloody Sunday, Parvus argued that in Russia only the workers were capable of making a revolution. The weak bourgeoisie could not be expected to provide revolutionary initiative, nor could the amorphous and anarchic peasantry be relied upon to form a "consolidated revolutionary army." Consequently, the "revolutionary provisional government" which would issue from the revolution could only be a government of the "workers' democracy." Unless Social Democracy were prepared to remain an "insignificant sect," it must take the lead and form a "Social-Democratic government." This government could not bring about a "socialist transformation" in Russia immediately, but the process of liquidating the autocracy and establishing a democratic republic could give it a "congenial basis for political activity." Parvus anticipated that this scheme might lay him open to the charge of "opportunist Jaurèsism," and therefore insisted that ministerialism and Millerandism had always been objected to, not on the ground that a socialist minister's only business was to make a "social revolution," but because, "remaining in a minority in the government and with insufficient support in the country, he would not be capable of doing *anything* at all and would only serve the capitalist government as a lightning conductor of our criticism."[86]

This would not be the case with a Social Democratic provisional government: it would be a "homogeneous" government with a Social Democratic majority, created in a revolutionary moment when the power of the state was very great. It would be supported by a revolutionary army of workers who would emerge elated and filled with extraordinary political energy from the revolution they had just made and it would have before it at the outset political tasks of a kind which would unite the entire Russian people.[87] Parvus did not ask what would happen when the revolutionary honeymoon was over. Still, he had given an unequivocal answer to the question of who should form the revolutionary government, in the slogan, "No tsar, but a workers' government!"

When Trotsky re-examined the question of power in 1905 and 1906, he had traveled a long way since his *Nashi politicheskie zadachi* of August, 1904. Urging the important role of the state either as a "lever of a deep revolutionary transformation or as an instrument of organized stagnation," Trotsky gave short shrift to the Menshevik self-denying ordinance: "Every political party deserving the name aims at seizing governmental power and thus putting the state at the service of the class whose interests it represents."[88] Like Parvus, Trotsky insisted that in Russia only the proletariat was capable of revolutionary initiative and leadership and urged Social Democrats who were "honest revolutionaries" not to shirk the "menial work" of the revolution but to organize an "all-Russian uprising" *and* form the "revolutionary provisional government":[89]

> Our liberal bourgeoisie is already behaving in a counterrevolutionary manner, even before the revolutionary climax; at every critical moment our democratic intelligentsia demonstrates nothing but its impotence; the peasantry as a whole constitutes a rebellious anarchic element *[stikhiia]* – it could be made to serve the revolution only by the force which takes governmental power into its hands. The proletariat remains.[90]

The working class, facing the formidable resistance of autocracy and the deliberate passivity of the bourgeoisie, would develop into an impressive fighting force and would push on:

> There is no stage in the bourgeois revolution where this fighting force, driven forward by the steel logic of class-interests, could come to rest. *Uninterrupted revolution becomes for the proletariat its law of self-preservation as a class.*

In the course of realizing basic democratic objectives and consolidating its political dominance it will be facing purely socialist objectives:

> Between the minimum and maximum programs of Social Democracy a revolutionary permanence (continuum) is established. This is not one single blow; it is not a month, it is a whole historical epoch. It would be absurd to predict its duration.[91]

Yet, while investing the Russian proletariat with colossal revolutionary qualities, Trotsky obviously realized that while it was one thing for a revolutionary proletariat to seize power, it was another to hold power in a backward, peasant country unattuned to socialist objectives. While he expected the peasantry to turn against the socialist minority government, he also expected a general European socialist revolution to rescue Russia.

But however breathtaking Trotsky's vista of permanent revolution might be, its answer to the Russian Social Democrats' dilemma of power was no real answer: it represented, in effect, a gamble on the intervention of a *deus ex machina* in the form of "immediate state support from the European proletariat."[92]

While Trotsky had resolutely thrown overboard the doctrine of bourgeois revolution, Lenin stopped half-way and tried only to divorce it from its complement, the commitment to abstain from power. Lenin agreed with Martynov that in Russia a bourgeois revolution and a democratic republic were on the agenda, but insisted that this did not absolve Social Democrats from the "duty to participate in a provisional revolutionary government after the overthrow of Tsarism." Only thus could they "see the revolution through" and make sure that the minimum program of Russian Social Democracy (i.e., the establishment of a republic and a citizen army, separation of church from state, full democratic liberties, and radical democratic reforms) would be realized. Lenin put his finger on the basic contradiction in the Menshevik revolutionary scheme when he castigated Martynov for his gloomy forewarnings:

> Martynov wants the proletariat to be the vanguard in the democratic revolution, and *therefore* clever Martynov *frightens* the proletariat with the prospect of participation in a provisional revolutionary government.[93]

However, while Social Democrats had a *duty* to join the "provisional revolutionary government" it was *"out of the question"* that they monopolize power and make it into a homogeneous "workers' government" à la Parvus.

> Only a revolutionary dictatorship which is supported by the vast majority of the people can be lasting. . . . However the Russian proletariat at present constitutes only a minority of the population of Russia. It can become a vast, overwhelming majority only if it unites with the mass of half-proletarians, half-proprietors, i.e., with the mass of the petty-bourgeois urban and rural poor.[94]

A "social basis" so structured must "inevitably" be reflected in a "heterogeneous" revolutionary government, including a wide variety of representatives of the "revolutionary democracy" who might even be the predominant group.[95] Such a government would be perfectly capable of realizing the minimum program of Russian Social Democracy, while the maximum program, i.e., the "full emancipation of the working class," was, in view of the backwardness of Russia, not yet realizable. In answer to the more impatient maximalists, Lenin insisted that the road to socialism led through the "democratic republic"; there was no road other than that of "political democratism."[96]

Lenin had certainly resolved the dilemma of power (Social Democrats would lead the revolution *and* participate in the provisional revolutionary government) and of minority (the revolutionary government would be a broadly-based coalition of Social Democrats, agrarian socialists, and radicals: a "revolutionary-democratic dictatorship of the proletariat and the peasantry"). But this revolutionary government, which would surely consist of a majority of socialists, was committed to self-limitation–to realizing no more than the minimum program demanded, i.e., bourgeois-democratic objectives. The paradox is ingenuously illustrated in an article published in Lenin's *Vpered:*

> Step aside you generals and dignitaries, professors and capitalists: the proletariat is advancing to build you your bourgeois republic; but it will build it so that it can be easily converted to socialist foundations when the *desired* hour arrives. . . .[97]

One wonders whether in the circumstances "generals and dignitaries" would not have insisted on doing the building themselves; more important still, was it likely that a revolutionary proletariat led by revolutionary socialists, having made a successful revolution and having attained state-power, would be capable of such self-restraint and self-limitation? Lenin had indeed thrown overboard the *self-denying* ordinance, but had replaced it with a *self-limiting* ordinance.

Though in the 1905 debate on power the Mensheviks claimed to have Marxist orthodoxy on their side (a claim that was only half-heartedly disputed by Trotsky and less than convincingly by Lenin[98]) it is interesting to note that the theoretical leaders of German and European Social Democracy endorsed neither the Menshevik version of "bourgeois revolution" nor their self-denying ordinance. Franz Mehring, in an article significantly called "Permanent Revolution," expressed views which came closer to those of Parvus than to those of the Mensheviks.[99] Worse still, Karl Kautsky (though a close friend of Aksel'rod and Plekhanov and on record as having been clearly on the Menshevik side in the Bolshevik-Menshevik feud of 1903-1904[100]) took a position scarcely distinguishable from that of Lenin.

In 1906 Plekhanov sent a questionnaire to western Social Democrats asking their opinions on the "general character of the Russian revolution," and specifically, whether a "bourgeois or a socialist revolution" was on the agenda, and what tactics should be adopted with regard to "bourgeois democracy" and the "bourgeois oppositional parties" in the Duma.[101] Kautsky thought the Russian revolution was neither a "bourgeois" nor a "socialist" revolution but something in between, proceeding on the "borderline between bourgeois and socialist society." He urged that "the era of bourgeois revolution, i.e., of revolutions in which the bourgeoisie was the chief driving force, had passed, even in Russia." For the proletariat was now too powerful and independent to allow the bourgeoisie to be revolutionary. Since this ruled out the bourgeoisie as a driving force in the contemporary revolutionary movement, there could be no bourgeois revolution. Nor could the Russian revolution be a socialist revolution when the proletariat was still too "weak and undeveloped" to hold and exercise power all by itself. While the proletariat must fight for victory, i.e., for power, it must share the revolutionary struggle and the power with the peasantry. The revolution was not likely to succeed without the active support of the peasantry, nor could the peasants be expected to become socialists, so that a strengthening of small-scale land ownership would result from the revolution. Therefore it could not be a socialist revolution. Nonetheless, Russian Social Democrats must fight for victory and power.[102]

Answers similar to that of Kautsky were returned by Filippo Turati, Harry Quelch (Social Democratic Federation of Britain), and Edgar Milhaud (Switzerland). Only Édouard Vaillant, a former Communard and Blanquist, saw Russia heading for a *social* revolution and urged its socialist party to lead the proletariat, the disinherited masses, and the idealistic intelligentsia "to the final battle and to victory." While Paul Lafargue (Marx's son-in-law), Enrico Ferri (leader of the Italian "Integralists") and Émile Vandervelde (chairman of the Bureau of the Socialist International) diagnosed the Russian revolution as "bourgeois," they endowed it with "strong socialist tendencies" and saw it marked with "the sign of the socialist proletariat." Of all those who replied to Plekhanov's questionnaire (and whose answers were published), Theodore Rothstein alone (and he was really a Russian if not a Menshevik emigre living in London) endorsed unreservedly the Menshevik view.[103]

It is difficult to decide which of the three revolutionary schemes proposed by Russian Social Democrats in the 1905 debate on power could claim to be truly Marxian, or more Marxian than others.

There seems to be no precedent in the writings and practice of Marx and Engels for Trotsky's "permanent revolution," i.e., a workers' government (which could then only be a minority dictatorship) trying to survive in backward and possibly hostile peasant Russia by way of a rescue operation coming from the state-power of a victorious socialist proletariat in the West. Even in their brief Blanquist period of 1849, when Marx and Engels toyed halfheartedly with the scheme of a "social republic" in Germany, they expected it to be established under the revolutionary impact of and in conjunction with a social revolution in France, rather than to precede it.

As for the Menshevik scheme which prescribed abstention from supreme power in the stage of bourgeois revolution and assigned to Social Democracy the role of extreme opposition until the social revolution, it had some precedent in Marx's *Address of the Central Bureau to the Communist League*. However, Marx's revolutionary strategy of 1850 was designed for Germany which had, at the time, a very weak socialist movement and a small and inexperienced working class, but a powerful radical-democratic movement. Marx expected these radical democrats to play the major role in the revolution *and* to form the government after victory had been achieved, while he told the German working class and its communist leaders to lend independent support to the democrats during the revolution and to confront their government as an irreconcilable opposition party after the revolution was victorious. In the Russian situation the balance of forces was very different, certainly as seen by Russian Social Democrats. They all agreed to assign the working class the role of vanguard in a Russian revolution; they had moreover done their best to organize it into a political force as effective as any which could be mustered by their rivals. There was no "natural" or practical reason why this vanguard, having been the "driving force" in a victorious revolution, should not take part in the government which issued from the revolution. What stood in the way was, rather, a self-denying ordinance, according to which the time to hold *state power* and govern could not be at hand until objective conditions were ripe for the realization of *socialism*.

From the notion of the *vanguard* function and position of the working class in the Russian revolution, Lenin derived the conclusion that the working class and its socialist leaders had a *duty* not only to make and lead the revolution but also to assume state-power and see the revolution through. From the realization or assumption that socialism could not yet be on the Russian agenda, he argued that the working class and its socialist leaders had sufficient *democratic* objectives in common with a potentially revolutionary peasantry, the urban poor, and other democratic elements to form a broadly-based "revolutionary-democratic dictatorship" committed to radical reforms, i.e., some sort of popular front government. In reply to the Menshevik taunt that this was nothing less than Millerandism, Lenin pointed out that it was one thing for Millerand to join the bourgeois government of Waldeck-Rousseau in association with General Gallifet, the butcher of the Paris Commune, and quite another for the Internationalist Varlin to enter the Executive Council of the revolutionary Paris Commune on which Blanquists and radicals had an overwhelming majority.[104]

It may be difficult, if not futile, to decide which revolutionary scheme was more Marxian. But it does seem to me that in 1905 Lenin (granting he meant what he said, and there is no convincing reason to think he did not) had the better in the debate with his Menshevik and Trotskyist opponents. His resolution of the dilemma of power confronting Marxists in Russia was more realistic than either the Mensheviks' self-denying ordinance or Trotsky's gamble on a socialist revolution in the West. While the Marxist heritage with regard to the question of power was ambiguous and could be interpreted in a number of ways, it was unequivocal in its injunction never to repeat the performance of Louis Blanc and join a bourgeois-democratic government as a *minority*. This injunction was reiterated at congresses of the Socialist International in the form of denunciation of "ministerialism" or Millerandism. Whatever justification there may have been in the Mensheviks' criticism of Lenin's organizational principles or of his *putschism*, his scheme for a "revolutionary-democratic dictatorship of the proletariat and the peasantry" could by no stretch of the imagination be interpreted as a plan for a *bourgeois* coalition government. Nor were the Social Democrats, whom Lenin expected to join the provisional revolutionary government as representatives of the vanguard which had made revolution successfully, cast for the role of junior partners à la Louis Blanc.

If one examines the behavior of the Russian Social Democrats in the 1917 Revolution, one finds, on the question of power, that only Trotsky adhered consistently to his 1905 position, working indefatigably from the moment of his arrival in Petrograd on May 3, for seizure of power and the establishment of a socialist dictatorship in an all-out gamble on a European socialist revolution. In a speech to Social Democratic delegates to the First Congress of Soviets early in June, 1917, Trotsky lashed out against the doubting Thomases who regarded "hope for a European revolution—a Utopia":

> We reply: if there is no revolution in Europe then Russian liberty will be crushed anyway by the united strength of both our Allies and enemies. All the social experiments which the course of events imposes on us constitute a threat to European capital. Will it not attempt by the use of universal violence to liquidate the Russian revolution? He who does not believe in the possibility of the European revolution, must expect our entire freedom to go up in smoke. . . .[105]

As for the majority-Mensheviks, the so-called "revolutionary defensists" led by Tsereteli and Dan, Skobelev and Liber assumed the role of opposition until the April government crisis: they entrenched themselves in the Soviets and gave critical and conditional support to the bourgeois Provisional Government. While this was not exactly traditional Menshevik revolutionary strategy, which had postulated a tougher, more "irreconcilable" and more "revolutionary" opposition role, still it was no flagrant departure from it. It was after the April crisis, when the Provisional Government had proved unwilling or incapable of pursuing democratic policies that the majority-Mensheviks led by Tsereteli abandoned their self-denying ordinance and joined a bourgeois coalition government. They thus proved guilty of that Millerandism with which they had self-righteously branded Lenin's revolutionary scheme of 1905, and acted à la Louis Blanc, ignoring the unequivocal warnings of Marx and Engels. True, in justification of the Mensheviks' entry into the coalition government Tsereteli invoked both the authority of Engels *and* the general will.[106] Confronted with the alternative either of taking power themselves or of entering a coalition government, the Mensheviks, according to Tsereteli,

> could not do the first because then we would have committed the mistake against which Engels had already warned, speaking of the tragic position of a proletariat which seized power at a time when the objective conditions for the realization of a proletarian program were still absent. This point of view was shared by the vast majority of the democracy represented by its most authoritative institutions.[107]

Whatever one may think of Tsereteli's interpretation of Engels' warning, he perhaps went too far when claiming that the decision not to take power themselves but to enter the *coalition* government was "the greatest victory for that brand of realistically revolutionary tactics of which Menshevism had always been the representative in Russia." [108]

Martov and Martynov and their small band of Menshevik-Internationalists certainly disagreed with Tsereteli's interpretation.

> It is wrong to interpret the Menshevik understanding of bourgeois revolution in the sense of absolute support and unconditional alliance with the bourgeoisie. Menshevism stood for supporting the bourgeoisie during the period of the struggle against tsarism and during the destructive phase of the revolution. To interpret this alliance as extending to all the steps and phases of the revolution is not in accordance with the traditional Menshevik understanding of the driving forces of the revolution.[109]

The Menshevik-Internationalists remained true to their commitment to the self-denying ordinance and opposed coalition until the July Days when, after the walk-out of the four Kadet ministers from the coalition government, they realized that the Russian bourgeoisie was *revolutionsmüde* and abstention from power made no sense. Martov then agitated for a government of the "revolutionary democracy," that is, for something like Lenin's revolutionary scheme of 1905, but rather belatedly and with little gusto, as if the assumption of power by socialists in Russia was a tragic necessity.

Lenin, too, abandoned his 1905 scheme—a broadly-based revolutionary-democratic dictatorship—when he prodded his reluctant "Old Bolsheviks," to whom this scheme made far better Marxist and Russian sense, into seizing power and establishing a Bolshevik dictatorship. He discarded his self-limiting ordinance, determined as he was to take Russia "to the *commune,*" for "no other aims" was he now prepared to serve.[110] Whether Lenin's narrow Bolshevik dictatorship was a gamble à la Trotsky on revolution in the West, or whether it expressed his new belief that the possession of state-power would make the plunge into socialism possible, even in backward Russia, is difficult to decide. It may have been a combination of both. Perhaps the example of Ludendorff's *Kriegskommunismus* in Germany may have impressed Lenin with the great possibilities of state-power.[111]

Neither Bolsheviks nor Mensheviks could justly claim to have acted in accordance with Marxist theory, precedent or prescription—certainly not the majority-Mensheviks under Tsereteli. Why they acted the way they did and failed calls for detailed investigation beyond the scope of this paper, but it may have had little to do with Marxist precept or precedent. Both Mensheviks and Bolsheviks had been good revolutionaries when it was a matter of overthrowing Tsarism: what distinguished the former from the latter was their underestimation of the importance of state-power. This fear of revolutionary state-power proved to be their undoing, for seizure of power is an integral part of revolution-making.

If underestimation of the importance of state-power as expressed in their self-denying ordinance was the Mensheviks' fatal weakness, Lenin seems to have overestimated the creative omnipotence of state-power; he abandoned his self-limiting ordinance and those democratic principles he had defended in 1905; he yoked backward, peasant Russia under a tough Bolshevik minority dictatorship and plunged the team into socialism.

This inquiry into a series of Marxist debates on power has endeavored to show that Marxism, from its earliest practical revolutionary beginnings, was bedevilled by a dilemma of power which can be traced from the Marx-Weitling clash in Brussels, to the debate of Plekhanov with the populists, and to the debates of the Bolsheviks and Mensheviks in 1905 and 1917. That dilemma of power can be seen as a reflection and illustration of the tension between Marxian scientific socialism and the Marxist revolutionary will.

None of the revolutionary schemes which Russian Social Democrats devised and argued in 1905, and abandoned, modified, or applied in 1917, succeeded in resolving that tension. Even Lenin's tremendous revolutionary will, which resolved the dilemma of power by cutting the Gordian knot in October, 1917, and creating Soviet state-power *(sovetskaia vlast')* has so far been tragically frustrated. The basic flaw in Lenin's, Stalin's, and Mao's schemes of socialist revolution from above after the seizure of power, is their overestimation of the creative potentialities of state-power. It still bedevils the part of the world which professes Marxism-Leninism and honors Lenin not only as a great revolutionary but also as the founder of *sovetskaia vlast'.*

WALTER SABLINSKY

The All-Russian Railroad Union and the Beginning of the General Strike in October, 1905

THE HISTORICAL BACKGROUND

The revolution of 1905 was a watershed in Russian history. Lenin called it a "dress rehearsal," while to many supporters of the regime it portended a new "Time of Troubles." In 1905 Russia was still economically as well as socially backward; its political structure was inefficient, and it was losing a humiliating war to what was thought to be an inferior enemy. Significant strides towards technological modernization had been made in the preceding decades, but this led only to greater dislocation within the social structure and further accentuated the socio-economic contradictions, creating new sources of irritation and discontent between the defenders of the old society and the rising forces of the new.

The spark came sooner than most had anticipated. On January 9, 1905 (or "Bloody Sunday," as it came to be known), processions organized by strikers and led by a priest were fired upon and dispersed as they tried in vain to deliver a petition of their grievances to the Emperor. The volleys of Bloody Sunday ushered in a period of unprecedented revolutionary struggle, culminating in October, 1905, in a great general strike which paralyzed the entire country. Public support for the strike was so overwhelming that the Emperor had little choice but to grant his subjects political rights and a national representative body—measures bitter to his taste and judgment. These concessions were embodied in the famous Manifesto of October 17.

The revolution was a product of mass participation and mass spontaneity; its leaders and forms were more the result of improvisation than of conscious direction. Popular demands were expressed through a variety of organizational forms and action; this diversity can be seen in the strike movement, as well as in union-organizing activities throughout the year and in the soviets, the best known form of workers' organization of that period.

Political parties found fertile ground for their activities, for the revolutionary atmosphere was affecting larger and larger segments of the population, opening them to propaganda and indoctrination. Social Democrats, both Mensheviks and Bolsheviks, were heartened to find workers developing "class consciousness" and "revolutionary militancy"[1]; still, the means had to be found and the course of action defined to harness and direct the movement. The Social Democrats made great strides in winning over adherents during the course of the year, but as late as October, 1905, the revolutionary movement was still running ahead of the party leaders. At the beginning of the October general strike, one of the Menshevik leaders in Moscow, P. Garvi, related his own bewilderment that despite complete involvement in revolutionary activity and constant participation in party work, "the party committees somehow missed the beginning of the general strike"; several days passed before they began to grasp the full meaning of events: "Our party committee, caught almost by surprise by the spontaneous growth of the general strike, was barely keeping up with the developments."[2]

While scholarly treatment of the 1905 Revolution in the West has been regrettably meager, the history of the revolutions, including that of 1905, obviously constitutes a major field of interest for Soviet scholars. A vast amount of printed material on 1905 has appeared in the Soviet Union over the years, with peaks of publication in 1925 on the occasion of the twentieth and, in 1955, the fiftieth anniversaries of the revolution. To indicate the scope of this enterprise it will suffice to mention that in 1930 the Communist Academy published an excellent annotated bibliography on the revolution of 1905 which ran to 715 pages of large format.[3] In 1955 the USSR Academy of Sciences began publication of a documentary series on the 1905 revolution which at present has reached seventeen volumes.[4] This series was preceded and has been accompanied by countless articles in periodicals and scholarly journals, monographs, conferences, papers, and various other forms of discussion. On the whole, the volume of Soviet literature on 1905 is very impressive and is constantly growing.[5]

Close examination of the more recent Soviet publications confirms once again the role historical writing plays in serving the political views of the Communist Party. In an effort to build for itself a revolutionary past and mythology, the party greatly overstates its role in the events of 1905, claiming leadership and initiative which in reality belonged elsewhere. From January through October, 1905, the Bolsheviks were anxious, although hopeful, swimmers with the current, not yet leaders of any significant movement of their own. In its attempts to build a position of dominance and leadership for the Bolsheviks, Soviet historiography tends to play down the role and independence of any action on the part of organizations that were products of the spontaneous participatory activity of the masses. It simply treats such manifestations as bourgeois aberrations, particularly if their policies conflicted with those of the Bolsheviks. Nonetheless, the revolution of 1905 was a product of mass upheaval, and the popular organizations which emerged then and which played an important role in determining the course of events were, indeed, genuine expressions of mass discontent and popular democracy.

This essay will focus on the role that one such organization, the All-Russian Union of Railroad Employees and Workers (henceforth referred to as the Railroad Union), played in instigating the October general strike—an event that represented the highest point of national unity, purpose, and achievement in the 1905 Revolution.[6] The history of the Railroad Union has not as yet received adequate attention. Most of its records were destroyed in the turbulent days of 1905. The union tried to take a neutral position among the political parties by refusing to support any party program; it represented the center between the liberal professional unions and the more radical proletarian unions, which were usually under the control of the socialist parties. The union embraced all railroad workers from station masters to switchmen, but it drew its strength primarily from among the "employees," i.e., a group made up largely of salaried workers who received better pay and enjoyed more privileges than the average railroad worker and thus stood closer to middle-class professional elements than to the proletariat.

THE EXPANSION OF RUSSIAN RAILROADS

During the second half of the nineteenth and the first years of the twentieth century, the Russian government authorized a vast program of railroad construction. In 1855, Russia had approximately 660 miles of railroad track; by 1881, 14,000 miles; by 1896, 32,500 miles. Almost 10,000 miles of lines were added in the last years of the century; and by 1905, Russian railway lines exceeded 40,000 miles, organized into thirty-two major lines, and largely state-owned.[7]

This rapid development had its effect on the growth of the railway labor force. From 1860 to 1905, the number of railwaymen increased 68 times, while the number of workers in Russian industry only quadrupled; in the decade prior to 1905, the railway labor force nearly doubled in size. In 1905, the total number of railroad workers for the entire Russian Empire was over three-quarters of a million.[8]

A rapidly expanding industry usually presents better than average opportunities for advancement and somewhat better pay in order to attract the desired number of workers; to some extent this was true for Russian railroads.[9] Although it is generally agreed that railwaymen's working conditions were somewhat better than those employed in industry, these conditions were far from satisfactory. Improvement of their economic position was very important to the railroad men and it frequently constituted their principal demand during strikes.

In the first years of the twentieth century, strikes by railwaymen were not infrequent and played an important part in paralyzing the economy of the country or of a given region.[10] In a number of instances railway strikes triggered general strikes, as for example in Rostov-on-Don in November, 1902.[11] The events of January, 1905, signaled a wave of strikes throughout Russia, particularly on the railroads. The Riazan-Ural Railroad was partially struck on January 12, and in a period of one week, the strikers gained a series of important concessions. Other railroads soon followed suit.[12] The demands of the workers were primarily economic, and the managements of the railroads struck consented to give favorable consideration to them.[13] On February 8, 1905, the Minister of Transportation approved new regulations permitting the workers to elect representatives to negotiate with the administration, and the administrations of railroads were given authority to grant certain concessions to their workers.[14]

On the other hand, the government began taking stern measures to prevent further unrest, placing all railroads under martial law, a status which gave railroad administrators the authority to imprison workers for a period of seven days, and to impose jail sentences of four to eight months for quitting or failing to show up for work without proper excuse.[15] However, these regulations were not very strictly enforced and consequently they had little effect on the strikes.

On March 11-16 a conference of the managers of railroads met to discuss the existing conditions of the railroads and, as a result, produced a vague and ambiguous statement, promising gradual improvement through a "fair approach to the needs of the workers, to be worked out in due process and time."[16] At the same time, this conference recommended that more resolute measures be taken to put a stop to railroad disorders. On March 29, a circular was issued by the Minister of Transportation which in effect retracted most of the concessions already won by the strikers. The circular reaffirmed the necessity for the maintenance of regular railway service and forbade all violations of discipline by railwaymen. Demands of the workers which required new expenses were termed economically unfeasible, while demands dealing with local matters and grievances not requiring special legislation were promised to be taken under consideration. Finally, the circular prohibited any permanent form of workers' organization, nor would it permit the establishment of a "workers' bureau."[17]

RUSSIAN SOCIAL DEMOCRATS AND THE ORGANIZATION OF THE RAILROAD UNION

The circular of March 29 took away from the railroad workers all that they had gained through strikes, but the strikes had taught the workers a great deal in terms of potential effectiveness; a well-organized strike involving an army of three-quarters of a million railway workers could indeed be a powerful weapon. The consensus among those who ultimately became involved in organizing the Railroad Union was that the circular provided the impetus for a national railroad workers' union.[18] Besides, spontaneous union activity in Russia was rapidly developing, and unions of the most diverse professions with or without party affiliations and programs were springing up like mushrooms.[19] The labor-organizing activity in Moscow was centered in the Museum of Labor Assistance *(Muzei sodeistviia trudu),* where delegations from various parties strove to lend their assistance to unions, as well as to establish their influence among them.[20] It was here, at a meeting of a group of railroad employees, that the idea of a railroad union took shape. The four principal instigators of the movement called a conference of representatives from railroads in and around the Moscow center to consider the establishment of a railroad union. V. N. Pereverzev, an engineer by profession, was to draft the preliminary program for the proposed conference.

According to its organizers, the Railroad Union's program was to be based on the general currents of opinion expressed in the programs of other unions and political parties. The union was to be non-partisan. However, its program would contain, as a primary aim, certain political goals, acceptable and common to all the opposition parties, most importantly, the convocation of a constituent assembly and the winning of political and civil rights. All economic and legal demands were to be subordinated to the achievement of the above minimal political program. The inclusion of these minimum political demands would permit the union to unite all employees and workers of the railroads, whose composition, class status, and party affiliation were widely diverse. The aims of the union program drafted by Pereverzev reflected the following considerations: 1) professional struggle on railways on a local basis was ineffective, since local concessions gained by strikes were cancelled by higher authorities; 2) demands must therefore be directed against the highest authority, i.e., the Ministry of Transportation; 3) this was possible only if a centralized organization of all railroad workers was established; 4) such an organizational project would require extensive propaganda work, meetings, etc.; and 5) since it would be impossible to carry out the latter under the existing political conditions, the economic professional struggle could begin only with the attainment of political concessions. The union could not accept any narrow political program if it were to unite the entire body of railroad employees and workers, nor could the program contain any provisions which would be contrary to the aims of some opposition parties.[21]

The program drawn up by Pereverzev was submitted to representatives of the Socialist Revolutionary party and both factions of the Social Democratic party and received their approval. The first conference (or congress as it later became known) of railroad workers was held secretly on April 20-21 and was attended by between fifty and sixty representatives of ten railroads, of which seven were from the Moscow center and three from outside it, with representatives of the Socialist Revolutionary and Social Democratic parties present, having an advisory vote.[22] The program submitted by Pereverzev was approved by the delegates.[23] It defined the basic goals of the union as the "improvement and defense of the economic, legal and cultural interests of railroad employees and workers of all categories," which could be attained only under the conditions of a democratic regime.

Since the center of the Russian railway network was Moscow, where most lines had their terminals and home offices, Moscow was also to become the center of the organizing activity and the source of most of the Union's leadership. The involvement of the Social Democrats in the Union reflected the strength of party alignments in that city. Despite the 1903 ideological split in the party, organizational separation on the local level generally did not take place until 1905. The party organization in Moscow was a bulwark of Bolshevik strength, and the Moscow Committee of the RSDRP was composed almost exclusively of Bolsheviks.[24] Social Democratic representation in the Union, therefore, was predominantly Bolshevik. The Moscow Mensheviks, who were considerably weaker than the Bolsheviks, did not separate into an independent organization until June, 1905.[25] Both Mensheviks and Bolsheviks had a large following among railroad workers, particularly workers in the depot shops, and were confident that their support would increase in time. However, the conceptions of the role of trade unions in the revolutionary struggle held by both factions were coming into conflict with the professed aims and goals of the union.

The Bolsheviks' view of trade unions was set forth by Lenin in *What Is To Be Done;* he expressed distrust of spontaneous action on the part of the masses, leading only to bourgeois trade-unionism and distracting workers from their primary interest—political struggle. "The task of Social Democracy," wrote Lenin, "is to *combat* spontaneity, and to divert the labor movement from this very spontaneous tendency of trade unionism to nestle under the wing of the bourgeoisie, and to bring it under the wing of the revolutionary Social Democracy."[26]

Although the conditions that led to the extensive trade union movement in 1905 compelled the Social Democrats to give careful consideration to the problem of their relationship to the labor unions, the Bolsheviks by and large remained true to the views of Lenin. There was some groping for a labor policy, but on the whole the question of political upheaval was given chief priority, and the labor movement was looked upon mainly as a means to the attainment of the above goal. In mid-July, 1905, an article in *Proletarii* on the relationship between the party and trade unions stated that the aim of the party was to unite workers in professional unions for struggle against the employers, and to "unite these unions under the leadership of the party."[27] This line of reasoning led to the promotion of party trade unions and the printing of a model constitution for such a union. *Proletarii* commented:

> Our task is to influence economic unions, to assure ourselves leadership over them in order to impregnate them with ideas of proletarian class consciousness. Our task is to make these unions Social Democratic in the sense of their acceptance of party leadership and program.[28]

By the beginning of October, the differentiation between unions and the party became sharper. According to a party directive, unions catered only to a small part of the total needs of the workers and therefore should restrict themselves to economic activity.[29]

The Mensheviks were considerably less preoccupied with the necessity of establishing effective control over workers' organizations. The basic aim of each faction—the political overthrow of the government, as well as the view of history as class struggle—were common to both factions. The Mensheviks were still smarting from the effects of "Economism" and were very conscious of the dangers of trade unionism. Yet they favored trade unions in the belief that they would create excellent conditions and means of propagandizing and attracting workers to the political struggle. At the same time they were aware of the possibility that leadership in such unions might fall into the wrong hands, and most significantly they also strove to promote unions on a class basis. Not excluding the possibility of cooperation with the radical bourgeoisie in the revolution, the Mensheviks nevertheless considered the sharpening of class antagonisms and struggle as a normal course of events. The labor unions would provide a means of propagandizing the workers and developing proletarian consciousness. The underlying assumption here was that the workers would realize the nature of their interests and instinctively follow the Social Democrats. Thus, the Mensheviks were in favor of promoting the widest possible trade union activity, in which the unions would either be politically neutral or accept party leadership and become a party organization. In neither case did the Mensheviks consider it appropriate that political leadership among workers be in the hands of bourgeois elements.[30]

Consequently, both factions of the RSDRP were vitally concerned with preventing the spread of liberal or Socialist Revolutionary influence among the workers. Both factions combined, the Social Democrats had the most representatives of any political party at the April 20-21 congress, but the joint forces of the liberals and Socialist Revolutionaries outnumbered them. The Social Democrats wanted to emphasize class interests, sharpening political and class differences between workers and employees, whereas their opponents argued for the promotion of common interests. The issue came to a head over the question of whether the union should be a political or an economic one. The Social Democrats proposed that it should be political, since it was pursuing political aims. In that case, it was bound to end up with the Social Democratic party, since it represented the working class. Their opponents held for the designation of the union as economic, arguing that its immediate political aims were only a prerequisite for economic struggle. When the matter was submitted to a vote, the Railroad Union was proclaimed to be economic.[31]

The congress then elected a Central Bureau, which was to direct the work of the union. Elections were by secret vote, with the results, for conspiratorial reasons, made known only to the elected. Seven persons were elected to the Central Bureau with the right to co-opt additional members as required. V. N. Pereverzev was elected chairman of the Central Bureau and V. Romanov, an engineer, vice-chairman. In addition to these two, the following were elected as regular members: K. D. Namitnichenko, a legal advisor in the central administration of the Moscow-Kursk Railway; I. I. Bednov, a telegraph technician from the Moscow-Kazan Railroad; an accountant, Voronin; and two workers, one of whom, L. I. Grishin, was sympathetic to the Social Democrats, while the other, whose name is not recalled by any source, soon ceased to be active in the union. Later, the Central Bureau co-opted G. B. Krasin, head of the technical department of the Moscow-Iaroslavl-Archangel Railroad; M. I. Bogdanov, a pension fund manager; accountants Trofimov and Zabulovskii; bookkeeper Bruevich; an engineer, Zhenishek; and Pechkovskii and Ukhtomskii, train enginemen, both Socialist Revolutionaries, who were co-opted before the December uprising.[32]

Thus the Central Bureau originally consisted of five members of the professional intelligentsia and two workers. Of the latter, one leaned towards the Social Democrats, while the other was an anarchist; however, the latter's association with the Union was very brief. Of the remaining five, three favored the Socialist Revolutionaries, one was of Menshevik sympathies and another leaned towards the Bolsheviks.[33] Pereverzev, Chairman of the Central Bureau, referred to himself as a Socialist Revolutionary; his contemporary, a member of the Moscow Bolshevik group, characterized him as a "non-party democrat, very energetic and full of initiative."[34] A member of the Bolshevik Moscow Committee of the RSDRP called him "half SR, half Kadet."[35] Social Democratic sympathizers in the Bureau included Grishin, Namitnichenko (a Menshevik) and, later, Krasin and Romanov, both of whom, according to one Bolshevik, did not "formally belong to the party, but were considered 'our men'."[36] Certainly in its composition the Central Bureau was closely aligned with the radical parties.

The Central Bureau was to work out a program of union activity which it was to submit to the next congress for approval. The Bureau (with the permission of the censors) printed twenty thousand copies of the union program and also published it in the major daily newspaper, *Russkie vedomosti.*[37] Having established contacts with all the political parties in Moscow, the Central Bureau next joined the liberal Union of Unions, although its participation in this organization was not very extensive.[38] This association proved fruitful; the Railroad Union was still relatively new but the Union of Unions was better known and could provide better means of communication between the Central Bureau and the newly formed local committees. The organizational work of the Bureau proceeded as well as could be expected under the circumstances. Upon hearing about the union, railwaymen in various places organized local committees, and these strove to establish contact with the Central Bureau.

The Central Bureau had its hands full; the means at its disposal were meager and the job colossal. To make matters worse, the Social Democrats were endeavoring to promote their own rival organizations among the railwaymen. They did not trust the liberal-Socialist Revolutionary leaning of the union's leaders and intended either to capture the union or to split it along class lines.

In order to gain a predominant position within the Railroad Union, the Moscow Committee announced that a "party union of the Moscow Committee of the RSDRP" had been formed. The leaflet announcing the formation of the party union was dated April 8, i.e., before the congress of the Railroad Union, and the notice of its existence appeared in *Vpered* (No. 18) on May 5, with editorial comment welcoming its establishment:

> We are firmly convinced that the start made by the "Union of the Employees of the Moscow Center" will attract the attention of the multitude of their fellow railwaymen, hastening them to unite under the banner of the Russian Social Democratic Labor Party in other areas as well.[39]

The founding of the Social Democratic union seems to have been promoted as a counteraction to the proposals to establish the All-Russian Railroad Union. The organizational strength of the Social Democrats among the railwaymen at the time was not extensive, and the move was designed, in the words of its organizer, "to wrest the leadership of the union from the hands of the liberals."[40] Even the name of the union emphasized "employees" rather than workers.

Following the First Congress of the Railroad Union, Moscow Social Democrats launched a concerted effort to promote union organizations among the railroad workers. A separate Railroad District (the Moscow Committee was subdivided into *raiony* or districts) was established to coordinate this activity. At first, A. V. Shestakov (Nikodim) and then N. N. Mandel'shtam (Mikhail Mironovich) were in charge of organizing the district.[41] Its strongholds were among the workers of the railroad depots, where the Social Democrats were busily involved in promoting class organizations,[42] and also on several railroad lines. The Bolsheviks organized a small number of workers' circles in the shops of the Moscow-Kursk line, and established contacts among the workers of the Nizhnii-Novgorod railroad depot, as well as some connections in the administration of the Moscow-Kursk and Moscow-Kazan railroads.[43] The Mensheviks had a "considerable group of tens of workers" in the main Aleksandrov shops as well as a large following in the shops of the Moscow-Brest railway—the last was referred to as "our Menshevik citadel" by one of the Menshevik organizers.[44]

Social Democratic opposition hampered the efforts of the Railroad Union to unify all railwaymen on the basis of their common interests.[45] Although the hostility of the Social Democrats discouraged many workers from joining the Railroad Union, their influence was not sufficiently strong to persuade these same workers to join the party union instead. The latter remained for the time being a skeleton organization, "organized . . . along the lines of the Railroad Union, so that we would have corresponding organs and thus be able to gain control of the union."[46] Denied a mass following, the Social Democratic organizations on the Moscow railroads remained essentially party organs.

The remaining railwaymen—administrative personnel, line workers, employees, etc.—were generally inclined towards the Railroad Union. In fact, the Social Democrats' opposition to the union made the employees more willing to join it, so that most of the new membership was drawn from these categories.[47] The Socialist Revolutionaries had a large following in a number of Moscow depots, particularly among the workers on the line, and they were willing to accept and follow the Railroad Union.[48] The St. Petersburg railroad center was divided between the Socialist Revolutionaries and liberals, both equally strong in drawing support from administrative personnel.[49] This, in short, was the situation facing the Central Bureau in the summer of 1905.

THE RAILROAD UNION AND A GENERAL RAILROAD STRIKE

The organizing efforts of the union were directed initially towards railroads that would have the greatest significance in the execution of a general railroad strike. The First Railroad Congress was concerned with the founding of the union and had not dealt with the details of organization nor with a plan of action. Yet the unrest among railroad workers demanded some concrete measures as soon as possible. The Central Bureau in Moscow formed a committee of 167 delegates from the different professional levels and railroads of the Moscow railroad center. This committee, which was representative of the opinions and attitudes of all workers and employees, strongly favored a general railroad strike.[50] The Central Bureau, in order to consolidate its organizational gains, to clarify its program, to write a permanent constitution, and to formulate a plan of action, convened a Second Railroad Congress in Moscow on July 22-24.[51] Of the thirty-two more important Russian railroads, the union counted nineteen among its members and had informational ties with three others, while ten still remained outside the union.[52] In all, twenty railroad units with voting rights were represented at the congress; three others, under the control of the Social Democrats, had advisory votes, as did the representatives of the Socialist Revolutionaries, Social Democratic parties, and Jewish Bund.[53]

The first session of the Second Congress was spent on reports from various railroads. On the second day, the representative of the Polish railroads, a member of the Polish Socialist Party (PPS), stated that delegates of the Polish railroads had met in Vilno in May and had decided to join the Railroad Union, but only on the condition that the union would include in its program a provision that the general strike would not be terminated until Poland was granted national autonomy.[54] The Social Democrats ardently objected to such a policy, claiming it to be a political one and opposed to their own program.[55] The Socialist Revolutionaries, on the other hand, felt that this was a demand for national self-determination, a fundamental democratic demand, which could be accepted by the union.[56] A third group argued against the inclusion of this provision on the grounds that it was a political one and that it conflicted with the program of one of the revolutionary parties. Despite the determined opposition of a considerable number of delegates, the Polish representatives remained adamant. In order to avoid open conflict, the vote on this thorny question was postponed, ostensibly to allow a committee to prepare a resolution. The maneuver allowed the congress to proceed with other business at hand.

The organization of a general railroad strike was the next point on the agenda and required little discussion. After several speakers were heard, the following principles were accepted: 1) to begin immediate agitation for a general strike on all railroads; the strike, once begun, was to last until the demands were accepted; 2) the strike was to be declared by the Central Bureau at the time the latter considered most appropriate, depending upon the general political situation in the country; the Central Bureau did not have to make preliminary arrangements with local committees; 3) the possibility of receiving aid from revolutionary parties was to be considered at the time of the declaration of the strike.[57]

A number of technicalities involved in the initiation of a strike were then brought up, and it was decided that damage to railway property and violence were to be avoided during the conduct of the strike. These measures then received unanimous approval.[58] The question of membership in the Union of Unions was not debated, and the union's current status was accepted by acclamation. The next point on the agenda concerned organizational matters. It was decided to retain the present composition of the Central Bureau and to empower it to draft a constitution for the Railroad Union, which was to go into effect as soon as it was ready, but which was to be submitted for approval to the next railroad congress.[59]

The congress ended its business by voting on the nationality question proposed by the PPS. The measure, that would require the general strike to continue until Poland had attained autonomy, was passed with twelve delegations favoring it, three opposed, three abstentions, and one neutral (the votes of the delegation were split). The twelve votes in favor consisted of six Polish railroads committed to the support of the resolution, and six railroads supporting the Socialist Revolutionary position. At this point, both factions of the RSDRP jointly declared that under such conditions they could no longer remain in the union. They were joined in their walkout by the organizations under their control on the grounds that the nonparty status of the union had been compromised.[60] The Polish resolution also antagonized conservative elements in the union through the infusion of the nationalist issue.

Realizing the seriousness of the situation and wishing to avoid a split within the union, and to placate the dissenting minority, the Central Bureau organized a referendum explaining the situation and asking all local organizations of the union to vote on the question. With the exception of the Polish railroads, local organizations voted against the Polish proposal, allowing the bureau to circumvent the decision of the congress by rescinding the resolution. The Polish railroads withdrew from the union and formed their own national organization. This pacified the majority of the dissenters, who withdrew their resignations, with a few exceptions including the Moscow Social Democratic contingent.[61] This fact pleased at least one quarter; the Moscow City Prefect was happy to inform the Police Department that "although the workers of the Moscow railroad center decided on a political strike, the withdrawal of the extreme revolutionary group from the All-Russian Railroad Union will postpone a strike on the railroads to the distant future."[62]

The debate over national autonomy affirmed party lines and indicated the alignment of the railroads behind the Railroad Union. Among the railroads which sided with the Socialist Revolutionaries' views were the Riazan-Ural, Nikolaev, Moscow-Iaroslavl, and Moscow-Kazan. The compromise proposed by the Central Bureau was accepted by all the Moscow railroads and the railroads south of Moscow. These railroads supported the Central Bureau in July and were to follow its leadership in the October strike. The Polish railroads established federated relations with the union, while the St. Petersburg group split: the Socialist Revolutionaries supported the Central Bureau, while the liberal wing opposed it, especially in regard to the manner in which the nationality problem was handled.[63]

The results of the Second Congress ended the Social Democrats' hopes of capturing the leadership of the Railroad Union, and the vote on the nationality question compelled them either to accept the majority decision and cooperate with the union or to withdraw from it altogether. Romanov, vice-chairman of the Central Bureau, a Bolshevik, felt that if all the Social Democrats had been united, they would have had the largest party representation. But, in fact, the combined forces of opposition were proving to be stronger, and furthermore, union leadership was gaining strength among the Social Democratic adherents. The union was embarking on an independent policy in pursuit of a clearly political aim, namely, the execution of a general railroad strike, designed to gain liberal concessions.[64] The Social Democrats looked upon the general strike only as a means of armed insurrection. Their belief that the union was falling under the sway of bourgeois liberalism raised the fear that a successful general strike executed by the Railroad Union might seriously hamper and retard the revolutionary uprising. In this regard, Soviet historians have alleged that the union leadership would have deliberately tried to prevent an uprising by seeking a compromise with the government.[65]

To the Social Democrats, fear of the growing influence of liberal-Socialist Revolutionary tendencies in the Railroad Union raised the spectre of the Railroad Union emerging as a potent, political, and independent force, capable of uniting all oppositional elements on the railroads. Rather than risk allowing the workers to fall under bourgeois influences, the Central Committee of the RSDRP decided to withdraw from the Railroad Union and concentrate on its party organizations among the railway workers. However, there was considerable hesitation among Social Democrats about leaving the union; indeed, many chose to remain, including several who kept their positions in the Central Bureau.[66] The Railroad Union still enjoyed substantial support from all segments of the railroad professions, despite its estrangement from the Social Democratic party. Immediately after the Second Railroad Congress, the party union issued an appeal for a conference of all Social Democratic organizations of railwaymen to be held in mid-August, to clarify its attitude towards a general strike and its relationship with the Railroad Union, but nothing came of the appeal.[67]

THE BEGINNING OF THE GENERAL RAIL STRIKE

The unrest begun on Bloody Sunday continued throughout 1905. The earlier wave of strikes subsided during the summer months, but a new wave of primarily economic strikes began at the end of September, after the printers in Moscow struck in a dispute over working conditions. They were joined by factory workers and then by the printers of St. Petersburg, who declared a three-day "solidarity" strike in support of their Moscow co-workers. The daily papers were full of accounts of the ratification of the Portsmouth agreement. Debates over the Bulygin Duma and the Zemstvo and Municipal Conference (September 12-16) were followed by student unrest.

On September 25 the government quietly convened a congress of railroad employees in St. Petersburg in the hope of pacifying this body with some concessions. The congress was to deal with pension funds and was attended by managers of pension funds and delegates, one delegate per twelve thousand employees, elected by indirect vote. The majority of the representatives at the congress were from professional groups; workers constituted only a small minority, and even these were mostly engineers, a group which was considerably better paid than the average railroad worker.[68] Thus the government anticipated a relatively conservative representation.

The congress, however, rebelled against the government. It voted to allow only elected delegates the right to vote, and it elected its own chairman. The government was indecisive and, fearing dire results, strove to conciliate the congress. The election of delegates to the Pension Congress, as it came to be called, provided a forum and helped unite all railwaymen, since the congress did after all represent the entire body of railroad workers. A stream of congratulations and expressions of confidence from various organizations and railroads poured into St. Petersburg. In a very real way, the Pension Congress served to channel the opinions of railroad workers. Rather moderate in its composition, the congress was primarily oriented towards obtaining economic concessions. While the mood of the congress was far from being submissive (there were a number of radicals among its members, and a prominent Bolshevik, Elizarov, served as vice-chairman), it was not adverse to cooperating with the government. The Ministry of Transportation undoubtedly preferred to deal with this body rather than the Railroad Union.

However, the agitated feelings among those whom they represented were not without effect on the members of the congress, as an avalanche of messages from local bodies and committees of railwaymen exerted leftward pressure on the delegates.

Initially, the Central Bureau of the Railroad Union opposed the Pension Congress and called for a boycott of its elections. But it soon came to view the congress as a potential sounding board and a means of unifying the railwaymen.[69] It was felt that the increasing radicalization of the Pension Congress might lead to repression on the part of the government, a move which would mobilize railway workers in support of a strike. Furthermore, in case of a strike at this time, the Pension Congress could act as spokesman for the Railroad Union and the railwaymen. Such speculation prompted the Central Bureau to consider whether the time for the long-awaited strike had arrived.

Unrest was so widespread by this time that local rail strikes were occurring frequently. Until the Pension Congress, however, the Central Bureau had exerted considerable pressure to prevent these uncoordinated strikes, seeking to avoid the dissipation of energies in order to concentrate them on a major undertaking. At the end of September the situation in Moscow was highly unstable. The Moscow-Brest railway shops went on strike on September 27 (partially in sympathy with strikes in nearby factories) and presented a list of economic demands.[70] With difficulty, the Central Bureau held back the Moscow-Riazan, Moscow-Kazan, and Riazan-Ural railroads from joining the Moscow-Brest strike.[71] The Bureau had hoped to time a general railroad strike to coincide with some important event that would crystallize unrest, such as the election of the Bulygin Duma or the anniversary of Bloody Sunday. But now, after consultation with its Moscow committee, the Bureau decided to launch the general railroad strike without further delay.[72]

The Central Bureau was certain that a properly initiated strike would be supported by most railwaymen, but that timing and strategy were of crucial importance to its success. Having had no experience with large strikes, the Central Bureau approached the revolutionary parties, who were better versed in such matters. Meetings with representatives of all revolutionary groups and some trade unions were arranged. The Social Democrats were represented by the Moscow contingent, with Bolsheviks playing the dominant role. The Menshevik stronghold, the shops of the Moscow-Brest railway, was out on strike, but it was not certain how long the strikers would hold out. A representative of the Social Democrats, according to the testimony of several officers of the Central Bureau, said that his group was willing to provide the initiative in several railroad shops where the Social Democrats had a large following, but that the Moscow Committee considered the time inappropriate for a general railroad strike in view of the overall decline of the strike movement. He agreed to issue an appeal, but for a local strike only, "leaving everything else to the consideration and responsibility of the union."[73]

The Railroad Union began dispatching telegrams to the various lines, warning them to prepare for a general strike to begin on October 4.[74] The Bolshevik organization issued a leaflet addressed to railwaymen, calling them to strike,[75] and ending with the words, "We are awaiting your answer." The effectiveness of the appeal can be judged partly by the fact that no record of this leaflet was preserved; we know of its existence because it was mentioned in the subsequent appeal of the Moscow Committee.[76] There was no response from the workers to this appeal. The contention of the Social Democratic representative that the timing was inappropriate seemed borne out.

A large number of enterprises were involved in strikes, but there was little unity and organization among the strikers, whose numbers were considerable, partly because the issues involved were largely local. The strikes had picked up momentum at the end of September, when the printers in Moscow went on strike, but by the first week of October, the strike wave was clearly on the decline. Although large segments of the population still remained in a state of agitation, the crisis had abated for the time being. On October 3 most St. Petersburg papers carried a dispatch from Moscow that the strike wave in the old capital was over, and this well reflects the views of those who were intimately involved in the events.[77] The Moscow *Okhrana,* in a secret report to the Governor-General of Moscow, assured him that it "had reason to believe" that by Monday, October 3, most strikers would return to their jobs.[78] This was the not very promising situation facing the Central Bureau when the Bolshevik attempt to start a Moscow railroad strike on October 4 failed.

Within the Central Bureau there was still considerable support for an immediate attempt to call a general railroad strike. On October 4, at the second meeting of the newly formed "Council of Representatives of the Five Professions," a representative of the Central Bureau stated that the strike would start at four p.m., October 5, on the Kazan-Moscow railroad, and that plans had already been made to have other lines join it.[79] But the strike did not start on October 5. On that day the Central Bureau called a joint meeting of the entire committee of the Moscow railroad center.[80] The majority of those present supported an immediate general railroad strike, but not without first overcoming considerable opposition. Those arguing against a strike felt that immediate action was inadvisable because of: 1) insufficient preparation, 2) decline in the strike movement, and 3) fear that the authorities would react to the strike by arresting the union's leadership, thereby crippling the union.[81] After heated debate, the meeting accepted a plan proposed by some employees of the Moscow-Kazan railway–telegraph operator Bednov, a member of the Central Bureau, and engineers Pechkovskii and Ukhtomskii (both members of the Socialist Revolutionary party). According to their plan, on October 7 they would stop the movement of trains on their line and call for support from depot workers and administrative personnel. Once the strike on the Moscow-Kazan line had begun, telegraph operators would immediately notify union organizations on other lines, in the hope that they would then support the strike. The meeting decided that the strike was to be called to support general political demands: freedom of speech, press, assembly, trade unions and strikes, and the convocation of popular representatives, freely elected by universal, equal, secret, and direct vote. More specific demands would be worked out later. The list of basic demands was published in the local newspapers.[82]

The actual strike began shortly after twelve noon on October 6, when freight engineers on the Moscow-Kazan railways stopped movement of trains on their trunk.[83] With the approach of darkness, two groups of engineers—one under Bednov, the other under Ukhtomskii—proceeded to neighboring railway stations on their line, calling railwaymen to join the strike. At Perovo, where the stationmaster was a member of the union, the strikers dispatched a prearranged telegram to signal the start of the strike. All night long the instigators of the strike moved from one part of the line to the other, spreading news of the strike. By early morning the strikers had interrupted telegraph communications in the main station of the Moscow-Kazan railway; however, before the night was over, several strike leaders were arrested, and in the morning gendarmes seized Bednov and Pechkovskii.[84]

But the strike was already set into motion, and the arrest of the leaders, instead of pacifying the strikers, served only to enrage them. When a crowd of strikers assembled before the police station and demanded the release of those arrested, police officials thought it prudent to let them go. At noon, a crowd of rail employees gathered in the hall of the main administration building of the Moscow-Kazan railroad and elected Bednov to chair an impromptu meeting. An account of the strike and its progress was followed by a reading of the demands worked out by the Railroad Union. The meeting voted to support the strike; upon dispersing, its participants spread news of the strike to other parts of the line, calling on their co-workers to join.[85] The authorities hint of coercion, i.e., many had to quit lest they be molested by the strikers, but probably closer to the truth is that there was support among railwaymen for the strike, and the appearance of mobs of strikers provided most with a convenient excuse for quitting work. The initial push was gaining momentum, as the call to strike by the engineers of the Moscow-Kazan railway quickly engulfed the entire line and soon the whole Moscow railroad center. Usually the initiative for the strike came from the administrative personnel and then spread to other railroad workers.[86]

The strikers usually expressed sympathy with the demands of the Railroad Union and walked off without presenting their own specific conditions. The Central Bureau issued a leaflet calling for a strike and instructing its supporters to back the demands worked out by the union, and also to be sure not to give up their struggle until their political program was attained.[87] Another leaflet, "What is to be done?" addressed to the strikers, advised them to continue the strike until the demands of the union were accepted.[88] By October 10, the Central Bureau could feel satisfied with its efforts, as the railway movement in the Moscow center, the heart of the Russian railway system, came to a complete halt.

THE LEADERSHIP OF THE STRIKE MOVEMENT

The evidence, then, clearly indicates that the initiative and execution of the massive railroad strike of early October, 1905, was the result of a planned effort on the part of the Central Bureau. Police documents substantiate the key role of the Central Bureau in starting the strike.[89] Until the advent of Stalinism, Soviet writers generally accepted the leading role of the Railroad Union in starting the strike and tended to criticize the hesitancy of the Social Democrats to join in the call for a general strike. The extensive study of the 1905 Revolution edited by M. N. Pokrovskii summarized the situation in the following comment: "The Petersburg and Moscow Bolshevik committees took a waiting attitude; it is apparent that they overdid their cautiousness *(pereborshchili v ostorozhnosti).*"[90]

How different this is from the more recent view that "the October strike was prepared and executed by the Russian proletariat under the leadership of the Bolsheviks."[91] Soviet authors have gone to great lengths in their efforts to create for the Bolsheviks the legend of leadership in the revolution of 1905. One of the most commonly repeated variations relates that:

> On October 6, a joint session of the MC [Moscow Committee] and representatives of district committees decided on a general strike. The same day, the Bolshevik workers of the Kazan shops held a meeting at No. 4 *Krasnoprudnyi pereulok;* present as well were representatives of the Iaroslavl and Kursk railroads, and leaders of the Railroad District. It was decided to begin the strike at noon on October 7. The workers of the Kazan shops struck at exactly the prescribed time.[92]

That there was a meeting of Bolshevik railroad workers is not surprising, since the strike was already in progress, and the Bolshevik organization had to clarify its policy towards it. The Bolshevik railroaders, like their co-workers, were in sympathy with the strike, whereas, Soviet assertions to the contrary notwithstanding, the committeemen were not in favor of coming out for a general strike at that time.

The majority of the members of the Moscow Committee were very dubious about the timeliness of immediate action, due to the failure of their previous calls to arouse sufficient support for a general strike. According to one member, such an appeal in June by the Moscow Committee "failed to get the support of a single enterprise."[93] A majority of the Bolshevik Moscow Committee was opposed to calling for a general strike; the comment of one party member that "we have suffered a fiasco and must not repeat it,"[94] typified the prevailing mood.

However, the growth of the railroad strike was forcing the hand of the professional revolutionaries. While the Bolshevik committeemen hesitated to commit the prestige of the party to the call for a general strike, the mass activity of the railwaymen was finding a broad response among all segments of the population. The Bolsheviks' vacillations were overcome only on October 10, four days after the railroaders had initiated their strike. On the tenth, the course of developments in Moscow and throughout the country prompted the Moscow Committee to call a general meeting of the entire Moscow Bolshevik organization. It was this meeting that finally convinced the Bolshevik leadership to declare support for the burgeoning strike movement.[95] The meeting was highly animated as rank-and-file Bolsheviks, reflecting the temper of the time, demanded more resolute action on the part of their leadership. There was a cry that the agenda be altered so as to make the question of a general strike the first order of business. Delegate after delegate spoke about the attitudes of fellow workers and of their anxiety regarding the failure of the Bolshevik organization to come out in support of the strike. The Bolshevik railwaymen were most outspoken, demanding support for the strike. As one witness recounts, "after a report on the railroad strike was read by the organizer of the Railroad District, there were shouts for the declaration of a general strike, and soon unanimous approval for a general strike was given."[96] It was decided that an appeal be issued for a general strike to start the next day, October 11, five days after the railroad strike was begun by the Central Bureau of the Railroad Union.

Among the Mensheviks the situation likewise provoked hesitation and bewilderment. One of the principal Menshevik leaders later recalled:

> Only on October 10 did the general view of the movement become clear to us. Our party committees, taken practically unawares by the spontaneous growth of the general strike, were barely keeping up with developments. A proclamation calling for a general strike was printed, it seems, when the general strike was already a reality.[97]

THE OCTOBER STRIKE AND THE RAILROAD PENSION CONGRESS

In St. Petersburg the course of the railroad strike initiated by the Central Bureau was inevitably influenced by the position of the Railroad Pension Congress, then still in session. This was due in part to the fact that the highest bureaucracy of the railroads, reflecting fairly moderate political views, was concentrated in the capital; it was also because the influence of the Central Bureau and its contacts with organizations in St. Petersburg were weak. In any case, and not surprisingly, the initial reaction of the Pension Congress to the strike was one of caution. Rumors were rife that the strike had been called because the congress delegates had been arrested.[98] Consequently, in an attempt to postpone the strike, congress representatives were dispatched to various locations to squelch the rumors of their arrest. Nonetheless, the Pension Congress maintained contact with the Central Bureau, whose vice-chairman, Romanov, made a report on the strike. The cautious attitude of the congress was perhaps best reflected by the rather moderate statements of Romanov, who justified the beginning of the strike because "postponement was impossible, since the railroad workers could have gone on strike at any moment."[99]

The course of the strike, however, had its effect on the delegates to the Pension Congress, and within the first few days they took up the cause of the strikers. Joining forces with union leadership, the congress presented the railwaymen with a national forum and began preparing a list of demands based on common grievances and a program for the railwaymen. The congress confirmed all political demands advanced by the Railroad Union and, having developed some fairly detailed economic demands, voted unanimously for their acceptance.[100]

Whereas the Central Bureau viewed the strike as a means of compelling the government to accept its demands,[101] the Pension Congress began to look upon itself as an intermediary between the strikers and the government. On October 11 the congress selected two five-man delegations, one to be sent to the Chairman of the Council of Ministers, S. Witte, and one to the Minister of Transportation, Prince M. I. Khilkov. The delegations were to convince these officials to accept their demands and to call a constituent assembly "in order to avoid a blood bath." They underscored that "the country must not be brought to an armed rebellion, and blood must not be allowed to spill."[102] Although Witte treated the delegation, led by Orekhov, with respect, he argued that acceptance of its demands by the government would be tantamount to complete capitulation on its part. In conclusion, he could only suggest that "at first, things will have to settle down, and then [we will talk about] reforms"; that is, Witte wanted the strike to end before any discussion could begin.[103]

After his interview with Witte, Orekhov reported to the congress and then addressed a meeting of railroad workers convened at St. Petersburg University. To an already agitated audience, he related the outcome of his talk with Witte, and when he reached the latter's final admonition, a "prolonged period of laughter broke out . . . which then turned into the roar of a crowd of three thousand. The task was accomplished. The strike was decided upon." The decision of the Pension Congress to support the strike and Orekhov's words swayed the railwaymen of St. Petersburg, and they unanimously voted to strike the next day.[104]

The Bolshevik Committee in St. Petersburg, not unlike its counterpart in Moscow, was vacillating and did not declare its support for a general strike until the night of October 12-13, i.e., at least two days after the railwaymen in the capital joined in a virtual shutdown of rail traffic in the Russian Empire.[105]

THE RAIL STRIKE BECOMES GENERAL

The strike on the railroads continued to spread until by October 16 every line was on strike; the railwaymen were joined in ever increasing numbers by workers and other oppositional elements until the autocratic regime reluctantly agreed to a series of political concessions embodied in the Manifesto of October 17. The October Manifesto promised the possibility of significant changes that could transform the autocratic regime into a real constitutional monarchy, but few, even among the progressive elements of the middle class, had genuine faith in the willingness of the regime to fulfill the promise. The Pension Congress passed a resolution condemning the Manifesto as inadequate and calling for complete fulfillment of its program.[106] But, despite reservations, the majority of railwaymen as well as their leaders were pacified by the Manifesto. Already by October 18 the Moscow union organization, as well as the Central Bureau, had decided to end the strike.[107]

During the 1905 Revolution, railroaders in European Russia had the highest rate of participation in strikes (100 percent) of any category of workers. All major strikes on railroads were carried out under the direction of union organizations or strike committees.[108] The success of the Railroad Union was also its failure. Its ideological and political inclinations tended towards middle class liberalism, while its methods relied heavily on the radical means of a general strike. The strike therefore was the ultimate weapon that was to bring about political compromise with the regime. The basis of the compromise was to be broad enough to include all strata of political opinion, a situation that demanded moderation on the one hand and promise of action on the other. It is difficult to see how such a position could be maintained by the Union with any hope of permanence.

The railroad strike "was only a match set to powder," and this was what the Central Bureau intended it to be. It concentrated its efforts on key personnel, thus hoping to provide the nucleus that would unite the opposition sentiment and galvanize it into decisive action. The sensitivity of the Central Bureau to the prevalent currents of public opinion and its reliance on them were what made it so effective. Its judgment was correct, and even when the more active leaders of the Central Bureau were arrested, the strike not only did not cease but continued to spread at a faster pace.

In the course of the October strike, the Railroad Union became closely tied to various strike organizations and radical elements. All revolutionary groups, however, had tended to regard a general strike only as a preliminary step towards an armed insurrection. The October general strike was the zenith of the influence and achievement of the Railroad Union. It failed to attain the full measure of its desired aims, and the government, once it regained its equilibrium, began taking determined steps to crush the union. Faced with the necessity of carrying on a struggle against the government, the union was nonetheless apprehensive about its ties with the revolutionary elements which were gaining in ascendancy, as the revolutionary wave crested in the direction of an armed uprising. Somewhat reluctantly, the union leadership continued a leftward course, albeit with less and less enthusiasm. When in December, 1905, it was confronted with the decision of the St. Petersburg and Moscow soviets for a general strike, to be followed by an insurrection, the Railroad Union found it impossible to refuse to lend its support in view of the paramount role the railroads would have in the success or failure of such an undertaking.[109]

Participation of railroads in the December strike was haphazard, and the principal railway connecting St. Petersburg and Moscow remained open, allowing the government to bring in troops to crush the insurrection. Commenting on the failure of the railroads to join the strike, one Bolshevik leader in Moscow wrote: "We proved to be correct in our distrust towards the liberal Railroad Union, against which we carried on an unremitting struggle ever since the October strike."[110]

The December uprising crippled the Railroad Union as a non-party organization. Alienated from the left, the union bore the burden of reaction, as countless numbers of its members were fired from their jobs, its leaders arrested, and its existence outlawed. Military punitive expeditions dispatched along the railroad lines to quell the rebellion summarily executed large numbers of union supporters.[111] The December uprising eliminated from the Russian political scene the force that had been so effective in precipitating the October general strike.

BRUNO KALNIŅŠ

The Social Democratic Movement in Latvia

Although Latvia constituted a small part of the Russian Empire, it played a leading role in the revolutionary movement of Tsarist Russia. Latvia's Social Democratic Party exerted considerable influence in the struggle between Bolshevism and Menshevism in the ranks of the Russian Social Democratic Workers' Party (RSDRP). Up to the present, foreign literature has paid little attention to these problems, and Soviet party sources assume a rather biased attitude when describing the Latvian Social Democratic movement.[1] It is the purpose of this paper to give an outline of the history of the Latvian Social Democratic Party and, above all, to throw light on its relation to Russian Menshevism.

THE BEGINNING OF THE LATVIAN SOCIAL DEMOCRATIC MOVEMENT

The Latvian Social Democratic movement, dating back to the 1890s, was formed under the influence of German Social Democracy. In spite of the fact that Latvia was a part of the Russian Empire, there had been no connection between Latvian Social Democrats and Russian socialists. The Latvian Social Democratic movement started with the activities of students who, upon graduation from German high schools, continued their studies at the Baltic University at Dorpat (Tartu). Under the influence of socialist books available at German bookstores in the Baltic cities, one of the student circles legally issued a volume of essays entitled *Pūrs* (1892), in which socialist ideas were expounded. *Dienas Lapa,* an important daily published in Riga, was also in their hands. Since 1891 it had been edited by the young jurist Jānis Pliekšans, known later by his pen-name Rainis.[2]

In 1893 Rainis went to Zürich to take part in the Third Congress of the Socialist International, where he became acquainted with the leader of German Social Democracy, August Bebel. Bebel discussed the principles of German Social Democracy with Rainis, presented him with a large assortment of socialist literature in German, and told him about his experience in transporting illegal literature across the border. Rainis brought German

All dates in this chapter are new style.

socialist literature to Riga without difficulty in a suitcase with a double bottom made specially for him by a Zürich craftsman.[3]

It should be stressed that in Zürich Rainis had been in touch only with Bebel; he did not look for G. Plekhanov or P. Aksel'rod, representatives of the Russian "Group for the Emancipation of Labor" who had also been in Zürich. As a result, he brought home only German socialist literature.

In the autumn of 1893, after Rainis' return from Zürich, socialist agitation spread in students' and workers' circles in the cities of Riga, Liepāja, and Jelgava. In a somewhat camouflaged form it appeared on the pages of the legal paper *Dienas Lapa* and in legal workers' organizations for mutual assistance that had existed in Riga since 1867. In 1894 and 1895 three illegal conferences of the first activists of the new movement were held in Riga. During the period 1893-97 this movement was known as the "New Current" *(Jaunā strāva).*[4]

However, in May, 1897 tsarist censorship and the police took action. The homes of 138 persons who had taken part in the movement were searched and 77 persons were arrested and under administrative procedure were sentenced by the Minister of the Interior to various terms of exile. In spite of this devastating blow, the "New Current" had laid the ideological foundations for the further development of the Social Democratic movement in Latvia.

THE FOUNDING OF THE LATVIAN SOCIAL DEMOCRATIC WORKERS' PARTY

Those members of the "New Current" who managed to escape abroad established their own presses, first in the United States and later in London and Berne, and began to publish Social Democratic proclamations and journals. In Boston, where there were a considerable number of Latvian immigrants, the monthly *Auseklis* was published from 1898 to 1901.[5] In London the *Latviešu strādnieks* was published from 1899 to 1900 and the *Sociāldemokrats* from 1900 to 1902. The latter monthly was then moved to Berne where it appeared from 1903 to 1905. In Berne, too, a series of Social Democratic pamphlets, originals as well as translations, was published. They were mostly the works of August Bebel, Karl Kautsky, and other German Social Democrats. In all, twenty-five pamphlets had been published up to 1906. The illegal transportation of these pamphlets to Latvia was well organized, and they exerted a great influence on the development of the Latvian Social Democratic movement.

At the same time, illegal circles of workers began to arise, first in Riga and then in other cities. Latvia was then one of the most industrialized provinces of Tsarist Russia, with a total industrial labor force of 140,000, chiefly in large plants, and with 70 percent of the workers concentrated in Riga.

As a result of the growing economic demands of workers and a violent general strike in Riga in May, 1899, known as the "Rebellion of Riga," workers began to organize socialist circles; the first conference of these circles took place in August, 1899, in Riga. The Riga Committee, charged with leading the circles, was formed in 1901. Jānis Ozols,[6] then a student at the Polytechnical Institute of Riga, was the principal leader of the committee. In 1901 Social Democratic organizations were founded in Jelgava; these became known as the "Group of Latvian Social Democrats in Kurland" and were headed by the young physician, Dr. Pauls Kalniņš.[7] In 1902 similar organizations were also formed in other cities. These organizations, with the exception of the Kurland group, formed one common Baltic Latvian Social Democratic Organization at a conference in Riga in 1902. However, controversies of a personal and organizational character were soon settled and the Kurland group joined the others to form the Latvian Social Democratic Workers' Party (LSDSP).

This event took place at an illegal congress which was held from June 20 to June 23, 1904, in Riga. The Congress was attended by eleven delegates, representing five party organizations with a membership of 2,500.[8] Given the conditions of the time this was a large membership and the LSDSP immediately became one of the leading organizations of the then weak Russian Social Democratic movement. The characteristic feature of the Latvian party was that more than 70 percent of its members were workers, whereas the membership of the Russian Social Democratic Party came mostly from the ranks of the intelligentsia. The LSDSP retained this character of a genuine workers' party throughout its existence.

The party declared the paper *Cīņa* and the journal *Sociāldemokrats* to be its official organs. The former had been printed illegally since March, 1904 in Riga and the latter was published abroad, in Berne. The congress elected a Central Committee in which leading roles were played by Jānis Ozols, a publicist Jānis Jansons,[9] and a worker Voldis Rikveilis.[10] A draft of the party's program was submitted to the congress, but its adoption was postponed until the next congress.

The LSDSP was formed on a national basis as a Latvian party. However, the congress considered it desirable to unite all the national Social Democratic parties of Tsarist Russia within the ranks of the Russian Social Democratic Workers' Party. This was to be accomplished on a *federative* basis. Thus the LSDSP supported the Bund's point of view and opposed the decisions of the Second Congress of the RSDRP. In addition, the congress of the LSDSP voted to consider the Bund "the only representative of the Jewish workers."[11] Later, this decision evoked Lenin's attacks against "Latvian federalists."

After the congress, in order to coordinate work with the Bund, which had organizations in Riga and other Latvian cities, a special Federative Committee was formed which included representatives of both parties. The Russian Bolsheviks and Mensheviks did not join this committee because they did not approve of the federative principle. In particular, M. Litvinov, leader of the Riga Committee of Russian Bolsheviks, was vigorously opposed to the idea of federation. It should be emphasized, however, that the federative principle was supported unanimously by all the delegates to the First Congress of the LSDSP, including P. Stučka who in 1907 was to become the leader of the Latvian Bolsheviks.

At the same time it should be mentioned that as early as 1904 the Latvian Social Democratic press rejected Lenin's views on the question of the organization of the party. In biting and ironic language, *Sociāldemokrats* came out against Lenin's ideas, as expressed at the Second Congress of the RSDRP, calling for an "omniscient and all seeing Central Committee" which should have the right to "expel from the party all those whom it does not like and respect those who show good behavior." The article stressed that it was imperative for the Latvian Social Democrats to support "the minority of the Russian Party [i.e. the Menshevik faction] which since the [Second] Congress [of the RSDRP] has been vigorously opposing such [i.e. Lenin's] bureaucratism."[12]

THE LATVIAN SOCIAL DEMOCRATIC PARTY IN THE REVOLUTION OF 1905

In Latvia the revolution of 1905 was more successful than elsewhere in Tsarist Russia. Latvia was one of the most industrially developed provinces in Russia, and the large factories of Riga and Liepāja became the main centers of the revolutionary movement. The strength of the movement was not the result of political and social factors alone, however; the 1905 Revolution in Latvia was also a *nationalist* revolution—a Latvian revolution against Russian-German oppression. Moreover, Latvia had a well-organized, well-disciplined, and strong illegal party, the LSDSP, which assumed leadership from the first day of the revolution.[13]

The well-organized character of the revolutionary movement became evident as early as the January strike, which opened the revolution of 1905 in Latvia. In contrast to the demonstrations of workers in St. Petersburg, led by the orthodox priest Gapon who was not affiliated with any political party, the Central Committee of the LSDSP asked Latvian workers to launch a general strike to protest the shooting of workers in St. Petersburg. Political and social demands were also stated. These included, for example, the demand for a democratically elected national assembly, political freedoms, an eight-hour day.[14]

The appeal of the LSDSP met with enormous success. Eighty thousand workers went on strike in Riga and 12,000 in Liepāja; strikes occurred in other Latvian cities as well. The total number of strikers in Latvia reached more than 100,000. In Riga, large demonstrations also took place. One of them, the demonstration of January 26, was attacked by troops; 73 demonstrators were killed, 200 wounded. After this event the revolutionary movement grew even stronger.

By decision of the LSDSP Central Committee, a new general strike broke out on May Day. The revolutionary movement also spilled into villages, drawing into its ranks laborers and peasants. Villagers met in Lutheran churches where representatives of the LSDSP delivered speeches, and from there marched to the buildings of local authorities and confiscated arms and the properties of German landlords.

At the climax of the developing revolution, the Second Congress of the LSDSP was held from June 24 to June 26 in Riga. Seventeen delegates represented 7,000 members of the party; 2,750 of these were members of the Riga organization, which was divided into 273 circles. Twelve thousand copies of *Cīņa* were published. Approximately 800,000 copies of 530 proclamations were issued in the course of 1905-1906.[15] These facts were illustrative of the remarkable growth of the party and its influence.

The Second Congress adopted a party program, based on the Erfurt Program of the German Social Democratic Party. In matters of political principle, it is important to stress that the congress refused to accede to the demand for a dictatorship of the proletariat, thus adopting a position quite different from that of the Russian Social Democratic Workers' Party. Concerning the national question, the program demanded "wide political and economic autonomy" and the introduction of the Latvian language to schools, courts, and governmental and municipal authorities. Their ideology concerning the national political problem was still undeveloped. The demand for autonomy within a federative Russia or even for an independent Latvian state had not yet ripened.

At the same time, the Second Congress agreed on the necessity of the existence of "separate national parties" in Russia. Union with the RSDRP would be possible only under the condition that the internal independence of the LSDSP be preserved and representation in the Central Committee of the RSDRP be granted. In practice, relations with the Russian Bolshevik and Menshevik organizations in Riga in 1905 were not very friendly. These two Russian organizations had only 600 members and their role in the Latvian revolutionary movement was insignificant. They acted separately, refusing to participate in the Federative Committee (formed in 1904) and thereby refusing to coordinate their work with the LSDSP. The Committee of Russian Bolsheviks issued pamphlets criticizing the LSDSP for tactics which were characterized as too moderate. *Cīņa* repeatedly waged a polemic with the Russian groups, accusing them of disrupting the revolutionary struggle, commenting ironically on the struggles between Bolsheviks and Mensheviks, who were fighting against each other and against the national Social Democratic parties instead of "fighting against tsarist autocracy." The paper stressed the fact that tiny Latvia with its population of two million had founded an illegal Social Democratic Party that had 7,000 well-organized members, issued *Cīņa,* which was printed in Riga and not abroad, and had 12,000 paying subscribers. On the other hand, the Bolsheviks and Mensheviks, with a Russian population of 130 million people to work with, had only 15,000 party members, and their journals *Iskra* and *Proletarii,* which were published abroad, had only 20,000 subscribers in all of Russia.[16] *Iskra* had also published several polemical articles against the LSDSP. In one of them it was stated that "Leaders of the Latvian Party play a reactionary role. They are afraid of the possibility of an uprising and of the destruction of the Latvian organization."[17] The latter was characterized by *Iskra*, however, as very strong and well-organized.

At any rate, it is difficult to take seriously this show of radicalism on the part of the Russian groups in Riga. An uprising in Latvia alone, without an uprising in St. Petersburg and Moscow, would have been put down immediately by the Tsarist Army. An uprising organized at the wrong time would undoubtedly have led to the complete destruction of the Latvian movement. The Second Congress of the LSDSP admitted that "the proletariat of Central Russia is still very weakly organized and not prepared for an armed uprising," and it therefore refused to ask the people of Latvia to take "such an irresponsible step." The congress determined that further revolutionary activities should take the form of earnest political agitation, strikes, demonstrations, agitation among the troops, and "partisan actions" against reprisals by the police. By accepting these tactics, the LSDSP rejected the Bolshevik strategy of preparation for an armed uprising and Lenin's demand for the formation of a "workers' and peasants' government." Therefore, statements of Communist Party historians that the Second Congress of the LSDSP "acted under the influence of the Bolshevik resolutions of the Third Congress of the RSDRP (Bolshevik)" have no foundation at all.[18] The further development of the revolution vindicated the cautious tactics of the Latvian Party.

The revolutionary activity of the LSDSP continued throughout the summer and autumn following the Second Congress. By October, the party had 18,200 members, of which 7,200 were in the Riga organization.[19] For an underground organization, this constituted an enormous power. There were as many organized Social Democrats in Riga alone as there were in St. Petersburg with its population of two million.

Revolutionary activities continued to spread in Latvian villages. From August 8 to August 11, the first general strike of agricultural laborers took place in southern Latvia. Thirty thousand people participated in this strike, the first of its type in the Russian Empire. The authorities retaliated by declaring the Kurland (Kurzeme) *guberniia* to be under martial law.

The peak of revolutionary activity was reached at the end of October, when a general strike of railroad workers gripped the whole of Russia and Latvia as well. The Manifesto of Tsar Nicholas II, promising political freedoms, ushered in a two-month period of real freedom in Latvia. Large rallies were held in Riga and in all cities and country districts, with representatives of the LSDSP addressing the crowds. The daily attendance was approximately 60,000. Papers were published without censorship. The Social Democratic paper *Dienas Lapa* was edited by Jānis Jansons, one of the *de facto* leaders of the revolution and a brilliant speaker at the rallies. In Riga, actual power passed into the hands of the Federative Committee which had been recognized by the governor, and which issued binding decrees and organized its own militia for the maintenance of order.

It was during this period that the first free trade unions were organized. Thirty-nine unions were formed with a total of 32,000 members.[20] Members of the LSDSP also participated actively in the convening of a Congress of Latvian Teachers, which was attended by 1,000 teachers. The congress voted to stop teaching in Russian immediately and to start teaching in Latvian.

At the same time, the agrarian revolution was spreading and intensifying all over Latvia. In all districts power was taken over by the revolutionaries, district authorities were dispersed, police disarmed, and German landlords expelled. With the participation of LSDSP representatives, for the first time in Latvian history local executive committees were elected in general elections, on the basis of universal suffrage [including women]. These 352 committees became the revolutionary organs of the people's power. They organized a militia in every district. On December 2 and December 3, a congress of executive committees' delegates was held in Riga. It operated under the political leadership of LSDSP representatives and was attended by 1,000 delegates. During the peak period of the revolution, power passed into the hands of Social Democrats in several Latvian cities, among them Tukums, Ventspils, Kuldiga, and Talsi. Apart from Latvia, the revolutionary movement achieved a comparable success only in Georgia.

A characteristic feature of the Latvian Revolution of 1905 was that it did not follow the Russian model, namely, no Soviets of Workers' Deputies were organized either in Riga or in other Latvian cities. Soviets were formed in many Russian cities because the RSDRP was still weak and unable to represent the masses of workers. In Latvia, on the other hand, the LSDSP had circles in all factories and plants which were considered by the workers to be their representatives. When necessary, Federative Committees in Riga and Liepāja convened meetings of these Social Democratic representatives. The revolutionary movement in both these cities was actually led by the Federative Committees, and the leadership of the revolution throughout Latvia was in the hands of the Central Committee of the LSDSP.

In Russia at this time, worker support for the revolution was much weaker. In December the political situation changed in favor of the tsarist government. Members of the Petersburg Soviet of Workers' Deputies were arrested on December 16, and the workers of Petersburg did not come to their defense. When a hopeless armed uprising broke out in Moscow on December 24, a meeting of representatives from all the Social Democratic circles in Riga decided to support the Moscow workers by instigating a general strike in Latvia. The strike lasted from December 25 to December 29, 1905. At the same time, the Riga Bolshevik Committee demanded that the Federative Committee start an armed uprising in Riga. This demand was rejected, because it was felt that Russian troops were not yet ready to lend their support to an uprising; the workers of Moscow had already been defeated and no other uprisings had occurred elsewhere in Russia. The general strike was terminated on December 29, 1905, by a decision of the Central Committee of the LSDSP.

After the defeat of the Moscow uprising, the revolution of 1905 was suppressed in all the Russian provinces. Punitive expeditions were sent to Latvia. The Lifland (Vidzenu) *guberniia* and Riga were declared to be under martial law, and the 19,000 soldiers who had been sent to Latvia treated it like an enemy country. Field courts martial and military courts were active in Latvia until 1908. In all, 2,556 Latvians were killed, 2,041 of them by punitive expeditions without any trial, and 8,000 people were exiled to Siberia and Northern Russia. More than 5,000 people emigrated, many of them to the United States, where a strong organization of Latvian Social Democrats came into existence in 1906-1907.[21]

THE UNION OF THE LSDSP WITH THE RSDRP

The defeat of the revolution in Russia strengthened the urge to concentrate and coordinate the forces of the workers' movement in the ranks of a united All-Russian Social Democratic Party. The events of 1905 proved that without a victorious revolution in Russia itself, any revolution in a small country like Latvia would be ultimately doomed to defeat no matter what its initial successes. The idea of union was also furthered by the temporary merger of Bolsheviks and Mensheviks in the RSDRP and by the readiness of Russian Social Democratic leaders to make concessions to the demands of the national parties for their preservation as autonomous territorial organizations. Thus the principle of federalism was actually accepted by the RSDRP.

A conference of the LSDSP which took place in March, 1906, decided to present to the RSDRP a project for union. According to this project, the LSDSP was to be the only Social Democratic Party in Latvia. Russian and Lithuanian Social Democratic organizations which had previously existed in Latvia were to be dissolved and their members were to join the organizations of the LSDSP. The party was to retain its Central Committee, its congresses, and its whole party apparatus. It would also retain the right to solve its organizational problems independently. The Latvian Party was to have representatives in the united Central Committee of the RSDRP and in delegations sent by the RSDRP to international socialist congresses. *Cīņa* commented that the Latvian Social Democrats refused to be dispersed within the ranks of the RSDRP and demanded union on a federative basis. Petr Stučka,[22] the future leader of the Latvian Bolsheviks who in 1906 was still a moderate and a national socialist, wrote that it was time for Russian Social Democrats to get rid of their hostile attitude toward the existence of independent national Social Democratic Parties in Latvia, Lithuania, Estonia, Armenia, and the Ukraine, and toward Jewish socialists in the ranks of the Bund.[23]

The union of the LSDSP and RSDRP took place at the Stockholm

Congress of the RSDRP held from April 23 to May 8, 1906. At the twenty-fourth session of this congress, which was presided over first by Lenin and then by Dan, M. Litvinov reported on the question and moved for the approval of the agreement on union which was based on the demands of the LSDSP. The Latvian Party was represented in Stockholm by J. Ozols, A. Buševics, and V. Dermanis.[24]

In the ensuing discussion, the Russian Bolshevik, M. Vaniushkin (Borodin), representative of the Riga Committee of the RSDRP, criticized the motion and suggested that all points concerning the federative basis be eliminated and that the LSDSP be transformed into a regional organization of the RSDRP. However, these amendments were rejected by the congress. Vaniushkin's amendment, that the LSDSP not be called the "Social Democratic Party of the Latvian Province" (or "of Latvia" as it was expressed in the Latvian translation), came closest to acceptance. Vaniushkin argued that this was not a suitable name, because there were workers of other nationalities living in Latvia but this motion was rejected by a vote of 28 to 22. Vaniushkin's proposal that the Latvian Party not be allowed to have representatives in the United Central Committee was also rejected by 42 to 22 votes. The Congress did approve the motion of the Bolshevik Surenin (Shaumian) that "representation [in the Central Committee] is granted temporarily until the next Congress of the RSDRP." At that point, Rybak (Buševics), representative of the LSDSP, declared that this decision was "unacceptable to us." After new arguments concerning a motion by the Bolshevik Bazarov, the congress decided to disregard Shaumian's motion. After a round of applause Buševics said that "now the project of our agreement will be accepted" by the Latvian Party. The entire project of union was adopted almost unanimously.[25]

The decisions made at the Stockholm Congress had to be approved by a Congress of the LSDSP, which took place illegally in and near the city of Riga on June 18 to June 21, 1906. This Third Congress of the LSDSP was attended by 51 delegates, representing 14,000 organized party members of which 6,000 were from Riga. In spite of the fact that the congress took place at the height of the activities of the punitive expeditions, the number of party members had decreased only slightly in comparison with 1905, a year of rising revolutionary activity. The congress unanimously approved the project of union with the RSDRP. In connection with this the party changed its name. Henceforth it called itself "Latvijās Sociāldemokratija," the Social Democracy of Latvia (SDL). Its Russian publications were issued under the heading "Social Democracy of the Latvian Province." Russian and Lithuanian organizations existing in Latvia before the union were dissolved and their members joined the SDL. For the purpose of agitation in the Russian language an illegal paper *Bor'ba* was published during 1906-1909. *Cīņa* remained the central organ of the SDL. A newly elected Central Committee issued a special manifesto in which it explained the recent union with the RSDRP.[26]

LATVIAN SOCIAL DEMOCRACY IN THE YEARS OF TSARIST REACTION (1906-1910)

The union with the RSDRP immediately introduced the Bolshevik-Menshevik conflict into the ranks of the SDL. A group of Bolsheviks took part in the First Congress of the SDL in 1906 and severely criticized the moderate tactics of its Central Committee during the revolution of 1905. The group demanded technical preparation for a new armed uprising, the purchase of arms, and the adoption of the tactic of individual terrorism ("partisan actions") against police and government officials. Moreover, they wanted to grant the terrorist organization autonomous rights within the party.

After the congress, radical tendencies were strengthened even further. Many members demanded that the party react against the punitive expeditions and executions of revolutionaries with systematic terrorist attacks. In order to avoid being caught, about 1,000 armed party members continued their revolutionary activity in the forests. In the autumn of 1906 these so-called "Forest Brethren" began to stage raids on private citizens and "confiscate" their property. As a result, a conference of village organizations of the SDL decided in November, 1906, to put an end to this guerrilla warfare and to liquidate the organization of "Forest Brethren."

Anarchic tendencies were also very strong at the time in the city organizations of the party. In the summer of 1906 a group of "fighters" broke away from the Riga organization and formed an independent organization of Latvian anarchists which was, however, liquidated by the police a few months later. The Central Committee of the SDL was fighting against these anarchistic tendencies and even published a special brochure for that purpose. But the Bolsheviks were not willing to adopt stern measures against the anarchic inclinations of some party members, because they themselves shared many of these ideas. This led to a conflict between the majority of the Central Committee and P. Stučka who demanded a more severe attitude toward anarchic tendencies. The conflict resulted in Stučka's resignation from both the Central Committee and *Cīņa's* editorial board in November, 1906.[27] Stučka soon left Riga and until 1914 he did not take any active part in illegal work.

After Stučka's departure, the Central Committee recalled two intellectuals, Pauls and Klara Kalniņš, from their exile in Switzerland and asked them to take charge of *Cīņa.* Both were known for their moderate opinions and their close relationship to German Social Democracy. They played an outstanding role in defining party ideology and it was largely because of their political influence that the SDL joined the camp of Menshevism in 1911. But this ideological redirection was a slow and gradual process. The first success came when J. Ozols, a member of the Central Committee, was elected to the Second State Duma in February, 1907; 55.1 percent of the votes were cast in his favor. In the Duma he sided with the Mensheviks and became a member of the Presidium of the Social Democratic faction as well as its secretary. On the floor of the Duma, Ozols made two interpellations: the first concerned the use of torture by the secret police in Riga, and the second concerned the activities of the punitive expeditions in Latvia.

In May, 1907, 26 delegates represented the SDL at the Fifth Congress of the RSDRP in London. Shortly afterwards, June 3 to June 7, the Second Congress of the SDL was held in London. Of the 26 delegates, 10 were Bolsheviks, 2 Mensheviks, and 17 Centrists-Conciliationists, the majority of whom were closer to the Mensheviks than to the Bolsheviks. The congress elected a Central Committee in which the Bolsheviks prevailed but which also contained some Mensheviks, among them P. Kalniņš. At the same time it was decided that the party would embark upon a campaign of agitation among the masses, take part in the elections to the Third Duma, and support the re-establishment of legal trade unions.[28] The Duma election brought victory to an SDL candidate, the physician Andrei Priedkalns.

In October, 1908, the Third Congress of the SDL took place in Helsinki. It was attended by 14 delegates of local organizations and representatives of the Foreign Committee of the party which was active in Brussels. Between 1907-1908, 804,500 copies of illegal newspapers and proclamations were published. Nevertheless, the party suffered a great deal from police repression and infiltration by its agents. The total number of SDL members, which had reached 17,000 in 1907 (8,467 in Riga), decreased to 5,000 (3,500 in Riga). This congress in Helsinki marked a departure from the radical Bolshevism of 1906-1907 and a return to realistic tactics adjusted to the new, post-revolutionary conditions. Among other things, the congress declared the formation and development of legal labor and cultural associations to be one of the most important tasks of the party. This resolution was approved despite the opposition of the Bolsheviks, whose attitude toward legal associations was strictly negative. The congress elected a new Central Committee, composed largely of Mensheviks and Centrists. The organ of the Russian Mensheviks characterized the Third Congress of the SDL as follows: "It strengthened the reversal of the SDL's tactics which became gradually more and more noticeable after the London Congress [of the RSDRP]. The Third Congress showed that the party had survived its internal crisis; that all the Blanquist and anarchist tendencies had been defeated."[29]

Between 1908-1910, the new Central Committee succeeded in re-establishing a considerable number of trade unions. These organizations united 2,000 workers in 1908, and as many as 3,700 workers in 1910. In 1909, an illegal Central Bureau of these legal trade unions was established. Including cultural associations, membership in these legal organizations reached 8,000. In this way, an open labor movement began to operate within the legal framework of Tsarist Russia under the Duma regime.

At the same time, the party itself suffered continually from persecution because it was never granted the status of a legal organization. It could not officially and legally maintain offices, publish newspapers, or compete in elections even though it did in fact sponsor candidates to the Duma. The Social Democrats in the Duma spoke openly as representatives of Social Democracy, but they were not legal representatives of a legal Social Democratic party. As a result of the repressive police regime, party membership continued to decrease. In 1909, it had 3,500 members (2,500 in Riga); in 1910 only 2,000 members (1,461 in Riga).[30] In spite of this, the SDL remained the strongest illegal organization in Russia throughout the years of reaction. According to Stalin,[31] there were no more than 400 members in the St. Petersburg organization of the RSDRP in 1909; that is, one-sixth of the number of members in the capital of Latvia.

THE MENSHEVIK PERIOD OF THE SDL (1911-14)

The SDL's transition to Menshevism was completed in 1910-11, when all its leading organs came under the control of the Mensheviks. In 1910, the central organ *Cīņa* was transferred to Brussels. Its board of editors consisted of two Mensheviks, K. Eliass and F. Menders, and a Conciliationist, J. Jansons. In September, 1911, a party congress assembled in Helsinki but was forced to recess after a few hours when it was discovered by the secret police.[32] Nevertheless, it did succeed in electing a new Central Committee in which there was not a single Bolshevik. The party leadership passed into the hands of worker Mensheviks; it was headed by the worker V. Rikveilis, the Central Committee's new secretary. Before the congress, early in 1911, the Central Committee replaced a Bolshevik delegate to the Foreign Bureau of the RSDRP Central Committee with K. Eliass,[33] a steadfast Menshevik, who supported all the motions of the Russian Mensheviks. The Foreign Committee of the SDL and the Central Board of Propagandists, a branch of the party Central Committee, also passed into the hands of Mensheviks. During 1910-14, the Riga Committee and four of the five District Committees of the Riga organization of the SDL consisted of Mensheviks and, at the same time, exclusively of workers. This was an extremely important fact, because the Riga organization constituted the majority of the party. (In 1911 it represented 1,153 of the 2,000 members.)

During its Menshevik period, the SDL took advantage of all the legal possibilities available under the Duma monarchy. Aided by the growth and development of Latvian industry between 1910 and 1914, a wide labor movement developed throughout Latvia under Menshevik leadership. In 1913, there were 138,000 industrial workers; together with those engaged in the transport and building industries there were about 190,000 workers. In 1914, there were 14 active trade union organizations with 7,800 members.[34] Associations of consumers and a number of cultural organizations emerged at the same time, while the older associations of mutual assistance continued to exist. Part of the SDL's agitation activities was now conducted within the framework of these organizations and thus could be carried on legally.

In all, in 1914, about 25,000 members were united in these various organizations; that is, eight times as many as were in the illegal SDL. Of considerable importance were the elections of workers' representatives and members of the Board of Health Insurance Funds which took place in 1913 on the basis of the Labor Insurance Act of 1912. In 1914, there were 82 active health insurance funds in Latvia, in which 88,661 workers participated. To the governing boards of these funds the workers elected Social Democrats.

All this broad organizational work was done by Menshevik organs alone. Moreover, they had to struggle not only against passivity but also against the open opposition of the Latvian Bolsheviks. In 1911, for example, a Party District Conference of the fourth district of Riga, the only one then controlled by the Bolsheviks, requested that all party members break away from legal organizations, which "were no longer of any importance." Only afterwards, in 1913, did the Latvian Bolsheviks change their tactics and begin to work in legal organizations.[35]

The Menshevik leaders of the SDL also established a legally published labor press. *Arodniēks,* a trade union journal, appeared in 1909. *Laika Bālss*, a Social Democratic paper, began to appear in 1911. These papers were frequently confiscated by the authorities and banned by the courts. Nevertheless, they would soon reappear under a slightly different name.

The Russian Social Democratic papers, the Menshevik *Rabochaia gazeta* and the Bolshevik *Pravda* maintained correspondents in Riga and were to some extent distributed throughout Latvia.[36] A well-known Menshevik activist, I. Isuf, in Riga in exile during 1913-15, maintained close contact with the Menshevik leaders of the SDL.

Party activity within the legal workers' organizations considerably raised the political consciousness of their members and produced a new type of activist within the labor movement. Professional revolutionaries were replaced by workers capable of leading large social organizations.[37]

The Menshevik Central Committee also changed the political tactics of the SDL. Instead of the Bolsheviks' radical and politically unrealistic demands, the party concentrated its agitation on demanding the reforms necessary for a gradual democratization of the country. In 1911, following the example of the Russian Mensheviks, the Central Committee organized a "petitionary campaign" in favor of "the freedom of coalitions," by which was meant freedom of association, press, and speech. "Freedom of coalitions," K. Eliass, one of the Menshevik leaders wrote, "is the most important and most proletarian demand included in our program. A labor movement can exist without a democratic republic, but it can never and nowhere exist without the right to coalitions."[38] During the pre-war years, this Menshevik slogan of "freedom of coalitions" became the mainstay of party policy. The petitionary campaign was unanimously approved by the Riga City Conference in December, 1911. The signed petitions were sent to Dr. A. Priedkalns, the Riga Social Democratic Duma deputy, and published in the workers' press.

In 1912, the party organized a broad campaign in connection with the elections to the Fourth Duma. Political freedoms were again the major plank of the electoral campaign. In December, 1911, the conference of Riga party organizations unanimously approved the Menshevik political platform. This platform was approved once more in Riga in June, 1912, by the Seventh Conference of the SDL. On this occasion, Latvian Bolsheviks, following the directives of the Russian Bolsheviks, tried to oppose the Menshevik policies but their efforts failed. The conference accepted the platform by a majority of 9 votes to 2 and declared the Menshevik tactics of the Central Committee to be correct. This was a great defeat for the Bolsheviks and it revealed their weakness in this period.[39]

The elections to the Duma brought more votes for A. Priedkalns, the candidate of the SDL, than for either of the other two candidates. Nevertheless, he did not obtain an absolute majority. In the second round of elections, his opponents united, and a Russian, Mansyrev, member of the Kadet Party, was elected by a narrow majority.

A new growth of the labor movement in Russia had begun in 1912 and had influenced Latvia particularly strongly. In 1912, 63,000 workers were on strike; in 1913, 180,000; and in the first half of 1914 the number of strikers reached 370,000. The strikes had an economic as well as a political character. In many cases the economic demands were connected with several political demands, especially the demand for political freedoms. This new and very strong growth of the labor movement was developing in Latvia under the political leadership of the Menshevik Central Committee of the SDL. In terms of the sweeping dimensions which the Latvian strike movement had assumed, particularly in Riga, Latvia was once more ahead of Russia.

Along with the strike movement, the illegal SDL also grew stronger. The Menshevik Central Committee did not have the slightest intention of "liquidating" the party, as the Bolsheviks had alleged, but had merely transferred part of the political work to legal workers' organizations. The whole party apparatus, its seven regional organizations, and its organ *Cīņa* continued to exist, illegal proclamations of the Central Committee and local committees continued to be issued, and conferences and illegal meetings of members took place regularly. The size of the SDL began to increase under Menshevik leadership. In 1911, there were 2,000 members; in 1912, 2,500; in 1913, 3,000; and in 1914, 3,500 members. As before, the Riga organization maintained its leading position during these years, with two-thirds of the party members belonging to it. It is especially important to stress the results of party statistics (the only statistics of this type in the entire RSDRP), gathered in 1913: in Riga, 97 percent of all members were workers, with only 3 percent belonging to the intelligentsia. No city organization of the Russian party had a comparable social composition. The Latvian Party was a purely *workers'* party. As to their age, 76 percent of the members were under 30. They joined the party after the 1905 Revolution and grew up in the conditions of the post-revolutionary period. Only 19.8 percent of the members had belonged to the party in 1905.[40] Among the veteran party members were the main Menshevik leaders and most active organizers of the party, V. Rikveilis and V. Caune.[41]

LATVIAN SOCIAL DEMOCRACY AND THE SPLIT WITHIN THE RSDRP

In spite of its clearly Menshevik policy, the SDL assumed at the beginning a conciliatory position concerning the dispute about the organizational question within the RSDRP. In 1911, K. Eliass published a long ironical essay entitled "How the Russian Comrades 'Unite,' or A Fairy Tale About a White Bull-Calf." In it he characterized fractional disputes as merely the arguments of exiled intellectuals quarreling because the party organization in Russia itself had been smashed by the tsarist reaction. The task of Russian workers, he wrote, "is to throw off the unbearable tutelage of these groups from abroad" and, following the example of the SDL, take the party leadership into their own hands.[42] In 1911, in order to emphasize its nonfractional and conciliatory line, the Central Committee of the SDL financially supported Trotsky's *Pravda,* which was issued in Vienna, because it "always made efforts to stand apart from fractional strife"[43] and distributed it among Russian members of the SDL. This conciliatory line was a logical result of the policy of the SDL which was based on the principle of strict organizational unity and consistent opposition to any fractional groups. The Latvian Social Democrats demanded that the RSDRP, too, follow this line even though their political sympathies were with the Mensheviks.

Nevertheless, towards the end of 1911, the SDL had to define more clearly its position concerning the split within the RSDRP. At that time, Lenin's fraction was organizing a conference, and its representative, G. Ordzhonikidze, sent two letters to the Central Committee of the SDL (dated November 14 and December 16) requesting it to send delegates to the conference. Moreover, S. Spandarian, a member of Lenin's Organizational Committee, came to Riga in November, 1911, and, with the help of Latvian Bolsheviks, penetrated the Propaganda Committee without the SDL Central Committee's knowledge,[44] provoking some confusion there. However, a conference of the Riga organization rejected a Bolshevik motion to send delegates to Lenin's conference and declared as "entirely correct" the anti-Leninist policy of the Central Committee. The delegates openly charged that one of the Latvian Bolsheviks, E. Zvirbulis, who had arrived from Berlin, "had come as Lenin's agent and was acting with the help of dark money."[45] The Central Committee of the SDL did not send any delegates to the Leninist conference, which took place in Prague in January, 1912. This conference, as is well known, put a formal end to the unity of the RSDRP.

After the Prague conference, in March, 1912, the Central Committee of the SDL adopted a special resolution stating that "this 'conference' is only a conference of Lenin's group and in no case an All-Russian conference."

The resolution pointed out that with the exception of Kiev alone the alleged "delegates" did not represent any genuine organizations and that the conference had not been attended by all national party organizations. Outstanding ideologists of Russian Social Democracy, such as Plekhanov, Martov, Trotsky, Dan, and others, had protested the convening of this conference. The resolution also stressed that Lenin's "conference" willfully adopted not only the name of an All-Russian conference, but also dared to declare itself "the supreme organ of the party" and to take decisions on problems it did not have the slightest right to discuss. In conclusion, the Central Committee declared that it "expresses the sharpest protest" against this "conference" and "proclaims categorically" that the SDL had nothing in common with its "decisions."[46]

In December, 1911, several months before this resolution, the Central Committee of the SDL had decided "to take the initiative and convene a meeting" of national organizations active in Russia.[47] This conference took place in January, 1912, and was attended by representatives of the SDL, the Bund, and the Caucasian District Committee. These three groups were the only Social Democratic organizations that were really operative at the time in Russia. The SDL had 2,500 members, the Caucasus (the Georgians) 1,300, and the Bund 475 members.[48] The conference decided to ask all Social Democratic organizations to elect delegates to a joint conference to be held in Vienna in August, 1912.

Towards the end of June, 1912, the Seventh Conference of the SDL took place in Riga and approved the Central Committee's policy by a majority of 8 votes with 2 opposed and 1 abstention. It also decided to send delegates to the joint conference in Vienna.[49] These decisions were a serious defeat for the Latvian Bolsheviks.

The Vienna Conference of August, 1912, was attended by representatives of almost all the non-Leninist organizations. At this conference, the SDL was represented by four delegates with full voting privileges and a fifth delegate, K. Eliass, sent by the Central Committee, who had an advisory vote only. Among the Latvian delegates, Rudolfs Lindīņš, head of the Central Board for Propaganda and particularly devoted to the Menshevik point of view, was elected to the seven member Organizational Committee of the RSDRP.[50]

After the Vienna Conference, the situation within the SDL grew more and more tense. Lenin began to interfere actively with the internal affairs of the Latvian Party. Early in 1912, he had published "A Letter from Riga" in his *Social Democrat,* in which he advised Latvian Social Democrats "to go over the heads of the intriguers in the leading organs" and to support the Russian Bolsheviks. The Central Committee severely criticized this article for "urging members to breach party discipline."[51] But the Latvian Bolsheviks disregarded the position of their Central Committee, and in June, 1912, without the Central Committee's knowledge, they organized a secret Bolshevik Center at a clandestine meeting in Riga. The task of the Center was to combat the Menshevik Central Committee and to win over Menshevik-led organizations of the party. Roberts Eiche, who later became Soviet Commisar of Agriculture, was one of the leaders of this secret Bolshevik Center.[52] At the same time, the Latvian Bolsheviks living in exile formed a Bureau of SDL organizations abroad, the task of which was to oppose the Menshevik-controlled Foreign Committee of the SDL and *Cīņa.* This Bolshevik Bureau was headed by an old Leninist, Jānis Bērziņš, who later became Secretary of the Comintern.[53] The Bureau issued its own Bulletin, *Biletens Latwijas Sozialdemokratijas Ahrsemju Grupu Biroja isdewums,* directed against the Central Committee of the SDL and published with Lenin's financial assistance.[54] Lenin was pleased by the formation of this organization of Latvian Bolsheviks and expressed his delight in one of his letters: "Latvian Bolsheviks have started to wage war against their Central Committee!"[55]

The Latvian Mensheviks, who in 1912 controlled all the leading party organs, did not take any organizational measures against these separatist Bolshevik activities, which undermined the party discipline and contravened its statutes. The Central Committee had the right to expel the Bolshevik factionalists from the party. Nevertheless, it did not do so because it feared that this might cause a formal split within the party. This hesitation had fateful consequences because it enabled the Bolsheviks to seize control of the party leadership a few years later.

THE BRUSSELS CONGRESS OF THE SDL IN 1914

In 1913, the Central Committee of the SDL decided to convene its Fourth Party Congress. At first the intention was to hold the Congress secretly in Latvia. However, the Russian Menshevik leader F. Dan, who had met with V. Caune, the SDL Central Committee's representative in St. Petersburg, warned against this plan. If the Congress were held in Latvia, the Bolshevik Duma faction would send as its delegate the provocateur Malinovskii, who would certainly report the meeting to the police. It was decided that the Fourth Congress would take place abroad, in Brussels.

The Bolsheviks mounted an energetic campaign to obtain a majority of votes at the congress. Lenin and the Russian Bolsheviks supported the Latvian Bolsheviks' struggle against their Central Committee. In 1913, Lenin corresponded with Latvian Bolsheviks and prepared a draft of a political platform for them. On October 14, the Bolshevik Central Committee voted to appropriate 100 rubles for the support of the Latvian Bolsheviks.[56] At that time, however, the Latvian Bolsheviks were still independent enough to reject the chapter concerning the national question in Lenin's draft of the platform. Among other things Lenin wrote in this chapter: "We are against any national culture, which we consider to be one of the slogans of bourgeois nationalism. The congress has to reject the slogan of cultural autonomy and the federative principle in the organization of the party as well."[57] In 1913, the Latvian Bolsheviks did not accept these views and that is why their *Biletens* (Bulletin), No. 9-10 of November 7/20, 1913, when publishing the Leninist draft of the platform, dropped the paragraph concerning the nationalities question and shortened and changed several other paragraphs. Indeed, it is characteristic that this draft was published anonymously under the title, "Our Platform for the Fourth Congress," thus keeping Lenin's authorship secret. The Latvian Bolsheviks feared that Lenin's open interference in Latvian party affairs would cause dissatisfaction among the members of the SDL and would seriously harm Bolshevik agitation during the campaign to elect delegates to the party congress.

Police repression, striking at Menshevik leaders of the SDL in June, 1913, proved to be a great help to the Bolsheviks during the election campaign. On June 10, the entire Propaganda Board of the SDL Central Committee was arrested, including its head R. Lindīnš. On June 14, almost all members of the Central Committee were arrested as well. It took several months to form a new Central Committee and to re-establish contacts with regional organizations. These arrests wrecked the whole campaign on the part of the Menshevik Party leadership against the Bolsheviks. The police did not arrest Bolshevik propagandists at that time, and they were able to continue their campaign against the SDL Central Committee. The Menshevik arrests were later revealed to have been the result of treachery by a Liepāja party worker, P. Augulis.

The Fourth Congress of the SDL was held at a "people's house" on the outskirts of Brussels from January 26 to February 8, 1914. It was attended by 18 delegates with voting rights; of these 9 were Mensheviks and 9 Bolsheviks. All the Riga districts except one sent only Menshevik delegates. Thus Riga, the most developed and most Europeanized center of the Latvian labor movement, supported the Menshevik line by an overwhelming majority. A minority of the Riga delegates (5 of 13) and the delegates from the Latvian countryside, where the labor movement still stuck to obsolete radicalism, were Bolsheviks.

The outcome of the congress depended upon the vote of the delegate from Liepāja, P. Augulis, ostensibly a Menshevik with conciliatory tendencies. His organization directed him to side with the Mensheviks on all decisive questions. Had he done so, the votes would have been evenly divided and the Bolsheviks would not have obtained a majority. As it turned out, the delegate from Liepāja was a provocateur, who had been registered with the secret police since January, 1913 under the assumed name "Leshii." His switch-over to the Bolsheviks was prepared in accordance with orders from the Police Department in St. Petersburg which at that time followed the policy of supporting the Bolsheviks everywhere in Russia. In the opinion of the Police Department, placing the leadership of the SDL in the hands of the Bolsheviks would lead to a split in the party and thus to a weakening of the Latvian labor movement. The police also assumed that after his switch to the Bolsheviks, Augulis would be elected to the new Central Committee of the SDL; this had been promised to him by the Bolshevik delegates. Thus, for the first time in the history of Latvian Social Democracy the police would have an agent in the highest organ of the party.[58]

During the opening days of the congress, Augulis remained with the Mensheviks and was elected one of three co-chairmen of the congress. After several meetings, and upon receiving orders from the Police Department, he suddenly switched from the Mensheviks to the Bolsheviks. Augulis explained this unexpected action by saying that the arguments of the Bolshevik speakers, especially those of Lenin, had "convinced" him and "made" him change his opinions. At the congress, the Russian Bolsheviks were represented by Lenin, the Menshevik Organizational Committee was represented by Semkovskii, the Bund by Iudin, the Menshevik fraction of the Duma by Chkhenkeli, and the Bolshevik fraction by R. Malinovskii, another agent of the Police Department who supported Lenin at the congress in a very rude fashion.[59]

Twenty speakers addressed themselves to the first point of the program, a report on the activities of the Central Committee, which were attacked by the Bolsheviks. Nevertheless, the debate ended with the adoption of a moderate resolution, appreciating the Central Committee's merits, on the one hand, while criticizing in a restrained manner its support of the Russian Mensheviks, on the other. A resolution demanding the re-establishment of unity within the Social Democratic fraction in the Fourth Duma was adopted unanimously.

However, sharp and prolonged arguments concerning the attitude of the SDL toward the split within the RSDRP ensued. F. Menders, speaking for the Central Committee, moved that the SDL continue to adhere to the Menshevik August Bloc in the future. J. Jansons took a moderate line, maintaining that the SDL should remain neutral and not join either the Russian Bolsheviks or Mensheviks. In a long speech, Lenin appealed to the SDL to join the Bolshevik Party and was supported by the Latvian Bolsheviks who spoke after him. The Bolshevik motion was accepted in principle by 10 votes to 8. Following this, J. Jansons delivered an able and hard-hitting speech accusing Lenin of wrecking Latvian Social Democracy; he declared he would take no further responsibility for the work of the congress and resigned from its chairmanship.

After Jansons' resignation, a flood of amendments to the resolution was proposed. The Mensheviks proposed twenty amendments of which only five were adopted. The major Menshevik victory was the adoption of an amendment forbidding the SDL to become affiliated organizationally with either the Russian Bolshevik Center or the Mensheviks. This amendment was approved by a majority of 14 out of 18 votes. Eight Mensheviks and, to Lenin's great displeasure, 6 of the 9 Bolsheviks supported it. During all of these proceedings Lenin himself was stationed in the lobby, giving continual instructions to the Latvian Bolsheviks. In spite of this, and at the decisive moment, the Latvian Bolsheviks, fearing that the Mensheviks might leave the congress and thus split the party, did not follow Lenin. In 1914, the Latvian Bolsheviks still valued the unity of their party and in this respect differed from the Russian Leninists. Referring to this after the congress, Lenin wrote: "The Latvians acted like reconciliators. . . . The Latvians remained neutral. They have not yet gotten rid of hopes for reconciliation."[60]

On other matters concerning practical policy the congress acted unanimously. But when electing the Central Committee, Lenin succeeded in persuading the Latvian Bolsheviks to make use of their majority to elect only Bolsheviks. In this way all the power in the party passed into their hands. This had fateful consequences, however, for it gave the Bolsheviks the opportunity to use the party apparatus to Bolshevize the SDL in the course of 1914-15. The Bolsheviks ignored the two Mensheviks who were alternate members of the SDL Central Committee, refusing them membership on the Central Committee when, after the Congress, some of its Bolshevik members were denounced by the agent Augulis and arrested. Augulis was elected a member of the Central Committee and remained in it until 1917.

After the congress, the Menshevik delegates held a separate consultative meeting at which J. Jansons appealed "not to give the party to the Bolsheviks," but to break away from them and found a new, non-Bolshevik party. He predicted, and quite correctly, that after handing over the party apparatus and the press to the Bolsheviks, the Mensheviks would never be able to get them back again. But the majority of the Mensheviks still nurtured the old and strong tradition of standing for the unity of the SDL and clung to the illusion that by playing the role of a Menshevik opposition within the party, they could again gain the majority.[61]

The Brussels Congress of the SDL represented a sudden change in the policy of the Latvian Party. All power was handed over to the Bolsheviks and to an agent of the Police Department, who proceeded to destroy the once strong and united party.[62]

WORLD WAR I, THE REVOLUTION OF 1917, AND THE SPLIT WITHIN THE SDL

In 1914 the Bolshevik Central Committee still adhered to the semi-neutral line which the Brussels Congress had approved. Lenin was quite displeased by this and when the Central Committee of the SDL applied for a loan of 300 rubles to publish the records of the Fourth Congress, the Central Committee of the RSDRP, which was then controlled by Lenin, refused on the ground that in Brussels the Latvian Bolsheviks had followed a conciliatory line.[63] At that time, Lenin was not yet sure of the Latvian Bolsheviks' full support. This is attested by a letter of May 23, 1914, written to Lenin by Jānis Bērziņš, a leading Latvian Bolshevik: "We shall hardly support you everywhere and in everything, but it is nevertheless extremely valuable to you that at least sometimes your side is supported by such a solid and, more importantly, *neutral* organization as the SDL."[64] In July, 1914, Lenin wrote to J. Hermanis, another Latvian Bolshevik: "I am very much alarmed by the fact that some of the Latvians back the Bund's federalism, or remain hesitant. . . ." He mentioned further that the Latvian party would have to struggle against "liquidationism," nationalism and federalism. If the Latvian Bolsheviks were not able to follow his advice, Lenin considered it "better to postpone" bringing the two parties closer.[65]

Although the Latvian Bolsheviks did not follow Lenin in every respect, they began to use all means to take over the Menshevik-dominated district organizations of the Latvian party. Augulis, the police agent in the Central Committee, helped them a great deal. The Menshevik leaders, including V. Rikveilis and V. Caune, were denounced and arrested a few weeks after the Brussels Congress. Moreover, the legal as well as the illegal party press and the whole party apparatus were now in the hands of the Bolsheviks. Thus it is not surprising that among the delegates to the Riga SDL Conference in June, 1914, there were 13 Bolsheviks and only 3 Mensheviks. The Mensheviks now congregated in the legal cultural association "Ungus" (Fire). In December, 1914, the Riga Bolshevik Committee declared a boycott of this association and in March, 1915, it expelled from the party all those active in the association's affairs. At the same time, many Mensheviks themselves withdrew from the party. By now, the Bolsheviks were free to act as they wished and in November, 1914, they sent an SDL delegate to the All-Russian Conference of Bolsheviks in St. Petersburg. In so doing, they willfully ignored the decision of the Brussels Congress on the neutrality of the SDL. Thus the breakup of the Latvian Party started within a year after the Brussels Congress.

However, in 1914 the Bolsheviks did not have a majority among the workers of Riga. This can be seen in the election of workers' representatives to the provincial commission on workers' insurance held in the spring of 1915. These representatives were elected by the delegates of the Health Insurance Funds which had been established by the Workers' Insurance Act of 1912. Associated in these funds were 88,000 industrial workers; when their delegates voted in March, 1915, the Mensheviks obtained a majority (40 to 31), and as a result, only Mensheviks were elected members of the commission.

Further development of the SDL was interrupted by World War I. In 1915, the German Army occupied Kurland (Southern Latvia) and tsarist authorities evacuated almost all Riga factories, their machines, and their workers to various cities in Russia. In 1916 only 3,400 of the city's 87,000 industrial workers remained in Riga. In 1914, the SDL had 3,500 members; in 1916 only 360 members remained. Latvian Social Democrats who had been evacuated to Russia either joined the Russian Mensheviks or Bolsheviks, or else remained outside the party since in many Russian cities there were no party organizations at all.

After the February, 1917 Revolution the SDL became legal in Riga and in Latvian territory that had not been occupied by Germans. The final split was delayed for a year, because the Menshevik-Internationalists and the Bolsheviks followed a common, anti-war line.[66]

THE PERIOD OF AN INDEPENDENT LATVIA

The final split occurred in Latvia as late as May, 1918. At that time, an illegal SDL conference expelled all the Mensheviks who declared themselves to be against the Bolshevik dictatorship in Russia and who demanded the foundation of an independent and democratic Latvia. On June 17, 1918, the Mensheviks convened a conference and founded their own party under the old name (dating from 1904) "Latvijās Sociāldemokratiska Strādnieku Partija" (the Latvian Social Democratic Workers' Party or LSDSP). It was actually a Menshevik party. P. Kalniņš and F. Menders were elected to its Central Committee as was the present author, who was elected Secretary.

The LSDSP played a decisive role in the creation of the Latvian Republic, which came into existence on November 18, 1918. From 1919 to 1920 the LSDSP also took an active part in Latvia's war of liberation against German militarists and against the Red Army.[67]

During the period of Latvia's independence, the LSDSP was the strongest political party in the country. In 1932, it had 12,089 members and was the political leader of all branches of the labor movement. In the elections to the Constituent Assembly in 1920, the LSDSP obtained 38.9 percent of the vote, and in the ranks of the army as much as 65 percent. In the four democratic parliamentary elections (1922-34), the LSDSP obtained 20.7 to 32.1 percent of the vote. It was always the strongest fraction in the Latvian Parliament and twice its representatives became members of the Latvian Government (1923 and 1926-28). Dr. Pauls Kalniņš headed the Parliament and was Vice-President of the Republic. Dr. F. Menders, an old Menshevik, was the last president of the LSDSP. The party was a member of the Socialist International and took part in all its congresses.[68] During the democratic period of independent Latvia (1918-34) and under the influence of the LSDSP, a democratic constitution was adopted and a radical agrarian reform was carried out. Also due to LSDSP's influence, Latvia's social legislation in the 1920s ranked among the most advanced in Europe.

During these years, the LSDSP remained on friendly terms with the Russian Mensheviks, whose center had been in Berlin since 1920. Menshevik representatives were invited to take part in the LSDSP's congresses in Riga. In 1922, F. Dan, B. Nicolaevsky and a group of other leaders of the Menshevik Party crossed Latvia on their way abroad and were received in a friendly manner. With the help of the LSDSP, G. Kuchin and other Menshevik activists were able to cross the Soviet-Latvian border illegally and continue to Berlin. The LSDSP also helped Kuchin and Eva Broido return to Russia in order to work there illegally for the Mensheviks. In the twenties, several hundred copies of each issue of the *Sotsialisticheskii vestnik* were sent by Latvian diplomatic mail to the Latvian Embassy in Moscow, again with the help of the LSDSP. There, J. Vigrabbe, who was Secretary to the Embassy at that time, distributed the Menshevik journal to representatives of the Menshevik organization (still existing at that time in the Soviet Union).

The LSDSP's free activities were interrupted by a fascist coup and by the introduction of the dictatorship of K. Ulmanis in May, 1934. The LSDSP was banned and all its leaders were arrested.[69]

In 1942, the party illegally resumed its activities and played a leading role in the democratic resistance. During the period of the first Soviet occupation (1940-41) and during the Nazi occupation (1941-45), many members of the LSDSP were arrested by the NKVD and the Gestapo and were sent to concentration camps, where they perished. During the period of Stalinist terror which followed the second Soviet occupation in 1945, many workers were again sent to concentration camps. Those who survived, among them F. Menders,[70] were set free by the amnesty of 1955.

Some of the LSDSP's members fled Latvia in 1944-45, and formed a party organization abroad. Since 1948 a Foreign Committee of the LSDSP has been working in Stockholm where a party organ, *Brīvība* (Freedom), is issued monthly. As far as is possible, contact is maintained with Soviet Latvia. Democracy and freedom for all nations, the traditional slogans of Menshevism, have until now remained the demands of the Latvian Social Democrats in exile.

ROBERT C. TUCKER

Stalin's Revolutionary Career Before 1917

Stalin joined the Georgian Social Democratic organization in 1898 at the age of eighteen, while attending the theological seminary in Tiflis. Not long after his expulsion from the seminary the following year, he went underground. Thus his entire adult life was devoted to the movement. He knew no other calling than that of revolutionary politics, and he endured his full share of the experience of prison and exile that normally befell those who pursued this hazardous profession in Russia.

His long and arduous revolutionary career was not, however, a distinguished one. For more than a decade he remained a provincial revolutionary operating in his native Transcaucasus. He had no dramatic anti-tsarist exploits to his credit. With the exception of his short treatise on *Marxism and The National Question* (1913), he contributed no writings that helped shape Bolshevism as an ideological current. Stalin was one of the party's practical workers: a committeeman, organizer, conspirator, propagandist, and journalist. But his services to the movement in these capacities, and subsequently as one of the party's leaders during the revolution and the civil war, were not of such magnitude or brilliance as to make him a figure of renown among the Bolsheviks. Lunacharskii, for example, did not include him among the ten subjects of his widely read *Revolutionary Silhouettes* (1923), and his name was notably inconspicuous in the authoritative party histories that began to appear in the mid-1920s. He was not once mentioned, for example, in a lengthy essay by Andrei Bubnov on the history of the party from its founding to the death of Lenin, and merely mentioned in the pioneering works on party history by V. I. Nevskii.[1] In the early twenties he was still all but unknown to the Soviet public, and not at all well known to the rank-and-file membership of the very party of which he was already General Secretary. "I will probably not sin against the truth," remarked Khrushchev in his secret report to the Twentieth Party Congress in 1956, "when I say that 99 percent of the persons present here heard and knew very little about Stalin before the year 1924. . . ."[2] Stalin was a political figure who accumulated great power before he acquired fame.

 This essay is drawn from a larger work in progress on Stalin and Russian Communism. I am grateful to Stephen F. Cohen for critical comments on the original version.

It was on the morrow of Lenin's death that he began to embellish his revolutionary biography. At a memorial meeting of the Kremlin military school on January 28, 1924, he told the cadets that he had first made contact with Lenin by correspondence from Siberian exile in 1903. Writing to a close friend then living abroad as a political exile, Stalin had expressed enthusiasm for Lenin as the party's outstanding leader. At the end of 1903 he had received a reply from his friend and a simple but profoundly expressive message from Lenin himself, to whom the friend had shown his letter. Lenin's message had contained both a criticism of the party's practical work and a concise plan for its operations in the immediate future. Commenting that he could not forgive himself for having yielded to the habit of an old underground worker and consigned Lenin's letter to the flames, Stalin said: "My acquaintance with Lenin dates from that time." He then added that he had first met Lenin personally at the time of the Bolshevik conference in Tammerfors in December, 1905.[3]

Quite apart from the fact that no copies of the alleged correspondence were ever found in the party's archives or those of the tsarist police and published, Stalin could not have received the letters in question at his place of exile, where he remained only a month before escaping. Prisoners never knew in advance to which place they would be banished, and there could not have been enough time to write from Siberia and receive a reply.[4] It has been conjectured that Stalin's story about a message from Lenin may have had a real basis in the fact that hectographed copies of a Lenin document entitled "Letter to a Comrade" were then circulating in Siberia, where a copy may have come into Stalin's hands. That hypothesis is all the more plausible in view of the contents of "Letter to a Comrade," which resemble Stalin's description of the supposed message from Lenin.[5] It is also a fact that Stalin expressed great admiration for Lenin in two letters that he wrote to a Georgian Bolshevik friend living in Leipzig. Those letters were written, however, from Kutais, a provincial town in Georgia, in the fall of 1904. Thus, what he did in his talk to the military cadets was to weave historical facts into a fantasy that predated his relationship with Lenin to 1903, the year of Bolshevism's beginnings as a political current within the Russian Marxist movement. He thereby bolstered symbolically his qualification for the succession.

In June, 1926, while on a visit to Tiflis, Stalin gave a sketch of his revolutionary biography as he liked to view it. Replying to acclaim from workers of the local railway shops, he chided them for flattery. It was quite an unnecessary exaggeration, he said, to picture him as a hero of the October Revolution, leader of the party and Communist International, a legendary warrior-knight, etc. That was how people usually spoke at the graveside of departed revolutionaries—and he had no intention of dying yet. The true story of his revolutionary career, he explained, was one of apprenticeship, of learning from worker-teachers first in Tiflis, then in Baku, and finally in Leningrad. In 1898, when he was put in charge of a study circle of workers from the Tiflis railway yards, elder comrades like Djibladze, Chodrishvili and Chkheidze, who perhaps had less book learning than he but possessed more experience, had given him practical instruction in propaganda activity. That was his first "baptism" in the revolutionary struggle. Here, among his first teachers, the Tiflis railroaders, he had become an "apprentice of revolution." Then in the years 1907-1909, spent in Baku, he had learned to lead large masses of workers in the oilfields, and had received his second baptism in the revolutionary struggle; he had now become a "journeyman of revolution." And in Leningrad in 1917, operating among the Russian workers and in direct proximity to the great teacher of the proletarians of all countries, Lenin, in the maelstrom of class war, he had learned what it means to be one of the leaders of the party. That had been his third revolutionary baptism. In Russia, under Lenin's leadership, he had become a "master-workman of revolution." He concluded that: "such, comrades, without exaggeration and in all conscience, is the true picture of what I was and what I became."[6]

This revealing essay in revolutionary autobiography laid the groundwork for a full biography of Stalin by his assistant, Ivan Tovstukha. Prepared for a special volume of the *Granat Encyclopedia* containing the autobiographies or authorized biographies of some 250 Soviet leading figures, the Tovstukha biography was also published in 1927 as a separate fourteen-page pamphlet in an edition of 50,000 copies. Iosif Vissarionovich Stalin (Djugashvili), it began, was born in 1879 in Gori, a Georgian by nationality, son of a Tiflis shoemaker and worker at the Adelkhanov shoe factory who was listed in his passport as a peasant from the village of Didi-Lilo in Tiflis province. After completing the Gori theological school in 1893, Stalin entered the Tiflis Orthodox theological seminary, then a hotbed of student radicalism. In 1897 he took the lead in the Marxist circles in the seminary and participated in illegal meetings of workers in the Tiflis railway yards. The following year he formally joined the Tiflis Social Democratic organization, and was later expelled from the seminary for "unreliability." In 1899-1900 he devoted himself to propaganda activity in worker circles, and became a member and one of the outstanding leaders of the new Tiflis Social Democratic Committee, championing the side of the younger elements who wanted the movement to go beyond the old clandestine propaganda methods into a new "street" phase based on mass agitation. In 1901 he had to go underground to evade arrest. In Batum, where he moved at the end of 1901, he founded the Batum Social Democratic Committee, led strikes at the Rothschild and Mantashev plants, and organized the political demonstration of Batum workers in February and March, 1902. He was arrested a month later.

While in prison in 1903—the Tovstukha biography went on—Stalin learned of the Bolshevik-Menshevik division at the Second Party Congress and resolutely espoused the Bolshevik position. Following his return to Tiflis in January, 1904, after escaping from Siberia, he resumed party work as a member of the Transcaucasian Union Committee. Throwing himself into the struggle against Menshevism, he made the rounds of the main Transcaucasian centers in 1904-1905, debating the Mensheviks both *orally* and in the press. He took his place at the head of the Transcaucasian Bolsheviks, directed the underground Bolshevik paper *Proletariatis brdzola,* and agitated for Bolshevik slogans of the revolution during the upheavals of 1905 in the Transcaucasus. At the end of 1905 he finally met Lenin while attending the Tammerfors party conference as a delegate of the Transcaucasian Bolsheviks. In Tiflis during the ensuing period of reaction, he was at the center of the fight against Menshevism and the anarcho-syndicalist elements active in the movement at that time: his series of articles, "Anarchism and Socialism," written in Georgian, was aimed at the latter group. He went to Stockholm in 1906 and to London in 1907 to attend the Fourth and Fifth Party Congresses, both times as a delegate of the Bolshevik section of the Tiflis organization.

On his return from the London Congress he settled in Baku, edited the illegal Bolshevik paper *Baku Worker,* and ran a campaign for a collective contract between the oil workers and employers. His successful fight against Menshevik influence secured the complete victory of Bolshevism in the Baku organization and made the oil city a citadel of Bolshevism. Arrested in March, 1908, he was held in prison for eight months and then banished for three years to Sol'vychegodsk in Vologda province, but escaped some months later and returned to underground work in Baku. Another round of arrest and exile in 1910 was followed by another escape in 1911, after which he settled in Petersburg on instructions of the party Central Committee. *Between successive further rounds* of arrest and exile, he was elected *in absentia* a member of the Central Committee at the Prague Bolshevik conference in 1912, took a leading part in the founding of *Pravda* in Petersburg, went abroad to meet with Lenin in Cracow, produced his work on the national question, and participated in directing the Bolshevik fraction in the Duma. Arrested once again in the spring of 1913, he was this time exiled to the Turukhansk territory in northeastern Siberia, where he remained until early 1917.[7]

Reading this account of Stalin's pre-1917 years, and comparing it with the careers of other prominent Bolsheviks recounted in the same biographical volume, one is struck by several distinctive features of Tovstukha's treatment. True, it followed a general stylization that was visible in this Bolshevik "lives of the revolutionaries"; in substance it was a laconic listing of revolutionary actions participated in, conferences attended, punishments suffered, etc. What distinguished the Stalin biography from the others was a solemnity of tone, a reaching for superlatives, and even in places a certain grandiloquence that deviated from the volume's general tendency to understatement. Stalin, for example, did not simply move at one point to Baku. Rather, "From 1907 commences the Baku period in the revolutionary activity of Stalin," and his arrival in Petersburg in 1911 marked the beginning of "the Petersburg period in the revolutionary activity of Stalin." This is the three-stage progress to "master-workman of revolution" which Stalin had related to the Tiflis railroaders in 1926; we sense that a revolutionary biography is being recast in retrospect according to certain canons of drama. It is notable too that Tovstukha's portrait modified historical reality in a number of ways flattering to its subject.

First, Stalin had not become by 1900 "one of the outstanding leaders" of the Tiflis Social Democrats. His friends Lado Ketskhoveli and Alexander Tsulukidze were seniors and mentors to him even within the radical minority. Nor is it true, as Tovstukha clearly suggested without actually saying, that he was elected a member of the Tiflis Social Democratic Committee when it was organized in that year. He was at that time a rather minor figure among Tiflis Social Democrats, and did not become a member of the Committee until the fall of 1901.[8] His move from Tiflis to Batum shortly afterward took place under circumstances which, although not fully clarified to this day, did not reflect credit upon him. Emigre Georgian Menshevik sources have persistently reported that he moved after being expelled from the Tiflis organization by a party tribunal on charges of intrigue and slander against a senior comrade, Sylvester Djibladze.[9] According to another version, the move was precipitated by an altercation over the admission of workers to membership in the Tiflis Committee, Stalin having unsuccessfully opposed this on the grounds that it would complicate conspiratorial operation and that the workers themselves were not yet sufficiently developed for the role of committeemen.[10] Furthermore, it is not clear that Stalin, after moving to Batum, actually played the part of strike-leader and demonstration-leader that Tovstukha ascribed to him. No reference was made to him, for example, in the detailed description of the Batum events of February-March, 1902, in Makharadze's authoritative history of the revolutionary movement in the Transcaucasus.[11]

Whether or not one accepts Tovstukha's assertion that Stalin espoused Bolshevism while in prison in 1903, when the party schism was still merely nascent, the evidence does indicate that he gravitated to the Bolshevik position without hesitation as soon as the issues became clear to him.[12] If he did in fact become acquainted with Lenin's views by reading the "Letter to a Comrade" during his first short sojourn in exile, he must have returned to Tiflis in early 1904 primed to join the intra-party fray on the side of Bolshevism, as in fact he did; and his own "Letters from Kutais" in the autumn of that year show him as an ardent Leninist.[13] On the other hand, Tovstukha's biography misrepresented fact when it stated that Stalin took his place "at the head of the Transcaucasian Bolsheviks" upon his return from exile. He did not at first even become a leading figure among them. Kamenev, who had spent his boyhood in Tiflis, was at that time Lenin's principal envoy and Bolshevik organizer in the Transcaucasus; and the other leaders of first rank included Leonid Krasin, Stepan Shaumian, Alyosha Djaparidze, Alexander Tsulukidze, and Mikha Tskhakaia. It is a measure of Stalin's relative unimportance that he was not one of the fifteen delegates from local groups who gathered in Tiflis in November, 1904, for the first conference of Transcaucasian Bolsheviks. Nor did he travel to London in April, 1905, as one of the four Transcaucasian delegates to the All-Bolshevik Third Party Congress, which has been described as "the constituent congress of Bolshevism."[14] The Tammerfors meeting later that year marked his debut in higher Bolshevik councils.

Tovstukha also inflated the significance of Stalin's Baku period. The founders of the Social Democratic organization in Baku at the beginning of the century were Abel Enukidze, Lado Ketskhoveli, and Leonid Krasin. When Stalin settled there in 1907 following the London congress, he was only one of several leaders of the Baku Bolsheviks. The principal Bolshevik organizer of trade union activity in Baku at that time was Djaparidze rather than Stalin; Shaumian, too, played a major role in the worker movement.[15] Moreover, Stalin's Baku period appears to have been clouded by a rivalry that developed between himself and Shaumian, and he was reportedly suspected by local Bolsheviks of causing Shaumian's arrest in 1909 by informing on him to the police.[16] However that may have been, Tovstukha had no basis for depicting Stalin as supreme leader of the Baku Bolsheviks in 1907-10. Nor was Baku itself transformed during that time into a "citadel of Bolshevism." There, as elsewhere, party activity and the revolutionary movement were in a state of depression.[17]

A comment on the moot question of Stalin's relations with the police is appropriate at this point. The report just mentioned is one of a number—chiefly emanating from Georgian Menshevik circles—which show that Stalin was suspected in certain quarters of informing the police about persons whom he wished to see removed from the scene. According to Semeon Vereshchak, a one-time member of the Socialist Revolutionary party and a fellow political prisoner of Stalin's in the Bailov prison in Baku in 1908, Stalin began the practice of informing (although not in this instance to the police) shortly after leaving the Tiflis theological seminary in 1899. In reminiscences published in a Paris Russian paper in 1928, Vereshchak cited other prisoners who had been schoolmates of Stalin as sources for the story that soon after being expelled he caused the expulsion of the other members of his secret socialist group in the seminary by reporting their names to the rector. According to these sources, he admitted his action and justified it to the expelled boys on the ground that they would become good revolutionaries now that they had lost the opportunity for careers as priests.[18] Although further evidence of Stalin's involvement is lacking, we do have confirmation that a group of forty or so students was forced to leave the seminary in the fall of 1899 in a manner very strongly suggesting that the school authorities found them to be engaged in forbidden clandestine activities.[19]

Stalin came to maturity in an extremely rough political milieu, and his lack of squeamishness in the choice of means is well attested. The above-mentioned suspicions do not, therefore, strain our credulity. In his early years as a revolutionary he may have resorted to police informing now and then for political purposes of his own. But we can make allowance for this possibility without accepting the view–to which two Western writers have devoted whole books in recent years–that he became a professional *agent provocateur* in the service of the tsarist police. No evidence of such a relationship was turned up by the Extraordinary Investigatory Commission of the Provisional Government which from March to November, 1917, investigated the relations between the *Okhrana* and the revolutionary movement. Stalin's name did not appear on the detailed list of police agents which the Commission compiled on the basis of its study of the archives and interrogation of prominent former police officials.[20] The only specific documentary evidence so far advanced in support of the thesis that Stalin was a police agent is the so-called "Yeremin document," which has been convincingly shown to be a forgery.[21] For the remainder, the case rests upon a series of speculative interpretations of Stalin's early actions and events in his life. To cite an illustrative example, it has been argued that the Tiflis Gendarme Administration may have approached Stalin shortly after his departure from the seminary in May, 1899, with a proposal that he become a secret agent; and that he, being unemployed, penniless, alone and friendless, had no alternative but to accept the proposal. The six-month period of his unemployment, it is added, would have been about the right amount of time for the training of the new recruit by one of the Tiflis gendarme officers.[22] But there is no proof that Stalin was so down and out at that time, and so bereft of the companionship of friends, that it would have been possible for the police (assuming they did approach him) to force him to enter their service. Nor, given his bitterly rebellious attitude toward the established order, can we imagine him doing such a thing unless compelled to it for the sake of survival. To this it may be added that according to the testimony of a companion in the seminary who later wrote as a hostile witness, in the period after he left the seminary, some of his former comrades "stood together to support him now and then in his need."[23]

That Stalin in the early years of his career had some connections with the Tsarist police, connections that he tried to use to his own and the movement's advantage while the police tried to use them to their advantage, seems probable. That he became a professional secret police agent working against the movement from within is an hypothesis that remains unsolved and seems quite improbable.

Since Stalin's early revolutionary career was not an outstanding one, the question arises: how did he come to be elevated to the Bolshevik Central Committee? To be sure, he was not elected to this post *in absentia* by the Prague Bolshevik conference of January, 1912, as asserted by Tovstukha, but coopted by the Central Committee elected there.[24] Since this was Lenin's doing, the question touches upon the history of his relationship with Stalin. How did he come to regard Stalin as suitable for membership in the inner circle of Bolshevik leaders?

There is a story, possibly but not necessarily apocryphal, that Stalin first came to Lenin's attention when the enthusiastically pro-Lenin letters that he wrote from Kutais in late 1904 were forwarded by his Leipzig friends to Lenin, who in reply called their Georgian correspondent "the fiery Colchian."[25] Direct correspondence dates from May, 1905, when Stalin, writing as a member of the Transcaucasian Union Committee, reported to Lenin on the comparative influence of Bolsheviks and Mensheviks in the party organizations of the region.[26] Meanwhile, he came out as a zealous disciple of Lenin in polemics against the Georgian Mensheviks. In *Briefly about the Disagreements in the Party,* a pamphlet issued in Georgian, Armenian, and Russian in the spring of 1905 by the Avlabar underground printing press in Tiflis, he assailed the leader of the Georgian Mensheviks, Noah Zhordania, for criticizing the views that Lenin had presented in his "remarkable book" *What Is To Be Done?* The chief issue was Lenin's contention that revolutionary (as opposed to trade-unionist) consciousness had to be instilled in the working class by organized social democracy. Marshalling quotations from Karl Kautsky and from Marx and Engels, Stalin stoutly maintained that Lenin's position was not in fundamental contradiction with Marxism, as Zhordania had argued, but fully in accord with it. In July, Krupskaia wrote from abroad to Tiflis requesting copies of the pamphlet, from which we may surmise that Lenin was informed about it. In August, Stalin returned to the subject in a polemical refutation of Zhordania's reply to his pamphlet. This so pleased Lenin that in his contribution to a review of the Russian-language edition of the Georgian party paper in which Stalin's second piece had appeared, he especially praised, and then paraphrased, its "splendid formulation of the question of the celebrated 'introduction of consciousness from without.' "[27]

What impression Stalin made upon Lenin when they first met face to face is not known. But he must have made a definite (if not wholly happy) impression when, at the Stockholm congress in 1906, in a session over which Lenin presided, he took the floor in the debate on agrarian policy to support neither the platform of land nationalization, which Lenin favored, nor the Menshevik platform of municipalization, but rather the confiscation and division of the landed estates among the peasants—a position that received majority support in the Bolshevik delegation though not in the congress as a whole.[28] In spite of, and perhaps also because of, their difference over the question at hand, Lenin may have come to realize by this time that in "Ivanovich" (Stalin's pseudonym at the congress) he had a forceful and incisive young Georgian follower who was worth watching.

Such a reaction would have been all the more understandable in view of a further general circumstance: Bolshevism's failure in Georgia. There the Mensheviks emerged from the revolution of 1905 as the dominant Social

Democratic faction, and their decision to contest rather than boycott the subsequent Duma elections enhanced their position in Georgian public life. The result was that five of the eight Georgian deputies to the first Duma, and all of the deputies to the second Duma, were Mensheviks. The special success of Georgian Menshevism derived in part from its more nationalist orientation and in part from the fact that its principal representatives were more genuinely revolution-minded than the Russian Menshevik leaders. So overwhelming was the Menshevik influence among Georgian Social Democrats that the sixteen delegates elected from Georgia to the Stockholm congress included but one Bolshevik–Stalin himself. Moreover, at the London congress the following year, *all* the voting delegates from Georgia were Mensheviks. Lacking sufficient local bases of support for similar mandates, Stalin and Tskhakaia, the two Bolshevik representatives from Georgia, were admitted only in the lower category of delegates with advisory vote, and at that only over protests from the Menshevik side.[29]

In addition to the fact that Stalin stood out as one of the few prominent Georgian Social Democrats adhering to Bolshevism, he appears to have shown his usefulness to Lenin in a practical way at this time. During the 1905 upheaval, fighting groups of the party carried out a series of so-called "expropriations," i.e., armed robberies of banks, mail coaches, etc. in various sections of the country, including the Transcaucasus. Despite the fact that these armed operations aroused much opposition in the party, especially from the Mensheviks, Lenin approved and relied heavily upon them as a source of funds to finance political activity. With his connivance they continued in the aftermath of 1905 despite the passage of a Menshevik-sponsored resolution forbidding them at the Stockholm congress. One of the most notorious was a raid carried out in the Erevan Square in Tiflis in June, 1907, which netted a huge sum of money for the Bolshevik treasury. The Tiflis operation was led by a daring adventurer, S. A. Ter-Petrosian ("Kamo"). Stalin, however, is believed to have played a covert directing role in this and other "exes" in the Transcaucasus. It is true that neither Tovstukha nor any of his later official biographers ever alluded to this facet of his revolutionary career, and that he himself evaded a direct reply when Emil Ludwig, interviewing him in 1931, observed: "Your biography contains instances of what may be called acts of 'highway robbery'."[30] Nonetheless, it is fairly well attested that Stalin, while never a direct participant, played a part behind the scenes as planner and organizer of various "expropriations."[31] He must have thereby recommended himself to Lenin as an underground worker who could safely be entrusted with secret assignments of great delicacy and importance.

Such an individual was all the more certain to come to the fore in Lenin's circle under the conditions of party crisis that prevailed from 1907 to 1912. The period of post-revolutionary reaction saw a catastrophic decline in party fortunes. Discouragement, apathy, and political quietism took over. The party practically fell apart as erstwhile activists deserted it *en masse* and arrests took a heavy toll of those still willing to carry on. By the summer of 1909, not more than five or six of the Bolshevik underground committees were still functioning regularly in Russia.[32] Meanwhile, those in the party whom Lenin contemptuously dubbed "liquidators" took the view that instead of rebuilding the illegal party, Social Democrats should now concentrate on such limited legal activities—in the Duma for example—as conditions allowed. It was a time, then, when Lenin felt an acute need for men who were absolutely unswerving in their dedication to revolutionary politics and to the illegal party as its organizational medium; in short, for men like Stalin, who during those years, between arrests and periods of exile, went on doggedly working in what was left of the underground organization to prepare for a new revolutionary period. And writing now in the Russian language in party organs read by Lenin, Stalin strongly espoused the cause of orthodox revolutionary politics. To make the party's activity as legal as possible and abandon revolutionary demands, he wrote in the *Baku Proletarian* in August, 1909, would bury the party rather than renovate it. In order to overcome the present state of party crisis, it was necessary, first, to end the isolation from the masses and, second, to unify party activities on a nationwide basis. And writing like the Lenin of *What Is To Be Done?*, Stalin suggested that the latter objective could best be achieved by creating an all-Russian party newspaper. There was, however, one difference: Stalin insisted upon the paper's being based inside the country rather than abroad, where party organs, being "far removed from Russian reality," could not effectively fulfill the unifying function.[33]

A seasoned professional revolutionary, a completely committed Bolshevik whose whole world lay in party affairs and who found his element in clandestine activity, Stalin was too rare a resource for Lenin to ignore. Nor did Stalin permit himself to be ignored. The proposal for a Russian-based party organ carried an overtone of self-nomination to the editorial role that Stalin in fact came to play when *Pravda* was founded in Petersburg three years later. And in a resolution of January 22, 1910, written by Stalin, the Baku party committee not only repeated the proposal for an all-Russian party organ but called for "the transfer of the (directing) practical center to Russia."[34] The implicit bid for inclusion in such a practical center became virtually explicit in a letter that Stalin sent abroad at the end of 1910 from his exile in the town of Sol'vychegodsk. Although addressed to a Comrade Simeon, the letter was clearly meant for Lenin, to whom Stalin at the outset sent hearty greetings. He argued in it that there was urgent need to organize a central coordinating group in Russia, to be called something like "Russian section of the Central Committee" or "auxiliary group of the Central Committee," and he offered his services upon expiration of his term of exile in six months' time, or sooner if necessary.[35] The proposal may have taken on added weight from the fact that Stalin by this time had been appointed an "agent" of the Central Committee, that is, a roving official maintaining liaison with and giving guidance to local party organizations on behalf of the

Bolshevik center.[36] In any event, when the Bolshevik faction was recast as a separate party at the Prague conference in 1912, the Central Committee, now exclusively Bolshevik in composition, not only coopted Stalin but also elected him as one of the four members of a "Russian Bureau" for direction of party activities inside Russia. Indeed, it is possible that Lenin brought Stalin into the Central Committee primarily so that he could become a member of this auxiliary organ whose creation he had persistently solicited.[37]

Lenin appears to have had certain reservations concerning the young man he was sponsoring for these high posts. For he had learned of some letters of Stalin's commenting on developments in the emigration in a way that he found objectionable. Writing in June, 1908, to Mikha Tskhakaia, who was then living in Switzerland, Stalin had characterized Lenin's philosophical polemics with the Bogdanov group over Machism ("empiriocriticism") as a "tempest in a teacup," and had found some "good sides" in Machism itself. Later, after *Materialism and Empiriocriticism* came out, he had written to a certain M. Toroshelidze (also in Switzerland) a letter in which, while praising Lenin's book as a compendium of the tenets of materialist epistemology, he also commended Bogdanov for pointing up some "*individual* faults of Ilich," and for correctly noting that "Ilich's materialism differs in many ways from Plekhanov's, which Ilich, contrary to the demands of logic (for diplomatic reasons?) tries to cover up." Then, on January 24, 1911, Stalin had written a letter from Sol'vychegodsk to Vladimir Bobrovskii saying:

> We have of course heard about the "tempest in a teacup" abroad: the blocs of Lenin-Plekhanov on the one hand and Trotsky-Martov-Bogdanov on the other. So far as I know, the workers' attitude toward the first bloc is favorable. But in general the workers are beginning to look upon the emigration with disdain: "Let them crawl on the wall to their hearts' content; but as we see it, let anyone who values the interests of the movement work, the rest will take care of itself."[38]

Ordzhonikidze, while attending the party school at Longjumeau in the summer of 1911, learned directly from Lenin that Stalin's letters had come to his attention and had vexed him greatly. While strolling with Ordzhonikidze one day, Lenin suddenly asked him whether he was familiar with the expression "tempest in a teacup abroad." Ordzhonikidze, who knew about the letters and immediately saw Lenin's point, tried to defend his Georgian friend from Baku days, but Lenin continued: "You say, 'Koba is our comrade,' as if to say, he's a Bolshevik and won't let us down. But do you close your eyes to his inconsistency? Nihilistic little jokes about a 'tempest in a teacup' reveal Koba's immaturity as a Marxist." Lenin softened the reproof by saying that he had the most favorable memories of Stalin and had commended some of his earlier writings from Baku, especially the previous year's "Letters from the Caucasus."[39] In view of this, and the fact that Ordzhonikidze was about to return to Russia, it seems likely that Lenin was taking the opportunity to communicate to Stalin his strong feeling about the letters. Perhaps he hoped to clear the way for collaboration with a man whom he saw as very valuable for the movement even if immature as a Marxist.

Not long after Stalin's cooptation into the new all-Bolshevik Central Committee, his political relationship with Lenin was cemented by their joint work on the national question. This question was very much on Lenin's mind when Stalin came to Cracow in November, 1912, to confer with him on party business. Lenin had written an article that same month expressing adamant opposition to what he called "the adaptation of socialism to nationalism" and an "Austrian federation" within the party.[40] The latter phrase referred to the situation in the Austrian Social Democratic party, which had evolved over the years into a federation of autonomous Social Democratic groups organized along national lines (German, Czech, Polish, Ruthenian, Italian, and South Slav). Lenin feared that a similar tendency could gain the upper hand in Russia. There the Social Democratic party had originally been conceived as a nonfederal association of workers of all nationalities in the Russian Empire.[41] In practice, however, the Jewish Workers' Bund (after its return to the party fold in 1906) and the Social Democratic organizations of Poland, Latvia, and Lithuania had enjoyed autonomy within the Russian party, introducing into the latter what a resolution of the Bolshevik conference in Prague called "a federation of the worst type." And now, in 1912, attempts were being made in certain Social Democratic quarters, notably the Bund and the Georgian Mensheviks, to gain acceptance by the Russian party of the Austro-Marxist slogan of "national-cultural autonomy." Lenin, for whom national separatism had no place within Social Democracy, was infuriated at what he saw as one more manifestation of "liquidationism." Any move to divide Russian Social Democracy along national lines could only hurt it as a class-conscious revolutionary movement against Tsarism. All Social Democrats regardless of nationality should work together in the party organization of their territory. The Transcaucasian organization, uniting revolutionaries of Georgian, Armenian, Russian, and other nationalities, could be taken as a model.[42]

Stalin's arrival in Cracow at just this time must have struck Lenin as very opportune. For if views being fostered by non-Russian "nationals" of the Social Democratic movement needed combating, other "nationals"–being least suspect of indifference to the concerns of national minorities–were good ones to do it. Moreover, Lenin may have seen in Stalin a potential source of light on the complexities of the nationality problem in the Transcaucasus. If so, he was not disappointed, for Stalin was well informed on this subject. More important (as Lenin may now have learned for the first time), he had a long record of opposition to local nationalism in the Transcaucasian revolutionary movement. In what was probably his first published article, he had taken a strong stand against the nationalist tendencies of certain Georgian and Armenian socialist groups, and championed the idea of a centralized Russian *("Rossiiskaia")* Social Democratic party that would gather the proletarians of *all* Russia's nationalities under its banner and work to destroy the national barriers dividing them.[43] He had continued to adhere to this position when, in 1906, a group of Social Democrats from Kutais raised the question of national-cultural autonomy at a Transcaucasian regional party conference; and again, in 1912, when Zhordania and the Georgian Mensheviks veered in that same direction. So Lenin encountered in Stalin a "national" who would eagerly take his side in the fight over the national question and do so out of long-standing personal conviction. The gratification this gave him was reflected in his well-known letter of February, 1913, to Maxim Gorky: "About nationalism, I fully agree with you that we have to bear down harder. We have here a wonderful Georgian who has undertaken to write a long article for *Prosveshchenie* after gathering *all* the Austrian and other materials. We will take care of this matter."[44]

Stalin wrote the bulk of the work during his stay in Vienna in January, 1913. After a theoretical section defining the concept of nation and surveying the characteristics of national movements, he opened fire on the Austro-Marxist concept of "national-cultural autonomy" as developed by its two chief exponents, Karl Renner and Otto Bauer. It was not the business of Social Democrats to organize nations or to "preserve and develop the national attributes of peoples" (as the Austrian Social Democratic program expressed it), but to organize the proletariat for class struggle. "National-cultural autonomy" was a masked form of nationalism, and (here Stalin mixed his metaphors) all the more dangerous because it was encased in socialist armor. It was an anachronism in an age when, as Marx had prophesied, national barriers were everywhere falling. Moreover, it created the psychological prerequisites for a division of a single workers' party into a group of parties organized on national lines, and for similar national separatism within a country's trade union movement. Such had been the experience of Austrian Social Democracy, and menacing tendencies in that direction were visible in Russia. Although Marx, Kautsky, and even Bauer had envisaged for the Jews not nationhood but assimilation, the Bund had broken with internationalist Social Democracy in an effort to take the Jewish workers of Russia down the road of national separatism. Now some Transcaucasian Social Democrats were raising a demand for national-cultural as well as regional autonomy for their area.

Trying to reduce such a demand to an absurdity, Stalin argued that it would entail the granting of national-cultural autonomy also to many small Transcaucasian nationalities of primitive culture, like the Osetians and Mingrelians, which in turn would reinforce them in their cultural primitivism and assist the local forces of political reaction. *Regional* autonomy was acceptable for the Transcaucasus because it would help the backward nations there to cast off the shell of small-nation insularity. But *national-cultural* autonomy would work in the opposite direction, shutting up these nations in their old shells. The national question in the Transcaucasus could only be resolved by drawing the backward nations and nationalities into the common stream of a higher culture. As for the argument that the demand for national-cultural autonomy was not in contradiction with the right of national self-determination proclaimed in the Social Democracy's program, it was of course true that nations have a right to arrange their affairs as they please. But Social Democracy, while proclaiming and upholding this right, ought nevertheless to fight and agitate against harmful institutions and inexpedient demands of nations, just as it ought to agitate against Catholicism, Protestantism, and Orthodoxy while upholding the right of all people to freedom of religious worship. The duty of Social Democracy was to influence the will of nations to arrange their affairs in a manner in keeping with the interests of the proletariat. For example, Social Democrats would agitate against Tartar secession or against cultural-national autonomy for the Transcaucasian nations. The correct general solution for the national question in Russia was regional autonomy, with full provision for national minorities in every region to use their native language, possess their own schools, and so on. And on the party side, the workers should not be organized according to nationality. Workers of all nationalities should be locally organized within the single integral party, thus becoming conscious of themselves not primarily as members of a given nation but as members of one class family, the united army of socialism.[45]

In a conversation with Milovan Djilas in 1948, Stalin said that he had expressed Lenin's views in *Marxism and the National Question,* and that Lenin had edited the work.[46] It is very likely, indeed, that Stalin, in addition to writing it on Lenin's suggestion, benefited greatly from the discussions in Cracow on the nationality problem and even incorporated various specific points that Lenin had made in those discussions. On the other hand, there is no good reason to credit Lenin (as Trotsky has done) with virtual authorship of the work.[47] Stalin's polemic against national-cultural autonomy flowed easily from views on the national question that he had expressed in writing as early as 1904. The language of the work and its style of argumentation are consistently recognizable as Stalin's. Footnotes to the work show that most of the required Austrian materials on the national question were available to him in Russian translation.[48] And he certainly needed no assistance in those important sections of the work that dealt with the Bund and the national question in the Transcaucasus. Finally, Lenin, although he had begun intensive thinking on the national question by 1912, had not yet produced any writings on it and may not yet have worked his thoughts into a systematic whole. And when he came out in 1915 with his most significant contribution, *The Right of Nations to Self-Determination,* his treatment of the national question was strikingly different from Stalin's in underlying emphasis. The theme of national self-determination—in the meaning of secession and the formation of an independent nation-state—was not at all stressed by Stalin. Indeed, he seemed to give it no more than a grudging recognition in those very few passages of the work that spoke of this right.

Marxism and the National Question was basically Stalin's, and it is a moot question which one–Lenin or Stalin–benefited most from the collaboration. Lenin, at any rate, was greatly pleased by the work. When Troianovskii suggested that it be published in *Prosveshchenie* under the editorially non-committal heading "discussion" (explaining that his wife, E. Rozmirovich, was for national-cultural autonomy!), Lenin wrote to Kamenev: "Of course, we are absolutely against that. The article is *very good.* The issue is a fighting one and we will not surrender one iota of our principled opposition to the Bundist trash."[49] Clearly, Stalin was no longer an immature Marxist in Lenin's eyes.

By his work on the national question Stalin established himself in Lenin's eyes as a developed Marxist. It may be more than a fanciful comparison to say that he presented his mentor with a successful dissertation. Yet this coming together of the two men, milestone though it was in Stalin's party career, was not yet the beginning of a close personal association. Stalin was arrested at a St. Petersburg concert hall before seeing his work in print, and spent the next four years in Siberian exile. His name appears a few times in Lenin's wartime correspondence, but in a manner that illustrates the absence of a close relationship. "Koba" and "Koba Ivanovich" were the names by which Lenin had come to know Stalin, who only in 1912-13 began to use the pseudonym "Stalin" in signing his articles. He had only a vague memory of Stalin's real last name. "Do you remember the last name of Koba?," he inquired in a letter of 1915 to Zinoviev, and later that year he wrote the following to V. A. Karpinskii: "Big request: find out (from Stepko or Mikha, etc.) the last name of 'Koba' (Joseph Dj . . . . . . ? ? have forgotten). It's very important! ! "[50]

Furthermore, Stalin's arrest in February, 1913, removed him for a long time from the role in the Bolshevik command that he had finally achieved only a year earlier. And this led to an embarrassing episode on his reappearance in the capital in March, 1917. By then the party was emerging from underground, and its directorate, the Russian Bureau of the Central Committee, was taking in various leading figures as they returned from prison or exile. Protocols of its meetings, first published in 1962, show that the question of Stalin's admission came up during the meeting of March 12. The Bureau heard a report that Stalin had earlier been an agent of the Central Committee and would on that account be desirable as a Bureau member. However, "in view of certain qualities inherent in him, the Bureau expressed itself to the effect that he should be invited with advisory vote."[51] The protocols did not elaborate on the nature of Stalin's objectionable qualities.

ALEXANDER RABINOWITCH

The Petrograd Garrison and the Bolshevik Seizure of Power

Under the tsarist regime the Petrograd garrison was a powerful military force, inevitably a major and sometimes a decisive factor in the political history of the Russian state.[1] In the 1905 Revolution the garrison had remained loyal to the Tsar and in so doing had insured the preservation of the Russian monarchy. In February, 1917, Nicholas II's fate was sealed when Petrograd-based military units, one after the other, joined the side of rebelling towns-people. Similarly, developments in the garrison were crucial to the defeat suffered by the Bolsheviks in July and to their subsequent triumph in October. Because of this a detailed knowledge of the Petrograd garrison's composition, of the process by which it was transformed from a bulwark of autocracy to an ally of popular revolt, and finally, of the political impact of the garrison in 1917 is indispensable to an understanding of the Russian revolution. Unfortunately, relatively little work has been done on the make-up and role of the Petrograd garrison in 1917, on the Soviet side because of preoccupation with the importance of the workers during the revolutionary period, and in Western accounts because of a shortage of reliable published data.[2]

THE COMPOSITION AND IMPORTANCE OF THE GARRISON

There is no doubt that far reaching changes in the composition of the Petrograd garrison took place during the devastating first three yaers of World War I. In normal times the guards regiments, which formed the backbone of the garrison, had been specially trained units recruited almost exclusively from the peasantry. However, this traditional core had been squandered in the campaigns of 1914-16 on the battlefields of East Prussia and Galacia. Consequently by 1917 most of the troops stationed in and around Petrograd, including those in regiments of the guard, were poorly trained wartime recruits, still predominantly peasant by background.[3] Military discipline was foreign to these soldiers; a high percentage had already had their fill of duty at the front (the fourth company of all reserve infantry regiments was made up exclusively of rehabilitated evacuees[4]). In the aftermath of the February Revolution they removed officers who had openly opposed the revolution as well as those with reputations for particular severity, watched suspiciously for any sign of a return to the old order, and awaited the compromise peace they felt certain would be arranged by the newly created Petrograd Soviet.

Command of the Petrograd garrison during tsarist times was exercised by the Commander of the Petrograd Military District, and so it remained until late August, 1917, when troops in the capital were placed under the strategic authority of the Commander of the Northern Front. At the time of the February Revolution the major force controlled by the Petrograd Military District consisted of sixteen guards infantry regiments of 4,500 to 7,500 men each and six army reserve infantry regiments of 10,000 to 19,000 men each. Although popularly referred to as regiments and despite their substantial size, these units were actually reserve battalions of regiments at the front; their primary task was to train replacement companies for front line duty. The guards infantry regiments included the Preobrazhenskii, Semenovskii, Izmailovskii, Egerskii, Moskovskii, Pavlovskii, Finliandskii, Litovskii, Keksgolmskii, Petrogradskii, and Volynskii Regiments, all quartered in Petrograd. Also included among guards infantry units were four reserve rifle battalions (two located in Petrograd and two in Tsarskoe Selo). The six army reserve infantry regiments included the First and 180th Reserve Infantry Regiments in Petrograd, the Third Reserve Infantry Regiment in Peterhof, the 176th Reserve Infantry Regiment in Krasnoe Selo, the First Reserve Machine Gun Regiment in Oranienbaum (from the time of the February Revolution until after the July days the bulk of the First Machine Gun Regiment was actually billeted in the Vyborg District in Petrograd), and the Second Reserve Machine Gun Regiment in Strelna. All the above regiments were quartered within twenty miles of the capital. Among other important elements making up the Petrograd garrison in February, 1917, were the First and Fourth Don Cossack Regiments, spread throughout the city and its suburbs, a number of reserve engineer and artillery units, and various military schools. Technically, the huge Kronstadt Naval Base located outside the capital in the Gulf of Finland was not part of the Petrograd garrison, though in 1917 it consistently and actively supported the latter in political questions.

The composition and numerical strength of the Petrograd garrison were fluid throughout the Provisional Government period, the most significant movement of troops occurring in late May and June (in preparation for the Kerensky offensive) and in late July and August (after the July uprising). In July special units were brought into Petrograd to help maintain order while hundreds of soldiers who had participated in the July days were gradually shipped to the front (this movement of "Bolshevized" troops to the front was speeded up considerably in mid-August, 1917, on the eve of the Kornilov affair). Largely as a result of these continuing shifts and because of lack of uniformity in defining what troops should be included in the garrison, published estimates of the Petrograd garrison's size in 1917 vary enormously. A figure of 215,000 to 300,000 soldiers stationed in and around Petrograd at the time of the February Revolution would seem to be a fair approximation. During the summer of 1917, transfers from the front to the capital ran far behind troop movements in the opposite direction so that by fall this figure may have dropped to about 150,000. There were substantial differences in the level of armament of these troops, and in general many of them were well below strength in equipment, arms, and ammunition. Still, it is clear that large numbers of garrison soldiers were quite well armed, and more importantly, were in close proximity to several major weapons and munitions plants and depots which promised access to ample supplies of military hardware.

The size and armament of the Petrograd garrison at the time of the February Revolution, then, insured that local military forces would be a major factor to be reckoned with in the crucial months immediately following the collapse of the old regime. It is perhaps no exaggeration to say that until such time as control over the Petrograd garrison could be re-established, the Russian government was at the garrison's mercy. Moreover, to make matters even more difficult for the government, the disintegration of the traditional police apparatus made post-tsarist administrators in Petrograd unduly dependent on military troops for the maintenance of public order.

THE STRUGGLE FOR THE GARRISON

Because of the garrison's enormous potential political significance, a contest for influence there was inevitable in the post-February period among the Provisional Government, the Petrograd Soviet, and the major Russian political parties. During the first weeks of March, 1917, the Provisional Government sought to re-establish the authority of the Petrograd Military District and its officers over the forces of the garrison. Moreover, the government appointed commissars to major units of the garrison as a further means of exercising its influence. However, the efforts of the Provisional Government were quickly overshadowed by those of the more broadly-based Petrograd Soviet. Important steps toward assuring the allegiance of the garrison were taken by the Soviet on February 28, when army units were invited to elect representatives to participate in the work of the Petrograd Soviet (a special Soldiers' Section was established to deal with the problems of the armed forces) and on March 3, when Soviet pressure forced the Provisional Government to include in its initial proclamation a provision that troops taking part in the revolution could not be disarmed or removed from Petrograd. Even more significant was the publication at about the same time of the Soviet's Order Number One regarding behavior in the armed forces. Among other things, the order authorized the immediate election of soldier and sailor committees with broad but vaguely defined administrative authority in all military units, placed control of all weapons in the hands of these committees, announced that orders of the Duma Military Commission (that is, orders of the future Provisional Government) should be obeyed only if they did not conflict with the orders of the Soviet, and proclaimed full civil rights for soldiers when not on duty.[5]

The practical effect of these provisions was to make garrison units look to the Petrograd Soviet for ultimate authority and to all but destroy traditional codes of behavior in the armed forces. Moreover, the fact that the Petrograd Soviet's stand on the war corresponded more closely to the soldiers' yearning for peace than did the patriotic declarations of the Provisional Government contributed to the popularity of the Soviet in the initial weeks of the revolutionary period. In the first half of April, ostensibly for strategic reasons but certainly also because of the impossibility of re-establishing firm control over the troops, the Provisional Government formulated plans involving the shipment of a major portion of the garrison to the front, a move which only weakened its position further. Striking proof of the Provisional Government's impotence in the garrison was furnished as early as the April crisis, when a few military regiments joined in popular demonstrations against the Provisional Government's foreign policy. The troops ignored orders from General Kornilov, then Commander of the Petrograd Military District, to return to their barracks, finally halting their protest in response to directives from the Executive Committee of the Petrograd Soviet.[6] Subsequently, in matters concerning the garrison, the Provisional Government was forced to act in concert with the Soviet.

In addition, the Kadets, Mensheviks, Bolsheviks, and Socialist-Revolutionaries competed among themselves for influence in the Petrograd garrison, the latter possessing an initial advantage by virtue of the support which they commanded among the more literate peasant-soldiers. But more than any other party the Bolsheviks, alone bent on overthrowing the Provisional Government and seizing power, devoted attention and an enormous expenditure of effort to the garrison. Indeed, while all of the major Russian political parties ultimately established special military branches, it seems apparent that only the semi-autonomous Bolshevik Military Organization was really active among troops of the garrison.[7] Alone among the major Russian political parties, the Bolsheviks sought to challenge the Soviet as spokesman for the garrison's seething discontent and to obtain absolute control of major garrison regiments, establishing party cells at battalion and even company levels as a means of attaining this objective. The party's interest in the garrison was threefold. Most important, garrison regiments were viewed as a major element in the armed force that would be needed to overthrow the bourgeoisie; among Bolshevik Military Organization leaders it was all but axiomatic that to control the Petrograd garrison was to control Petrograd and that to win the capital was to obtain a dominant position in the struggle for power in Russia. Secondly, the indoctrination of replacement companies in the garrison was to serve as a funnel for the Bolshevization of the front. Finally, the spread of Bolshevik ideas to the soldier-peasants of the garrison was viewed as an important means of winning over the countryside.[8]

Bolshevik attempts to gain a foothold in the Petrograd garrison were not immediately successful. In March such efforts were hampered by a shortage of trained agitators and in early April widespread criticism of the Bolsheviks aroused by Lenin's return passage through enemy Germany increased the difficulty of conducting anti-war propaganda in the garrison. In this respect developments such as the April crisis and, later, preparations to resume active military operations at the front marked a turning point in Military Organization fortunes. From then on the revolutionary Bolshevik program attracted a steadily increasing mass following. "Club Pravda," a "non-party" soldiers' club opened by the Military Organization in the basement of the Kshesinskaia mansion, became a magnet for the most extreme elements in the armed forces. Garrison rallies staged by the Military Organization drew crowds numbering into the thousands. *Soldatskaia pravda,* the Military Organization's special soldiers' newspaper and probably its most successful enterprise, quickly attained a circulation of 50,000, half of which was distributed in the Petrograd garrison and the remainder sent to the front.[9]

Advertising itself as the soldiers' own organ, *Soldatskaia pravda* focused attention on political issues of particular interest to the troops and on the hardships of everyday life in the armed forces. In a simple and direct style that contrasted sharply with the Central Committee's *Pravda, Soldatskaia pravda* issued a steady stream of propaganda on important aspects of the Bolshevik program: the removal of the Provisional Government, the transfer of all power to the Soviets, the confiscation of farmland, and immediate peace. *Soldatskaia pravda's* inaugural issue launched a campaign to encourage fraternization at the front, and in subsequent articles practical ways of initiating fraternization were discussed in detail. Each day except Monday, from April 15 to July 5, *Soldatskaia pravda* articles, often written by the soldiers themselves, attacked government attempts to re-establish a minimum of discipline in Petrograd regiments and to transfer soldiers from the garrison to the front, while an endless stream of letters and resolutions from frontline soldiers sketched a disturbing, albeit distorted, picture of conditions there.

By mid-May the effect of such propaganda was observable. To be sure, soldiers committees in most regiments remained under the control of non-Bolshevik moderates as they had been from the first days of the revolution. Moreover, there were some garrison units still relatively free of Bolshevik influence; generally speaking, such was the case in cavalry and cossack forces. However, party cells were flourishing in many units of the garrison and these were represented in the central Bolshevik Military Organization. Military Organization membership in Petrograd already totaled well over one thousand.[10] Support for the Bolshevik program was quite strong in such large units as the Grenadier and Moskovskii Guards Regiments, the First Machine Gun Regiment, the 180th Reserve Infantry Regiment, and the Sixth Engineer Battalion. Probably facilitating Bolshevization in the latter unit was the fact that among the engineers were a relatively high percentage of industrial laborers. Among factors contributing to rapid Bolshevik success within several other regiments were the presence in some of these units of dynamic young officer-Bolsheviks (this factor was particularly significant in the 180th Reserve Infantry Regiment) and their location in seething factory districts of Petrograd, often in close proximity to Bolshevik Party headquarters. Bolshevik influence was also great among sailors at the Kronstadt Naval Base. Particularly bitter memories of the harsh injustices of the tsarist regime, the relatively high percentage of sailors of working class origin, and the existence of a strong revolutionary tradition harking back to 1905 appear to have aided the Bolshevik cause among the sailors. At Kronstadt, the local Soviet passed a resolution rejecting the authority of the Provisional Government on May 16. Yet for the Bolshevik Party this early success was a mixed blessing; while it increased the potential of the Bolsheviks to influence the course of political events in Petrograd, it tied the party's fortunes to some of the most impatient, irresponsible, and generally anarchic elements in Russian society. The very significant problems which this situation posed for the Bolsheviks were reflected in the period immediately preceding the July days.

THE GARRISON AND THE JULY UPRISING[11]

In late May, measures taken by the Provisional Government to restore a semblance of order and authority in the armed forces and the threat of imminent transfer to the front stirred unrest in several regiments of the garrison. Dissatisfaction was particularly acute in precisely those units in which Bolshevik influence was greatest. Under pressure for immediate revolutionary action from its garrison followers, desperate lest the socialist revolution occur too late to save them from death at the front, and bolstered by the confidence inevitably inspired by substantial armed force, the Bolshevik Military Organization appealed to the party Central Committee to authorize a march of Petrograd soldiers and workers to protest the policies of the government and to demonstrate support for the transfer of all power to the Soviets. Although L. B. Kamenev and other moderate Bolsheviks opposed such action on both ideological and strategic grounds, a Central Committee majority led by Lenin favored the proposal.[12] On June 8 a mass protest march, to be organized in secret, was scheduled for June 10; however, intervention by the Congress of Soviets forced Lenin to cancel this demonstration at the eleventh hour. And, apprehensive about the danger of a premature uprising in the capital (which the more conservative provinces and the front would oppose), Lenin now insisted on the immediate need for organization, patience, and discipline. He emphasized this point in a heated address to the Petrograd organization of the party on June 11;[13] this was Lenin's theme in some editorials which appeared in *Pravda* and the crux of his message to a session of the All-Russian Conference of Bolshevik Military Organizations, where demands for the immediate overthrow of the Provisional Government were particularly emphatic.[14]

However, Lenin's policy of trying to control revolutionary unrest in Petrograd proved unsuccessful for several reasons, the most important of them connected with developments in the garrison. In the first place, on June 18 the Bolsheviks successfully turned a mass street demonstration sponsored by the Congress of Soviets into an impressive expression of support for the Bolshevik program. To rank-and-file Bolsheviks in Petrograd military units and factories and in Kronstadt, and to many junior level party leaders in the Bolshevik Petersburg Committee and Military Organization, this seemed evidence enough that the forces at the disposal of the party were more than adequate for the seizure of power.[15] On this same day, Russian military forces on the Southwestern front launched their long-heralded offensive. Orders for sizable shipments of men and arms to the front now received by regiments of the Petrograd garrison triggered efforts by rank-and-file Bolsheviks in the most rebellious unit, the First Machine Gun Regiment, to organize an immediate uprising with or without the authorization of the party center.[16] Although the leaders of the Bolshevik Military Organization cooperated in squelching this movement on June 20, there is evidence that on June 22, Military Organization leaders, genuinely concerned about losing the support of the masses to the more militant Anarchists if the party proved unwilling to act, began to lay plans for an uprising of their own.[17]

Eleven days later, on July 3, the First Machine Gun Regiment responded to new orders to send men and arms to the front by touching off the July uprising, aimed at overthrowing the Provisional Government and forcing the Soviet to take power. Organized with the help of Bolshevik Military Organization members in the regiment,[18] it was almost immediately supported by all of the military units in which Bolsheviks had been most active and by large numbers of factory workers. Evidently only after the leadership of the Military Organization and the Petrograd organization of the party had approved participation in the movement, and then only very belatedly and reluctantly, did the Central Committee agree to stand at its head.[19]

Lenin's judgment as to the untimeliness of immediate revolutionary action had been correct. To be sure, during the height of the July uprising the Provisional Government and the Soviet were completely at the mercy of demonstrating workers, soldiers, and sailors, with almost no garrison troops willing to come to the government's rescue. However, such regiments as the Litovskii, Volynskii, Petrogradskii, and Preobrazhenskii Guards, who had been among the first to rebel in February, failed to respond to Bolshevik appeals to go into the streets. The effective support of several other units lasted only a few hours. Moreover, after receiving news that loyal troops would soon be arriving from the front and after the release of evidence purporting to show that Lenin was a German agent, previously neutral regiments were persuaded to come to the aid of the government.

The July uprising culminated in a serious defeat for the Bolshevik Party. The Provisional Government, now headed by Kerensky, appeared determined to destroy the party's influence in the garrison and disband those regiments in which Bolshevization was most advanced. According to a plan drawn up by General G. D. Romanovskii and approved by Kerensky on July 11 (with the pencilled notation, "agreed, but I demand that this be forcefully carried out without deviation"), regiments of the Petrograd garrison were divided into three categories, depending on the extent of their involvement in the July movement. To the first category were assigned units participating in the demonstrations in full or close to full strength. Included in this group were the Grenadier Regiment, the First, Third, 176th, and 180th Reserve Infantry Regiments, and the First Machine Gun Regiment, together constituting the core of Military Organization strength in the garrison. These units were to be completely and permanently disbanded, their personnel (with the exception of those in jail) to be transferred to duty at the front. To the second category were assigned units in which only individual companies took part in the demonstrations. The Moskovskii, Pavlovskii, Third Rifle, and Second Machine Gun Regiments and the Sixth Engineer Battalion were assigned to this group. Only guilty elements in these units were to be dissolved. Finally, the third category was composed of units not taking an active part in the demonstrations but containing guilty individuals. This group was ordered to conduct a thorough housecleaning of subversive elements. By this plan Romanovskii proposed to reduce the garrison by one hundred thousand of its most unreliable elements.[20] The Military Organization's *Soldatskaia pravda* was banned; much of the Military Organization's apparatus in the garrison was damaged; the Military Organization's junior level leadership was decimated by arrests. The list of garrison personnel jailed in the course of the Provisional Government's investigation of the July uprising read like a Bolshevik Military Organization "Who's Who."[21] In short, the Bolsheviks were forced to pay dearly for their early successes in the garrison.

A number of factors, however, permitted the Bolshevik Party to make a rapid recovery from its defeat in July and to emerge in the fall of 1917 with renewed strength and stature in the Petrograd garrison. First, the spirit of indignation toward the Bolsheviks among troops of the garrison did not last long. This was in large part because even after the collapse of the July offensive the Provisional Government and the General Staff, fully supported by the Soviet, continued to give top priority to restoring the discipline and fighting capacity of the armed forces and to seeing the struggle against the Central Powers through to a successful conclusion. Whether Russian military leaders were right in believing that a triumphant attack would arrest disintegration in the armed forces is problematical; what seems clear is that in the garrison word of the massive German breakthrough at the front brought further discredit to the war effort, the Provisional Government, and the Soviet. Among the major Russian political parties only the Bolsheviks remained uncompromised by support for the war.

Moreover, for a variety of reasons the Provisional Government's efforts to deal forcefully with the Bolsheviks were also of short duration. The policy of disarming unreliable troops and removing them from the capital, for example, was only partially carried out. Quite naturally, most field commanders were not at all interested in receiving such replacements. Persuasive evidence regarding the Bolshevik role in the organization of the July uprising gathered by a special, high level investigating commission was not made public, and none of the many Bolsheviks arrested in the aftermath of the July days was ever brought to trial. Actually, the top leaders of the Bolshevik Military Organization somehow managed to evade arrest. A bit wiser and more cautious, but exhibiting remarkable resilience and energy, they were able to supervise rebuilding of the Military Organization in the garrison. Finally, despite restrictions on the Bolshevik press, *Soldatskaia pravda,* albeit under a new title, was circulating among the troops after a post-July days interruption of short duration.[22]

It appears clear that the Bolsheviks had already recouped many of their July losses by the time of the Kornilov affair in late August. However, relevant sources leave no doubt that a direct consequence of that blundering attempt by the High Command of the Russian army to establish a military dictatorship with or without Kerensky's cooperation was a new upsurge in Bolshevik fortunes in the garrison. This was not only because to defend themselves from the danger on the right, the Provisional Government and the Soviet were forced to free imprisoned Bolsheviks and to authorize the issue of arms to Bolshevik supporters in the garrison and the factories. The Kornilov episode contributed immeasurably to the internal disintegration of the garrison. It shattered whatever moral authority the officers still possessed and as a result, the carrying out of even the most routine functions became virtually impossible for them. By seeming to demonstrate the validity of pre-July Bolshevik warnings in regard to the threat of counterrevolution and by putting the Bolsheviks in the position of appearing to be the chief defenders of the revolution, the Kornilov affair enormously enhanced Bolshevik prestige in the garrison. At the same time the Kornilov experience destroyed whatever loyalty the troops still had to the Provisional Government in general and Kerensky in particular. In his memoirs, W. S. Woytinsky, then Commissar of the Northern Front, focuses attention on this factor, recalling that every soldier knew that the conflict between Kerensky and Kornilov had been preceded by negotiations between them; that discussed in these negotiations were the reimposition of capital punishment, the curbing of soldiers' committees, the return of power to officers, in short, a return to the ways of the "old regime." Consequently, to the average soldier the *Kornilovshchina* appeared as a conspiracy against himself and against the revolution on the part of the Military High Command *and* Kerensky.[23]

In the several weeks between the Kornilov affair and the October Revolution a second purge of officers was carried out in many regiments. Military Organization membership in the garrison rose significantly, and Bolshevik collectives were successfully organized or expanded in most of those military units heretofore relatively free of Bolshevik influence—in the Egerskii, Petrogradskii, Izmailovskii, Preobrazhenskii, Volynskii, and Litovskii Guards Regiments, for example—and even in scattered military schools. Concomitantly, control of a number of regimental committees passed from more moderate elements into the hands of the Bolsheviks.[24] This change in the power position of the Bolsheviks was reflected in the fact that even soldiers in those garrison units which had been most instrumental in putting down the July uprising now passed Bolshevik-sponsored resolutions calling for transfer of all power to the Soviets.

This is not to suggest that in the aftermath of the Kornilov affair the Bolsheviks had already attained their goal of winning absolute control over the major elements of the Petrograd garrison. In September, 1917, only a fairly small percentage of soldiers in individual garrison regiments appear to have been politically active; these were the people who consistently participated in protest demonstrations and meetings and who ultimately played active roles in the overthrow of the Provisional Government. On the whole, garrison troops were more an unstable mob concerned most of all with avoiding transfer to the front than a disciplined Praetorian Guard. The soldiers viewed the Provisional Government and the General Staff with the greatest bitterness and suspicion (was not Kerensky—the same Kerensky who had conspired with Kornilov—now Commander-in-Chief as well as head of the Russian government?). Further, in the eyes of the average soldier the majority socialist leadership of the Executive Committee of the All-Russian Congress of Soviets, because of its close association with the policies of the Provisional Government, had been similarly compromised. However, the organs of the Soviet still embodied revolutionary legitimacy. In part because of this Lenin's rallying cry from April on had been "All Power to the Soviets," not "Power to the Bolsheviks."[25] Consequently, what political loyalty the mass of garrison soldiers possessed was less to the Bolshevik Party than to the Bolshevik-dominated Petrograd Soviet. This was precisely what a Bolshevik district organization leader had in mind when at a party gathering in mid-October he reported that at the request of the Soviet the masses in his district would come out against the Provisional Government, but that at the request of the party few would act.[26] All this did not mean, of course, that garrison troops were not to be a decisive factor in the Bolshevik seizure of power; however, to assess properly the significance of the garrison in October it is necessary to consider, if only briefly, the broader problem of Bolshevik preparations for the overthrow of the Provisional Government.

THE BOLSHEVIKS PREPARE

Not long after the Kornilov affair Lenin, then still in hiding in Finland, appealed to his followers in Petrograd to overthrow the Provisional Government without delay. This action was not a direct response to the events of late August. Indeed, influenced by the open rift that had developed between the majority socialists and the Kadets during the Kornilov affair, Lenin apparently acquired some "constitutional illusions" of his own. In an article written for *Rabochii* on September 1, he momentarily ignored the course toward an armed uprising set by the Sixth Bolshevik Party Congress in late July; to him, the establishment of a government of Socialist Revolutionaries (SR's) and Mensheviks responsible to the Soviets and a peaceful transition to socialism now seemed possible. However, in a postscript which Lenin added to this article two days later, after learning of a Central Executive Committee pledge of support to a five-man ruling Directory organized by Kerensky, Lenin wondered whether it was not already too late for this.[27] Moreover, subsequent Bolshevik triumphs in Soviet elections in Petrograd, Moscow, and other Russian cities made negotiation with the majority socialists increasingly unattractive. The effect of these victories on Lenin, coupled as they were with the Provisional Government's announcement of coming elections to the Constituent Assembly, was electrifying.

On September 12 and September 14 Lenin began peppering his followers in Petrograd with frantic appeals to seize power.[28] The Germans were then consolidating their position in the Baltic; soon Russian naval forces would be forced out of the Gulf of Riga, leaving the approaches to Kronstadt and Petrograd unprotected. Taking note of the German advance, Lenin claimed that the Provisional Government was about to surrender the capital after which Bolshevik prospects for the seizure of power would be "one hundred times less favorable." Pointing to Bolshevik victories in local Soviets, Lenin argued that the party had the support of a majority of peasants, workers, and soldiers. At the same time he repeated again and again that Russia was experiencing a revolutionary upsurge, that vacillation among Bolshevik enemies was enormous, and hence that the optimum moment for the seizure of power had arrived. Left unstated, though probably very real, was the fear on Lenin's part that waiting to seize power until the opening of the Congress of Soviets (scheduled for October 20) or until after the convocation of the Constituent Assembly would cripple possibilities for an immediate revolutionary dictatorship.

At any rate, in his September letters from Finland Lenin sought to demonstrate that an organized rebellion (in his words, "the treatment of insurrection as an art") was a fundamental tenet of Marxism. Treating insurrection as an art, the Bolsheviks "were to organize a headquarters of insurgent detachments, distribute their forces, surround the Aleksandrinskii theater [the meeting place of the Democratic State Conference], occupy the Peter and Paul Fortress, seize the telephone and telegraph exchanges, and arrest the General Staff and government," all this "without losing an instant!"

Yet nothing on this order was attempted for several weeks. For the Bolsheviks this was probably extremely fortunate because an armed coup of the kind advocated by Lenin at this time might well have been disastrous. We have Stalin's word that after the revolution Lenin himself acknowledged this.[29] The Bolsheviks were saved because of the stubborn opposition to the course advocated by Lenin on the part of those moderately inclined Bolsheviks who had warned against precipitous action in June and July. To them the debacle of July attested to the danger of going too far too fast, while the gains registered by the Bolsheviks in the aftermath of the Kornilov affair seemed proof enough that the development of the revolution was working to their advantage. It is not surprising, then, that the Bolshevik Central Committee's initial response to Lenin's messages of mid-September was not much different from that which had greeted Lenin's "Letters from Afar" six months earlier. The Central Committee evidently considered burning the letters; indeed, in a 1921 speech Bukharin maintained that the Central Committee resolved unanimously to do so.[30] According to the published protocols the committee voted to preserve one copy of each letter and to take steps to prevent a movement into the streets.[31]

Further pressure by Lenin, including an offer to resign from the Central Committee, brought some party leaders to Lenin's side. And at its historic session in Sukhanov's apartment on October 10, the Bolshevik Central Committee, with only Zinoviev and Kamenev in opposition, "resolved to place an armed uprising on the order of the day."[32] While this resolution said nothing about a possible date for an insurrection, it is clear that Lenin viewed it as authorization for an armed uprising at the earliest possible date before the opening of the Second Congress of Soviets, then scheduled for October 20. Yet even now the Petrograd Bolsheviks did little about actually preparing an immediate uprising, except talk. In his letters of early October and in a personal appeal to the Central Committee on October 10, Lenin argued that the Northern Congress of Soviets provided an eminently suitable institution for the organization of an insurrection against the Provisional Government.[33] Yet the Bolshevik-dominated Northern Congress was convened in Petrograd on October 11, sat for three days and dispersed, having limited itself to the passage of the usual collection of militant-sounding resolutions. More important, it appears that as late as October 18, when the Central Executive Committee announced that the opening of the Second Congress of Soviets was to be postponed until the twenty-fifth, the Bolsheviks were not much closer to starting an armed uprising than they had been on the tenth. Available evidence suggests that the primary reason for this was that the deep divisions among the leaders of the Bolshevik Party in regard to both ideology and tactics were not eliminated by the vaguely worded formal agreement of October 10.

The categorical opposition to the seizure of power by people like Kamenev and Zinoviev has already been mentioned, and there is no doubt that their actions after October 10 slowed preparations for an immediate armed uprising. Actually, in the aftermath of the Central Committee meeting of October 10, Kamenev and Zinoviev composed a memorandum for circulation to lower party organizations outlining the reasons for their opposition to the overthrow of the Provisional Government,[34] in the immediately succeeding days they agitated actively against such action, and on October 18 Kamenev all but made public Bolshevik plans in Gorky's newspaper, *Novaia zhizn'*. Following this, even Lenin, to judge by his letters, began to think that the moment to strike had been lost.[35]

However, there was another attitude, much more widely shared than that of Zinoviev and Kamenev, that helps to explain Bolshevik hesitancy and procrastination in October. The fact is that many lower-level Bolshevik leaders who in principle were fully as committed as Lenin to an early seizure of power were apprehensive about the tactical feasibility of the classical popular armed uprising advocated by Lenin. To be sure, it would be misleading to suggest that the views of lower-level Bolshevik leaders regarding immediate direct action after October 10 were uniformly pessimistic. Protocols of two major meetings at which reports from Bolsheviks working at the district level and in the Military Organization were heard (a meeting of the Petersburg Committee on October 15 and a session of the Central Committee with representatives of lower party organizations the next day) indicate that such was not the case.[36] For example, at the October 15 Petersburg Committee meeting M. Ia. Latsis of the all-important Vyborg District lavished praise on preparations by the workers in his area for the seizure of power and expressed confidence that they could be counted on, while I. A. Rakhia, speaking for the Finns, declared that their attitude toward an uprising was "the sooner the better." Similarly, at the Central Committee meeting on the sixteenth, N. A. Skrypnik declared that an urge for practical action and a dissatisfaction with mere resolutions could be distinguished among the masses everywhere.

On the other hand, the general picture of the state of affairs in the factories and barracks that emerged at the important Bolshevik meetings of mid-October was often so unpromising that it could not but have had a dampening effect on the mood of party members. Perhaps the most alarming factor brought out at these discussions was the apparent lethargy of large numbers of Petrograd workers and soldiers. Thus, of nineteen district representatives at the Petersburg Committee meeting of October 15, only eight felt that the masses were in a "fighting mood" and ready to act immediately, apparently six representatives viewed the prevailing spirit as indefinite, while five referred explicitly to the lack of any desire to "come out." The Military Organization leader V. I. Nevskii, while acknowledging that the whole of the Petrograd garrison would join workers in support of an uprising organized by the Soviet, asserted that among the workers there was no fighting spirit and that in this respect the soldiers were even more hopeless. M. M. Kharitonov said that among the masses he could distinguish no mood to fight, that in Kronstadt the mood had fallen sharply, and that he had witnessed widespread drunkenness even among Bolsheviks. An unidentified trade union representative felt that the mood of the masses was such that if they were attacked by the counterrevolution a rebuff would be given, but that the masses would not attack by themselves.

Similar observations were made at the Central Committee meeting of October 16. N. V. Krylenko revealed that reports to the Military Organization's All-Russian Bureau from local representatives suggested that the revolutionary mood was falling, while I. Schmidt, speaking in behalf of the party's trade union representatives, commented that the influence of the Bolsheviks predominated in the trade unions but warned that fear of layoffs acted as a brake on revolutionary action by the workers. A. G. Shliapnikov, representing the Metalist Union, commented in a similar vein and added that among metal workers rumors of a "coming out" had resulted in panic. Toward the end of the same meeting, M. V. Volodarskii, the Petersburg Committee's top agitator, declared: "If the question of a coming out is being posed as a matter for tomorrow, then we must honestly say we are not ready. I have been making public appeals daily but must acknowledge that the masses have responded to our appeal with bewilderment." A few local level Bolshevik leaders were a bit more optimistic than they had been a day earlier, a fact which did not escape A. V. Shotman, an opponent of immediate action. In an apparent dig at speakers who were allowing themselves to be swayed by Lenin's enthusiasm he warned that "at the City Conference [the Third Bolshevik Petrograd City Conference in session from October 7 to October 11], in the Petersburg Committee, and in the Military Organization the mood was much more bleak than it is now being pictured."

Apparent mass apathy was by no means the only important problem contributing to the pessimistic picture emanating from below on the eve of the proposed Bolshevik seizure of power. The local reports of October 15 and 16 revealed widespread concern about a general absence of technical preparations for an insurrection; indeed there were few speakers who did not note either serious organizational problems in connection with the Red Guards or critical shortages of arms and ammunition, and from the reports taken together it is clear that an apparatus for the seizure of power was still to be created. At the Petersburg Committee meeting of October 15, one of the bluntest statements regarding Bolshevik unpreparedness for an immediate uprising was issued by Nevskii, who, as a leader of the Military Organization, was most directly concerned with overall technical preparations for the seizure of power. Nevskii's report on this occasion testifies to the enormous impact of the July experience on Military Organization leaders.[37] Warning that absolutely nothing had been done to prepare the provinces for the overthrow of the Provisional Government and that the Bolsheviks were in fact just beginning to gain a foothold in the countryside, he declared that peasants in several provinces had stated that in the event of an uprising they would withhold bread. Nevskii also pointed out that such vitally important factors as the support of the railroad workers and the Fifth Army on the Northern Front had not been secured. In general, technical preparations for an uprising had yet to be initiated; as matters stood there was no assurance that the Bolsheviks would have that initial preponderance of strength necessary for victory over the Provisional Government. For all these reasons Nevskii called the Central Committee's resolution of October 10 "premature."

Judging by the published protocols, Nevskii's views were shared by the most important leaders of the Bolshevik Petersburg Committee and Military Organization; within the Bolshevik Central Committee their chief adherent appears to have been Trotsky. Some Soviet historians suggest that such attitudes were the result of timidity and "constitutional illusions," to use Lenin's phrase. However, in retrospect they seem to have been based on a realistic appraisal of the prevailing mood and correlation of forces in Petrograd, the provinces, and at the front. In opposing the "immediate bayonet charge" advocated by Lenin, tactically more cautious Bolsheviks such as Trotsky argued that the prestige of the Soviets dictated that they, rather than the organs of the party, be utilized for the seizure of power. Confident that the Bolsheviks would have a majority in the Second Congress of Soviets, these Bolsheviks maintained that the probability of success would be greatly increased if the seizure of power could be linked with and legitimized by the decisions of the Congress. Some Bolsheviks sharing these views also urged that for maximum support any attack on the Provisional Government be masked as a defensive operation on behalf of the Soviet and the revolution, hence, that action be delayed until a suitable pretext for giving battle presented itself. At the Bolshevik strategy session of October 16, Krylenko was quite specific. He followed his pessimistic report on the mood of the garrison with the observation that some sort of immediate motivating factor was needed to mobilize the masses. He added that a fresh attempt by Kerensky to move unreliable troops out of the capital (several garrison units received orders to prepare for transfer to the front on October 9) provided just the issue around which a decisive struggle against the Provisional Government could be waged.[38]

THE ROLE OF THE GARRISON IN OCTOBER

The unwillingness of garrison troops to accept transfer to the front in early summer, 1917 (during preparations for the ill-fated Kerensky offensive) and the problems which this created for the Provisional Government have already been touched upon. A similar situation developed in late September and early October, when it appeared that the Germans might attempt to take Petrograd. To judge by the report of the Commander of the Northern front, General Cheremisov, at a staff meeting on October 11, Russian military leaders did not take the possibility of an early attack on Petrograd seriously.[39] What appears clear is that the Kerensky government viewed the apparent German threat as an excellent excuse to rid the capital once and for all of the more unruly elements in the garrison.[40] On October 5 Kerensky directed General Polkovnikov, Commander of the Petrograd Military District, to prepare his troops for transfer to the front and the following day

Polkovnikov issued preliminary instructions to key commanders.[41] According to Woytinsky, Cheremisov himself had little taste for such an operation, feeling that transfers of troops from Petrograd would only hasten complete catastrophe at the front. Be that as it may, on October 9 Cheremisov issued a supplementary order drafted by Woytinsky reaffirming General Polkovnikov's directive on the grounds that such action was absolutely vital to the defense of the capital from the Germans.

There is nothing surprising in the response of the troops once these directives became public. With encouragement from the Bolsheviks they quickly concluded that Kerensky, still in league with the generals, was once again bent on stifling the revolution. Rumors which had begun to circulate earlier that the Provisional Government was making preparations for a move to Moscow (these were later substantiated) served to reinforce the popular conviction that the revolution was in danger. As early as the spring of 1917, at the time of the April crisis, scattered elements of the garrison initiated protest demonstrations against the Provisional Government's foreign policy; in June and July close to half of the garrison ranged itself against the government. Now as if with one voice garrison troops proclaimed lack of confidence in the Provisional Government and demanded transfer of power to the Soviets. On this occasion virtually all of the major garrison regiments which had refused to follow the Bolsheviks in July rejected the Provisional Government and pledged support to the Petrograd Soviet.[42] Moreover, those units in which the government was most confident—for example, Cossack forces and the regiments rushed to Petrograd from the front after the July days—now either affirmed their neutrality in the struggle between the Petrograd Soviet and the military authorities or openly sided with the Soviet.

This new crisis involving the garrison erupted in the second week of October, and the Bolsheviks exploited it to the fullest. In the press, in the Petrograd Soviet, and most importantly, in factories and barracks, the Bolsheviks trumpeted the slogan, "the All-Russian Congress is in danger," fanning popular fears of a "second Kornilov." Thus on October 11 the lead editorial in *Rabochii put'* ridiculed the argument that garrison forces were being ordered out of Petrograd for strategic reasons, arguing that ostensibly the offensive of June 18 had been "organized in the name of strategic necessity; yet later leading SR's and Mensheviks had openly acknowledged that the offensive was initiated for political reasons—in order to take the army in hand." The same pattern, *Rabochii put'* implied, had been repeated in August. "The Kornilov 'reforms,' capital punishment, and the suppression of army organizations had been justified by the need to raise the fighting capacity of the army to fight the foreign enemy. Yet later it became clear to everyone that all of Kornilov's strategy had been aimed at fighting the revolution. Before the Kornilov uprising," the editorial went on, "the conspirators demanded the transfer of a whole group of regiments from Petrograd, for strategic necessity of course. The Bolsheviks had told the soldiers, you are being destroyed. But the soldiers still trusted the SR and Menshevik windbags—they left to dig trenches and the revolution nearly fell into the pit then being dug for it by Kornilov."[43]

The government attempted to counter these arguments by presenting the dangers of a German attack in ever more alarming terms. The most important allies the government could count on in its conflict with the garrison were embittered front line troops, themselves long impatient to move to the rear. Consequently, in the days between October 9 and the fall of the Provisional Government, military authorities attempted to utilize the pressure of army committees at the front to force garrison regiments to accept transfer. However, at a conference in Pskov on October 17, garrison representatives temporarily dodged a direct rebuff from the front and the move failed. Actually, so great was the popular mistrust of the Provisional Government's intentions at this time that even the majority socialists were forced to recognize that garrison troops could not be expected to respond to orders not in some way controlled by the Soviet. Hence at a session of the Petrograd Soviet's Executive Committee on October 10 the Menshevik Mark Broido, while appealing to the soldiers to prepare for transfer to the front, proposed that a special committee be established by the Soviet to clarify the problem of Petrograd's security and to draw up a plan for the defense of the city which could be popularly supported. Under Bolshevik supervision, this committee officially came into being on October 16 as the Military Revolutionary Committee.[44] Ostensibly created to organize the defense of Petrograd from the Germans and to save the Second Congress of Soviets from the counterrevolution, it became the directing body for the Bolshevik seizure of power.

The Military Revolutionary Committee was a formally elected organ of the Petrograd Soviet; among its approximately 66 members were Soviet officials and representatives of worker, soldier, and party organizations, Left SR's, and Anarchists, as well as Bolsheviks. Actually, the Military Revolutionary Committee's first chairman was a young Left SR, P. E. Lazimir, selected by the Bolsheviks with an eye toward maintaining the committee's "non-party" character. However, beginning on October 20, when the Military Revolutionary Committee launched operations, its activities were effectively controlled by Trotsky and the central leadership of the Bolshevik Military Organization. As numerous historians have emphasized, the Military Revolutionary Committee's efforts were handicapped by continuing self doubt and internal wrangling; yet on the whole the patient, cautious attack which Bolshevik strategists now managed to mount against the Provisional Government, the attention which they paid to retaining and expanding the support of the Soviet and the masses, and in this connection, the pains which they took to mask each forward step as a defense of the revolution and the Second Congress of Soviets contrast strikingly with the confused and erratic behavior of the party leadership in July.

In its first day of operation the Military Revolutionary Committee began substituting its own representatives with extensive command authority for government commissars in major garrison units, arms depots, and other militarily important points. A high percentage of these new commissars were well-known members of the Bolshevik Military Organization; many were young officers only recently released from the prisons in which they had languished since July. Now on October 20-22, with almost no exceptions, they were received by the troops with genuine enthusiasm. Somewhat earlier, an ad hoc conference of garrison delegates had been created to operate alongside the Military Revolutionary Committee, and during crucial stages in the seizure of power this conference of soldier delegates, the Military Revolutionary Committee's commissar system, and regular company and regimental committees were effectively utilized to coordinate the activities of the troops in the struggle against the government.

By the evening of October 21, under intense pressure from Lenin, the Military Revolutionary Committee was ready for a test of strength with the government. On that date the committee sent a delegation to Colonel Polkovnikov with the demand that it be given the right to validate orders to the troops.[45] Not surprisingly, Polkovnikov rejected this demand, after which the Military Revolutionary Committee secured agreement from virtually the whole garrison that troop orders not countersigned by the Military Revolutionary Committee would be considered invalid.[46] It might be argued that for practical purposes, all this only confirmed procedures established much earlier; at least from the time of the April crisis the Provisional Government had been forced to take the attitudes of the Soviet into account in dealing with the troops. However, heretofore the majority socialists who dominated the Soviet supported the Provisional Government on fundamental political questions; hence only very rarely did it question orders from the Petrograd Military District. Now the situation was radically different; the authority of the Petrograd Soviet over the garrison meant that ultimate control of the troops was vested in a body openly committed to the immediate overthrow of the government.

Early on the morning of October 24, Kerensky initiated steps aimed at averting a coup d'état. Among other things, the Bolshevik newspapers *Rabochii put'* and *Soldat* were raided and closed. According to official Soviet historiography concerned most of all with portraying the October revolution as a well-organized mass uprising and glorifying Lenin's role in it, technical preparations were completed and the Bolshevik seizure of power commenced around midday, October 24, when the Military Revolutionary Committee openly resisted Kerensky's belated effort to squelch the Bolsheviks and shortly before Lenin came out of hiding to take personal command of Bolshevik forces. During the following twenty-four hours, the Bolshevik newspapers were forcibly reopened and the telephone exchange, post office, state bank, railroad stations, main bridges, etc. were seized by Bolshevik-led workers, soldiers, and sailors on orders from the Military Revolutionary Committee. In the standard Soviet view, the overthrow of the Provisional

Government culminated on the evening of the twenty-fifth with the storming of the Winter Palace, the arrest of government ministers, and the proclamation of the Soviet regime at the Second Congress of Soviets.

Yet when studying the development of the October Revolution, one is left with the feeling that the classic uprising directed by Lenin on October 24 and October 25 was supplementary in character.[47] This is not to imply that this armed insurrection may not have had great significance; in his detailed study, *Red October,* Robert V. Daniels, for one, argues persuasively that the decisive break with the majority socialists which resulted from the events of the twenty-fourth and twenty-fifth freed Lenin's hands for the creation of an all-Bolshevik dictatorship which otherwise would have been impossible.[48] It is probably also true that until Kerensky's counterattack of the twenty-fourth most of Lenin's followers, Trotsky included, were more concerned with maintaining the defensive and "legal" appearance of the Military Revolutionary Committee's operations than with overthrowing the Provisional Government *before* the opening of the Second Congress of Soviets. Nonetheless Trotsky does not seem far off the mark when he suggests that the outcome of the insurrection of October 25 was "three-fourths, if not nine-tenths, settled" after the Military Revolutionary Committee assumed command of the garrison and control of arms distribution (i.e., on October 23),[49] for in a very real sense the Provisional Government and the All-Russian Central Executive Committee were disarmed without a shot being fired. In fact, a good case could probably be made for the argument that it was not until after the Military Revolutionary Committee had consolidated control of the garrison that the success of the classic general mass insurrection advocated by Lenin was assured.

What, then, was the significance of the crisis over the garrison for the Bolshevik seizure of power? Coming at the end of several weeks during which Lenin had tried with such little effect to prod his party into seizing power, at a time when prospects for overthrowing the Provisional Government before the Second Congress of Soviets appeared nil, and when the Bolshevik Party's state of disarray was hardly distinguishable from that of its opponents, the conflict between the Provisional Government and the Petrograd Soviet over the removal of the Petrograd garrison provided a perfect immediate "cause" around which a decisive struggle with Kerensky could be waged. With the Kornilov affair fresh in mind, Petrograd soldiers needed little prodding from the Bolsheviks to see the proposed transfer of garrison troops as an attempt to disarm and destroy the revolution. In the Military Revolutionary Committee the garrison crisis provided an ostensibly non-party apparatus for the seizure of power; in addition, the fact that the battle against the government was to be waged over the removal of troops to the front insured that in its struggle with the Bolsheviks, the Provisional Government would receive no support from the garrison, inevitably its first and perhaps most important line of defense.

This is not to exaggerate the importance of the garrison in 1917. As it turned out, the overthrow of the Provisional Government did not require much military force. Moreover, the Bolshevik struggle to retain power was to reveal that when it came to actual fighting, both the sailors of the Baltic Fleet and the worker Red Guards were more reliable and effective than the troops of the garrison. The importance of developments in the Petrograd garrison in the summer of 1917 lies less in the garrison's positive military contribution to the Bolshevik victory than in the disastrous effect that the demoralization of the garrison had upon attempts to reestablish public order and governmental authority and ultimately in the elimination of garrison troops as a significant military force on the side of the Provisional Government. Had the Bolsheviks been opposed by a few well armed and disciplined military units, it is not at all certain that they could have seized power; the crucial point is that by October there were almost no troops upon which the government could rely. That a similar process of disintegration had occurred in the provinces and at the front sealed the fate of the Provisional Government. Of course, the source of the government's continuing difficulties with the garrison lay in its attempt to maintain Russia's commitments in the war. This objective was behind Kerensky's continuing and ultimately catastrophic efforts to restore a measure of order and discipline in the armed forces and initially, at least, to transfer a major portion of the garrison to the front. At the same time the Bolsheviks must be credited with having been the only major Russian political group to recognize the enormous potential significance of the garrison and to make a serious effort to obtain its support. As we have seen, the Bolshevik policy of tailoring the party's program to the aspirations of the soldier and of attempting to make use of discontent among the troops of the Petrograd garrison in order to seize power was not without risk, as the July experience demonstrated. But undoubtedly this policy was of crucial significance to the Bolshevik triumph in October. At the time of the October Revolution the vast majority of Petrograd soldiers were not Bolshevik in the sense of supporting the creation of an exclusively Bolshevik government. The soldiers were anti-war and pro-Soviet; most of all they feared a second Kornilov. Hence the importance of Trotsky's tactics. The soldiers of the Petrograd garrison supported the Bolsheviks in the struggle for transfer of all power to the Soviets because only the Bolsheviks were untainted by support for the war effort and only the overthrow of the Provisional Government seemed to offer them hope of avoiding a return to the injustices of the tsarist military system and death at the front.

STEPHEN F. COHEN

In Praise of War Communism: Bukharin's The Economics of the Transition Period

When hopes and dreams are loose in the streets, it is well for the timid to lock doors, shutter windows and lie low until the wrath has passed. For there is often a monstrous incongruity between the hopes, however noble and tender, and the action which follows them. It is as if ivied maidens and garlanded youths were to herald the four horsemen of the Apocalypse.

Eric Hoffer, *The True Believer*

The Economics of the Transition Period, Nikolai Ivanovich Bukharin's eulogistic and controversial analysis of war communism, appeared in May, 1920, just as those extremist civil war policies of the Bolshevik government were reaching their apogee. It was destined to be the least circulated, but among the most famous of all his major theoretical works. That, unlike Bukharin's other important writings, *The Economics* had no further Russian editions[1] was due to the rush of events: its domestic programmatic implications were made largely obsolete by the collapse of war communism and the introduction of the New Economic Policy (NEP) in March, 1921. That the book nevertheless continued to be influential and admired—the doyen of Soviet historians, M. N. Pokrovskii, cited it in 1928 as one of the three great Bolshevik achievements in "social science" since the revolution[2]—was due to its theoretical content, which is the subject of this essay.

I

Like most revolutionary documents, *The Economics* is not fully comprehensible apart from the events that prompted its writing. The time, it will be remembered, was not ideal for leisurely theorizing. The civil war raged; and Bukharin, in addition to his duties as a Central Committee member, editor of *Pravda,* and a chief executive of the Communist International, was a candidate Politburo member and thus one of the eight party leaders who constituted the real government of Soviet Russia. Two circumstances seem to

 This article is drawn from a larger study on Bukharin and Russian Bolshevism, 1888-1938, undertaken with the support of the Research Institute on Communist Affairs, Columbia University, and to be published by Alfred A. Knopf in 1972.

have prompted his lengthy excursion into abstract Marxist theory during these turbulent days: the improvised nature of the regime's domestic policies, and his own special role in the Bolshevik leadership.

The first circumstance involved the origin and development of the policies which in retrospect became known collectively as war communism: wholesale nationalization of almost all manufacturing enterprises; regimentation of labor; rationing, state-controlled distribution of goods, and the disappearance of institutionalized market relations; forcible requisitioning of grain from the peasantry; and, as a result and most characteristic, the extensive "statization" *(ogosudarstvlenie)* of the country's economic life. These spectacular policies originated not in the party's 1917 ideology or program (as is frequently assumed), but in response to the perilous military situation that suddenly confronted the Bolsheviks with the outbreak of civil war in the summer of 1918. Encircled by white armies and foreign troops, blockaded and cut off from major sources of supplies, the fragile government abandoned the relatively moderate economic policies then in force and sought through a series of frantic, makeshift measures to lay its hands on all available human and material resources. In short, war communism was born and took shape in the crucible of military expediency and the Bolsheviks' desperate efforts to survive as the government of Soviet Russia.[3]

During the next two years, however, as the tide of war turned in their favor, these policies acquired a higher rationality in the minds of many Bolsheviks. They came to be regarded not only as necessary, but as principled—as comprising a valid, if painful, road to socialism. But the sanctification of measures that had begun as siege expedients, and which were in important respects contrary to previous Bolshevik expectations, and which were attracting the criticism of foreign socialists and Bolshevik doubters, created an increasingly awkward situation. By 1919-20, given the Bolsheviks' commitment to ideological tidiness, a serious attempt to make theoretical sense of the party's radical policies and their social consequences was long overdue.

It was this task that Bukharin undertook in *The Economics.* That it fell to him is explained by his gradual emergence as the man responsible for the theoretical integrity of Bolshevism. A significant body of work completed before 1917 had established him as the party's leading theoretical economist. After 1917, his arterial love of theory, his plethora of pedagogical and literary activities, and the instant canonical status of popular works such as *The ABC of Communism,*[4] written with Evgenii Preobrazhenskii and published in 1919, had already begun to cast him, at the age of thirty-one, in his familiar role of the 1920s as the official theorist of "orthodox Bolshevism."[5] A seeker of ideas ill-suited to serve as their embalmer, it was a mantle Bukharin neither sought nor wore with ease. But war communism demanded theoretical treatment. And, as Lenin had said in 1919 of another problem, "if anyone could do this, it is most of all Comrade Bukharin. . . ."[6]

If *The Economics* represented Bukharin's attempt to rationalize policies of dubious origin, it also memorialized a change in his own thinking. Before the summer of 1918 he had neither advocated nor envisaged economic policies similar to those of war communism. While to the left of Lenin on economic issues during the early months of Bolshevik rule, his own recommendations had for the most part been moderate.[7] What is important here is not that he came to embrace war communism as a viable road to socialism but that he was not alone in this. The notion (promoted by the Bolsheviks themselves after 1921) that only a few dreamers and fanatics accepted war communism as enduring policy is incorrect. It was, in fact, the sentiment of the party majority; few resisted the general euphoria.[8] What set Bukharin apart from the others, what made him seem to be the most convinced, was his literary monument to the collective folly, *The Economics of the Transition Period,* a tract which partook in the worst error of the period—the belief that "Civil war lays bare the true physiognomy of society. . . ."[9]

II

Bukharin intended *The Economics* to be the theoretical half of a two-volume study of "the process of the transformation of capitalist society into communist society." The second volume, projected as "a concrete, descriptive work on contemporary Russian economics," never appeared. Originally, he planned to co-author the study with another young Bolshevik and close friend Iurii Piatakov, but "practical tasks" (Piatakov was at the front during most of the civil war) made this impossible and the latter contributed directly to only one chapter.[10] Written rapidly and in extremely abstract language—as Bukharin noted apologetically, "almost in algebraic formulas"[11] —key ideas and concepts were frequently not fully explained and occasionally inconsistent. But as a first and audaciously brilliant attempt to go beyond the existing body of Marxist thought, the book was an immediate and lasting *succès d'estime.*

It is possible to be generous or overly critical in judging *The Economics.* Western historians have tended to dismiss it as a theoretical apology for war communism, which it was, though Bukharin's notion that it was a Marxist duty to analyze contemporary reality is surely a mitigating factor. Something more, however, accounted for its enduring esteem and for the fact that several of the book's arguments outlived war communism. Very generally, Bukharin dealt with three broad subjects or themes: the structure of modern capitalism on the eve of proletarian revolution; society in the midst of revolutionary breakdown, or the revolutionary "disequilibrated" society; and the process of establishing a new societal equilibrium out of the chaos as a phase in the transition to socialism. He mentioned Russia very rarely, but it was clear from his treatment of the second and third subjects that the Bolshevik experience since 1917 was foremost in his mind. Just as Marx had posited his findings on English capitalism as general laws, so did Bukharin believe that he was formulating universal laws of proletarian revolution.

Bukharin's treatment of neo-capitalism in *The Economics* was largely a restatement of his earlier writings on the subject. For our purposes, it is necessary to observe only that he found contemporary capitalism to be profoundly unlike the *laissez-faire* economy Marx had analyzed in three important respects. First was the widespread monopolization and trustification of economic life. Second, and closely related, the bourgeois state had become directly and actively involved in the economy as an owner and organizer. And third, as a result of these two processes, a "merging" or "fusing" of political and economic functions in capitalist society had occurred, a development which transformed the advanced capitalist economy "from *an irrational system* into *a rational organization.*" Since the major characteristic of this new system was the interventionist role of the modern state, he called it state capitalism.[12]

As he had done in his pre-1917 writings, Bukharin portrayed the state capitalist economy as an imposing assembly of productive, technological, and organizational achievements. This, however, raised a serious question about the desirability of revolution, which, in the case of Russia, had reduced economic production to a virtual fraction of the 1913 level.[13] In addition to the direct casualties of the civil war, thousands of people were dying from the most primitive of causes, hunger and cold. Consequently, the Bolsheviks were being assailed by European Social Democrats, particularly Karl Kautsky, as destroyers not builders. Marxists regarded themselves as harbingers of a socially just abundance, and this accusation hurt. A number of Bolshevik polemics had been produced in response,[14] but the charge required a more substantial and reasoned answer. *The Economics* sought to provide that answer by formulating "the costs of revolution" as a law of revolution.

Bukharin had observed earlier that the charge was reminiscent of the one leveled by the Girondins against the Jacobins, and which had driven Charlotte Corday to murder Marat.[15] His point was that great revolutions were always accompanied by destructive civil wars. His favorite illustration was that when barricades are constructed out of railway cars or telegraph poles the outcome is economic destruction.[16] But he was more intent on proving that a proletarian revolution inevitably resulted in an even greater temporary fall in production than did its bourgeois counterpart. Lenin's *State and Revolution* (and Bukharin's own writings before 1917) had established the doctrine that the bourgeois state apparatus had to be destroyed during the revolutionary process. Bukharin now argued that the merger of political and economic functions under capitalism, and the fact that the proletariat aimed at a fundamental restructuring of "production relations," meant that the onslaught against the state had to become an onslaught against the economic apparatus of capitalism. "The hierarchical relations of capitalist society" are undone; "the *disorganization* of the 'entire apparatus'" results.[17]

Bukharin enumerated four "real costs of revolution": the physical destruction or deterioration of material and living elements of production, the atomization of these elements and of sectors of the economy, and the need for unproductive consumption (civil war materials, etc.). These costs were interrelated and followed sequentially. Collectively they resulted in *"the curtailment of the process of reproduction"* (and "negative expanded reproduction") and Bukharin's main conclusion: "the production 'anarchy' . . . , 'the revolutionary disintegration of industry,' is an historically inevitable stage which no amount of lamentation will prevent."[18]

This may appear to have been an obvious point, but it apparently came as something of a revelation to many Bolsheviks. It was directly opposed to the prevailing Social Democratic assumption that the transition to socialism would be relatively painless. Kautsky and the Austrian Marxist Rudolf Hilferding had fostered this belief, particularly the latter with his argument that if the proletariat seized the six largest banks it would automatically control the economy.[19] Even some "older"—a euphemism for less radical—Bolsheviks accepted Bukharin's law only in connection with Russia, arguing that in England, for example, no serious fall in production would occur.[20] Bukharin disagreed, insisting on its universal applicability. After the introduction of NEP in 1921, he claimed that this was the basic point of *The Economics:* "The central thought of the whole book is that during the transition period the labor apparatus of society inevitably disintegrates, that reorganization presupposes disorganization, and that therefore the temporary collapse of productive forces is a law inherent to revolution." He had proved, he said in summary, "the necessity of breaking an egg to obtain an omelette."[21] Profound or not, Bolsheviks generally came to accept the "law" and to regard it as a significant discovery by Bukharin.[22]

Bukharin's law solved another problem as well. Marxists were accustomed to believing that the "objective prerequisites" of socialism "ripen" within the envelope of capitalist society, and that revolution occurs only after considerable "ripening." Maturation was measured in terms of "the level of concentration and centralization of capital" of "the aggregate 'apparatus' " of capitalist economy; the new society, it seemed, arrived as a *"deux ex machina."* By arguing that this apparatus was invariably destroyed in the process of revolution, and that therefore "*in toto* it cannot serve as the basis of the new society," Bukharin subtly dismissed the nagging question of peasant Russia's relative backwardness (unripeness). He emphasized the "human" rather than the "material" apparatus as the essential criterion of maturity: the decisive prerequisite was a certain level of "the socialization of labor" (the existence of a proletariat) and the revolutionary class's capacity to carry out "social-organizational" tasks.[23]

This argument led Bukharin to the heart of the dilemma of Bolshevik rule in an underdeveloped society, and to the previously unarticulated proposition that was to be at the center of the intra-party controversies of the 1920s—"building socialism." He rejected the traditional Marxist assumption that socialism attains almost full maturity in the womb of the old order, and thus adapted Marxism to backward Russia. He contrasted the growth of socialism to the growth of capitalism:

> They [the bourgeoisie] did not build capitalism, it built itself *[stroilsia]*. The proletariat will build socialism as an organized system, as an organized collective subject. While the process of the creation of capitalism was spontaneous *[stikhiinym]*, the process of building communism is to a significant degree a conscious, i.e., organized process. . . . The epoch of communist construction will therefore inevitably be an epoch of planned and organized work; the proletariat will solve its task as a social-economic task of building a new society. . . .[24]

III

Up to this point, Bukharin was describing a disequilibrated society, presenting a sophisticated and frequently ingenious account of the multiple rupturing of societal connections and interrelationships. Now he had to treat the emergence of a new equilibrium. The concept of equilibrium runs through most of Bukharin's theoretical work, from *The Economics* to *Historical Materialism* (1921), where he explained Marxist dialectics and social change in terms of the establishment and disturbance of equilibrium, to his famous 1928 attack on the first Five Year Plan in "Notes of An Economist." It is important to note here only that he meant a "dynamic" or "moving" equilibrium, not a static system, and that the practice of viewing society (or at least economic systems) as being in a state of equilibrium had a geneology, albeit a somewhat subterranean one, in Marxist thought. It was implicit in volume two of *Capital,* where Marx had employed static and dynamic models to explain capitalist accumulation and reproduction, and explicit in one chapter of Hilferding's *Finance Capital,* where he had used the concept and the term to expound the second volume of *Capital.*[25]

Bukharin's reliance on this precedent, and his understanding of equilibrium as a state of "evolution and growth," was spelled out in *The Economics:*

> In theoretically mastering the capitalist system of production relations, Marx proceeded from *the fact of* its existence. Once this system exists it means . . . that social demands are being satisfied, at least to the degree that people are not only not dying off, but are living, acting, and propagating themselves. In a society with a social division of labor . . . this means that there must be a certain *equilibrium* of the whole system. The necessary quantities of coal, iron, machines, cotton, linen, bread, sugar, boots, etc., etc., are produced. Living human labor is expended in accordance with all of this in the necessary quantities in relation to production, utilizing the necessary means of production. There may be all sorts of deviations and fluctuations, the whole system may be enlarged, complicated, and developed; it is in constant motion and fluctuation, but, in general and in its entirety, it is in a state of equilibrium.
>
> To find the law of this equilibrium is the basic problem of theoretical economics.[26]

Analyzing an existing equilibrium (or disequilibrium), however, was not the same as explaining how a new one was to be forged out of the wreckage of the old.

Bukharin's answer was to endorse the coercive measures of war communism and give them theoretical expression. The new equilibrium was established by replacing the destroyed links between elements of production with new ones, by restructuring "*in a new combination the dismantled social layers* . . . ." This operation was performed by the proletarian state, which statizes, militarizes, and mobilizes the productive forces of society. "The process of socialization in all of its forms" was "the function of the proletarian state."[27] Bukharin carefully pointed out that while there was a "formal" similarity between the proletarian system and state capitalism (since capitalist property was being transformed into "collective proletarian 'property' "), they were "diametrically opposite in essence."[28] Since it was no longer "surplus profit" but "surplus product" that was being created, "any sort of exploitation" was "unthinkable" *(nemyslimyi)* under the dictatorship of the proletariat. Labor conscription, for example, which under state capitalism was "the enslavement of the working masses," was now "nothing other than the . . . self-organization of the masses."[29]

Beneath this elaborate construction was the crux of Bukharin's argument: force and coercion *(nasilie* and *prinuzhdenie)* were the means by which equilibrium was to be forged out of disequilibrium. He did not avoid the harsh conclusion; an entire chapter on " 'Extra-Economic' Coercion in the Transition Period" defended the proposition:

> In the transition period, when one productive structure gives way to another, the midwife is revolutionary force. This revolutionary force must destroy the fetters on the development of society, i.e., on one side, the old forms of "concentrated force," which have become a counter-revolutionary factor—the old state and the old type of production relations. This revolutionary force, on the other side, must actively help in the formation of production relations, being a new form of "concentrated force," the state of the new class, which acts as the lever of economic revolution, altering the economic structure of society. Thus on one side force plays the role of a destructive factor; on the other, it is a force *(sila)* of cohesion, organization, and construction. The greater this "extra-economic" power is . . . the less will be "the costs" of the transition period (all other things being equal, of course), the *shorter* will be this transition period, the faster will a social equilibrium be established on a new foundation and the quicker will the . . . production curve begin to rise.

Here, too, revolutionary coercion was unlike previous " 'pure force' of the Duhring type," because it led toward "general economic development."[30]

The ugly potentialities of Bukharin's reasoning are easy to emphasize. All kinds of abuses could be and were rationalized with the argument that exploitation of the working class was not possible under a dictatorship of the proletariat. To argue that a workers' state could not by definition exploit a worker was to condone one set of evils because they were "progressive." Less obvious, perhaps, is the cogency and historical validity, at least within limits, of Bukharin's statement on the role of coercion in laying the foundations of a new social order. History has provided few (if any) examples of a society in revolutionary upheaval being stilled or restored to harmony without the use of considerable force. Unfortunately his argument was beclouded and therefore weakened by one supplementary theoretical digression and by one omission.

The digression dealt with his belief that political economy and its traditional categories were not applicable to post-capitalist society, an assumption which gave his treatment of the economics of the transition period an ultra-radical gloss. Marxism, in other words, employed "a dialectical-historical" methodology: categories and economic laws discussed by Marx related only to capitalist commodity production. Bukharin explained:

> as soon as we take an organized social economy, all the basic "problems" of political economy disappear: problems of value, price, profit and the like. Here "relations between things" and social economy are regulated not by the blind forces of the market and competition, but consciously by a . . . *plan.* Therefore here there can be a certain descriptive system on the one hand, a system of norms on the other. But there can be no place for a science studying "the blind laws of the market" since there will be no market. Thus the end of capitalist commodity society will be the end of political economy.[31]

This understanding of political economy was shared by many Marxists and, by the mid-twenties, by a majority of Bolshevik economists. It remained something of a "dogma," but also a topic of lively debate, until the 1930s when it was officially repudiated in the search for "a political economy of socialism."[32] But despite its currency, Bukharin's attempt to apply the proposition in 1920 caused considerable headshaking. In the chapter written with Piatakov, he observed that in analyzing the transition period "the old understandings of theoretical economics instantly refuse to serve"; they even "begin to misfire." Examining each category (commodity, value, price, wages), and finding each theoretically obsolete, he proposed new concepts (instead of wages, "a social-labor ration"; instead of commodity, "product"; and so forth).[33]

As a result, *The Economics* sounded more radical than it was. For while Bukharin carefully stressed that the subject of political economy—commodity production—still existed in the transition period, and that therefore the old categories were still of practical value, his theoretical glimpse into the future seriously disturbed some readers. Two problems were involved: by discarding political economy, Bukharin seemed to be saying that man was no longer constrained by objective economic laws. Although he did not argue this point, his failure to specify new objective regulators left him open to the charge of "voluntarism." Second and related was his disconcerting habit of discussing the future in the present tense.[34] In both respects, his presentation reflected the "leap-into-socialism" ideas associated with war communism.

But the most serious flaw in regard to the programmatic implications of *The Economics* was Bukharin's failure or inability to distinguish clearly between the period of disequilibrium and the period following the re-establishment of equilibrium. He spoke of the transition period as the transition to socialism, and also as the transition to a new social equilibrium, from which society would move on to socialism. Left unclear was whether the extreme measures employed to forge a new equilibrium would continue to be the norm after equilibrium was established. Occasionally he implied that this would be the case.[35] But his periodization of the transitional process distinguished between an initial period of mobilizing the fragments of the collapsed order, which he called "the economic revolution" or "primitive socialist accumulation" (a term borrowed from Vladimir Smirnov and made famous in the 1920s in a different context by Preobrazhenskii), and a subsequent period of "technical revolution," which would witness an evolutionary, harmonious flowering of production.[36]

Put another way, Bukharin's understanding of equilibrium seemed to be in conflict with his analysis of the transition period. If a state of equilibrium, capitalist or otherwise,[37] implied proportionality between the elements and spheres of production, then the measures of war communism would have to become obsolete at some stage in the transition period. Bukharin's explanation, in which he tried to have it both ways, illustrated the confusion:

> *The postulate of equilibrium* is invalid . . . . There is neither proportionality between production and consumption, nor between different branches of production . . . nor between human elements of the system. Therefore it is radically wrong to transfer to the transition period categories, concepts, and laws adequate to a state of equilibrium. One may object that insofar as society has not perished, there is equilibrium. Such reasoning, however, would be correct if the period of time we are examining was conceived of as being of great length. A society cannot live *long* outside equilibrium, it dies. But this social system for a certain time can be in an "abnormal" state, i.e., outside a state of equilibrium.

This was open to two interpretations: either the transition to socialism would be relatively brief; or Bukharin meant only the transition to an equilibrated state from which socialism would evolve. It is reasonable to assume that in 1920 he believed the former. After 1921, however, he offered the second interpretation.[38]

The dilemma implicit in Bukharin's reasoning was particularly evident in his remarks on agriculture. Like most Bolsheviks, he previously had said little that was meaningful on the peasant's role in the new society. The enormity of the agrarian problem was now clear to him. The need to re-establish equilibrium between town and country, he explained, was "decisive for the fate of mankind . . . the most important and *complex* question."[39] His solution hardly suited his description of the problem. Here, too, he formulated the key role of coercion, especially in the forcible requisitioning of grain. It was most crucial, however, at an early stage of the revolution, while the transition period as a whole was to be characterized by *"a secret or more or less open struggle between the organizing tendencies of the proletariat and the commodity-anarchical tendencies of the peasantry."* He did not specify the form of this struggle or its arena. Significantly, however, he did exclude collective forms of agricultural production as the primary means of bringing the peasantry into the "organizing process," arguing instead that "for the main mass of *small producers,* their drawing into the organized apparatus is possible mainly through *the sphere of exchange. . . .*"[40]

The remark was a tantalizing adumbration of Bukharin's later theory of "growing into socialism" through the market, the lynchpin of his cautious, evolutionary agrarian policies of the 1920s–but without its essential mechanism. For while he excluded meaningful collectivization, he also excluded market ("free trade") and "monetary-credit" links between town and country. In 1920, he still accepted the state "organs of distribution and procurement" as the basic intermediary between the industrial city and the small-peasant countryside.[41] The problem should have been clear: without a commodity market, what was to encourage the peasant to produce and deliver a surplus? Bukharin spoke of the middle peasant's "two souls"–one inclined toward capitalism, one toward socialism–and presumably hoped that the good soul would volunteer surplus grain. The alternative to this dubious likelihood was a system of permanent requisitioning. One of the book's rare pessimistic notes suggested that Bukharin saw the quandary: "The Revolution [in Russia] triumphed easily because the proletariat, striving toward communism, was supported by the peasantry, who moved against the landlord. But this same peasantry turns out to be the greatest brake in the period of constructing communist production relations."[42] That, of course, was the Bolshevik dilemma, and the blind side of war communism.

IV

Final judgment on a book like *The Economics*–so much a child of its time–should take into account its reception as well as its contents. That its esteem outlived war communism was due to Bukharin's innovative treatment of themes which were compatible with the post-1921 view of war communism as a regrettable but necessary episode: the structure of neocapitalism, the "costs of revolution," the concept of "building socialism," and the historical limitations of political economy. Although some Bolsheviks regarded parts of the book as "debatable from a Marxist point of view," none questioned its considerable influence.[43] Indeed, in one quarter of the party, it was greeted with undisguised hostility, because it did promise to be influential.

A scathing attack by M. S. Ol'minskii, one of the older, less radical party leaders edged aside in 1917 by the young Bolshevik Left (of which Bukharin was the most prominent representative), appeared shortly after the introduction of NEP. It burned with resentment. Ol'minskii accused Bukharin of having abandoned Marxist political economy for "the Bukharinist method of penal servitude and shooting," and of "revising Marxism from the Left." In the campaign to give the book the status of *The ABC of Communism,* he saw the further machinations of "that part of the party" who were delirious with "the enthusiasm of power," and for whom "nothing was impossible."[44] Bukharin, to his credit, responded in a light vein, reprimanding Ol'minskii for his charges of "revisionism."[45]

With war communism then in the process of being dismantled and discredited, Ol'minskii scored some easy points; but he was mistaken or disingenuous in identifying the book's stance on war communism with Bukharin's generation, as was vividly illustrated by Lenin's private notes on *The Economics* and his *"recensio academica,"* written on May 31, 1920, for the Communist Academy, which had published the book. Lenin's evaluation was subsequently distorted by the circumstances surrounding the publication of his notes, which rested in an archive until Stalin's victory over Bukharin in 1929, when they were hastily disinterred as part of the campaign to destroy Bukharin's theoretical credentials.[46] Stalinist commentators naturally dwelt on the negative comments, of which there were many, but this spoke more of the dissimilarities of Bukharin and Lenin as intellectuals than of the book itself.

The great majority of Lenin's objections centered on Bukharin's terminology. He particularly disliked what he called the use of "Bogdanovist gibberish"—a reference to the lapsed Bolshevik philosopher Aleksandr Bogdanov—instead of "human language," and, closely related in Lenin's mind, Bukharin's penchant for the words "sociological" and "sociology." Over and over he greeted them with "ugh!," "ha, ha," *"karaul,"* "eclecticism," and at one point, "it is good that the 'sociologist' Bukharin finally puts the word 'sociologist' in ironical quotation marks! Bravo!"[47] Lenin's terminological reprimands reflected the very different intellectual orientation of the two men: Bukharin was deeply interested in and influenced by contemporary sociological thought (as *Historical Materialism* would show), and regarded Bogdanov's recent work on "organizational science" as "interesting"; Lenin instinctively distrusted modern schools of social theory and had an abiding dislike for anything associated with Bogdanov.[48] When Bukharin said something was "theoretically interesting," Lenin retorted with scorn. Lenin's other objections were more substantial: some related to previous areas of disagreement such as the structure of modern capitalism; and some rightly focused on those parts of Bukharin's argument which were too abstract and in need of clarification or empirical evidence. They were pertinent comments from a friendly and sympathetic critic.

But all Lenin's reservations paled against his ecstatic praise for the most "war communist" sections of *The Economics.* Almost every passage on the role of the new state, statization in general, militarization and mobilization met with "very good," often in three languages, as did Bukharin's formulation of disequilibrium and "building socialism." Most striking, Lenin's greatest enthusiasm was reserved for the chapter on the role of coercion. He filled these margins with superlatives and at the end wrote, "Now this chapter is superb!," a judgment more representative of his overall evaluation.[49] He concluded his summary review with the hope that "small" shortcomings "will disappear from following editions, which are so necessary for our reading public and which will serve to the even greater honor of the Academy; we congratulate the Academy on the splendid work of its member."[50] Ol'minskii feared the book's influence; Lenin looked forward to future editions. There were to be no other editions, and Lenin's review was not published.

V

Bukharin once said of Pokrovskii's historical work, "he who makes no mistakes, does nothing."[51] It was a fitting epigram for *The Economics.* Its critical shortcoming reflected the defect in war communism. Bukharin's analysis was mute on what were to be the long-term economic problems of Soviet Russia and his own chief concerns after 1921: the problems of investment and accumulation, of the relationship between industry and agriculture, and of expanding the entire economy, quantitatively and qualitatively. The "prose of economic development," as Ol'minskii put it, was absent. Hosannas to the advent of a "conscious regulator" did not constitute an economic program. *The Economics* was really about disequilibrium and the costs of revolution; and Bukharin's error, as he was soon to realize, was to generalize on this experience for the entire transition period. His charge against the Social Democrats applied to him as well; for while he added a destructive stage in the transformation process, he, too, left the impression that socialism would come as a *deus ex machina.* It was indeed "as if ivied maidens and garlanded youths were to herald the four horsemen of the apocalypse."[52]

WIKTOR SUKIENNICKI

An Abortive Attempt at International Unity of the Workers' Movement (The Berlin Conference of the Three Internationals, 1922)

I. UNITY IN THEORY AND PRACTICE

Unity in thought and deed, a complete solidarity of all people in common action, is one of the most tempting ideals of humanity. It has never been achieved in the past, and will hardly be achieved in the future. Human beings are still rather quarrelsome and bellicose, and the angelic salutation of nearly twenty centuries ago: "Peace on the earth to men of goodwill" is far from being realized in practice. In wartime, however, close unity within each of the opposing camps is even more important than it is in times of peace. Thus, the great apostles of class war, Marx and Engels, preached unity and coined the popular slogan: "Workingmen of the world, unite!"

The first attempt to apply this slogan failed after roughly a decade. The so-called First International, the International Workingmen's Association, established in 1864, was officially dissolved in 1876 as a result of a fundamental split between the Bakuninists and the Marxists. Re-established in 1889, the Second International did not pass the crucial test of the First World War, when individual national solidarities prevailed over international working-class solidarity. After the war, great efforts were made to reassemble the former International which had disintegrated further into groups supporting the war effort (the right-wing), those who opposed it (the left-wing), and those who remained neutral (center). Many were against the re-establishment of a Second International to be led by those who had failed the test in 1914 and had "betrayed" the working-class cause. During the war, the oppositionists met in Zimmerwald (September, 1915) and Kienthal (April, 1916) to discuss possible unity, but did not dare to proclaim formally the foundation of a new Third International. However, after the first attempts at reconstitution of the broken Second International had been made, and a conference for this purpose had gathered in Geneva from February 3 to February 10, 1919, the leaders of the victorious Russian Revolution made the fateful move and the creation of the Third International was officially proclaimed in Moscow in March, 1919.

Hence the problem of the workers' "unity" became even more complicated because of the rivalry of the two "unifying" centers to which a third—the intermediate "Second-and-a-half International"—was promptly added.

II. "UNITY" BASED ON THE RUSSIAN MODEL

The proclamation of the establishment of the Third International in March, 1919, was, in fact, a repetition on an international scale of Lenin's strategy and tactics in the Russian socialist movement. From its beginning, the Russian socialist movement was, in theory, pledged to "the workers' unity," "the proletarian unity," and "the socialist unity." But in practice it had always been split into multiple factions quarrelling and fighting with each other.

The first attempt to unify all Russian Marxists into one organized party had been made in March, 1898, at a conference in Minsk. The following year Bernstein's famous book was published in Germany starting the world-wide "revisionist" schism among the Marxists. Lenin, exiled in Siberia at the time, carefully observed the events in the socialist movement, studied the appropriate materials, and reflected upon adequate methods of implementing his theoretical conceptions of a radical transformation of the whole social, political, and economic order. Lenin's idea of a paper, published uncensored abroad (born at this time), was shared by two of his closest friends, Martov and Potresov, as well as by the leaders of the Russian Social Democratic movement abroad, Plekhanov, Aksel'rod, and Zasulich; in August, 1900, they formed the editorial board of *Iskra* (Spark).

On behalf of the board, Lenin wrote in a declaration on the proposed publication that its aim would be to "establish and consolidate unity among all Russian Social Democrats." However "before we can unite, and in order that we may unite, we must first of all draw firm and definite lines of demarcation. Otherwise, our unity will be purely fictitious, it will conceal the prevailing confusion and hinder its radical elimination."[1] After a year and a half of preparatory work, during which the editorial board of *Iskra* was often divided on many issues, a congress was summoned in July, 1903. The result of the congress was not the intended unification of all Russian Social Democrats but the momentous split into the Bolsheviks and the Mensheviks.

Although at the end of the congress the majority (Bolsheviks) seemed to be on Lenin's side, shortly afterward he was abandoned by nearly everybody. Deprived of *Iskra,* Lenin, with Bogdanov-Malinovskii and his brother-in-law, Lunacharskii, founded another paper, *Vpered* (Forward), and succeeded in constituting a "Bureau of the Majority's Committees" at a meeting of twenty-two persons, in August, 1904, in Geneva. This Bureau summoned the pure-Bolshevik "Third" Congress, in April, 1905, in London, attended by twenty-four persons. A larger Menshevik conference was simultaneously convened in Geneva.

Further discords with his new friends and the fact, revealed during the 1905 Revolution in Russia, that Bolshevik influence was hardly predominant there among the working masses striving spontaneously for "workers' unity," made Lenin a little more cooperative. He agreed to call a new "unity congress" with the Mensheviks, in April, 1906, in Stockholm; among its 112 delegates, the Bolsheviks formed a minority of forty-six.

According to subsequent reminiscences of Lunacharskii, at the time of the preparatory work for the congress Lenin, with "his subtle smile," had said to him:

> If we have the majority in the Central Committee or on the editorial board of the central organ, we will demand the strictest discipline. We will insist on complete subordination of the Mensheviks for the party's unity. If their petty-bourgeois nature will not allow them to go with us, let them take the responsibility for the split *(odium rasriva)* in the party's unity, which was achieved at such a high price. Then, certainly, they will take from the united party considerably fewer workers than they brought in.

When Lunacharskii asked what Lenin's tactics would be if, after all, the Mensheviks got the majority at the congress, Lenin answered with a "somewhat mysterious smile": "it depends on the circumstances. In any case, we will not permit a noose to be put around us because of unity, and we will by no means allow the Mensheviks to lead us on a rope."[2] According to Bertram Wolfe, "Lenin considered himself 'the only true master and exponent of an infallible science called Marxism'," and "was not merely ready to split any organization on any difference that he had come to think important; he was ready to split and discredit and wreck every organization he could not control."[3]

When, in connection with the electoral campaign to the Second Duma in 1907 Lenin was accused by the Central Committee before a party court of honor of using a "poisoned weapon" against his "Menshevik comrades," he declared that he "will *always conduct* a struggle of *extermination*" against the "political enemies."[4]

At that time and during the following decade, it was just a literary metaphor, but, after 1917, it could be—and was—a genuine reality.

The fictitious "unity" of the party was tolerated by Lenin for some five years. In January, 1912, he gathered fifteen of his most trusted partisans in Prague and called the gathering a general congress of the party. This "congress" formally excluded from the party all but Lenin's groups and "elected" a new Central Committee with Lenin at its head. On Trotsky's initiative, a conference of the "excluded" groups was called in August, 1912 in Vienna, and they decided to indict Lenin for this peculiar *coup d'état* before the International Socialist Bureau in Brussels. In an attempt to straighten out their mutual relations, the Bureau summoned the representatives of all Russian socialist groups to Brussels on June 16, 1914. Fourteen groups were present; only one was Bolshevik.[5]

The coming of World War I and the subsequent Russian Revolution not only destroyed those plans for socialist unity in Russia but resulted in Lenin becoming the head of the Soviet Russian state. In this state, the soviets, not the party, theoretically "united" all the working people and in the initial stage of the revolution, they represented all shades of leftist socialist opinion. At first, the "anti-Bolshevik bloc" held the majority in them, including their leading organs (with all groups and parties being represented on a proportional basis). This method was so firmly established that after the October upheaval many Bolsheviks were of the opinion that the new Soviet government should be formed in a similar way and should be a "coalition" socialist government. Lenin did not share this opinion and did his best not only to keep his "political enemies" out of the government but also to reduce at first, and then to eliminate, their representation in all the soviet and other official organizations.

The non-Bolshevik socialist parties and groups were for some years tolerated in the Bolshevik-dominated state under the official assumption that they represented insignificant minorities of the "working people's" opinion. Although most of them accepted the basic idea of the Soviet state and were ready to collaborate with the Bolsheviks on a democratic basis, many of their leaders and most of their active workers were arrested during the Civil War by state security organs, on charges of connection or sympathy with the counterrevolutionary Whites. Such was the practical application of the theory of the "poisoned weapon" in "a struggle of extermination" against all "political enemies" formulated by Lenin as early as 1907.

At the Eighth All-Russian Congress of Soviets on December 23, 1920, Lenin said in a speech following the debates on his report on foreign and domestic policy that

> now we actually saw that in the epoch of the social revolution the proletariat can only be united by an extreme revolutionary Marxist party, only through a ruthless struggle against all other parties. (Stormy applause.)[6]

It was after the Civil War that Lenin completely eliminated all the dissidents from the party and formally outlawed all the non-Bolshevik socialist parties in Russia. In March, 1921, after the Kronstadt revolt, at the Tenth Party Congress, his famous resolution on party unity prohibited the formation of any faction or group. In a booklet, *O prodovol'stvennom naloge*, written in April and published in May, 1921, he stated the necessity for a regime of terror.

> After the imperialist war of 1914-1918 . . . it is impossible not to apply terror despite hypocrites and phrasemongers. It is either . . . White-Guard bourgeois terror, or it is the Red proletarian terror. There is no in between. There is none and there will not be any of the "third" side. . . .[7]

He also publicly announced that he would keep all the non-Bolshevik Russian Socialists–the Mensheviks and the Socialist Revolutionaries–"carefully in prison" or banish them "to Berlin, to Martov."[8] These were the last steps on the long road of building a "monolithic" party and achieving the "complete unity" of the working people in Russia.

According to Lenin's speech at the Third Congress of the Comintern, on July 1, 1921, a similar pattern was to be applied in all other countries.[9]

III. THE WESTERN SOCIALISTS AND SOVIET RUSSIA

The Russian Revolution and the subsequent establishment of the "First Workers' and Peasants' State" made a deep impression throughout the world, particularly among the "working people"; socialist and labor parties became basically pro-Russian. Several of them were reluctant to take part in attempts to re-establish the former International, for practically nobody wanted to separate himself from the Russian comrades. At the first post-war international socialist conference in Berne (February 3-10, 1919),[10] there had been differences of opinion on the socialist attitude towards democracy and dictatorship, although everybody expressed great sympathy and interest in the Russian Revolution, and the conference agreed to send a special commission to Russia "to study carefully the political and economic situation in Russia, and to present to the International a detailed and objective report." While the minority at the conference, led by F. Adler and J. Longuet, had done their best not to shut the reconstituted International's door in the faces of the Russian Bolsheviks, the latter refused categorically to have anything in common with any "betrayer of the working class." They not only hurried to establish their own Third International in March, 1919, but at its Second Congress in 1920 put a padlock at the entrance in the form of the "Twenty-one Conditions."[11]

Such an attitude hardly facilitated the efforts of the partisans of "an honorable compromise" in the quest for a genuine "unification of the world-wide forces of socialism and democracy." The *Constitution and Rules* of the British Independent Labor Party (ILP) explicitly stated that it worked for this end "in co-operation with the Socialist International."[12] Ramsay MacDonald, the leader of this party after August 4, 1914, "did not fear to declare war on war," and also publicly stated in *L'Humanité* of April 14, 1919, that he was "very much distressed" by the foundation of the independent Moscow International:

> The Socialist International at the present time is sufficiently wide for all types of socialist thought, and in spite of all the theoretical and practical differences created by Bolshevism, I see no reason why the Left Wing should break away from the Center and form an independent group.[13]

Neither MacDonald's article nor Lenin's answer to it, written in rather abusive language,[14] brought any definite solution. According to Philip Snowden, the Chairman of the ILP in the 1918-20 period, the ILP membership (which in 1919 was estimated at "not less than 80,000")[15] was "acutely divided" on the question of the International: a moderate section supported the rebuilding of the Second; "a not inconsiderable section, composed in the main of young men and women" was for the Third; and there was "a third section dissatisfied with both the moderate policy of the Second International and the extreme [policy of the Third]." "It looked at one time as though these divisions would disrupt the ILP."[16] This did not happen, and at their next conference in Glasgow in April, 1920, after animated debates the ILP by a majority of 529 to 144 decided to sever all its connections with the Second International and, without affiliating itself immediately to the Third (206 delegates voted for this solution), to inquire and consult with Moscow and every other left party before the next special conference of the ILP assembled in order finally to solve this problem.[17]

The situation in several other important socialist parties–Italian, Swiss, American, German Independent, etc.–was very similar to that of the British ILP; they refused to send their representatives to the conferences in Berne (February, 1919), Amsterdam (April, 1919), and Lucerne (August, 1919) in order to reconstitute the former International, but were willing to go to Moscow, where the Second Congress of the Third International was summoned in the summer of 1920.

On December 10, 1919, an extraordinary British Trade Union Congress passed a resolution demanding from the British Government "the right to an independent and impartial inquiry into the industrial, political, and economic conditions in Russia." British passports and Soviet entry-visas were issued to members of the special delegation of the Trade Union Congress and the Labor Party (seven men and two women, one of whom was Mrs. Snowden) and to the two delegates of the ILP and some journalists (among whom was Bertrand Russell) accompanying them.[18] This delegation left England on April 27, 1920, and spent over a month in Russia, returning to England in several individual groups in the second half of June or July, 1920. As this was the first official foreign delegation to Russia, a special train was sent from Petrograd to the frontier to meet them. According to Mrs. Snowden's report it was

> gaily decorated with red bunting, fervent mottoes, and the green branches of trees. The train was attended by a number of Red Guards and Bashkir cavalrymen in gorgeous purple uniforms, with wonderful cloaks and long swords. From Reval to Narva we had been just a plain, ordinary Cook's Tourist Party. From the Russian frontier to the end of our visit we were the Royal Family![19]

After a few days in Petrograd, the party went on to Moscow where it was officially welcomed at the railway station by Kamenev; its members dined with Chicherin and met with Trotsky at the Bolshoi Opera and Ballet Theater. The next day, May 18, a military parade of the Moscow garrison was organized in honor of the foreign guests, and in the evening a solemn meeting of the Moscow Soviet took place in the Bolshoi Theater at which a Menshevik, R. Abramovich, was given the floor, along with several Bolsheviks and guest speakers.

During their stay in Russia the members of the British delegation had no difficulty in meeting, not only with representatives of the Soviet authorities and the Bolshevik Party, trade unions, Red Army and Navy, and the Third International, but also with the official representatives of the Mensheviks, the Socialist Revolutionaries and other parties, as well as "a very large number of private persons . . . representing the professional classes and many of the former bourgeoisie and nobility."[20] The non-Bolshevik Russian socialists provided the British guests with several memoranda on the political and economic situation in Russia, on the situation of Russian workers, on the trade unions, on the activities of the *Cheka* etc.; some of these memoranda and statements influenced or were included in the delegation's official *Report.*[21]

In order to give the members of the delegation a more intimate acquaintance with the actual situation in Soviet Russia, they were invited to attend a meeting of the Moscow printers' trade union which, like the trade unions of chemists and civil servants, was not yet dominated by the Bolsheviks. The Moscow printers' meeting was in honor of the British guests and was open to the public. It was officially advertised and widely publicized and on May 23, 1920, the great hall of the Moscow Conservatory of Music was filled to overflowing. There was a rather critical report by M. S. Kefali-Kammermacher on the condition of the printers in Soviet Russia: "As in the time of the Czar's government, the printers are forced to print, not their own thoughts, but calumnies against themselves."[22] This was followed by no less critical speeches (among others by a representative of the Menshevik Central Committee, F. I. Dan), which were enthusiastically corroborated by the audience. Then, at the end of the meeting, its chairman, a printers' union officer, A. F. Deviatkin, announced that there was one more speaker who could not reveal his name because he was hunted by the police. The audience loudly demanded that the floor be given him, and—as reported in the delegation's *Report:*

> in response to tremendous applause and shouts for his name, [the anonymous speaker] came down to the front of the platform, at the conclusion of the speech, and announced: "I am Tchernoff." The meeting sprang to its feet and cheered. Tchernoff then escaped, while the entrances to the hall were guarded to prevent pursuit. . . .[23]

This incident created a great impression and was widely commented on; it brought about rather serious consequences both for the Moscow printers and the Soviet people in general: the printers' union was dissolved and most of its former officers were arrested during the night of June 17.[24] Subsequently the other trade unions had to submit to more severe control and in the following few months the last remnants of political freedom in Soviet Russia were liquidated.

Before the latter process was completed or, rather, while it was still in its early stages, the Second Congress of the Comintern gathered in Moscow. It was attended by a large number of foreign delegates, not all of whom were communists. Some of them established contact not only with the official Comintern and Bolshevik representatives in Moscow but—like the British delegation before them—also with the remnants of the Russian non-Bolshevik socialists. Most of the Italians, Serrati excepted, were not impressed by their informal meetings with members of the Menshevik Central Committee, but the German Independent Socialists, Dittmann and Crispien, were so impressed by their talks with Martov and Abramovich (who spoke German fluently), that they asked them to come to the German Independents' Congress to be held in Halle in October, 1920. This congress was to decide definitely the problem of the Independents' adherence to the Comintern; Zinoviev and Lozovskii from the Bolshevik side were also invited.

After the invitation was formally confirmed by the German USPD, the Mensheviks decided to accept it, announced this decision in an "Open Letter" delivered to most of the delegates to the Comintern Congress, and asked for passports to go abroad. The Soviet authorities hesitated, and the question was brought before the Bolshevik Central Committee for a decision on principle. According to rumors in Moscow, despite opposition from several Central Committee members, Lenin's opinion prevailed that the removal of the "minority opposition" leaders from Moscow and from Russia in general would facilitate the ultimate "unification" of the "working people" under Bolshevik leadership, and the question of passports was decided affirmatively. Martov left Russia at the end of September, 1920; Abramovich, who was accompanied by his family, received his passport a few weeks later. In both cases it was explicitly stated on the passports that they had been issued "according to the decision of the RKP(b) Central Committee."[25]

Several foreign delegates who attended the Second Congress of the Comintern were not impressed by either their personal experiences in Russia or by the rigid "Twenty-one Conditions" voted upon by this congress, and, after returning home, publicly stated disapproval. In particular, Dittmann's articles on the experiences of the German workers who voluntarily emigrated to the "First Workers' and Peasants' State," first published in Berlin in *Freiheit* on August 31 and September 1, 1920 and then reprinted in several other languages, had worldwide repercussions.[26] On September 2 a correspondent of the London *Daily News* named Segrew dispatched a radiotelegram to Lenin in which he said:

> The reports of the French and German Socialist Delegations, who recently returned from Russia, did more damage to your cause, than the whole anti-Bolshevik propaganda during the last years . . . . The report published here by the German Independent Socialist Dittmann is even more harmful to you.[27]

In his direct answer to Segrew, written on September 8, Lenin said:

> it is obvious that the Kautskyites, like Crispien and Dittmann, do not like Bolshevism. It would be sad if such men did like us. . . . The Third Com-

> munist International would be poor if it accepted in its ranks the Dittmanns of Germany, France or any other type. . . .

On September 24, in a "letter to the German and French workers on account of the debates at the Second Congress of the Communist International," he stated that

> only the split with such and similar people [as Crispien and Dittmann] will create the international unity of the revolutionary proletariat *against* the bourgeoisie and for its abolition.[28]

Even more violent language was used by Radek in a pamphlet, *The Mask Has Fallen,* published by the Communist International in Germany:

> Your reports become weapons not only of the Anti-Bolshevik League . . . but also of the international bourgeoisie which directs them against Soviet Russia; they become weapons which are to activate cannons and tanks against the Russian workers. . . . Hands off Soviet Russia, you hypocrites and traitors! No honest worker believes you when you lie about Soviet Russia, and no honest worker will believe you when you feign sympathy for Soviet Russia. . . . Our slogan is not an understanding with you but a struggle against you until your destruction—you slaves and lackeys of the bourgeoisie, you traitors to the German and Russian proletariat![29]

The style and tone of the publications supporting the foreign delegates' position were quite different. An active USPD worker, Tony Sender, wrote in a pamphlet entitled *The Dictatorship Over the Proletariat or the Dictatorship of the Proletariat:*

> Is the Communist International *the* real *de facto* International? With most painful regret we say that this is not so. . . . This is why it must be once more underscored that the question is not "for or against Moscow" but "for or against the conditions," and our answer is: for Moscow, but against the impossible conditions which hinder the revolution.[30]

IV. INTERNATIONAL WORKERS' UNION—THE "SECOND-AND-A-HALF" INTERNATIONAL

The verbal duel between Zinoviev and Martov, the latter handicapped by illness, at the Congress of Halle in October, 1920, was followed by a split in the USPD: 236 delegates voted for the acceptance of the Comintern's "Twenty-one Conditions," 156 against.[31]

The example of the Germans proved decisive for the French and Italian parties at their congresses held respectively in Tours in December, 1920, and in Leghorn in January, 1921. The majority of Frenchmen joined the Comintern unconditionally. The majority of Italians, led by Serrati, while professing unfaltering allegiance to the program of the Comintern, refused to depart from the party tradition of tolerance for divergent opinions and did not accept the twenty-first "condition." After their inquiry in Moscow, the

British Independents, at their conference at Southport in March, 1921, also refused to accept the "Twenty-one Conditions," by 521 votes against 97, a decision which resulted in an exodus of some 5,000 of their members who joined the "United" Communist Party of Great Britain established at a conference in Leeds in January, 1921.[32]

Refusal to accept the Comintern's "Twenty-one Conditions" was by no means an indication of acceptance of the program of the rebuilders of the Second International. Neither French and Italian Socialists nor German and British Independents took part in the Geneva Congress of July-August, 1920, at which the Second International was formally reconstituted. As partisans of genuine unity of the world proletariat, they deplored its division between the two Internationals, and most of them welcomed an initiative put forward as early as the fall of 1919 by a leader of the Swiss Socialist Party and participant at the Zimmerwald and Kienthal conferences, Robert Grimm. He advocated the "reconstruction" of the real International, which would absorb the old Second and the new Third Internationals. In particular, at their Glasgow Conference of April, 1920, the British Independents formally seconded the Swiss initiative and invited

> the Swiss Party to arrange for a consultation regarding the possibility of the re-establishment of one' all-inclusive International for the purpose of formulating a basis for an International which, while making a quite definite announcement of our Socialist objective, would allow the national sections to adapt their politics to the differing political and industrial conditions in the various countries.[33]

On their part the German Independents decided, on October 29, 1920, to invite all the socialist parties not belonging to either International to a conference in Berne to take place on December 5, 1920; the Austrian Social Democratic Congress passed a resolution on November 7, 1920, offering Vienna as a place for a conference which would "not establish a new Fourth International but would look for ways and means leading to the establishment of a world organization of the working class in which the class-conscious proletariat of all countries is united."[34]

The result of these conferences was the establishment in 1921 of the International Working Union of Socialist Parties, "not an International embracing the whole revolutionary proletariat, but a means to create such an International," according to paragraph 1 of its *Rules.*

The Russian Social Democratic Labor Party (Mensheviks) became an outstanding member of the so-called Vienna Union (or Second-and-a-half International), along with the British and German Independents and the French and Austrian socialists. Martov and Abramovich did not return to Russia after their trip to Halle, but settled in Berlin. They established contact with those of the former Russian socialist emigres who did not return to Russia after the revolution, constituted the party's Delegation Abroad, and started the publication of *Sotsialisticheskii vestnik* (Socialist Courier–the first issue appeared in February, 1921, the last in 1965), which during its more than forty years of existence was one of the world's leading socialist papers. Despite their precarious situation of exile from their own country, the Mensheviks' actions were sometimes very successful and, owing to the generally pro-Russian attitude in Western left-wing circles, were not without their effect on the Kremlin. In particular, their vigorous political campaign of protest against the imprisonment of the Mensheviks in Russia was so effective that Moscow decided by the middle of January, 1922, to give most of the arrested Mensheviks a "free choice" between the two alternatives suggested by Lenin in the spring of 1921. (See above p. 207.) Several of the prisoners, as for example, G. Y. Aronson, F. I. Dan, B. I. Nicolaevsky, S. M. Schwarz and others, preferred banishment and went "to Berlin, to Martov" where they substantially reinforced the *Sotsialisticheskii vestnik* and the Delegation Abroad, and also the "Second-and-a-Half International."

V. THE SECOND INTERNATIONAL'S ATTEMPTS FOR "UNITY" THROUGH THE BRITISH LABOR PARTY

Having proclaimed the formal reconstitution of the Second International, the 1920 Geneva Congress did not consider its work completed. It voted upon a special resolution in which "in order to obtain a complete exploration of the possibilities of securing a representative International," it appealed to its

> British Section to accept the responsibility of acting as a negotiating body charged with the duty of approaching national Socialist and Labor bodies not represented at this Conference, and taking such steps as may be considered necessary to secure their adherence.[35]

After some hesitation, the British Labor Party accepted this "responsibility" and, in December, 1920, addressed a letter "to the Socialist and Communist Parties of the World" in which it pleaded for a "Unified International" and expressed its readiness to "conduct some preliminary consultations and then consider how we can best fulfill the responsibilities imposed upon us by the Geneva Conference." [36]

According to the *Report* presented at the British Labor Party Congress in Brighton in June, 1921,

> There has been no response to this appeal from the parties which seceded from the Second International in order to negotiate with the Communist International. On the contrary, the divisions in the International Socialist movement have been consolidated by the formation of the Vienna Union . . . [and] the French Socialists, the German Independents and the British I.L.P. are associated with it . . . [and] have engaged not to enter into any separate negotiations for joining with other International organizations.[37]

After the debates on this *Report,* the Brighton Congress passed a resolution

> that in view of the present position of the Labor Movement throughout Europe and the changes in the International Socialist Secretariat, [which was transferred to London], this Conference instructs the Executive to take steps to secure that the position of the Second International shall be strengthened, that its democratic foundations as opposed to dictatorship shall be accepted, and that invitations shall be sent out to all Labor and Socialist bodies throughout the world, inviting them to attend a conference from which a comprehensive International may arise; this Conference also calls for a consultation between the Vienna International Committee and the Executive of the Second International Committee to promote unity and prevent further division.[38]

This resolution was communicated without delay to the Vienna Union and the Second International. The latter replied positively while the former debated the problem at an enlarged meeting of its Bureau in Frankfurt, on July 8-11, 1921.[39] In a letter addressed to the British Labor Party on July 14, 1921, the Vienna Union replied that, in principle, it was in agreement with the object of creating a comprehensive Labor International. The International, however, could only be created on the basis of fundamental conceptions common to all, and unfortunately, in their view, this community of fundamental conceptions did not yet exist.

> An obvious symptom of this, is the antagonism existing between the principles of the Second International and those of the Parties affiliated to our . . . Union . . . , which [antagonism] is, in a word, to be traced back to the antagonism between the reformist and revolutionary conceptions of the class struggle.

For these reasons, the Vienna Union considered that the time for convoking a conference on an extended basis had not yet come. On the other hand, they willingly accepted the British Labor Party invitation to meet and discuss this entire problem, independent of the planned general conference.[40]

The consultative meeting between the Labor Party Executive and the Vienna Bureau took place on October 19-20, 1921 in London. The Vienna Union members insisted that the Communist parties be invited to any proposed general conference on the restitution of the International, while the British Labor Party did not propose, for the moment, to invite the Communists because their methods were so different as to make any cooperation impossible. No agreement was reached. The two points of view were subsequently embodied in a written declaration by the Vienna Union and a rejoinder by the Secretary of the British Labor Party.[41]

On November 22-23, 1921, at a meeting of the Second International Executive in Brussels, the report of the British Labor Party's meeting with the Vienna Union was discussed and it was agreed that, in view of the unsettled differences of opinion, no immediate results of the negotiations initiated by the British Labor Party were to be expected; the obstacles to international unity were still very serious.[42] However, they were to continue to try to create a frame of mind favorable to the re-establishment of unity by common action, in Western Europe at least, between the parties affiliated to the different Internationals. Since the problem of reparations was one of those that most directly concerned the working people of the war-devastated countries, it was agreed that if the French Socialist Party would take the initiative in calling a conference of all the workers' parties of the countries directly affected, the parties belonging to the Second International would not refuse to attend. Thus, the right-wing opposition to any direct contact with the Communists was, at least partly, overcome.

VI. THE COMINTERN'S "NEW TACTICS"

The Comintern leaders in Moscow carefully watched all the moves of the British Labor Party for a rapprochement between the Vienna Union and the Second International. On August 1, 1921, the so-called "Little Bureau" of the Comintern's Executive Committee decided to publish a manifesto "For the Unification of the World Proletariat, against the Social-Traitors' Union," denouncing both the attempts to reach an agreement and their failure and appealing to the workers to unify under the Communist banner: "They wish to exploit the workers' tendency for unity for their dirty little business, for a filthy union of the Social-patriotic and independent leaders. . . . Let yourself go with us; . . . against Jouhaux and Renaudel, against Noske, Scheidemann and Ebert, against Renner and Vandervelde, against Dittmann and other bourgeois valets! . . . Down with their unity, directed against the revolutionary struggle of the proletariat."[43]

The Communist leaders realized, however, that such appeals and manifestos did not work in practice, and where real, concrete issues were at stake (for example, the problems of the famine in Russia or of the "White Terror" in Spain and Yugoslavia), they did not hesitate to approach the European socialists, proposing common action. These precedents were quoted by Zinoviev when, at the full Executive Committee of the Comintern session of December 4, 1921, he inaugurated the great debates on a radical change in the Comintern's tactics with regard to the question of the proletarian "united front."

According to Zinoviev, the "revolutionary tide" in the West had reached its ebb and the reflux had begun; the masses, which had been passive and inclined to the right, now were anxious for action and were inclined to the left. They were demanding the unification of all forces for this action, and viewed the "united front" of workers' organizations as a condition for success. The Communists could not ignore this spontaneous tendency of the masses; they must exploit it for their own aims. After a short analysis of the actual situation in Germany, Italy, France, England, Switzerland, and the United States, Zinoviev came to the conclusion that "Menshevism and

Bolshevism are international phenomena," and that the lessons of the Russian experiences of 1905-1906 and 1912-13 might be useful to other countries. "Our enemies are trying to discredit us in the eyes of the masses as professional splitters. That is why, in such a situation as the present, we must strongly support the demand for a united front, and know how to exploit it for the aims of Communism."[44]

Zinoviev also saw the dangers connected with such a strategy. "To be a strategist," he said, "to execute a definite maneuver, it is necessary to have a clear head and to stand on strong feet, not made of clay. This means that we must have genuine Communist parties. . . . On the surface we may even make some concessions, but only on the surface. This will be very dangerous in the countries where our Communist parties are weak."

Zinoviev had no doubt that the leaders of the Second International would be aware of the real meaning of the Communist maneuver, but thought that the Communists must openly put down some definite conditions for unification, the most important being their complete independence and full liberty to criticize the Second and Second-and-a-half Internationals. There could, in fact, be unity of action of the separate forces, but by no means full organizational unity. When organizing an anti-war demonstration, for example, the Communists should propose to "those gentlemen" that they also take part in it. If they refused, they would appear to the masses as the splitters and saboteurs of the working masses' unity.

In the debates following Zinoviev's report, the representatives of the Western Communist parties expressed doubts and stressed the dangers of the new tactics which they felt would not be comprehensible to their members. Only Radek and Bukharin (and Lozovskii) agreed unreservedly with Zinoviev, although they polemicized with each other.

Bukharin contested Radek's opinion that the new tactics might be more or less stable. He felt that they could be changed in twenty-four hours to meet demands of changing situations. He stressed that there was no contradiction between the former and the present tactics; the former demanded splits which were absolutely necessary and extremely important; the latter did not demand the preventing of splits or the reconstitution of unity, but only proposed to form a bloc with the splitter groups. The results of the new tactics might be twofold: if the Communist proposal were rejected, then this fact would be exploited in order to stigmatize the Social Democrats, to unmask them; if the answer were positive, the Communists must do their best to take into their hands the general leadership and the positions strategically most important.

Radek then agreed that complete confusion *(polnaia nerazberikha)* could arise if the theoretical premises of the Communist tactics were not carefully thought over and the working masses properly informed.

Zinoviev summarized the discussion, saying that the tone of the polemics with the socialists should be even more rude *(muzhitski)* than before, and that mistakes were inevitable. He suggested that before the appropriate theses on the new policy were adopted they be discussed by a special commission.

On December 18, 1921, Zinoviev, reporting on the work of this commission, suggested that the draft theses "on the United Front" be submitted for further discussion to the enlarged plenary session of the Comintern Executive Committee, called for the beginning of February, 1922. Radek proposed that the Executive Committee adopt the theses and immediately start both "wide-scale organizational work in the [Communist] parties and negotiations with the adversary." After a short discussion, the draft-theses were in principle unanimously adopted by the Comintern Executive, and on December 25 the Comintern Presidium debated on their practical execution.[45] It was decided that the theses should be publicized in the *Communist International* and in *Internationale Korrespondenz* (Berlin) and published in a separate brochure together with relevant materials; that a special appeal to the international proletariat should immediately be drafted by Souvarin, Radek, and Zinoviev, explaining the essence of the theses, and that confidential letters should be sent by the Comintern Secretariat to the Italian, German, French, Polish, and Czechoslovak parties with concrete suggestions. Radek's drafts of the appeal and the confidential letter to the German party were adopted by the Comintern Presidium on December 27, 1921.[46]

The twenty-five theses "On the United Workers' Front and on the Attitude Towards the Workers Who Are Members of the Second, the Second-and-a-half, and the Amsterdam Internationals, as Well as Towards the Workers Who Are Supporting the Anarcho-Syndicalist Organizations" repeated in their argumentation the principal ideas of Zinoviev's report of December 4. The most important was thesis 20 which stated in part:

> . . . The leaders of the Second, the Second-and-a-half, and the Amsterdam International have proved by their behavior until now that they renounce, in fact, their watchword of unity when the question is practical action. . . . However, the refusal of the leaders . . . will not incite us to drop the proposed tactics which have deep roots among the masses and which we must know how to develop systematically and without hesitation. In the instances when our proposals of joint struggle are rejected by our adversaries, it will be necessary that the masses know this, and thus realize who actually is the splitter of the united workers' front. In the cases when the proposal is accepted by the adversary, it is necessary to aim at the gradual deepening of the struggle and its elevation to a higher level. . . .[47]

The most important concluding chapters of Radek's appeal stated that past experience should have convinced "even blind people" of the correctness of the Comintern program and ended: "Since you could not make up your minds . . . to struggle with arms in hand for power, for dictatorship, . . . then, at least, unite among yourselves for the struggle for bare existence, for a piece of bread, for the struggle for peace. . . . When you start the fight, you will see that in order to win you will need the sword of dictatorship."[48]

VII. THE VIENNA UNION'S INITIATIVE AND THE GENOA CONFERENCE

When, at the beginning of January, 1922, the French Socialist Party sent invitations to all the leftist parties of Great Britain, France, Italy, Belgium, and Germany for a joint conference in Paris on February 4, 1922, the British Labor Party and the Belgian Socialist Party accepted without reservation, in accordance with the Second International Executive's decision. The Vienna Union's Bureau formally approved the French initiative and even spread it by publicizing in an appeal "To the Workers' Parties of All Countries" its intention to enter into negotiations with the Executive Committees of both the Second and Third Internationals in order to arrange by mutual agreement of all the international central organizations a general all-embracing conference in the spring of 1922 with an agenda limited to the most imminent questions:

1. The economic situation and the struggle of the working class;
2. The defensive struggle of the proletariat against reaction.[49]

None of the Communist parties accepted the French invitation despite the Moscow December debates and theses on the "united front." Since the internal situation prevented the representatives of the Italian Socialist Party, and the railway strike the representatives of the German parties from coming to Paris on February 4, 1922, only the French and Belgian Socialists and the British Laborites attended. Those present considered it inopportune to proceed with the proposed debates on reparations and disarmament and decided to refer the memoranda on these subjects, submitted by the French Socialist Party, to a special commission; the remainder of the conference was spent discussing the proposal of the recent appeal of the Vienna Union. An informal exchange of views between the Executive members of the Vienna Bureau and the Second International then took place.[50]

The Vienna Union appeal had also been discussed in Moscow, at the Comintern Executive's Presidium meeting on January 10, 1922, and it was decided that in principle the Communist parties should answer positively, with a reservation that the ultimate decision would be reached at the enlarged Comintern Executive meeting, which it decided to call on February 21.[51]

Representatives of the non-Communist leftist parties of nine Western European countries had gathered in Frankfurt on February 23, 1922. The parties affiliated to the Second International were represented by Vandervelde and Huysmans from Belgium; Shaw, Jowett, and Tillett from Great Britain; Braun and Wels from Germany; Andersen from Denmark; Vliegen from Holland. The parties of the Vienna Union were represented by Wallhead from Great Britain; Ledebour and Crispien from Germany; Longuet and Bracke from France; Adler from Austria; Grimm from Switzerland. The Russian Left SR's were represented by Schreider. Serrati, a representative of the Italian Socialist Party not affiliated to any international, was also in Frankfurt and took part in one of the joint meetings.[52]

In addition to separate meetings of each group, two joint meetings were held on February 23 and February 24, 1922. The representatives of the Second International declared that no question of principle divided them from the Vienna Union, and that they were ready to make some concessions with regard to persons and organization in order to make possible the fusion of the two bodies. With regard to the Comintern, they said that they did not completely reject the idea of a general conference with a definite agenda; however, they had doubts concerning the good will of the Communists. They said that certain preliminary questions should be put to the Communists in order to ascertain whether they wanted a general conference to prepare for genuine common action or rather to provide themselves with a platform to enable them to fight "the Social-Traitors" better. Finally, the representatives of the Second International still reserved complete liberty of action with regard to the proposed general conference, and said that their final decision would depend on the impression they received from a preliminary joint meeting of the representatives of the three international bodies, "with the object of examining the possibility of a joint convocation of this conference." When agreeing to take part in the preliminary meeting with the Communists, the representatives of the Second International openly stated that they intended to raise the questions of political prisoners in Russia, of the Red Army invasion of Georgia, and of the right of peoples to self-determination, as well as the question of Communist methods of creating their clandestine "cells" and provoking divisions and splits in the workers' organizations. All these points were explicitly mentioned in a formal letter handed to the representatives of the Vienna Union as an official reply of the Second International to the Union's public appeal.[53]

In Moscow, the New Economic Policy, officially adopted in the spring of 1921, was followed by a New International Policy of trade and negotiations with capitalist states; on October 28, 1921, Chicherin suggested an economic "general conference." This suggestion was accepted by the Allies' Supreme Council at its meeting in Cannes on January 6, 1922, and the prompt convocation of such a conference in Genoa was decided. The Cannes decision was formally transmitted to the Moscow government by Italian Prime Minister Bonnoni and on January 17, 1922, it was discussed by the Politbureau.

Despite some objections against the place of the proposed conference,[54] the Politbureau decision was in principle positive; the unusually large fifteen-man Soviet delegation to Genoa was designated, and unofficial talks about possible mutual concessions followed.

The Communists intended to go to Genoa as "businessmen." "We are going there as merchants," said Lenin in a public speech on March 6, 1922, and he added:

> If upon this basis [business] should be superimposed many various political talks, proposals and projects, it is necessary to realize that this is

only a minor super structure, quite often artificially constructed, invented and executed by those who have an interest in it.[55]

Thus, when on January 20 Chicherin asked Lenin if it would be possible "for a decent compensation" to agree to a "small change" in the Soviet constitution and give some limited political rights to all Soviet citizens, Lenin considered such a proposition proof of Chicherin's overwork, if not insanity.[56]

In his opinion, there was no price for a genuine political concession on the Soviet principles of extermination of all "parasite" elements and detention of all political opponents "carefully in prison." On January 21, 1922, in a telephone message to Trotsky, Lenin said that he had no doubt "that the Mensheviks are increasing now, and will increase, their most malicious *(zlostnaia)* agitation. I think therefore that it is necessary to increase both the supervision and the reprisals against them." Further on in the message Lenin suggested that Trotsky should start "immediately an open struggle" with the Mensheviks through the press *(poshli nemedlenno v otkrytyi boi v pechati).*[57] The following day, January 22, in a most confidential note to the Politbureau members, Lenin wrote that "here in Moscow, we are surrounded by Menshevik and semi-Menshevik *spies*"[58] and a few days later in letters to Unszlicht, at that time the acting chief of the political police, he suggested that the newly created revolutionary tribunals should be packed with "'your' men," and that the "speed and the *strength* of reprisals" should be increased, particularly "against the Mensheviks."[59]

Such was the political atmosphere in Moscow when on January 19, 1922, the Vienna Union sent to the Comintern their official proposal of an invitation to "a general conference of workingmen's organizations." On the one hand, it fitted well into the Comintern's "new tactics of a United Front" as well as into the Soviet New International Policy and the proposed Genoa Conference; on the other hand it was a rather delicate matter in view of the domestic policy described above.

While postponing the official answer to the Vienna Union invitation until the ultimate decision of the enlarged plenum of the Comintern's Executive which had been summoned, Zinoviev approached Lenin and asked him to deliver personally a report on the delicate matter of "the united front" at this plenum. He also asked Radek, who at that time was in Berlin,[60] to conduct unofficial preliminary talks on the proposed "general conference." However, Lenin, for reasons of ill-health, declined to give such a report, despite Zinoviev's repeated insistances.[61] Moreover, Radek's activities in Berlin, although positive with regard to both the proposed "general socialist conference," and the Soviet-German rapprochement, caused some displeasure to both Chicherin and Lenin. The former objected to Radek's interview with a correspondent of the Parisian *Le Matin* as undiplomatic. The latter, in a note of January 30, 1922, to the Politbureau members, suggested officially rebuking Radek "for his compliant attitude *(podatlivost')* toward the Mensheviks" and [at the same time] proposed to increase reprisals against the Mensheviks, asking Trotsky "to hasten with all his forces the furious attack on the Mensheviks with regard to Georgia."[62]

All this by no means meant that Lenin was against participating in the "general conference" sponsored by the Vienna Union. Quite the contrary; he took this participation for granted, but with no concessions to the Mensheviks. On February 1, 1922, Lenin addressed a telephone message to Bukharin and Zinoviev asking them to look for the "most pungent" *(naibolee zubastykh)* people as candidates for delegates to this conference and to think over the main strategic and tactical questions connected with it. On his part Lenin suggested limiting the agenda of the proposed conference to the questions most directly related to the practical common action of the working masses in those fields that were considered by all three Internationals. However, said Lenin, "In the case that the yellow gentlemen raise controversial political questions as, for example, our relations with the Mensheviks, Georgia, etc., we should apply the following tactics": insist that the general conference agenda be unanimously accepted by its participants and declare that the Communists would be ready to discuss any controversial question under the strict condition *(pri obiazatel'nom uslovii)* that simultaneous discussions would also take place on such questions as: 1) the socialists' betrayal of the anti-war Basle Manifesto; 2) their indirect participation in the assassination of R. Luxemburg, K. Liebknecht, and other German Communists, as well as 3) the murders of many revolutionaries in the colonies, etc. A full list of such counter-questions should be prepared in advance, and the proper persons designated to report on them at the general conference. During its debates, Lenin instructed further, an occasion should be found to declare officially that the Communists consider both the Second and the Second-and-a-half Internationals to be "inconsequent and hesitant" members of the international "bourgeois bloc." It should be made known that the Communists were negotiating with them not only in order to reach, possibly, a practical unity of mass action, but also to unmask their wrong political line before the masses (just as the socialists hoped not only to achieve practical unity in direct mass action, but also to unmask the political incorrectness of the Communist attitude).[63]

On February 3, Bukharin wrote Lenin that both he and Zinoviev fully agreed with Lenin's suggestions with regard to the three Internationals' projected conference[64] and a day later, on February 4, Lenin sent a telephone message to Bukharin, Zinoviev, and all the Politbureau members suggesting that the problem of "the struggle against war" be put on the agenda of the enlarged plenum of the Comintern Executive and an extended propaganda campaign be started in the Soviet press recalling the Basle anti-war manifesto and its betrayal by the socialist leaders.[65]

After having ultimately refused to report on the "united front" at the Comintern meeting, he did not keep his semi-promise to draft the theses on this problem nor even to complete an article on it.[66] Neither was Lenin enthusiastic about the draft-resolution prepared by Zinoviev for the proposed meeting of the three Internationals. On February 23, 1922, in a telephone message addressed to Molotov but to be communicated to all Politbureau members, Lenin suggested that some changes be made in the draft-resolution and, in particular, insisted that the words describing the leaders of the Second and Second-and-a-half Internationals as "the helpers *(posobniki)* of the world bourgeoisie" be omitted. "This is quite obvious," said Lenin, and "it is absolutely nonsensical to risk a break of an extremely important practical achievement in order to have once more the pleasure of chiding the scoundrels *(obrugat' merzavtsev)* whom we chide, and will chide, a thousand times more in another place."

In conclusion, Lenin suggested that the resolution could be adopted by the enlarged plenum by a majority of votes, instead of unanimity, and added in brackets: "those voting against we will later on submit to a special, serious, and popular lesson in common sense *(umu-razumu)*."[67]

Practically at the same time Lenin formally disqualified Radek as a diplomat in a telephone message of February 20 to the Politbureau members, and in a letter of February 21 to Kamenev and Stalin.[68]

Parallel to his preoccupation with Comintern problems, Lenin was active with the preparatory work for the Genoa Conference. In several messages he insisted on speeding up the conclusion of economic and other agreements with the Germans,[69] drafted detailed instructions for the Soviet delegation to Genoa,[70] and argued with Chicherin who had shown some opposition when instructed eventually to promote the "petty-bourgeois pacifist illusions" that "I [Chicherin] have cursed all my life."[71] It seems that, in sum, Lenin attached more importance to and worked harder for the Genoa Conference than for the conference of the three internationals.

VIII. THE FIRST ENLARGED SESSION OF THE COMINTERN EXECUTIVE (FEBRUARY 21-MARCH 4, 1922)

A double representation of each party had been invited for this first enlarged session, and 105 delegates gathered in Moscow on February 21, 1922; this included delegations from thirty-six countries (the Poalei Syon delegates from Palestine were not admitted) as well as representatives of international Communist organizations such as trade unions, youth, women's, cooperative, and sport societies.[72]

At the first four meetings, on February 21 and February 22, the representatives of the Communist Parties of Germany, France, Czechoslovakia, Italy, England, America, Poland, and the Balkans reported on their internal situation; at the fifth meeting, Zinoviev made a report on the Comintern Executive's activities and Radek reported on his negotiations in Berlin with the representatives of the Second-and-a-half International.[73] On the same evening, at the sixth meeting, Zinoviev presented a report on the "Tactics of the United Front."[74]

Zinoviev started his report by denying that the "Tactics of the United Front" were new or that the change in tactics was influenced by the interests of the Soviet state. In his opinion, "the historical and deep interests of the first victorious proletarian state corresponded to those of the working class of the whole world." The tactics on the united front had been preached by Lenin in 1920 in his *Infantile Disease;* Zinoviev quoted long passages and stressed that Lenin had then been very frank and had said, as Zinoviev had said later, "that the tactic of the united front is just a tactical maneuver in order to unmask the socialist leaders: 'You should support Henderson and MacDonald in the same way as a cord supports a hanged man.'"

Historically, Zinoviev discerned three different periods: 1919-20 when the masses were revolutionary but the leaders were lacking; 1920-21 when Communist parties were being organized in most of the countries but the masses had ceased to be revolutionary; and the most recent period when in the face of the capitalists' offensive the masses of workers were ready to fight for their interests and desired to do so through a united front. This latter tendency was not quite clear at the time of the Third Congress of the Comintern; it had become so since.

Zinoviev said that both the tendency for unity and the readiness to fight were objectively revolutionary factors and even the Christian workers, who did not wish to hear anything about communism, when they supported a strike were following a Communist policy without knowing it. On the other hand, the Communists supporting the watchword, "united front," proved that they were not "professional splitters." Now, said Zinoviev, "the time has come to change roles, since the Second and the Second-and-a-half Internationals will appear before the working class as the splitters, and not we."

After having refuted the arguments of the French and Italian parties who, for different reasons, were against the new tactics and in particular against the general conference proposed by the Vienna Union, Zinoviev affirmed that, in fact, all the socialist leaders realized that a united front would be disastrous for them, and that Serrati and Martov were "furious" and were saying that the Communist tactics were immoral. This, according to Zinoviev, was not true.

At the seventh meeting, on February 25, the floor was given to the French and Italian oppositionists. Speaking on behalf of the former, Renault started by stressing that, although the French Communist Party was a "particularly disciplined" member of the Comintern, it would use its right of free internal discussion to present to the enlarged session "an opposing thesis, a thesis which rejects the propositions of the Executive."[75]

The French Socialist "splitter" Party had, according to Renault, no influence among the masses, and the tactics proposed by the Executive would give it such an influence.

Renault suggested that the question of the Executive proposal be passed over to the next Comintern congress for final decision and with regard to Radek's proposal for a preparatory conference for the "general conference" he said:

> . . . We believe that the international proletariat does not understand this rapprochement between the leaders of the Third International and the Russian Revolution on one side and the men who have fought most against communism and the Soviet Republic on the other. . . . We believe that the directors of the Second and Second-and-a-half Internationals will gladly profit from the occasion that will present itself to hear the calumnies of international Menshevism to which the representatives of the Third International will surely respond with the necessary energy. We strongly doubt that such discussion would be a useful preface to the Conferences of Genoa or of Rome.

Renault concluded his speech by saying that it would be easy for the French Communists to declare that they, as disciplined members of the Comintern, would submit to its decisions and do their best to apply these decisions in France, and then report that in practice these decisions were inapplicable. Instead of this formal and hypocritical method, they preferred to try to persuade the majority with their arguments.

Although Renault had been formally authorized by the *Comité Directeur* of the French party to present at the meeting a view opposing the Executive's theses, there were some French Communists who supported the theses. On behalf of them, Kerr, Souvarin, and Treint presented a written declaration in which they dissociated themselves from Renault's point of view, as allegedly based on a wrong interpretation of the Executive's theses, and reserved for themselves the right to present their arguments orally. On February 27, Treint was given the floor, and he affirmed that, despite the arguments of the *Comité Directeur,* an important minority, "environ le quart de nos Fédérations," had correctly understood and supported the Executive's theses on the united front.

The Italian delegates who, on several other problems, had been even more divided than the French, did not disagree among themselves on the question of the Executive's theses. They had received mandatory instructions to oppose them, confirmed by a special telegram from Italy. Their point of view was presented on February 25 by Roberto and Terracini. The former said that it was Zinoviev's report that had ultimately convinced him that the Executive had drawn the wrong conclusions from a correct evaluation of the actual world situation. According to Roberto, no unity of action was possible between the Social Democrats who held strictly to legality and the Communists who were ready "to go outside the limits of law, to fight illegally, and to apply violence."

Terracini, in his speech, reported on the theses that had been drafted in Italy and finally edited by the Italian delegation in Moscow. He expressed doubts as to whether it was worthwhile to sacrifice principles in order to win the masses. He believed that any accord with Vienna or Amsterdam would be a great mistake. If the Italian theses were rejected (Terracini thought this quite probable) and the Executive's theses approved by the majority, they would be inapplicable in many countries, according to Terracini.

On February 26 the partisans of the Executive had the floor: Lunacharskii, Radek, McManus (Great Britain), Thalheimer (Germany), Burian (Czechoslovakia), Walecki (Poland), Trotsky, and Marshall (USA). As there were twenty-nine more persons on the speakers' list their number was limited to no more than one speaker from each delegation. On February 27 six more speakers pleaded for the Executive's theses, and on February 28, after more discussion by the French and Italian delegates, the debate was closed, following a concluding speech by Zinoviev.[76] In a last effort to reach an agreement with the oppositionists, he proposed not to pass to a vote but to nominate a commission. Kolarov then proposed that any partisan of the oppositionist view should be able to take part in the deliberations of this commission. During four days of deliberations no agreement was reached by the commission, and finally, on March 4, at the seventeenth meeting of the enlarged Executive session, individual draft resolutions were presented by the majority and the minority on both the general problem of a united front and the proposed "general conference."[77] The general draft resolutions were rather short: the majority stressed the fact that the tactics proposed by the Executive by no means signified any attenuation of the opposition to reformism, and formally approved the theses adopted by the Executive in December; the minority insisted that no rapprochement should take place with "political parties" and did not mention the theses.

On the proposed "general conference," the minority's draft resolution suggested rejection of the Vienna Union's invitation for the proposed general conference; the majority pronounced itself for participation in this conference and suggested enlargement of the number of organizations to be invited in order to have "an effective and universal representation of all the workers' organizations of the world." The majority's draft resolution proposed also to add to the agenda of the general conference the following points: struggle against new imperialist wars; assistance for the rehabilitation of Soviet Russia and for the reconstruction of the regions devastated by war; the imperialist Versailles Treaty. It also stressed the importance of the workers' world conference being held simultaneously with the planned Genoa conference.

Of the twenty-two delegations that took part in the voting, nineteen (with a total of forty-six votes) voted for the majority; three delegations (with ten votes) voted for the minority. After the voting, Cachin, on behalf of the three minority delegations (Italian, French, and Spanish), read a declaration, which stated that having carried out their instructions, having given their arguments and having defended them up to the vote, the minority would loyally follow the majority's decision.[78]

Zinoviev, on behalf of the newly elected Presidium, said that they would accept this declaration and, without referring directly or indirectly to Lenin, added that "some comrades" had demanded that the leaders of both the Second and the Second-and-a-half Internationals be asked to explain several essential problems at the proposed general conference. In particular "many Russian comrades" demanded that Vandervelde be indicted for violation of the Basle Congress decisions, and eventually be charged for this crime before the Russian revolutionary tribunal; "our Russian comrades" asked also that the Russian Socialist Revolutionary Party leaders be accused for the part they played in the attempts against Lenin's and Trotsky's life and in the assassination of Volodarskii; "the comrades from Georgia" requested an explanation from Henderson for his meddling in Georgian affairs; "the Yugoslav comrades" sought an explanation from the Yugoslav Social Democrats for their united front with the police and the reaction; "several German comrades" questioned Scheidemann and Noske on their role in the assassination of Rosa Luxemburg and Liebknecht and on V. der Goltz's action in Baltic provinces; "the Polish comrades" sought an explanation from Daszynski for assisting "the Polish and French counterrevolution." Far from rejecting all these claims, Zinoviev said that they must be postponed for another time and place; at the proposed general conference only the most important question of a united front of the working class against the offensive of the capitalists should be raised and solved. "Ultimately, the proletariat's victory over the bourgeoisie will put its seal on the judgment of all the traitors."[79]

IX. THE BERLIN CONFERENCE OF THE EXECUTIVES' DELEGATES FROM THE THREE INTERNATIONALS

Due to ill health in March, 1922, Lenin's work was curtailed but he continued to supervise Soviet policy, both domestic and foreign, and in particular the preparatory work for the planned international conferences. His original objections to Chicherin's policy notwithstanding, he came to the conclusion that the latter had successfully adapted himself to the political line drawn in Moscow. In particular he was fully satisfied with Chicherin's plan of action in Genoa; he found it "excellent" *(prevoskhodno; prekrasno; verno; pravilno)* and wrote: "It will be both virulent and 'by mutual understanding' *('po dobromu')*, and will help to split the enemy . . . . We will disgrace them and will spit upon them 'by mutual understanding' *(Osramim i opliuem ikh 'po dobromu')*."[80]

On March 27, 1922, at the Eleventh Russian Party Congress, Lenin once more expressed his satisfaction with the "Genoa delegation," saying that it was composed "of our best diplomats" and armed with carefully prepared, detailed instructions.[81]

He was much less satisfied with the preparatory work for the second "general conference." Although all his remarks and instructions transmitted to the Politbureau members on February 23 had been taken fully into consideration in the final version of the majority's resolution of the enlarged plenum of the Comintern Executive and were corroborated in Zinoviev's closing speech, Lenin's recent conflict with the Comintern leaders undoubtedly left little confidence in and bitter feelings toward Zinoviev and Radek, in particular. On March 14, Zinoviev asked Lenin for his opinion of a draft of instructions for the Comintern delegates to the meeting of the representatives of the Executives of the three Internationals. Lenin was dissatisfied with the draft on the whole, and in particular with a point about the proposed change of attitude toward the Mensheviks. He was also not satisfied with the list of delegates which the Comintern Executive nominated on March 17.[82]

By that time it had become evident that a new, delicate, and rather complicated matter would be introduced by the non-Communists at this meeting: the problem of the Russian Socialist Revolutionaries. Whereas, in accordance with Lenin's instructions, most of the Mensheviks and anarchists were, in the early spring of 1922, given a "free choice" between jail or banishment, on February 28, 1922, a GPU (State Political Administration) decision was published announcing that several Socialist Revolutionary leaders and activists imprisoned in Russia would be indicted before the Revolutionary Tribunal for counterrevolutionary terrorist crimes. The announcement made a great impression in the West, and after the Socialist Revolutionary emigre paper *Golos Rossii* on March 11 published an appeal "To the Socialist Parties of the Entire World" asking them to protest the probable death sentences pronounced by the Revolutionary Tribunal, several Western socialist leaders, Vandervelde among them, sent telegrams to Lenin, Zinoviev, and Chicherin asking them for a postponement of the Socialist Revolutionary trial.

On March 17 Lenin instructed Zinoviev that the reply to these telegrams (which he would draft) should be sent by the Soviet Minister of Justice, D. I. Kurskii. On the same day, he made an urgent proposal to the Politbureau containing instructions to the "Comrades who are going abroad," stressing the need for "great restraint in declarations and discussions about the Mensheviks and Socialist Revolutionaries on the one side, and on the other a most ruthless struggle against them and a complete lack of confidence (because they are *de facto* the most dangerous assistants to the White-Guardists)."[83]

There is no doubt that Lenin's proposal represented his immediate reaction to the news that Radek was to be nominated as the Comintern's chief delegate. Lenin's position was not easy: he had advised looking for "the most pungent people" as delegates for the proposed conference; Radek's extraordinary "pungency" was notorious, but Lenin doubted his qualities as a diplomat and even as a politician: he had explicitly objected to his "softness" *(podatlivost)* with regard to the Mensheviks on January 30.

His proposal was duly voted by the Politbureau on March 18, and without contesting Radek's formal nomination, Bukharin was designated as Radek's unofficial adviser and "political commissar." He was later to share a large part of the blame for the result of the Berlin meeting.

A nine-man body composed of official delegates of the three Internationals met in Berlin on April 1, 1922, and agreed that at the formal meeting on April 2 each of the three Executives was to be allowed 10 delegates with deliberative voices; in addition all members of the Executives were to be admitted as guests; parties not affiliated to any of the three Internationals were not to be admitted, with only one exception: the Italian Party was to have the right to one delegate with a deliberative voice and two guests; the nine representatives of the Executives were to form a Committee of Nine[84] acting throughout the whole conference; and Tom Shaw, Clara Zetkin, and Friedrich Adler would in turn be in the chair. French, German, and English were *al pari* with De Man from Brussels and Grimm from Berne acting as translators. After some deliberation, Radek's proposal that the conference be open to the press was not accepted; only a limited number of journalists, sponsored by any of the three Executives, was admitted.[85]

The first formal meeting was opened on Sunday, April 2, 1922, in the Berlin Reichstag, by F. Adler. In the opening speech he said in part:[86]

> . . . We have no illusions, we know that each of the three groups present here entered this conference with considerable reservations. . . . Each of the three sides will give some such expression of their views. . . . In spite of these differences an attempt can be made to lead the way towards common action within definite limits . . . it is no part of our present task to try to bring about any fusion . . . . I think I may say that the chief reason which has brought us together . . . is that the International of capitalist imperialism is now gathering for a conference in Genoa. . . . We will discuss the problems, the difficulties and obstacles, which lie before us all. . . . We will not be dismayed if at first we deal honestly, differences manifest themselves. We think that on the ground of these differences and in spite of these differences a common struggle on the part of the international proletariat can be waged for certain concrete ends. . . .

After Adler's speech, Clara Zetkin read a statement on behalf of the delegation of the Third International, written in unexpectedly cautious and moderate language:

> . . . Until labor bands together in a common struggle for its interests against international capital, until labor breaks with the policy of coalition with capital, until labor rises to the fight for political power, there will always be the disunity within its ranks which is one of the principal sources of capital's strength . . . . The Communist International demands of the working masses that they unite for the struggle against the present offensive of capital, and that they carry on that struggle in the most

> energetic manner without consideration as to their differences of opinion upon the way leading to the final victory and the means of assuring this way. . . . It considers this proposed International Labor Congress a means for the uniting of the coming labor struggles. . . . The delegation of the Communist International is ready to do all in its power for the united struggle of the international proletariat, without concealing for a moment what separates it from the reformist and semi-reformist parties. . . . The delegation of the Communist International . . . proposes that this International Conference only deal with such questions as concern the immediate practical united action of the working masses, questions which do not divide it, but unite it. . . .[87]

The Communists' unexpected moderation induced the representatives of the other two Internationals to postpone their declarations and ask for an adjournment of the meeting.

At the afternoon session under T. Shaw's chairmanship, Vandervelde made some personal remarks on the Comintern declaration and then said in the name of the Second International:

> . . . The exchange of views about to take place will show us whether this [general] conference is actually possible or impossible. . . . There must be between us a minimum of agreement upon the common action, accompanied by mutual confidence. . . . I will explain why we are filled with suspicions and apprehensions. Certain documents have been published recently which justify these apprehensions.

Here Vandervelde referred to Radek's "confidential" letter ("with which you are all familiar") and to the December Comintern public appeal (see above p. 218), and said:

> An appeal is made for union, for the realisation of the united front, but no secret is made of the intention to stifle us and poison us after embracing us. . . . I know very well that one has to take these things in the Pickwickian sense; that in Communist circles to call a man a traitor simply means that you disagree with him in principle . . . you told us this morning, in very moderate and careful language, not only that you were ready to unite with us in conference, but that you were anxious to do so. . . . Under these conditions, we are bound to reply to you: Before we go to a general conference, we must have certain guarantees; . . . guarantees against attempts at *noyautage;* guarantees for freely elected delegations from the peoples whose territory you are now occupying; finally, guarantees of rights of defense for the prisoners. Such are our conditions; . . . At a general conference we must all feel ourselves on the basis of equality, we cannot have as allies in the deliberations gendarmes and executioners.[88]

In concluding his speech, which later was qualified by E. H. Carr[89] as "highly provocative," Vandervelde affirmed that he had tried to express himself without bitterness and not to reply with insults for the "often received insults," and stressed the historic significance of the meeting:

For the first time since 1914 we are united here. A sight like this is not without a certain grandeur, to see to-day in this assembly, whether as journalists or delegates, such men as Chernov, Dan or Martov, side by side with Radek or Bukharin. We are united . . . . Can we not, in spite of everything which separates us, unite . . . and by international action prepare the way for the coming of Socialism.

After Vandervelde's speech a short declaration on behalf of the Vienna Union was read by Paul Faure:

The formation of a really united Labor Front . . . can only succeed if the conflicts between working class parties are conducted exclusively with intellectual and moral weapons, and are not poisoned by terroristic methods of combat of one workers' party against the other. . . . Equality of political rights shall be restored to Socialist Parties of Russia, the freedom of political and economic activity to the workers and peasants of Russia, and the right of self-determination to the toiling people of Georgia. . . . The carrying out of death sentences against members of the SR Party of Russia . . . would make the continuation of the action started by this conference morally impossible. . . .

In its final paragraphs, the declaration of the Vienna Union stated that the right-wing socialists in the Western countries were also guilty for their part in the "brutal persecutions" of left-wingers and Communists and stressed "an indispensable necessity for a united proletarian front" to use "all their power to restore the full freedom of expression" also in the West.[90]

After the three Executives' statements were delivered, a general debate was opened. Radek, MacDonald, and Serrati asked for the floor. The chairman, Tom Shaw, proposed to give it to Radek and to postpone the other two speakers until the next meeting.[91]

The general tone of Radek's speech was quite different from the written declaration read by Clara Zetkin. He started by stressing that the Communists had come to the conference based on the Vienna Union invitation, and "refrained from settling past accounts." To Vandervelde's demand of "a minimum of agreement . . . accompanied by mutual confidence," Radek answered with brutal frankness:

Not a pennyworth of confidence! . . . we stand here to-day as enemies and have to try to find the way to an understanding; and if you come to us with phrases about confidence we say to you plainly: "No." . . . we sit down at the same table with you, we will fight with you, and this fight will decide whether it is a maneuvre, as you say, . . . or a stream which will unite the working class. . . . If you fight with us and with the proletariat of all lands . . . against further world ruin . . . we will try to fight together, not for love of you, but because of the unprecedented need of the hour which drives us and compels you to confer in this hall with the very Communists you have treated as criminals.[92]

Radek rejected the "conditions put by Citizen Vandervelde" and offered instead a kind of trade in political prisoners: the Russian SR's for the supporters of the Bavarian Soviet republic.

The general tone of Radek's speech nearly broke up the conference. Although the Sunday afternoon meeting was explicitly adjourned by the chairman "until 10 o'clock to-morrow morning,"[93] there were no official meetings on Monday but only negotiations behind the scene. According to E. H. Carr, Radek, who alone of all those present at the conference was informed of the advanced state of the negotiations between the Soviet and German governments that were soon to be completed at Rapallo, was "unshakeably" determined to avoid a final break, and "his public polemics were matched by extreme conciliatoriness behind the scenes."[94] Ultimately the official meetings were resumed on Tuesday, April 4; Clara Zetkin was in the chair, and MacDonald and Serrati were given the floor.

Ramsay MacDonald's speech was correct in form but peremptory in content. In his opinion the position of the Second International had been "perfectly clear." As long as "we feel that every Communist," when co-operating with socialists, "has a dagger concealed behind his back," no honest and genuine cooperation is possible. Radek's rejection of a demand that political prisoners in Russia be tried by "an international tribunal" is justified, but not his "cynical gesture" in suggesting a trade in prisoners.

In order to avoid any "misunderstanding about our position," MacDonald read during his speech a written and carefully worded official declaration of the Second International, stating that "a general conference with a limited objective must be preceded by the acceptance of the following conditions by the Third International: (1) Renunciation of the *'noyautage'* tactics; (2) Nomination of a commission . . . for the examination of the case of Georgia and other states similarly circumstanced . . . ; (3) The liberation of prisoners detained for political reasons, and the trial of those who are the objects of a criminal accusation before a court of justice with rights of defense under the control of International Socialism."[95]

To the surprise of some listeners, Serrati rallied to the Comintern point of view. He started by stressing his strange situation of a "guest" admitted "simply because it was said that the general conference might be held in Genoa or Rome." Passing to the heart of the matter, he said:

> . . . We are surely not here to set ourselves up as judges one of another. We have all committed many errors. . . . It is not possible to play the part of accusers, when we are simply the slaves of circumstances. We do not rule history; we follow it. . . . I am persuaded that the Bolshevist comrades will eventually form a coalition: that you Bolshevists, you Menshevists, you Social Revolutionaries, will unite one day to defend the proletarian revolution against the attack of the capitalist bourgeoisie. Our duty should be to understand and to try to act in such a way as not to embitter discussions; not to deepen wounds, but to seek to cure them as far as we can . . . . I believe that the conference will be more successful than is

> expected. . . . What is this *noyautage*? It is something that we all do when we want to get together those comrades who are in agreement with us in order to carry out some special task of propaganda in the general situation. It is true that the Bolshevists have sometimes carried it out in a very malicious way. . . . But *noyautage* will be stronger if we are divided than if we are united. I believe there will be no more *noyautage* when our Bolshevist comrades no longer find themselves alone to defend their cause. . . .[96]

At the afternoon meeting O. Bauer, a representative of the Vienna Union, did not share Serrati's opinion that "all moral considerations" should be eliminated in the debates of the politicians.

> . . . I agree with MacDonald that we must also seek moral conditions for co-operation. . . . Let the masses first fight together, whatever their different political convictions may be, then I am convinced that *in this common struggle,* on the common battlefield, the feeling of comradeship and solidarity will develop, until no proletarian Party will allow itself to oppose the fulfillment of these moral conditions. *(Applause from Vienna and Moscow)* . . . . I am quite convinced that the actual conditions of the proletariat . . . and a difficult, tragic situation of the Soviet Republic will compel the Third International to abandon any maneuvres they are contemplating and . . . I believe that the conditions put by the Second International are such that no one can seriously oppose them. . . . All we can do is appeal to both sides. If either side thinks that we can help in the task of mediation, we place our services at your disposal; for our part we are convinced that the need of the proletariat in this hour demands sacrifices from us all. . . .[97]

After Bauer's speech Radek was given the floor once more. His second speech was full of irony and pungency. He attacked personally MacDonald and Vandervelde, as well as England and the Vienna Union, and refused to make any concessions:

> England always stands for small peoples, unless she has conquered them. . . . England considers also the Baku petroleum wells as an integral part of Western civilization. . . . I understand the position of the Vienna International. It sits between us and the Second International, . . . and speaks like God himself, like Justice with her balance distributing exhortations on the right and on the left. . . . The good faith does not consist in this, that we have forgotten anything we have said about you and will swear that we will not fight you anymore . . . . Now the concrete conditions . . . the renunciation of cell-tactics. . . . If you ask us to give up the struggle against Reformism we shall answer flatly: "No." . . . We will fight against Reformism in the Trade Unions, so long as we exist. . . . [As to] examination of the question of Georgia and the other States "in similar circumstances," . . . we agree to this condition, . . . I would like to ask, whether in "similar circumstances" the attitude of the Labor Party towards the Egyptian question, the Irish question, and the Indian question ought to be examined . . . the liberation of prisoners . . . the accused have the right

to choose the defense they want. . . . And as far as our delegation from the Communist International is concerned, we can promise that we cordially accept the suggestion that you [Vandervelde] should be granted the right to appear as lawyer for the defense. . . . We can satisfy you by allowing you to take as many stenographic reports as you like, and to examine all documents and letters. . . . I repeat again: we accept no conditions. . . . *We stand for the united front of the proletariat without conditions.*[98]

Radek's speech concluded the public debates. Before closing the meeting, its chairman, Adler, stated the general wish to complete the conference "before tomorrow night," and announced a meeting of the Committee of Nine in the morning and a plenary meeting to be held the following afternoon. There were rumors that the talks had been completely broken off when the plenary meeting did not convene on schedule. Finally, at 11:45 p.m. Friedrich Adler opened the meeting and reported on the results of the work behind the scenes:

. . . there is no reason why we should hide from you the fact that again and again our attempts were nearly wrecked. . . . But, comrades, . . . we have in the end reached an agreement such as we had dared not hope for at the beginning of the proceedings. *(Bravo)* We can say that, after years during which it has been impossible even to meet in common debate, we have at least succeeded in passing a common resolution of the Executives. Each of the three Executives has put on one side its own special views with regard to certain paragraphs in the resolution, and its wishes with regard to the insertion of further points, and the representatives of all three Executives will set forth in a protocol separate declarations on such points . . . [which] will be published in order to give the whole proletariat a chance of understanding existing differences. But, comrades, in spite of these differences, we have, after long and troublesome deliberations, arrived at a resolution which will express the common will of all three Executives.[99]

The most important parts of the resolution which was finally agreed upon are as follows:

. . . The conference . . . proposes that the Executives should agree to the setting up of an Organisation Committee of Nine, which shall undertake preparations for further conferences of the three Executives, as well as conferences on a wider basis . . . . In this Organisation Committee no majority resolutions will be allowed, its task will be to express the general point of view of the three Executives as far as this is declared . . . .

The conference notes the declaration of the representatives of the Communist International that the 47 S-R's who are to be tried will be allowed any defenders they wish; that, as already announced in the Soviet Press before the conference, no death sentences will be inflicted in this trial; that . . . the trial will be public . . . .

The conference declares that all the three Executives have expressed their

> readiness to collect and examine the material . . . on the question of Georgia . . . .
>
> The conference agrees in principle upon the necessity for calling a general conference as soon as possible. . . . The conference, therefore, calls upon the workers of every country to organise great mass demonstrations, with as much unity as possible, during the Genoa Conference, either on the 20th of April, or, where this is technically impossible, on the first of May:
>
> For the eight-hour day;
> For the struggle against unemployment . . . ;
> For the united action of the proletariat against the capitalist offensive;
> For the Russian revolution, for starving Russia, for the resumption by all countries of political and economic relations with Russia;
> For the re-establishment of the proletarian united front in every country and in the International.[100]

Except for a few interventions by Radek, nobody else took the floor; on Radek's proposal the declaration was proclaimed adopted without a formal vote;[101] and at midnight the conference was formally closed. To its official proceedings separate declarations were annexed.

The delegation of the Comintern Executive stated that they agreed to the joint declaration "after much hesitation" because it did not pronounce itself against the Treaty of Versailles. In addition they renounced their demand for an inquiry into the murders of Luxemburg, Liebknecht and other German Communists; into the persecution of Communists in Latvia, Poland, Yugoslavia, and Hungary; into the attitude of the Labor Party towards Ireland and the Colonies, all because of their "desire to further, and not to obstruct, the slightest advance in the direction of the united front." The Communist declaration concluded by expressing a conviction "that unless there is a break with the policy of coalition with the bourgeoisie, which is at the root of all this trouble, a real united front of the working class will be impossible," and that "the pressure of events will compel the working masses to battle, and will teach them to force their reformist leaders to change their policy if they do not wish to be set aside by the working classes."[102]

The Executive of the Vienna Union stated that the opposition of the Comintern delegates prevented the insertion of a passage on "the immediate release of all political prisoners in their own countries," into the joint declaration, and noted that the Communists "considered of such importance the further detention of socialist prisoners in Russia that they were prepared to abandon their struggle for the freedom of the proletarian political prisoners languishing in capitalist state prisons."[103]

The Executive of the Second International in its "final declaration" "whilst accepting the principle of a general conference as soon as a common ground of action can be found," insisted upon the necessity of "a written and precise answer" from the Comintern to their three "conditions."[104]

In addition to these separate declarations by the three main parties, declarations on behalf of the German Social Democrats and the Georgian Socialists, by Otto Wels and I. Tsereteli respectively, were published. The former protested in vigorous language Radek's reference "to the tragic events of January, 1919, in Berlin" and "allusions to the victims of the March Putsch in Central Germany in 1921," stressed Radek's personal involvement in German events, and concluded that his "immoral and horrible" proposal, "which amounts to blackmail," of a trade of political prisoners in Russia and in Germany "does not lack a certain symbolic meaning: for both are . . . the victims of the Moscow International."[105] The latter stressed the fact of Radek's public admission that the Bolsheviks had occupied Georgia by military force in order "to secure access to the naphtha regions," and emphasized that the Georgian Socialists were always ready "to take into account as widely as possible the economic needs of Russia."[106]

X. AFTERMATH OF THE BERLIN CONFERENCE

On the very day that the Berlin Conference of the three Executives began, a large Soviet delegation arrived in Berlin on their way to the Genoa Conference. On April 3, 1922, its leaders, Chicherin and Litvinov, paid a formal visit to the German chancellor and foreign minister Wirth and lunched with Rathenau. On April 4, Wirth and Rathenau met with Chicherin, Litvinov, Rakovskii, and Radek. Their talks were friendly and fruitful; officially it was announced in *Pravda,* April 5, that the German government had decided to pass over to the Soviet government the premises of the former Russian embassy in the central part of Berlin[107] which until then was in the possession of non-Bolshevik Russians. The most essential part of the talks on the prospective Russian-German collaboration—economic, political, and in the military field in particular—was not publicized. Agreements in the first two areas were kept secret until the Rapallo treaty; agreements in the military field remained secret much longer.[108]

Thus, this part of Lenin's manifold policies on the eve of the Genoa Conference went very smoothly, and Lenin found himself quite satisfied with Chicherin's "diplomatic ability." In general, the Soviet press gave a great deal of publicity to the coming Genoa Conference, whereas the Berlin meeting of the three Executives was left in silence. The first news about it was published in the aforementioned April 5 issue of *Pravda,* on the second page, in the form of ROSTA's (Soviet news agency) wire from Warsaw, dated April 3. On the next day, i.e. two days after the completion of the conference, the wires from Berlin, dated April 3, were published saying that the "fate of the conference hangs in the air," along with an unsigned *Pravda* editorial stating that in this "first meeting with the splinters of former Social Democracy" the question of the summoning of an international conference of the workers' organizations for the struggle against capitalist reaction is being debated, that the Socialists "are trying to break up *(sorvat')* this practical accord *(sgovor),*" but "their plans will be unmasked." The editorial concluded among other items the following:

> . . . the King's minister, Vandervelde, . . . thinks that if we are entering into trade relations with foreign capital, we will, probably, choose him as a go-between and will pay him a commission. He is absolutely wrong *[neprostitel'noe zabluzhdenie]*.

On April 7, *Pravda* published on the front page a more detailed report on the conference of the three Executives, giving the abstracts of MacDonald's, Serrati's, Bauer's, and Radek's speeches delivered on April 3 and 4, and on April 9, it printed a wire from Berlin, dated April 6, that "an agreement had been reached" and another from Hannover with an abstract of the "general declaration."

This scarcity of delayed news in the Soviet press was by no means a result of lack of information. Technically the communication between Berlin and Moscow was in order and the latter was duly informed on the happenings at the conference. Politically, however, Lenin continued to be rather cool and dissatisfied with regard to the Comintern action, and he decided to squash it completely. On April 9, 1922, he dictated an article to be published immediately in the Soviet press and in a separate note asked the Politbureau members: Not to oppose publication of the article in *Izvestiia* and *Pravda;* To instruct the Soviet and the Party press to evaluate the Berlin agreement from this point of view; To increase the propaganda against the S-Rs and the Mensheviks under the guidance of Trotsky; and To instruct Radek to return immediately to Moscow "with all the proceedings of the Berlin conference."[109]

On April 10, the Politbureau agreed with Lenin's proposals, and on April 11 both *Izvestiia* and *Pravda* published his front-page editorial: "We paid too dearly."

Lenin stated plainly that, in his opinion, Radek, Bukharin, and the other Comintern representatives had made a mistake in accepting two conditions in particular: 1) that there would be no death penalties in the trial of the forty-seven SRs; and 2) that the representatives of all three Internationals would be admitted to this trial.

According to Lenin, both these conditions were nothing but political concessions made to the reactionary bourgeoisie by the revolutionary proletariat, and no reciprocal concessions were made. Thus, the "bourgeois diplomats" "this time" were much more clever than "ours," concluded Lenin, and he stressed that in the future no concessions should be made by the Communists without getting something equivalent in return.

As a result of the Berlin mistake, Lenin foretold the possibility of a strengthening of the Italian and French Communists' opposition to the united front. With some irony he also predicted that "two or three" attempts might be made by the enemies of Soviet Russia on the lives of Communist leaders, which "might be successful," since now they know in advance that they can shoot at the Communists and have a chance that the Communists will be prohibited from shooting at them.

On the other hand, Lenin stressed the partial success of Radek in "unmasking" the Second International's positive attitude toward the Treaty of Versailles, and in making "some kind of breach into a closed hall," and came to the final conclusion that the signed agreement should not be repudiated *(rvat' podpisannoe soglashenie nam ne sleduet).*[110]

On the same day, April 11, Zinoviev asked for Lenin's approval of a draft resolution to be voted upon by the Comintern Executive with regard to the Berlin Conference and agreement:

1. To increase the campaign against the Mensheviks and the SR's in the international Communist press;
2. To use systematically the materials of the Berlin Conference and to attack all the weak points of the opponents;
3. For the time being the [Committee of] Nine should not publish any joint appeals;
4. During the demonstrations of April 20, to criticize the opponents without restraint *(ne stesniat'sia);*
5. The separate sections [of the Comintern] should act according to local conditions;
6. Any moves of the [Berlin] delegation will be postponed until the questions of the ratification of the Berlin results are decided.[111]

In general, Lenin agreed with Zinoviev's draft but made a few remarks and suggestions:

a) to make more precise point (1) by stressing the identity of the leaders of the Second and Second-and-a-half Internationals, with the Russian Mensheviks and Socialist Revolutionaries and the latter's contact with "the general front of the landowners and the bourgeoisie against the Soviets";
b) point (3) is doubtful; in some cases (as defending the interests of Soviet Russia) joint appeals would be useful;
c) to ratify the Berlin agreement as soon as possible;
d) to be more careful in propaganda among the workers who support the Second and the Second-and-a-half Internationals, to avoid "sharp words" and to explain patiently the Communist policy and its differences as compared with that of the Socialists.[112]

On the following day, April 12, *Pravda* published an editorial by Zinoviev on "The Prospects of the United Proletarian Front." In it Zinoviev agreed with Lenin's opinion that "unnecessary concessions" had been made in Berlin, but expressed his conviction that the agreement would "undoubtedly" be ratified by the Comintern Executive. Further on, Zinoviev stressed that the Communists have "complete independence" in choosing the slogans for the joint demonstrations of April 20 and May 1, because "the united front is not a feast of reconciliation with the leaders of the Second and Second-and-a-half Internationals. It is not covering up *(zatushevyvanie)* of the differences. It does not blunt *(prituplenie)* the contradictions."

On April 20, 1922, the Comintern Executive formally ratified the Berlin agreement and nominated its representatives to the Committee of Nine: C. Zetkin, Frossard, and Radek as full members and Heckart (Germany) and Bukharin as deputy members. At the same meeting the text of a "manifesto" was adopted which affirmed that the whole idea of the united proletarian front was in danger, because of an effort of the leaders of the Second and Second-and-a-half Internationals to kill it at birth, as had allegedly been proved at the Berlin Conference.[113] According to *Sotsialisticheskii vestnik,*[114] on the same day, April 20, the Soviet People's Commissar of Justice, D. I. Kurskii, broadcast "to the whole world" that "the Moscow Court is in no way limited by an obligation taken by the Russian C.P. to withhold the death penalty" in the SR trial.

Kurskii's statement was not mentioned in the Soviet press, which, at that time, was full of news and articles on the Genoa Conference and Soviet-German treaty which was signed at Rapallo, on April 17, 1922. This treaty not only greatly surprised world public opinion but also radically changed the entire political situation, and influenced the "united front" demonstrations fixed for April 20 and May 1. Many leftists, particularly in Germany, were greatly shocked by the fact that the Soviet government had become an "ally" of the German Government which, until then had been bitterly fought by the Communists.

On the eve of May Day, *Pravda* reported on Zinoviev's speech at a Petrograd Soviet meeting, dealing with the Genoa Conference, in which he said that the Rapallo Treaty was an event "of the greatest historical importance" and, until then, the only achievement at Genoa. According to *Pravda,* Zinoviev said that "This is the germ of a close working alliance between a multi-million agricultural nation and a multi-million technical country. This alliance marks a new stage in the history of humanity."

All this was carefully watched by the leaders of the Second International who waited in vain for any sign from the Comintern that they were putting into effect the three Berlin "conditions." In order to discuss the entire situation in detail, they summoned their Executive and addressed a demand to the representatives of the other two Internationals to postpone the first meeting of the Committee of Nine, fixed for May 7, in Düsseldorf.

On behalf of the Comintern delegation, Radek replied by publishing a statement in the Berlin *Rote Fahne* of May 7, accusing the leaders of the Second International of breaking the Berlin agreement by sabotaging the idea of the World Workers' Congress. Then, on behalf of the Vienna Union, Adler addressed a circular letter to all the members of the Committee of Nine, refuting Radek's accusations and stating that Vandervelde had asked for a short postponement of only a week. At the same time, Adler's letter stated that the renewed persecutions of the socialists in Russia after the

Berlin Conference and the recent Communist split-activities among the Scandinavian (Norwegian) trade-unionists, did not make it easier to reach a final understanding on the prompt summoning of the World Congress.[115]

On May 11, *Pravda* published an editorial, "Our Answer," to the letter received by the Soviet authorities from the Second International with the list of names of the ten persons who, according to the Berlin agreement, intended to come with Vandervelde to Moscow as the defense counselors at the coming Socialist Revolutionary trial. Among them were three Russian lawyers, Sukhomlinov, Kobiakov, and Gurevich. The tone of *Pravda's* editorial was extremely bitter and aggressive; it called the list "shameless" and "provocative" because the names of undoubted "spies" and "conspirators" were included in it, and concluded that, although in accordance with the Berlin agreement, everybody, even the most notorious spies and anti-Soviet agents, would be admitted to the court room during the Socialist Revolutionary trial, the Soviet authorities would take the necessary precautions to prevent them from spying and conspiring outside the court room. The full text of the official Soviet answer to the letter of the Second International was published in *Pravda* on May 31 in an interview with the People's Commissar of Justice Kurskii. The opening of the Socialist Revolutionary trial was fixed for June 1 and the entire Soviet press started an abusive campaign against the accused and their would-be defenders.

On May 10, Adler informed Clara Zetkin by telegram of MacDonald's proposal to call a meeting of the Committee of Nine on May 22 at Cologne. He repeated this proposal on May 14, in a letter to the Communist members of the Committee of Nine, and, at the same time, wrote in some detail about the increased persecutions of socialists in Russia and the hunger strikes of the latter in Soviet prisons, and asked them not only to collect and present at the meeting of the Committee of Nine all relevant materials but also to intervene immediately with the Soviet authorities in order to stop the "shame of the hunger strikes."[116]

On May 18, *Pravda* published an article by Zinoviev, dated May 17, and entitled "When Will the World Workers' Congress Take Place?" Zinoviev affirmed in this article that there was no doubt that the World Congress would take place *(sostoitsia neizbezhno),* the only question was when. Until now, according to Zinoviev, the leaders of the Second and Second-and-a-half Internationals have been sabotaging the summoning of this congress and their resistance must be broken. A definite answer must be received "at any price" *(vo chto by to ni stalo)* by May 21; either the leaders of the Second and Second-and-a-half Internationals will agree to summon the World Congress in the immediate future or will not have anything to do with the Committee of Nine. There could be no question of any kind of "organic union" and cooperation between the Communists and the reformists.

On May 19, *Pravda* published a letter addressed to the Comintern Executive and signed by Stalin on behalf of the Russian Communist Party, stating that since the papers edited by the Second International affirmed that the tactics of the "united front" were nothing but a Machiavellian Russian move to exploit the workers' world movement in the interests of the foreign policy of the Russian state, the Central Committee of the Russian Communist Party was ready to withdraw all watchwords calling for Russia's defense, in any joint appeals or declarations. In the same issue of *Pravda* a lengthy Comintern Executive statement on the Socialist Revolutionary trial was published, stressing the alleged monstrosity of the crimes involved and appealing to all workers to follow the development of the trial. At that time, the Soviet press in general was full of propaganda against the accused and their would-be defense counselors; under the influence of such official propaganda, demonstrations were staged along the lawyers' train route to Moscow.[117]

While the Socialist Revolutionaries' defense counselors were traveling to Moscow, the Committee of Nine gathered for their delayed first meeting in Berlin's Reichstag on May 23, 1922.[118] A declaration submitted by MacDonald was read, containing evidence that none of the "three conditions," which had been considered indispensable for united action, had been fulfilled by the Communists. It came to the conclusion that:

> The present situation forces the Second International to stress the pure imperialist and capitalist character of activity of the delegation of the Soviet government in Genoa, and to emphasize most strongly the differences between the Second and Third Internationals in fundamental conceptions of socialist liberty and methods, and to declare that a General Conference would be possible only when the difficulties pointed out had been removed.

After an interval, Radek read a lengthy declaration on behalf of the Comintern delegation, full of counteraccusations against the Second and Second-and-a-half Internationals. With regard to the question of Georgia, it stated that the Third International would only agree to put the promised documents before the Committee of Nine when the General Conference had been convoked, and declared that if the latter were not convoked within the shortest possible time, the Committee of Nine would have lost all justification for its continued existence. The declaration concluded that, in any case, the freedom of defense granted by the Soviet government for the trial of the Socialist Revolutionaries would not be curtailed, and that the "Comintern will double its effort in the struggle for a united front, and, if the non-Communist working masses succeed in changing the attitude of their leaders toward the united front, the Executive of the Third International will always be ready to send back its representatives to a common organ of the three Internationals."

Adler then read a statement in which, after having quoted Zinoviev's article of May 17 in *Pravda* and several other statements of both the Third and the Second Internationals, he said that the Vienna Union, which started the action for unification, to its deep regret had realized that the latter was impossible at the present moment. Its Executive agreed that at the present time no agreement existed between the Second and the Third Internationals either for summoning a General Conference or even for the continuation of the activity of the Committee of Nine. He asked that the three delegations should report to their Executives for possible changes in their standpoints.

After a short exchange of arguments, Radek officially announced that the Comintern withdrew from the Committee of Nine, which, in consequence, ceased to exist. On May 27, *Pravda* published an unsigned editorial "The Social-Traitors Are Breaking the United Front (The Decomposition of the Nine)." A wild campaign in the Soviet press, in the streets of Moscow, and in the court room forced Vandervelde and the other Western lawyers to renounce the defense, in full accordance with the defendants, and to leave Soviet Russia before the end of the trial. Despite a flood of protests the Moscow court passed 12 death sentences. For a long time they were neither commuted nor executed; the prisoners were held as hostages to prevent any anti-Communist action.

On the other side, on May 24, 1922, the Vienna Union delegates to the Committee of Nine published an appeal "To the Workers of All Countries" in which they accused both the Second and Third Internationals of breaking off the negotiations on the united front, expressed their hope that the break would be only temporary and announced their intention of continuing their efforts on behalf of the united front.[119] After a year of labor, they ultimately gave up their hopes of reaching any agreement with the Communists and, in May 1923, united with the Second International at a congress in Hamburg to form the Labor Socialist International without Communist participation.

ALEXANDER DALLIN

The Kaminsky Brigade: A Case-Study of Soviet Disaffection

I. VOSKOBOINIKOV: A PRELUDE

The responses which the German-Soviet war evoked among Soviet citizens ranged from wholehearted defense of the fatherland to determined struggle against the Bolshevik regime.* While certain groups, such as the Soviet partisans and the Vlasov movement, have been studied in some detail, others have received little serious notice. A few of these smaller units are of considerable interest—not because they were typical of the country as a whole, but because they exemplify variations in popular attitudes and reactions.[1]

One extreme manifestation of this kind has become known by the name of its leader, Kaminsky. It is generally known only as a group of Russian

*The author wishes to express his gratitude to the Russian Research Center, Harvard University, for enabling him to conduct the interviews with Soviet refugees which constitute a substantial part of the source material for this paper, and for supporting the research which resulted in an earlier, unpublished version of this report. He is also grateful for the technical assistance provided by the Russian Institute, Columbia University, and for the comments and advice from his former colleagues on the staff of the War Documentation Project, Columbia University.

Interviews with refugee informants (conducted in the main in 1950-51, in Germany, as part of the Project on the Soviet Social System, Russian Research Center, Harvard University) are cited by informant code number. Those with former German officials were held from 1951 on. Several manuscripts by eyewitnesses have been of substantial value; these were procured through or commissioned by the Russian Research Center, Harvard University, the Research Program on the USSR, New York, or individual intermediaries.

In addition to published Soviet sources, the documentation stems largely from German wartime records. Other than the author's own files, the major collections used were:

- Centre de Documentation Contemporaine Juive (CDCJ), Paris, France;
- Hoover Institution on War, Revolution and Peace, Stanford, California;
- Institut für Zeitgeschichte, Munich, Germany;
- International Military Tribunal (IMT) and Nuremberg (U.S.) Military Tribunals (NMT), records, documents submitted in evidence, and proceedings;
- Jewish Scientific Institute (YIVO), Archive, New York;
- National Archives of the United States, Washington, D.C.;
- U.S. Army, The Adjutant General's Office, Departmental Records Branch, Captured Records Section, Alexandria, Va.

bandits working for the SS and taking an active part in the German sack of Warsaw during the Polish uprising of 1944. In fact, the biography of the Kaminsky movement is far more complex and intriguing.

After the German troops advanced into Soviet territory in the summer of 1941, large areas of occupied territory behind the front lines remained under military rule. It was in such an area between Orel and Kursk that the Kaminsky movement had its birth. So quickly did the invaders drive through, in the early summer of 1941; so numerous were the Soviet armed forces cut off; and so auspicious was the terrain for concealing isolated units, that the Germans were never able to effectively comb out the wide spaces of the Briansk forests. Where later large partisan units made their headquarters, at first Red Army men hid out in the woods, drifting about hungry but armed. Eventually some of these banded together to form gangs as yet unconnected with the Soviet command; properly speaking, these were marauders afraid to surrender to the Germans, whose mistreatment of prisoners of war was rapidly becoming known. At times these bands would attack German truck convoys or kill a soldier. The Germans would then take quick revenge on the civilian population, with the result that increasing numbers of local inhabitants would take to the woods—not for political reasons but in self-defense against the terror of the occupying forces.

The Germans, unable to exercise more than sporadic or nominal control, encouraged the formation of "native" local governments. This was also the case in the area controlled by Second Army and, more particularly, in the *raion* of Lokot'.[2] The prewar population of Lokot' was only a few thousand; the district had perhaps 35,000 inhabitants, of whom many had been drafted into the army; hundreds of other residents, including local Communist Party and government officials, had been evacuated eastward as the German armies approached. It was still a predominantly agricultural district, barely touched by modernization.

The first mayor of Lokot' under the Germans is something of a legendary figure. While there is dispute over his biography, the following seems established: Konstantin Pavlovich Voskoboinikov had been a junior officer in the tsarist army during the First World War. In 1917 he supported the Socialist-Revolutionaries. In the 1920s, in Moscow, he was an engineer in charge of an office of weights and measures. He was arrested in 1930 or 1931 and sent to a Novosibirsk concentration camp until 1935. Because of his "political" past he had difficulty finding a suitable job; for a while he evidently taught at a small *tekhnikum.* It was in some engineering capacity that he came to Lokot' before the war. When the Red Army retreated, he remained.[3] Whether he began working on his own or received preliminary sanction from the German commandant in the region is not known. Evidently a hardworking and skillful organizer, he rapidly set out to introduce "reforms" in local government.

Because of its fairly isolated location, Lokot' was well-suited to become the object of some administrative experimentation. The German military was

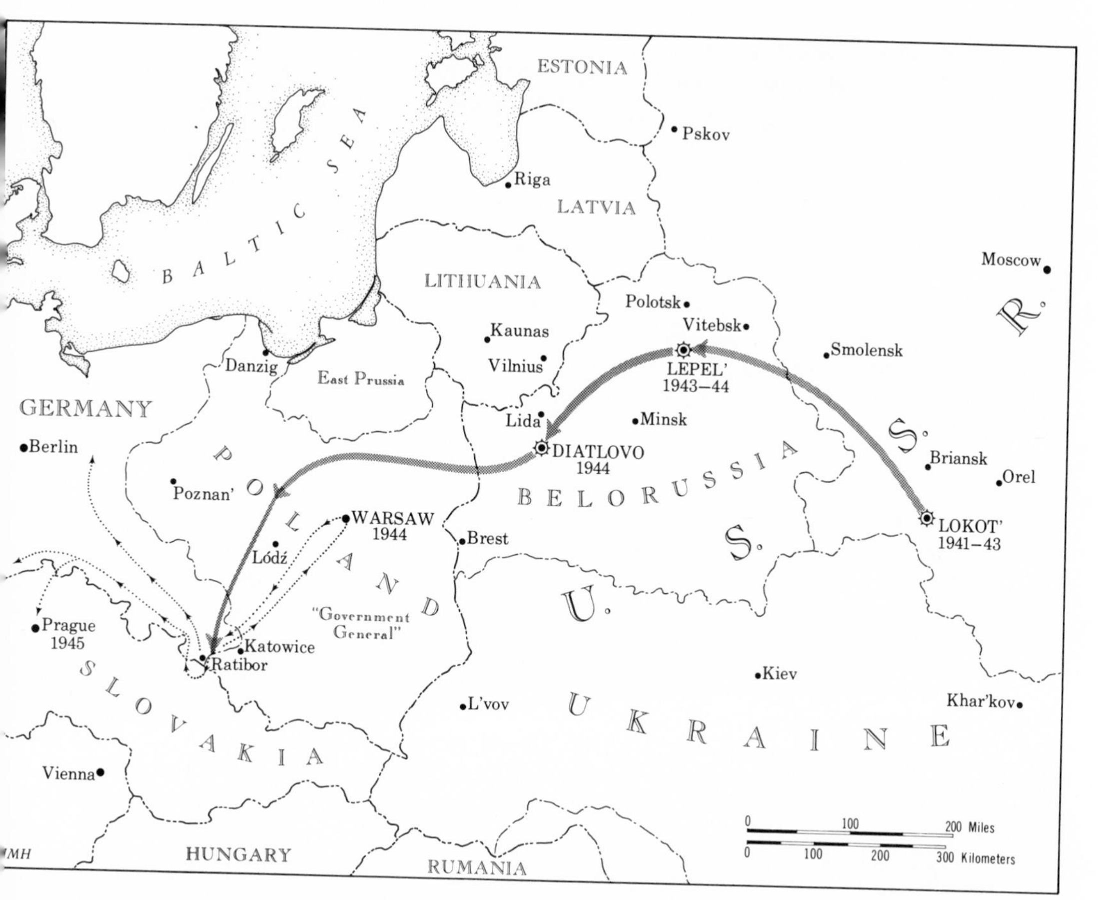

ROUTE OF THE KAMINSKY BRIGADE

content to leave the region alone as long as the local authorities rendered it secure from Soviet marauders and furnished the German army with the requisite amounts of food. Here was the basis of the peculiar "live and let live" policy which the military area commander sanctioned in regard to this venture.

Thus Voskoboinikov was free to initiate a policy which ran counter to Berlin's directives for the treatment of the Eastern *Untermenschen.* Voskoboinikov, with five aides, formulated a "Manifesto," which (along with an Appeal and Order No. 1) was published on November 25, 1941. These documents represent a curious mixture of principle and accommodation. The Manifesto opened with the announcement that "as of this date, the Popular Socialist Party of Russia[4] has begun its work." Its origin was traced back to the "underground in the concentration camps of Siberia." The movement did not hesitate to assume responsibility for the fate of Russia and to demand a government that would assure "law and order and all the conditions necessary for the peaceful flourishing of labor in Russia, for the upholding of her honor and dignity."

There are in these documents echoes of the old Russian *narodnichestvo* that made the peasant the center of its concerns. In the labor camp Voskoboinikov had adopted the nickname of *Zemlia,* or "Soil," and in the fall of 1941, as self-appointed spokesman for the rural masses, he again signed his Manifesto "Engineer Zemlia," followed by his initials, K.P.V. The twelve-point program called for the "complete destruction of the communist and kolkhoz system in Russia." About half the document dealt with questions of landholding and farming, calling for

> the free transfer in perpetuity of farm land to the peasantry, with the right to lease, exchange, and will, but without the right to sell. . . . The free award and use in perpetuity by each citizen of Russia of a garden plot, with the right to exchange and inherit, but not to sell. . . . All enterprises shall grant two months' leave a year so as to enable the beneficiaries to work on their own garden plots. . . . Free distribution of timber from state holdings, for the purpose of housing construction. . . .

Landholding in central Russia was to be set at about ten hectares, the garden plot at about one hectare per household.

The program also promised amnesty for all Komsomol members, Heroes of the Soviet Union, and rank-and-file party members "who have not sullied themselves by abusing the People." It contained no provisions for elective organs of government. But the most jarring note is the article calling for the "ruthless liquidation of Jews who were commissars." One may suspect that these points were either urged upon the authors or else volunteered by them with an eye to their acceptability by the German authorities. (But what about Jews who were not commissars? and what about commissars who were not Jews?) "Free labor, private property within the limits determined by law, state capitalism complemented and corrected by private initiative, and civic valor are the bases for the construction of a new state order in Russia," the Manifesto said. All railroads, forests, natural resources, and all "basic" factories would remain state-owned. In line with its attempt to appeal to national traditions and religious sentiments, the NSPR proclaimed the image and flag of St. George as its symbols.

The other documents were even less elegant of thought or expression. These may have been composed in cooperation with, or at the behest of, the Germans. The Russian soldier must surrender, and (he was told in what was a tip-off to the German paternity of the order) if he did so, his life would be spared. "The Stalin regime is doomed and will perish under all circumstances, but millions of innocent lives must be saved."

Voskoboinikov's actual practices and policies are largely unknown. It is a fact that he appealed to former communists for help; in the villages he fostered the return to a system of elective elders *(starosty)*. He seems to have continued social services, taking for granted public responsibility for "welfare" obligations. Some hospitals, elementary schools, and churches were reopened, and special grants-in-aid were provided for families whose heads were in the army.

The collective farms were not chaotically dissolved and looted, as was frequently the case on occupied soil, but rather were declared "people's property." In name at least, each peasant household became the owner of a piece of land. Agricultural equipment, however, remained communal property, with the peasants as joint owners of what was left of kolkhoz and MTS* equipment and machinery. In the future the peasants presumably would be free to leave the cooperatives if they desired.

As was true elsewhere on occupied territory, a local police detachment was set up to keep "law and order." In Lokot' it initially consisted of twelve men; a number of peasant boys and stragglers from the Red Army soon joined its ranks, and by the end of the year the "self-defense" force had grown to over two hundred men.[5]

On Voskoboinikov's relations with the Germans we have only the report of the German Foreign Office liaison officer, Anton Bossi-Fedrigotti, who visited Lokot' in the spring of 1942. Voskoboinikov, he reported, dispatched one of his deputies, Mosin, to the German army headquarters on two occasions; the second time he requested permission for the operation of his party. The army side-stepped this request; instead it sent Voskoboinikov a series of questions revealing the new German preoccupation on occupied soil: "(1) What is Voskoboinikov's attitude toward the partisans? (2) Is Voskoboinikov prepared to conduct propaganda against the partisans? (3) Is Voskoboinikov prepared to participate actively in the struggle against the partisans?" Mosin affirmed Voskoboinikov's willingness to fight the partisans

*Machine-Tractor Station.

and promised to provide further data sought by the intelligence section of Second Army.[6] Soon Second Army moved on, and Second Panzer Army took over the Briansk-Orel area.

Lokot' was more independent and more progressive than most areas under the Germans. It was also more active in recruiting peasant support in the surrounding region and blanketed the area with oral and written propaganda. By the end of 1941 Soviet partisans began to pay special attention to Voskoboinikov's "republic." The same factors which had enabled him to gain a measure of autonomy—weakness of German personnel and organization, terrain, and general disorganization—had made it possible for pro-Soviet stragglers to band together, too. By December, 1941, some of these groups had re-established contact with the Soviet side, which soon began to provide some direction and reinforcements in men and matériel.

In December, a group of partisans was dispersed near Lokot' by the new "self-defense" force. On January 8, 1941, another group attacked and briefly seized Lokot'. Some of Voskoboinikov's men were on leave; others were drunk over Russian Christmas. While sustaining heavy losses themselves, the partisans inflicted considerable casualties on the Lokot' forces—ostensibly, about fifty men—and shot up Voskoboinikov's headquarters. Voskoboinikov himself was wounded in the attack and died soon after.[7]

The most detailed (though distorted) accounts of this encounter come from Soviet sources. They betray some awkwardness in dealing with this unit. An early postwar memoir on the Briansk forests partisans relates how Voskoboinikov, "by training a pedagogue, by profession a counterrevolutionary,"

> . . . authored a "declaration of the rights of the peoples of Russia" [strictly speaking, an incorrect ascription], which he spread among the population. Often he would himself drive out to villages and *khutors,* conducting conferences or making speeches at markets and fairs. . . .[8]

Soviet partisan headquarters, these accounts make clear, considered him enough of a menace to order an early raid on Lokot'. Voskoboinikov was to be captured alive. Under the command of Alexander Saburov (later a leading partisan general) several detachments combined forces to carry out the raid.

In his own memoirs, Saburov deals with this episode in greater detail. According to his version, a partisan agent was sent to Lokot', where he managed to become deputy commander of the headquarters guard. Somehow the Germans managed to intercept a messenger sent by him to the partisans, whereupon Saburov threw his men into immediate attack on Lokot'. The raid succeeded: the core of the officers' cadres was smashed and the party leadership destroyed.

In his postwar account, Saburov was faced with the problem of how to explain the "experiment," for the Lokot' enterprise could not be written off as a Nazi endeavor. In the 1953 Soviet version (reprinted essentially unchanged in later editions), Voskoboinikov and his sponsors emerge as creatures of United States intelligence! This convenient fiction provides an explanation for the "peculiarities" of Voskoboinikov's program, while simultaneously linking American programs of anti-Soviet intervention with those of the Nazis.[9] To the analyst, the Soviet linkage of the Voskoboinikov enterprise with American goals or values constitutes an additional piece of evidence in support of the hypothesis that the Lokot' adventure indeed had aims which differed markedly from those of Moscow and Berlin alike.

II. LOKOT' AND THE GERMANS

The man who replaced Voskoboinikov was Bronislav Vladislavovich Kaminsky. His father was a Pole who, Kaminsky later alleged, had married a *Volksdeutsche* girl (a story which, though oft-repeated, cannot be accepted since it is likely to have served merely to make Kaminsky more "equal" to the Germans). Before the Revolution the family lived rather comfortably on an estate in the Vitebsk area, where Bronislav was born on June 16, 1899. In the 1920s he was trained as a chemical engineer in Leningrad. Like others with a Polish background, he was arrested around 1935 and reportedly charged with liaison with Polish and German agents. He was sentenced and shipped to the Nizhnii-Tagil'sk concentration camp, in Cheliabinsk *oblast'*. Among the camp inmates were a number of intellectuals, including a group he later characterized as Bukharinites. Opposition to the kolkhoz system was common among them. In 1940 Kaminsky was released and assigned to "forced residence" in Lokot' as an engineer at the local liquor distillery.[10]

He impressed friends and foes as basically nonpolitical though obviously anti-Bolshevik and as inordinately ambitious and frustrated. Now at last his thirst for authority and assertion seemed to find an outlet. A former associate of his describes him as "an adventurer, stupid and self-centered, conceited, and politically illiterate." He liked to picture himself in the role of "an omnipotent executive who made order in his realm in defiance of all difficulties, as well as the military commander of a force which . . . he would time and again lead to victory." An official German visitor found Kaminsky to be "a pompous ignoramus who enjoyed and hence overdid his warlording."[11]

One suspects that Kaminsky had been in some contact with the Germans even before Voskoboinikov's death; in January, 1942, he requested their confirmation of his authority as his successor. He had survived the partisan raid because he lived at some distance from the Lokot' headquarters; apparently he had turned down a subsequent partisan appeal to join them.

Little is known of his early dealings with the Germans. Mikhail Oktan, another leading demagogue and collaborator in the occupied area, testified later:

> I was invited to the headquarters of Army Group Center and asked to take over the administration of Orel. At headquarters I met Kaminsky, who had been called there in connection with the death of the chief of the Lokot' district, Voskoboinikov. We lived in the same room, and I had

occasion to attend several meetings between Kaminsky and General Hamann, who commanded the rear area of Third [Second?] Army, and to act as interpreter. Kaminsky promised, in return for a mandate to run the district, to bring it into closer ties with the German military administration, to militarize it so as to protect the rear of the German army, and to increase the food supply to the German troops.[12]

German approval came promptly. At a moment of demoralization and in the absence of other "leader" types, Kaminsky stood out. He was sufficiently aware of "public opinion" to depict his assumption of authority as a native act. He persuaded Voskoboinikov's widow, a local schoolteacher, to endorse his succession.[13] Thus began the first phase of Kaminsky's reign: until July, 1943, he was *Oberbürgermeister* and commander-in-chief of the Lokot' forces.

The German army soon concluded that the Kaminsky experiment was a success: he kept order, fought the partisans, and supplied the army with the requisite quantities of food. A variety of his new measures were aimed at tightening discipline and giving the "police force" special privileges as incentives for loyal performance. One order proclaimed a "state of war" and authorized the village elders to draft any man between seventeen and fifty years of age for essential tasks. Another decree forbade travel among the villages of the district, barred public gatherings, imposed a curfew, and temporarily placed the Lokot' market and the church of Brasovo off limits—evidently in anticipation of a new partisan attack. An announcement reported that a policeman had been shot for "drunkenness, robbery, and disgrace." And Order No. 33 stipulated that

> . . . in order to preserve peace and order, I decree that within three days the residents of Lipovaia Alley and Vesenii Pereulok [in Lokot'] be moved to other streets. The apartments thus freed are to be assigned to the families of policemen. . . .[14]

In February Kaminsky ordered his troops reorganized into the "First Russian National Army" in anticipation of "major" antipartisan operations.

The Germans' willingness to support him was increased by the absence of political objections to his reign. "Kaminsky does not spread Russian national propaganda," one German officer summed it up: "he runs his administration by the prestige of his own personality; and he claims to be a 'faithful thane of the Germans,' who come to free the Russian people from Bolshevism." "For our purposes, the new mayor is a good collaborator," concludes another reconnaissance report. Kaminsky gave promise of being a useful instrument precisely because he depended on his German masters for help, or so they believed. The German Foreign Office observer, Bossi-Fedrigotti, sent home a detailed report after visiting Lokot' in April, 1942:

> Kaminsky openly grants that without the consent of German political officialdom he will not proceed to make his combat unit into a political instrument. At the moment he understands that his tasks are of a purely military [i.e., antipartisan] nature. . . . Above all, it seems that with clever

> political handling Kaminsky could be made serviceable for German plans to reorganize the East. This man can surely become a propagandist of the German new order in the East, provided one does justice to certain demands of Russian mentality.[15]

A few months later a German propaganda official, after investigating the situation, concluded:

> After a number of conversations, I believe I can say with assurance that Kaminsky has no political ambitions, that he wants to become neither "*Gauleiter* of Lokot' " nor "tsar of Russia." This experiment . . . proves that it is possible . . . to use Russians under a watchful German eye for the benefit of our war effort.[16]

Kaminsky's lack of political ambitions may have been a German misconception. His impact on German policy-makers, however, was clear: he must be supported in his district and in his paramilitary operations.

Two letters from Second Panzer Army on February 23, 1942, reflected the German decision to "promote" Kaminsky. One authorized him to appoint village elders and majors within his district. The other entitled him to give awards, in the form of landholdings, for anti-partisan exploits (normally two but in exceptional cases up to ten hectares of land), and to proceed with at least a tentative distribution of the available horses and cows.[17] His district was soon considerably expanded to encompass several neighboring *raiony* (including two from adjacent Kursk *oblast'*).[18] On July 19, 1942, Colonel General Rudolf Schmidt, of Second Panzer, formally charged Kaminsky with "self-government in the administrative district of Lokot' and appointed him commander of the militias of this area, with the rank of brigade commander."[19]

While there was some autonomy, there was no popular sovereignty. Lokot' was Kaminsky's midget realm in which he ruled as a dictator. And yet, compared with German conduct in other occupied areas, Lokot' constituted a significant exception. It was (excluding the short-lived Karachai and Azov Cossack districts) virtually the only area in which the Germans agreed to place the administration in indigenous hands.

Characteristically, the experiment, which ran counter to basic Nazi policy, was neither stopped nor extended to other areas. It was not the "men of good will" in Berlin–i.e., the advocates of a more generous policy toward Russia, like Schulenburg, Strikfeld, or Hilger–who backed the Kaminsky venture, but primarily the German military, such as General Schmidt and later Field Marshal von Kluge, the ambivalent commander of Army Group Center. Concerned with efficient control, they were scarcely disposed to support a Russian national movement and in all likelihood would have scuttled Kaminsky if he had displayed any independence contrary to the program of his protectors. But Kaminsky did what they wanted him to.

Sooner or later the "autonomous district" had to be sanctioned by higher authority. An early opportunity was created when Kaminsky, after only a few weeks in office, addressed a letter to Hitler. (Apparently it had been carefully gone over by the German liaison staff.) In an accompanying letter to Army Group Center, requesting that the Kaminsky message be forwarded to Hitler, General Schmidt expressed the view that

> the ideas contained in the letter unquestionably correspond to the expectations and hopes of those parts of the population who are still in sympathy with us. . . . [He] has created an island within the extensive partisan area of Briansk-Dmitrovsk-Sevsk-Trubchevsk, which prevents the expansion of the partisan movement, ties up strong partisan forces, and offers an opportunity to spread German propaganda among the population. In addition, the district supplies food for the German troops. . . .
>
> The fact that, thanks to the successful deployment of Russian forces under Kaminsky's leadership, it was possible to invest no further German units and to save German blood in fighting the partisans prompts me to comply with this man's desire and to forward the letter addressed to the Fuehrer. Moreover, I believe that I may not withhold from the Fuehrer these ideas which are widespread among that part of the Russian population which is prepared to collaborate with Germany, but which are only rarely if ever written down by the Russians themselves.[20]

Kaminsky's letter was indeed a curious document. A "sense of obligation" to his native land, he wrote, led him to discuss why the war, once expected to be terminated victoriously within three months, still dragged on. The vast spaces and the weather were not adequate explanations. Red Army discipline and morale, after two decades of indoctrination, proved more formidable than anticipated. Above all, "propaganda, the strongest weapon in a war against the Soviets, had not been used." After prolonged saturation with Soviet "poison," Kaminsky continued, "there is a marked demand for the propagation of new ideas in harmony with the new [forthcoming] order of state and economy. The solution of these problems now, in wartime, is of great importance for the further conduct of the war."

Echoing Voskoboinikov's Manifesto, Kaminsky proceeded to summarize his program:

> Above all else, the peasant wants to have his own land. Therefore it should be divided now, before the spring sowing. . . . The best land should go to those who have fought, arms in hand, against the Soviet system. . . . The second important question for the peasants is the distribution of horses. . . . The third is the economic-industrial question. It is difficult to organize Russian private enterprise. Time is needed to effect the transfer from state to private economy, . . . No enterprise must be permitted to stay idle and its workers unemployed. However, the representatives of the new order have thus far shown very little interest in this problem.[21]

Army Group Center transmitted the letter to Berlin with a favorable endorsement. Hitler was evidently informed and at the end of March was reported to have approved the experiment, though it remains uncertain just how explicit his approval was.[22]

Most of the Germans' dealings with Kaminsky were handled by the liaison staffs assigned to Lokot' or operating nearby. Until May, 1942 no German troops were stationed there, and he dealt largely with army headquarters in Orel or with smaller units passing through. Even after that date no military government detachment was established in the district; and when the entire army rear area was reorganized into nine administrative units, one of them was the "Self-Governing District."[23]

A regular liaison officer was assigned to Kaminsky in July, 1942. Major von Veltheim was "to assist [Kaminsky] in an advisory capacity. Coordination with other parts of the Army Area is desirable."[24] While Veltheim's functions were primarily political and administrative, a military staff was responsible for the anti-partisan activities of Kaminsky's forces: General Bernhard, the commander of the "Rear Area" in which Lokot' was located, went to some trouble to explain that, though technically Colonel Rübsam was the equivalent of a German commandant for the Lokot' area, his tasks were primarily those of military coordination.[25]

Much of this carefully defined chain of command and authority was systematically disregarded by everyone, especially by Kaminsky himself. He was intent on minimizing the interference of the Germans while maximizing their contributions to him in the form of ammunition and weapons, and their recognition of his status by tokens such as letters of appreciation, cases of vodka, and medals of honor.

As time went on, other German agencies also sent their delegates or representatives to Lokot'. Army propaganda and economic agencies had their staffs there. Finally the SS, increasingly taking charge of anti-partisan warfare, was interested in cultivating relations with Kaminsky and—typically, given the power struggle among the Nazi *diadochi*—in wooing him away from the army. A Russian-speaking Baltic-German officer, Georg Loleit, was made SS liaison man to Kaminsky, apparently managing to win his confidence. In fact, the transfer of further neighboring districts to Kaminsky's jurisdiction took place with the joint approval of army and SS: these were areas where, in practice, the partisans were in control.

One may wonder why Kaminsky remained so faithful to the Germans. The reason seems to lie partly in his own vanity and ambition for power which, he realized, only German backing could provide. In addition, Kaminsky was virtually isolated from all opportunities to witness the abuse of prisoners of war and the humiliation of *Ostarbeiter* which so strongly affected captured Soviet officers and civilians. Nor did his men have to pass through the degrading phase of *Hiwi* battalions of auxiliaries. Kaminsky could explain away all shortcomings as due to the exigencies of war. He saw only a few Germans, and the personnel of the liaison staff consisted, more often than not, of clever and tactful men. Most of them were attuned to Kaminsky's foibles, and they made sure to "advise" him, not to order him around. They even catered to his inordinate urge for formal recognition.[26] Partly by accident and partly by intent, he was placed in a position in which it was relatively easy for him to "collaborate"—easier than for Soviet prisoners of war who remained adamantly anti-German, and for those collaborators who had a more realistic picture of Nazi goals and means.

III. LIFE IN THE DISTRICT

As time passed, Kaminsky became increasingly a military commander. His armed force was both an index and a source of his authority, and (at least to the Germans) the *raison d'être* of his regime. It began with the small militia detachments established in Lokot' under his predecessor in the fall of 1941. With the growth of the partisan movement in the Briansk forests, the Germans pressed Kaminsky to expand his own police unit into a fighting force. He needed little encouragement. In February, 1942, the police force was officially renamed the Russian Popular Army of Liberation—*Russkaia Osvoboditel'naia Narodnaia Armiia,* or RONA.[27] It expanded from 5,000 men in July, 1942, to about 8,000 in December, and over 10,000 in the spring of 1943.[28]

In mid-1942, 85 percent of its troops were local inhabitants; the others were deserters from partisan units, former prisoners released by the Germans, and a few Red Army men who had been hiding in the woods. With the passage of time the relative weight of nonlocal and nonvoluntary elements increased. A number of peasants became Kaminsky's men—some of them afraid of partisan retaliation. Late in 1942, with the consent of the Germans, Kaminsky toured prisoner-of-war camps in the Orel area to recruit a few officers, whom his brigade lacked. Gradually the assemblage of amateur policemen and opportunist pillagers was transformed into a fairly effective fighting force.[29]

As new men arrived, the original battalion swelled to five regiments with a total of fifteen battalions, of which fourteen were directly under Kaminsky and one was organized as a special German-trained "volunteer" combat unit.[30] In December, 1942, four of his battalions wore German uniforms. "The rest," a German visitor reported, "make the impression of a heap of wild bandits." Civilian dress and pieces of Red Army and German uniforms were worn in incongruous combinations. Often it was impossible to tell whether a soldier (or a whole unit) belonged to Kaminsky's troops or to the partisans.

The brigade was organized on the model of the Red Army. The men were encouraged to gather abandoned Red Army weapons and equipment; additional quantities were captured from the partisans. But there remained severe shortages of many goods, such as shoes, ammunition, and medical supplies, and the Germans were obliged to supply some of these items.

Kaminsky's men participated in anti-partisan operations with only a minimum of discipline. Indeed, one former RONA man asserts that "the absence of discipline was what kept the organization going. Usually there were no restrictions on looting." Kaminsky was evidently eager to tighten discipline, both to perform his mission and to impress the Germans.[31]

With all its serious deficiencies, this colorful horde proved relatively successful in fighting the partisans. The brigade was careful not always to accept battle. As a matter of policy it never seized towns, both because the Germans had effective control over urban areas, and because the partisans operated primarily in the countryside. Major encounters were usually accompanied by desertions in both directions. In 1942 the number of partisans joining Kaminsky seems to have exceeded that of RONA men switching to the Soviet side; this was due in large measure to RONA's better food and supplies.

Summary reports by Germans and RONA officers spoke of the brigade's accomplishments with praise, whereas individual contemporary documents tended to concentrate on failures and shortcomings. The missions assigned to the brigade appear to have become progressively more taxing and hazardous as the unit and its skill grew. In June, 1942, partisan pressure began to increase markedly; by September they had become reinforced by air from the Soviet side with specialist personnel, explosives, radios, and heavy weapons. Now even Kaminsky's newly recruited "volunteer battalion," albeit under German command, was thrown into action against them. Though morale in this unit was admittedly worse than in the older Kaminsky battalions, the following report on its performance is indicative of the general trend (allowing for its author's prejudices and ignorance of the Russian language):

> Despite severe prohibition, there was looting. . . . As officers took part in it, it was quite impossible to keep the men in check. At night the men on guard duty left their posts without cause. The rations issued for two days were consumed in their entirety during the first day; part of the bread was given as a gift to civilians—largely as a matter of convenience, so the men would not have to carry it with them. The following day there was frequent grumbling about lack of supplies. Occasionally uncomradely behavior was exhibited in the distribution of rations. One sought to gain special advantage and outdo the others. . . .[32]

In October, 1942, a German officer criticized the brigade's armor as inferior and recommended withholding fuel from the RONA tanks (given the German gasoline shortage). As partisan attacks increased, General Bernhard was constrained to admit that "in view of the state of its clothing and its local roots, the militia of Engineer Kaminsky would seem at present to be in no condition to fend off major attacks by itself."[33]

As the fortunes of war changed and the partisans picked up strength, the Germans began to respond with a series of major operations against the bands in the Briansk forests, with Kaminsky fighting essentially under German orders. In the words of a Nazi official, he and his men "wage a daily struggle against the partisans, thereby *saving the German command the use of one division.*"[34] Conditions were becoming more and more tense, and correspondingly the treatment of civilians by the Kaminsky troops—especially of residents outside his district—deteriorated further. If they refused to obey RONA orders, survivors recall, "the people were punished, beaten or shot."[35]

Given the general trend of events and the behavior of Kaminsky's men, it was small wonder that by mid-1943 the rank-and-file peasantry had frequently withdrawn what support it had previously given to the Lokot' experiment.

What authority Kaminsky enjoyed among his own troops and "subjects" is a more difficult question to answer. With those who depended on him he could be both exceedingly cruel and unexpectedly generous. In 1942-43 he appears to have been generally respected by his men. A man who joined his forces after fighting as a partisan for over a year put it briefly: "Kaminsky was popular because he permitted looting." While this was by no means the whole story, it is clear that the lack of discipline as well as the better material conditions demonstrated to the RONA men the advantages of belonging to it. Indeed, the kinds of "manpower" which Kaminsky and the partisans disposed of were fundamentally the same. "Most of them," one eyewitness reflected, "did not know what they were fighting for or against. One had to fight—that's all."

Kaminsky himself had become a full-fledged dictator. His will was supreme.[36] He and his staff acted with an arrogant haughtiness and self-assured disregard for the rights of others, which amazed and distressed their victims as well as some German observers. Major von Veltheim is said to have remarked that Kaminsky ruled "like an African chieftain who was prepared to use any means to prove everyone's dependence on him."[37]

To this picture must be added the extraordinary favoritism shown by Kaminsky and his aides. Partly because of the shortage of trained officers, partly on impulse, Kaminsky promoted soldiers who had been corporals or sergeants in the Red Army to majors and colonels by the stroke of a pen if he took a liking to them. The by-product of this "intuitive" promotion system was the advancement of incompetent sycophants and illiterate adventurers to positions of considerable authority.

> The Germans issued 22 rations daily for headquarters [a Kaminsky staff officer relates]. Furthermore, we had considerable supplies—chickens, ducks, meat—for headquarters personnel. We took hams and sausages instead of taxes from the peasants whenever we wanted. In general, headquarters lived well, taking any amount of food and supplies from the storeroom simply by signing for it. Later a special officers' club was built, and there were frequent drinking parties, to which sometimes a few enlisted men would be invited, usually from the headquarters guard battalion.[38]

By and large, the special privileges benefited only the top command of the brigade and a few of the civilian officials in the district. A (rather inferior) theater and ballet company was established in Lokot', and Kaminsky would make pompous appearances at gala performances there—to unending "spontaneous" applause from the soldier and peasant audience. For a while, there was both bread and circus. And then there was neither.

The administration of the district was neglected. Kaminsky, a German visitor discovered, was interested in his own prestige, in anti-partisan warfare, and in vague political plans, roughly in that order; "only in the last place is he interested in administration." Those who knew him doubted whether he would ever make a decent administrator. On the *raion* level, section heads, appointed by Kaminsky, had very little responsibility. He reserved the right to make decisions, using the "one form of persuasion [he knew] : an order." The file of orders issued as laws or decrees was an incredible hodge-podge:

> The tax law would be followed by the dismissal of a typist and the appointment of her successor; then comes a proclamation making the Lokot' newspaper, *Golos naroda,* the official organ of party and state; a subsidy of 50 kilograms of grain and 300 rubles is given to the family of a slain militia officer; there follows the introduction of daylight-saving time; and then the amnesty of [April 20, 1943]. All these orders are issued in the form of an official gazette.

The decrees, orders, and laws (no proper distinction was made among them) reflected Kaminsky's impulsive approach, uninhibited by traditional procedures and professional standards. In addition, there was the typical tendency to overstaff, both as a form of "conspicuous consumption" and as a way of breeding a sense of dependence and gratitude in a somewhat privileged stratum of officialdom. As of October, 1942, the civilian administration of the district alone included twenty sections with a total of over 500 employees—in addition to those on the *raion* and village levels.[39]

Some social services were provided—reflecting an axiomatic assumption of government responsibility—for such groups as surviving dependents of combat casualties. A number of schools were reopened—first, four-grade schools; then, in the fall of 1942, some seven- and ten-grade schools—but in these attendance tended to be small because of the competing demands on scarce manpower. In November, 1942, the eight *raiony* of the district were officially reported to have 284 schools in operation—all but 27 of these had four grades. One vocational school and a rudimentary teachers' college were also begun. German was taught from the fourth grade on. There was no religious instruction in the schools, but technically parents were free to decide whether or not they wanted their children to study religion. There were only two priests in the district (or, rather, two who collaborated with Kaminsky's authorities), and while apparently a Roman Catholic by background (though hardly an ardent believer), Kaminsky supported and attended the Orthodox church. A primitive hospital functioned in Lokot' under the guidance of two Russian physicians. In March, 1942, the Germans authorized regular publication of a newspaper, and from then on *Golos naroda* (Voice of the People) appeared every three days (initially, every ten days; later every week) in some 8,000 to 14,000 copies. Given the lack of other mass media, it was reportedly in great demand in the district.[40]

The judicial organs were confused by an absence of any definition of their competence. Military and civil jurisdiction overlapped. Courts-martial were convened whenever Kaminsky desired. The head of the brigade's investigative branch generally acted as prosecutor, and customarily a defendant was allowed an attorney. By special agreement, death sentences against militia members required the approval of the German liaison staff. Much of the judicial process was made ludicrous, however, because all sentences were subject to Kaminsky's personal review. He had the right to reduce or augment them. Only for minor misdemeanors were norms of punishment fairly well defined; a Justice of the Peace handled many of these as well as civil cases. Appeals were heard by the district court. A special agreement provided for turning over major political offenders to the Germans. In addition to fines, the local court could impose forced labor sentences. These were generally preferred by the population, for treatment in the three jails of the district was deemed to be far more severe.[41]

The representatives of "authority"—military and civilian alike—became a distinct caste, which, however, could be joined by peasants and former enemy troops. Indeed, thanks to a peculiar system of "military settlements" there was a considerable overlap of functions between army and peasantry.

Except for guard posts and a part of headquarters, the brigade was quartered in peasant huts throughout the district. In the intervals between fighting, the soldiers worked as farmhands. Later, at the suggestion of the Germans, married soldiers were given higher pay—with the result that the number of marriages increased.

The farm problem had been a major source of grievance and concern from the start. Voskoboinikov had appealed to those who were discontented with the kolkhoz; and German failure promptly to partition the collectives had helped antagonize many peasants. Under Kaminsky, too, there was no full return to private farming, but a make-shift system reflecting an accommodation to German desires and pressures as well as an effort to give the peasants some tangible improvement of their status. Those actively engaged in fighting "the Reds" were given top priority in the repossession of land.

Various forms of agricultural cooperation were adopted in many localities. The existing farm equipment was owned jointly by neighboring households. What cattle the peasants managed to find, they came to own and "use." Some MTS continued to exist but with only a minimum of equipment (most of the machinery having been wrecked or removed before the Soviet evacuation). Now the stations were attached to specific villages and no longer received the taxes they had levied under the Soviet regime.

In 1942 the peasants were, on the whole, not too badly off. As a result Kaminsky successfully collected a part of the harvest as taxes and deliveries for his own and for the German forces. Until June, 1942, the brigade lived off the land whenever it left the district and survived on partisan supplies it managed to capture. When these supplies were exhausted, however, it was necessary to assess the peasants in the district (with the politically astute proviso that no deliveries were to exceed 50 percent of what had been compulsory deliveries under Soviet rule). The dependents of brigade members received a subsistence allowance in food, also.

Kaminsky endeared himself to the Germans by the efficiency with which he fulfilled the delivery norms. The chief German agricultural expert states that the Lokot' district was more efficient in collecting grain than were the Germans themselves.[42] The peasants turned in the grain willingly for two reasons: the protection the brigade afforded them against partisan raids and the realization that the system forestalled direct German levies. Beyond the amounts paid as taxes, peasants and soldier-settlers could sell their produce on the market or turn it over to the local authorities for resale to the Germans.[43]

And yet, Kaminsky's rule was distinctly less popular with the civilians than with the soldiers, who were the architects of their own privileges under the new regime. People outside his district rarely heard of Kaminsky; neither Soviet nor German news media publicized his existence. The group which most decisively turned against him was the peasant population in the villages raided by his troops in cooperation with the Germans or other auxiliaries, and which it subjected to considerable privation, often to atrocities and murder. The upshot was a strange glorification of Voskoboinikov, his "well-intentioned" predecessor. As a bitter German officer reported in October, 1942,

> several persons acquainted with the situation (Major von Veltheim, Major Müller, 1st Lt. Buchholz) agree in maintaining, independently of each other, that the population still reveres the predecessor of Kaminsky, shot by the partisans, but that they hate Kaminsky. They "tremble" before him and ostensibly are kept in line only by fear.[44]

The situation was bound to become even more serious as the Germans suffered setbacks and the partisans continued to gain in strength.

IV. LEPEL', 1943-44

The German military situation deteriorated drastically after Stalingrad. Manpower and supply shortages became more telling. The newly-won Soviet victories and the sense of initiative fired the soldiers and partisans with daring and confidence. By 1943 the bulk of the population in the occupied Soviet areas—even those who had originally accepted the Germans without pronounced hostility—had turned sharply against them in reaction to their policies and behavior. In early summer of 1943, when a new Soviet offensive was unleashed along the Kursk-Orel front, Lokot' found itself close to the front lines. On September 5, Lokot' was reoccupied by the Soviet Army.

Late in July the German army completed its evacuation plans;[45] the entire "self-government" of Lokot' district was to be transplanted and re-established behind the so-called Panther position in Belorussia. Evacuation was begun in August and completed in September; the most reliable figures speak of a total of 6,000 soldiers and 25,000 civilians.[46] Meanwhile Army Group Center had informed the high command in Berlin that

> The transfer of the Self-Governing District of Lokot' to the area of Lepel' is being carried out for the following reasons:
>
> (a) The Lokot' District was established with the Fuehrer's specific sanction and has proved itself. It has always been an experiment, which one must in the last analysis consider to have succeeded, in spite of various difficulties.
>
> (b) The new area is economically very valuable and is capable of absorbing an additional 60,000 men.
>
> (c) Because of the lack of our own security forces and the unfavorable transportation situation, economic exploitation to date has been poor.
>
> (d) If the Self-Governing District under Kaminsky proves strong enough to pacify this presently partisan-threatened area (a development for which there is a good prospect in view of Kaminsky's energetic personality, his political outlook, and the ratio of forces of his militia [to the partisans]), the economic utilization of the area will be very valuable. If on the other hand the District should become unsafe, there would be no immediate threat to the military lines of transportation here. . . .[47]

Actually there was a good deal of disagreement over the brigade's prospects, even among the liaison staff. Captain Könnecke, who headed the army liaison staff at the new location, and Loleit, the SS aide, expected the Lepel' experiment to succeed, provided food could be found, evacuees settled, and military equipment supplied. Kraushaar, who represented Third Panzer Army, however, was dubious whether Kaminsky could take root in the new area and successfully fight the "red bands."[48]

Whatever the reservations, Kaminsky took over his new "Self-Governing District" on October 1. Though the area was to consist of five *raiony,* he was originally allocated only three (Lepel', Ushachi, and Chashniki); the other two (Senno and Beshenkovichi) were largely in partisan hands.[49] The German *kommendaturas,* which had previously ruled here, now withdrew.

Kaminsky's task in Lepel' was more military than it had been in Lokot'. The very reason the German command had selected Lepel' as his new headquarters was that the district had been virtually abandoned to the partisans. In the area of Ushachi, regular Red Army units remained concealed throughout the German occupation, built defense fortifications, maintained kolkhozes, and established a Soviet-type administration. Here the partisans had at their disposal several airfields through which the Soviet Staff for Partisan Warfare for Belorussia supplied them with arms, ammunition, radio, and other equipment.

Army Group Center officially acknowledged these difficulties:

> Kaminsky's position is not simple, and he himself looks upon it as serious. Conditions in the Self-Governing District of Lokot' were significantly different from those which now prevail at Lepel'. The new territory, thus far ruled for the most part by bands, and throughout infested by partisans, must first be conquered by Kaminsky and his men. Even if no one thus far has had reason to doubt Kaminsky's loyalty, his troops cannot any longer be deemed reliable.[50]

Thus the brigade had to fight its way into its new domicile. Even when it managed to dislodge the partisans, the civilian population was overwhelmingly hostile to this "band of outsiders." It was not so much the fact that it was a Russian group stationed on Belorussian soil—there is no evidence of chauvinism in the peasants' reaction—as the fact that the peasantry, having been exposed to German treatment for two years, had resolutely taken sides against the Nazis and their allies. Perhaps more important than political considerations (they had little affection for the marauding partisans who restored collective farms) was the fact that the arrival of the RONA brought a further deterioration of material conditions.

Kaminsky made no effort to win the good will of his new subjects. His men constituted an elite superimposed on an impotent population deprived of all support except from the Red partisans. Moreover, Kaminsky promptly antagonized those among the indigenous population who had collaborated with the Germans by ousting local residents from their houses, which he used as billets; next he replaced the indigenous administration with his own men.

The result was the first serious clash between Kaminsky and the German military. Third Panzer Army, in whose area Lepel' was located, sought to mediate between the brigade and the inhabitants. Kaminsky, however, indignantly insisted that the German command keep its promise that he would have the same prerogatives as he had had in Lokot'. Additional friction stemmed from the appearance of new German agencies at his side. German censorship over his printing presses was established. Economic agencies insisted that their (very small) yield from the Lepel' area must not be jeopardized by the brigade's arrival. Finally, a conflict developed when the Germans decided that Kaminsky was to secure "his" three *raions* in their entirety, while he sought to concentrate all his men in and around Lepel', apparently for the sake of greater safety. The upshot was continuous friction with the Wehrmacht—a development which was to foster his transfer to the SS.[51]

While thus waging a three-cornered fight against partisans, population, and (only "diplomatically") against the Germans, Kaminsky was faced with revolt in his own midst. Given the semi-anarchical way of life of his men and the continual interpenetration between partisans and RONA, it is not surprising that both Soviet-sponsored cells of dissidents and independently-dissatisfied groups willing to redefect to the "Reds" developed.

The trouble began in Lokot' in November, 1942, when three communist cells with a total of thirty-four members were uncovered. Other contacts had been established within Kaminsky's units by the Soviet partisan brigade, *Za Rodinu.* Among others, it was in touch with his chief of the Mobilization Section, Vasiliev, who had been a Red Army quartermaster officer. On one of his trips into remote areas of the Lokot' district, Vasiliev was evidently won over by the partisans and instructed to form a cell that might try to overthrow Kaminsky, help the partisans blow up railway tracks, and disrupt telephone lines around Lokot'. On March 26, 1943, the partisans were to come out of the forests and break through to the Soviet lines, some twenty miles away. Meanwhile Vasiliev was to arrest the officers of the RONA. But the plot was uncovered; all that took place on the prearranged date was a Soviet air raid on Lokot'. The summary court sentenced some 38 men to be shot. Characteristically, Kaminsky commuted the sentence of Vasiliev, his mother, and his wife—ostensibly because he had been on intimate terms with the nineteen-year old sister of Vasiliev's wife. Vasiliev evidently managed to stay behind when the brigade moved west; he was reported captured in Soviet-held Minsk and hanged there.[52]

No wholesale defections occurred during the brigade's move to Lepel'. But once it arrived, a new and more serious revolt was not long in coming. On September 20, 1943, the commanding officer of Kaminsky's Second Regiment, Major Tarasov, stationed at Senno, rebelled and prepared to defect to the partisans. Between September 20 and 23, over 250 soldiers actually did desert with heavy weapons and equipment. Kaminsky flew to Senno, where he apprehended Major Tarasov and three of his officers. Tarasov was promptly condemned to be hanged, his *politruk* and two aides to be shot. The sentence was carried out in the presence of the Kaminsky force in the Senno area, with Kaminsky attending in general's uniform with decorations. Following this, Kaminsky toured his remaining outposts; he was again master of the situation, but the revolt had done irreparable harm to his self-assurance and prestige.[53]

Rebellions and attempts on Kaminsky's life continued. The situation was such that terror against deserters caught in the act no longer sufficed to intimidate others. The general disorganization, defeat, and depression, accompanied by shortages and German encroachments, propelled many into the partisan camp, where safe-conduct and possible forgiveness were promised to those who returned voluntarily.

Still there was a hard core, both in the brigade and among the civilians, who firmly held that there was no returning to the Soviet fold. Out of fear, conviction, or a quest for adventure and gain, they were determined to stick it out under Kaminsky's command.

In this atmosphere of growing insecurity and hostility on all sides, the brigade continued its operations. Even less inhibited on alien soil, answering partisan terror with terror, treating the local inhabitants with unwarranted brutality, Kaminsky's men became the scourge of the land. Even the Germans had no illusions on this score. Kaminsky himself went so far as to "trap" political rivals whom he "invited" to Lepel'. The local residents spoke of him as an appanage prince. As for the spreading abuse and immorality, the worst offender was one of his henchmen, the chief of the Prosecutor's Section, Protsiuk, who was rumored to have been an NKVD man before the war.[54] For a long time Kaminsky, who knew of his aide's cruelty, made no effort to interfere.

The soldiers of the brigade were scattered throughout villages of the district but in larger groups than before. Fighting now absorbed a much larger proportion of their energies, so that the system of "military settlements" was far less efficacious than it had been in Lokot'. Typically enough for the growing conversion from a "government" to an "army," 50 percent of the rations were now supplied by the Germans. There was no longer any question of selling surpluses to them.

Kaminsky's troops had become an unruly horde of mercenaries. While discipline continued to deteriorate, the loyal elements relied even more heavily on their leader. "After the evacuation from Lokot'," a German observer notes, "relations between Kaminsky and his men and the camp-followers became even closer. Here, on alien soil, one felt more keenly that one was fully dependent on him and that one's own fate hung on Kaminsky's fate." Moreover, his men felt that, once they were branded as followers of Kaminsky, they could expect no pity from their erstwhile masters and had little choice but to fight to the end.

Even at this stage, however, there were still defections *to* the brigade as well. One informant, captured in January, 1944, describes his own decision:

> I was captured by Kaminsky's men and some Cossack units fighting with them. They mistreated us but our village elders within the Lepel' district vouched for us and got me released on parole. What was I to do? If I went home, the partisans would shoot me for having fallen into Kaminsky's hands. If I stayed around, I'd have to hide, and the frontline was right near-by. So I decided to stay with the Kaminsky Brigade. . . .

Another notes that

> . . . in Belorussia we no longer had orders to shoot the partisans. So we would bring them back with us. Of course they would be beaten and mistreated, perhaps struck with rifle butts. After a day, the headquarters company would release them, give them a rifle, and they'd be *kamintsy*. The men had no choice: they could not be neutral; and if they did not risk going back, they had to stay with the German-controlled police—or with Kaminsky.

Actual military operations became increasingly bitter. Kaminsky, in a new tactical departure, kept the bulk of his forces in a few populated centers. On operations the brigade now acted as one element in a combination of German-directed forces and suffered increasingly heavy casualties.[55] By January, 1944 the armored battalion and the 5th Regiment were utterly decimated.

Confronted with hostility in his own ranks, among the local inhabitants, from the German military, and by the Soviet partisans, by early 1944 Kaminsky could think of only one potential "ally" left to rely on: the SS.

V. WESTWARD TO WARSAW

From February, 1944 on, Kaminsky's men were absorbed in incessant battles, which were part of the intensive though often futile German anti-partisan campaign in Belorussia. On the whole, the Brigade still performed more acceptably than some of the other "Eastern" units on the German side. Yet the partisans usually managed to elude their foes until finally joining the advancing Red Army.

Kaminsky seemed to acquiesce gladly to the military functions being thrust on his brigade. The one demand he made of his German liaison officers was to move "his" civilians to safety. Lepel' was no longer secure, especially when the brigade was far away in the forests and swamps. The Germans, foreseeing further retreats, prepared a new district for Kaminsky farther west: on February 23, 1944, the first order was issued to prepare for a transfer to Diatlovo, near Lida, in (formerly Polish) Western Belorussia.[56] This migration was to be slower and more hazardous than the move from Lokot'. By the end of March, some 3,000 soldiers and about 10,000 civilians—peasants from Lokot' and the soldiers' families—along with some 2,000 horses and 1,500 cows had been moved, and the name, "Kaminsky Self-Government District," was attached to this third area in the brigade's history. The transfer of authority was to take place gradually as the move from Lepel' was carried out.[57] The remaining troops were soon to follow.

Meanwhile a serious tug-of-war was raging within the Nazi elite. The influence of the professional military had declined sharply, while the SS continued to take over new branches of government and economy, displacing both civilian and military authorities. After his tiffs with Third Panzer Army, Kaminsky appears to have sensed that the SS managed to obtain more arms and equipment than did the army. His shift of allegiance was facilitated by the fact that virtually the entire anti-partisan effort was now directed by the SS.

For the SS, Kaminsky was a welcome tool. By 1944 it had begun to recruit replacements in the Baltic states and in other occupied areas. Important elements of the SS leadership had become convinced, reluctantly, in the face of disastrous retreats, that the only "secret weapon" which Germany still had was the population of the USSR.

The efforts of two high SS officials sufficed to bring Kaminsky under the wing of the SS. They were von Gottberg, the "Higher SS and Police Leader" for Belorussia, and Gottlob Berger, who headed the SS "Main Office" and represented the SS in Rosenberg's "Ministry for the Occupied East."

Sometime in the early summer of 1944 Himmler approved the absorption of the Kaminsky Brigade into the SS; as of July the SS listed it as the 29th *SS Waffen-Grenadier-Division RONA (russische Nr. 1),* a designation suggesting a projected expansion in size and the planned integration of the brigade into the regular *Waffen SS* machine. And on July 31, Himmler personally received Kaminsky at his headquarters in East Prussia, formally made him a SS officer, and awarded him the Iron Cross, first class.[58]

For the men in the brigade, the shift of jurisdiction was of little practical significance. Outwardly, the only change was the adoption of SS uniforms, but bearing the familiar "RONA" insignia on the new black coats. Discipline in the division continued to deteriorate. There were instances of rape. Two men from the headquarters platoon—once the elite of the unit—broke into a priest's house and stole valuables from his cellar. In its path the division burned down whole villages and killed the inhabitants.[59]

The change which both the division and its leader had undergone is expressed in the memoirs of the SS officer attached to Kaminsky:

> Kaminsky viewed the tie binding his following increasingly from the point of sheer utility, as the distance in space and time from Lokot' increased. In Lepel' they still hoped for an early return to the home district . . . , but with the increasing transition of the Kaminsky action into a Russian mercenary operation and the simultaneous change in Kaminsky's own attitude, the moral assessment of Kaminsky by his subordinates declined. They recognized increasingly that now the motives for his behavior were personal ambition, lust for adventure, and finally, even thirst for profit.

In May the remainder of the division, with heavy losses, fought its way westward from Lepel' to Diatlovo. The situation was familiar: the division had to oust the local population and fight at every step to "establish" itself. But the stay in Diatlovo was shortlived, too. The Soviet breakthrough was faster and more decisive than anticipated. In July, 1944, the remnants of the division—three regiments of some 4,000 men, almost 10,000 dependents, and camp followers (variously estimated at up to 14,000 men, women, and children)—again moved on, leaving Soviet soil forever.[60] Continuing westward, they were slated to move to the Sokolów area of the Government-General of Poland, north of Warsaw.[61]

Kaminsky's band was now only one of several refugee problems the Germans faced. Many thousands of Belorussians, Cossacks, Caucasians, and others were on the move as the Red Army stormed into Bobruisk, Minsk, and Baranoviche. Indeed, the German command now had little use for the "29th SS." Rosenberg's official representative with the badly mauled Army Group Center opined:

> To what extent this rather depraved group, which moves across the countryside stealing and plundering, heeding nothing, can be made to settle in the Government-General and to fight against partisans, cannot as yet be judged.[62]

At the end of July the fate of Kaminsky's hordes was in doubt.[63] Most of the personnel was moved to Upper Silesia, to the area between Ratibor and Częstochowa. Meanwhile the Polish underground army rose in Warsaw on August 1, 1944. With the Red Army but a few miles away, across the Vistula, the Poles opened an attack on the Germans, expecting the Russians to join hands and liberate the Polish capital. But the Soviet troops remained immobilized on the far side of the river, standing by while the Germans defeated the Polish rebels.

To suppress the rising, the SS badly needed reinforcements. Among those sent to Warsaw were Turkestanis and Cossacks fighting on the German side; the Dirlewanger Brigade, consisting of criminals released from Nazi concentration camps; and Kaminsky's "29th SS."

It is understandable that the participants in this, the most shameful episode of the Kaminsky affair, have been silent about it. It is equally natural that various myths should have arisen about their participation. Many of Kaminsky's officers, finally out of the fighting area and looking forward to relative comfort, were apparently loath to go into action in Warsaw. One version even speaks of an understanding among them to oppose the Warsaw venture—evidently an overstatement.[64] Their reluctance may, however, account for the decision to send only a part of the division into Warsaw.

A special regiment was speedily activated with members drawn from all units of the 29th SS, in compliance with German orders. The diary of a Kaminsky soldier killed in Warsaw contains an entry that on August 2 all single men in his unit were ordered to Warsaw.[65] As early as August 3 and August 4 the regiment was rushed to the Polish capital and promptly thrown into action.[66] The appointment of Major Frolov as regimental commander supports the hypothesis that there was friction within the division: Frolov was an undistinguished officer at Kaminsky's headquarters. None of the more dashing and better-known officers was offered—or, at any rate, none held—the job.[67]

The regiment, some 1,700 men in all, went into action in the borough of Ochota and found itself in a crucial sector for at least a week; later it was moved north of the rebel stronghold and into the suburban area of Puszcza Kampinoska.[68] From August 5 to August 27 the regiment was engaged in such "action" as to make its name synonymous in the popular mind with plunder, abuse, murder, and rape.

How is one to explain this? The debauchery cannot be considered merely the logical culmination of a continuous deterioration in morals and morale; its enormity was out of all proportion to what had occurred previously. Several interpretations may be considered. The least convincing is that of

Kaminsky's German friends, who attribute this development to the absence of German liaison personnel, who (they insist) had invariably had a restraining effect on the unit. More significant is the general atmosphere in which the action took place. In the course of savage street fighting, house after house went up in flames, and whatever was not seized or stolen was demolished and burned. The very tempo and destructiveness of the battle encouraged disregard for property and decency.[69]

Even more important was the predisposition of the troops as they entered Warsaw. After the long, weary trek from Central Russia, they had realized finally that they were on the losing side. They knew they had nothing to hope for. Whatever the outcome of the war, they were doomed. Thus Warsaw provided them with one, perhaps the last, opportunity to live riotously and release all restraints of civility and morals. *Après nous, le déluge!*[70]

This attitude was abetted by the fact that Warsaw was the first contact which Kaminsky's men had with the wealth and comfort of the "West." Here the loot and opportunities were far richer than those they had encountered in the desolate and impoverished villages of the USSR.

The upshot was an orgy horrifying enough to turn even the most ruthless Germans against the Special Regiment. A German general on August 5 asked to be relieved of his command because of the behavior of the RONA regiment, but his request was turned down by higher headquarters. Army and SS admonitions to restore discipline in the unit were in vain.

After the war, von dem Bach-Zelewski, who had overall charge of the Warsaw operation, was to testify that he had seen Kaminsky's men cart off entire carloads of "stolen jewelry, gold watches, and precious stones." As he recalled it, "The capture of a liquor supply was more important for the brigade than the seizure of a position commanding the same street."[71]

An eyewitness claims to remember how "Kaminsky was seen sitting on a Warsaw balcony with a girl on each knee, drinking champagne." To anyone familiar with the mood during the life-and-death struggle raging in Warsaw, this vignette—if true—speaks eloquently. Small wonder that a member of the Special Regiment concluded:

> There were savage orgies there. They raped nuns and plundered and stole anything they could get their fingers on. Some returned from Warsaw with five kilograms of gold. It was the most shameful episode I know of.[72]

The Germans hastened to get the rebellion over with, hoping that the Poles would yield more readily once they realized that neither the Red Army nearby nor the Western Allies would or could give them material aid. Von dem Bach therefore demanded that the Turkestanis and Kaminsky troops be brought under control. By the end of August the regiment was moved out of the Warsaw area. Minus some sixty casualties, the Special Regiment counted its loot, slowly sobered up, and prepared to rejoin the rest of the brigade.

What happened next is shrouded in contradictions. Two Germans who were close to Kaminsky seem to supply the most reliable account. According to them, Kaminsky was called to a German headquarters for a conference designed to settle the fate of his civilians. Meanwhile von dem Bach-Zelewski had related the excesses to Guderian, the newly-appointed chief of the General Staff. SS General Fegelein, an intimate at Hitler's headquarters in the final stages of the war and himself no better than Kaminsky's men, in turn informed Field Marshal Jodl of the incidents. "Ten minutes later," Jodl testified at Nuremberg, "I reported this fact to the Fuehrer, and he immediately ordered the dissolution of the brigade."[73]

The fate of the division was thus sealed. When Kaminsky showed up before the German command and was reproached for his troops' "wild plunder," he sought to defend himself.

> Kaminsky was enraged [one of the German officers recalls] : firstly, before going into action his men had been promised a free hand; secondly, he failed to understand the German point of view: he and his men had, in years of fighting for the Germans, lost all they had—and now they would not even be allowed to compensate themselves at the expense of the treacherous and rebellious Poles?[74]

Serious altercations ensued, until a clearly disgruntled and fearful Kaminsky, "put in his place" by the Germans, was hurriedly called back to Warsaw. A few days later his men were informed that he had been killed.

The version first broadcast blamed the murder on Polish partisans who allegedly ambushed Kaminsky, his chief of staff, doctor, and driver in a car about twenty miles south of Warsaw. Soon different versions, contradictory regarding time, place, and circumstances of the assassination, began to circulate. While some claimed that Kaminsky was shot while trying to escape the Germans, others asserted that, far from fleeing, he was on his way from Warsaw to his troops. The vicinity of Warsaw, the road to Ratibor, the city of Cracow, and the Tatra Mountains have all been given as locales of the murder. All these versions appear to have been concocted in the aftermath of the leader's disappearance.

The officers of the Special Regiment, suspicious of the official account, insisted on investigating the circumstances on the spot. Ten days passed before the Germans let them visit the alleged place of the murder. What they found was Kaminsky's car, spattered with blood and riddled with bullet holes. No bodies were found. The investigation only reinforced their suspicions.[75]

Kaminsky was clearly shot on German orders. After receiving instructions to dissolve the division, von dem Bach evidently decided to dispose of Kaminsky.[76] He admitted the killing in a memorandum presented at the Nuremberg trials in 1946 and in later testimony before the Polish procuracy.

> My measures [Bach states with regard to the steps taken at the end of the Warsaw uprising] were . . . shooting of Brigade Commander Kaminsky

under martial law, as well as his staff, because they had sanctioned further plundering and requisitioning. . . .[77]

The execution is described by an SS officer who later read the top-secret SS file on the case. According to him, Kaminsky was arrested in connection with the removal of a truckload of jewelry and valuables from Warsaw. "The sentence was to be carried out in all secrecy by the Gestapo in Litzmannstadt [the Nazi name for Lódź]." On August 26, Kaminsky was "sentenced in Warsaw by a nominal court-martial at Bach-Zelewski's request, probably without formal trial." Supplementary oral information suggests that Kaminsky was shot in the back without warning while eating in Lódź.[78]

Thus Kaminsky disappeared from the scene as mysteriously as he had entered three years earlier. His troops, startled by this turn, accepted their leader's end without particular commotion. Perhaps they were relieved to see someone else take the blame for the atrocities of the Special Regiment.[79]

VI. PARTY AND POLITICS

In the chaos of 1941 Voskoboinikov had formed the nucleus of a "Popular Socialist" party. To him, the political and ideological aspects of the movement which he fancied himself as heading seemed to be of intrinsic importance. Not so for Kaminsky, even though he perpetuated the political shell that his predecessor had created. The fact that it is possible to trace the history of the Kaminsky "movement" without reference to political ideals is characteristic; fundamentally it was not a political movement at all.

Even after he had assumed Voskoboinikov's mantle as head of the "party," Kaminsky's relative indifference to issues remained striking. According to a German visitor, the 1942 elaborations of the party program seemed to amount to "a certain alignment with German ideas and institutions." In this rather more opportunistic form, the program of what was henceforth a Russian Nazi party amounted to: a complete liquidation of communism; reconstruction of a Russian government; friendship with Germany and the German Nazi Party, "cognate to us in spirit and ideas"; abolition of collective farms and free distribution of land; state ownership of forests, natural resources, railroads, and key industries; furtherance of private trade; and an extensive political amnesty, though not for "Jewish commissars, parasites, and scoundrels."[80]

Actually this program was of scant significance to the Kaminsky complex itself. The interests and motives of the leaders as well as the rank and file were overwhelmingly personal or material. Absorbed in day-to-day struggle with peasants and partisans, preoccupied with activities that often revolved around plunder, lacking politically sophisticated figures, isolated from intellectual and urban life in general, the brigade and the district seemed profoundly devoid of ideological convictions.

This feature distinguished Kaminsky from many of the other "movements" of former Soviet citizens on the German side. Most other groups—the Ukrainian separatists, the Vlasov movement, the "real" Russian Nazis, the conservative nationalists—had a cause for which they were prepared to fight. This is not to suggest that there were not large clusters of opportunists or confused victims of circumstances in all of these, nor that their alignment on the German side thereby assumes a different moral hue. Yet the difference is important for an understanding of the Kaminsky Brigade: it underscores the logic in the transformation of the Lokot' regime into a horde of unprincipled mercenaries.

It was no paradox that Kaminsky became the leader of a Russian Nazi Party. Under different circumstances he might have espoused a communist, monarchist, or any other cause—provided it promised to bring him prestige and power. In this regard Kaminsky, even though a victim of the Soviet system, typified the frustrated Soviet-bred technician, potentially a dangerous careerist, willing to subordinate his overt behavior to his drive for advancement—a drive inordinately fostered by the barriers endemic to Soviet life. Not at all the "new man" whom the Stalin era had sought to produce, he was rather the unbidden product of the regime, without any inhibitions that might keep him from becoming a turncoat, a "Bolshevik with a minus sign." His anti-communism was imbued with the same mores and attitudes that had characterized his earlier beliefs. Unable to differentiate except between extremes of black and white, he invariably sought to wind up on the winning side.[81]

While Kaminsky probably did desire a "free" and presumably non-communist (or at least non-Stalinist) Russia, he had no conception of what values or institutions this might require. His insistence on running things his own way was not motivated by national pride or disagreement with the Germans. As an SS official correctly stated,

> It was not political dogmatism but experience and utility that made him recommend to the Germans to leave the practical execution of administrative tasks and the command of troops to him and not to interfere in details. Then, and only then, he claimed, could he guarantee the fulfillment of German wishes.[82]

Never did he recommend to the Germans any measures to improve the lot of the Russian population. Never did he appeal for the respect of national traditions. Indeed, this was one reason why the Germans—or at least some Germans—would confidently entrust a district and a brigade to him.

Still his experience in Lokot' must have fostered Kaminsky's political ambitions. The designation of the RONA as an "army of national liberation" and references in his editorials to the "Russian national state" of which Lokot' was to be the nucleus, betray intentions beyond the scope of his own realm. His future political role was likewise enhanced by his intuitive sense (no doubt conditioned by his Soviet experience) of the importance of demagogy and propaganda. At an early date he established political sections in his brigade, after the model of the Red Army. His Political Administration prepared leaflets, which the Germans dropped behind enemy lines; another important phase of its work was the indoctrination of the Kaminsky troops themselves. In 1942 propaganda within the brigade and district appears to have lacked effective slogans and symbols, resting largely on vague anti-communism plus opposition to collective farming.[83]

Berlin would not allow a Russian party. Hence tacit sanction had to come from a lower level, in the form of *de facto* toleration rather than outright permission. In this regard, Kaminsky looked to General Schmidt as his protector. But when, in early April, 1943, Kaminsky sent him his Order No. 90 establishing a Party Committee and instructing it to draft a new program, Schmidt asked Kaminsky for restraint. The latter promised to submit his program before proclaiming it, adding that in reality no party had been founded yet. Meanwhile, however, *Golos naroda* published the appeal of the party's organizing committee as a *fait accompli.*[84]

For his German backers there was indeed reason for caution. The more highly-sponsored, propagandistically more promising, far less blatantly pro-Nazi "Vlasov action"—or rather, its first round—had just run its course and was soon to be called off entirely. It seems that this is precisely what stirred Kaminsky to insist that he had already established a tangible prototype of a non-Bolshevik Russia, whereas Vlasov could only talk and make promises for the future. Actually the Germans did succeed in getting Kaminsky to restrict his political activities to the Lokot' district. Neither the Russians nor the Germans knew much about his party, and almost the entire population of German-occupied Russia never heard of it. Thus the party is interesting as a curiosity, not as an effective force.

In the late spring of 1943, Kaminsky's political career appeared to be in the ascendant as the "political warfare" wing of the German military sought to promote a scheme calling for the establishment of some Russian government-in-exile. Kluge's memorandum of May 22, 1943, suggested that the chairmanship of the Russian National Committee, which he proposed to establish, go to Vlasov. Its other members were to include one or two Belorussians, the German-oriented mayor of Gomel'—and Bronislav Kaminsky. This was to be merely an advisory committee on administrative, cultural, and economic affairs, but gradually its functions were to be increased (even though Kluge made sure to recommend the inclusion of German secret informants in its midst).[85]

This put Second Panzer Army in an awkward position. While its staff favored the idea of a Russian Committee, the inclusion of Kaminsky as a member under Vlasov raised ticklish questions of "diplomacy." Second Panzer Army recommended the establishment of subcommittees in various cities; and it urged that the Orel committee be headed by Kaminsky.[86] As it turned out, the whole effort collapsed; on June 8, 1943, Hitler torpedoed the entire "Vlasov action" and with it, all alternative plans for the use of Russians in political warfare experiments.[87]

Kaminsky's ambition, even with his anti-Vlasov animus, thus did not suffice to blow life into the "Russian Nazi Party." It was to receive support from another, unexpected quarter. While Berlin recognized no Russian emigre group as its ideological ally in the war, various German agencies had availed themselves of the services of "activist," dynamic emigre organizations. Foremost among these was the so-called NTS *(Natsional'no-Trudovoi Soiuz*, or "Solidarists"), which took advantage of this collaboration to establish a modest network of its representatives in occupied Russia. Often through official channels, sometimes *sub rosa,* it placed a number of its men in responsible positions and won to its ranks some of the mayors, chiefs of police, and editors appointed by the Germans in occupied Russia. Kaminsky's abortive political movement struck the NTS as a suitable vehicle for the promotion of its goals. Indeed, several sources believe that the very idea of reviving the party was urged on Kaminsky by the first NTS official sent to him. Sometime in March, 1943, the NTS executive dispatched to Lokot' a young engineer, Georgii Efimovich Khomutov.

Khomutov had been captured by the Germans early in the war. He was soon sent to Wustrau, a special training camp of propagandists and government personnel for occupied Russia and collaborating troop units; its Russian section was in the hands of the NTS (which Khomutov had joined in 1942). Khomutov is roundly described as an attractive fellow. "He made the impression of an honest, decisive and convinced patriot and anti-Bolshevik," a seasoned observer recalled. "He looked upon the Germans as upon a temporary tool to be used in the struggle against Stalin, hoping that in the course of time the intrinsic strength and abilities of the Russian people would free it from German tutelage." His patriotism did not prevent him from becoming a German propaganda officer or from being a faithful representative of the NTS, in which he appeared to see the only available focus for Russian "national forces" in the German orbit.[88]

Khomutov evidently exerted considerable influence on Kaminsky. After the move to Lepel', Khomutov and his friends ran the ephemeral party, themselves residing in nearby Minsk at what was referred to (in good Soviet terminology) as the party's "*oblast'* committee." A number of other NTS men also became officers of the group. Through Khomutov the Central Committee soon provided an "interlocking directorate" with the NTS, in which Kaminsky would never have accepted a subordinate position.[89]

The program, by-laws, and manifesto, were modeled closely on those of the NTS, in some cases copied verbatim (such as the key formulae, "national revolution" and "land to the toiling peasants"). The manifesto appealed to all "Russian citizens" to reflect on the heavy casualties and untold suffering which their homeland was sustaining: "The peoples of Russia know that the sole guilty ones are the Bolsheviks, with the bloody Stalin at their head." After an unoriginal review of events since 1917, it called for the total defeat of the Bolshevik regime. In one version, the appeal repeatedly stressed the menace of "Judeo-Bolshevism" and promised "the total elimination of all

Jews from the territory of Russia." In another, it insisted instead: "History will not again grant us such a favorable moment, and if we fail to use it, Russia will perish and our children and their children will damn us." Hence only an organized party could properly unite all honest anti-Stalinists, "under the leadership of B. V. Kaminsky, the experienced fighter for Russia's happiness, the leader of the new power."

The party's goals were briefly described as the establishment of a new and sovereign Russian state; an end to the kolkhoz system; the recognition of private enterprise; a guarantee of work and minimal income to workers and intellectuals; social services such as old-age pensions, education, and vacations; and freedom of religion, conscience, speech, assembly, and press.[90]

The manifesto received some publicity outside the Kaminsky District, a reflection of the wider scope which the Germans tacitly allowed the NTS, especially by opening branch offices in a half-dozen Belorussian towns. Thus the appeals caused a minor ripple. At first, a former member relates, "as was to be expected, local officials flocked to it [the party]: members of the police, mayors, municipal clerks, including many shady characters. All of them were easily given entry into the party." Along with them, some idealists joined, in search of a movement "without *Sonderführer* or commissars."[91] The bulk of the political activists were men like Vasiukov, the secretary-general, who until the war had been a communist *raikom* secretary: a turncoat who had evidently maintained the basic patterns of Stalinist mentality.[92]

The Russian Nazi Party thus became a strange hybrid. It was a means of adding luster to the leader; it was a tool for the advancement of the NTS; it was a propaganda weapon exploited by the Germans. It remained largely ineffectual in all three functions, small in the scope of its activity, and overwhelmingly bereft of faith and inherent meaning. As for Kaminsky himself, there is no evidence that he, any more than his followers, genuinely believed its tenets.[93]

To the Germans, the evolution of the Russian Nazi Party raised some problems. The military high command (OKH) adopted an ostrich-like approach, promising directives from the Rosenberg Ministry "in several months." The latter, in essence, concluded that common sense militated against banning the party even if in principle it would be impermissible for the Nazis to give it open succor: the political vacuum created by a new ban, it argued, would redound to the benefit of the communists. But the SS objected: Kaminsky was under von Gottberg's command who (as an SS general) must be given a free hand to deal with the matter. In practice, any effort to secure von Gottberg's consent to a joint directive meant postponing the idea *sine die.*[94]

One other ministry, however, was prepared to back the miscellaneous efforts of various "Eastern" politicians and adventurers to set up little Nazi parties of their own: Goebbels' Propaganda Ministry. In particular, Eberhardt

Taubert, the head of its Soviet section, pursued this course through various subsidiaries. As early as the fall of 1942 an internal report of the ministry had spoken in laudatory terms of Lokot' as a "National-Socialist Russian Republic."[95] Thereafter the ministry tried to supply Kaminsky with equipment, newsprint, and slogans. In return, Kaminsky sent Goebbels a carload of vodka produced in his area. Similar shipments went to the major commanding the propaganda detachment to which Khomutov was assigned.[96] In practice, such efforts mattered little.[97]

When finally, at the end of 1944, Taubert summarized his work in a confidential memorandum to Joseph Goebbels, he stressed the virtues and advantages of Kaminsky's orientation as compared to Vlasov's. In terms suggestive of Taubert's own outlook, he concluded:

> The Vlasov movement is not National-Socialist. While National-Socialist ideology has the effect of dynamite in the [former] realm of Bolshevism, as has been demonstrated by the experience of Kaminsky, the Vlasov movement is a watered-down infusion of liberal and Bolshevik ideologies.[98]

Dmitrii Soshal'skii, chairman of the Minsk branch of the Russian Nazi Party, was the pseudonym of an historian who had taught at Moscow University.[99] An elderly man, educated in Germany before 1914, he was poorly acquainted with the substance of National-Socialism. Early in the war he went to work for a German propaganda agency in Smolensk and later in Minsk. Wholeheartedly on the German side, he applied every effort to rectify what he considered mistakes of German policy in the occupied areas. Typical in this connection is the lengthy memorandum which he submitted to the Germans in 1943. Aspiring to a future alliance between the Reich and Russia, Soshal'skii pointed to the inane measures that could not but arouse popular anger against the Germans.[100] Of course his memorandum had no effect on German conduct.

Though increasingly disappointed in the Germans, Soshal'skii kept hoping for an opportunity to do productive work and was therefore amenable to the role which Khomutov offered him in February-March, 1944. He became the head (or, Khomutov must have reasoned, figurehead) of the Minsk branch of the party. He was suited for this role both because of his age and background, and because he was on relatively good terms with Germans and Russians alike. In the next three months—from March to May, 1944—the Minsk branch attracted a few dozen individuals to its ranks. In practice, however, there was nothing for the party to do. During the entire period there were only two open meetings, each attended by some fifteen members. These included several former prisoners of war, a few society ladies, two or three newspapermen, and Russian employees of the local German agencies.

Before the Minsk "committee" ended its sterile existence, a minor coup was staged within it. The man behind the coup was one of the local party officials, Mikhail Bobrov. This was the assumed name of a former Soviet journalist who had worked on Moscow dailies and at the Comintern radio station. Under the Germans he had edited the Bobruisk newspaper, *Novyi put'* (later, *Rul'*). He withdrew with the German troops to Minsk, where he joined the "committee" at Khomutov's request. Probably by agreement with the NTS, which was tired of Soshal'skii's inaction and ceremoniousness, the ambitious and energetic Bobrov tried to take over the Minsk branch. After conferring with Kaminsky in Diatlovo in late May, he arranged with the German sponsors in Minsk to oust Soshal'skii from the chairmanship of the group.

In practice, the episode was farcical. A few days later Minsk was evacuated, and the "activity" of the Russian Nazi "movement" ceased once and for all. Khomutov urged Soshal'skii to join the brigade, but the elderly professor had become disappointed with the "uncouth youths." He fled to Germany, where he was involved on the fringes of the final Vlasov "action" at the end of 1944.[101] Bobrov too joined the westward evacuation and wound up as a Vlasovite propagandist in the final stages of the war. His otherwise trivial coup is interesting in that it exemplifies a type of Soviet-bred dynamic ambition and reflects the attitude then reigning in certain German and NTS circles.[102]

As the Germans withdrew, the NTS wound up its own work. At the printing shop of the brigade, NTS printers ran off, *sub rosa,* leaflets to Red Army troops, which were left behind as the units retreated. Khomutov stayed in territory reoccupied by the Soviet army; there is some dispute whether he meant to redefect, or to carry on "subversive" work. Rumors among emigres have it that he was shot by the NKVD in 1947.

However warped or naive their ideas and methods, Khomutov and Soshal'skii, in their very different ways, were basically sincere men who thought of themselves as idealists: something that could not be said of Kaminsky. In effect, the party slipped out of Kaminsky's hands. Under the circumstances, it had been doomed from the start.

VII. THE END

In Army Group Center, Kaminsky and Vlasov symbolized alternative experiments. It was natural that a profound gulf should develop between them and between their backers. A keen German observer who knew both men writes:

> The main argument of Vlasov and his followers was: "Kaminsky has put himself in the service of the Germans for a German cause. He has assumed German tasks without considering the interests of the Russian people as a whole and without seeking to lay down the conditions of future German-Russian relations. . . . His attitude can be explained only in terms of his personal ambitions."

The Vlasovites stressed that Kaminsky had never protested against German colonial and *Untermensch* policies in occupied Russia.

> He was reproached for waging the struggle against the Soviet regime in purely negative terms and for not offering the Russian people any constructive solutions, especially with regard to social questions.[103]

In return, a German officer reported from Lokot' in May, 1943, Kaminsky claimed to see in Nazism a common ideological basis for Germany and his movement, whereas "he for this reason opposes the national-Russian movement of General Vlasov, who he fears may one day turn against Germany."[104]

When the Kaminsky Brigade was transformed into the 29th SS Division, Vlasov objected (partly out of fear of being outplayed) and told his German friends that this sort of venture was "bound to be a failure, that he [Kaminsky] had no character, and that one could never make the Russian people into an ally against the Soviet regime by such measures."

In the spring of 1944 the OKW recognized that "in ideology and goals" Kaminsky's movement "diverged" from Vlasov's. It was only natural, however, that when elements in Berlin sought to step up the utilization of Vlasov, attempts would be made to bring the two men together. The First Corps, for instance, advised Sixteenth Army in May, 1944, that Kaminsky's party must be "reorganized" by the Reich as a measure of political confidence in the wavering Soviet population. In addition, "the Vlasov-Kaminsky dualism must be eliminated. The Vlasov idea must be absorbed in the new [Kaminsky] movement. A personal visit by General Vlasov would be of far-reaching significance."[105]

While Army Group Center was by then sober enough not to seek futile political experiments, Army Group North pressed for prompt action, stressing the psychological-warfare potential of the wholehearted promotion of an indigenous political movement.[106] By this time the course of military events had made such endeavors ludicrous. Before long, Kaminsky's men were in Poland. As his first echelons moving southward reached the Katowice area, on September 5, 1944, the anti-German partisans in Slovakia began an open revolt. While the Germans rushed reinforcements to suppress them, trainloads of Kaminsky's men and refugees piled up in Upper Silesia, in the vicinity of Ratibor, virtually abandoned by their preoccupied masters. Finally the *Gauleiter* of Upper Silesia threatened to court-martial the SS officer attached to the refugees if they did not move out of his province immediately.

The SS considered throwing the Kaminsky Division into action against the Slovaks; Gottlob Berger, the SS chieftain who had general authority over Kaminsky as well as the anti-Slovak campaign, reportedly favored this way out. However, opposition to the idea arose both within the SS and outside it.[107] By this time Himmler had been persuaded to receive General Vlasov in a final, quixotic "political warfare" maneuver. The Kaminsky Division was about to be dissolved. Its leader was gone; its men were restive. When their fate was weighed, the contemplated new "Vlasov divisions" suggested themselves as a natural and suitable destination for them.

A carefully staged "election" was held in the division. The man chosen as the new leader was Kaminsky's deputy, Lieutenant Colonel Belai. An honest fellow, Belai had been (according to one source) a senior lieutenant or (according to another) a junior *politruk* in the Red Army, and had been a partisan until his capture by Kaminsky's men. According to some, Belai had emphatically objected to the participation of the division in the Warsaw operation.[108] But Belai's assumption of command was purely nominal. The fate of the division was sealed.

While the families of the Kaminsky men were moved from Upper Silesia to Pomerania, the soldiers—between 6,000 and 8,000 men—remained at the training camp of Neuhammer. There, in the late fall of 1944, the division was absorbed into the new Vlasov complex.

One of the Vlasovite representatives recalls: "We were struck by the utter chaos that reigned there. It was a real gypsy camp. Horses ran about ungroomed. Uniforms were untidy. Equipment consisted of the queerest mixture of German and Soviet types. Still, they had twelve T-34 and two 'KV' tanks."[109] Vlasov's men were received coolly by the leaders of Kaminsky's division. "Secretary-General" Vasiukov threatened to lead his men off into the Carpathians rather than see the unit disbanded. Protsiuk, due to be arrested, disappeared, never to return.

However great the difficulties among the officers, the rank and file were anxious to identify themselves with the Vlasov movement. Without any overt trouble, some 6,000 men were transferred to Bavaria—first to Feldstetten, then to Münsingen, where Vlasov's "First Division" was being activated. After three months of screening and training, most of the officers and men, demoted to their actual ranks, joined the new division as regular troops. Many Vlasov officers were unhappy about the infusion of these elements who in their minds "compromised" the movement. Indeed, to the end the *kamintsy* remained an alien body even within this unit. Occasionally it took severe punishment to keep them in line.[110]

The reorganization had its ludicrous aspects. For all intents and purposes, Germany had lost the war. In March, 1945, some *kamintsy* participated in a small operation on the Oder front. Then they marched southward to Prague, defying German orders and, in the first days of May, fought with other Vlasov units against the SS on the side of the Czech rebels. But by then the Kaminsky forces were no longer an entity; they obeyed other—or no—authorities.

Most of the survivors were turned over to the Soviet armed forces in the general chaos of repatriation that followed the capitulation of the Reich. Others got to Plattling, from where they too were extradited to the Soviet Union a few months later. Only a handful remained in the West. About the fate of the thousands who fell into Soviet hands one can only speculate. Their lot was undoubtedly among the most severe meted out by Stalin's punitive organs.

VIII. KAMINSKY: A LAST LOOK

The sudden German occupation of vast areas of the Soviet Union permitted, for a short time, the emergence of local authority against the background of the accumulated frustrations and grievances of the prewar years. The rapid collapse of the Soviet control system over this part of the USSR set the stage for a range of "alternatives"—from microcosms of relatively untrammeled life on the village level to stringent and oppressive German dictation and terror. One such variant was the Kaminsky complex.

Against the titanic background of World War II, Kaminsky and his movement—district, party, and brigade—were but a petty episode. Their emergence did not alter the course of history. Had they never existed, neither military operations, nor German occupation policy, nor popular attitudes would have been materially different. And yet the Kaminsky phenomenon is illustrative of a curious and characteristic development.

He and his movement were accidents in the pattern of wartime policies. There was no logic in the fortuitous toleration of a measure of indigenous self-government which one German officer proferred while another forbade it; no reason why one cluster of villages should have organized local administration on their own while another did not. The role of individuals, in a situation of general paralysis from fear or inertia, is exemplified by the changes wrought as a result of the replacement of Voskoboinikov by Kaminsky. Whatever would have been the former's fate, had he not been killed, Kaminsky's rule wrote *finis* to all plans for a politically meaningful non-Soviet experiment. Less appealing than the Cossack atamans of yore; less daring than the pioneer leaders of the *vol'nitsa;* less splendiferous or competent than the Chinese warlords; less independent than the *condottieri*, in the latter stages of his career, Kaminsky was an opportunist *par excellence*.

From the German vantage point, the Kaminsky "formula" for occupation government arose almost accidentally through the realization of some of the military that effective occupation of an area as vast as the USSR was impossible, and especially hopeless without relying on some elements of the population. Yet the very effectiveness of a homegrown movement lies in its relative autonomy from the occupying power. It is more appealing to the inhabitants precisely because it has its own dynamics which the foreign power cannot expect to control—and which present this power with the dilemma of whether or not to support the movement at the risk of its potential deviation into "undesirable" channels.

Kaminsky was particularly well suited to the purposes of the Third Reich. Eschewing broad social movements as well as ideologically-oriented groups, the Germans in this instance chose to throw their backing to the non-ideological, ambitious opportunist. In a Russia that was to be a colony of Greater Germany, in a region that was not to be reconstructed socially or culturally according to the wishes of its population, the occupying power could afford to have a Kaminsky rule much as he pleased, so long as he was loyal to Berlin.

The Kaminsky "formula," however, as applied in Lokot' and Lepel' could work only under certain special conditions. If some part of the population backed Kaminsky in the early stages of his venture, this was due primarily to the fact that he was "one of them" and that he kept the Germans (and partisans) away. Others, with fewer drawbacks, also met these two conditions; Voskoboinikov is the most obvious example.

Kaminsky's approach was bound to be ineffective—indeed, it boomeranged with a vengeance—when applied within the framework of a broader, let alone national, policy of reconstruction or an extensive effort at political propaganda. Likewise, the Kaminsky formula became inapplicable if an overall plan of socio-economic and political engineering was to be implemented. One need only imagine a Russia ruled by a bevy of Kaminskies, each refusing to carry out the dictates of a central indigenous authority—and the result is ominously reminiscent of China ruled by feuding warlords, unwilling or unable to embark on large-scale reforms, pool economic resources for the common good, or establish anything more than mere "order."

Built on the quicksand of individual ambitions, the Kaminsky alternative to Soviet rule—without the cement of political, social, and national ideals—inevitably deteriorated as soon as it was transplanted outside its original area. "Administration" became terror; arbitrariness replaced law; looting took the place of orderly assessment, with the result that the population was transformed into bitter enemies; and in the end Kaminsky was more feared and hated by the peasants than the Germans were.

The Kaminsky movement was not effective in controlling cities, where at least part of the remaining intelligentsia demanded answers to questions which Kaminsky never even raised. Nor could the Kaminsky formula inspire a military movement of any scope: this conclusion is supported by a comparison with the Vlasov approach. With all the similarities of collaboration and all the moral compromises, the differences between the two types—and those whom they attracted—are persuasive.

A man of limited intellectual resources, Kaminsky successfully manipulated his environment for his own ends. Yet paradoxically in some of his ideas he was closer to an "old emigre" of pre-1917 vintage, even if his program mirrored contemporary grievances of Soviet men. Kaminsky's outlook in political affairs (or perhaps, the absence of such an outlook) further aroused some of the politically-motivated or socially-responsible defectors against him.

Kaminsky charged the Vlasov men with having remained communist in their ideals; Vlasov accused the *kamintsy* of having remained Bolsheviks in morals and behavior. Within limits, both were right. With regard to ideology and political orientation, moreover, the Vlasovites could castigate Kaminsky as a puppet

> . . . who would build the future Russia unilaterally on the basis of German power, rather than seek the forces needed for this reconstruction in the power inherent in the peoples of Russia. Like the Germans and the old Russian emigres, he [Kaminsky] negated everything that had taken place in the Soviet Union since 1917.

More fairly, one might say, Kaminsky neither negated nor approved recent socio-political change: he ignored it. He was far more at home as a minor tyrant than as a politician, let alone as a theorist laying plans for a better tomorrow.

Not all the men in his "movement" shared their leader's characteristics. While some of his henchmen, like Protsiuk, exceeded Kaminsky in cruelty and immorality, others, like Belai, were evidently more decent. Among the rank and file of peasants, prisoners, and partisans, there were men to whom—had they had a free choice—many of the associations which Kaminsky's name evoked would have been plainly repugnant. But once they had deserted the Soviet side, they had little choice. A hostile observer states that "among his officers there were efforts to find another leader, but under the circumstances this was bound to be chimeric."[111] And a former partisan who wound up in the brigade recalled years later:

> We would sometimes reflect that after all we were mistreating our own people. But then again the partisans were doing the same thing. I sometimes wished I could just get away from it all to the end of the world. We didn't care much for either side. . . .[112]

As in most units, the bulk of men were content to survive, with an occasional "good time" and by inertia, to follow the general pattern that was being shaped with blood and fire.

It had been a short road from the populist hopes of late 1941 to the savagery of Warsaw three years later. Ironically, as Kaminsky lost all his inhibitions, he became increasingly a tool of other men. His opportunism had helped him so long as he remained at the head of a relatively small, self-contained peasant area. Once he had left it, he was bound to fail. But then, the collapse of his enterprise was preordained as much by the general conditions under which he operated as by the organic weaknesses he and his movement possessed.

Kaminsky was representative of a personality type which persists in Soviet society. Ability and arrogance, ambition and mediocrity, nihilism and conviction merge to produce a prototype which must be placed close to one extreme and on the spectrum of potential counter-elite cadres of the Stalin era. Fortunately for the Soviet population—and for the world abroad—there are, increasingly, other and better types, too.

ROBERT M. SLUSSER

The Presidium Meeting of February, 1961: A Reconstruction

The Soviet political system has been deliberately devised to make penetration of its *arcana imperii* as difficult as possible for an outsider. Among the most closely guarded secrets of the Kremlin are the real nature of decision making in foreign policy and the existence of factional differences within the leadership over patronage and policy.

Non-Soviet scholars are coming to realize, however, that despite the obstacles put in their path by Soviet censorship, it is possible for them to achieve an understanding of Soviet policy making, provided they are willing to recognize the special character of the evidence and to devise suitable means for its interpretation. The present article is designed to illustrate and exemplify some of these means.

Close observation of organizational changes in the Soviet political machine—primarily the Communist Party of the Soviet Union (CPSU) and the All-Union and Union Republic governments—has by now established itself as an indispensable analytical tool. Correlation of organizational changes with policy statements by Soviet leaders, a technique employed with notable success by the late Boris Nicolaevsky, has enabled analysts to demonstrate the existence of well-marked factions in the Soviet leadership and to define their position on a number of important questions of policy.

The establishment of an accurate and detailed chronology as a means for the reconstruction of the specific historical context in which events and decisions have taken place has only recently been utilized as an analytical technique for "penetrating" the Kremlin's secrets. While the chronological approach has necessarily been employed to some extent by nearly every analyst of recent Soviet history, this has usually been done on a limited scale and with regard to specific circumscribed areas. Only when an attempt is made to reconstruct chronologically the total historical context of a given event in recent Soviet history, however, can progress be made towards identifying the hidden links between internal politics and foreign policy decisions. The method is somewhat arduous and necessarily slow, but the insights which it yields fully justify the effort.

An instructive example of the application of this method is provided by the study of a self-contained episode in Soviet political history, the agricultural tour undertaken by N. S. Khrushchev in the early months of 1961. In studying this problem, the principal areas from which evidence must be taken into account are the following: (a) the political struggle within the Soviet leadership between Khrushchev and his supporters on the one hand and his opponents on the other; (b) the differing views of Khrushchev and the opposition on policy towards the United States; (c) the scientific-military balance between the United States and the Soviet Union; (d) Soviet disarmament policy; (e) Soviet policy towards Germany, including Berlin; and (f) Soviet policy towards Communist China and its European satellite, Albania.

The conclusions obtainable from this approach, as will be seen, vary in their degree of probability from strongly supported to frankly hypothetical. At the same time it should be noted that even the hypothetical conclusions acquire a greater degree of solidity when considered as part of a longer chain of events and hypotheses. The episode selected for consideration takes its place as part of a historical sequence which derives its inferential strength precisely from the fact that it is an interconnected and continuous chain with its own compelling inner logic, rather than a disjointed succession of meaningless and incomprehensible happenings.

I

At the close of his final speech to the CPSU Central Committee plenum which met from January 10 to 18, 1961, Khrushchev revealed that he was planning to make a tour of some of the Soviet Union's principal agricultural regions, and that the trip had the approval of the Presidium:

> In the Central Committee Presidium we have agreed that I shall soon go to the Ukraine and visit the Northern Caucasus and Georgia; I plan also to go to Voronezh and the virgin lands of Siberia and Kazakhstan.[1]

Following the plenum, Khrushchev remained in Moscow for about a week. On January 21 he met with U.S. Ambassador Llewellyn K. Thompson to arrange the release of the surviving members of the crew of the U.S. RB-47 which had been shot down by Soviet interceptors on July 1 of the preceding year. He then turned his attention to the agricultural tour which he had announced at the plenum. On January 24 he arrived in Kiev for a plenum of the Ukrainian Communist Party Central Committee, held on January 26-28. From January 30 to February 1 he was in Rostov-on-the-Don for a conference of agricultural workers of the North Caucasus. From there he moved on to Tbilisi (February 4-7), for a similar gathering in the Transcaucasus. His next stop was Voronezh (February 9-11), in the Central Black Earth Zone of the RSFSR. On February 21-23 he was back in Moscow for a conference of the Central RSFSR. From February 28 to March 2 he was in Sverdlovsk, the Urals. From there he went to Kurgan for a ceremony awarding the Order of Lenin to Kurgan Province. On March 5 he arrived in Novosibirsk for a conference of Siberian farm workers which ended on March 8. His next stop was at Akmolinsk, capital of the Virgin Lands Territory, where a conference was held March 12-14. His final conference took place in Alma Ata, capital of the Kazakh SSR, on March 20-21. On March 24 he returned to Moscow. On the last day of each of the conferences Khrushchev delivered a speech, which was duly published in the Soviet press, though not immediately; his speeches were published only after delays which ranged from four to eight days. The delays cannot be explained as the result of any difficulty in transmission from remote locations, since one of the longest occurred with regard to the speech delivered on February 23 in Moscow.

According to Khrushchev, as we have seen, the Presidium had authorized him to make the tour. The delay in publishing his speeches suggests that they were being submitted to review before publication, presumably by the same Presidium which had agreed to the tour.

Analysis of Khrushchev's itinerary indicates that there was a ten-day interruption from February 11 to February 21, coinciding with the longest delay in publication of one of his speeches. We know that during part of this period, Khrushchev was in Moscow, since *Pravda* reported him as receiving the ambassadors from Tunisia and the United Arab Republic (February 14) and Turkey (February 15). During this period his closest ally in the Presidium, L. I. Brezhnev, was away on a good-will tour to Africa; *Pravda* announced the journey on February 3, and it lasted from February 9 to February 19. Following the interruption Khrushchev attended a conference in Moscow, which he had omitted from his advance description of the tour. His speech on this occasion was listened to by the full Presidium.

As a tentative hypothesis to account for these facts, let us assume a meeting of the Presidium during the period between February 11 and February 19, called on the initiative of Khrushchev's opponents. A consideration of the content of Khrushchev's speeches on the tour and of certain other events taking place during the same period will not only strengthen this hypothesis but also enable us to specify the principal subjects which the meeting was called to consider and the decisions it reached.

II

In each of his speeches on the tour, Khrushchev included a section devoted to one of his favorite themes, the prediction of victory for the Soviet Union in its economic rivalry with the United States. In his speech to the Ukrainian Central Committee plenum on January 28, for example, he assured his listeners that "The Ukraine, if it works as it should, can overtake America in per capita output of meat in two to three years—four at the most."[2] At Rostov-on-the-Don on February 1 he suggested that the names of workers who "made their contribution to accomplishment of the task of overtaking the U.S.A., the most highly developed capitalist country, in per capita output of meat and milk," should be inscribed in a Golden Book.[3] At Tbilisi on February 7 he predicted that the Soviet Union would overtake the U.S.A. in per capita industrial output by 1970.[4] At Voronezh on February 11 he issued a call for leadership to help in "building a communist society whose level of production must of course be higher than in the U.S.A."[5]

In each of his speeches up to this point, Khrushchev's rivalry-with-America theme had been couched in exclusively economic terms. Furthermore, he had taken special pains to emphasize the peaceful nature of the competition. For example, in his February 7 speech at Tbilisi, he said,

> . . . Our land of the Soviets will not only overtake but surpass you [the U.S.]! *(Prolonged applause.)*
>
> In saying this we do not threaten anyone. After all, we do not intend to take away your goods and wealth. Let this wealth remain with you. The social system in the U.S.A. rests on the American people, and our social and political system was established by the peoples of the Soviet Union. . . . Our successes and our growth do not harm other peoples.[6]

The Voronezh speech, as we have seen, was followed by the longest delay in publication and by an unexplained 10-day hiatus in the tour. When Khrushchev returned to the podium at the conclusion of the Moscow meeting of February 21-23, the rivalry-with-America theme had acquired an entirely new aspect:

> Recall, comrades, the comparatively recent time when the first atomic bomb was built in the U.S.A. The American imperialists began conducting an atomic policy of frightening the socialist countries, and above all the Soviet Union. This was a difficult time for us.

The Soviet people had risen to the challenge, Khrushchev continued, by developing atomic and thermonuclear weapons, and when the "American imperialists" surrounded the Soviet Union with military bases, Soviet engineers and scientists pioneered in the creation of intercontinental ballistic missiles. "All the advantages that the Americans had obtained by establishing their bases around our country," Khrushchev boasted, "they lost at the moment when our rocket soared and, flying thousands of kilometers, landed exactly in the area planned by our scientists, engineers, and workers."[7]

The military overtones to the rivalry theme became even more strident in Khrushchev's speech in Sverdlovsk on March 2. "What is the significance," he asked,

> . . . of surpassing the U.S. in per capita production of meat and milk? It means showing the whole world that a people that has taken power into its own hands can in a short time convert its country from a backward into an advanced one, develop its economy, industry, and agriculture, its science and culture—that it will be able to attain the level of the most highly developed capitalist country and thereby bring glory to its system, the socialist system.
>
> Capitalism's most farsighted ideologists already foresee this and are fearful that the socialist system will in the immediate future accomplish this task. But this is the inexorable law of our forward movement. Capitalism cannot halt this movement, cannot stem the development of the Soviet land, of its economy. The imperialists may try to halt the

> development of the Soviet economy by war. But to choose the path of war is to doom the capitalist system to perdition. The Soviet Union has the most powerful rocket weapons in the world and has produced as many atom and hydrogen bombs as are needed to wipe aggressors from the face of the earth should they try to settle the ideological, political dispute between the two world systems by war. *(Stormy applause.)*[8]

Thereafter, however, the rattle of rockets in Khrushchev's speeches faded away, and the former economic aspects of the rivalry theme reasserted their predominance. At Novosibirsk on March 11 he exulted in the performance of Soviet athletes in peaceful sport competition with Americans, but emphasized the greater importance of "competing [with the U.S.] in the name of a still greater rise in the people's well being."[9] And at Alma Ata on March 21, in the last speech of his tour, he sketched his favorite vision of the future:

> . . . To overtake the U.S.–the most highly developed capitalist country–in per capita meat production will be once again to demonstrate the great power of the socialist system. It will be a historic victory, a victory for the immortal doctrine of Marxism-Leninism. *(Applause.)*[10]

In concluding his speech, and with it his entire tour, Khrushchev sounded the themes of peace and disarmament:

> The Communists are not intimidating anyone, they are not threatening war. It is not through war that we are advancing to our great goal. On the contrary, we desire that there shall be no wars among states and among peoples, and we are fighting for this; we propose general and complete disarmament and will accept any terms of control over disarmament if the Western powers accept our proposals on disarmament. *(Applause.)*[11]

Surveyed as a whole, Khrushchev's tour thus falls into two halves not only chronologically, with the Moscow break separating the early phase from the later, but also thematically. Before the Moscow break, the theme of rivalry with the U.S. was presented in Khrushchevian economic terms–victory in the drive for supremacy in per capita output in agriculture. In the Moscow and Sverdlovsk speeches, the first ones delivered after the break, bellicose boasts about Soviet military power nearly drowned out the peaceful notes of the rivalry theme. These notes regained their strength, however, in the final stages of the tour.

Before drawing any conclusions from these observations it will be useful to take note of some concurrent developments.

III

While Khrushchev was on tour, the new administration of President John F. Kennedy was engaged in a review of the military balance between the United States and the Soviet Union. On January 30, in his first State of the Union message, the President informed the Congress that he had instructed the Secretary of Defense "to reappraise our entire defense strategy," and, pending the presentation of preliminary conclusions at the end of February, to take three immediate steps: an increase in U.S. military airlift capacity, in order to achieve greater mobility in preparation for unexpected developments, a step-up in the production of Polaris submarines, and an acceleration of the missile program.

Long-term policies initiated by the previous administration were meanwhile bearing fruit and significantly altering the U.S.-Soviet balance in favor of the United States. In November, 1960, the U.S.S. "George Washington," a nuclear-powered submarine carrying sixteen 1200-mm. Polaris missiles, became operational. In his farewell State of the Union message on January 11, 1961, President Eisenhower maintained that "the 'missile gap' shows every sign of being a fiction," and cited intercontinental ballistic missiles (ICBM's) and Polaris-armed nuclear submarines as evidence of America's growing power. On February 1 the first test launching was held of the Minuteman ICBM, a three-stage solid-fuel rocket with a range of over 6300 miles. It was estimated that quantity production of the Minuteman would follow in the near future and that large-scale deployment would be achieved by mid-1962.

In an off-the-record press briefing on February 6, Defense Secretary McNamara mentioned that studies carried out by the new administration had led to the tentative conclusion that there had been, in fact, no "missile gap." A report of McNamara's statement in the *New York Times* on the following day brought a prompt White House disavowal: at a press conference on February 8, the President said that it would be "premature" to try to tell whether there was in fact a "missile gap" favoring the Soviet Union, and expressed the opinion that only after completion of the review of U.S. strategic and tactical weapons which the Defense Department was currently conducting could an accurate assessment be reached.[12]

For the Soviet leadership, however, the changes in the strategic balance caused by U.S. rearmament, and—equally important—the changes in Washington's perception of the strategic balance and its growing realization that the U.S. had a clear preponderance in strategic power over the Soviet Union, constituted a sharp warning that it would be increasingly difficult for them henceforth to use the alleged Soviet lead in strategic striking power and military-scientific technology as an effective instrument of Soviet foreign policy.[13]

Soviet concern about growing U.S. strategic power was reflected on February 3, when Soviet Ambassador to Turkey N. S. Ryzhov handed Turkish Foreign Minister S. Sarper an official statement asking for clarification of recent press reports of U.S. plans to provide the Turkish army with Jupiter rockets, build rocket bases in Turkey, and give Turkey access to atomic weapons.[14]

On the following day the Soviets inaugurated their program of interplanetary exploration with the orbiting of Sputnik VII, a 6483-kg. satellite test vehicle from which a space probe towards Venus was to be launched. The probe failed to leave the parking orbit, however, and on February 26 the satellite was destroyed on re-entry.[15] Greater success attended the launching of Sputnik VIII, on February 12. This time the space probe, a 643.5-kg. rocket, was successfully launched from the parking orbit towards a planned rendezvous with Venus on approximately May 19.[16] The new technique employed in these shots was of great significance for future space exploration, according to M. V. Keldysh, President of the Soviet Academy of Sciences, because "(1) it eliminates the necessity of choosing specific dates for flights to the moon; (2) it makes possible the launching of heavier space vehicles towards Venus and the other planets; and (3) it removes the restrictions connected with the fact that not all points on the earth are equally advantageous for launching."[17]

On February 17 the Soviet government sent a long note to the Bonn government, restating the Soviet arguments in favor of concluding a peace treaty with Germany, and asserting the Soviet government's "unshakable determination . . . to bring the matter of peace negotiations with Germany to a conclusion." The note called on the government of the German Federal Republic, and on Chancellor Adenauer personally, to contribute to "a peaceful settlement with Germany and also to the strengthening of peace and security in Europe."[18]

On February 23, 1961, Soviet Armed Forces Day, the Soviet press carried significant statements by a number of Soviet military leaders. In a *Pravda* article entitled "Mighty Army of a Mighty People," Chief of the General Staff Marshal M. V. Zakharov maintained that "the main force of aggression is the imperialism of the U.S.A.," and warned that "the influence of the West German army in the aggressive NATO bloc is growing." He raised the specter of a new German war against the Soviet Union, "this time with nuclear weapons," but claimed that "the armament, composition, strength, and high combat readiness" of the Soviet Armed Forces "enable them to strike an immediate and crushing retaliatory blow at any aggressor who tries to disrupt the peaceful creative labor of the Soviet people."[19]

In Armed Forces Day speeches by two of Marshal Zakharov's colleagues, a new and meaningful shift appeared in Soviet military claims. Both Marshals K. S. Moskalenko, Commander-in-Chief of Rocket Troops, and I. Kh. Bagramian, Chief of Rear Services, characterized the number of available Soviet ICBM's as "sufficient" or "necessary"—apparently the first appearance of this formulation in place of earlier Soviet claims for superiority.[20] We have already noted Khrushchev's employment of a variant of this formula in his Sverdlovsk speech on March 2. The Soviet leaders' restraint is all the more striking in view of the new Soviet achievements in space exploration.

IV

We have postulated a meeting of the Presidium in mid-February 1961, called on the initiative of Khrushchev's opponents. On the basis of the data which have been cited, we can now attempt a preliminary reconstruction of the meeting.

The planning for the meeting can be dated to early February. The note to

Turkey about U.S. rocket bases and the announcement of Brezhnev's African tour, both on February 3, provide a firm date for the beginning of the build-up towards the meeting. By this time texts were available for the first two of Khrushchev's tour speeches, those in Kiev and Rostov-on-the-Don, and it was clear that he was taking a moderate line in foreign policy, emphasizing peaceful economic competition with the U.S. and saying nothing about military rivalry. Also available was the text of President Kennedy's January 30 State of the Union message.

For the opposition a new urgency was injected into the situation by McNamara's premature but accurate statement on February 6 that the "missile gap" might turn out to be a myth. The publicity given this statement in the United States led to no change in Khrushchev's handling of the Soviet-U.S. rivalry theme in his next two speeches, however (those at Tbilisi on February 7 and at Voronezh on the 11th).

The long delay in publishing the text of the Voronezh speech was a clear indication of high-level concern over its content. Khrushchev, as we have seen, was back in Moscow by February 14 at the latest. It is probable that one of the decisions taken by the Presidium at the meeting for which he was unceremoniously recalled to Moscow by his colleagues was that he would have to beef up the rivalry-with-America theme in subsequent speeches on his tour by giving it a military setting and emphasizing Soviet strategic power. The Venus shots of February 4 and 12, which must have been long in preparation, came at a favorable moment to provide new evidence and reason to strengthen this theme, and at an earlier time might well have given rise to new claims for Soviet strategic superiority. Instead, in the light of the strategic reassessment being conducted by U.S. leaders, it was decided that henceforth a new and less provocatively misleading formulation—"adequate" or "necessary"—would be substituted for the earlier claims of Soviet rocket superiority.

The moderate, verbose, and typically Khrushchevian note to West Germany on February 18 may be taken to indicate the terminal point for the meeting. It took another three days to complete preparations for the Moscow agricultural conference, which opened on the 21st with a sizable turnout of the top party leaders, including both of Khrushchev's most openly identified opponents and critics, F. R. Kozlov and M. A. Suslov. The Moscow conference can be viewed as an adroit improvisation which preserved the appearance of continuity on Khrushchev's agricultural tour and thus masked the high-level deliberations on foreign policy which were the real reason—in this reconstruction—for his premature return to Moscow.

V

The most important decisions reached at the February meeting of the Presidium concerned four closely interrelated issues of cardinal importance in Soviet foreign policy: Berlin, disarmament, relations with the United States, and the resumption of nuclear testing.

In early January, 1961, as the time neared for the inauguration of the newly elected President in Washington, a number of Soviet diplomats were busy dropping broad hints to their American opposites that it would be desirable for the new administration to reach agreement on disarmament with the Soviets without delay; otherwise, they warned, Khrushchev's position would be undermined by his internal opponents, who would prove less willing to compromise with the West if they should come to power.[21] In Washington these hints were ignored as transparent efforts to pressure the new administration into premature and unwise concessions. Instead, the Kennedy administration asked its diplomatic partners in the disarmament talks, Great Britain and the Soviet Union, for a delay in resumption of the talks, in order to give it time to review and revise the U.S. position.

When the test-ban talks resumed in Geneva on March 21, the Soviet mood had undergone a sharp change. In his opening statement the chief Soviet delegate, Semyon K. Tsarapkin, without even waiting to hear the revised U.S. position, presented a demand for acceptance by the Western powers of a three-man team *(troika)* to head the control board to be entrusted with monitoring a test-ban treaty, in place of the one-man neutral administrator on whom the three powers had earlier agreed.[22] The effect of Tsarapkin's demand was to freeze the disarmament negotiations at the very outset of the Kennedy administration and to block further progress towards agreement on a test-ban treaty.

During the summer of 1961 the Soviets mounted a major propaganda campaign designed to force the West to accept Soviet proposals for a change in the status of Berlin. Instead of making concessions, the U.S. responded by taking a series of measures designed to strengthen its military capacity. At the height of the ensuing tension the East German regime (August 12-13), began the construction of a wall bisecting the occupied city and physically sealing off the East Zone regime from West Berlin.

The sequel to these events was the Soviet announcement on August 30 that the Soviet Union would shortly resume the testing of nuclear weapons, thereby unilaterally breaking the *de facto* three-power moratorium which had been in effect since early November, 1958.[23] The new Soviet test series, which ran from September 1 to October 30, constituted the largest cumulative total of nuclear explosions in history.

At the time, it was clear to technically trained observers that the Soviet test series of autumn, 1961, must have been in preparation for a considerable period of time. According to Dr. Hans A. Bethe, a prominent U.S. physicist, "It is very likely that they [the Soviets] had started specific preparations by March of 1961 when the test-ban conference reconvened in Geneva."[24]

Ambassador Arthur H. Dean, chief U.S. delegate to the test-ban talks, had come to a similar conclusion independently, based on his observation of Soviet behavior at Geneva. In particular, he regarded Tsarapkin's *troika* proposal as a clear indication that the Soviets in March, 1961, were no longer interested in substantive negotiations on disarmament and were simply using the Geneva conference to mark time while preparations for the test series were under way.[25]

While it is impossible within the brief scope of this essay to present all the relevant data bearing on the significance of these events, the conclusion to which they point can be stated concisely: At the February meeting of the Presidium whose existence we have postulated, a majority in the Presidium, led by the opponents of Khrushchev's policy of rapprochement with the U.S., presented him with a clear-cut alternative: either obtain within six months a major concession from the West over Berlin, or accede to the resumption of nuclear testing by the Soviet Union. The Soviet note to West Germany on February 18 marked the launching of this propaganda offensive.

Khrushchev's failure in August, 1961, to obtain the diplomatic victory which he sought in Berlin was therefore followed, first, by the building of the Berlin Wall, satisfying the immediate need of the East German regime for the physical security of its territory, and second, by the Soviet resumption of nuclear testing.

VI

While Khrushchev and his colleagues were conferring in Moscow, the Albanian Party of Labor was holding its twice-postponed Fourth Congress in Tirana.[26] The congress keynote was struck on the opening day, February 13, in speeches by party boss Enver Hoxha and Chief of State Mehmet Shehu. Their militant opposition to Khrushchev's foreign policy of "peaceful co-existence" with the United States was veiled, as was characteristic at this stage of the Soviet-Albanian rift, under cover of denunciations of the Yugoslav Communists as "revisionist."

The Soviet delegation to the congress was headed by P. N. Pospelov, a veteran party functionary and ideologist whose career pattern and public statements indicate an affinity with Khrushchev. The second member of the delegation was Iurii V. Andropov, later to achieve eminence as Chairman of the Committee of State Security (KGB), but at this period a rising young functionary who had served in the Komsomol, the central party apparatus, the diplomatic corps, and the government. His career had been built without visible assistance from Khrushchev, but he could not be identified with the Kozlov-Suslov opposition either. If he had a patron in the party hierarchy it appears to have been the senior party figure O. V. Kuusinen, in whose home territory the early stages of Andropov's career were passed, and whose influence may have helped him get his appointment to the party Central Committee apparatus in 1957.

A year after the Albanian congress, on February 16, 1962, the Albanian party newspaper *Zëri i Popullit* denounced Andropov as a "professional

Soviet provocateur and Khrushchev's faithful spokesman," and accused him of having helped to organize a walkout by the Greek Communist Party delegation at the February, 1961, congress, an incident which precipitated a sharp clash among the delegates. As Andropov's collaborator in staging this incident, the Albanians named Rudolf Barák, head of the Czechoslovak Communist Party delegation to the congress, member of the Czechoslovak Communist Party Politburo, and Czech Minister of the Interior.[27]

Barák's speech at the Albanian congress did in fact provide strong evidence of an ideological link with Khrushchev. He warned the Albanians of the danger of isolation from the Soviet bloc, while paying tribute to Khrushchev as the principal architect of the Warsaw Pact of May, 1955, which, he said, "guarantees . . . the security and defense of the Albanian People's Republic." Barák also praised Khrushchev for his attack on the "cult of personality" at the Twentieth Congress of the CPSU in 1956 and for his behavior at the Fifteenth Session of the United Nations General Assembly in the autumn of 1960.[28]

At the close of the congress Hoxha received the Soviet delegation, together with the Soviet ambassador, I. V. Shikin. The communiqué issued to mark the occasion asserted that the discussion had been "very cordial and friendly,"[29] but according to a speech by Pospelov at the Twenty-Second CPSU Congress in October, 1961, the reality had been very different: stung by "a number of glaring instances of direct anti-Soviet attacks by prominent Albanian officials, instances of a humiliating, hostile attitude toward our specialists, geologists, and Soviet seamen," Pospelov had delivered a formal protest from the Central Committee of the CPSU, warning the Albanians that such actions "not only impede the development and strengthening of Albanian-Soviet friendship but also run counter to the interests of the entire socialist camp." "If these abnormal phenomena are not stopped in good time," the note concluded, "they may entail serious consequences."[30]

Pospelov's revelation that the Central Committee had sent a note of protest to the Albanians clinches the evidence for a meeting of the Presidium in mid-February, 1961, and enables us to add an additional point to the agenda which we have postulated, namely, the increasingly unsatisfactory state of relations between the Soviet Union and Albania. The note of protest delivered by Pospelov on February 20 represented the agreed policy of the Presidium, speaking in the name of the Central Committee.

The subsequent Albanian charges against Andropov and Barák, however, and their identification of Khrushchev personally as an influence making for Soviet-Albanian conflict, provide a basis for the speculation that Khrushchev, smarting under the attack on his policy towards the United States, may have instigated an intrigue designed to disrupt the Albanian congress and exacerbate the tension between Albania and the Soviet Union.

Forced by the internal opposition to adopt a more hostile tone toward the United States, did Khrushchev retaliate by sharpening the ideological conflict with the external opposition? The available evidence is too fragmentary to permit a definite answer to this question, but at least it can be noted as significant that three major developments in Soviet policy occurred at virtually the same moment: a decision on preparations for the resumption of nuclear testing, a sudden rise in bellicosity toward the United States, and a sharp deterioration in Soviet-Albanian relations.

JOHN L. H. KEEP

The Rehabilitation of M. N. Pokrovskii

Some years ago a Soviet historical journal published an article with the somewhat sensational title "Who Killed Rasputin and How?"[1] It was the sequel to a documentary series on the court of Nicholas II introduced by the late A. L. Sidorov, a leading Soviet historian. Although the article contained little that would have surprised those familiar with relevant sources published in the West, the choice of theme and the manner of its presentation constituted a sharp break with a tradition that dominated historical writing under Stalin, and to some extent survives today. Soviet historians have responded to recent changes in the political climate, although more reluctantly than their colleagues in fields such as economics, or creative intellectuals outside the academic world. Progress was slow until the Twenty-second Party Congress in 1961. Since then there has been vigorous activity, although the pace has diminished markedly since 1966. Today, despite the limitations that have been reimposed upon the choice and treatment of sensitive themes, several schools or trends of thought can be identified, all operating within a common ideological framework, but competing with one another for the allegiance of professional historians and the interested public.[2]

One significant aspect of these changes has been the rehabilitation of Mikhail Nikolaevich Pokrovskii (1868-1932), the leading Marxist historian in the early years of the Soviet regime. The purpose of this article is to examine the way in which this reform was carried through and to assess its significance for the evolution of Soviet historical thought. The problem is as much political as historiographical, for reasons that will be clarified below.

I

Pokrovskii, who was of middle-class background, studied history at Moscow University under Pavel Vinogradov and Vasilii Kliuchevskii, and took up a teaching career. His first works were influenced by the "legal Marxist" ideas much in vogue at the turn of the century, but his political affiliation was to the liberal constitutionalists. In 1904 he turned to the Social Democrats, largely, it seems, under the influence of the errant Bolshevik, A. A. Bogdanov, with whom he collaborated on the non-party legal journal *Pravda*. He was drawn to Bolshevism because it seemed to him the most activist of the many left-wing groups then competing for the support of progressive-minded intellectuals. In 1905 he engaged in propaganda work under the aegis of the Bolshevik-oriented Moscow Committee of the RSDRP and made a trip to Geneva, where he met Lenin; later he played a modest and nonviolent part in the Moscow insurrection. He was able to continue his journalistic activities, although a pamphlet which he wrote on *Economic Materialism* was impounded by the censor. In December, 1907, after the collapse of the first Russian revolution, he moved to the relative security of Finland, and in 1909 to Paris, where he lived until 1917. He joined Bogdanov and Lunacharskii in the *Vpered* group which opposed Lenin's leadership of the Bolshevik faction, and he later associated with the Trotskyists. When World War I broke out he became an Internationalist and in 1915, as a member of Trotsky's *Nashe slovo* group, attempted without success to bring together those Mensheviks and Bolsheviks who shared this point of view. Like Bukharin, Pokrovskii believed that the nation-state had outlived its day and that the coming revolution would be international in scope. This view led him to oppose Lenin over national self-determination.[3]

Although an emigre, he could still publish his work legally in prewar Russia, and it was at this time that he established his reputation as an historian. His four-volume *History of Russia from Ancient Times* (published between 1910 and 1912), was not well received by the critics. It was an obvious effort to produce a Marxist alternative to the work of Kliuchevskii, then at the height of his fame. Whereas his former master had illuminated Russia's social and economic history with erudition and profound knowledge of the primary sources, Pokrovskii operated with schematic sociological formulas and displayed a militant partisanship. The political aim of his work was painfully clear: to discredit both Russia's "ruling class" in all phases of its history, and the state which, he believed, acted merely in the interests of that class. He selected his facts to "prove" the theses, commonly accepted by Russian Marxists of the day, that economic causes were "basic" and all others derivative; that the class struggle was the motive force of history; that progress resulted, not from the will of individuals, but from "objective" socio-economic forces, operating in accordance with scientifically-determinable "regularities" *(zakonomernosti, Gesetzmässigkeiten);* and that the regular succession of "formations" which Marx had identified in Western European history was equally valid for Russia. In common with nearly all his party colleagues at this time, Pokrovskii was first and foremost a European. It was to the West that he looked for capitalist progress and proletarian revolution, which would bring emancipation to backward agrarian Russia. In Russia modern social classes were still in the process of development; feudal relics in economic life went hand in hand with an autocratic political system disguised in quasi-constitutional forms. He criticized without equivocation the aggressive imperialist foreign and colonial policies of the tsarist regime. Despite his obvious bias, superficiality, and intellectual arrogance, his writing at this time gave evidence of sincerity and an independent questing spirit. He was sympathetic to the long-suffering Russian masses and applied the Marxist historical method in an original way: although he treated factual evidence arbitrarily, he did not distort it beyond all recognition. A fruitful dialogue between a historian of his ilk and non-Marxist scholars was still possible.

The February Revolution surprised him at his studies in the Bibliothèque Nationale. It was some months before arrangements could be made for the return of Russian political emigres in France. When Pokrovskii got back to Moscow in August Trotsky's *mezhraiontsy* group, with which he had most in common, had just joined the Bolsheviks. Pokrovskii does not seem to have followed their example. In his unpublished memoirs he states vaguely that he "formulated his relations" with the Bolsheviks in September;[4] his position at this time can best be described as that of an enthusiastic sympathizer whom the local Bolshevik committee found very useful but did not completely trust. He joined the Moscow Soviet and represented it at the Democratic Conference, in which the Bolsheviks participated contrary to Lenin's express wishes. In October he wrote first-hand reports for the Moscow Committee on the fierce fighting that took place in the city. Pokrovskii believed, somewhat naively, that the Bolshevik Revolution would establish a more democratic system of government, resting on autonomous local soviets. It was in this idealistic spirit that he assumed the title of "People's Commissar for Foreign Affairs" in the Moscow Soviet, an office which, had it carried any power, would have directly challenged the authority of the new government in Petrograd. As the dictatorial nature of the "Soviet" regime became apparent, however, he had to modify his views. At Brest-Litovsk, where he participated in the peace negotiations, he did his best to resist German pretensions and, when his efforts failed, joined Bukharin and other leading Bolsheviks in calling for a "revolutionary war" against the invader. But Lenin overruled this "leftist" opposition; Pokrovskii lost his post on the Moscow Soviet (he had in the meantime become its chairman) and was transferred to the cultural field, where his deviant political opinions could do the party less harm.

As deputy to his old friend and associate Lunacharskii, the first People's Commissar for Education, and head of the State Council on Scholarship (GUS), Pokrovskii was entrusted with wide supervisory powers over the country's academic life, in so far as it continued at all at this time. The civil war and economic chaos almost totally disrupted the working of universities and other institutions of learning; scholars and teachers fled, were arrested, or eked out a precarious existence under the constant threat of denunciation. Pokrovskii brought the handful that were sympathetic to the new regime together in a Socialist (later Communist) Academy of Social Sciences, visualized as a body that would rival and supplant the prestigious Academy of Sciences. Other institutions of learning were reformed in such a way as to transfer effective power from the established administrative or academic authorities to the more militant elements of the student body, loosely supervised by the local party committee.

In few fields of learning were the changes more fundamental than in history, a subject to which the new regime, for obvious ideological reasons, attached the utmost importance. It was no coincidence that Pokrovskii, an historian, should have been given such broad responsibilities over all the social sciences, or that the borderline between history (and politics) and other subjects should have been deliberately blurred. Pokrovskii's inadequate understanding of historical materialism or Leninist doctrine was overlooked. He was virtually the only pro-Bolshevik scholar of any standing, as well as a man of immense energy, able and willing to impose his views. He saw it as his duty to permeate Russian intellectual life with Marxist ideas, and to ensure that all institutions of learning complied with the party's requirements. Lenin appreciated the practical value of his services and gave him more or less a free hand. Soon he acquired an impressive variety of functions which taxed even his tremendous strength.

The transition to NEP brought a change of perspective. The class struggle against bourgeois tendencies, in the cultural as in the economic sphere, was now seen as extending over a more prolonged, but indeterminate, period of time. In February, 1921, Pokrovskii formed the Institute of Red Professors (IKP) to train cadres of Marxist teachers and research workers in social-science subjects, and became director of this institute, at first situated incongruously in a former Moscow monastery. Most of the entrants were men of middle-class origin who had been educated under the old regime, so that their training consisted largely of political indoctrination. Until newly-trained Marxists could take over key posts, teaching and research were carried on by "bourgeois" elements under Pokrovskii's watchful eye. At first they continued to work at the universities to which they belonged and supervision was fairly lax. In 1924 six local bodies were brought together to form the Russian Association of Institutes for Scholarly Research in the Social Sciences (RANION). Pokrovskii was the most prominent member of its directing board, which was nominally headed by a leading non-Marxist scholar, the medievalist D. M. Petrushevskii. By the following year the IKP's cadres had grown sufficiently to permit an organization to be created specifically devoted to historical studies, the Society of Marxist Historians (OIM). This, too, was naturally headed by Pokrovskii. He edited its organ, *Istorik-marksist,* as well as other well-known journals, notably *Krasnyi arkhiv*. This was published by the Central Archive Administration of the People's Commissariat for Education, a body which had as its chief none other than the ubiquitous Mikhail Nikolaevich. Somehow Pokrovskii also found time to preside over seminars and give lectures at the IKP, the Sverdlov University and elsewhere, as well as to write books and articles.

Although he could now draw upon archival sources which had been denied him before the revolution, the quality of his scholarly work deteriorated in the Soviet period. He saw himself chiefly as a propagandist and a popularizer. His condensation of his four-volume work, *Russian History in Very Brief Outline,* first published in 1920, went through no less than ten editions in the author's lifetime. It was based on lectures and retained an enviable freshness, laced as it was with rhetorical flourishes; but it was also superficial. Complex problems were grossly simplified or evaded; it did not give a comprehensive Marxist evaluation of all Russian history. Pokrovskii could plead in extenuation that his purpose was to awaken among the semi-educated an interest in history, and more especially a proper positive attitude toward the revolution. To this end he struck a strong moral note and presented the whole of Russia's pre-revolutionary history as a logical build-up to October (although chronologically his work stopped in 1910). Emphasis was laid upon the succession of historical "formations" and on the masses' just and heroic struggle against wicked or incompetent rulers. Characteristically Pokrovskii gave a graphic picture of the cruelty and corruption inherent in Russia's administrative and judicial system prior to the "great reforms" of the 1860s; equally characteristically, he went on to say that matters had been no better in the conservative monarchies of central Europe.[5] For he still saw Russia's development as closely bound up with the international revolutionary process. She had lagged in her development because her bourgeoisie had been weaker and less radical than in the more advanced countries; as a result her revolution had been carried out by the proletariat, and had gone beyond "bourgeois democracy" to socialism. The impression he left was that this had been something of a distortion of the proper historical process, and that further proletarian revolutions in the West were essential to rescue Soviet Russia from her dangerous isolation. This could be interpreted—and was—as indicating a lack of faith in Russia's capacity to build socialism by her own unaided efforts. Although Pokrovskii dutifully accepted Stalin's thesis of "socialism in one country," and as early as 1922 joined in the chorus against Trotsky,[6] he retained ideological affinities with his one-time associate. Indeed, it could hardly be otherwise: he belonged to the "Old Bolshevik" generation, idealistic, romantic, and increasingly out of touch with the harsh practical necessities of power which Stalin understood so well. He could not accept the cynical argument that, to ensure the survival of the dictatorship, "politics must command," and that the economic interpretation of history he held dear would have to be stood on its head.

For the moment these differences remained latent. Pokrovskii's career reached its zenith in December, 1928, when he presided over the first All-Union Conference of Marxist Historians. It was a decisive turning-point in Soviet historiography, as it was in the history of the USSR in general. Stalin was launching his all-out drive for industrialization and collectivization of agriculture, which would bring in its train the full panoply of totalitarian rule. In the intellectual field this meant a campaign to eliminate the last remnants of "bourgeois" influence and the creation of a monolithic *apparat* able to control every expression of opinion. The time for "coexistence" and makeshift devices had passed. Pokrovskii was no longer indispensable. Although he was appointed director of the newly-founded Institute of

History in the Communist Academy and elected to the governing body of the USSR Academy of Sciences (now brought under party control), his ramshackle empire was in danger.

Hitherto one major sector of the "historical front" had remained outside his command: the history of the VKP(b) itself, for which he lacked the necessary political qualifications. Stalin's choice of commanding general—until he was ready to take on the job himself—was E. E. Iaroslavskii, an Old Bolshevik of considerable seniority, who had rendered him valuable support in his struggle for power. Iaroslavskii's *Istpart* machine was between 1922 and 1928 a department of the Central Committee; it took its line directly from the source of power, and had its own arrangements as regards finance, publication outlets, and the like. After 1928 institutional and personal rivalries developed which Stalin exploited with his customary skill. There is an ironic element in the developments that ensued. Pokrovskii was put in charge of the struggle against bourgeois historiography; but the more he attacked his old enemies, the more he himself came under fire as insufficiently "party-minded." Some of the cadres he had trained joined in the criticism. It has recently been stated that a "deliberate persecution" of Pokrovskii was organized by L. M. Kaganovich, secretary of the Central Committee.[7] Whatever the truth of this, the operation must surely have been master-minded by Stalin himself.

A major point of criticism concerned Pokrovskii's ideas on commercial capitalism, which he saw as the dominant force in the Russian economy, and the power behind the throne, from the mid-sixteenth to the nineteenth century. This chronology had enabled him to depict Russia as a relatively advanced European state, and therefore as less immature for socialism than the Mensheviks (and Trotsky) implied. But in 1931 he was obliged to admit that Russia had known only "commercial capital," not "commercial capital*ism*"; that "feudal" elements had survived longer than he had previously thought; and that the autocratic state had rested upon an alliance of landlords and capitalists rather than simply upon the latter. "In the first editions of my scheme," he confessed, "insufficient attention was paid to the relative independence of the political superstructure from the economic basis." But he still held to his general scheme, and contended that in nineteenth-century Russia the main conflict had been between commercial and industrial capital—more specifically, between small-scale merchant producers and large-scale manufacturers. The final picture was confused and contradictory, the more so since Pokrovskii did not adjust his views on tsarist foreign or colonial policy.

These revisions were due to political pressure. The reasons for the change in the party's ideological line at this time are fairly familiar.[8] Stalin's desperate attempt to construct "socialism" at a dizzying pace, relying on mass enthusiasm and terror, required that historians should stress Russia's uniqueness, her backwardness vis-à-vis the West; in this way the achievements of the Five-Year Plan would stand out in a still more glorious light. Related to this was the need to cultivate feelings of patriotism among the *apparatchiki* and the broad mass of the population, now that proletarian revolution abroad would clearly be postponed to the Roman *kalends* (or, to put it more precisely, that indigenous communist forces would have to be helped to power artificially by intervention on the part of a strong socialist state). Stalin realized that in totalitarian conditions national sentiment could serve as a useful means of binding the masses to their rulers. The internationalism of the Old Bolsheviks had become an archaic embarrassment. Equally awkward was their "objectivism"–i.e., their stress on the need to shape policy in accordance with environmental factors–which could only hinder the regime in its efforts to mobilize the masses for its purposes.

Pokrovskii never really grasped the measure of the men and forces that opposed him. Although he put up a valiant rearguard action, his days were clearly numbered. With some of his critics he dealt harshly, banishing them to minor provincial posts by administrative fiat. S. M. Dubrovskii, one of his pupils, was charged with "right-wing opportunism" on the grounds that he had presented the transition from feudalism to serfdom as a peaceful, gradual change. The actual cause of Dubrovskii's fall, however, seems to have been a work disputing the relevance of the Asiatic mode of production, which may have been written at Stalin's behest to aid the latter in his struggle against Trotsky over policy in China.[9] On the other hand, Pokrovskii was willing to adjust his views where he felt his opponents had a case. In 1929 only certain aspects of his work, such as the commercial capitalism theory, were under attack; by the winter of 1930-31 it was being said that his entire "historical conception" was un-Marxist. Thereupon, we are now told, "after careful preparation, on February 5, 1931, he sent a letter to the secretaries of the Central Committee of the VKP(b), in which he dissected and refuted the charges levelled against him."[10] The rather elementary exposition of his views which he gave makes painful reading today. The response which this petition evoked has not been revealed. It may be that at this moment Stalin was angry with Iaroslavskii for having mentioned in his party history Stalin's tactical errors in 1917, and that he took Pokrovskii's part. In any case in November, 1931, he dispatched his celebrated letters to the editors of *Proletarskaia revoliutsiia,* the main *Istpart* organ, condemning them for tolerating Trotskyist tendencies. This was the signal for a violent press campaign in which, however, Pokrovskii was spared; instead he "was singled out as the one Bolshevik historian correctly applying the Marxist conception of history."[11] But he could draw little comfort from this praise. Stricken with cancer, he had entered the Kremlin hospital in the summer of 1931. Bravely he continued writing to the last, but his strength was ebbing and on April 10, 1932, he died. He was buried with full honors, Stalin himself acting as one of the pallbearers.

Hardly had his ashes been laid to rest in the Kremlin wall than the attack on his legacy began. Already on March 15 the Central Committee had ordered a reorganization of scholarly work that would "place first the elaboration of key concrete problems connected with the party's current tasks and the class struggle of the world proletariat at the present stage." *Istorik-marksist*, the OIM organ, had to suspend publication for several months while organizational changes were carried through. In August, 1932, an official pronouncement criticized inadequacies in the teaching of history and other social sciences and ordered the preparation of new textbooks. In May, 1934, a decree set up a special commission to produce more acceptable versions, in which there should be "due emphasis . . . on important historical facts, the names of historical persons, and chronological dates," in place of the "abstract sociological schemes" that had hitherto prevailed. Several of Pokrovskii's works were published in posthumous editions, but in 1934 the body charged with this task, headed by the party historian A. S. Bubnov, unobtrusively ceased its labors. The universities reverted to what seemed to be a more conventional administrative structure; faculties of history, compulsory attendance at lectures, and regular curricula were restored; the earlier periods of history again became respectable. In 1936 Stalin demanded that historians shake off "the erroneous views characteristic of the so-called Pokrovskii 'school' " and portray the Russian past in a way that reflected credit on its national traditions; a new textbook compiled in conformity with these instructions finally received official sanction. Some of Pokrovskii's old associates, such as N. M. Lukin, P. O. Gorin, and S. A. Piontkovskii, were liquidated in the purges.[12] A few historians whom Pokrovskii had discredited as "bourgeois," notably E. V. Tarle[13] and R. Iu. Vipper, returned to positions of authority; other leading posts were filled by former RANION graduates such as M. V. Nechkina, N. M. Druzhinin, and V. M. Khvostov.

The nadir was reached in 1939 when a *Pravda* article by Iaroslavskii, one of the few Old Bolsheviks to survive the holocaust, inaugurated a further campaign against Pokrovskii's memory. The Institute of History rallied its leading collaborators to help compile a two-volume collection of essays, which exposed his erroneous treatment of various historical themes and put the worst construction on his early political deviations.[14] These outpourings reflected Stalin's paranoid fears for the security of the party leadership which he had purged into trembling docility. "It is with a heavy heart," writes the Soviet historian E. A. Lutskii, "that the author of this article now recalls this collection."[15] During World War II exponents of official "Soviet patriotism" such as Tarle attacked Pokrovskii for his cosmopolitan opinions, which he said had contributed to "the moral disarmament of the Russian people."[16] In the years that followed Pokrovskii's name was mentioned rarely, and then as a term of abuse. His works had long since been withdrawn from libraries and bookshops, and to the postwar generation of Soviet scholars he was less familiar than certain conservative historians of the nineteenth century. To all intents and purposes he had become "unpersoned."

II

The partial demolition of the Stalin myth at the Twentieth Party Congress in 1956 unleashed a ferment in Soviet intellectual life and created conditions in which Pokrovskii's ideas and achievements could be reassessed. Before discussing this matter one important point needs to be made. The drive for his rehabilitation was not the work of those younger historians who objected most strongly to the frauds and injustices perpetrated under the shield of the "personality cult," but of older men who had begun their careers in the 1920s and had in many cases suffered hardship on account of their association with Pokrovskii. Politically, these scholars identified themselves with the mild revisionism of Khrushchev; they welcomed such relaxations as the party permitted, but did not actively press for further concessions which might imperil the regime's stability. As thoroughly loyal elements, they cannot be regarded as sympathetic to "bourgeois" Western liberal values or modes of thought. Yet it is an elementary lesson of history that reforms often lead to results neither anticipated nor desired by those who initiate them. By casting doubt on previously accepted assumptions, the revisionists stimulate critical thought, which may become more radical as it meets resistance from conservative elements. This pattern could be illustrated from many aspects of Soviet intellectual life since Stalin's death.

One should perhaps enter a *caveat* here against the tendency to personalize intellectual conflicts of this kind, and say that the struggle is as much one within men's minds as one between individuals. For Soviet historians the tension is between their professional interest in elucidating the truth and their political interest in bolstering the official ideology, with its immutable and sanctified precepts.

The first indications of impending changes came in January, 1956, when Pokrovskii's name received favorable mention in an official statement: he was credited with important services in the struggle against bourgeois historiography, although he had also been guilty of "vulgarizing errors" which had been justly condemned.[17] The authorities seem to have planned a gradual revision of their line, carried out under close party control, but events moved too fast for them. E. N. Burdzhalov, editor of *Voprosy istorii*, provoked a crisis by questioning the legitimacy of the October Revolution. Not until this affair had been settled by his dismissal and a reconstitution of the journal's editorial board was it safe to take further steps towards Pokrovskii's rehabilitation. The revisionists (as we may call them) hoped that, by presenting him as a loyal Leninist who had been unjustly victimized by Stalin, they could improve their own image in the eyes of younger and more skeptically-minded historians. But it was not easy to overcome the conservatism of those brought up in the Stalin mold, who feared, not unreasonably, that any rethinking would encourage heretical ideas. Late in 1957 M. E. Naidenov could write that, although Pokrovskii had played a positive role in Soviet historiography during the 1920s, "his views upon a whole number of important questions concerning the October Revolution differed radically from the precepts of Lenin. He understood neither Lenin's teaching on imperialism nor his theory that the revolution could grow over from the bourgeois-democratic to the proletarian-socialist phase."[18]

The nettle was not grasped firmly until the following summer, when, apparently without any preliminary announcement in the press, a meeting was held at the Museum of the Revolution in Moscow to celebrate the ninetieth anniversary of Pokrovskii's birth. The main report was delivered by S. M. Dubrovskii, who thirty years earlier had been one of his fledglings. Later he had suffered under Stalin: an acknowledged authority on pre-revolutionary agrarian conditions, he published little or nothing between the late 1920s and 1956. The text of his report appears to have been circulated *na pravakh rukopisi,* as is the usual practice with politically sensitive documents, but its tenor can be reconstructed fairly well from materials published subsequently. In the autumn of 1958 a conference was held in the editorial offices of *Voprosy istorii,* the proceedings of which likewise remained in manuscript. Among those present was a lady who had once attended Pokrovskii's seminar in the IKP and now recalled sympathetically his efforts to correct his mistakes.[19]

The next phase in Pokrovskii's rehabilitation came in 1960-61, when the journal *Istoriia SSSR* began a lethargic and scholastic discussion on "the periodization of Soviet historiography." The participants labored under the hindrance of being unable to mention explicitly the role played by individual historians or politicians. The revisionists, led by the formidable M. V. Nechkina, drew heavily upon Pokrovskii's published writings as well as other materials of the 1920s, which had now evidently been made available again, at least to approved scholars. They also used some unpublished material, notably from Pokrovskii's personal archive, preserved in the Institute of History.

Their arguments can be summarized as follows. First, Pokrovskii had made a notable contribution to the struggle against "bourgeois" historians and deviant communists (e.g., Trotsky) in difficult conditions. Secondly, he deserved credit for his endeavors to acquire a wholly orthodox Leninist *Weltanschauung;* it was necessary to view his work "dialectically," in its process of development, rather than "statically" and dogmatically. Third, it was implied—but not clearly stated—that his political vacillations were not really relevant to his work as a historian, and that they were in some way offset by the political "mistakes" committed by his Stalinist critics. Finally, Pokrovskii's best-known work, his *Brief History,* had been approved by Lenin in a letter of 1920,[20] and indeed actually "commissioned" by him. (This letter had been frequently referred to when Pokrovskii's career was at its height, but had since either been passed over in silence or else cited selectively—a procedure that aroused much indignation.) An element of special pleading was involved here, since the relationship between party leader and scholar in Lenin's day was very different from what it was to become later, and the Bolshevik leader's attitude to Pokrovskii had actually been equivocal. But the maneuver was necessary because it at once indicated to potential critics that they should move cautiously.[21]

Had logic been given its due in this discussion, the conservatives might well have pointed to the inconsistencies in the revisionist position: it was still said that Pokrovskii's methodology and his erroneous views on periodization had "caused tremendous harm to historical science," yet the overall evaluation was positive. But they preferred more devious tactics. They argued, for example, that the early period of Soviet historiography ought rightfully to be named after Lenin rather than Pokrovskii, and that the real turning-point in its development had come in the mid-1930s.[22] Naidenov now admitted that Pokrovskii's role had been "indubitably progressive," but complained that Nechkina was divorcing the development of Soviet historiography from the political struggle in the country at large (which, however, neither of them could discuss frankly), and drew attention to Pokrovskii's sympathies for "Bogdanovism" and his "national nihilism."[23] The debate was inconclusive, and had to be settled at a higher level. In the summer of 1961 a hint was given in *Kommunist* that the Central Committee was about to intervene.[24]

At the Twenty-Second Party Congress in October, 1961, L. F. Ilyichov, the chief ideologist, stated authoritatively:

> In the period of the personality cult some quite inexplicable things occurred, such as suppressing the names of leading scholars. This was the fate of the eminent Marxist historian and Old Bolshevik M. N. Pokrovskii. In his scholarly and political activity there were no few mistakes. This is true and account should be taken of it. But it is well known that he defended Marxism and made a great contribution to the writing of Russian history.[25]

He proceeded to quote (in full) Lenin's familiar letter and to contrast his gentle paternalism with the brutal attitude of Stalin. So began the third phase in the rehabilitation process. The leading historians now fell into line, although some of them put up a kind of smoke screen to cover their retreat. At a meeting held in December, 1961, to discuss the implications of the party congress decisions, the man chosen to deliver the report was, significantly, Dubrovskii. He ended on a note of self-vindication:

> The decisions of the Twentieth and Twenty-Second Congresses, the exposure of the personality cult, . . . the crushing of the anti-party group of Molotov, Kaganovich, Malenkov and co. have created favorable conditions for . . . an objective assessment of our historiographical legacy, including Pokrovskii's works.[26]

I. I. Mints, whose position was somewhat delicate since he had succeeded Pokrovskii as head of the IKP, made the point that Dubrovskii had been the first to criticize Pokrovskii's entire conception of history in the 1920s—a remark which might be thought to imply that Dubrovskii was something of a weathercock.[27] M. P. Kim repeated the Stalinist argument that Pokrovskii had tried to build up for himself a monopoly position in the field of historical studies. On the other hand, A. L. Sidorov broke new ground by making the first public criticism of the two-volume critique of Pokrovskii, which he had helped to edit. Summing up the discussion, the chairman held out the prospect of a thorough investigation into Pokrovskii's work. One of the questions that needed to be answered was: "what were the consequences for Soviet historical scholarship of the struggle against Pokrovskii during the period of the cult?"[28]

One year later another conference was held to discuss the general subject of history teaching.[29] The debate had now broadened out into a general indictment of Stalinist methods—something of much greater significance than the question of Pokrovskii's merits or demerits, which were scarcely discussed at all. One of the few references to him was by Burdzhalov, the *enfant terrible* of 1956, who made a strong attack on Sidorov for having criticized Pokrovskii as late as 1955.[30] One might think that this was scarcely fair: after all, at that time such articles were quite in order, and in the last few years Sidorov had changed his line as fast as anyone else. But the radicals were playing the game by different rules; their main objection was precisely to what they felt was a hypocritical readiness on the part of leading historians to adjust their views to the political *koniunktura*. Burdzhalov was probably paying off an old personal score as well. In any case Sidorov did his best to make amends. In March, 1964, he published a revealing memoir in which he recalled his experiences as a member of Pokrovskii's seminar in the 1920s.[31] He mentioned that in 1929, "with the best of intentions and a clear conscience," he had rashly suggested to the great man that he make certain alterations in his *Brief History,* whereupon he had been sent to do practical work in Nizhnii Novgorod (now Gorky).[32] He had taken it in good heart and did not hold Pokrovskii himself responsible so much as his associates Gorin and Friedland. He had now been asked to give some advice to young scholars. "I should prefer that young people, reading my story, should draw from it the conclusions they think useful."[33] He ended by warning his colleagues against concentrating too heavily on collective works, which could inhibit them from expressing individual ideas; they should study the technique and methodology of bourgeois writers—as Pokrovskii had recommended.

Since 1962 Soviet historians have indeed tried to grapple with the legacy of the 1920s, although a thoroughgoing *Bewältigung der Vergangenheit* remains to be accomplished. A valuable but brief sketch of Pokrovskii's career has been given by E. A. Lutskii, and L. V. Danilova has discussed the contribution which he and other early Soviet scholars made to the study of feudalism.[34] O. L. Vainshtein has described, a little drily for one of his experience, the general historiographical scene in the 1920s.[35] Pokrovskii's selected works have appeared in a four-volume edition.[36] The first three volumes comprise his two major historical works; the last contains a rather uninspiring choice of his articles and book reviews, devoted mainly to such topics as Lenin, the Russian revolutionary movement, historiography, archive administration, and scholastic organization. Volume IV of the new official history of Russian historiography, published in 1966 under the chief editorship of M. V. Nechkina, contains an authoritative assessment, by L. V.

Cherepnin, of Pokrovskii's position in Soviet scholarship as the revisionists see it. It is not calculated to stimulate any intellectual interest in the Old Bolshevik's ideas. Cherepnin states unequivocally:

> Pokrovskii belongs to history. It is not a matter of restoring his conclusions, or idealizing his works or conceptions, but of establishing in an objective scientific way his role in the establishment and development of science.[37]

No comprehensive systematic study has been made, or is in present circumstances likely to be made, of Pokrovskii's thought and its implications for the contemporary Soviet historian.

In what way, then, if at all, one may ask, is his rehabilitation likely to change such historians' image of the world?

III

At first sight it may seem that the positive developments in Soviet historical writing during recent years represent a return to the relative freedom of the 1920s. Such a conclusion would, however, be superficial.[38] There are a number of common features between the Pokrovskii era and the present: greater variety in the institutional pattern, a more tolerant intellectual climate, increased contact with other countries and greater attention to combating "bourgeois ideology." But the historian's function today is still basically what it was in the Stalin era: to provide an intellectual legitimation for the existing regime and the order of society it has established. A great deal of scholarly effort is devoted to expounding fictions which substantiate the party's claims to be the authoritative interpreter of "the logical process of mankind's movement toward communism" (N. E. Fedoseev). The Soviet historian is not simply required to eulogize his political masters: he must adopt enthusiastically a *Weltanschauung* centered upon the collective experience of party and people in the "building of socialism and communism." When assessing any historical event, idea, or problem, however remote in time or space, he is to take as his criterion its "progressiveness"—meaning in effect the contribution it made to the events that led to the current might of the USSR and world communism. This creed governs his perception of historical facts, as well as his manner of interpreting them.

The spirit of official thinking is thus closer to that of the 1930s than the 1920s. Stalin's arbitrary despotism has gone, but the substance of his system remains. The party still sees itself as engaged upon a worldwide struggle which necessitates the consolidation and extension of its power at home and abroad. The revolutionary internationalism of the early Bolsheviks, to which Pokrovskii and even Lenin were committed, has little relevance to the position of post-Stalinist Russia.

There is thus an artificial quality about the rehabilitation of Pokrovskii: it is his reputation that is being salvaged rather than his ideas. The prime motive of the revisionists is to present a politically acceptable image of Soviet historiography, from Lenin to the present, as monolithically united in a relentless struggle against hostile ideas. But some Soviet historians with strong professional loyalties pursue a rather different aim: to right a tragic injustice, and so to arrive at a closer approximation to actual truth. The tension between these two purposes may be illustrated by reference to several specific problems.

The first is that of methodology. It is not surprising that the official revisionists should have said little favorable about Pokrovskii's historiographical technique, although this aspect of his work is probably of the greatest interest to the professionals. Stalin had indicted him in the first instance for methodological errors: for making broad generalizations unsupported by facts, for disregarding or confusing chronological details, and for a naive understanding of Marxism. But Stalin's own disciples had then substituted even crasser simplifications, had been even more selective in their choice of factual evidence, and had forbidden creative Marxist thought altogether. With almost diabolical cunning they accused Pokrovskii of the very sins that they were themselves committing on a far grander scale. He was said to have preached the necessity of "projecting politics into the past,"[39] although they themselves molded the historical record unashamedly in accordance with political expediency.

Two charges were fundamental in the Stalinist indictment. The first was that Pokrovskii retained, as the legacy of his early academic upbringing, a non-partisan respect for factual evidence. Wherever possible, he had based his more specialized work upon research in the primary sources; he set high standards for his pupils in this regard; and the collections of documents which he edited by and large conformed to normal scholarly standards. Naturally this respect for observed fact had its limits: he was not prepared to question the fundamental dogmas of Marx or Lenin, but he sincerely believed that scholarly analysis of objective evidence would validate the Marxian scheme. Such faith his Stalinist successors conspicuously lacked.

The second major point of criticism was that he made no secret of his political bias. He took the crude but intellectually honest view that all historical interpretation was politically motivated. The class struggle, which determined men's political beliefs, made non-partisan historiography impossible; one had to take one's stand on one side of the barricades or the other. This simple formula was inappropriate to totalitarian conditions. Intellectuals were now required to pretend that their *Weltanschauung* was truly scientific, while at the same time suspending all critical judgment in regard to the central core of their beliefs, loyalty to the party *(partiinost')*. Various formulas have been evolved in an attempt to reconcile the contradictory strains, one scientific and the other fideistic,[40] in Stalinist and post-Stalinist thought. It is argued, for instance, that true objectivity (as distinct from "bourgeois objectivism") can be attained only by partisanship, the two principles being allegedly "related dialectically": the party, intervening in the historical process, influences its objective regularities, to which its own actions naturally conform.[41]

The valiant efforts recently made by Soviet philosophers and historians to enrich their stock of theory have not brought its inherent contradictions any nearer solution, but have helped crystallize two points of view. The conservatives take a classic utilitarian stand. In effect they see it as the historian's job to provide evidence that will substantiate the current official analysis of the speed and direction of the historical process. They emphasize the general at the expense of the particular and are suspicious of mere "factography." The revisionists are more interested in the way that general regularities work themselves out in specific concrete conditions, and are more willing to let the facts speak for themselves. They would like to refine the concept of regularity in such a way as to distinguish between those laws that are applicable to broad sociological processes, e.g. the succession of socio-economic formations, and those laws that govern their implementation within a narrower frame of reference.[42] The revisionists emphasize the distinction between the social and natural sciences and come close to recognizing history's claims as an autonomous discipline, in which factual description and narrative have an important part to play. Thus the philosopher A. V. Gulyga argues:

> In branches of learning which pursue descriptive aims as well as that of generalization, factual material plays a special role, different from that in purely theoretical disciplines. The latter utilize factual data simply as an aid to generalization. These sciences go through the stage of accumulating empirical material, but their aim is always to establish a law, and when this has been done the empirical material loses its importance. Historical research also begins with the collection of facts. Here, too, facts are to an even greater degree the air which the scholar breathes . . . . Without a firm, assured groundwork of fact no historical generalization is possible. At the same time the historical fact is not simply material for generalization; it is not just an example which can be dropped or replaced, to illustrate the operation of a social law. Historical generalization is no substitute for fact. To a certain extent facts in history have a value in themselves.[43]

A provincial historian from Kalinin, A. Iu. Gurevich, has pleaded for a more sophisticated interpretation of the concept of regularity in the historical as distinct from the sociological context; quoting Sir Isaiah Berlin (although in a critical sense), he suggests that the laws of social development should be seen merely as trends *(zakony-tendentsii).*[44] Gurevich, in common with several other writers, also points to the role of probability and chance in interrupting or diverting the logical flow of events: a number of options are available to the decision-maker, and a given situation may have several possible outcomes. This new flexibility seems to reflect recent trends in mathematics. It certainly shows that some Soviet historians are dissatisfied with conventional doctrine, which asserts that "historical necessity makes its way through an endless multiplicity of fortuitous events," but does not explain *how* it does so.

Other revisionist writers have stressed the aesthetic aspects of the historian's craft, and held up for emulation the more sensitive approach of literary and other cultural historians. Excessive concentration on the typical, they point out, is liable to bore the reader, who is naturally interested in whatever is individual and unique. Such study is perfectly permissible, they maintain, since even the unique is socially conditioned and derives ultimately from the operation of general laws; the typical and the individual are not diametrically opposed categories, but are dialectically linked.

Truly the conservatives face an unenviable task in trying to stop all the loopholes in the official philosophy of history, which can be readily exploited by ingenious critics. Pokrovskii's legacy in this field could strengthen the revisionists' hand, by giving them an officially sanctioned example of creative Marxist thought. In a speech of 1928, for example, he too distinguished between sociological and historical interpretations of events.[45] This was not directly quoted by any participant in the recent discussion on methodology, but it is not surprising to find one leading historian complaining that his colleagues were still thrashing out the problems of thirty-five years ago.

Another fruitful field which they may wish to explore is Pokrovskii's concept of the role of the individual in history. Although he is usually regarded, not without reason, as a crass economic determinist, his attitude was really much more subtle. It is true that Pokrovskii minimized the role of Russian rulers, generals and saints, some of whom Stalin later resurrected and even glorified. But he was also willing to recognize that revolutionary leaders and elites could decisively alter the shape of events, and he regarded the October Revolution as a supreme example of this. We shall come back to this point in a moment.

Turning now from methodology to particular problems of Russian history, one may identify three fields in which, if and when the political climate again improves, Pokrovskii's rehabilitation may serve to accelerate the movement of opinion away from Stalinist traditions.

The first is the problem of pre-revolutionary Russian colonial and foreign policy. As a consistent internationalist, Pokrovskii emphasized the imperialist nature of tsarist diplomacy, particularly in regard to the Balkans and Near East; he even exaggerated the aggressiveness of Russia's drive for control of the Straits. In a popular sketch of 1926 he suggested—on the basis of very dubious evidence—that the Entente, not the Central Powers, was responsible for the outbreak of World War I.[46] In his *Brief History* he argued that the Russian state had been built up by the conquest of successive native peoples, from the Finns of the northern forests in Kievan days to the Moslems of Central Asia in the nineteenth century. Stalin, of course, changed all this and introduced into Soviet historiography a strident patriotic note. Emphasis was laid upon the positive effects of absorption into the Russian Empire for the minorities concerned. Parallels were drawn between the German invasion of 1941 and Napoleon's campaign of 1812, a subject which Pokrovskii had neglected: looking at it in a European perspective, he had roundly condemned the Russian role as reactionary and shown more sympathy for the relics of the Grande Armée than for the peasant guerrillas.

In recent years some of the worst nationalistic distortions have been discarded. Among the keenest advocates of revision, of course, are historians from the non-Russian (and especially non-Slavic) republics. The conservatives have their principal stronghold among military historians, who currently occupy an almost privileged semi-autonomous position.

The ramifications of this argument cannot be discussed in detail here.[47] In general it may be said that any thorough-going revision of historical doctrine on this issue is exceedingly unlikely. Characteristically, in the new edition of Pokrovskii's history virtually the only passages selected for editorial comment are those in which the author expressed his internationalist viewpoint. For example, where he criticizes Alexander II's government for seeking to liberate "brother Slavs" (the author's inverted commas!) in the Balkans, a discreet footnote refers the reader to a remark by the Bulgarian communist leader Dimitrov on the "liberation" of Bulgaria by "the Russian people" in the war of 1877-78.[48]

The party leaders know that national feeling, in its guise of Soviet patriotism, is a more important prop than ever. If spokesmen for the minorities go too far, they can easily be discredited as "bourgeois nationalists." They cannot look to Pokrovskii for support, since he took little direct interest in minority problems, but they may benefit if some other historians of the 1920s again become respectable. Russian revisionist historians have little incentive to recall Pokrovskii's views. Dubrovskii has pointed out in his defense that Pokrovskii had to combat the chauvinistic and nationalistic sentiments so widespread under the old regime. But Fedoseev, warning that Pokrovskii's rehabilitation should not be pressed too far, specifically mentioned his error in "not always indicating the significance of national traditions and permitting wrong evaluations in this regard."[49] To illustrate his point he referred to Pokrovskii's positive assessment of the thirteenth-century Tatar invaders of Rus'—which his percipient audience will have construed as a blow against certain pro-Chinese historians who have endeavored to rehabilitate Ghenghis Khan. The present moment is scarcely opportune for anyone to probe deeply into this aspect of Pokrovskii's legacy.

A related problem is that of the Russian revolutionary tradition. For Pokrovskii—as indeed for Lenin—Bolshevism was intimately linked with international left-wing socialism and "revolutionary Marxism." In the Stalin era, when the Comintern and all that it stood for lost importance, these connections were played down. Instead, emphasis was laid upon antecedents of Bolshevism in the Russian past—in the "men of the 1860s," the Decembrists, and even the peasant uprisings of the seventeenth and eighteenth centuries. One link in the chain, however, was conspicuously missing: the revolutionary populists, who were influenced either by Bakunin's anarchism or the "Blanquist" Jacobinism of Zaichnevskii, Nechaev and Tkachev. The populists were presented as reactionary and anti-Marxist. One reason for this was that during the 1920s a number of writers, some former Mensheviks, had sought the antecedents of Leninism among these radical populists, and for this had been sharply condemned. For example, in 1925 the journal *Katorga i ssylka* published an article by S. Mitskevich on "the roots of Bolshevism," which had been rejected by the more orthodox *Proletarskaia revoliutsiia;* six years later, after Stalin reproved the latter journal for its laxity, the editors of *Katorga i ssylka* apologized for having "granted a rostrum to those who had no right to it."[50] Pokrovskii did not go quite so far as Mitskevich. But in a course of lectures delivered in 1923-24 he stated that Tkachev "undoubtedly had a Marxist concept of history" and, referring to Nechaev, went on:

> . . . already at the end of the 1860s there was formed in Russian revolutionary circles a plan which the Mensheviks later mocked so greatly and which was put into effect almost literally on October 25, 1917—the plan for an *appointed* revolution.[51]

Pokrovskii considered the populist Jacobins both naive and "petty-bourgeois," but saw a continuity between them and the Bolsheviks in that both had built up a conspiratorial party with the deliberate object of seizing power.

In recent years Soviet historians, following the initiative of the late B. P. Kozmin, a distinguished authority on the period, have sought to present populism in a truer perspective. The artificial and illogical distinction between the radicals of the 1860s and of the 1870s has been discarded. V. A. Tvardovskaia has criticized those historians, of whom Nechkina was the *doyenne*, who exaggerated the revolutionary role of the peasantry in post-reform Russia.[52] A noteworthy feature of this rehabilitation is that it concentrates on the *narodovol'tsy* at the expense of those identified with anarchism or Jacobinism.[53] One party historian has angrily rebutted the suggestion of a link between Tkachev and Lenin.[54] The specific problem of Bolshevik antecedents has been gingerly taken up by V. V. Shirokova,[55] but her article seems to have evoked no response.

Future writers on this theme will welcome the access now granted to the historical literature of the 1920s. But they will have to go carefully in citing such sources on later stages of revolutionary history, where a conflict is likely with the Leninist canon. Pokrovskii, discussing the events of 1905, minimized the role of the peasants as an active and "conscious" revolutionary force; in his treatment of 1917 he maintained that the February Revolution had already brought the working class to power *de facto,* and that the Bolsheviks did no more than establish the proletarian dictatorship *de jure.*[56] These assertions reflected the Trotskyist affiliations which he had shared at one time. Yet despite the obvious difficulties involved, Soviet historians *are* today revising their views on the revolution itself, partly as a natural consequence of destalinization, partly in response to recent developments in world politics.

The significance of this will become clear if we turn to our third specific problem, Russia's social and economic development in the pre-revolutionary period. Pokrovskii, as we have seen, was forced by the Stalinists to modify his views on the chronological dating of Russia's transition from feudalism to capitalism, and a new doctrine on this point became established in the 1930s. It was somewhat closer to the facts than Pokrovskii's scheme, and was probably accepted with relief by specialists on this period. They could now give the landowning nobility its due in an epoch when it was dominant, and recognize, at least in part, the achievements of those monarchs, officials, or capitalists who had promoted Russia's economic advance. But some historians still considered that less than justice was being done to business enterprise among the peasants prior to the Great Reforms, and once discussion again became possible they pressed for the onset of capitalism to be backdated. A long and arid debate ensued, in which the weight of opinion came down in favor of the accepted late dating, approximately in the mid-nineteenth century. If the issue is raised again, the revisionists will be able to draw upon Pokrovskii's arguments in support—with their implication that imperial Russian society was closer to that of Western countries than the Stalinists cared to admit.

The same issue is raised by the attempt to fix chronological limits for the supposed "imperialist" phase in Russian history. Pokrovskii first took the view that this could be dated only from 1914, when Russia had entered the "imperialist war," but later pushed it back to 1890. In his view the main criteria involved were protective tariffs and an expansionist foreign policy; and in the 1890s Russia had had both. The existence of trusts and syndicates he considered a less important characteristic, for these had been much weaker in Russia than in more advanced countries such as Germany or the United States. It was only in the immediate prewar years that Russia had developed a "finance capital" of her own, since previously she had depended heavily upon foreign investment. An economic satellite could hardly be imperialist in the economic sense. Pokrovskii's views were quite reasonable and in the 1920s the question was debated fairly on the basis of objective evidence. Some of his pupils emphasized the role of native capital more than Pokrovskii did. Others were more inclined to portray Russia as a colony of foreign investors. Pokrovskii had greater sympathy for the latter view, which carried the implication that the revolution had been as much a national anti-imperialist movement as a social one, and which cast doubt upon the existence of any objective basis for socialist construction in the USSR.

Stalin first beat all these historians into silence with the stick of orthodox Leninism, pointing out dogmatically that Lenin had dated imperialism from 1900, and then appropriated their opinions himself. In 1934 he stated that pre-revolutionary Russia had been a "semi-colony" of Western capital. This theme was much stressed in the post-World War II years, when the anti-cosmopolitan drive was at its height.

Destalinization in this field got under way shortly before the Twenty-Second Party Congress, when a conference for this purpose was held in Leningrad; its sponsor was a body known rather grandly as the Section on Regularities and Particularities of the Development of Russia under Imperialism, a sub-group of the Council on the History of the Russian Revolution.[57] The "semi-colonial" theory was explicitly discarded, freeing the way for a rehabilitation of native Russian capital.

It seems that there emerged two schools of thought, each of which sought to provide a more up-to-date and credible historical legitimation for the October Revolution. This was no academic issue, for as one historian observes:

> . . . the rise and development of the world socialist system after the Great Patriotic War has made particularly topical the problem of the regularity of the transition from capitalism to socialism, which began in October 1917.[58]

One tendency, represented by A. P. Pogrebinskii and Ia. I. Livshin, emphasizes the dominant position of monopolistic trusts and syndicates in Russia's economic and political life prior to 1917, and especially their responsibility for the outbreak and prolongation of the war. The reader is left with the impression that Russia's privileged groups formed a powerful and united reactionary bloc, which could be overthrown only by a still mightier union of the popular masses, and that such a national union came about in opposition to the war, into which the people were dragged by domestic and foreign business interests. Seen in this perspective, 1917 appears as the forerunner of the "anti-colonial" revolutions in China and other developing countries. The political implication is that Russia's historical experience entitles her to a vanguard role in the emergent peoples' struggle against "Western imperialism," from which she was the first to emancipate herself.

The second tendency views the revolution in a European rather than an Asian perspective, and is closer to the Western standpoint than to the Chinese. Spokesmen for this tendency are of course totally opposed to the evaluation of Bolshevism given by "bourgeois" scholars. But they do not contest too strongly the argument that the Bolsheviks' victory was largely a matter of superior leadership and organization. They conceal this deemphasis of the role of the masses behind loud endorsement of the current extravagant cult of Lenin. The implication of this line of thinking is that, but for Lenin and his party, Russia would have had to develop along the road of Western "bourgeois democracy." The alternative to Bolshevik rule is thus seen as limited progress rather than outright reaction. It is further suggested that Russia had been prepared for such progress by her previous history: her industrial progress prior to 1914 was quite significant; monopolistic restrictions were not all-important; the role of foreign investment was not exclusively negative; the ruling groups were divided among themselves. The chief obstacle to Russia's advance, it is implied, was not so much the capitalists, native or alien, as the court camarilla and other archaic "feudal" survivals within the privileged elite. Hence Sidorov's interest in Rasputin. In short, this school inclines toward a more sophisticated–and in Western eyes realistic–understanding of the causes of the Russian Revolution, even though the explanation given might not satisfy non-Marxists.

Among those who have intervened on this side of the debate are the late A. L. Sidorov, I. F. Gindin and V. K. Iatsunskii,[59] who worked with Pokrovskii in the 1920s. The latter's rehabilitation should reinforce their position, and may encourage younger, more questing spirits to urge greater frankness in discussing this key problem. How far can the pendulum swing toward a less standardized interpretation of October? Will Soviet historians be able to refine the concept of *zakonomernost'* to a point where they can accept Pokrovskii's view (which many early Bolsheviks would have shared) that it was an "appointed" revolution, carried out in contravention of "narrow economic laws"?

The answer to these questions cannot be given by the historians alone. In the last resort their evaluation of the past depends upon the politicians. In the decade 1956-66 the party permitted a notable advance both in methods of research and in quality of analysis. If and when the present "freeze" is over, these progressive trends may reassert themselves.

GEORGE FISCHER

Political Monism and Cultural Duality: A Soviet Model of Modern Society?

When the world marked the fiftieth anniversary of the Bolshevik Revolution not long ago, it made good sense to ask once again: what are the lessons of October?

A major lesson of October, I believe, is that the Bolshevik Revolution and Russia's development since 1917 may point to a new model of a fully modern society. In a tentative way, I propose to argue here that the USSR of today does suggest a model of modernity quite different from the Western, "pluralist" model on which we tend to focus when we now speak of modern society.

Specifically, we can see in the Soviet case at least two main elements that the Western model of modernity is said to do without: the element of monism in the political sphere, and the element of duality in the cultural sphere. Just as we are apt to tie modern politics to pluralism (in the sense of a plurality of autonomous social forces), we think of modern society in terms of a single dominant culture—what Raymond Williams in *Culture and Society* calls "a whole way of life"—and not two or a "dual" culture. That half a century after the Bolshevik Revolution Russia may in fact be a fully modern society, and yet lack a Western type of political pluralism and cultural integration, could indeed be one of the great lessons of October.[1]

Generally speaking, modernization involves three main processes: industrialization, the building of a nation-state, and the rise of a new culture. The new culture, less traditional than any in the past, must be more adaptable to change—an endemic and ubiquitous kind of change that science and technology help to set off and then to keep up. A fully modern society is one that has an industrial economy, a viable national state, and a culture that puts stress on new technical modes and skills. When a society has moved to this stage, we can say that it has become "modern."[2]

In regard to Russia, where should one draw the hazy but all-important line between the process of becoming modern and actually being modern? I would put the hazy line in the quite recent past. The term "modernity" is not used here to cover the years before or during Soviet industrialization and administrative consolidation, Stalin's Iron Age of the 1930s. Nor does it cover the difficult years of World War II and the great economic reconstruction that followed. It is not until the 1950s that this generally most advanced of the communist countries began to cross the line. Only then, it seems, did the USSR begin to face the tasks and needs of becoming modern.

Along with a modern stage of development, each type of modern society is characterized by a distinct historical path. Most comments today link Russia with one such path, and the West with another. The way a country industrializes marks the difference between the two paths. In the West, primacy has been given to a private-sector economy. The business entrepreneur dominates the economy. Russia, along with many countries today, has put stress on a public-sector economy. The state dominates the economy. More than that, as has often been said of Russia, the state dominates society. The West alone showed the reverse pattern as it came to be "modern."[3]

I. POLITICAL MONISM

If up to 1917 Russia was ruled by a hesitantly modernizing absolute monarchy, its political system in 1967 is geared to heavy emphasis on continuing and quite drastic social change. Much of this "induced" change from above centers on the economy, all of which is directed by the state and its political leaders. But no less intensive care is given by the political system to a vast program of cultural and social transformations, the end result of which (before the close of this century) is to be an advanced stage of the ideal, communist social system. Not only the ruling group, the leaders of the party, but also their established creed, can be said to focus on this change-oriented, and future-oriented, kind of politics. Both the leaders and their creed, in other words, define the society's task in terms of unceasing state-directed modernization. This shapes the political monism of which I speak.

As an ideal type, a second, non-pluralist model of modernity covers all those social systems in which the state is dominant and where it rules by means of public economic power.

To run a fully modern society well, any kind of monist system will have to meet two basic needs which, in a way, run counter to each other. On the one hand, a monist system must take great care to keep the state dominant. On the other hand, it must give a good deal of leeway to the many complex and specialized elements that make up a modern society.

Hence total control of other spheres, notably the economy, is not essential to monist politics. It would be more accurate to say that in a new model the state has the final say about all economic matters at the apex of the entire system. Below the apex, a monist system need not (and most likely cannot) limit the economic division of labor much more than a pluralist society of the capitalist sort. Thus a good deal of professional leeway within key groups such as managers, scientists, and the military is still possible. Nor does a monist system like the Soviet rule out a degree of organizational leeway in many parts of economic life. To be sure, this administrative type of autonomy stops short of social autonomy under which major social groups are more or less free of state control. Yet we should not equate that fact with a total lack of leeway within major groups and spheres.

In general, it should be clear by now that *both* the monist and the pluralist models allow for more and more functional specialization of the kind that marks all of life today. Nor does either model rule out the ever greater role of the state as a coordinating and integrating element in any modern society. Most of all, neither model denies that a modern society may indeed carry within it very strong pulls toward social autonomy. These key aspects of potential social development fit both models.

The models go different ways not on the question of such overall development, but on what they mean for a modern society. Thus, proponents of the pluralist model imply not only that the overall development will take place, but also that in its main spheres a modern society *must* give (or keep up) large amounts of social autonomy. This consequence, and not the development itself, is what an examination of the possibilities of a monist model casts doubt on. I would argue that much functional specialization, much state power, and some pressure toward social autonomy can coexist effectively with little *actual* social autonomy.

More specifically, the two models clash on the mechanisms, the organizing devices, that are to be found at the core of a modern society. In the pluralist model, the vast complexity and boundless change of modern life can be dealt with by one mechanism alone: pluralism, as a mechanism of large-scale social autonomy. In this model, social autonomy gives a share of real power to a set of autonomous groups, so that they can act more or less on their own within one or more spheres of life. The pluralists maintain that only such division of labor–and division of power–make a modern society adaptable enough to cope with endemic and ubiquitous change.[4]

In contrast to that view, the monist model holds that some mechanisms other than social autonomy can serve to pull together a vastly complex society. We know all too little about how such alternate mechanisms might look or work. But any new model of modernity rests on the assumption that they will emerge.[5]

These last points suggest that the monist model is not unlike the "imperfect" totalitarianism of which Gordon Skilling speaks. As Skilling puts it, the Soviet system today "is not genuine pluralism, nor is it pure totalitarianism; it is rather an imperfect monism in which, of the many elements involved, one–the party–is more powerful than all others but is not omnipotent."[6]

However, what Skilling terms "imperfect monism" amounts to one form only, a limited form. As has been stressed already, limited monism is central to a monist model of modernity. For limited monism calls for administrative *tutelary* autonomy. A "pure totalitarianism"–we can call it full monism–lacks this tutelary autonomy. Hence full (totalitarian) monism does not fit a modern society.

The monism that does fit modernity covers a wide range of systems. It includes the Soviet Union as it is now, a system of "imperfect" totalitarianism. But *limited* monism, the reader should note, includes other forms that the Soviet system took in the past—or might yet take—and all sorts of systems that lack most things Soviet. Thus it includes some modern or modernizing systems that are not totalitarian but authoritarian. In quite a few of the new states of Asia and Africa as well, we see authoritarian systems that have a good deal of tutelary autonomy. They too give clear primacy to public power over private. Yet they leave more room for private power than "imperfect" totalitarianism.

Just as monism can take two forms—full and limited—so can a model in which private power plays a big part. Here the distinction lies between a society that mixes social autonomy for its major groups with tutelary autonomy, and one which rests on social autonomy alone.

The distinction draws a line between authoritarian (limited) pluralism—such as Franco Spain—and the democratic (full) pluralism that many American writers associate with the West. I have argued that tutelary autonomy could meet the minimal needs of a highly complex modern society. In so far as that view is valid, only full monism fails to fit modernity at all. For the rest, the main contrast lies between social and tutelary autonomy.[7] The following figure brings that out.

MONIST AND PLURALIST MODELS OF MODERN SOCIETY

			Tutelary Autonomy*	
			+	–
Pluralist Model		+	Limited Pluralism	Full Pluralism
	Social Autonomy**			
Monist Model		–	Limited Monism	Full Monism

*Tutelary Autonomy: the state grants some autonomy in professional and personal life, in technical activities (including the economy), and in some parts of law and public affairs.

**Social Autonomy: wide autonomy from the state is enjoyed by major social groups in the society.

II. CULTURAL DUALITY

When Disraeli wrote of the "two nations" in the England of the mid-nineteenth century, he had in mind most of all an economic gulf, the gulf between rich and poor. In regard to Russia, Western observers have long been apt to draw a similar line. But the line they draw divides Russia not so much in economic terms, but in moral or cultural terms. For example, an

American political scientist juxtaposed an alien, energizing "state" to a passive, exploited "society." And a British psychiatrist pointed to an unpredictable alternation, in the widespread peasant culture among Russians proper, between submissiveness to authority and sudden, extreme outbursts of rage and violence against it.[8]

This duality has to do with a deep cultural cleavage within the main nationality of the country, the Russians. In 1917, the cleavage set apart rulers from ruled. In yet another way, the cleavage divided a highly educated, "Western" minority of the population from a majority deeply rooted in a particularistic and ascriptive peasant culture.

By itself, such a cleavage is neither unusual nor necessarily harmful to the fuller integration of a national society. From recent research in social science, we learn more and more that a host of diverse kinds of cultural ties tend to persist in the same group (and in the same individual) no matter how far modernization may have gone. Something else makes the cleavage among Russians distinctive. Despite a relatively high level of development in the country's urban centers, one of the cultures involved—the traditional or peasant culture—seems to have been a good deal more resistant to adapting to the more modern and urban culture than was the case in Western Europe, the initial area of modernization. Prior to 1917, we can see this pattern best when we look at the main transmitters of culture in the society: education, religion, family.

At the turn of the twentieth century, illiteracy was widespread in both rural and urban areas of Russia. True, a sizable network of schools had developed under government, church, and "zemstvo" (rural self-government) auspices. Some 10 percent of the total number of children between the ages of five and fifteen (most of them boys) were attending school. A little over 1 percent of the population went beyond grade school (1.4 million out of about 125 million). Of this number, the urban areas had a much larger share than the rural. While in urban areas 6 percent got an education beyond grade school, in rural areas less than half of one percent did. The same pattern sets apart a minority of the urban population from the peasantry as far as higher education goes.

By 1900, the major cities of Russia featured a network of nine universities and numerous specialized professional and vocational schools. University training was pretty much out of the question for students of lower class origin. Access to higher education was open, however, to lower middle class families (notably from the priesthood, schoolteachers, and lesser civil servants). Along with this significant upward mobility by means of university education, though, the mass of the population had little or no access to the educational system.

Inevitably, this situation gave all the more weight to the social role of religion. For most Russians, this meant the established church of the country, Russian Orthodoxy. Official figures at the time claimed that 70 percent of the population belonged to the Orthodox church. But this count included a lot of dissenting sects and also the many lapsed intellectuals and factory workers who had been born into the faith. Nonetheless, the Orthodox church both reflected and shaped the widespread peasant culture far more than did the other major religions of Russia. To the peasantry, the church preached submission to established authority and also the doctrine of collective responsibility *(sobornost')*. Throughout the Orthodox church, from top to bottom, longstanding ritual and folk custom held primacy over the intellectual and individualistic theology that played such a modernizing role in Western Europe. In all of these ways, Imperial Russia's established church and main religion did a lot to reinforce Russia's anti-modern peasant culture.

At the fringes of the established church, and in some of Russia's other religions as well, reforming and modernizing currents did make some inroads both among peasants and in the cities. Some of these dissenting groups bore a resemblance to the individualistic and puritan Western sects of early modern times. Although these currents were strikingly numerous and widespread, they remained only deviant cases in the face of the continuing hold on most believers of the Mother Church.

Nowhere in the Russia of 1917 does the cultural cleavage stand out as clearly as in family life. While the urbanized Russian family was becoming "modern," no such change marked the peasantry or the many city dwellers with closer ties to peasant ways than to the national society. Most importantly, the prevalent Russian family put local over national values, collectivism over individualism, submission to authority and attachment to established custom over striving and innovation. To be sure, a gradually spreading market economy, as well as military service and the recruitment of peasants into the industrial labor force, all made inroads into the peasant culture. But the resilience of this culture, and the uneven gains being made by the city-based national culture, combined to keep up the deep cleavage in education, in religion, and in the organization of the family.

Fifty years after the October Revolution, a cultural duality still stands out. As in 1917, the Russian culture of 1967 is divided between a more modern and urban culture and a peasant culture. In overlapping but different ways, the intelligentsia and the party are actively committed to a modern national culture. That culture itself reflects the vigor and integration brought on by the Soviet form of modernization. Yet though the peasant culture had become less insulated, and an even larger share of the people came to divide their attachment between the two cultures, the persistence of the peasant ways and values is remarkable in light of the country's giant strides toward modernity. Despite all the inroads of industrialization, education, and urban living, peasant mores continue to loom large not only in the countryside but among a significant portion of the urban population.

Such attachment does not involve conscious or active opposition to the national society. But it does mean that norms and attitudes live on which go against some of the main prerequisites of full national integration. Thus many a Soviet citizen has failed to adopt the standards of work discipline, or the acceptance of occupational and geographic mobility, which matter so much in modern living. Nor is a significant share of the people as open to the impact of formal education and mass communication, although they partake of both, as they would be if the national culture did not have to coexist with a still highly particularistic and generally premodern second culture.

Along the same lines, it should be noted that for its top party posts the Soviet system continues to seek and attract men whose fathers were workers or peasants. This fact bears directly on the far-reaching cultural duality of the USSR. If in the United States men of plebeian origin take on white collar ways on their way up,[9] a far more limited change takes place among Soviet leaders. On the level of cognitive learning, many shifts can be found as Soviet people move up from lower class origin. In Soviet schooling, one can discern three distinct mechanisms that operate to bring about these shifts. These socializing mechanisms consist of the set but many-sided fare of official doctrine, a wide reading of Russian and also Western classic literature, and expertise in some field of knowledge. On the level of norms and values, though, much of the Soviet leaders' culture still comes from the lower classes and most of all the peasantry.[10]

Within this persisting cultural duality, education is still the main means by which the state teaches the population how to act in the Soviet kind of national society. The educational system is not only vast and attendance in it more or less universal; it has become accepted and even revered as the society's major path of upward social mobility. As does the Soviet system in general, the schools combine a stress on disciplined and collectivist devotion to country and work with indoctrination and technical training. By now, the evidence suggests, this Stalin-era combination has become quite routinized and thus in part lacking in moral and intellectual appeal. Nor has all of the youth gotten the schooling and jobs they had been led to expect. By and large, though, this does not undercut the role of Soviet education as an imposing method of socializing the population and channeling youth into the openings the state has for them.[11]

The persistence of peasant culture suggests that religion has retained more of a place in Soviet life than might be expected in the light of the state's outlook and its resolute actions against both religious institutions and religious beliefs. As of now, the brunt of official opposition is against the numerous local and regional dissenting sects. These had taken advantage of the relative easing of state controls in the wake of de-Stalinization, and evidently found a good manv new adherents among the people. This is true both in the countryside and in the cities. In their outlook, these proselytizing sects range from chiliastic to quietist creeds. But some of the most successful emphasize the virtues of personal discipline, virtue, and the like which one associates with puritan and post-puritan currents in Western religion. The strength and variety of these religious manifestations would seem to reflect an incomplete attachment to the Soviet type of national society, since all of them serve as (and officially are seen as) rivals to both the established creed and the modern national culture.

The family reflects both of the cultural elements in Soviet society. Compared to the Russian family before 1917, that of 1967 is smaller in size and nuclear rather than extended in structure. As a rule it puts a good deal of emphasis on the educational and social mobility of children. And it passes on to them a good deal of the established creed. The role of women has become much more equal than it had been. Soviet families have come to know the high divorce rates, too, characteristic of modern urban life.

At the same time, both the persistence of a peasant culture, and the limits on income, living space, and material comforts, have led to a continued reliance on extended and multi-generational family ties which recall the peasant family of old. For the same reasons, the official emphasis on disciplined devotion to work and civic effort finds less complete acceptance in many Soviet families than the state would like. Nor have the formal ways of urban living, such as conformity to laws, contractual obligations, and the like.

If cultural duality marks the Russia of 1967, as well as 1917, a contrast stands out, too. The modern, more national culture is now in the ascent and on the offensive, much more so than it was before the revolution. In a noteworthy way, the peasant culture still to be found in abundance may not be as contrary to the Soviet form of modernization as to the individualistic and capitalist one in the West. For the Soviet system and the peasant culture share an emphasis on collectivism. And both presume a powerful central authority and a submissiveness to it by the bulk of the population. Whether this compatibility will hold for the near future, when further complexity and affluence may lead to more rationalization and individualism in public and economic life, remains to be seen.[12] Meanwhile, though, the persistence of a local peasant culture next to a modern national culture turns out to be not just dysfunctional for the Soviet type of modernization, but in some ways to help it as well.

Russia's process of change in the course of the past half century has been vast and at times grandiose. A new mode of social change brought forth a mix of swift industrialization and imposing social innovations with totalitarian rule and a change-oriented—and in part still revolutionary—creed. In the population, one finds a wide range of social wants and strains side by side with much acceptance of the established system. By the time of Stalin's death in 1953, the country had achieved an unheard of amount of economic strength and of worldwide power and recognition. And yet it lacked the social organization, and the political experience and self-confidence, to move with any speed away from Stalin's Iron Age.

A host of new as well as old problems thus sustain a good deal of the duality between modern and peasant culture. These problems keep up, too, much of the political monism that marked Imperial Russia and still more so the age of Stalin. The outcome points to a new model of modern society which lacks the pluralism of the first. As long as political monism and cultural duality stay intact, the case of Russia will show that the second model (unlike the first) calls for no full break with the old ways of a non-Western country.

ANNA M. BOURGUINA

The Writings of B. I. Nicolaevsky: A Selected Bibliography

Nicolaevsky's literary and journalistic career began in 1904. His first historical article focused on the Russian critic and publicist N. Shelgunov (*Samarskii kur'er,* December, 1904). During his lifetime Nicolaevsky wrote hundreds of articles on history, historical literature, and politics; it would be impossible to enumerate all of them. With a few exceptions, this is a bibliography of works written by Nicolaevsky as an emigre. Even so, the list is incomplete. Many journals and newspapers in which his articles appeared were not available to this bibliographer. Moreover, among Nicolaevsky's papers are many clippings which bear neither the name nor the date of the periodical in which they appeared; there was no way these items could be included. Finally, it should be pointed out that in addition to the articles in Russian, English, French, and German listed below, a great number of Nicolaevsky's writings were published in Dutch, Polish, Latvian, Czech, Hungarian, Yiddish (the latter especially in *The Forward,* New York), and other languages.

The entries in this bibliography are arranged by periodical in roughly chronological order, so as to reflect Nicolaevsky's foci of interest at various stages of his career. Where relevant the city of publication for journals and newspapers is included. In a few cases, because the sources were unavailable, it has been impossible to supply complete bibliographical data.

Nicolaevsky's writings did not always appear under his full name. Particularly in the pre-revolutionary period but after 1917 as well, many of his articles were published anonymously or under a pseudonym (N. Borisov and Gr. Golosov were the most common). Often he used a shortened form (B. N-skii or B. N.). Some of these pen names are indicated in the present bibliography. Particularly numerous are Nicolaevsky's signatures in the *Sotsialisticheskii vestnik,* where much of his material appeared either anonymously or designated by one or two initials (A., B., B. A., I., N., S., or X., for example). In establishing Nicolaevsky's authorship, this bibliographer was aided by information from Nicolaevsky himself as well as by use of a set of the *Sotsialisticheskii vestnik* in which many of the authors' names have been marked.

As regards Nicolaevsky's journalistic career during his years in Russia, the following is at best an approximate list of the periodicals (journals and newspapers) in which he published articles prior to his expulsion in 1922; it is based on a list jotted down shortly after his arrival in the United States in 1940:

Samarskii kur'er (Samara), *Samarskaia gazeta* (Samara), *Novaia zhizn'* (St. Petersburg), *Vpered* (illegal), *Tovarishch* (St. Petersburg), *Den'* and its literary supplement (St. Petersburg), *Volzhskoe slovo* (Samara), *Ufimskii krai, Ural'skaia zhizn'* (Ekaterinburg), *Arkhangel'sk, Izvestiia Arkhangel'skogo obshchestva izucheniia russkogo severa* (Arkhangel'sk), *Iuzhnaia zaria* (Ekaterinoslav), *Baku, Kaspii* (Baku), *Nashe slovo* (Baku), *Eniseiskii krai* (Krasnoiarsk), *Sibir'* (Irkutsk), *Golos Sibiri* (Novo-Nikolaevsk), *Sibirskaia zhizn'* (Tomsk), *Nashe delo* (Irkutsk), *Dal'nevostochnoe obozrenie* (Vladivostok), *Sibirskii rassvet* (Barnaul), *Sibirskii rabochii* (Irkutsk), *Sibirskie zapiski* (Krasnoiarsk), *Nevskii golos* (St. Petersburg), *Nash golos* (Samara), *Luch* (St. Petersburg), *Rabochaia gazeta* (St. Petersburg), *Nasha zaria* (St. Petersburg), *Russkoe bogatstvo* (St. Petersburg), *Vpered* (Moscow), *Iskra* (Petrograd), *Vsegda vpered* (Moscow).

BOOKS

Konets Azefa. Introd. by V. I. Nevskii. Leningrad: Gosizdat, 1926. 2nd ed. Berlin: Petropolis, 1931.

Istoriia odnogo predatelia (E. Azef). Terroristy i politicheskaia politsiia. Berlin: Petropolis, 1932.

Asew. Die Geschichte eines Verrats. Berlin: Verlag Der Buecherkreis, 1932.

Aseff the Spy. Russian Terrorist and Police Stool. New York: Doubleday, 1934.

Nicolaevsky, B. I., and Maenchen-Helfen, O. *Karl and Jenny Marx. Ein Lebensweg.* Berlin: Verlag Der Buecherkreis, 1933.

Nicolaevsky, B. I., and Maenchen-Helfen, O. *Karl Marx.* Paris: Gallimard, 1937. Second edition: *La Vie de Karl Marx. L'Homme et le lutteur.* Paris: Gallimard, 1970. Other editions: *Karl Marx. Man and Fighter.* London, 1936 (Penguin edition to be published in 1972); *Karl Marx. Man and Fighter.* Philadelphia, 1936; *Karl Marx. Mens en Strijder.* Leiden, 1949; *Karl Marx. Eine Biographie.* Hannover, 1963.

Letter of an Old Bolshevik. The Key to the Moscow Trials. [Signed Y. Z.] New York: Rand School Press, 1937.

Dallin, David, and Nicolaevsky, Boris. *Forced Labor in Soviet Russia.* New Haven: Yale University Press, 1947. [Appeared in several foreign editions.]

"Men'sheviki v dni oktiabr'skogo perevorota." Mimeographed. New York: Inter-University Project on the History of the Menshevik Movement, 1962.

Power and the Soviet Elite. "The Letter of an Old Bolshevik" and Other Essays. Edited by Janet D. Zagoria with an introduction by George F. Kennan. New York: Praeger, 1965. French edition: *Les Dirigeants soviétiques et la lutte pour le pouvoir.* Paris: Les Lettres nouvelles, 1969. Japanese edition: 1970.

WORKS EDITED AND ANNOTATED

Iz arkhiva P. B. Aksel'roda (1881-1896). Edited by V. S. Voitinskii, B. I. Nikolaevskii, and L. O. Tsederbaum-Dan; annotated by B. I. Nikolaevskii. Berlin: Russkii Revoliutsionnyi Arkhiv, 1924.

Pis'ma P. B. Aksel'roda i Iu. O. Martova (1901-1916). Edited by F. Dan, B. Nikolaevskii, and L. Tsederbaum-Dan; annotated by B. Nikolaevskii. Berlin: Russkii Revoliutsionnyi Arkhiv, 1924.

Perepiska G. V. Plekhanova i P. B. Aksel'roda. Edited and annotated by P. A. Berlin, V. S. Voitinskii, and B. I. Nikolaevskii. 2 vols. Moscow: Izdanie R. M. Plekhanovoi, 1925.

Sotsial-demokraticheskoe dvizhenie v Rossii. Materialy. Edited by A. N. Potresov and B. I. Nikolaevskii; annotated by B. I. Nikolaevskii. Moscow-Leningrad, 1928.

Doklady sotsial-demokraticheskikh komitetov vtoromy s"ezdu R.S.-D.R.P. Annotated by B. I. Nikolaevskii. Moscow, 1930.

The Crimes of the Stalin Era. Special Report to the 20th Congress of the Communist Party of the Soviet Union by Nikita S. Khrushchev. Annotated by Boris I. Nicolaevsky. New York: The New Leader, 1962.

INTRODUCTORY ARTICLES

"A. N. Potresov. Opyt literaturno-politicheskoi biografii," in A. N. Potresov, *Posmertnyi sbornik proizvedenii.* Paris: n.p., 1937.

"P. A. Garvi v Rossii," in P. A. Garvi, *Vospominaniia sotsial-demokrata.* New York: n.p., 1946.

"V. M. Chernov (19 noiabria 1873–15 aprelia 1952)," in V. M. Chernov, *Pered burei. Vospominaniia.* New York: Chekhov Publishing House, 1953.

"I. G. Tsereteli i ego *Vospominaniia,*" in I. G. Tsereteli, *Vospominaniia o fevral'skoi revoliutsii.* 2 vols. Paris-Hague: Mouton, 1963.

ARTICLES AND REVIEWS

Byloe (Petrograd-Moscow):

- "Novoe o proshlom." No. 7 (1918).
- "Novoe o proshlom." No. 8 (1918).
- "L. N. Tolstoi v departamente politsii." No. 9 (1918).
- "Novoe o proshlom." No. 9 (1918).
- "Kladbishche pisem. (1) A. D. Mikhailov v dni ozhidaniia kazni. (2) Poslednie pis'ma A. I. Barannikova. (3) Poslednie pis'ma M. V. Teterki." No. 10/11 (1918).
- "Kazn' N. E. Sukhanova. Arkhivnye dokumenty." No. 10/11 (1918).
- "Novoe o proshlom. Po tiur'mam i ssylkam." No. 12 (1918).
- "Programma pervogo v Rossii s.-d. kruzhka. Iz materialov po istorii s.-d. dvizheniia v Rossii." No. 13 (1918).
- "Skorbnye stranitsy shlissel'burgskoi letopisi." No. 13 (1918).
- "S. M. Ginsburg v Shlissel'burge." No. 15 (1919).
- "Novoe o proshlom (Iz proshlogo v Sibiri)." No. 15 (1919).
- " 'Pervoe prestuplenie' M. Gor'kogo (Iz ocherkov po arkhivnym materialam). S primechaniiami M. Gor'kogo." No. 16 (1921).

"S.-Peterburgskoe okhrannoe otdelenie v 1895-1901 g.g." No. 16 (1921). [Unsigned.]

"Ivan Okladskii v Tiflise." No. 25 (1924). [Signed B. Fedorov.]

"Zhertvy l-go marta 1887 g." No. 32 (1925).

Novaia russkaia kniga (monthly critical-bibliographical journal, ed. A. S. Iashchenko, Berlin):

Articles:

"Iz nedavnego proshlogo russkoi literatury. (Literatura o L. N. Tolstom)." No. 8 (1922).

"Iz nedavnego proshlogo russkoi literatury. (Gertsen i Korolenko v Viatskoi gubernii.—Vospominaniia o Nekrasove A. S. Suvorina i E. A. Riumling-Nekrasovoi.—Turgenev o Dostoevskom. M. E. Saltykov v svoei sem'e)." No. 9 (1922).

"Vozrozhdenie tolstogo zhurnala." No. 1 (1923). [Signed G. G—ov.]

"Iz nedavnego proshlogo russkoi literatury. (Vospominaniia o V. G. Korolenko v zarubezhnoi pechati.)" No. 2 (1923).

"Iz nedavnego proshlogo russkoi literatury. (Vospominaniia ob A. A. Bloke.)" No. 5/6 (1923).

Reviews:

Byloe, No. 18 (Petrograd, 1922). No. 3 (1922).

Dela i dni, Istoricheskii zhurnal, kniga vtoraia (Petrograd: Gosizdat, 1921). No. 3 (1922).

Vpered. Sbornik statei, posviashchennykh pamiati P. L. Lavrova, edited by P. Vitiazev (Petrograd: Izd. "Kolos," 1920); *Sotsial'naia revoliutsiia i zadachi nravstvennosti. Starye voprosy,* by P. L. Lavrov, annotated by P. Vitiazev (Petrograd: Izd. "Kolos," 1921). *Materialy dlia biografii P. L. Lavrova,* edited by P. Vitiazev. Vyp. 1 (Petrograd: Izd. "Kolos," 1921). No. 4 (1922).

Istoriia bol'shevizma v Rossii ot vozniknoveniia i do zakhvata vlasti (1883-1903-1917), by General A. I. Spiridovich, s prilozheniem dokumentov i portretov (Paris, 1922). No. 4 (1922).

Nachalo, Al'manakhi, Vyp. 1, 2/3. (Ivanovo-Voznesensk, 1921, 1922). No. 5 (1922).

Zapechatlennyi trud, by Vera Figner, Chast' 1 (Moscow: Izd. "Zadruga," 1921). No. 6 (1922).

Literaturnye zapiski. Nos. 1, 2, Literaturno-obshchestvennyi i kritiko-bibliograficheskii zhurnal, edited by B. I. Khariton (Petrograd: Izd. "Logos," 1922). No. 6 (1922).

Krasnaia Golgofa, Sbornik, posviashchennyi pamiati tovarishchei, pogibshikh za raboche-krest'ianskoe delo, edited by I. Zhukovskii and Z. Mokin (Blagoveshchensk: Izd. redaktsii gazety *Amurskaia pravda,* 1920). No. 6 (1922).

Zapiski devochki, by V. Naryshkina-Vitte (Leipzig: Izd. avtora, 1922). No. 6 (1922).

Tragediia severnoi oblasti (iz lichnykh vospominanii), by N. P. Zelenov (Paris, 1922). No. 6 (1922).

Golos minuvshego, Zhurnal istorii i istorii literatury (Moscow: Izd. "Zadruga," 1920-1921). No. 7 (1922).
Kniga i revoliutsiia, Ezhemesiachnyi kritiko-bibliograficheskii zhurnal (Petrograd: Gosizdat, 1922). No. 7 (1922).
Russkaia letopis', Kn. 1 (1921); Kn. 2 (1922) (Paris: Izd. "Russkii ochag"). No. 7 (1922).
Iakov Mikhailovich Sverdlov, Ego zhizn' i deiatel'nost' (1885-1919), by B. Ivanov (Petrograd: Gosizdat, 1921). No. 7 (1922).
Grafika satiricheskikh zhurnalov 1905-1906 g.g., by P. Dul'skii (Kazan': Tatgosizdat, 1922). No. 8 (1922).
Zapiski sotsial-demokrata, Kn. 1: *Nakanune,* by Iu. Martov (Berlin: Izd. Grzhebina, 1922). No. 9 (1922).
Zapiski sotsialista-revoliutsionera, by V. Chernov, Kn. 1 (Berlin: Izd. Grzhebina, 1922). No. 9 (1922).
Nechto fantasticheskoe, by V. Shul'gin (Sofia: Izd. "Ros.-Bolg. Izd.," 1922). No. 10 (1922).
Zadruga, Desiat' let: 1911-1921 g.g., Otchet Chrezvychainogo Obshchego Sobraniia chlenov t-va "Zadruga" i obshchestvennykh organizatsii v den' desiateletnego iubileia 25 dek. 1921 g. (Petrograd, 1922). No. 10 (1922).
Pis'ma k Lunacharskomu, by Vladimir Korolenko (Paris: Izd. "Zadruga," Zagranichnyi otdel, 1922). No. 11/12 (1922).
Po tiur'mam i etapam, by I. Genkin (Petrograd: Gosizdat, 1922). No. 11/12 (1922).
Za tri goda (vospominaniia, vpechatleniia i vstrechi), by L. A. Krol' (Vladivostok: T-vo izd. "Svobodnaia Rossiia," 1922). No. 2 (1923).
Pogromy na Ukraine (Period dobrovol'cheskoi armii), by N. I. Shtif (Berlin: Izd. "Vostok," 1922). No. 2 (1923).

Letopis' revoliutsii (Berlin):

"'Pis'mo Plekhanova' v redaktsiiu *Rabochei gazety*." Kn. 1 (1923).
"Istoricheskie zhurnaly v Sovetskoi Rossii." Kn. 1 (1923).
Review of *Chto chitat' po istorii ruskogo revoliutsionnogo dvizheniia,* by A. A. Shilov (Petrograd, 1922). Kn. 1 (1923).

Katorga i ssylka (Moscow):

Articles:

"Butyrki v dni dekabr'skogo vosstaniia 1905 g." No. 3 (1922).
"K biografii odnogo iz osnovatelei 'Severo-russkogo rabochego soiuza'. I. A. Bachin i ego drama." No. 13 (1924). [Signed G. Golosov.]
"Pamiati poslednego iakobintsa-semidesiatnika." [Gaspar-Mikhail Turskii.] No. 23 (1926).
"Iz dokumentov po delu K. G. Neustroeva." No. 24 (1926).
"Pis'ma P. A. Kropotkina k V. N. Cherkezovu." No. 25 (1926).
"Varlaam Nikolaevich Cherkezov (1846-1925)." No. 25 (1926).
"Novoe o proshlom v zarubezhnoi russkoi pechati." [Obzor literatury o Bakunine. K istorii partii "Narodnaia volia."] No. 26 (1926).
"Neizdannoe pis'mo A. I. Gertsena." [K. Adol'fu Kolacheku.] No. 27 (1926).

"K istorii 2-go s"ezda RSDRP." No. 28/29 (1926).
"Eshche o Bachine i Iuzhakovoi." No. 28/29 (1926).
"Novoe o proshlom v zarubezhnoi russkoi literature." [Obzor literatury o dekabristakh.] No. 28/29 (1926).
"Novoe o proshlom v zarubezhnoi pechati. K istorii 1917 g.: martovskie dni." No. 30 (1927).
"Poslednii nomer *Izvestii Peterburgskogo Soveta rabochikh deputatov* 1905 g." No. 31 (1927).
"Novoe o proshlom v zarubezhnoi pechati." [K istorii revoliutsionnogo narodnichestva.] No. 31 (1927).
"RSDRP o soglasheniiakh s oppozitsionnymi i revoliutsionnymi partiiami v 1904 g." [Vopros o mezhpartiinoi konferentsii v sovete partii.] No. 32 (1927).
"Tsentral'nyi komitet bol'shevikov o zadachakh partii v oktiabre 1905 g." No. 33 (1927).
"Eshche o No. 11 *Izvestii Peterburgskogo Soveta rabochikh deputatov* 1905 g." No. 33 (1927).
"Iz epokhi *Iskry* i *Zari* (Po neizdannym materialam)." Nos. 35, 36 (1927).
"Novoe o proshlom v zarubezhnoi russkoi pechati (Iz vospominanii o revoliutsii 1905 g.)." No. 35 (1927).
"N. A. Ishutin na katorge." No. 38 (1927).
"O vospominaniiakh L'va Tikhomirova." No. 38 (1927).
"K istorii l-go s"ezda RSDRP." No. 40 (1927).
"K biografii G. V. Plekhanova." No. 42 (1928).
"Novoe o proshlom v russkoi zarubezhnoi literature." [O Gertsene, Ogareve, Bakunine i Chernyshevskom.] No. 51 (1928).
"K istorii 'Partii russkikh sotsial-demokratov' v 1884-86 g.g. (Po neizdannym dokumentam)." No. 54 (1929).
"Iz literaturnogo nasledstva V. I. Zasulich." No. 55 (1929).
"Gde byl napechatan No. 1 zhurnala *Zerno* [1880 g.]?" No. 65 (1930).
"Bakunin epokhi ego pervoi emigratsii v vospominaniiakh nemtsev-sovremennikov." No. 69/70 (1930).
"N. L. Sergievskii kak istorik 'Partii russkikh sotsial-demokratov' (1884-1887 g.g.)." No. 74 (1931). [Signed B. Ivanov.]

Reviews:

Russkie v Amerike, by M. Vil'chur (New York: Izdanie "Pervogo russkogo izdatel'stva v Amerike," n.d.). No. 12 (1924).
Iz moei zhizni za 40 let, by Ia. L. Teitel' (Paris, 1925). No. 19 (1925).
Rabota tainoi politsii, by P. P. Zavarzin (Paris, 1924). No. 19 (1925).
"Pri tsarskom rezhime," by A. I. Spiridovich, in *Arkhiv russkoi revoliutsii,* Vol. 15 (Berlin, 1924). No. 19 (1925).
Ein Blatt der Erinnerung von Konrad Haenisch, by "Parvus" (Berlin, 1925). No. 20 (1925).
Sviatye i greshnye. Vospominaniia byvshego cheloveka, by A. V. Bolotov (Paris, 1924); *Gospodin Velikii Novgorod, Vospominaniia* (Paris, 1925). No. 20 (1925).
Rossiia i Don, by S. G. Svatikov. No. 22 (1926).

Der Vorfruehling der Anarchie, by M. Nettlau. No. 22 (1926).
Arkhiv russkoi revoliutsii, edited by I. V. Gessen. Vol. 16, No. 23 (1926).
Sobranie sochinenii, by M. A. Bakunin. No. 26 (1926).
Golos minuvshego na chuzhoi storone, zhurnal istorii i istorii literatury. Edited by S. P. Miakotin and T. I. Polner. Nos. 1, 2 (1926); No. 26 (1926).
Leitenant Shmidt ("Krasnyi admiral"), Vospominaniia syna, by E. Shmidt-Ochakovskii (Prague, 1926). No. 27 (1926).
Giuseppe Mazzini e l'emigrazione polassa, by Adam Lewak (Casale, 1925). No. 27 (1926).
A travers la République, Mémoires, by Louis Andrieux (Paris, 1926). No. 33 (1927).
Gruppa "Osvobozhdenie truda." Iz arkhivov G. V. Plekhanova, V. I. Zasulich i L. G. Deicha, Sborniki Nos. 4, 5 (Moscow: Gosizdat, 1926). No. 34 (1927).
Geschichte der oesterreichischen Sozialdemokratie, by Ludwig Bruegel (Vienna, 1922-1925). No. 36 (1927).
Iz perezhitogo (1887-1921), by O. A. Ermanskii (Moscow-Leningrad, 1927). No. 37 (1927).
Rabochii, by N. L. Sergievskii. No. 45 (1928).
Moi vospominaniia, by D. Blagoev. No. 45 (1928).
Arkhiv russkoi revoliutsii. No. 47 (1928).
Sbornik *Revoliutsiia 1905 g. i samoderzhavie.* No. 49 (1928).
Golos minuvshego na chuzhoi storone, No. 6. No. 49 (1928).
Gruppa "Osvobozhdenie truda," No. 6. No. 50 (1928).
Portrety, by Petr Ryss. No. 50 (1928).
Zapiski narodovol'tsa, by A. N. Bakh (Leningrad, 1929). No. 54 (1929).
Osteuropaeische Bibliographie fuer das Jahr 1923 (Bresiau: Osteuropa-Institut, 1928). No. 54 (1929).
Russkii istoricheskii arkhiv, Sbornik 1, and A. A. Kizevetter, *Na rubezhe dvukh stoletii.* No. 60 (1929).
Moi zhiznennyi put', by A. Posse. No. 63 (1930).
Sbornik *Nikolai Vasil'evich Chaikovskii,* and S. P. Mel'gunov, *N. V. Chaikovskii v gody grazhdanskoi voiny.* No. 65 (1930).
Sborniki *Vol'naia Sibir'* and *Sibirskii arkhiv.* No. 65 (1930).
Bibliografia pamietnikow polskich; polski dotyczacych, by Edward Maliszewski (Warsaw, 1928). No. 67 (1930).
Katalog Rekopisow Biblioteki Narodowei, I. Zbory Biblioteki Papperswilskiej, 1 (Warsaw, 1929). No. 67 (1930).

Na chuzhoi storone (Prague):
"Ustav Ispolnitel'nogo Komiteta 'Narodnoi Voli'." Vyp. 7 (1924).
"General Novitskii o samom sebe." Vyp. 8 (1924).
"Zarubezhnaia kniga." [Review of *Trudy Komiteta russkoi knigi,* vyp. 1 (Prague, 1924).] Vyp. 8 (1924).
"(1) Tkachev i Lavrov. (2) S. M. Kravchinskii i P. L. Lavrov." Vyp. 10 (1925).

"Konflikt v redaktsii *Vestnika Narodnoi Voli* (Pis'mo P. L. Lavrova L. A. Tikhomirovu)." Vyp. 12 (1925).

Golos minuvshego-Na chuzhoi storone (Paris):

"Pokushenie na imperatora Aleksandra III. (K istorii dela 1 marta 1887 g.): (1) Vospominaniia O. M. Govorukhina; (2) Zapiska I. D. Lukashevicha." No. 3 (16) (1926).

Letopisi marksizma (Moscow):

"V. I. Ul'ianov-Lenin v Berline v 1895 g." No. 1 (1926).

"K istorii peterburgskoi sotsial-demokraticheskoi gruppy 'starikov'." No. 3 (1927).

"Neizdannoe stikhotvorenie I. S. Turgeneva." [Posviashchennoe K. A. Farngagenu fon-Enze 1847 g.] No. 4 (1927).

"M. M. Kovalevskii o knige Bel'tova." No. 5 (1928).

"O pis'makh V. I. Zasulich k G. V. Plekhanovu. Sborniki *Gruppa 'Osvobozhdenie truda'*, t.t. 4 i 5." No. 5 (1928).

"Pis'mo N. I. Sazonova k Gervegu." No. 6 (1928).

"Pis'mo Zhorzh-Zand k M. A. Bakuninu." [K istorii stolknoveniia M. A. Bakunina s redaktsiei *Novoi reinskoi gazety.*] No. 7/8 (1928).

"Vzgliady M. A. Bakunina na polozhenie del v Rossii v 1849 g." [Zabytaia broshiura Bakunina.] No. 9/10 (1929).

"Anonimnaia broshiura M. A. Bakunina 'Polozhenie v Rossii'." No. 9/10 (1929). [Introduction and annotation by B. Nikolaevskii.]

"Pis'ma P. L. Lavrova k Germanu Iungu." No. 12 (1930).

Arkhiv K. Marksa i F. Engel'sa (Moscow):

"Russkie knigi v bibliotekakh K. Marksa i F. Engel'sa (Materialy dlia izucheniia ikh otnosheniia k Rossii)." Kn. 4 (1929).

Die Gesellschaft (Internationale Revue fuer Sozialismus und Politik, Berlin):

Articles:

"Marx und das Russische problem." July, 1924.

"Karl Kautsky in Russland." 1924. Ein Sonderheft der *Gesellschaft* zu Karl Kautskys 70. Geburtstag.

"Aus der Geschichte der ersten Internationale." No. 11 (1925).

"Aus dem nachgelassenen Briefwechsel von Marx und Engels. Marx und Engels ueber das Gothaer Programm." No. 8 (1927).

"Karl Marx ueber proletarische Revolution. Ein Brief von Marx an F. Domela-Nieuwenhuis." No. 7 (1931).

"Jenny von Westphalen-Marx. Zu ihrem 50. Todestage." No. 12 (1931).

"Karl Marx und die Berliner Sektion der 1. Internationale." No. 3 (1933).

Reviews:

Ausgewaehlte Werke. Der Kampf und die soziale Revolution, by Wladimir Iljitsch Lenin (Berlin: Verlag fuer Literatur und Politik, 1925). No. 10 (1925).

Anarchisten und Sozial-Revolutionaere. Die historische Entwicklung des Anarchismus in den Jahren 1880 bis 1886, by Max Nettlau (Berlin: Asy-Verlag, 1931). No. 5 (1932).

Geschichte der sozialistischen Ideen in der Schweiz, by Robert Grimm (Zurich: Verlag Dr. Oprecht u. Helbing A.-G., 1931). No. 10 (1932).

International Review for Social History (The International Institute for Social History, Leiden):

M. A. Bakunin in der Dresdner Zeitung (Eine Episode aus der Geschichte des politischen Kampfes in Deutschland in den Jahren 1848-49." 1 (1936).

Review of *Geschichte der deutschen Handwerkervereine in der Schweiz 1836-1843. Die Wirksamkeit Weitlings (1841-1843),* by Otto Brugger (Bern and Leipzig, 1932); Julius Fröbel. *Seine politische Entwicklung bis 1849. Ein Beitrag zur Geschichte des Vormärz,* by Ernst Feuz (Bern and Leipzig, 1932); *Karl Heinzen (1809-1880). Seine politische Entwicklung und publizistische Wirksamkeit,* by Hans Huber (Bern and Leipzig, 1932); *Die politischen Verlangsanstalten und Druckereien in der Schweiz 1840-1848. Ihre Bedeutung für die Vorgeschichte der deutschen Revolution von 1848,* by Hans Gustav Keller (Bern and Leipzig, 1935). 1 (1936).

"Deux billets inédits de Marx et d'Engels." [A. V. Smirnov.] 3 (1938).

"Toward a History of 'The Communist League' 1847-1852." 1 (1956).

Bulletin of the International Institute for Social History (Leiden):

"Historique de la presse périodique de l'émigration socialiste russe, 1917-1937." No. 1 (1938).

"V. M. Chernov (1873-1952)." No. 3 (1952).

Russkie zapiski (monthly journal, ed. P. N. Miliukov, Paris):

Review of *Adolf Hitler, ses aspirations, sa politique, sa propagande et les "Protocoles des Sages de Sion,"* by Ruben Blanc with a preface by Paul Milioukoff (Paris, 1938). Kn. 12 (1938).

Review of *Arkhiv Mikhaila Dragomanova,* 1: *Listuvannia kiivs'koi Staroi Gromadi z M. Dragomanovim (1870-1895 r.r.)* (Izdanie Ukrainskogo Nauchnogo Instituta v Varshave, 1938). Kn. 15 (1939).

Sovremennye zapiski (Paris):

Review of *Vremennik Obshchestva druzei russkoi knigi,* Vyp. 4 (Paris, 1938), Kn. 67 (1938).

"Iz perepiski deiatelei pushkinskoi epokhi (Neizdannye materialy iz arkhiva F. V. Bulgarina)." Kn. 68 (1939).

"Tsvetnye knigi." Kn. 70 (1940).

Miscellaneous (1917-1941):

"Delo Malinovskogo." *Rabochaia gazeta* (Petrograd), Nos. 63, 67, 83, 85, 87 (1917). [Unsigned.]

"Iz proshlogo nashei partii." [O pervykh s.-d. gazetakh.] *Iskra* (Petrograd), No. 6 (1917).

"Delo *Russkogo bogatstva* (Iz materialov arkhiva byvshego Departamenta politsii)." *Russkoe bogatstvo* (Petrograd), Nos. 1, 2, 3 (1918).

"Pervyi Irkutskii provokator-dobrovolets (Iz ocherkov po neizdannym materialam)." *Sibirskii rabochii* (Irkutsk), Nos. 8, 9 (1919).

"Chernyshevskii v Viliuiske." *Sibir'* (Irkutsk, 1919).
"Pervye dekabristy v Irkutske (Iz ocherkov po neizdannym materialam)." *Sibirskie zapiski,* No. 3 (1919). [Part of this sketch appeared in the Irkutsk newspaper *Novaia Sibir'* before it was closed.]
"Otkliki 14 dekabria 1825 g. v Sibiri." *Sibirskii rassvet* (1919).
"Perevod dekabristov iz Chity v Petrovskii zavod." *Dal'nevostochnaia okraina* (Vladivostok, 1919).
"Iz zapisnoi knizhki arkhivista (po arkhivnym dokumentam): (1) K istorii obrashcheniia Vandervel'da k russkim sotsialistam [1914]; (2) Avtor znamenitogo russkogo prem'era [Pis'mo E. Mednikova]; (3) Nachalo odnoi kar'ery [E. Azef v 1893 g.]; (4) Pis'mo B. N. Kokovtseva k Nikolaiu II [Sent. 1911 g.]." In *Sbornik materialov i statei,* under the editorship of the journal *Istoricheskii arkhiv.* Vyp. 1. Moscow: Glavnoe upravlenie arkhivnym delom, Gosizdat, 1921. [Signed B. N.]
"Die historische Literatur in Russland waehrend der Revolution." *Archiv fuer die Geschichte des Sozialismus und der Arbeiterbewegung,* edited by Gruenberg. 12 (1926).
"Iz narodovol'cheskikh vospominanii S. A. Ivanova (Pis'ma S. A. Ivanova k P. V. Karpovichu)." In *Narodovol'tsy 80-kh i 90-kh g.g.,* Trudy kruzhka narodovol'tsev pri Vsesoiuznom obshchestve politkatorzhan i ssyl'no-poselentsev. Vyp. 2 (Moscow, 1929).
"August Becker, Dem Gedaechtnis eines Pioniers des deutschen Sozialismus." *Der Abend* (Berlin), March 25, 1931. [Also in *Volkstimme* (Mannheim), May 3, 1931; *Hess. Volksfreund* (Darmstadt), March 26, 1931.]
"August Willich, Ein Soldat der Revolution von 1848." *Der Abend,* May 4, 6, 1931.
"Agentenbericht ueber Friedrich Engels. Auffindung eines wichtigen Dokuments." *Der Abend,* May 10, 1931.
"Pioniere der Internationale. Zum Kongress der Sozialistischen Arbeiter-Internationale in Wien." *Der Abend,* July 25, 1931.
"Die erste sozialistische Zeitschrift in Sachsen." *Volkstimme* (Mannheim), November 14, 1931.
"Karl Marx persoenlich. Erinnerungen eines Zeitgenossen." *Vorwaerts* (Berlin), January 14, 1932.
"Max Stirners Trauung. Nach unveroeffentlichten Dokumenten." *Vossische Zeitung,* September 11, 1932.
"Prag in den Tagen des Slavenkongresses 1848 (Ein vergessener Artikel von A. Meissner)." *Germanoslavica* (Prague, 1932).
Review of *Bakuninstudien,* by J. Pfitzner (Prague, 1932) in *Zeitschrift fuer slavische Philologie* (Leipzig), No. 3/4 (1934).
"Der neuzeitliche Antisemitismus und die 'Protokolle der Weisen von Zion'." *Zeitschrift fuer Sozialismus* (Zurich), No. 22/23 (1935).
"Contributions à l'histoire de la naissance du Parti socialiste en France. Une lettre de Jules Guesde à Karl Marx." *Le Combat marxiste,* No. 19 (1935).
"Moses Hess's Letters to Berthold Auerbach, 1839-1843." *Historische Shriften fun Yivo* (Wilno, 1937). [Introduction in Yiddish, Hess's letters in German.]

The New Leader (New York):
"Comintern Apparatus Now Part of Berlin's 'Fifth Column' Ministry." April 27, 1940.
"French Pacifist Bloc Joined in 'Peace Front' Run by Secret Nazi Agent." January 11, 1941.
"French Pacifists Capitulate to Hitler." February 22, 1941.
"De Man Utilizes Old Socialist Slogans to Win Belgian People for Hitler." March 29, 1941.
"Underground against Vichy." May 17, 1941.
"Russian Foreign Policy, 1917-1941." July 19, 1941.
"The Roots of Russian Foreign Policy." July 26, 1941.
"Dormoy's Assassination." August 2, 1941.
"Soviet Policy 1934-1939." August 23, 1941.
"The Price that Stalin Paid." August 30, 1941.
"Japan Waits." September 13, 1941.
"Petain Resorts to Extra-Legal Powers to Try Blum, Reynaud." November 15, 1941.
"Petain's Failure at Riom." November 22, 1941.
"The Axis Starts a New Front–Why?" December 20, 1941.
"The Protocols of Zion." September 12, 1942.
"The Decline and Fall of Minister Togo." September 26, 1942.
"French Underground Press." November 14, 1942.
"Ten Years of Hitler." February 6, 1943.
"The Future of China and Japan." March 27, 1943.
"Putsch or Purge?" July 29, 1944.
"Japs Prepare for Negotiated Peace." August 12, 1944.
"Will Gaullism Go Democratic?" September 23, 1944.
"De Gaulle and the Communists in France." November 11, 1944.
"The Conflict in France: Communists vs. De Gaulle." December 2, 1944.
"The Socialist Congress in Paris." January 13, 1945.
"Freedom of the Press According to Stalin." February 24, 1945.
"Stalin's Plan for Asia." March 10, 1945.
"Russian Church and Power Politics." April 7, 1945.
"Russian Policy in the Far East." April 21, 1945.
"*Pravda* against Ehrenburg." May 12, 1945.
"Manuilski on American Imperialism." May 19, 1945.
"Free Japanese Committee." June 23, 1945.
" 'Dalstroi'–A Slave Labor Camp in the Far East." December 22, 1945.
"American and Soviet Policy in Japan." January 5, 1946.
"National Minorities in Soviet Russia. Why Have Five 'Autonomous' Soviet Republics Been Abolished?" February 16, 1946.
"New Developments in Postwar Soviet Russia." February 23, 1946.
"Stalin's New Government." May 18, 1946.
"The Fate of Zhukov." September 28, 1946.
"Soviet Science and the Purges." December 14, 1946.
"As Moscow Views the American Press." January 4, 1947.
"The NKVD and the Russian Army." February 22, 1947.
"Palace Revolution in the Kremlin." March 19, 1949.
"Moscow Awaits Changes." April 23, 1949.

"Fate of I. S. Babel." November 19, 1949.
"The Coming Soviet Purge." February 18, 1950.
"Stalin's New War on the Peasants." January 1, 1951.
"The Split in Soviet Farm Policy." May 21, 1951.
"Soviet Communists Meet–to Dissolve." October 6, 1952.
"Malenkov: His Rise and His Policy." March 23, 1953.
"How Malenkov Triumphed." March 30, 1953.
"How Did Stalin Die?" April 20, 1953.
"Russia Purges the Purgers." December 28, 1953.
"For What Did Beria Die?" January 4, 1954.
"The Return to Stalinism." April 19, 1954.
"The New Soviet Spy Directors." June 21, 1954.
"The Strange Death of Mikhail Ryumin." October 4, 1954.
"The Abakumov Case." January 10, 1955.
"The Role of the Soviet Army." February 21, 1955.
"Soviet Tightens Grip on East Germany." December 5, 1955.
"Atomic Weapons and Soviet Diplomacy." December 26, 1955.
"The Trial in Tiflis." January 16, 1956.
"Soviet Communists Meet. Behind the 20th Party Congress." February 6, 1956.
"Soviet Party Congress." March 12, 1956.
"The 20th Congress and Soviet Foreign Policy." March 19, 1956.
"A Major Triumph for Zhukov." April 2, 1956.
"Is Bulganin Finished?" April 23, 1956.
"Behind the Great Purge." June 25, 1956.
"The Crimes of the Stalin Era. Report to the 20th Congress by Nikita S. Khrushchev (annotated by B. I. Nicolaevsky)." July 16, 1956.
"Poland and Hungary. Two Different Revolutions." November 12, 1956.
"Four Years of Struggle. Inside the Kremlin." November 26, 1956.
"Malenkov Comes Back." February 11, 1957.
"The Party Men and the Managers." July 29, 1957.
"The Rise and Fall of Lavrenti Beria." August 5, 1957.
"Malenkov's Heyday and Deposition." August 12, 1957.
"Molotov Loses to Tito." August 19, 1957.
"The Surprise of the 20th Congress." August 26, 1957.
"The Meaning of Khrushchev's Victory." September 2, 1957.
"Kremlin Battle (Letter to the Editor)." October 7, 1957.
"The Fall of Zhukov." November 11, 1957.
"Communism's Terror Machine." [Review of *The Soviet Secret Police*, ed. Simon Wolin and Robert M. Slusser (New York: Praeger, 1957).] February 17, 1958.
"Russia Five Years After Stalin. The Communist Party." March 31, 1958.
"Soviet Police (Letter to the Editor)." April 7, 1958.
"New Fight in the Kremlin (Khrushchev vs. the Ideologists)." June 23, 1958.
"The Soviet Scandals." [Prof. G. F. Alexandrov and M. A. Leonov.] October 13, 1958.
"Khrushchev's Victory." February 16, 1959.

"Khrushchev's Foreign Policy." May 4, 1959.
"Khrushchev Visits Peking." October 26, 1959.
"Maneuvers in the Kremlin." [The Summit Meeting in Paris.] May 30, 1960.
"In Memoriam: W. S. Woytinsky." June 20, 1960.
"Agriculture and Khrushchev's Power Struggle." August 29, 1960.
"Khrushchev at the UN." September 26, 1960.
"Is Khrushchev Slipping?" November 21, 1960.
"Mao Checks Khrushchev." January 16, 1961.
"'Khrushchevizing' the Party." May 29, 1961.
"Purging the Party Apparatus." January 22, 1962.

Novyi zhurnal (New York):
"Vneshniaia politika Moskvy (Stat'ia pervaia)." Kn. 1 (1942).
"Smeshchenie fel'dmarshala von-Braukhicha." Kn. 2 (1942).
"Vneshniaia politika Moskvy (Stat'ia vtoraia)." Kn. 3 (1942).
"Vneshniaia politika Moskvy (Stat'ia tret'ia)." Kn. 4 (1943).
"Sovetsko-iaponskoe soglashenie 1925 goda (Iz ocherkov po istorii vneshnei politiki Moskvy)." Kn. 5 (1943).
"Revoliutsiia v Kitae, Iaponiia i Stalin (Iz ocherkov po istorii vneshnei politiki Moskvy)." Kn. 6 (1943), and Kn. 8 (1944).
"'Za vashu i nashu vol'nost'!' (Stranitsy iz istorii russko-pol'skikh otnoshenii)." Kn. 7 (1944).
"Pamiati S. O. Portugeisa (St. Ivanovich)." Kn. 8 (1944).
"P. A. Garvi-Bronshtein (1881-1944)." Kn. 8 (1944).
"P. B. Struve (1870-1944)." Kn. 10 (1945).
"Gertsenovedenie v Sovetskoi Rossii." [Review of *Literaturnoe nasledstvo,* vols. 39/40 and 41/42; *A. I. Gertsen* (Moscow: Izd. Akademii nauk SSSR, 1941, 2 vols.).] Kn. 10 (1945).
"Kak Iaponiia prishla k voine." Kn. 11 (1945), and Kn. 12 (1946).
"Vospominaniia V. N. Ipat'eva." [Review of *Zhizn' odnogo khimika,* by V. N. Ipat'ev.] Kn. 13 (1946).
"Sovetskaia katorga na Kolyme." Kn. 15 (1947).
"Porazhenchestvo 1941-1945 godov i gen. A. A. Vlasov (Materialy dlia istorii)." Kn. 18, 19 (1948).
"Otvet G. Ia. Aronsonu. Pis'mo v redaktsiiu." Kn. 21 (1949). [See Aronson's letter, "Po povodu statei B. I. Nikolaevskogo o vlasovskom dvizhenii," in the same issue.]
"Novyi pokhod protiv derevni v SSSR." Kn. 24 (1950).
"Porazhenie Khrushcheva." Kn. 25 (1951).

Griadushchaia Rossiia, Biulleten' Ligi bor'by za narodnuiu svobodu (Supplement to the newspaper *Novoe russkoe slovo,* New York):
"Dvortsovaia revoliutsiia v Kremle." [Otstavka Molotova i Mikoiana.] No. 1, March 13, 1949.
"O nepredreshenchestve." No. 4, April 24, 1949.
"Liga i sotsialisty." No. 7, June 5, 1949.
"Na putiakh k politicheskomu samoopredeleniiu." [K voprosu ob ob"edinenii poslevoennoi emigratsii.] No. 12, October 23, 1949.
"'Osnovnye polozheniia' Ligi i ikh kritiki." No. 13, November 6, 1949.

"Pervaia politicheskaia aktsiia n'iu-iorkskikh monarkhistov." No. 14, November 20, 1949.
"Problema novykh sovetskikh bezhentsev." No. 21, March 5, 1950, and No. 23, April 2, 1950.
"'Vnutrenniaia liniia' i kap. K. A. Foss." No. 24, April 16, 1950.
"Rech' B. I. Nikolaevskogo na kongresse 'V zashchitu Svobody i Kul'tury' v Berline." No. 30, July 9, 1950.
"Tragediia bezhentsev–antibol'shevikov." No. 32, December 3, 1950.
"Na putiakh ob"edineniia demokratii." No. 37, December 24, 1950.

Narodnaia pravda (Organ ob"edineniia demokratov, Izdanie rossiiskogo narodnogo dvizheniia, Paris):
"Stalin pishet svoe zaveshchanie." No. 1 (1948).
"Razoblacheniia A. Rekhberga." No. 5 (1949).
"Uroki 'Tresta'." No. 7/8 (1950).
"Provokatorskaia rabota 'Vnutrennei linii'." No. 11/12 (1950).

Na rubezhe (Paris):
"Nashi zadachi." No. 1 (1951).
"Taina dela Tukhachevskogo." No. 1 (1951).
"Pamiati ushedshikh: A. Kagan, G. P. Fedorov." No. 1 (1951).
"Natsional'nyi vopros i demokratiia." No. 2 (1952).
"Smysl 'ezhevshchiny' v armii." No. 2 (1952).
"V. M. Chernov kak ideolog." No. 3/4 (1952).
"Nachalo kar'ery Malenkova." No. 5 (1952).
"Problemy nashei radio-propagandy." No. 5 (1952).

Novoe russkoe slovo (New York) [Partial list]:
"O platforme Koordinatsionnogo Tsentra." November 23, 1952.
"K sporam vokrug 19 s"ezda KPSS." December 7, 1952.
"Eshche o platforme Koordinatsionnogo Tsentra." December 21, 1952.
"Na putiakh k russko-ukrainskomu soglasheniiu." January 4, 1953.
"Chego zhdat' ot Malenkova." March 29-31 and April 1-4, 1953.
"Dvortsovyi perevorot v Kremle." April 17-19, 1953.
"Chto bylo v Miunkhene." [Problema politicheskogo ob"edineniia emigratsii.] September 20-25, 1953.
"Otvet g. A. Kerenskomu. Pis'mo v redaktsiiu." October 25, 1953.
"V chem znachenie dela Beriia?" December 27, 1953, and January 3, 1954.
"O roli politsii v sovetskom gosudarstve." February 20, 1954.
"Spory vokrug dela Beriia." February 28, 1954.
"O terrore v nachale voiny." March 30, 1954.
"Novyi etap v bor'be. Rasstrel Abakumova i dr." January 2, 1955.
"K istorii dela Beriia." January 30, 1955.
"Otstavka Malenkova." February 13, 1955.
"A. Kerenskii o dele Beriia." March 13, 1955.
"Rasprava s 'agentami' Beriia v Gruzii." January 8-9, 1956.
"Itogi XX s"ezda KPSS." March 11, 18, 1956.
"Likvidatsiia 'stalinskogo naslediia'." March 25, 1956.
"Vneshniaia politika diktatury i zadachi emigratsii." April 21, 1956.

"Pervye itogi s"ezda KPSS." February 13, 1959.
"Pamiati I. G. Tsereteli." May 24, 1959.
"Chetvert' veka nazad." [Istoriia 'Pis'ma starogo bol'shevika' — soobshchenie o svoem avtorstve 'Pis'ma'.] December 6, 1959.

Sotsialisticheskii vestnik (Berlin, Paris, New York):
"L. Martov-Iu. O. Tsederbaum (Biograficheskie daty)." Special edition, 1923.
"Istoricheskaia spravka (Pervyi s"ezd RSDRP)." No. 5/6 (1923). [Unsigned.]
"Na s"ezde RKP (Pis'mo iz Moskvy). No. 15 (1923). [Unsigned.]
"Iu. O. Martov (Pervyi opyt biograficheskogo kalendaria)." No. 7/8 (1924). [Unsigned.]
"Pamiati rabochego kommunista." [Iu. Kh. Lutovinov.] No. 11 (1924). [Signed I.]
"S"ezd RKP i zaveshchanie Lenina." No. 15 (1924). [Signed I.]
"Chto bylo v Gruzii." No. 19 (1924). [Signed Andreev.]
"Gospodin Krasikov o Solovkakh." No. 21 (1924). [Signed B. Andreev.]
"Novoe ob Azefe." No. 5 (1925). [Signed B. N.]
"P. B. Aksel'rod (Osnovnye cherty politicheskoi biografii)." No. 15/16 (1925).
"Pered s"ezdom RKP." No. 23/24 (1925). [Signed I.]
"Monarkhisty, ikh terror i bol'shevistskaia provokatsiia." No. 20 (1927). [Signed Andreev.]
"Zhiznennyi put' P. B. Aksel'roda." No. 8/9 (1928).
"Daty k politicheskoi biografii F. I. Dana." No. 20 (1931). [Unsigned.]
"Nakanune reshaiushchikh sobytii na Dal'nem Vostoke." No. 16 (1932).
"K iubileiu M. Gor'kogo." No. 17/18 (1932). [Signed X.]
"Bor'ba za GPU (Pis'mo iz Moskvy)." No. 14/15 (1933). [Signed Iv.]
"Diktator Sovetskogo Soiuza (Pis'mo iz Moskvy)." No. 19 (1933). [Signed Iv.]
"Blizhaishee okruzhenie diktatora (Pis'mo iz Moskvy)." No. 23 (1933). [Signed Iv.]
"Sovremennyi antisemitizm i 'Protokoly Sionskikh mudretsov'." No. 12 (1935).
"Kak podgotovlialsia moskovskii protsess (Iz pis'ma starogo bol'shevika)." No. 23/24 (1936) and No. 1/2 (1937). [Signed Y. Z.]
"O lozunge 'bor'ba za legal'nost' ' i o lozungakh voobshche." No. 9/10 (1938).
"Stalin i Gitler v poslednie dni avgusta 1939 g." No. 23/24 (1939).
"Sovremennaia voina i zadachi demokraticheskogo sotsializma." No. 1/2 (1940).
"Rol' Stalina v sovremennoi voine." No. 4/5 (1940).
"Frantsuzskaia sotsialisticheskaia partiia v period obshchego obvala." No. 13 (1940) and No. 1/2 (1941).
"Iz zhizni rabochikh organizatsii v stranakh okkupatsii (Bel'giia, Gollandiia, Frantsiia)." No. 3 (1941).
"Konets Krivitskogo." No. 4 (1941).

"O klassovoi strukture totalitarnykh gosudarstv." Nos. 6, 7, 8, 9, 10 (1941).
"Na novom etape." [Stalin-Gitler.] No. 13 (1941).
"Po Rossii. V dni voiny." No. 14 (1941).
"Marks Dormua." No. 14 (1941).
"Na poroge Tikhookeanskogo perioda voiny." No. 15 (1941).
"O roli kommunistov i o pugale 'antibol'shevizma'." No. 20/21 (1941).
"Na ser'eznye temy po ne-ser'eznomu povodu." [O tseliakh voiny—polemika s F. I. Danom.] No. 22 (1941).
"Itogi i uroki." [Gitler i Iaponiia.] No. 22 (1941). [Signed Gr. Golosov.]
"Na puti k edinomu rukovodstvu voinoi." No. 1 (1942).
"Riomskii protsess." No. 6/7 (1942).
"Chto takoe sotsializm." No. 9/10 (1942).
"Pamiati cheshskikh sotsialistov." No. 11/12 (1942).
"Teni dalekogo proshlogo (Pamiati V. N. Figner)." No. 13/14 (1942).
"O sotsializme i fashizme." No. 15/16 (1942).
"Krest'ianstvo i kolkhozy." Nos. 17/18, 19/20 (1942).
"Pamiati V. L. Burtseva." No. 19/20 (1942).
"Sovremennaia voina i kapitalizm." No. 21/22 (1942).
"Iubilei tret'ego raikha (10 let diktatury Gitlera)." No. 3/4 (1943).
"Pamiati S. I. Ingermana." No. 5/6 (1943).
"P. N. Miliukov." No. 9/10 (1943).
"O 'pilatovskom voprose'." [Polemika s F. I. Danom po voprosu: chto takoe sotsializm.] No. 9/10 (1943).
"Pamiati N. N. Minor." No. 9/10 (1943).
"Spor eshche ne vzveshennyi sud'boi (K 25-letiiu smerti G. V. Plekhanova)." No. 11/12 (1943).
"75-letie Ia. M. Dzhemsa." No. 21/22 (1943).
"P. A. Garvi (Cherty k politicheskoi biografii)." Nos. 5/6, 7/8 (1944).
"Iu. O. Martov i s.-r. (Istoricheskaia spravka)." No. 9/10 (1944).
"Eshche raz Martov i s.-r." No. 11/12 (1944).
"Voina i taktika sotsial-demokratii." No. 13/14 (1944).
"Itogi odnogo spora." [K voprosu o smysle voennogo soiuza Gitlera s Iaponiei.] No. 17/18 (1944).
"Voina i taktika sotsial-demokratii." No. 23/24 (1944).
"Kongress frantsuzskikh sotsialistov." No. 1/2 (1945).
"Krymskaia konferentsiia i Dal'nii Vostok." No. 3/4 (1945).
"O 'svobode pechati' v Sovetskoi Rossii." No. 3/4 (1945).
"Russkaia tserkov' na novom etape." No. 5/6 (1945).
"Russkaia emigratsiia v Parizhe." No. 11/12 (1945).
"Maks Nettlau." No. 13/14 (1945).
"Sovetizatsiia pravoslavnoi tserkvi." No. 15/16 (1945).
"'Termidor' russkoi revoliutsii." No. 15/16 (1945).
"Pamiati A. P. Aksel'roda." No. 15/16 (1945).
"O tseliakh i metodakh sovetskoi diktatury." No. 17/18 (1945).
"P. I. Kalnin." [Nekrolog.] No. 17/18 (1945).
"'Vossoedinenie tserkvei v rasseianii sushchikh'." No. 19/20 (1945).
"Pravda o diktature (Otvet E. D. Kuskovoi)." No. 21/22 (1945).

"Krov'iu omytoe sovetskoe zoloto . . . ('Dal'stroi'–sovetskaia katorga v Kolymskom krae)." No. 21/22 (1945).
"Pochemu i kak unichtozheno piat' sovetskikh respublik." No. 1 (1946).
"Iz letopisi sovetskoi literatury. (Stalin v 'potaennoi literature'.–'Prestuplenie i nakazanie' poeta O. Mandel'shtama.–Sud'ba 'sovetskogo Gogolia': N. Erdman i ego neuvidevshaia stseny p'esa *Samoubiitsa*)." No. 1 (1946).
"Ideologicheskaia perestroika VKP(b)." No. 2 (1946).
"Sud'ba Checheno-Ingushskoi ASSR." No. 3 (1946).
"Novoe pravitel'stvo Stalina." No. 4 (1946).
"Novaia emigratsiia i zadachi russkikh sotsialistov." No. 4 (1946).
"Na komandnykh vysotakh Kremlia (Svodka)." No. 5 (1946).
"Na komandnykh vysotakh Kremlia. G. M. Malenkov i 'malenkovtsy'." No. 6 (1946).
"Opala marshala Zhukova." No. 7/8 (1946).
"Smutnye dni russkogo Parizha (Svodka po pis'mam)." No. 7/8 (1946).
"Sud'ba fizika P. Kapitsy." No. 12 (1946).
"Teoreticheskoe zaveshchanie R. Gil'ferdinga (K shestoi godovshchine so dnia ego smerti)." No. 1/2 (1947).
"O 'novoi' i 'staroi' emigratsii." Nos. 1, 2 (1948).
"Zloveshchaia figura staroi Rossii." [Markov 2-oi.] No. 1 (1948).
"Znachenie dela Beriia." No. 1 (1954).
"O korniakh sovetskogo imperializma." No. 2 (1954).
"Restavratsiia stalinizma." No. 3/4 (1954).
"Amerikanskii Komitet i demokraticheskaia emigratsiia iz SSSR." No. 5 (1954).
"General'nyi shtab kommunisticheskoi diversii." No. 6 (1954).
"Politicheskie zametki: S. P. Mel'gunov i ego voinstvuiushchii 'antimarksizm'." No. 6 (1954).
"Rasstrel Riumina." No. 8/9 (1954).
"Novaia rabota po istorii kommunizma." [Review of *Ukrainian Communism and Soviet Russian Policy*, by Yurij Lawrynenko (New York, 1954).] No. 11 (1954).
"Iz istorii ezhovshchiny: Padenie Postysheva." No. 12 (1954).
"Amerikanskii Komitet i rossiiskie demokraty." No. 12 (1954).
"Delo Abakumova." No. 1 (1955).
"Otvet V. G. Chemberlinu." [Ob Amerikanskom Komitete.] No. 1 (1955).
"Bulganin (Kontury politicheskoi biografii)." No. 2/3 (1955).
"Itogi dvukh let. Ot Malenkova k Bulganinu." Nos. 4, 6 (1955).
"SSSR i Kitai." No. 5 (1955).
"Bor'ba za vlast' v partii (Podgotovka XX s"ezda KPSS)." No. 7/8 (1955).
"Problema mezhnatsional'nogo soglasheniia." No. 9 (1955).
"Marks i Chernyshevskii." Nos. 10, 11 (1955).
"Sovetskaia diktatura i germanskaia problema." No. 10 (1955).
"Sovetskaia diplomatiia i atomnye vzryvy." No. 12 (1955).
"Lenin mezhdu Marksom i Chernyshevskim." No. 12 (1955).

"S"ezd zakrepleniia pobedy Khrushcheva i Bulganina (Nakanune XX s"ezda KPSS)." No. 1 (1956).
"K pred"istorii *Sotsialisticheskogo vestnika* (Voina s Pol'shei i men'sheviki v 1920 godu)." No. 2/3 (1956).
"Bor'ba za vlast' v KPSS (K itogam 20-go s"ezda)." No. 4 (1956).
"Stalin i ubiistvo Kirova (Zametki dlia budushchei istorii)." Nos. 5, 10, 12 (1956).
"Khrushchev o prestupleniiakh Stalina (Opyt istoricheskogo kommentariia)." No. 6 (1956).
"Bol'shaia igra Khrushcheva." No. 11 (1956).
"Chto proiskhodit v Moskve?" [Posle sobytii v Vengrii i Pol'she.] No. 1 (1957).
"Stranichka proshlogo: Pamiati Ia. L. Delevskogo." No. 1 (1957).
"Vokrug iubileia G. V. Plekhanova." No. 2/3 (1957).
"Stalin i Kirov (Eshche raz o konflikte 1932-34 g.g.)." No. 4 (1957).
"Legenda ob 'utaennom pis'me' Marksa." [Pis'mo K. Marksa k V. Zasulich ot 8 marta 1881 g.] No. 5 (1957).
"Gosudarstvennyi perevorot Nikity Khrushcheva. (1) Partapparatchiki i parttekhnokraty; (2) Bor'ba za stalinskoe nasledstvo; (3) Razgrom partekhnokratov 'kak klassa'." Nos. 8, 9/10 (1957).
"Iubilei organov gosbezopasnosti." No. 1 (1958).
"Sovetskaia diktatura na novom etape." No. 2/3 (1958).
"Pervaia popytka istorii mashiny sovetskogo terrora." [Review of *The Soviet Secret Police,* edited by Simon Wolin and Robert M. Slusser (New York: Praeger, 1957).] No. 2/3 (1958).
"K istorii 'Ezhovshchiny'." No. 5 (1958).
"Khrushchev protiv 'ideologov' (Novyi etap bor'by na verkhushke diktatury)." No. 6 (1958).
"Stranitsy proshlogo. K 80-letiiu L. O. Tsederbaum-Dan." Nos. 6, 7/8 (1958).
"Khrushchev ishchet novykh soiuznikov." No. 9 (1958).
"V mire merzosti i zapusteniia (Nravy na verkhushke diktatury). Delo G. F. Aleksandrova. Delo M. A. Leonova." No. 9 (1958).
"Kitai i SSSR." No. 10 (1958).
"K istorii Stalinskikh 'chistok'. Dopolnitel'nyi (51-yi) tom *Bol'shoi Sovetskoi Entsiklopedii.*" No. 11 (1958).
"Pered XXI s"ezdom KPSS." No. 12 (1958).
"K itogam XXI s"ezda kompartii." No. 2/3 (1959).
"T. I. Vulikh (1886-1959)." No. 2/3 (1959).
"Vneshniaia politika Khrushcheva." No. 4 (1959).
"Pamiati G. I. Uratadze." No. 4 (1959).
"Pervyi s"ezd RSDRP (1898 g.) i ego sovremennye kommunisticheskie istoriki." No. 5 (1959).
"K istorii 'krasnogo terrora'." No. 5 (1959).
"I. G. Tsereteli (Stranitsy biografii)." Nos. 6, 7, 8/9, 10, 11, 12 (1959), and No. 2/3 (1960).
"Iz istorii mashiny sovetskogo terrora." No. 8/9 (1959).
"Khrushchev i Mao." No. 10 (1959).
"Diktatura na putiakh k 'vysokomu urovniu'." Nos. 4, 5 (1960).

"Khrushchev pod perekrestnym ognem." No. 6 (1960).
"Khrushchev i mirovaia revoliutsiia." No. 7 (1960).
"Nakanune bol'shogo vystupleniia Khrushcheva?" No. 8/9 (1960).
"V. S. Voitinskii (12. XI. 1885-11. VI. 1960)." No. 8/9 (1960).
"Khrushchev v ON i 'krizis rukovodstva' v Moskve." No. 10 (1960).
"M. A. Suslov. Opyt biograficheskoi spravki." No. 11 (1960), and No. 1 (1961).
"Ob obshchestvennom i lichnom (Vynuzhdennyi otvet N. Ul'ianovu)." No. 11 (1960).
"Na putiakh k vossozdaniiu Kominterna. Khrushchev i Mao v 1960 g." No. 12 (1960).
"Kitaiskaia versiia o prichinakh konflikta Khrushchev-Mao." No. 12 (1960).
"Sorok let tomu nazad." [Men'shevistskaia partiia v 1920-1921 g.g.] No. 2/3 (1961).
"N putiakh k XXII s"ezdu KPSS." No. 4 (1961).
"Pis'mo v redaktsiiu." [K voprosu o predkakh Lenina.] No. 5 (1961).
"Kto iskazhaet istoriiu?" No. 6 (1961). [In response to an article by E. P. Kandel' in *Voprosy istorii;* this is the concluding part of a piece by Nicolaevsky in *Proceedings of the American Philosophical Society,* April, 1961.]
"Marshal N. S. Konev (Opyt biograficheskoi spravki)." No. 8/9 (1961).
"XXII s"ezd KPSS (Pervye itogi)." No. 10/11 (1961).
"Bor'ba za vlast' na XXII s"ezde (Itogi i perspektivy)." No. 12 (1961).
"Posle XXII s"ezda KPSS." No. 3/4 (1962).
"'Neozhidannosti' XXII s"ezda i bor'ba za vlast' v Kremle." No. 3/4 (1962).
"M. D. Shishkin (1886-1962)." No. 3/4 (1962).
"A. S. Enukidze, ego 'prestuplenie' i ego 'reabilitatsiia'." No. 5/6 (1962).
"Pavel Abramovich Berlin (1877-1962)." No. 5/6 (1962).
"Mikhail Markovich Ravich (1881-1962)." No. 5/6 (1962).
"I. G. Tsereteli i ego *Vospominaniia* o 1917 g." Nos. 7/8, 9/10 (1962).
"Novyi krutoi povorot Khrushcheva." No. 11/12 (1962).
"Moskva v poiskakh novoi vneshnei politiki?" No. 1/2 (1963).
"Mezhdu Vostokom i Zapadom. Vokrug pan-aziatskogo naslediia Stalina." No. 3/4 (1963).
"Pamiati L. O. Dan." No. 3/4 (1963).
"Khrushchev i 'vnutrennie kitaitsy'." No. 7/8 (1963).
"Padenie Frola Kozlova (Iz istorii bor'by na verkhushke diktatury)." No. 9/10 (1963).
"O sushchestve spora (Otvet B. K. Suvarinu)." [K voprosu o bor'be za vlast' v Kremle.] No. 11/12 (1963).

Sotsialisticheskii vestnik, Sborniki:
"Na zare kominterna. Rasskaz 'tovarishcha Tomasa'." Sbornik Nos. 1, 2 (1964).
"Iu. P. Denike. Opyt politicheskoi biografii." Sbornik No. 3 (1965).
"Klara Kalnin." [Nekrolog.] Sbornik No. 3 (1965).

"Problema destalinizatsii i delo Bukharina." Sbornik No. 4 (1965).

"Bukharin ob oppozitsii Stalinu. Interv'iu s B. I. Nikolaevskim." Sbornik No. 4 (1965).

Miscellaneous (1941-1966):

"A Study of Polish-Russian Socialist Relations." *New Europe,* No. 10 (1941).

"The Crisis in the German High Command." *New Europe,* No. 5 (1942).

"Japan under the Black Dragon." *New Europe,* No. 7 (1945).

"Rudolf Hilferdings theoretisches Vermaechtnis." *Neue Volkszeitung* (New York), June 21 and July 5, 1947.

"Stalin's Eldorado." *Fortune,* August, 1947. [Forced labor in the Kolyma goldfields.]

"Stalin's Secret Sickness." *This Week Magazine,* November 7, 1948.

"Nature de l'État Soviétique. Capitalisme? Socialisme? Ou quoi?" *La Revue socialiste* (Paris), December, 1947.

"Russia, Japan, and the Pan-Asiatic Movement to 1925." *The Far Eastern Quarterly,* May, 1949.

"The New Soviet Campaign against the Peasants." *The Russian Review,* April, 1951.

Review of *Mouvements ouvriers et socialistes* (Chronologie et bibliographie): *La Russie,* Vol. 1, 1725-1907; Vol. 2, 1908-1917 (Paris, 1956). In *Le Contrat social* (Paris), No. 3 (1958).

"France–French Socialism in the 20th Century." *Encyclopedia Americana.* 1969 ed., Vol. 11.

"Who is Distorting History? (*Voprosy istorii* and Karl Marx in 1848-1849)." *Proceedings of the American Philosophical Society,* April, 1961.

"Les premières années de l'Internationale communiste. D'après le récit du 'camarade Thomas'." *Contributions à l'histoire du Comintern,* edited by Jacques Freymond. Geneva, 1965.

"Secret Societies and the First International." *The Revolutionary Internationals 1864-1943.* Stanford: Stanford University Press, 1966.

Notes

B. I. Nicolaevsky: The Formative Years

1. The most important single written source for this biographical article is a long manuscript of some one hundred pages which Nicolaevsky dictated to a journalist friend in 1953. Also helpful are shorter autobiographies, written at various times and for various purposes; letters to his old friends; and interviews which Boris Ivanovich recorded in the early 1960s with Professor Leopold Haimson, Director of the Inter-University Project on the History of the Menshevik Movement. Still, I have learned most about his general outlook from Nicolaevsky himself while I was Associate Director of the Menshevik Project (1959-64), and then when I, like him, moved to Stanford to work in the archives of the Hoover Institution (1964-66). It was during this latter period that I began to collect material for a *festchrift* in his honor. Copies of all the above mentioned sources are deposited with the Nicolaevsky Collection in the Hoover Institution, Stanford University, and I am grateful to Anna M. Bourguina, the Curator of the Collection, for helping me in my research. A brief biography of Nicolaevsky was published shortly after his death (see Ladis K. D. Kristof, "Boris I. Nicolaevsky, 1887-1966," *Russian Review,* 25, No. 3 (July, 1966), 324-27.

2. One brother, Vsevolod, died in his teens and one, Mikhail, who became a doctor, sympathized with the revolutionary movement but remained politically uncommitted. One sister, Alexandra, the oldest (born 1885) and closest to Boris Ivanovich, was a Socialist Revolutionary and switched later, in the post-1905 period, to the anarchists among whom her husband, Nikolai P. Fedoseev, was quite prominent in the Urals. The other sister, Natalia, was a Social Democrat with Menshevik orientation. The second oldest brother, Vladimir (born 1889), began his revolutionary career in 1905 in Ufa as a Bolshevik but later, partly under the influence of Boris Ivanovich (with whom he was in exile in Arkhangelsk *guberniia*), became a Menshevik; he was married to a sister of the Bolshevik leader A. I. Rykov who was to succeed Lenin as Prime-Minister of the Soviet Union. He lived with Rykov in Moscow after 1920 and was protected by him until the two were arrested and perished together in 1938 during the Great Purges. The youngest brother, Viktor (born 1898), joined the Bolsheviks upon graduation from high school in 1917, made a career in the Red Army, and was a staff officer, but died in his early thirties. Whatever their political differences, the members of the Nicolaevsky family remained on good terms with one another.

3. The Tatars were much more accepted than the Chuvash but even so the children of Russian parents and those of Tatar parents tended to engage in quite rough games of war against each other on the streets of Belebei. Boris Ivanovich remembered it as something rather unusual that he occasionally "went over" to the Tatar side of the "front" to rescue some lonely Tatar boy against whom several Russian boys had ganged up.

4. Lev Nikolaevich Kremer (Kreiner?) was also to join the revolutionary movement

but died around 1905. He was the son of a railroad official who himself had been involved in some illegal political activities. He lived with his divorced mother who, while she apparently had a low opinion of the revolutionaries and their propaganda literature, encouraged her son and his friends to read the writings of the so-called revolutionary democrats whom she appreciated as serious authors.

5. On the whole, Boris Ivanovich's friends tended to be of somewhat higher social origin than he and certainly better off materially than he was after his father's death.

6. "K istorii Bolgar" was Boris Ivanovich's first publication. As far as he remembered, three issues of the mimeographed *Podsnezhnik* came out, all of them in the first half of 1903. He contributed only to the first one.

7. He was not greatly impressed by it, which was rather characteristic given his temperament and intellectual outlook.

8. Six years later Boris Ivanovich was to share a prison cell and become good friends with a Socialist Revolutionary, Mikhail Vedeniapin, and to learn that it was he who had authored the leaflet while a student at Samara Teachers' College. In 1922 Vedeniapin was among the accused in the famous Moscow trial of the Socialist Revolutionaries while Boris Ivanovich was among those making frantic efforts to mobilize socialist public opinion in Western Europe to intervene with the Bolsheviks and save the lives of the defendants.

9. Boris Ivanovich often mentioned that one of the most self-defeating of the tsarist policies for suppressing the revolutionary movement was that of exiling the activists into the four corners of the Empire. Indeed, nothing promoted the spread of subversive ideas from the capitals and universities into the farthest, quietest, and most loyal provincial towns so much as this policy of banishing into their midst professional political agitators whose every word carried the weight of authority attributed to anybody who had arrived from the main cultural centers of Russia.

10. When V. P. Artsybushev died in 1917 Boris Ivanovich published a fairly long, unsigned biography of him in *Rabochaia gazeta.*

11. See B. I. Nikolaevskii, "75 letie Ia. M. Dzhemsa," *Sotsialisticheskii vestnik*, November, 1943.

12. Iakov Markovich Lupolov, a native of Kostroma, first fled Russia in 1891 and settled two years later in the United States where, under the name of James, he became active in the Boston, and later New York, socialist movement. In 1900 he returned to Russia for illegal party work, was active in Perm, worked as a correspondent for *Iskra*, etc. Between 1900 and 1907 he was repeatedly in and out of Russia, three times falling into the hands of the tsarist police. In 1907 he was an organizer of the illegal passage through Finland of the delegates going to the London Party Congress. After that Lupolov returned to New York but remained an active party (Menshevik) worker.

13. Boris Ivanovich was aware at this point of the basic differences between the Social Democrats and the Socialist Revolutionaries, and he had close friends among both groups. Thus his choice was based on a definite preference, however limited the knowledge upon which that preference was based.

14. The Ufa Social Democratic group was centered in the local *zemstvo* administration. Among its leaders was Petr N. Grigor'ev.

15. Boris Ivanovich's school bench mate, Vasilii Gorelov, the son of a railway conductor and with no contacts with the movement prior to his recruitment into the circle, was to become a local revolutionary hero when, together with another member of Ufa's Social Democratic "fighting organization," Mikhail Kadomtsev, he held up a train and took 300,000 rubles.

16. Mikhail Kozlov was the son of "Nadezhda" Kozlov in whose private library Boris Ivanovich had been studying populist literature. The father was a respected old time revolutionary and the son was himself an SR and thus familiar with, and bound by, the code of secrecy. Why then did young Kozlov readily admit to the police that

he had received the proclamation from Boris Ivanovich and that he had heard the latter acknowledge its authorship? Why did he not simply say that he had found the proclamation? Boris Ivanovich never quite overcame the grief which this incident caused him, not so much because of the consequences which he had to suffer, but because it dishonored and raised all kinds of doubts about a revolutionary, one whom he knew personally and would have regarded as above suspicion.

17. Actually it was a whole series of articles which Chernov published in 1900 in *Russkoe bogatstvo* on the subject of the capitalist versus agrarian type of evolution. The articles were published under a pseudonym and Boris Ivanovich did not know at the time the true identity of the author.

18. Aleksei Fedorovich Ogorelov, born about 1881, was then (1904) a Bolshevik but like Boris Ivanovich he was to switch to the Mensheviks in the post-1905 period. After the 1917 Revolution he was for a time mayor of Vladivostok. Later he worked for the Soviet Government as an economist yet when he came once to Berlin he talked at length and freely with Boris Ivanovich.

19. This activity in the rural areas was, however, something quite new for the Social Democrats. The Socialist Revolutionaries had far more solid ties in this milieu. "Wherever we would go into the villages," Boris Ivanovich recalled, "we would find that the Socialist Revolutionaries had preceded us and already established agents. The teacher, the *fel'dsher,* often the more intelligent shopkeeper as well as the *zemskii* functionary, and the doctor, these were the pillars of the Socialist Revolutionaries."

20. The other Samara newspaper, the *Samarskaia gazeta,* was the mainstay of the Socialist Revolutionaries. Since it was an old and well-established paper, Boris Ivanovich first went there to look for a job but was refused because his Social Democratic sympathies were already known at the time. The Marxist *Samarskii vestnik* had been shut down several years before.

21. The situation here described was characteristic not only for Samara, or the Volga-Urals region, but for all Central Russia and Siberia. In fact, to a large extent it was the same all over Russia and contrasted sharply with the situation in the emigration. Echoes of the deep divisions and animosities within the party which developed abroad immediately after the Second Congress were noticeable in Russia in the 1903-1905 period only in the centers of old anti-*Iskra* sentiment (i.e., mainly in a few towns of southwest Russia) and where the influence of the emigre leadership was more direct (i.e., in St. Petersburg and Moscow) or where the influence of the Bund was strong. This geographical pattern of varying intensity in the Bolshevik-Menshevik animosities largely maintained itself also in the period 1906-17 as the split within the party became increasingly deep and open. The further east, the further away from the emigration, the capitals and the western and southern fringes of the Empire inhabited by national minorities, the less intense was the struggle between Bolsheviks and Mensheviks. Despite the influence of colonies of exiles who imported their quarrels with them, some Social Democratic organizations in Siberia remained united as late as the second half of 1917.

22. The only two members of the Central Committee in Russia who escaped arrest were L. B. Krasin and A. I. Liubimov. Both of them (and especially Krasin) were at the time "conciliators" *(primirentsy)* but Lenin succeeded finally in persuading them to support the idea of a purely Bolshevik Third Party Congress, in which they participated. Later Liubimov was to lapse once more into the conciliatory attitude, and by 1917 he was completely alienated from Bolshevism and had become a follower of Plekhanov.

23. The leader of the Samara Social Democratic Committee was Boris Pavlovich Pozern (known as "Zapadnyi"), son of a wealthy local pharmacist. He was quite a prominent Bolshevik who later became an aide of Kirov. He was shot during the Great Purges.

24. That demonstration, which followed a noisy eruption into a public meeting about local educational matters, was organized by I. A. Konovalov ("Nikolai") who was to become a police agent in the ranks of the St. Petersburg Bolsheviks. The townspeople complained bitterly at the time that the revolutionaries had broken up the meeting at which there was a unique chance to ventilate grievances against the school system. In retrospect, Boris Ivanovich admitted that they were right, but at the time the revolutionaries were too youthful, and too impatient for action to ponder the consequences of these actions.

25. Petr Voevodin, a few years Boris Ivanovich's senior, can still be seen in photographs in *Pravda* when the oldest party members are feted. He is listed as a "party member since 1898."

26. Boris Ivanovich pointed out that the Samara organization of the Union of Liberation, which was considerably to the left of the broad spectrum of those who called themselves liberals, had within its ranks an impressive number of intellectuals who also occupied respected social positions. The Samara Social Democratic Committee, on the other hand, had only two men, the above mentioned B. P. Pozern and V. M. Pototskii, who were in this category, and since the political activities in which they engaged were considered criminal they had to lead a double life.

27. The Black Hundreds in Samara were attempting to capitalize on the discontent caused by widespread unemployment which had followed the summer railroad strike. They blamed the Jews, the intelligentsia, and the revolutionaries in general for this unemployment. The Social Democrats were able to counteract this propaganda through the contacts they had established among the workers' teenage sons.

28. After the revolution was crushed, the reactionaries took revenge on Colonel von Galin. He was court martialed, stripped of his rank, and sent to prison for four years.

29. The mood, activity, and in general the whole course of the 1905 Revolution was affected by the youth of the participants. In Samara the average age of the Social Democratic activists was probably only slightly above that of Boris Ivanovich (who became eighteen in October). A few were in their mid-twenties (I. F. Dubrovinskii, the ranking Social Democrat of Samara was twenty-eight) and from all those whom Boris Ivanovich could recall not more than one or two were over thirty. Even the very youthful contemporary revolutionary movements of Latin America, Africa, and Asia seem to be older in terms of the age of most of the activists.

30. There was in Samara a small separate Menshevik organization headed by Vladimir Trapeznikov, a physician and a Social Democrat since the 1890s.

31. V. I. Lenin, "O sovremennom polozhenii i blizhaishikh zadachakh sovetskoi vlasti," *Sochineniia,* 3rd ed. (Moscow, 1932) 24, pp. 357-58. Boris Ivanovich's speech, "Chto takoe kolchakovshchina?" was given in the Polytechnical Museum of Moscow on July 3, 1919.

32. From among the Menshevik leaders, besides Boris Ivanovich only R. A. Abramovich and D. Iu. Dallin supported the League. Boris Ivanovich also strongly advocated the drawing of the new Soviet emigration towards Menshevism. To the end of his life he considered that that was the only chance of revitalizing Menshevism and its press, even if only in emigration for the time being. But most of his party colleagues were either cool or downright opposed to the idea because they were suspicious of the background and motives of these Soviet emigres. Boris Ivanovich considered such an attitude unfair towards people who had grown up under the totalitarian Soviet system, had had to survive somehow the era of terror of the "Ezhovshchina" and were finally confronted with the necessity of making at least an outward choice between Stalin and Hitler while caught in a crossfire of propaganda, perhaps never in their whole lives having had access to any objective source of information. He was not ready to dismiss or even suspect out of hand the sincerity or integrity of an emigre merely be-

cause he had been a member of the Communist Party of the Soviet Union, joined the Vlasov units, published some articles, or the like.

33. "Organic work," which was favored by the Mensheviks, especially the *likvidatory,* meant day-to-day practical party work among the masses with emphasis on organization and the so-called "small deeds," whether economic or political, which were understandable and of immediate concern to the workers and with which they themselves could deal. Its aim was to build up a network of grassroots workers' organizations managed and led by the workers themselves which in turn would build up their class consciousness and self-confidence and make them independent of the intelligentsia.

34. Boris Ivanovich recalled how he used to contrast the power and effectiveness of the strike to that of acts of terror. The former was awesome, virtually irresistible because it reduced the opponent—the state—to powerlessness. Moreover, it could be rationally planned, its consequences foreseen, and thus used purposefully. Terror, on the other hand, was a puny weapon that was at the same time capable of causing unforeseen consequences. Briefly, it was an irrational weapon wholly incompatible with Marxism and its attempt to control and rationalize the historical process.

35. Actually, Boris Ivanovich's pro-Georgian sympathies preceded his arrival in Transcaucasia. Reading about the Guriia Uprising in 1904, he was impressed by the fact that the Georgian peasants had turned *en masse* into Social Democrats and unanimously adopted their resolutions; nothing could have been more important to Boris Ivanovich than the idea that somehow the peasantry and Social Democracy could be brought together.

36. Boris Ivanovich was for all practical purposes *the* center from which the party organization was rebuilt. He formed a new Social Democratic Committee, which, to the great chagrin of Lenin, became Menshevik dominated. In April, 1912, as leader of the Baku Social Democratic Committee, he founded a small weekly, *Nashe slovo,* of which seven issues appeared. He was aided in editing the journal by Anshlius, a Menshevik, and Stepan Iakushev, a Bolshevik *primirenets.* Boris Ivanovich also wrote one or two reports on the situation in Baku for *Zvezda,* which he signed Likvidator.

37. When Boris Ivanovich was arrested the police knew nothing of his activities; the only thing they had against him was that he was not Grigorii Nikolaevich Golosov, whose passport he was using, since the real owner had declared it invalid. After admitting his identity, Boris Ivanovich was sent back to the north to complete his original term of exile without any additional punishment.

38. Incidentally, it was in the Vologda jail that Boris Ivanovich first heard that Malinovskii, who was just then (July, 1912) running as a Social Democratic candidate to the Fourth Duma with the support of both factions, was suspected of being a police agent. V. G. Chirkin, who lived in exile in Vologda, came to see Boris Ivanovich and told him about these suspicions which dated back to 1910, when he (Chirkin) and a group of others, among them Malinovskii, were arrested in Moscow; all were sent into exile except Malinovskii who inexplicably was promptly released.

39. He remained a *primirenets* even after his Transcaucasian experience (e.g. in 1913-14 when he worked in St. Petersburg with the Social Democratic fraction) though he gradually became less and less sanguine. In any case he never passed blanket judgments and even after 1917, there were individual Bolsheviks (e.g., Riazanov, Rykov, Liutovinov, etc.) who for various reasons commanded his respect and friendship.

40. This is not to imply that on principle he preferred to collaborate with the Bolsheviks rather than with the Plekhanovites; quite to the contrary, but it simply happened that he had no contact among the Plekhanovite group while he did have a friend among the Bolsheviks, Enukidze, and this was reason enough for him to seek affiliation with the latter's organization.

41. Boris Ivanovich was also convinced that members of Stalin's old squad of *kochi* from Baku were instrumental in Kirov's assassination.

42. Boris Ivanovich failed to secure any hard evidence against Stalin and the trial ended (even before Boris Ivanovich returned from his trip) inconclusively with both sides claiming victory.

43. The "Letters" were published under the signature Iv.

44. Babel visited Western Europe at that time and had a series of secret meetings with Boris Ivanovich. Whether the G.P.U. found out about these meetings and, if so, whether this contributed to the decision to liquidate Babel a few years later is unknown.

45. It should be mentioned here that Soviet sources are mistaken when listing Boris Ivanovich as a delegate to the London Party Congress of 1907. Whoever participated in that congress under the name of Volosov or Golosov was not Boris Ivanovich.

46. Boris Ivanovich remembered writing speeches for Tuliakov and reports for *Rabochaia gazeta* about meetings with constituents during the summer of 1913 for Iagello, Khaustov, Man'kov and Tuliakov.

47. Malinovskii, it must be recalled, was a very close collaborator of Lenin and the main instrument of his Duma policy. Without him Lenin would probably not have succeeded in splitting the Social Democratic fraction.

48. The police were attempting at that time to provoke the Social Democrats into extreme statements and actions in order to discredit them in public opinion as an irresponsible element and justify their complete elimination from public life at a future date. Thus in various direct and indirect ways the police supported the radicals, namely the more extreme Bolsheviks, banking on the proposition that they would dig the grave of the whole movement. Most Mensheviks agreed with this analysis.

49. In his later years, Boris Ivanovich admitted that probably not all of the Mensheviks' suspicions at this time were justified.

50. For several months, in spring and summer, 1917, Martov was on the left flank of, and in opposition to, the majority (led by Tsereteli, Dan, Chkheidze, etc.) within the Menshevik party and was toying with the idea of splitting off his group of Menshevik Internationalists.

51. Boris Ivanovich pointed out that many an underground party activist was shocked when he went abroad for a brief visit to discuss the revolution with party leaders and found them living in conditions of relative well being and/or steeped in various un-revolutionary intellectual pursuits. Martov generally evoked sympathy because he often lived in poverty; but he, too, had broad intellectual interests which distracted him from total devotion to party affairs.

52. In Boris Ivanovich's opinion Martov was at least able to generate warm feelings and deep attachment among those with whom he had face to face contacts. Dan, on the other hand, was not really liked personally even within inner party circles, Martov included, though he was respected and appreciated as a hard and efficient party worker.

53. This is not to imply Boris Ivanovich withdrew from party activity. In 1920 he became a member of the Central Committee.

54. In the Soviet Union, however, Boris Ivanovich remains *persona non grata*. Thus in *Literaturnaia gazeta* of April 19, 1967, there was an article on Gorkii in which a long passage described sympathetically Boris Ivanovich's correspondence with Gorkii and other writers. A few issues later (no. 24/1967) the same paper printed a letter with a rebuke for having called Boris Ivanovich a well-known historian of Social Democracy when in fact he was an enemy of the Soviet Union.

55. Friedrich Adler, "Das Apriori des Sozialismus," *Neues Forum,* 13, No. 154 (October, 1966), 604-605.

Boris Nicolaevsky: The American Years

1. Louis Fischer, rev. of *Power and the Soviet Elite,* by B. I. Nicolaevsky, *New York Times Book Review,* November 21, 1965, p. 3.

2. Fritz T. Epstein, "The Nikolaevskii Collection at Indiana," *Indiana Library News Letter,* 1, No. 4 (April, 1966), 1-2.

3. Anna M. Bourguina, *Russian Social Democracy: The Menshevik Movement; a Bibliography,* Hoover Institution Bibliographical Series, No. 36 (Stanford, 1968).

4. Boris I. Nicolaevsky, *Power and the Soviet Elite: "The Letter of an Old Bolshevik" and Other Essays,* ed. Janet D. Zagoria (New York, 1965).

Russian Youth on the Eve of Romanticism: Andrei I. Turgenev and His Circle

1. Serious study of the Society was started only after the archives of the Turgenev family (in Paris until the first years of the twentieth century, when they were turned over to the Russian Academy of Sciences) were made available to scholars. The first detailed account was in A. N. Veselovskii, *V. A. Zhukovskii (Poeziia chuvstva i "serdechnogo voobrazheniia")* (St. Petersburg, 1904). See also M. Sukhomlinov, "A. S. Kaisarov i ego literaturnye druz'ia," *Otdelenie russkogo iazyka i slovesnosti Akademii Nauk, Sbornik,* 65, No. 5 (1897), 1-33; A. Fomin, "Andrei Iv. Turgenev i Andrei Serg. Kaisarov—novye dannye o nikh po dokumentam arkhiva P. N. Turgeneva," *Russkii bibliofil,* January, 1912, pp. 7-39; "Andrei Sergeevich Kaisarov (Novye materialy dlia biografii i dlia kharakteristiki ego literaturnoi deiatel'nosti iz arkhiva P. N. Turgeneva)," ibid., April, 1912, pp. 5-33. In the two decades preceding and following the Russian Revolution, V. M. Istrin made an extensive study of the Turgenev archives in preparation for their publication. See V. M. Istrin, *Zhurnal Ministerstva narodnogo prosveshcheniia* (cited hereafter as *ZMNP*), n.s., 26 (March, 1910), 1-36; 28 (July, 1910), 80-145; 28 (August, 1910), 273-307; 32 (April, 1911), 205-37; 44 (March, 1913), 1-15. Istrin gave an overall account and interpretation of the Turgenev circle in the long introduction to *Pis'ma i dnevnik Aleksandra Ivanovicha Turgeneva gettingenskogo perioda (1802-1804) i pis'ma ego k S. A. Kaisarovu i brat'iam v Gettingene (1805-1811), Arkhiv brat'ev Turgenevykh,* vypusk 2 (St. Petersburg, 1911). The same source was summarized by V. I. Rezanov, *Iz razyskanii o sochineniiakh V. A. Zhukovskogo,* vyp. 2 (Petrograd, 1916). During the next two and one-half decades there were no further sources or monographs published on the Turgenev circle. A revival of interest in it occurred in the 1950s as reflected in e.g. Iu. M. Lotman, "Andrei Sergeevich Kaisarov i literaturno-obshchestvennaia bor'ba ego vremeni," *Uchenye Zapiski Tartuskogo gosudarstvennogo Universiteta* [Tartu Riikliku Ülikooli Toimetised], vyp. 63 (Tartu, 1958), and in his *Puti razvitiia preddekabristskoi obshchestvenno-politicheskoi mysli,* Diss. 1961 (Leningrad University). Although some material quoted below is cited in works referred to in this note, we shall give references to the originals because our viewpoint and interest differ in many ways from that of previous scholars and the excerpts quoted do not quite overlap.

2. The fullest account of Turgenev's life is in Istrin, *Arkhiv brat'ev Turgenevykh,* vyp. 2.

3. E. I. Tarasov, "K istorii russkogo obshchestva vtoroi poloviny XVIII st.-mason I. P. Turgenev," *ZMNP,* n.s., 51 (June, 1914), 129-75.

4. Akademiia Nauk, Institut istorii russkoi literatury (Pushkinskii Dom), Leningrad, Arkhiv Turgenevykh, fond 309 (hereafter cited as F 309). Additional materials are to be found in the Rukopisnyi otdel, Gosudarstvennaia publichnaia biblioteka imeni Saltykova-Shchedrina, Leningrad, Arkhiv V. A. Zhukovskogo, F 286. Individual items may also be found in the *fondy* of the main participant literary figures such as Voeikov, Merzliakov.

5. F 309, No. 271, Journal entry 22.XI.1799, p. 10 ("Do good according to your ability, do your duty, act for the good of others and your own, exhaust yourself in activity . . ."); No. 272, Journal entry 14.III.1802, p. 40 ("To what purpose is now

the main striving of my spirit: to be known in literature?"). Also his letter to Zhukovskii, 19.VIII.1799, quoted by Veselovskii, *V. A. Zhukovskii,* p. 64, and the last lines of his poem, "I vetkhomu poddevicheskomu domu A. F. V[oeiko]va," in Iu. M. Lotman, ed., *Poety nachala XIX veka,* Biblioteka poeta, malaia seriia, izdanie tret'e (Leningrad, 1961), p. 261 (hereafter cited as *Poety nachala*).

6. F 309, No. 1239, Journal entry 16/28.IX.1802, p. 13 ("Activity, it seems, is higher than liberty. For what else is liberty? Activity endows it with all its value. . . . Put chains on man and leave him a free spirit and a clean conscience, he will not stop being active in his mind. . . . Activity is the stairway to perfection."); F 309, No. 840, Letter to Andrei S. Kaisarov, no pl., n.d. (from Vienna?), ("If *idealisieren* means to make oneself ideals for future life, i.e., make plans, and if one is not to expect their fulfillment, then man has also another goal, the most virtuous and useful for him and for others: he can be active, he must be active. For what is the use of sleep without tiredness and of entertainment without work? As for contemplation that has no influence on the activity of life, it is nothing but an empty condition of the soul–it brings neither labor nor tiredness. Look how philosophical I have gotten!").

7. For example, *Utrenniaia zaria (Trudy vospitannikov Universitetskogo blagorodnogo Pansiona),* Bk. 1 (1800), 193-211 (Rech' o liubvi k otechestvu); Bk. 2 (1803), 235-50 (Rech' o tom kakov dolzhen byt' blagorodnyi vospitannik); Bk. 3 (1805) (Rech' o istinnykh dostoinstvakh blagovospitannogo cheloveka); Bk. 5 (1807), 5-81 (O vospitanii); P. S. Zheleznikov, ed., *Sokrashchennaia biblioteka v pol'zu gospodam vospitannikam pervogo kadetskogo korpusa,* 2 (St. Petersburg, 1802), 241 ff; 3 (1804), 381.

8. F 309, No. 542, Letter of I. P. Turgenev to Andrei Turgenev, 1.X.1793 (". . . a dedicated striving to please God and serve men will open the world to you . . ."); also a curious book given as a present to Nicholas Turgenev by his father for good progress in studies: *L'Ami de l'Enfance ou Contes moraux à la portée des enfants et des adolescents de l'un et l'autre sexe,* Du Laurent (Paris, 1795), F 309, No. 549. Cf. also first writing exercise of Alexander Turgenev, March-May, 1790, Gosudarstvennaia publichnaia biblioteka im. Saltykova-Shchedrina, otdel rukopisei, Bumagi V. A. Zhukovskogo, F 286, No. 316 (hereafter cited as Zhukovskii, F 286).

9. F 309, No. 271, Journal entry 9.XI.1799, pp. 5, 7 (sight of peasant woman and three children); entry of 3.XII.1799, pp. 23-24 (sight of soldiers dragging away drunk man); No. 745 (Nekotorye chuvstva i mneniia moi), entry 28.VIII.1799, p. 5 (sight of old procuress and young prostitute); F 309, No. 271, entry for 3.XII.1799 tells the story of a non-commissioned officer whose wife was seduced by an officer and who had to accept this outrage, which reminds him of the plot of *Kabale und Liebe* ("This flaming, sensitive heart–crushed and tortured by the hand of despotism–deprived of all rights! . . . Oh, if I could only express all that moves my heart. If I could only describe this silence!").

10. F 309, No. 271, entry 15.II.1800, p. 36 (Daydreams about living alone, independent, with modest income without having to serve); No. 272, entry of 14.III.1802, p. 40 (daydreaming about family bliss on voyage to Vienna). We are reminded of Alexander I's daydreaming that he would retire on the banks of the Rhine in quiet private family bliss.

11. F 309, No. 272, entry 25.I.1802, p. 38; entry 14.III.1802, p. 40 ("With such lively feelings [of love for Catherine Sokovnin] I will not be able to occupy myself with literature and poetry"); entry 10.V.1801, p. 6 ("I shall live in the past, I shall weep over the past, I shall revive [the past] with renewed strength in my memory."); No. 840, Letter to A. S. Kaisarov 26.XII.[1802] 7.I.1803.

12. The mood is well summarized in his poem "I v dvatsat' let uzh ia dovol'no ispytal," *Poety nachala,* p. 263. Characteristic of this mood is the design of Andrei Turgenev's seal: a flower on a short leafy stalk with the motto: "jusqu'à son retour."

F 309, No. 276, entry for September, 1799, p. 33; entry for June, 1797, p. 59-60 (draft of a poem: "I net otrady mne ni v chem"); entry for 15.VIII.1797, p. 73 ("Liubvi minuta est' nagrada / Za god unyniia i slez"); No. 272, entry for 10.V.1801, p. 5. See also the poems "Uma ty svetom ozaren" and "Moi drug! Kol' mog ty zabluzhdat'sia," *Poety nachala,* pp. 262, 274; journal entries of Zhukovskii, Zhukovskii, F 286, I No. 1 b, p. 5 ("Ach das *dort* ist niemals hier!").

13. The theme is given poetic form in his Elegy, the most significant of his literary efforts, *Poety nachala,* pp. 267-70; also F 309, No. 272, pp. 41-42.

14. F 309, No. 272, pp. 16-37 (dated 13.XII.1801) contains copies of letters of Catherine, the following pages contain many references to the affair, expressions of regret, hesitations, etc. The affair is summarized (with a different interpretation) by Istrin in *Arkhiv brat'ev Turgenevykh,* vyp. 2; see also the interesting parallel to Evgenii Onegin's Tatiana drawn by Veselovskii, *V. A. Zhukovskii,* p. 82.

15. Catherine died unmarried in 1809.

16. F 309, No. 840, Letter to A. S. Kaisarov from Vienna, no date, and No. 1239, entry for 10/22.I.1803.

17. And which, *mutatis mutandis,* would also hold true of the German scene about two generations earlier, when the traditional Protestant and authoritarian framework was called into question.

18. For example the literary works on which Andrei Turgenev's generation was reared, *Detskoe chtenie dlia serdtsa i razuma* (Moscow, 1785-89); *Detskii sovetnik prepodaiushchii iunoshestvu Pravila, kak blagorazumno v svete postupat',* Ia. Beliavskii, ed. (St. Petersburg, 1789); *Sokrashchennaia biblioteka,* 3 (1804), 370-81.

19. *Detskoe chtenie dlia serdtsa i razuma,* 1 (1785), 8 ff ("Povest' o Seleme i Ksamire"), 3 (1785), 8-16 ("O podrazhanii roditeliam"). The theme is strongly emphasized in Ivan P. Turgenev's own book, *Kto mozhet byt' dobrym grazhdaninom i vernym poddannym* (Moscow, 1796), pp. 1-28 *passim.*

20. Was this not the burden of the lesson which Radishchev drew from his experiences and which impelled him to write his *Journey?*

21. It had also become clear that the nobility did not (or perhaps could not) take advantage of the opportunities for useful local life as paved by the acts of 1775 and 1785. This also explains the bitter sarcasm with which the average provincial nobleman and his way of life were satirized by this generation. The irony is more cutting than the smiling ridicule of eighteenth century satire; it presages Griboedov, the gloomy picture of Gogol', and the angry outbursts of Saltykov-Shchedrin, cf. examples in E. G. Ermakova-Bitner, ed., *Poety satiriki kontsa XVIII–nachala XIX v.* (Leningrad, 1959) and A. Fomin's attribution of "Brakosochetanie Karamzina" to A. S. Kaisarov (*Russkii bibliofil,* January, 1912, pp. 30-39). There were exceptions, of course, but they were few, which explains the admiration which was heaped on a man like I. V. Lopukhin.

22. See Andrei Turgenev's diary in Vienna, F 309, No. 1239 with his plans for study and excerpts from historical books, also his letters to parents from St. Petersburg and Vienna, F 309, Nos. 1231, 1238 *passim,* in which he announces his new objects of study (English, reviewing of Latin, etc.). No doubt, a similar point of view accounts for the orientation towards technical training as preparation for *meaningful* service which we note in Alexander and Nicholas Turgenev's letters and diaries from Goettingen.

23. F 309, No. 544, Letter to his friend Vasilii Stepanovich (?) 9.XI.1794, from Selo Turgenevo.

24. F 309, No. 840, Letter from 7.IX.1799. On the reaction to Andrei's death see the full documentation by V. Istrin, "Smert' Andreia Iv. Turgeneva," *ZMNP,* 26 (March, 1910), 1-36.

25. F 309, No. 271, entry for 1.XII.1799. The most significant stanzas in this

context are: ". . . Bruder!/ Bruder, nimm die Brüder mit,/ Mit zu deinem alten Vater,/ Zu dem ewgen Ozean,/ Der mit ausgespannten Armen/ Unser wartet,/ Die sich, ach! vergebens öffnen,/ Seine sehnenden zu fassen . . ." and "Und so trägt er seine Brüder,/ Seine Schätze, seine Kinder/ dem erwartenden Erzeuger/ Freudebrausend an das Herz."

26. F 309, No. 840, Letter 1.X.1799. See also the allusively revealing remark by Catherine Sokovnin in a letter, 26.XII. 1801: "Il ne faut pas se sacrifier tout à fait aux autres, mais nous leur devons des ménagements. Osobenno vy vashemu batiushke. Il a des droits bien forts sur vous." (F 309, No. 272, p. 32). Cf. also his long description of the relationship between Prince Kozlovskii and his father, from whose clutches he wants to free him, F 309, No. 1231, letter of 25.XII.1801.

27. We need only compare F 309, Nos. 840 (to Kaisarov) and 1231, 1238, 1237 (to parents).

28. See the curiously revealing entry in Turgenev's Diary, 8.IV.1802 (F 309, No. 272, p. 46): "My mother's character has a great deal of influence on mine, on my morality, and on my happiness. She confines my soul. How frequently did she not permit the development of some joyful, elevated feeling; how often she smothered that which already was there. If it had not been for her, my soul would have been freer, more joyful, more enterprising, and consequently better, nobler . . . ."

29. The expressions of a sense of incompleteness and futility pervade all the writings of Andrei Turgenev and his friends. His poetry is the best introduction for it. Most frequently in diary for the Vienna period, F 309, No. 1239. Andrei's youngest brother, Sergei explained more fully the social-political dimensions of this feeling of futility in his diary for 1814: "Denn ich zweifle sehr ob das Vaterland oder der Mensch Nummer eins ist. Das höchste Ziel des Menschen ist sein Glück, der Staat ist ein Mittel zur Erreichung desselben; und das Vaterland scheint nur eine Folge des Staates zu sein [. . . illegible] haben kein Staat und kein Vaterland. Und was bekümmert mich ein Staat wo ich kein Bürger bin, und ein Vaterland welchem ich nicht dienen kann ohne sich [illegible] manches gefallen zu lassen, was der Würde des Menschen zuwider ist . . ." (No. 16, pp. 75-76).

30. There are no elaborate descriptions of friendship in general terms in Andrei Turgenev's papers. The sentiment is reflected in his poetry. A more general definition is given by Zhukovskii in a letter to Alexander Turgenev, remembering the early circle of friends (quoted by Sukhomlinov, *Sbornik,* 65, No. 5 [1897], 1-2): "Our friendship, yours, mine, Merzliakov's, Kaisarov's, was based on imagination . . . . Brothers, let us be friends; we'll *do* much more. . . . Even now I am not very active, but at any rate I see the necessity of being higher, higher: for this I demand the help of my friends. Brothers, together, together let us go to everything that is good! It is not an enthusiast, childish and fiery, who speaks this, but cold reflection. . . . We must be inspired by one thing, supported by one thing! In a word, our life must be *cause commune.*" An elegiac expression of the same feeling was given by Andrei Turgenev in a letter to Zhukovskii (Fomin, *Russkii bibliofil,* January, 1912, p. 12 note): ". . . I would wish that on the festive days [of our Society]–1 or 7 April, the other I don't remember–each one of us would celebrate it, wherever he may be. This would be pleasant to many of us; others might do it out of consideration to the others. Imagine that one of us would be in Paris, the other in London, the third in Sweden, the fourth in Moscow, the fifth in St. Petersburg, and that on these days they are together in spirit. Each one will know that . . . every one of his spiritual friends is thinking of him. This thought is worth something." A. F. Merzliakov gave a comprehensive and accurate expression to this conception of friendship in several of his poems, *Stikhotvoreniia,* Iu. M. Lotman, ed. (Leningrad, 1958), pp. 198, 229.

31. The entire correspondence between Andrei Turgenev and Andrei Kaisarov illustrates this, F 309, Nos. 840, 50. The only clear reference to a homosexual attachment among members of this generation encountered by this writer is the case of

A. Kh. Vostokov. Cf. "Zametki A. Kh. Vostokova o ego zhizni," *Sbornik statei chitannykh v otdelenii russkogo iazyka i slovesnosti Akademii Nauk,* 70 (St. Petersburg, 1901).

32. F 309, No. 840, Letter 15.VI.1797(?); "I found on the road wonderful forget-me-nots, your favorite flower. I picked them and put them in my pocket, and as soon as I saw them I remembered you, and then later also S[andunova?]." Also No. 50 (5.V.1802).

33. Cf. the frequent reference to the lines from Schiller's *An die Freude:* "Wem der grosse Wurf gelungen,/ Eines Freundes Freund zu sein."

34. F 309, No. 840, 15.VI.1797(?); ibid. from Moscow, New Year's eve, 1800. Even more dramatic are the self-doubts of Kaisarov, who waits with trepidation for Andrei's letters as a sign that he still loves him, without him he is "an orphan" (F 309, No. 50).

35. The revealing confession of their friend I. F. Zhuravlev that he slept with a prostitute (or courtesan) in Vilno, F 309, No. 1213, 31.VII.1798.

36. F 309, No. 840, Letter to A. Kaisarov, 2.IX.1799. ("For example, I determined that you have a good heart, tender and kind, which makes those whom it loves happy, and that it loves me.")

37. F 309, No. 50, Letter of A. Kaisarov to Andrei Turgenev, 8.V.1802. No. 276, entry for 14.VIII.1799, p. 34.

38. For example, *Kabale und Liebe* and *Die Verschwörung von Fiesko.*

39. The practice of organizing societies for the pursuit of cultural and social goals (largely to make up for the inadequacies of educational, religious, and government institutions) became popular in the second half of the eighteenth century, particularly as a result of the efforts of the freemasons. A. Prokopovich-Antonskii sponsored the organization of a society for literary and cultural pursuits among the pupils under his care at the Noblemen's Pension of the University of Moscow. Of course, the Corps of Cadets had set a precedent for this kind of activity in a private school for children of the nobility. But Prokopovich-Antonskii's foundation had a much more purposeful moral and didactic orientation, consonant with the sentimental religiosity and philanthropy of the late eighteenth century. It helped give a new institutional framework to Russian cultural life, which conveniently replaced the traditional associations based on family, church, and class solidarities.

40. The works of Istrin, Lotman, and Rezanov are the best introduction to the history of the society. See also Iu. M. Lotman, "Stikhotvorenie Andreia Turgeneva 'K otechestvu' i ego rech' v 'Druzheskom literaturnom obshchestve'," *Literaturnoe nasledstvo,* 60, pt. 1 (Moscow, 1956), 323-38. The members were as follows: A. F. Merzliakov, A. I. Turgenev, M. S., A.S., and P. S. Kaisarov, V. A. Zhukovskii, Alexander I. Turgenev. S. E. Rodzianko and A. Ofrosimov joined the group later. The rules of the Society have been published by N. Tikhonravov, "Zakony Druzheskogo literaturnogo obshchestva," *Sbornik obshchestva liubitelei rossiiskoi slovesnosti na 1891 g.* (Moscow, 1891), pp. 1-14.

41. F 309, No. 618, "Rechi druzheskogo obshchestva 1801" (hereafter cited as "Rechi"). This is not a transcript but a copy (incomplete) of the speeches (probably from the final drafts submitted by the authors). Not all speeches have titles.

42. "Rechi," 19.I.1801, pp. 11-24.

43. Ibid., 27.II.1801; with stress on the closeness of friendship to love, a theme that he repeated in his speech, "On Passions," 12.IV.1801(?), 75-77. Also note the significant statement of Andrei Turgenev: "Even a criminal can fall in love. But to feel friendship, this only a virtuous heart can do." F 309, No. 271 (entry for 30.VII.1800, p. 63).

44. "Rechi," 15.III.1801(?), "O tom, chto esli by chelovek s samogo rozhdeniia ostavlen byl na neobitaemom ostrove; to mog li by on otlichat' v posleduiushchee vremia porok ot dobrodeteli?" pp. 60-63.

45. Ibid., 1.VI.1801, "O tom, chto mizantropov nespravedlivo pochitaiut bezchelovechnymi."

46. Ibid., "O tom, chto liudi po bol'shei chasti sami vinovniki svoikh neschastii i neudovol'stvii sluchaiushchikhsia v zhizni," pp. 115-18.

47. Ibid., 22.IV.1801, pp. 83-89, echoed by M. Kaisarov, 26.I.1801, "O tom, chto voobrazhenie dostavliaet nam bol'she udovol'stvii nezheli sushchestvennost'," pp. 31-35.

48. Ibid., 26-30, not dated. The most recent scholar on the subject, Iu. M. Lotman, has argued strongly that the speech was a direct allusion to the reign of Paul I (by contrast) on the basis of the hypothetical date of January 19 on which it may have been delivered. True or not, the point is of no essential consequence.

49. The language best known in the Turgenev circle was German. Andrei Turgenev refers to his readings of German literature from the earliest diary entries. (See also E. Bobrov, *Literatura i prosveshchenie v Rossii v XIX v. [Materialy issledovanniia i zametki]*, 2 [Kazan', 1902], p. 120 [letter of G. P. Kameneva, Nov. 26, 1800, relating visit with I. P. Turgenev].) He played the major role in introducing Schiller to the group, and his and his friends' writings are filled with references or quotations (often incorrect and not very varied) from Schiller. What M. Malia says about the appeal of Schiller for the generation of the 1830s could apply also to the Turgenev circle, perhaps even more so. It seems to us that Malia is underestimating the dynamic role of the early vogue for Schiller ("Schiller and the Early Russian Left," *Russian Thought and Politics,* H. McLean, M. E. Malia, and G. Fischer, eds., *Harvard Slavic Studies,* 4 [1957], pp. 169-200; cf. also Hans-Bernd Harder, Schiller in Russland–Materialien zu einer Wirkungsgeschichte (1789-1814). Frankfurter Beiträge zur Germanistik 4, Bad Homburg-Berlin-Zürich, 1969.

50. Zhukovskii, F 286, 2, No. 327.

51. F 309, No. 272, entry for 24.V.1802; No. 840, letter to Kaisarov, 27.III.1803.

52. "Rechi," 5.IV.1801(?), "O poezii i o zloupotreblenii onoi," pp. 71-74; 19.IV.1801, "O russkoi literature," pp. 78-82.

53. Note the parallelism to Schiller, although I could find no evidence of their being acquainted with his philosophic and aesthetic essays. For a recent study of Schiller which brings out very well those aspects of the poet's work that would appeal to Andrei Turgenev and his generation, see Emil Staiger, *Friedrich Schiller* (Zurich, 1967), especially the chapters, "Fremde des Lebens" and "Freiheit."

54. Andrei Turgenev noted, for instance, in his diary, 15.VIII.1797 (F 309, No. 276), p. 75: "Il n'y a plus aujourd'hui de Français, d'Allemands, d'Espagnols, d'Anglais même, quoiqu'on en dise, il n'y a que des Européens."

55. See Andrei Turgenev's draft of a speech on patriotism, *Literaturnoe nasledstvo*, 60, pt. 1 (1956), 334-36. It may be worth pointing out that in the language of the time, reference was to *otechestvo* (neuter, derived from *otets,* father) when speaking of the country Russia. The current term *rodina* (feminine) was used only with reference to the specific place or region of birth. The hunt for psychoanalytical interpreters is open!

56. *Arkhiv brat'ev Turgenevykh,* vyp. 2, p. 198 and *passim.*

57. F 309, No. 1238, letters of 8/20.VI.1802 (the play was *Das Mädchen von Marienburg*) and 29.VI.1802 (the name of Czech scholar is torn off): "I spoke to him as it behooves a Russian to speak about the Russians, praised to him our epic poems, mentioned Derzhavin and [illegible] poets, did not forget also Karamzin, Dmitriev and mentioned Izmailov, finally I promised to send him Russian tea and took my leave. . . ."

58. The most readily available introductions to this society are V. Orlov, *Russkie prosvetiteli 1790-1800kh godov* (Moscow, 1950), and V. Bazanov, *Uchenaia respublika* (Moscow-Leningrad, 1964).

59. See Lotman's biography of A. S. Kaisarov mentioned in note 1 above; also Iu. M. Lotman, "Pokhodnaia tipografiia shtaba Kutuzova i ee deiatel'nost'," in *1812 god–K stopiatidesiatiletiiu Otechestvennoi voiny* (Moscow, 1962), pp. 215-32, and

R. E. Al'tshuller and A. G. Tartakovskii, eds., *Listovki Otechestvennoi voiny 1812 goda, Sbornik dokumentov* (Moscow, 1962).

60. Edward J. Brown, *Stankevich and His Moscow Circle 1830-1840* (Stanford, 1966). Incidentally, the *kruzhok* is one form of "adolescent society" as we know it in the West today, and the two have a similar causal dynamics, i.e., the problem of identification with the father. See Kenneth Keniston, *The Uncommitted-Alienated Youth in American Society* (New York, 1960), and, more generally, the theoretical discussion of the need to take into account the particular historical and total social contexts in Erik H. Erikson, *Identity–Youth and Crisis* (New York, 1968).

61. See Veselovskii, *V. A. Zhukovskii,* p. 95; the vast amount of evidence in Istrin, *ZMNP,* n.s., 26 (March, 1910), pp. 1-36, and this confession of Alexander Turgenev: "I am becoming an empty man. The more I reflect on the fate of my brother, the more cause I find to envy him. He died at the very moment of life when we stop being enthusiastic, enjoying life, and when there approaches that emptiness which unavoidably must fill the second half of our life." (F 309, No. 1210, letter of 25(?).VI.1805 to Sergei A. Kaisarov). Still later, Kaisarov was to write to Sergei Turgenev, 8.VII.1810 (F 309, No. 386, p. 4): "Sometimes he [Andrei Turgenev] would lighten my ills by his affectionate kindness, but now I am completely alone . . . and it seems as if I am condemned to spend the whole life alone, far from everything that is dear to me and loving."

62. On Russia's "pedocracy" see the very suggestive, albeit overly critical, remarks of A. S. Izgoev, "Ob intelligentnoi molodezhi–Zametki ob ee byte i nastroeniiakh," *Vekhi, Sbornik statei o russkoi intelligentsii,* 3rd ed. (Moscow, 1909), pp. 97-124.

Voluntarism, Maximalism, and the Group for the Emancipation of Labor (1883-1892)

1. I. Deutscher, *Stalin: A Political Biography* (London, 1961), pp. 28-29 (first published 1949).

2. S. M. Schwarz, "Populism and Early Russian Marxism on Ways of Economic Development of Russia," in E. J. Simmons, ed., *Continuity and Change in Russian and Soviet Thought* (Cambridge, Mass., 1955), pp. 40-62; R. Pipes, "Russian Marxism and Its Populist Background," *Russian Review,* October, 1960, pp. 316-37.

3. *Russian Review,* October, 1960, p. 322.

4. In Simmons, ed., *Continuity and Change,* p. 53.

5. J. L. H. Keep, *The Rise of Social Democracy in Russia* (Oxford, 1963), pp. 22-26; S. H. Baron, *Plekhanov: the Father of Russian Marxism* (London, 1963), pp. 112-16.

6. F. Bystrykh, "Ob agrarnoi programme gruppy 'Osvobozhdenie Truda'," *Proletarskaia revoliutsiia,* No. 5 (88) (1929), pp. 60-94; V. Rakhmetov, "K voprosu o men'shevistskikh tendentsiiakh v gruppe 'Osvobozhdenie Truda'," ibid., No. 9 (80) (1928), pp. 26-56, 33.

7. V. Vaganian, *G. V. Plekhanov: opyt kharakteristiki sotsial'no-politicheskikh vozzrenii* (Moscow, 1924).

8. Keep, *The Rise of Social Democracy,* p. 23.

9. Baron, *Plekhanov,* p. 115.

10. V. I. Nevskii, "Gruppa 'Osvobozhdenie Truda' " in Nevskii, ed., *Istoriko-revoliutsionnyi sbornik,* 2 (Leningrad, 1924), p. 45.

11. "Polemicheskaia bespomoshchnost', ili serdit, da ne silen," in Plekhanov, *Sochineniia,* ed. D. Riazanov (Moscow, 1923-27), 19, p. 242; (hereafter referred to as *Sochineniia*).

12. N. Riazanov (pseudonym of D. V. Gol'dendakh), *Materialy dlia byrabotki programmy* (vyp. 2: *Proekt programmy "Iskry"*) (Geneva, 1903), pp. 4-12, 100-104.

13. "Programma sotsial-demokraticheskoi gruppy 'Osvobozhdenie Truda' " (1884), in *Sochineniia,* 2, p. 361.

14. "Proekt programmy russkikh sotsial-demokratov" (1884) in B. Nikolaevskii, "Programma pervogo v Rossii s.-d. kruzhka," *Byloe,* No. 13 (1918), p. 48. In a letter to Plekhanov and his comrades, the *Blagoevtsy* contrasted their own basically negative attitude to political assassination with that of the Group which, they wrote, "unswervingly declares its sympathy for the terrorist campaign against the government." (Ibid., p. 49.)

15. "Vtoroi proekt programmy russkikh sotsial-demokratov" (1885?), in *Sochineniia,* 2, pp. 402-403. The dating of this, the second draft program produced by the Group, has caused some difficulty. First published in 1888 and sent to the press in 1887, it was apparently written in 1885 in response to a request from the *Blagoevtsy.* See N. Sergievskii, "Kogda i po kakomu povodu byl napisan Plekhanovym Proekt programmy russkikh sotsial-demokratov," *Proletarskaia revoliutsiia,* No. 1 (72) (1928), pp. 85-101.

16. Plekhanov, *Sochineniia,* 2, pp. 360-61 (italics here and throughout are those of the source quoted).

17. Nikolaevskii, *Byloe,* No. 13 (1918), pp. 46-47.

18. "Ot izdatelei," *Rech' P. A. Alekseeva* (Geneva, 1889), p. v.

19. Plekhanov's introduction to *Pervoe maia: chetyre rechi rabochikh* (Geneva, 1892), p. viii.

20. Plekhanov's introduction to *Vademecum dlia redaktsii "Rabochego Dela"* (Geneva, 1900), p. xxxiii.

21. P. B. Aksel'rod, *K voprosu o sovremennykh zadachakh i taktike russkikh sotsial-demokratov* (Geneva, 1898), pp. 9, 15.

22. In Nikolaevskii, *Byloe,* No. 13 (1918), p. 51.

23. Plekhanov, *Sochineniia,* 2, pp. 360-61.

24. Ibid., p. 402.

25. Plekhanov, "O sotsial'noi demokratii v Rossii" (1893) in A. Tun, *Istoriia revoliutsionnykh dvizhenii v Rossii* (Geneva, 1903), p. 279.

26. Nikolaevskii, *Byloe,* No. 13 (1918), p. 46.

27. Plekhanov, *Sochineniia,* 2, p. 402.

28. In *Literatura sotsial'no-revoliutsionnoi partii "Narodnoi voli,"* p. 885.

29. "Mezhdunarodnyi rabochii sotsialisticheskii kongress v Parizhe, 14-15 iulia 1889," *Sotsial-Demokrat,* 1 (1890), p. 29.

30. "Pis'mo k tovarishcham" (1884) in N. Sergievskii, "Gruppa 'Osvobozhdenie Truda' i marksistskie kruzhki," *Istoriko-revoliutsionnyi sbornik,* 2, p. 181. For the identification of P. B. Aksel'rod as the author, see L. G. Deich, "V mesto bibliografii," *Gruppa Osvobozhdenie Truda,* 3 (Moscow, 1925), pp. 354-55.

31. P. B. Aksel'rod, *Zadachi rabochei intelligentsii v Rossii* (Geneva, 1893), p. 11 (first published 1889).

32. Aksel'rod, "Politicheskaia rol' S.-D. i posļednye vybory v germanskoi reikhstage," *Sotsial-Demokrat,* 4, pt. 2 (1892), p. 26 n.

33. Plekhanov, "Polemicheskaia bespomoshchnost'," *Sochineniia,* 19, p. 236.

34. Plekhanov, "Komediia oshibok (otvet i sovet A. Martynovu)," ibid., p. 54.

35. In Plekhanov, ed., *Vademecum,* pp. 38, 53.

36. A. Martynov (pseudonym of A. S. Pikker), "Kto likvidiroval ideinoe nasledstvo?" *Golos sotsial'demokrata,* No. 18 (1909), p. 9.

37. E.g. N. L. Sergievskii, *Partiia russkikh sotsial-demokratov i gruppa Blagoeva* (Moscow, 1929), pp. 113-15.

38. Plekhanov's introduction to *Vademecum,* p. xlii.

39. Marx-Engels, *Selected Works* (Moscow, 1962), 1, p. 46.

40. Plekhanov, "Polemicheskaia bespomoshchnost'," *Sochineniia,* 19, pp. 233-34, 240.
41. Ibid., p. 247.
42. "Otvet P. B. Aksel'roda na pis'mo I. P. Prisetskii" (December, 1881) in *Istoriko-revoliutsionnyi sbornik,* 2, p. 84; "Pis'mo k tovarishcham," ibid., p. 176.
43. Plekhanov, "Sovremennye zadachi russkikh rabochikh" (1885), *Sochineniia,* 2, p. 372.
44. N. Riazanov, *Materialy,* p. 237.
45. *Arkhiv K. Marksa i F. Engel'sa,* ed. D. Riazanov (Moscow, 1924), 1, p. 269.
46. Plekhanov, *Sochineniia,* 2, p. 86.
47. V. Zasulich's introduction to F. Engel's, *Razvitie nauchnogo sotsializma* (Geneva, 1884), p. v.
48. "Nashi raznoglasiia" (1884), in *Sochineniia G. V. Plekhanova* (Geneva, 1905), pp. 511-12.
49. The introduction by Marx and Engels to the Russian edition (1882) of the *Communist Manifesto* quoted by Plekhanov in "Sotsializm i politicheskaia bor'ba," *Sochineniia,* 2, p. 47.
50. Ibid.
51. Plekhanov, "Sotsializm i politicheskaia bor'ba," *Sochineniia,* 2, p. 86.
52. Marx-Engels, *Selected Works,* 1, p. 65.
53. "Nashi raznoglasiia," *Sochineniia G. V. Plekhanova,* p. 512.
54. *Sochineniia,* 2, p. 86.
55. V. Zasulich's introduction to Engel's, *Razvitie,* pp. iii-iv.
56. Ibid., p. v.
57. "Sotsializm i politicheskaia bor'ba," *Sochineniia,* 2, p. 86.
58. Plekhanov, *Sochineniia,* 2, pp. 361-62.
59. "Sotsializm i politicheskaia bor'ba," *Sochineniia,* 2, p. 77.
60. L. Tikhomirov, "Chego nam zhdat' ot revoliutsii?" *Vestnik Narodnoi voli,* No. 2 (1884), p. 237.
61. "Nashi raznoglasiia," *Sochineniia G. V. Plekhanova,* p. 428.
62. Plekhanov, "Polemicheskaia bespomoshchnost'," *Sochineniia,* 19, pp. 233-34.
63. "Nashi raznoglasiia," *Sochineniia G. V. Plekhanova,* pp. 475, 482-83.
64. Ibid., p. 475.
65. V. Zasulich's introduction to F. Engel's, *Razvitie,* pp. v, vii.
66. "Nashi raznoglasiia," *Sochineniia G. V. Plekhanova,* pp. 524-25. Lenin, of course, advanced similar views in 1902 during the debate among the editors of *Iskra* about the draft Party Program.
67. V. Zasulich, "Revoliutsionery iz burzhuaznoi sredy," *Sotsial-Demokrat,* 1, pp. 68, 72.
68. "Nashi raznoglasiia," *Sochineniia G. V. Plekhanova,* p. 487.
69. E.g. Plekhanov, "Kak dobivat'sia konstitutsii" (1890), *Sochineniia,* 3, pp. 21-23.
70. Plekhanov, *O zadachakh sotsialistov v bor'be s golodom v Rossii* (Geneva, 1892), pp. 76-77, 87-88.
71. Ibid., p. 86.
72. F. Bystrykh, "Ob agrarnoi programme gruppy 'Osvobozhdenie Truda'," *Proletarskaia revoliutsiia,* No. 5 (88) (1929), p. 82.
73. Marx-Engels, *Selected Works,* 1, p. 112.
74. Plekhanov, *Sochineniia,* 2, pp. 402-403.
75. Quoted in Vaganian, *G. V. Plekhanov,* p. 377.
76. *Perepiska G. V. Plekhanova i P. B. Aksel'roda,* eds., P. A. Berlin, V. Voitinskii, and B. I. Nikolaevskii (Moscow, 1925), 1, p. 44.
77. N. Riazanov, *Materialy,* pp. 288, 295.
78. Lenin, "Chto takoe 'druz'ia naroda' " (1894), *Polnoe sobranie sochinenii,* 1 (Moscow, 1960), p. 299.

Russian and Jewish Social Democracy

1. General accounts of the Jewish movement, although not very satisfactory for our purposes, may be found in V. Akimov, *Materialy dlia kharakteristiki razvitiia rossiiskoi sotsial-demokraticheskoi rabochei partii* (Geneva, 1905), N. A. Bukhbinder, *Istoriia evreiskogo rabochego dvizheniia v Rossii* (Leningrad, 1925), and *Materialy k istorii evreiskago rabochego dvizheniia* (St. Petersburg, 1906). The data used in this article are primarily from memoir accounts, many of which are included in the important collection, *Revoliutionnoe dvizhenie sredi evreev* (Moscow, 1930), edited by S. Dimanshtein. Hereafter this work will be referred to simply as Dimanshtein. By far the most informative full-length recollections are those of Iulii Martov, *Zapiski sotsial-demokrata* (Berlin, 1923) and P. A. Garvi, *Vospominaniia sotsial-demokrata* (New York, 1946).

2. The best account of the origins of the Vilna Social Democratic group is that of Kopel'zon in Dimanshtein, pp. 65-80.

3. Kopel'zon reports the entreaties of the P.P.S. representative, Joseph Pilsudski (later the founder of the Polish republic), to adopt Polish as their operating tongue and states that he "threatened us with pogroms against Jews by the Polish masses" if the Russifying policy were not abandoned. (Ibid., pp. 72-73.)

4. The best treatment of the cultural and social development of Russian Jews is still S. M. Dubnow's *History of the Jews in Russia and Poland,* 3 vols. (Philadelphia, 1916-20). A more recent, but less detailed work is Salo Baron, *The Russian Jew under Tsars and Soviets* (New York, 1964). Understandably such treatments focus primarily on the Jewish traditions rather than on the phenomenon of assimilationism. See Dubnow, 2, pp. 209-11, 221, and *passim.*

5. Dimanshtein, p. 71.

6. See the memoir fragment by Sponti in the collection S. I. Mitskevich, ed., *Na zare rabochego dvizheniia v Moskve* (Moscow, 1932), pp. 41-47.

7. See Martov, *Zapiski,* pp. 221-22.

8. *Ob agitatsii* (Geneva, 1897), pp. 9, 16.

9. Martov states this unequivocally in *Zapiski,* p. 233. The best accounts of the introduction of agitation in Vilna are ibid., pp. 224-54, and S. N. Gozhanskii in Dimanshtein, pp. 81-95.

10. See S. I. Mitskevich, *Revoliutsionnaia Moskva* (Moscow, 1940), pp. 147-48.

11. Garvi, *Vospominaniia,* p. 76.

12. See Martov, *Zapiski,* pp. 252-53.

13. Martov's long list of Vilna products who were later active in the Russian Social Democratic movement (pp. 196-212, 250-54) is supplemented by another participant of the following period, V. Tsoglin (David Kats) in Dimanshtein, p. 135.

14. See accounts of Ginzburg and Vilenskii in Dimanshtein, pp. 96 and 131 ff., and more detailed versions in the collection, M. A. Rubach, ed. *Istoriia ekaterinoslavskoi sotsial-demokraticheskoi organizatsii (1889-1903)* (Ekaterinoslav, 1923), pp. 78-92, 141-168 (cited hereafter as Rubach).

15. On Ioffe's career, see the police report reprinted in "Delo kharkovskogo rabochego soiuza," *Letopis' revoliutsii,* No. 4 (1923), pp. 206-207, and Garvi, *Vospominaniia,* pp. 101-103.

16. Rubach, p. 150.

17. A. Notkin's recollections in V. I. Nevskii, ed. *K dvadtsatipiatiletiiu pervogo s"ezda partii (1898-1923)* (Moscow, 1923), p. 161.

18. Grigorii Aronson, *Revoliutsionnaia iunost': Vospominaniia 1903-1917,* Inter-University Project on the History of the Menshevik Movement (New York, 1961), p. 11.

19. See Garvi, *Vospominaniia,* pp. 3-18.

20. For two years he participated in underground Menshevik committees in Russia,

finally becoming one of the chief organizers of the Moscow uprising of December, 1905. Thereafter, he was a prominent "liquidator" and trade union leader and an internationalist during the war. After February, 1917, he adhered to the majority line in the Menshevik Party and was active in emigre Menshevik circles from 1923 until his death in 1946.

21. In surveying the composition of the Ekaterinoslav Committee from 1896 to 1903, one finds that the Jewish contingent always constituted at least half, and at times virtually the entire organization. Jewish Social Democrats were even more in evidence in the subordinate activities, handling the manifold practical tasks such as propaganda, communications, transport, printing leaflets, and maintaining secret quarters. The materials in Rubach make possible such a survey for Ekaterinoslav from the early 1890s to 1903. The less complete sources for Kiev, Rostov, Kremenchug, and Kharkov give the same impression.

22. Cited by Tsoglin-Kats in Dimanshtein, pp. 143-44.

23. Ibid., p. 444.

24. See Martov, *Zapiski,* pp. 244-47 and L. I. Gol'dman, *Organizatsiia i tipografiia "Iskry" v Rossii* (Moscow, 1928), pp. 4-5. Gol'dman was one of Martov's model pupils who was denied entrance to Russian schools and was forced to learn the printer's trade (his brother, "Gorev," gained entrance to the university). Criticizing Martov for his concessions to "nationalism," Gol'dman later operated a secret press for *Iskra* in Kishinev (1901-1902); another brother Mikhail (Liber) by 1903 was one of the leaders of the Bund and defended the Jews' rights to "national autonomy" at the Second Congress where his chief adversary was Martov. To Martov's embarrassment his speech of 1895 was printed by emigre Bundists in 1900 to justify their turn toward national particularism *(Povorotnyi punkt v evreiskom rabochem dvizhenii [Geneva, 1900]).*

25. On the founding of the Bund and its role in the First Congress of the RSDRP see Kremer, "Obosnovanie Bunda," *Proletarskaia revoliutsiia,* No. 2 (1922), pp. 50-56, and the article "Pervyi s"ezd Bunda," by Tsoglin-Kats in Dimanshtein, pp. 131-48.

26. See Dimanshtein, p. 137 and *passim.*

27. See the decisions of the Congress in Dimanshtein, pp. 157-58. Tsoglin-Kats was a delegate at the First Congress and discusses it in illuminating detail. Other accounts of the First Congress are V. Akimov, "Pervyi S"ezd," *Minuvshie gody,* No. 2 (1908), pp. 128-68 and B. L. Eidel'man, "K istorii vozniknoveniia r.s.-d.r.p.," *Proletarskaia revoliutsiia,* No. 1 (1921), pp. 26-66.

28. See Dimanshtein, p. 147.

29. See Ginzburg's account in Rubach, pp. 155-60.

30. See "K istorii Belostokskoi konferentsii 1902 g.," *Proletarskaia revoliutsiia,* No. 101 (June, 1930), pp. 132-48. Here a coded letter of Dan to *Iskra* headquarters reporting on the conference is reproduced.

31. Letter of June 22, 1903 in V. I. Lenin, *Sochineniia,* 3rd ed. (Moscow, 1936), 28, p. 140.

32. P. N. Lepeshinskii, *Na povorote (ot kontsa 80-kh godov k 1905 g.)* (Leningrad, 1925), p. 128.

33. The pertinent excerpts from *Iskra* from the Bund's *Posledniia Izvestiia* are reprinted in *Vtoroi S"ezd R.S.-D.R.P.–Protokoli* (Moscow, 1959), pp. 726-29.

Marxist Revolutionaries and The Dilemma of Power

1. Boris Nicolaievsky and Otto Maenchen-Helfen, *Karl Marx, Man and Fighter* (London, 1936), especially Chs. 10-15.

2. John Plamenatz, *German Marxism and Russian Communism* (London, 1954), p. 211; E. H. Carr, *The Bolshevik Revolution 1917-1923,* 1 (London, 1950), p. 41.

3. Wilheim Weitling to Moses Hess, March 31, 1846, in Edmund Silberner, ed., *Moses Hess, Briefwechsel* (The Hague, 1959), p. 151.

4. [Pavel Annenkov], "Eine russische Stimme über Karl Marx," *Neue Zeit*, Erster Jahrgang (Stuttgart, 1883), pp. 238-39; also see Max Nettlau, "Londoner deutsche Kommunistische Diskussionen, 1845," in Carl Gruenberg, ed., *Archiv fuer die Geschichte des Sozialismus und der Arbeiterbewegung*, 10 (Leipzig, 1922), pp. 368-70, 380, 382-83.

5. Moses Hess, *Sozialistische Aufsätze 1841-1847, Herausgegeben von Theodor Zlocisti* (Berlin, 1921), pp. 229-30; Edmund Silberner, *Moses Hess, Geschichte seines Lebens* (Leiden, 1966), pp. 278-80.

6. Karl Marx and Friedrich Engels, *Werke*, 4 (Berlin, 1959), p. 314.

7. Ibid., pp. 338-39.

8. Ibid., p. 339.

9. Ibid., p. 392.

10. See also Ibid., pp. 49, 51.

11. Ibid., pp. 502-503.

12. Nicolaievsky and Maenchen-Helfen, p. 171.

13. See *Werke*, 5, pp. 6-7, 22-24.

14. Ibid., pp. 96-97, 249, 282-83.

15. Ibid., p. 456; 6, p. 152.

16. Ibid., 6, p. 109.

17. Ibid., 5, p. 457.

18. Ibid., 6, pp. 124, 206, 217, 504-506.

19. Ibid., pp. 233, 257.

20. Ibid., p. 528.

21. Ibid., pp. 584, 588.

22. Ibid., 7, pp. 245-500.

23. Ibid., pp. 253-54.

24. Whatever claims Engels and later "orthodox" Marxists may have made for "scientific socialism" by analogy with and in imitation of the exact sciences, Marx himself provided a more modest definition of his scientific socialism in his notes on Bakunin's *Staatlichkeit und Anarchie*. He insisted he had used the term "only by contrast with Utopian socialism which wants to foist new fantasies on the people instead of confining its science *[Wissenschaft]* to the cognition of the social movement made by the people itself" (*Werke*, 18, pp. 635-36); in other words, Marx used "scientific" in the broad, inclusive German sense of the word *Wissenschaft*, i.e., rigorous *study* of objective conditions.

25. *Werke*, 7, pp. 440, 514; 8, pp. 590-91.

26. Ibid., 8, p. 598.

27. Ibid.

28. Ibid., pp. 598-99.

29. Ibid., 7, p. 563.

30. Ibid., 8, p. 599.

31. Ibid., p. 600.

32. Ibid., p. 461.

33. Ibid., p. 600.

34. Ibid., 7, pp. 400-401.

35. Marx and Engels, *Selected Correspondence* (Moscow, 1965), pp. 468-72.

36. Ibid., pp. 471-72.

37. Ibid., p. 472.

38. *Werke*, 18, pp. 556-57.

39. Ibid., p. 557.

40. Ibid., p. 634.
41. Ibid., pp. 476-77.
42. Ibid., pp. 492-93.
43. Ibid., 36, pp. 54-55.
44. Ibid., 8, pp. 589-90.
45. The relevant documents in English are available in Paul W. Blackstock and Bert F. Hoselitz, eds., *Karl Marx and Friedrich Engels: The Russian Menace to Europe* (London, 1953), pp. 203-41, 273-84.
46. Ibid., p. 284.
47. *Werke,* 18, pp. 633-34.
48. Knowing how anxious Plekhanov was for Engels to come out against populist maximalism, Vera Zasulich is said to have played a practical joke on Plekhanov, breaking the news to him that a letter from Engels to that effect had arrived. Interview with Lydia O. Tsederbaum-Dan, New York, 1962.
49. G. V. Plekhanov, *Izbrannye filosofskie proizvedeniia,* 1 (Moscow, 1956), pp. 100, 101, 105, 106-107, 110.
50. Ibid., pp. 100, 107.
51. Ibid., p. 127.
52. Ibid., pp. 164, 216, 345-46.
53. Ibid., p. 353.
54. Ibid., p. 375; both points, the terrorist struggle and the seizure of power, were omitted in the second draft of 1887.
55. Ibid., p. 421; while the wording of the passage is somewhat different in the first draft of the speech (see ibid., p. 419), the emphasis is the same.
56. *Pervyi s"ezd RSDRP, Dokumenty i materialy* (Moscow, 1958), p. 80.
57. *Leninskii sbornik,* 2 (Moscow-Leningrad, 1924), pp. 18-19, 60-61, 64.
58. Ibid., pp. 85-87.
59. P. Aksel'rod, "Ob"edinenie rossiiskoi sotsialdemokratii i eë zadachi," *Iskra,* No. 55, December 15, 1903; No. 57, January 15, 1904.
60. N. Trotskii, *Nashi politicheskie zadachi* (Geneva, 1904), pp. 101-107.
61. Ibid., p. 107.
62. "Otvet na pis'mo Ts. O. predstavitelei Ufimskogo, Sredne-Ural'skogo i Permskogo komitetov," supplement to *Iskra,* No. 63, April 1, 1904. Boris Nicolaevsky identified the author of the Ural Manifesto as M. A. Trilisser who later became a leading Chekist and had ample opportunity to practice what he had preached.
63. Quoted in A. Martynov, *Dve diktatury* (Geneva, 1905), p. 4, and dated December, 1903.
64. Martynov, *Dve diktatury,* p. 4; Trotskii, *Nashi politicheskie zadachi,* p. 106.
65. Martynov, Trotskii, and Plekhanov used it for that purpose; Plekhanov in his critique of the Ural Manifesto ("K voprosu o zakhvate vlasti," *Iskra,* No. 96, April 5, 1905) took issue with the "dictatorial" propensities of the Ural Bolsheviks but ignored entirely their commitment to the seizure of power.
66. *Dve diktatury* was written at the end of 1904 and published early in 1905; it was republished in a revised edition in 1917.
67. Martynov, *Dve diktatury,* pp. 10-11.
68. Ibid., pp. 53-57.
69. Martynov, "Revoliutsionnye perspektivy," *Iskra,* No. 90, March 3, 1905; No. 95, March 31, 1905; L. Martov, "Na ocheredi. Rabochaia partiia i 'zakhvat vlasti' kak nasha blizhaishaia zadacha," *Iskra,* No. 93, March 17, 1905; Plekhanov, "K voprosu o zakhvate vlasti (Nebol'shaia istoricheskaia spravka)," *Iskra,* No. 96, April 5, 1905; Martynov, "V bor'be s marksistskoi sovest'iu," *Iskra,* No. 102, June 15, 1905; No. 103, June 21, 1905.
70. Martov, *Iskra,* No. 93, March 17, 1905.
71. Martynov, *Iskra,* No. 95, March 31, 1905.

72. Martov, *Iskra,* No. 93, March 17, 1905.

73. Ibid.; Martynov, *Iskra,* No. 95, March 31, 1905.

74. Plekhanov, "K voprosu o zakhvate vlasti," *Iskra,* No. 96, April 5, 1905. Plekhanov paraphrased Engels' letter thus: "And *after victory* it would be extremely dangerous ('Questo é il pericolo piú grande')," says Engels, "if socialists entered the government." Yet the burden and emphasis of Engels' warning referred specifically (certainly in the Italian version available to Plekhanov published in *Critica Sociale,* February 1, 1894) to the acceptance of *"minority"* status in the "new government" à la Louis Blanc.

75. Martynov, "V bor'be s marksistskoi sovest'iu," *Iskra,* No. 102, June 15, 1905.

76. See *Pervaia obshcherusskaia konferentsiia partiinykh rabotnikov, Iskra,* No. 100, May 15, 1905, appendix, pp. 23-24.

77. Plekhanov, "K voprosu o zakhvate vlasti," *Iskra,* No. 96, April 5, 1905.

78. See L. M.[artov], "Na ocheredi. 'Boikot' Dumy i revoliutsionnoe samoupravlenie naroda," *Iskra,* No. 109, August 29, 1905.

79. See Martov, "Chernomorskoe vosstanie," *Iskra,* No. 104, July 1, 1905; also his "Voennaia sila na sluzhbe revoliutsii," *Sotsial'demokrat,* No. 8, June 24, 1905.

80. *Pervaia obshcherusskaia konferentsiia partiinykh rabotnikov,* p. 21.

81. See J. L. H. Keep, *The Rise of Social Democracy in Russia* (Oxford, 1963), pp. 214-15.

82. See Martov, *Iskra,* No. 109, August 29, 1905, and ibid., No. 104, July 1, 1905.

83. See Martov, "Das russische Proletariat und die Duma," *Arbeiter Zeitung* (Vienna) No. 233, August 24, 1905, for a more detailed discussion of the Mensheviks' scheme of dual parliament; also Israel Getzler, *Martov, A Political Biography of a Russian Social Democrat* (Melbourne and Cambridge, 1967), pp. 107-109.

84. *Pervaia obshcherusskaia konferentsiia partiinykh rabotnikov,* p. 21.

85. Martov to Aksel'rod, end of October, 1905, *Pis'ma P. B. Aksel'roda i Iu. O. Martova 1901-1916* (Berlin, 1924), p. 146; also see D. Sverchkov, *Na zare revoliutsii* (Moscow, 1922), p. 92; Oskar Anweiler, *Die Rätebewegung in Russland 1905-1921* (Leiden, 1958), p. 85.

86. N. Trotskii, *Do deviatogo ianvaria, s predisloviem Parvusa* (Geneva, 1905), pp. 11-12.

87. Ibid.

88. N. Trotskii, *Nasha revoliutsiia* (St. Petersburg, 1906), pp. 244-45.

89. T.[rotskii], "Politicheskie pis'ma," *Iskra,* No. 93, March 17, 1905, reprinted in L. Trotskii, *Sochineniia,* 2, pt. 1 (Moscow-Leningrad, 1925), p. 236.

90. N. Trotskii, "Sotsialdemokratiia i revoliutsiia," *Nachalo,* No. 10, November 8/25, 1905.

91. Ibid.

92. Isaac Deutscher, *The Prophet Armed, Trotsky 1879-1921* (London, 1954), p. 159.

93. Lenin, *Polnoe sobranie sochinenii,* 10 (Moscow, 1960), pp. 12-13.

94. Ibid., p. 18.

95. Ibid.

96. Ibid., 11, p. 16.

97. Quoted in Martynov, *Iskra,* No. 95, March 31, 1905.

98. See Trotskii, *Nasha revoliutsiia,* pp. 245-46; Deutscher, *The Prophet Armed, Trotsky 1879-1921* (London, 1954), p. 154; Lenin, *Polnoe sobranie sochinenii,* 10, pp. 8, 130, 134.

99. Franz Mehring, "Nepreryvnaia revoliutsiia," *Nachalo,* No. 10, November 25, 1905.

100. See Kautsky's letter to M. N. Lyadov, published in *Iskra,* No. 66, May 15, 1904, under the heading "Kautskii o nashikh partiinykh raznoglasiiakh."

101. For the text of the questionnaire, see Lenin, *Sochineniia* (Moscow, 1935),

p. 494. Kautsky's reply is in his "Triebkräfte und Aussichten der russischen Revolution," *Neue Zeit,* Jahrgang 1906/7, 1 Band, pp. 331-33.

102. *Neue Zeit,* Jahrgang 1906/7, 1 Band, pp. 331-33. Martov's critique of Kautsky's views, "K. Kautskii i russkaia revoliutsiia," *Otkliki,* 11 (1907), pp. 3-24, adds little to the 1905 debate.

103. "Mneniia zapadno-evropeiskikh sotsialistov o sovremennom obshchestvennom dvizhenii v Rossii," *Sovremennaia zhizn',* November, 1906, pp. 206-25.

104. Lenin, *Polnoe sobranie sochinenii,* 10, pp. 8, 238-39.

105. L. Trotskii, *Sochineniia,* 3, pt. 1 (Moscow, 1925), p. 108; also see ibid., p. 251.

106. Tsereteli's speech of May 7, 1917 at the All-Russian Conference of the RSDRP in Petrograd is quoted in full in V. L. L'vov-Rogachevskii, *Sotsialisty o tekushchem momente; Materialy velikoi revoliutsii 1917 g.* (Moscow, 1917), pp. 197-200.

107. Ibid., pp. 198-99.

108. Ibid., p. 199.

109. See Martov's speech at the "Unification Congress" of the Menshevik party in August 1917, *Novaia zhizn',* No. 107, August 22, 1917.

110. See Lenin to A. M. Kollontai, March 17, 1917, and Lenin to A. V. Lunacharskii, March 25, 1917, Lenin, *Polnoe sobranie sochinenii,* 49, pp. 402, 411.

111. Viktor Chernov, *Rozhdenie revoliutsionnoi Rossii* (Paris-Prague-New York, 1934), p. 237.

The All-Russian Railroad Union

1. J. L. H. Keep, *The Rise of Social Democracy in Russia* (Oxford, 1963), p. 218.

2. P. A. Garvi, *Vospominaniia sotsial demokrata* (New York, 1946), pp. 555-56.

3. Kommunisticheskaia akademiia, *Pervaia russkaia revoliutsiia: Ukazatel' literatury* (Moscow, 1930).

4. A. M. Pankratova, ed., *Revoliutsiia 1905-1907 gg. v Rossii: Dokumenty i materialy* (Moscow, 1955–). Two volumes deal with the October general strike: L. M. Ivanov, ed., *Vserossiiskaia politicheskaia stachka v oktiabre 1905 goda* (1955).

5. A brief summary of Soviet writings on the 1905 Revolution appears in I. F. Ugarov and N. N. Iakovlev, "Pervaia russkaia revoliutsiia 1905-1907 gg. v sovetskoi istoriografii" in M. B. Nechkina et al., eds., *Ocherki istorii istoricheskoi nauki v SSSR* (Moscow, 1966), 4, pp. 411-27. More prominent among the recent works pertinent to this paper are the following: F. D. Kretov et al., eds., *Bol'sheviki vo glave pervoi russkoi revoliutsii 1905-1907 gg.* (Moscow, 1956); G. D. Kostomarov, ed., *1905 v Moskve* (Moscow, 1955); A. M. Pankratova and G. D. Kostomarov, eds., *Ocherki istorii SSSR: Pervaia russkaia burzhuazno-demokraticheskaia revoliutsiia 1905-1907 gg.* (Moscow, 1955); I. V. Spiridonov, *Vserossiiskaia politicheskaia stachka v oktiabre 1905 g.* (Moscow, 1955); V. Kirillov, *Bol'sheviki vo glave massovykh politicheskikh stachek v period pod"ema revoliutsii 1905-1907 gg.* (Moscow, 1961); A. V. Piaskovskii, *Revoliutsiia 1905-1907 gg. v Rossii* (Moscow, 1966); L. K. Erman, *Intelligentsiia v pervoi russkoi revoliutsii* (Moscow, 1966).

6. It should be noted that at an earlier date some Soviet historians considered the October days to be the high point of the 1905 Revolution; contemporary Soviet interpretations, however, view the Moscow December uprising as its peak. See brief discussion in Ugarov and Iakovlev, pp. 415-18.

7. The figures on railroad mileage are taken primarily from P. I. Liashchenko, *Istoriia narodnogo khoziaistva SSSR,* 4th ed. (Moscow, 1956), 2, pp. 120-21, 130-31, 152, 412-13; also from "S"ezd predstavitelei promyshlennosti i torgovli, dekabr', 1906 g.," *Kratkii otchet o rabotakh proizvedennykh Sovetom s"ezdov po zheleznodorozhnomu voprosu* (St. Petersburg, 1907), pp. 17-18, 20-23; see also J. N. Westwood, *A History of Russian Railways* (London, 1964), p. 143 and Appendix 2, p. 304; Appendix 7, pp. 308-309.

8. This figure is from *Statisticheskii sbornik Ministerstva putei soobshcheniia,* No. 89, table xii, p. 11, cited in I. M. Pushkareva, "Zarabotnaia plata zheleznodorozhnikov nakanune revoliutsii 1905-1907 gg.," *Istoriia SSSR,* No. 3 (July-August, 1957), p. 159; see also A. G. Rashin, "O chislennosti i territorial'nom razmeshchenii rabochikh v period kapitalizma," *Istoricheskie zapiski,* 46 (1954), pp. 129-32.

9. On the question of wages of railwaymen see M. B. [M. Bogdanov], *Ocherki po istorii zheleznodorozhnykh zabastovok v Rossii* (Moscow, 1907), pp. 5-6; Pushkareva, *Istoriia SSSR,* No. 3 (1957), pp. 160-164, 168; K. A. Pazhitnov, *Polozhenie rabochego klassa v Rossii,* 2nd ed. (Leningrad, 1925), 3, pp. 10, 47, 52; *Kratkii otchet,* p. 50; also see S. G. Strumilin, *Izbrannye proizvedeniia* (Moscow, 1964), 3, pp. 318 ff. In addition to wages permanent employees were covered by pension funds. Their operation is discussed by V. V. Sviatlovskii, *Professional'noe dvizhenie v Rossii* (St. Petersburg, 1907), pp. 42-47. Inadequacy of the pension plans is summarized by A. D. Pokotilov, Chairman of the Railroad Pension Congress, in *Novoe vremia,* September 23, 1905, p. 4.

10. A. El'nitskii, *Istoriia rabochego dvizheniia v Rossii* (Kremenchug, 1924), 2, p. 7.

11. L. Martov, "Razvitie promyshlennosti i rabochee dvizhenie s 1893 do 1903 g.," *Istoriia Rossii v XIX veke* (St. Petersburg, 1907-1911), 8, pp. 125-26.

12. V. N. Pereverzev, "Pervyi vserossiiskii zheleznodorozhnyi soiuz 1905 goda," *Byloe,* No. 4 (32) (1925), pp. 38-39. See also N. Rostov, "Zheleznodorozhniki v pervoi revoliutsii," in *Proletariat v revoliutsii 1905-1907 gg.* (Moscow, 1930), pp. 131 ff.

13. M. B., *Ocherki,* pp. 19-20; also Pereverzev, *Byloe,* No. 4 (32) (1925), p. 39.

14. Text of regulations is in N. Trusova et al., eds., *Revoliutsionnoe dvizhenie v Rossii vesnoi i letom 1905 goda: aprel'-sentiabr'* (Moscow, 1957), 1, pp. 866-69, note 25; also p. 871, note 47, from the series A. M. Pankratova, ed., *Revoliutsiia 1905-1907 gg. v Rossii: Dokumenty i materialy.*

15. Ibid., p. 874, note 68; enacted as law on December 14, 1905. *Polnoe sobranie zakonov Rossiiskoi imperii,* sobranie 3-e, Vol. 25, 1905, Otdel 1, No. 27043 (St. Petersburg, 1908), pp. 887-89.

16. M. B., *Ocherki,* pp. 21-22.

17. Pereverzev, *Byloe,* No. 4 (32) (1925), p. 39.

18. M. B., *Ocherki,* p. 25; Pereverzev, *Byloe,* No. 4 (32) (1925), p. 40; also V. Romanov, "Dvizhenie sredi sluzhashchikh i rabochikh russkikh zheleznykh dorog v 1905 g.," *Obrazovanie,* No. 11 (1906), p. 26.

19. See D. Kol'tsov, "Rabochie v 1905-1907 gg.," in *Obshchestvennoe dvizhenie v Rossii v nachale XX-go veka,* L. Martov et al., eds. (St. Petersburg, 1909), 2, pt. 1, p. 230.

20. S. I. Mitskevich, *Revoliutsionnaia Moskva* (Moscow, 1940), pp. 357-63; see also Pereverzev, *Byloe,* No. 4 (32) (1925), pp. 40-41.

21. Pereverzev, *Byloe,* No. 4 (32) (1925), pp. 42, 45; Romanov, *Obrazovanie,* No. 11 (1906), pp. 29-30.

22. For an enumeration of the railroads attending this first congress see Romanov, *Obrazovanie,* No. 11 (1906), p. 28, and No. 6 (1907), p. 23, n. 2.

23. The text of the program is in Pereverzev, *Byloe,* No. 4 (32) (1925), p. 42; see also Romanov, *Obrazovanie,* No. 11 (1906), pp. 32-34; M. B., *Ocherki,* pp. 25-28.

24. A prominent Bolshevik, A. Shlikhter, was one of the Social Democratic representatives, and he seems to have been their principal voice. He chaired some of the meetings and played an important role in the proceedings. Since the leadership of the union showed "liberal bourgeois" tendencies, both factions often acted in common and issued joint declarations. For example, in *Iskra,* No. 109 (1905), the Mensheviks express their solidarity with Bolshevik views on the Railroad Union and praise the speech of the Bolshevik representative at the congress.

25. See Garvi, pp. 519 ff; a brief summary of the activity of the Social Democrats in Moscow is in David Lane, *The Roots of Russian Communism* (Assen, 1968), pp. 94-132.

26. "Chto delat'?" in V. I. Lenin, *Polnoe sobranie sochinenii,* 5th ed., 6, pp. 39-40.

27. "Professional'noe dvizhenie i sotsial-demokratiia," *Proletarii,* No. 8 (July 4/17, 1905).

28. V. Vorovskii, "Pervye shagi professional'nogo dvizheniia," *Proletarii,* No. 11 (July 27-August 9, 1905); also see Erman, *Intelligentsiia v pervoi russkoi revoliutsii,* pp. 89-90.

29. M. Borisov, "O professional'nom dvizhenii i zadachakh sotsial-demokratii," *Proletarii,* No. 21 (October 4/17, 1905).

30. For discussions of the difference in attitudes between Mensheviks and Bolsheviks, see Keep, pp. 188-91; E. Mil'shtein, "Politicheskie techeniia v rossiiskom profdvizhenii 1905-1907 gg.," in *Proletariat v revoliutsii 1905 g.,* pp. 443-70; and S. M. Shvarts [Schwarz], *Bol'shevizm i men'shevizm v ikh otnosheniiakh k massovomu rabochemu dvizheniiu* (Inter-University Project on the History of the Menshevik Movement), published in an English version as *The Russian Revolution of 1905: The Workers' Movement and the Formation of Bolshevism* (Chicago, 1967).

31. Romanov, *Obrazovanie,* No. 11 (1906), p. 29.

32. Ibid., p. 31; Romanov says that five members were elected, and then soon after, five more were co-opted. By the Second Congress, the Central Bureau consisted of twenty persons. Pereverzev (*Byloe,* No. 4 [32] [1925], p. 43) says that seven were elected; however, in an earlier account, *Zheleznodorozhniki v 1905 g.* (Moscow, [early 1920's]), p. 9, he also stated that the elected number was five. See also Rostov, *Proletariat,* pp. 136-37.

33. Pereverzev, *Byloe,* No. 4 (32) (1925), p. 43.

34. Mitskevich, p. 391. Rostov (*Proletariat,* p. 157) calls Pereverzev a Socialist Revolutionary.

35. M. I. Vasil'ev-Iuzhin, "Moskovskii sovet rabochikh deputatov v 1905 godu," *Proletarskaia revoliutsiia,* No. 5 (40) (1925), p. 114.

36. Mitskevich, p. 391. The party affiliation of Romanov is questionable; in his own account, he expresses himself against the Social Democrats' attitude towards the union. He remained a stalwart supporter of the union. Nonetheless, in many subsequent works he is referred to as a Bolshevik, e.g., Rostov, *Proletariat,* p. 137.

37. Pereverzev, *Zheleznodorozhniki v 1905 g.,* p. 9.

38. Pereverzev, *Byloe,* No. 4 (32) (1925), p. 47; also Romanov, *Obrazovanie,* No. 6 (1907), p. 29.

39. The text of the leaflet appears in *Listovki moskovskikh bol'shevikov v period pervoi russkoi revoliutsii* (Moscow, 1955), Doc. 56, p. 128.

40. N. N. Mandel'shtam, "Iz proshlogo," in the collection, *Piatyi god,* ed. S. Chernomordik (Moscow, 1925), p. 78.

41. Ibid.

42. L. K. Erman, "Uchastie intelligentsii v oktiabr'skoi politicheskoi stachke," *Istoricheskie zapiski,* 49 (1954), p. 363.

43. Mandel'shtam and Kotliarenko in *Piatyi god,* pp. 83, 95.

44. Garvi, pp. 523, 547.

45. Romanov, *Obrazovanie,* No. 11 (1906), pp. 39-41, 43, and Pereverzev, *Byloe,* No. 4 (32) (1925), p. 43.

46. Mandel'shtam, *Piatyi god,* pp. 83-84.

47. Pereverzev, *Byloe,* No. 4 (32) (1925), p. 46.

48. Ibid., p. 42; see also Mandel'shtam, *Piatyi god,* p. 83.

49. Romanov, *Obrazovanie,* No. 11 (1906), pp. 42-43.

50. Ibid., No. 7 (1907), p. 70.

51. Agenda for the meeting and the constitution prepared by the Central Bureau, as well as several other documents pertaining to the union, are in Chapter IX of A. Kats

and Iu. Milonov, *1905: Professional'noe dvizhenie,* from the series *1905: Materialy i dokumenty,* ed. M. N. Pokrovskii (Moscow-Leningrad, 1926).

52. Romanov, *Obrazovanie,* No. 11 (1906), p. 43.

53. Ibid., No. 7 (1907), p. 66, contains a complete list of railroads attending the congress.

54. Ibid.

55. The Social Democratic position is summarized in *Iskra,* No. 109 (August 29, 1905), p. 3.

56. The Socialist Revolutionary position is summarized in *Revoliutsionnaia Rossiia,* No. 73 (August 15, 1905), pp. 24-25.

57. Romanov, *Obrazovanie,* No. 7 (1907), p. 70. A writer in *Iskra* (No. 109) asserts that the decisions on the strike were "thrust upon" *(naviazany)* the congress by the Social Democrats.

58. Ibid., pp. 70-71.

59. Ibid., p. 72; the text of the proposed constitution is on pp. 81-83; see also Pereverzev, *Byloe,* No. 4 (32) (1925), pp. 48-49; M. B., *Ocherki,* pp. 28-30. For the constitution of the union see V. Ivanovich, *Rossiiskie partii, soiuzy i ligi: Sbornik program, ustavov . . .* (St. Petersburg, 1906), pp. 227-29.

60. Romanov, *Obrazovanie,* No. 7 (1907), p. 74; *Iskra,* No. 109.

61. Romanov, *Obrazovanie,* No. 7 (1907), pp. 75-78; Pereverzev, *Byloe,* No. 4 (32) (1925), pp. 48-49; *Iskra,* No. 109; Erman, *Istoricheskie zapiski,* 49 (1954), p. 363; Mitskevich, p. 391.

62. From a police report in Kats and Milonov, *1905: Professional'noe dvizhenie,* p. 254; also cited in Erman, *Istoricheskie zapiski,* 49 (1954), p. 361. Although most sources indicate that the party union withdrew from the Railroad Union, several authors claim that the Social Democratic Union remained a member; see Rostov, *Proletariat,* p. 146; Piaskovskii, p. 123.

63. Romanov, *Obrazovanie,* No. 7 (1907), p. 78.

64. Ibid., No. 6 (1907), pp. 51-52; No. 7 (1907), pp. 72-73.

65. For example, see Erman, *Istoricheskie zapiski,* 49 (1954), pp. 369 ff.

66. Mitskevich, p. 391; Romanov, *Obrazovanie,* No. 7 (1907), pp. 72-74, 78.

67. Rostov, *Proletariat,* p. 147.

68. G. Khrustalev-Nosar', "Istoriia Soveta rabochikh deputatov," *Istoriia Soveta rabochikh deputatov* (St. Petersburg, date unk.), p. 56.

69. Rostov, *Proletariat,* p. 149.

70. *Vserossiiskaia politicheskaia stachka,* 1, Doc. 60, pp. 85-86. See also Garvi, pp. 547-48.

71. L. Trotskii, "Stachka v oktiabre 1905 g.," in *Revoliutsiia i RKP(b) v materialakh i dokumentakh,* M. Vasil'ev-Iuzhin, ed. (Moscow, 1926), 3, p. 272; also Romanov, *Obrazovanie,* No. 7 (1907), p. 85.

72. Pereverzev, *Byloe,* No. 4 (32) (1925), p. 49; Romanov, *Obrazovanie,* No. 7 (1907), p. 84.

73. Pereverzev, *Byloe,* No. 4 (32) (1925), p. 50, and *Zheleznodorozhniki v 1905 g.,* p. 10. See also A. Shestakov, "Vseobshchaia oktiabr'skaia stachka 1905 goda," in M. N. Pokrovskii, ed., *1905: Istoriia revoliutsionnogo dvizheniia v otdel'nykh ocherkakh,* Vol. 2: *Ot ianvaria k oktiabriu* (Moscow-Leningrad, 1925), p. 277. J. L. H. Keep (p. 221, n.1) is incorrect in assuming that the Mensheviks represented the Social Democrats in these negotiations. The evidence clearly indicates that the representatives were Bolsheviks.

74. Rostov, *Proletariat,* p. 151.

75. Pereverzev, *Byloe,* No. 4 (32) (1925), p. 50.

76. *Vserossiiskaia politicheskaia stachka,* 1, Doc. 333, p. 415, and note 193, p. 678.

See also Akademiia nauk SSSR, *Istoriia Moskvy* (Moscow, 1955), 5, ed. A. M. Pankratova, L. M. Ivanov, and V. D. Mochalov, p. 138; A. M. Pankratova and G. D. Kostomarov, eds., *Ocherki istorii SSSR: Pervaia russkaia burzhuazno-demokraticheskaia revoliutsiia 1905-1907 gg.* (Moscow, 1955), p. 147. Another author says that the Moscow Committee issued an appeal for a general strike on October 2; L. M. Ivanov, "Vserossiiskaia oktiabr'skaia stachka i sovety rabochikh deputatov," in Akademiia nauk SSSR, *Doklady i soobshcheniia Instituta istorii* (Moscow, 1956), 9, p. 12. The role of other parties and unions in calling for a general strike at this time is not clear, but at least one author maintains that it was the Socialist Revolutionaries that tried to start such a strike but failed; Rostov, *Proletariat,* p. 151.

77. L. Trotskii, *1905* (Moscow, 1922), pp. 89-90; Khrustalev-Nosar', *Istoriia Soveta rabochikh deputatov,* p. 55; Mitskevich, p. 390, and Garvi, pp. 553-56.

78. *Vserossiiskaia politicheskaia stachka,* 1, Doc. 69, p. 98; see also Docs. 330, 331, pp. 409-13 for official figures on strikers.

79. Extracts from minutes of the meeting of October 4 in *Materialy po professional'nomu dvizheniiu rabochikh,* No. 1 (February, 1906), p. 15. The "Council of Representatives of Five Professions" was formed on October 2 to coordinate the strike activities among printers, workers in mechanical production, tobacco workers, carpenters, and the Railroad Union.

80. Pereverzev, *Byloe,* No. 4 (32) (1925), p. 51; M. B., *Ocherki,* pp. 31-32.

81. *Vserossiiskaia politicheskaia stachka,* 1, secret *Okhrana* report, Doc. 332, p. 414.

82. Pereverzev, *Byloe,* No. 4 (32) (1925), p. 51; Rostov, *Proletariat,* p. 152. Also see the leaflet issued by the union calling for the strike in *Vserossiiskaia politicheskaia stachka,* 1, Doc. 134, pp. 201-202; and *Russkie vedomosti,* No. 263 (1905).

83. *Vserossiiskaia politicheskaia stachka,* 1, Docs. 140, p. 210; 144, p. 217; and 394, p. 488.

84. Ibid., Docs. 140, p. 210; 394, p. 488; Rostov, *Proletariat,* p. 152.

85. *Vserossiiskaia politicheskaia stachka,* 1, Doc. 196, p. 268; Doc. 394, p. 488; Doc. 195, p. 267; Doc. 197, p. 270.

86. For example, see ibid., Doc. 140, pp. 210-13; Doc. 144, pp. 217-20. (Doc. 144 gives a day-by-day account of the strike's progress from October 6 to 16.)

87. Ibid., Doc. 134, pp. 201-202.

88. Ibid., Doc. 135, p. 202.

89. For example, see ibid., Doc. 197, p. 270.

90. A. Shestakov in *1905: Materialy i dokumenty,* 2, p. 290.

91. Erman, *Istoricheskie zapiski,* 49 (1954), p. 367.

92. G. D. Kostomarov, ed., *1905 god v Moskve* (Moscow, 1955), p. 84.

93. Account of N. N. Mandel'shtam in *Piatyi god,* p. 85.

94. Mitskevich, p. 389; account of B. A. Breslav in *Piatyi god,* p. 158.

95. *Piatyi god,* p. 158.

96. Mitskevich, p. 392.

97. Garvi, p. 556.

98. This was a widely held version, and most Menshevik writers ascribed the beginning of the strike to this. For example, see L. Martov, et al., *Obshchestvennoe dvizhenie v Rossii v nachale XX veka,* Vol. 2, pt. 2, pp. 78, 232.

99. *Zheleznodorozhnik,* No. 127 (1905), (*Biulleten' Pervogo vserossiiskogo delegatskogo s"ezda zheleznodorozhnykh sluzhashchikh,* No. 10).

100. *Vserossiiskaia politicheskaia stachka,* 1, Doc. 136, pp. 203-206. See also Rostov, *Proletariat,* p. 154.

101. Ibid., Doc. 135, p. 202.

102. *Syn otechestva,* No. 207 (October 12, 1905); *Zheleznodorozhnik,* No. 127 (1905), p. 8.

103. Orekhov, *Zheleznodorozhniki v 1905 g.*, pp. 10-15, contain his account of the interview with Witte.

104. Letter of the St. Petersburg Governor-General, D. F. Trepov, to the Minister of Education concerning the meeting of October 11 on the premises of St. Petersburg University in *Vserossiiskaia politicheskaia stachka,* 1, Doc. 285, p. 355.

105. On this see Schwarz, *The Russian Revolution of 1905,* pp. 138-40.

106. Text in *Vserossiiskaia politicheskaia stachka,* 1, Doc. 137, p. 207.

107. Rostov, *Proletariat,* p. 156.

108. Amal'rik, *Istoricheskie zapiski,* 52 (1955), p. 148 and table 29, p. 178f.

109. Pereverzev, *Byloe,* No. 4 (32) (1925), p. 63; also P. V. Kokhmanskii, ed., *Moskva v dekabre 1905 g.* (Moscow, 1906), pp. 10-11; Rostov, *Proletariat,* pp. 163-65.

110. Vasil'ev-Iuzhin, *Proletarskaia revoliutsiia,* No. 5 (40) (1925), pp. 114-15.

111. Rostov, *Proletariat,* pp. 166-68. For specific examples, see V. Vladimirov, *Karatel'naia ekspeditsiia otriada leibgvardii Semenovskogo polka v dekabr'skie dni na Moskovo-Kazanskoi zheleznoi doroge* (Moscow, 1906), p. 159.

The Social Democratic Movement in Latvia

1. The following works deal with the history of the Social Democratic movement in Latvia: F. O. Ames, *The Revolution in the Baltic Provinces of Russia, A Brief Account of the Activity of the Latvian Social Democratic Workers' Party* (London, 1907); J. Aberbergs, *Latvijas Sociāldemokratiskā Strādnieku Partija* (Riga, 1929); B. Kalniņš, *Latvijas Sociāldemokratiskā Strādnieky Partijas, 50 gadi* (Stockholm, 1956); B. Kalniņš, "Lettlands Sozialdemokratie," in *Sozialdemokratie in Europa,* ed. H. Wehner (Hannover, 1966). From the Bolshevik point of view, the history of Latvian Social Democracy is commented upon in the collective work, V. Miške, ed., *Latvijas Komunistikās partijas vēstures apcerējumi,* 1, 1893-1919 (Riga, 1961), published in both Latvian and Russian. The subject is also treated in the volume of essays, *LKP–25 gadi* (Moscow, 1929).

2. Jānis Rainis (1865-1929), an outstanding Latvian poet and ideologist of Latvian independence, later became a member of the Central Committee of the LSDSP, a delegate to the Constituent Assembly, a member of the Latvian Parliament, and Minister of Education.

3. J. Rainis, *Dzīve un darbi, 9. sējums* (Riga, 1925), p. 14.

4. For detailed information on Rainis' activity in the "New Current" see the essay by B. Kalniņš, "Rainis kā brīvības cinitajs," in J. Rainis, *Darbi,* 17 (Västerås, 1965). See also the memoirs of other members of the "New Current," such as Klāra Kalniņš (1874-1964), *Liesmainie gadi* (Stockholm, 1964), and J. Kļava (1876-1956), *Der Rebell, Das Leben eines lettischen Bauersohnes* (Aarau, 1958). Information concerning the "New Current" may also be found in the manuscript "Obzor vazhneishikh doznanii proizvodivshikhsia v zhandarmskikh upravleniiakh za 1897 god" (St. Petersburg, 1902), pp. 68-155, a copy of which is in the B. I. Nicolaevsky Collection, Hoover Institution, Stanford, California.

5. A complete collection of *Auseklis* may be found at the Public Library, Boston, Massachusetts.

6. Jānis Ozols (1878-1968), graduated from the Faculty of Economy of the Technical College in Riga. He was an alert conspirator and organizer, a member of the Second Duma and secretary of its Social Democratic fraction, and a Menshevik. When the Second Duma was dissolved, Ozols emigrated to the United States where he received a Ph.D. from Harvard University.

7. Dr. Pauls Kalniņš (1872-1945), graduated from the Medical School of Dorpat (Tartu) University. In 1903, in order to avoid imprisonment, he left for Switzerland,

where he remained until 1907. In the years of tsarist reaction he was a member of the Central Committee of the SDL and the editor of party publications. A Centrist at first, he later became a Menshevik. One of the founders of the Latvian Republic in 1918, Kalniņš was the Presiding Officer of the Parliament for many years and became a leader of the democratic resistance during World War II. A memorial volume to Kalniņš, *Tautai un brīvībai,* was published in Stockholm in 1952.

8. J. Ozols (J. Zars), *Brīvība,* No. 52-53 (Stockholm, 1954).

9. Jānis Jansons (1872-1917). A student of the Faculty of Law at Dorpat University, he became one of the leaders of the "New Current," the best known leader of the revolution of 1905, and a publicist and editor of party publications. In the years of reaction he was a member of the SDL Committee in Brussels as a Centrist. Jansons was the author of several works on history and politics.

10. Voldis Rikveilis (1874-1940) was a worker (painter) and a member of the Central Committee of the SDL for many years. An excellent organizer and conspirator, he was frequently arrested; he later became one of the leaders of the Latvian Menshevik "Liquidators."

11. For more details see B. Kalniņš, *Latvijas Sociāldemokratiskā,* pp. 42-43.

12. *Sociāldemokrats,* No. 27 (Berne, 1904), pp. 1-10.

13. This was also admitted by Lenin (*Sochineniia,* 2nd ed., 14 [Moscow, 1935], p. 339) and by L. Martov ("To the Jubilee of *Cīņa," Cīņa,* No. 100, 1910). See also J. L. H. Keep, *The Rise of Social Democracy in Russia* (Oxford, 1963), pp. 41, 257-58, 267.

14. The complete text of the appeal is in *Latvijas sociāldemokratisko organizāciju lapiņas pirmās revolūcijas laikā* (Riga, 1955), pp. 25-26. This volume contains 74 of the 2000 leaflets issued in the years of the revolution (1905-1907).

15. All facts and quotations of the decisions of the Second Congress are according to *Paziņojums par LSDSP otro kongresu* (Berne, 1905).

16. See the series of articles on relations with the RSDRP in *Cīņa,* June, September, and November, 1905.

17. *Iskra,* Nos. 88, 110 (1905).

18. *Latvijas komunistiskās partijas vēstures apcerējumi,* 1, p. 103.

19. F. O. Ames, *Revolution,* p. 22, and B. Kalniņš, *Latvijas Sociāldemokratiskā,* pp. 90-91.

20. B. Kalniņš, "The Latvian Trade Union Movement," in *Labor in Exile* (Paris), No. 11 (1966), and No. 1 (1967).

21. For more details on the role of the LSDSP in the revolution of 1905 see J. Jansons, *Baltijas revolūcija* (Brussels, 1912); P. Kleinberg [Pauls Kalniņš], "Aus der Geschichte der lettischen Arbeiterbewegung," in *Neue Zeit* (Berlin, 1905), pp. 85-90, 116-25; P. K. [Pauls Kalniņš], *Revoliutsionnaia sotsial-demokratiia v Pribaltiiskom krae* (St. Petersburg, 1906); B. Kalniņš, *Latvijas Sociāldemokratiskā,* pp. 48-132; *1905, gads Latvija* (Riga, 1966); *Revoliutsiia 1905-1907 gg. v Latvii, Dokumenty i materialy* (Riga, 1956). The communist point of view is given by Ia. P. Krastynsh, *Revoliutsiia 1905-1907 gg. v Latvii* (Moscow, 1952).

22. Petr Stučka (1865-1932); counselor at law; 1894-1906 a national Social Democrat, later theorist of the Latvian Bolsheviks. In 1917-1918 Soviet Commissar of Justice. In 1919 head of the Soviet Government in Latvia. In 1923-31 President of the Supreme Court of the RSFSR in Moscow and a member of the Control Commission of the Communist International.

23. *Cīņa,* No. 32 (1906), and a special pamphlet, *Kā apvienoties Krievijas sociāldemokratikjai?* (Berne, 1906).

24. Ansis Buševics (1874-1943), counselor at law, was one of the leaders of the revolution of 1905 in Latvia. In 1906-1914, he was a moderate Menshevik and member of the Central Committee of the LSDSP. During the period of Latvian independence

he was a member of Parliament and Minister of Finance. In 1940 he joined the Bolsheviks. Vilis Dermanis (1875-1938), a teacher, was one of the first Latvian Mensheviks. In 1908 he was sentenced to four years in a labor camp. In 1914 he fled from Siberia to the United States and returned to Latvia in 1920. He became a member of the Central Committee of the LSDSP and of the Constituent Assembly, but he left the LSDSP and was sent to the USSR where he became a Communist (1921). Dermanis was shot in 1938. His biography is described from the Bolshevik point of view in J. Kipurs un M. Šacs, *Kvēlais tribūns* (Riga, 1964).

25. *Protokoly ob"edinennogo s'ezda RSDRP* (Moscow, 1926), pp. 285-92.

26. *Cīņa,* No. 47 (1906).

27. Ibid., Nos. 48, 50, 60 (1906).

28. Ibid., Nos. 76, 77 (1907).

29. *Golos sotsial-demokrata,* No. 15 (1909).

30. *Der Tätigkeitsbericht der Sozialdemokratie Lettlands pro Jahre 1907-1909* (Brussels, 1910).

31. Stalin, *Darbi* (Riga, 1947), p. 138.

32. A confidential report of the Police Department to F. A. Zvein, Governor General of Finland (August 19, 1911) and a secret report of the chief of the St. Petersburg Provincial Headquarters of the Gendarmerie, dated September 1, 1911. These documents may be found in the State Archives of Finland in Helsinki. The provocateur was the congress delegate "Dakters," who was shot in 1919. Later, this congress was designated an unofficial one.

33. Kristaps Eliass ("Švarc," "Socius," and "Čipus") was a member of the LSDSP from 1903 and took an active part in the revolution of 1905. Elected a member of the Central Committee of the LSDSP at its Third Congress in 1906, Eliass was arrested in December, 1906, and sentenced to life banishment in the province of Irkutsk. In 1907 he fled to Belgium, where he became editor of *Cīņa,* and a member of the Foreign Committee of the LSDSP (1908-1914). At this time he was the principal leader and publicist of the Latvian Mensheviks. After the Revolution of 1917 he returned to Latvia and became a member of the Riga Soviet and Iskolat (Executive Committee of all the Soviets of Latvia). From 1918 to 1934 he was editor of the *Sociāldemokrats* in Riga and a member of all the democratic Latvian Parliaments. In 1949 he was arrested by the MVD, sentenced to 10 years in a concentration camp, and sent to the Province of Irkutsk for the second time. He was set free after the amnesty of 1955 and returned to Riga, where he died in 1963 at the age of 77.

34. More details on the trade union movement in Latvia can be found in Brūno Kalniņš' articles in *Labor in Exile,* No. 11 (1966), No. 1 (1967).

35. Ia. N. Netesin, *Rabochee dvizhenie v Rige v period stolypinskoi reaktsii* (Riga, 1958), p. 172.

36. The present author was a correspondent of *Rabochaia gazeta* and other Menshevik newspapers in Riga (1913-15). His articles were published under the pen name "Tangens."

37. *Dzīves Balss* (Riga), December 5, 1913.

38. *Cīņa,* No. 120 (1912).

39. Ibid., Nos. 122, 123 (1912).

40. *Latvijas komunistiskās partijas vēstures apcerējumi,* 1, p. 201.

41. Voldemars Caune (1890-1944) was a member of the military organization from 1906 to 1913 and in 1910-13 one of the leaders of the legal associations and a member of the Central Committee of the SDL. He published his articles in the Menshevik press under the pen name "Ant." In 1914 Caune was banished to Narym Province. One of the leaders of the Latvian Menshevik Organizations in Russia in 1917-18, he returned to Latvia in 1918. Due to illness he was only a member of the Control Commission of the LSDSP and chief of the party archives.

42. *Cīņa,* No. 109 (1911).
43. *Pravda* (Vienna), No. 21 (1911).
44. Netesin, *Rabochee dvizhenie v Rige,* p. 174.
45. Ibid.
46. The resolution of the Central Committee of the SDL on Lenin's Prague Conference was printed in Latvian and Russian in March, 1912. A French translation was given to the International Bureau of the Socialist International. At present it is in the archives of C. Huysmans.
47. *Pravda* (Vienna), No. 23 (1911), and the notification *(Izveshchenie)* about the conference by the organizations of the RSDRP (Vienna, 1912), p. 3.
48. *Cīņa,* No. 122-123 (1913).
49. *Die Lage der Sozialdemokratie in Russland* (Berlin, 1912), pp. 21-22.
50. Rudolfs Lindiņš (1887-1944), the son of a peasant, was a journalist and propagandist for the SDL. He was banished to Northern Russia in 1913-15. During the period of Latvian independence he was a member of the Constituent Assembly, a member of Parliament, and deputy Minister of Agriculture. He was deported in 1941 and died in a Stalinist concentration camp.
51. *Cīņa,* No. 119 (1912).
52. Roberts Eiche (1890-1941), took an active part in the revolution of 1905 at Jelgava. In exile from 1908 to 1911, he became a member of the Central Committee of the SDL in 1914. In 1915 Eiche was sentenced to exile in Siberia. In 1917 he again became a member of the Central Committee of the SDL and in 1919 was made commissar in charge of provisions and a member of the Soviet Government in Latvia. Later he became USSR Commissar of Agriculture and in 1935 a candidate member of the Politbureau of the Central Committee of the Communist Party. He was arrested in 1937 and executed in 1941.
53. Jānis Bērziņš (1881-1939), a teacher, was a party member from 1902. In 1903 he was banished to the Olonets Province. In 1907 he became a member of the St. Petersburg Committee of the RSDRP. He emigrated to Paris in 1908 and was in contact with Lenin. In 1917 he became a member of the Central Committee of the RSDRP(b) and in 1919 was made a secretary to the Communist International. Bērziņš served in the diplomatic service from 1920 to 1932 and then became editor-in-chief of *Krasnyi arkhiv.* He was arrested in 1937 and executed in 1939.
54. *Latvijas komunistiskās partijas vēstures apcerējumi,* 1, p. 208.
55. Lenin, *Sochineniia,* 2nd ed., 29 (Moscow, 1933), p. 51.
56. A. M. Volodarskaia, *Lenin i partiia v gody nazrevaniia revoliutsionnogo krizisa, 1913-1914* (Moscow, 1960), p. 259.
57. Lenin, *Sochineniia,* 29, p. 51.
58. In 1914 Augulis became one of the most important agents of the tsarist police. So as not to reveal his activities, he had contact only with the Liepāja Gendarmerie Captain Dmitriev. Valuable information concerning the role of Augulis was obtained from the Archives of the Secret Police at the Hoover Institution. See also *Konspirātora piezīmes* (Riga, 1931) by V. Caune, a delegate to the Fourth Congress of the SDL; letter of August 28, 1965, written to the present author by B. I. Nicolaevsky; *Laikmetno mainā* (Stockholm, 1961), 1, p. 385, by F. Cielens who participated in the Congress and who was subsequently Minister of Foreign Affairs of independent Latvia. Communist historians evade the role of Augulis. Only in a few cases do they mention that he had turned provacateur. In 1919 Augulis was shot by Soviet authorities during the Civil War in Latvia.
59. The works of Bolshevik historians never mention Malinovskii's presence at the congress.
60. *Put' pravdy,* No. 62 (1914); also Lenin, *Sochineniia,* 2nd ed., 17 (Moscow, 1932), pp. 318-19.

61. F. Menders [F. Weiss], "S'ezd latyshskikh marksistov," *Nasha zaria,* No. 4 (1914).

62. A. Ezergailis, "The Bolshevization of the Latvian Social Democratic Party," *Canadian Slavic Studies,* 1 (1967), pp. 238-52.

63. *Istoricheskii arkhiv,* No. 6 (1958), p. 11.

64. Volodarskaia, *Lenin i partiia,* p. 343.

65. Lenin, *Sochineniia,* 5th ed., 48 (Moscow, 1964), p. 321.

66. F. Weiss [F. Menders], *Die baltische Frage im Weltkrieg* (Berne, 1917).

67. U. Gērmanis, "The Idea of Independent Latvia and Its Development in 1917," in *Res Baltica* (Leyden, 1968), pp. 27-87.

68. For more details on the activity of the LSDSP during Latvia's independence see B. Kalniņš, *Latvijas Sociāldemokratijas 50 gadi,* pp. 210-57; the memoirs of V. Bastjanis, member of the Central Committee of the LSDSP, *Demokratiskā Latvija* (Stockholm, 1966); F. Menders, "Die Probleme der Arbeiterbewegung in den baltischen Staaten," *Der Kampf,* 24 (Vienna, 1931).

69. For more details on this period see V. Bastjanis, *Gala sākums* (Stockholm, 1964).

70. Fricis Menders, born in 1885, Doctor of Law and Economy, graduated from the University of Berne. He joined the party in 1904, participated actively in the Revolution of 1905 in Riga, and was later active in the Russian Social Democratic Workers' Party in Kazan. In 1906 Menders was sentenced to life banishment in Turukhansk. From there he fled abroad in 1907. He became a member of the Foreign Committee of the SDL and was the leader of the Mensheviks at the Brussels Congress in 1914. During World War I as a Menshevik-Internationalist, he worked in Switzerland together with L. Martov. They returned to Russia after the Revolution of 1917. In 1917 Menders was a member of the Executive Committee of the Riga Soviet and of Iskolat. After the party split in 1918 he became a permanent member of the Central Committee of the LSDSP and was elected President of the party in 1929. Menders was a member of the National Council of Latvia which proclaimed the independent Republic of Latvia in 1918 and a member of the Constituent Assembly and of all four democratic Latvian Parliaments (1920-34). He was president of the Social Democratic faction of the parliament. In 1929 he became a member of the Executive Committee of the Socialist International. Menders was an excellent orator and publicist and was the author of several works on politics and economy written in Latvian and German. Menders took an active part in the democratic resistance during the Nazi occupation (1942-45). During the second Soviet occupation he was arrested and sentenced by the Ministry of the Interior to ten years in the concentration camp at Mordovlag. The Socialist International interceded on his behalf and he was set free after the amnesty in 1955, although not permitted to emigrate. Subsequently, Menders, a sick man, resided in Riga under the constant supervision of the KGB. In 1961 the KGB confiscated his memoirs (some 3,000 pages). In November, 1969, the eighty-four year old Menders was sentenced to five years imprisonment in a labor camp for "anti-Soviet propaganda" and deported from Latvia.

Stalin's Revolutionary Career Before 1917

1. A. Bubnov, *Osnovnye voprosy istorii R.K.P. Sbornik statei* (Moscow, 1924). V. I. Nevskii, *Istoriia RKP(b). Kratkii ocherk* (Leningrad, 1926), and *Ocherki po istorii rossiiskoi kommunisticheskoi partii,* 2nd ed., 1 (Leningrad, 1925). A brief biographical sketch of Stalin did appear, however, in a collection of official biographies of twelve Bolshevik leaders: Boris Volin, *Dvenadtsat' biografii* (Moscow, 1924).

2. N. S. Khrushchev, *The Crimes of the Stalin Era: Special Report to the 20th Congress of the Communist Party of the Soviet Union* (New York, 1962), p. S57.

3. Stalin, *Sochineniia* (Moscow, 1946-52), 6, pp. 52-54.

4. Leon Trotsky, *Stalin* (New York, 1967), pp. 48-49. The force of Trotsky's reasoning is not diminished by his possible error in dating Stalin's arrival at the place of exile in January, 1904. According to the official chronology in volume one of Stalin's *Sochineniia,* he arrived in the village of Novaia Uda, Irkutsk *guberniia,* on November 27, 1903, and escaped on January 5, 1904.

5. Bertram D. Wolfe, *Three Who Made a Revolution* (New York, 1948), p. 426. Particularly noteworthy is the further fact that the Lenin document was published by the Siberian Social Democratic Union in June, 1903.

6. Stalin, *Sochineniia,* 8, pp. 173-75.

7. I. P. Tovstukha, *Iosif Vissarionovich Stalin. Kratkaia biografiia* (Moscow-Leningrad, 1927), pp. 3-11. This authorized biography also appeared in volume 41 of the *Entsiklopedicheskii slovar' Granat.*

8. Isaac Deutscher, *Stalin: A Political Biography,* 2nd ed. (New York, 1966), p. 45. A problem of date also arises with respect to Stalin's membership in the Tiflis Committee's successor organization, the Transcaucasian Union Committee, which was formed in March, 1903, while Stalin was in prison. Tovstukha, as noted above, wrote that Stalin, after returning to Tiflis in January, 1904, resumed party work as a member of this Committee. Later Soviet sources stated that he was elected to it *in absentia* at the time of its original formation. Accepting that version, Deutscher commented that the rarity of such an election *in absentia* "suggests that at the age of twenty-two he was already some sort of 'gray eminence' in the underground of his native province. He was certainly not the undistinguished member of the rank and file, the nonentity, described by Trotsky" (*Stalin,* p. 50). Curiously, Trotsky also accepted this version of the facts, although without placing the same interpretation on it (*Stalin,* p. 44). A post-Stalin Soviet history of party organizations in the Transcaucasus has made it clear that the version was false. After listing the names of the nine members elected at the time of the Union Committee's formation, it mentions nine others, Stalin included, who entered it "at various times"; and says nothing of his having been elected to it *in absentia (Ocherki istorii kommunisticheskikh organizatsii zakavkaz'ia, pt. 1, 1883-1921 gg.* [Tbilisi, 1967], p. 72).

9. *Brdzolis khma,* No. 3 (Paris, 1930). Quoted by Bertram D. Wolfe, *Three Who Made a Revolution,* p. 420. See also N. Vakar, "Stalin po vospominaniiam N. N. Zhordaniia," *Poslednye novosti* (Paris), December 16, 1936, and Grigorii Uratadze, *Vospominaniia gruzinskogo sotsial-demokrata* (Stanford, 1968), pp. 66-67. Deutscher does not accept this story, but does suggest that Stalin's move was precipitated by personal and political antagonisms between himself and Djibladze (*Stalin,* p. 46).

10. This version, which is accepted by Trotsky, has its source in a history of Transcaucasian Social Democracy first published in Geneva in 1910 and republished in Soviet Russia in 1923: S. T. Arkomed, *Rabochee dvizhenie i sotsial-demokratiia na kavkaze (s 80-kh godov po 1903 g.),* 2nd ed. (Moscow-Leningrad, 1923), pp. 83-84. The second edition was unchanged save for the addition of notes and a preface. Arkomed, himself a Social Democratic participant in events recounted in the book, does not name Stalin directly. He writes that worker participation on the Committee was resisted by one young intellectual whom he describes as motivated by personal caprice and love of power. After being badly defeated in the Committee vote, the young man departed Tiflis for Batum, "whence the Tiflis workers received information concerning his improper behavior, his hostile and disorganizing agitation against the Tiflis organization and its members" (ibid.). Trotsky takes Stalin to have been the young man in question, stating that he was the only member of the Tiflis Committee who moved to Batum in the fall of 1901 (*Stalin,* p. 30).

11. Filipp Makharadze, *Ocherki revoliutsionnogo dvizheniia v Zakavkaz'i* (Tiflis, 1927), pp. 83-84. See also the memoirs of Baron (Bibineishvili), *Za chetvert' veka*

(Revoliutsionnaia bor'ba v Gruzii) (Moscow-Leningrad, 1931), pp. 65-66, where the same events are described without reference to Stalin's role in them.

12. For direct testimony to this effect, see the memoirs of Joseph Iremaschwili, *Stalin und die tragödie Georgiens* (Berlin, 1932), pp. 21-23, and Uratadze, *Vospominaniia,* p. 67. Trotsky's contention that Stalin began his activities as a Menshevik and only aligned himself with the Bolsheviks on the eve of 1905, after much hesitation, is unconvincing. Apart from some debatable psychologizing (*Stalin,* pp. 50-51), he offers in evidence only a tsarist police report, dated 1911, in which the following appeared: "According to newly obtained agent information, Iosif Djugashvili was known in the organization under the names of 'Soso' and 'Koba,' worked in the organization from 1902, first as a Menshevik and then as a Bolshevik, as a propagandist and head of District I (Railway District)." This police report was published in the Tiflis party paper *Zaria vostoka* on December 23, 1925, among reminiscences of Stalin by former comrades on the occasion of his forty-sixth birthday. A copy of the report is contained in the archives of the Imperial Russian Secret Police *(Okhrana),* the Hoover Institution, Stanford, California. Its authenticity is not in doubt, but its accuracy is. It was an obvious anachronism for the author of the report (chief of the Tiflis province gendarme administration) to ascribe Menshevism to Stalin from 1902. For Menshevism had its inception only in the following year in the aftermath of the Russian Social Democratic Party's Second Congress. The police officer might have been misled by the fact that most of the Social Democrats with whom Stalin was connected in Tiflis in 1902 subsequently became Mensheviks.

13. Stalin, *Sochineniia,* 1, pp. 56-61. The Bibineishvili memoir shows that Stalin was taking a Bolshevik position in the developing intra-party conflict when he came to Kutais in the summer of 1904 to head the local Social Democratic Committee (*Za chetvert' veka,* pp. 80-81).

14. Trotsky, *Stalin,* p. 59. The four were Kamenev, Tskhakaia, Djaparidze, and Nevskii. The Third Congress was convened by the Bureau of Committees of the Majority contrary to the desire of the Mensheviks, and it was at this Congress that the Bolshevik section of the party informally organized itself as a separate and independent unit. As regards Stalin, Tovstukha had to confine himself to saying that he "took a most active part in the organizing of the Third Congress of Bolsheviks."

15. Ibid., p. 115.

16. Uratadze, *Vospominaniia,* p. 67; and R. Arsenidze, "Iz vospominanii o Staline," *Novy zhurnal,* No. 72 (June, 1963), p. 224.

17. Trotsky, *Stalin,* p. 124.

18. Semeon Vereshchak, "Stalin v tiur'me (vospominaniia politicheskago zakliuchennago)," *Dni,* January 22, 24, 1928. The cited material appears in the first installment of the article.

19. V. Kaminskii and I. Vereshchagin, compilers, "Detstvo i iunost' vozhdia. Dokumenty, zapisi, rasskazy," *Molodaia gvardiia,* No. 12 (1939), p. 88.

20. Gregory Aronson, "Was Stalin a Tsarist Agent?," *The New Leader,* August 20, 1956, p. 24.

21. For the Yeremin document and the case built upon it, see Isaac Don Levine, *Stalin's Great Secret* (New York, 1956). In a later communication (*The New Leader,* October 1, 1956, p. 28), Mr. Don Levine admitted the possibility that this document might prove of "dubious origin." For cogent argumentation indicating its fraudulence, see Gregory Aronson, *The New Leader,* August 20, 1956, and Martin K. Tytell, "Exposing a Documentary Hoax," paper presented at the New York meeting of the American Association for the Advancement of Science, December 29, 1956.

22. Edward Ellis Smith, *The Young Stalin. The Early Years of an Elusive Revolutionary* (New York, 1967), pp. 67-68. This is the most voluminous study yet produced on Stalin's early life, and the major effort made so far to argue the thesis

that Stalin became a tsarist police agent. I do not consider the argument successful, for it is based throughout on circumstantial evidence which admits of other possible interpretations. The book contains the fullest bibliography on the young Stalin yet available in English. For an appraisal of the book by George F. Kennan, see *The American Historical Review* (October, 1968), pp. 230-32.

23. Iremaschwili, *Stalin*, p. 24. Iremashvili (to use the proper English transliteration) became a Menshevik after leaving the seminary, and emigrated from Russia in the early 1920s. Although the passage here quoted from his memoir does not specifically refer to the period *before* Stalin obtained part-time employment in the Tiflis observatory but to his post-seminary period generally, it is implausible to suppose that if Stalin's seminary friends were willing to help him on occasion after he obtained that job, they would not have done so earlier when his need was still greater.

24. Because Stalin entered the Central Committee "through the back door," Trotsky infers that his candidacy was opposed when put forward at the Prague conference (*Stalin*, pp. 136-37). Another possibility is that he simply did not receive a sufficient number of affirmative votes. The fact that he originally entered the Central Committee by cooptation was shown in official party documents published in the 1920s, and has been recognized in various Soviet official sources of the post-Stalin period, e.g., *Piatyi (Londonskii) s"ezd RSDRP. Aprel'-mai 1907 goda. Protokoly* (Moscow, 1963), p. 888.

25. Stalin, *Sochineniia*, 1, p. 396. "Colchian" derives from the name "Colchis," which the ancients used to designate the western part of Georgia. The reported source of the story is the reminiscences of D. Suliashvili, one of the Georgian Bolsheviks then living in Leipzig. According to Suliashvili, the letter of Stalin's that evoked Lenin's comment was the one in which he called Lenin a mountain eagle.

26. *Ocherki istorii kommunisticheskikh organizatsii zakavkaz'ia, pt. 1, 1883-1921 gg.*, p. 141.

27. Lenin, *Polnoe sobranie sochinenii* (Moscow, 1958-65), 11, p. 386. For Stalin's two articles, see his *Sochineniia*, 1, pp. 89-130, 160-72. Whether Lenin knew at the time that Stalin was author of the two articles is uncertain. The pamphlet appeared in the name of the Union Committee, and the second article (entitled "Reply to 'Social Democrat' ") originally appeared unsigned. Interestingly, Stalin began it with an unusual assertion of individual authorship: "I must note this: Many consider that the author of *Briefly About the Disagreements in the Party* was the Union Committee and not an individual. I must declare that the author of this pamphlet is myself. Only the editing of it comes from the Union Committee (Stalin, *Sochineniia*, 1, p. 160).

28. The position that Stalin supported was presented to the congress by the preceding Bolshevik speaker, S. A. Suvorov.

29. *Piatyi (Londonskii) s"ezd RSDRP*, pp. 226-32. When Lenin, who presided at the fourteenth session of the congress, called for a vote on the proposal of the credentials commission to admit Ivanovich (Stalin), Barsov (Tskhakaia) and two others with the right of advisory vote, Martov demanded to know "to whom an advisory vote is being given: who are these people, where are they from, etc.?" Lenin called for a vote on Martov's demand. Martov spoke up from his seat: "I point out that one cannot vote without knowing who is involved." Lenin then said: "That, in fact is unknown. But the congress can have confidence in the unanimous opinion of the credentials commission." Martov's motion was voted down and the credential commission's proposal was adopted by a majority of votes, with a considerable number of abstentions (*Piatyi Londonskii s"ezd RSDRP*, p. 241).

30. Stalin, *Sochineniia*, 13, p. 112. According to the Soviet transcript of the interview, Ludwig coupled the comment here quoted with a query on Stalin's view of Stepan Razin as an "ideological highwayman." Stalin took advantage of this opening and confined himself to the historical aspect of the question, denying an analogy between Bolsheviks and such leaders of *jacqueries* as Razin.

31. This is one of the points on which the non-Soviet biographers of Stalin are generally agreed. See, for example, Trotsky, *Stalin,* pp. 100-101; Deutscher, *Stalin,* pp. 87-88; Wolfe, *Three Who Made a Revolution,* pp. 390-91. Menshevik sources (e.g., Arsenidze, *Novyi Zhurnal,* No. 72 [June, 1963], p. 323) have alleged that Stalin was expelled from the party by the Transcaucasian organization for his part in the Tiflis raid of June, 1907. In March, 1918, Martov wrote in his Moscow newspaper that Stalin at one time had been expelled from his party organization for having something to do with expropriations. Stalin thereupon brought charges against Martov before a party tribunal, and denied that he had ever been tried or expelled by his party organization. But he did not deny involvement in expropriations. On this episode see Trotsky, *Stalin,* pp. 101-102 and Wolfe, *Three Who Made a Revolution,* pp. 470-72.

32. L. Schapiro, *The Communist Party of the Soviet Union* (New York, 1959), p. 101. See also Wolfe, *Three Who Made a Revolution,* p. 486: "By 1909 the Party had crumbled away until Krupskaya could write 'we have no people at all.' In retrospect, Zinoviev, very close to Lenin then, would say, 'at this unhappy period the party as a whole ceased to exist'."

33. Stalin, *Sochineniia,* 2, p. 147.

34. Ibid., pp. 198-99.

35. Ibid., p. 211.

36. *Iosif Vissarionovich Stalin, Kratkaia biografiia,* 2nd ed. (Moscow, 1947), p. 50, where Stalin is said to have held the status of *agent* or *upolnomochennyi* of the Central Committee from 1910 to 1912. One might question the statement, especially in view of its absence from earlier versions of Stalin's official biography. It has been confirmed, however, in a footnote to protocols of the Central Committee Bureau's meeting in March, 1917 (*Voprosy istorii KPSS,* No. 3 [1962], p. 156).

37. Since the other members of the Russian Bureau (Ordzhonikidze, Spandarian and Goloshchekin) had all three been elected to the new Central Committee by the party conference, it would have been awkward to make Stalin a member of the Bureau without simultaneously coopting him onto the Central Committee itself.

38. These letters do not appear in Stalin's collected writings. The text of the third, which at the time of dispatch was intercepted by the tsarist police, was disinterred from police files and published among the materials on Stalin in the Tiflis paper *Zaria vostoka* for December 23, 1925. The full texts of the other two have not, so far as I know, been published. However, excerpts are quoted in I. Dubinskii-Mukhadze, *Ordzhonikidze* (Moscow, 1963), p. 93, and in *V. I. Lenin, Biografiia,* 3rd ed. (Moscow, 1963), pp. 179-80.

39. Dubinskii-Mukhadze, *Ordzhonikidze,* pp. 92-94.

40. "'Bol'nye voprosy' nashei partii: 'likvidatorskii' i 'natsional'nyi' voprosy," *Polnoe sobranie sochinenii,* 22, p. 230.

41. The use in its title of the term "*rossiiskaia,*" referring to the Russian Empire, rather than "*russkaia,*" which would have described the party as Russian in nationality, subtly conveyed this distinction. For Lenin's emphasis upon this transnational meaning of "*rossiiskaia,*" see his "Tezisy po natsional'nomu voprosu," in *Polnoe sobranie sochinenii,* 23, p. 320.

42. A brief summary of these views of Lenin's appears in his *Polnoe sobranie sochinenii,* 23, p. 59. For an expanded version of them, see ibid., pp. 314-22.

43. Stalin, *Sochineniia,* 1, p. 42. Entitled "How Does Social Democracy View the National Question?," this article originally appeared in the Georgian language paper *Proletariatis brdzola* on September 1, 1904, without signature. Although two other articles precede it in volume one of Stalin's collected writings, both originally published in the same Georgian paper in late 1901, also without signature, they do not read stylistically like products of Stalin's pen, whereas the article of 1904 on the national question does.

44. Lenin, *Polnoe sobranie sochinenii,* 48, p. 162.

45. Stalin, *Marksizm i natsional'nyi vopros,* in *Sochineniia,* 2, pp. 290-367. When originally published in the party's theoretical journal *Prosveshchenie* in the spring of 1913, the work was entitled (like Bauer's) *The National Question and Social Democracy.*

46. M. Djilas, *Conversations with Stalin* (New York, 1962), p. 157. Stalin made the remark in reply to a question from Djilas on the difference in meaning between "people" and "nation." An ambiguity in the English text at this point makes it unclear whether Stalin was referring to the distinction in question or the whole of *Marxism and the National Question* when he went on to say: "That was Ilich's–Lenin's view" (ibid.). I have been informed by Mr. Djilas that in his view Stalin was referring to the book as a whole.

47. Arguing that Stalin produced nothing of comparably high quality either before or after this work, Trotsky concluded that it "was wholly inspired by Lenin, written under his unremitting supervision and edited by him line by line." He also suggested that Bukharin and Troianovskii, whom Stalin met in Vienna at the time, selected the most important quotations from the Austrian materials (since Stalin did not know German), and that Bukharin was probably responsible for the logical construction of the work (Trotsky, *Stalin,* pp. 156-58). Others who have taken Stalin's work as basically a reflection of Lenin's thinking include Deutscher (*Stalin,* p. 117), Souvarine (*Stalin,* p. 133), and Wolfe (*Three Who Made a Revolution,* pp. 578-81). The contrary position, which I share, has been argued by Richard Pipes, *The Formation of the Soviet Union* (Cambridge, Mass., 1954), pp. 40-41, and by Robert H. McNeal in "Trotsky's Interpretation of Stalin," *Canadian Slavonic Papers,* No. 5 (1961), p. 90, and in his *Stalin's Works: An Annotated Bibliography,* pp. 43-44.

48. For example, Otto Bauer's *The National Question and Social Democracy* was used by Stalin in a Russian translation by M. Panin. Richard Pipes (*Formation of the Soviet Union,* p. 41) was the first to call attention to this fact in refutation of Trotsky. Stalin appears to have made at least a desultory effort to study German and knew a few words of it. Significantly, Stalin's footnote mentioning the Panin translation of Bauer's book does so by way of correcting a minor mistranslation of the German phrase *"nationalen Eigenart."* Stalin evidently wished to convey the impression that he knew German well. See his *Sochineniia,* 2, p. 321.

49. Letter of February 25, 1913, in *Polnoe sobranie sochinenii,* 48, p. 169. On March 29, he wrote again to Kamenev: "Koba has managed to write a big (for three issues of *Prosveshchenie*) article on the national question. Good! We have to fight for the truth against the separatists and opportunists from the Bund and from among the liquidators" (ibid., p. 173). And in an editorial of December, 1913, on the national program of the party, Lenin wrote that Stalin's article "stands out in first place" in the recent theoretical Marxist literature on the national question (ibid., 24, p. 223).

50. Lenin, *Polnoe sobranie sochinenii,* 48, pp. 101, 161. The first of the two letters appears here for the first time; the second was first published in *Leninskii sbornik,* 11 (Moscow, 1929). I am indebted to Abdurakhman Avtorkhanov for bringing these letters to my attention.

51. "Protokoly i resoliutsii Biuro TsK RSDRP(b) (Mart 1917 g.)," *Voprosy istorii KPSS,* No. 3 (1962), p. 143. The protocol on the Bureau's meeting of March 15 (ibid., p. 149) records that Stalin was on that day elected a member of the Bureau's presidium. By this time he must have acquired full voting rights.

The Petrograd Garrison and the Bolshevik Seizure of Power

1. The author is grateful to Indiana University Press for permission to use some material previously published in Alexander Rabinowitch, *Prelude to Revolution: The Petrograd Bolsheviks and the July 1917 Uprising* (Bloomington, 1968).

2. The most useful studies of the Petrograd garrison in the revolutionary period

are M. I. Akhun and V. A. Petrov, *Bol'sheviki i armiia v 1905-1917 gg.* (Leningrad, 1929); A. K. Drezen, "Petrogradskii garnizon v iiule i avguste 1917 g.," *Krasnaia letopis',* No. 3 (24) (1927), pp. 191-223; O. N. Chaadaeva, "Soldatskie massy Petrogradskogo garnizona v podgotovke i provedenii Oktiabr'skogo vooruzhennogo vosstaniia," *Istoricheskie zapiski,* No. 51 (1955), pp. 3-44; V. M. Kochakov, "Sostav Petrogradskogo garnizona v 1917 g.," *Uchenye zapiski Leningradskogo gosudarstvennogo universiteta,* Vyp. 24, No. 205 (1956), pp. 60-86; V. M. Kochakov, "Bol'shevizatsiia Petrogradskogo garnizona v 1917 godu," in Akademiia nauk SSSR, Institut istorii, Leningradskoe otdelenie, *Oktiabr'skoe vooruzhennoe vosstanie v Petrograde* (Moscow-Leningrad, 1957), pp. 142-83. A valuable collection of documents is A. K. Drezen, ed., *Bol'shevizatsiia Petrogradskogo garnizona: Sbornik materialov i dokumentov* (Leningrad, 1932).

3. V. M. Kochakov's detailed investigations of the social composition of the garrison in 1917 (*Uchenye zapiski LGU,* pp. 55-67) indicate that during World War I the number of workers recruited for service in units of the Petrograd garrison tended to increase. In 1917 the percentage of soldiers of working class origin differed significantly from unit to unit; for example, army reserve infantry regiments and particularly engineer units contained relatively greater numbers of workers than did guards infantry or Cossack regiments. However, it is significant that in the minds of Bolshevik leaders who were in close contact with garrison troops, there was no doubt that Petrograd based soldiers were primarily peasants. Bolshevik leaders in the garrison based their agitation on this assumption and, indeed, throughout the summer of 1917 they used it to explain the anarchic character of the troops.

4. Significant in this connection is the fact that the first garrison force to come out against the tsarist government in February, 1917, was the Fourth Company of the Pavlovskii Regiment.

5. For an analysis of the origins and content of Order Number One, see John R. Boyd, "The Origins of Order No. I," *Soviet Studies,* January, 1968, pp. 359-72.

6. An interesting view of the significance of the April events in the garrison as seen through the eyes of an official of the Provisional Government, A. I. Koz'min, is contained in V. Maksakov, "Iz zapisnoi knizhki arkhivista," *Krasnyi arkhiv,* No. 5 (60) (1933), pp. 149-50.

7. The works of S. E. Rabinovich contain valuable information on the Bolshevik Military Organization in 1917: "Bol'shevistskie voennye organizatsii v 1917 g.," *Proletarskaia revoliutsiia,* No. 6-7 (77-78) (1928), pp. 179-98; *Bor'ba za armiiu 1917 g.* (Leningrad, 1930); and "Vserossiiskaia konferentsiia bol'shevistskikh voennykh organizatsii 1917 g.," *Krasnaia letopis',* No. 5 (38) (1930), pp. 105-32. Especially useful memoir accounts include N. I. Podvoiskii, "Voennaia organizatsiia TsK RSDRP(b) i voenno-revoliutsionnyi komitet 1917 g.," *Krasnaia letopis',* No. 6 (1923), pp. 64-97, and No. 8 (1923), pp. 7-43; V. I. Nevskii, "V oktiabre: Beglye zametki pamiati," *Katorga i ssylka,* No. 11-12 (96-97) (1932), pp. 27-45; V. I. Nevskii, "Voennaia organizatsiia i oktiabr'skaia revoliutsiia," *Krasnoarmeets,* No. 10-15 (1919), pp. 34-44.

8. See, for example, Nevskii, *Krasnoarmeets,* No. 10-15 (1919), p. 34.

9. Akhun and Petrov, *Bol'sheviki i armiia,* p. 224.

10. This is a very rough approximation based on an estimate of Military Organization strength for mid-June in S. E. Rabinovich, *Krasnaia letopis',* No. 5 (38) (1930), p. 109.

11. A. Rabinowitch, *Prelude to Revolution,* and O. N. Znamenskii, *Iiul'skii krizis 1917 goda* (Moscow-Leningrad, 1964).

12. The protocol of this meeting was published for the first time in Akademiia nauk SSSR, Institut istorii, et al., *Revoliutsionnoe dvizhenie v Rossii v mae-iiune 1917 g.: Iiun'skaia demonstratsiia,* ed. D. A. Chugaev, et al. (Moscow, 1959), pp. 483-85.

13. Vsesoiuznaia Kommunisticheskaia partiia (bol'shevikov), Leningradskii istpart, *Pervyi legal'nyi Peterburgskii komitet bol'shevikov v 1917 g.: Sbornik materialov i protokolov zasedanii Peterburgskogo komiteta RSDRP(b) i ego Ispolnitel'noi komissii za 1917 g.*, ed. P. F. Kudelli (Moscow-Leningrad, 1927), pp. 153-54.

14. This speech is not in any editions of Lenin's complete works. The fullest record of it is contained in M. Kedrov, "Vserossiiskaia konferentsiia voennykh organizatsii RSDRP(b)," *Proletarskaia revoliutsiia,* No. 6 (65) (1927), pp. 216-31.

15. See *Pervyi legal'nyi Peterburgskii komitet,* pp. 185-205.

16. P. M. Stulov, "Pervyi pulemetnyi polk v iiul'skie dni 1917 g.," *Krasnaia letopis',* No. 3 (36) (1930), pp. 86-94.

17. V. I. Nevskii, "Narodnye massy v oktiabr'skoi revoliutsii," *Rabotnik prosveshcheniia,* No. 8 (1922), pp. 20-21.

18. The most thorough study of the organization of the July uprising in the First Machine Gun Regiment is Stulov, *Krasnaia letopis',* No. 3 (36) (1930), pp. 64-125. Pertinent documents from the Provisional Government's official investigation of the July uprising are contained in I. Tobolin, ed., "Iiul skie dni v Petrograde," *Krasnyi arkhiv,* No. 4 (23) (1927), pp. 13-26.

19. See, for example, the report of N. I. Podvoiskii at the Sixth Bolshevik Party Congress in Institut marksizma-leninizma pri TsK KPSS, *Shestoi s"ezd RSDRP (bol'shevikov) avgust 1917 goda: Protokoly* (Moscow, 1958), p. 65.

20. Akademiia nauk SSSR, Institut istorii, et al., *Revoliutsionnoe dvizhenie v Rossii v iiule 1917 g.: Iiul'skii krizis,* ed. D. A. Chugaev, et al. (Moscow, 1959), pp. 73-74.

21. Tobolin, *Krasnyi arkhiv,* No. 4 (23) (1927), pp. 6-15.

22. The fullest memoir account of the Military Organization's activities after the July uprising: N. I. Podvoiskii, "Voennaia organizatsiia TsK RSDRP(b) i voenno-revoliutsionnyi komitet 1917 g.," *Krasnaia letopis',* No. 6 (1923), pp. 64-97, and No. 8 (1923), pp. 7-43.

23. V. S. Voitinskii, "Gody pobed i porazhenii: 1917" (Berlin, 1922-1923), Nicolaevsky Collection, The Hoover Institution, Stanford, California, pp. 295-99.

24. A. L. Khokhriakov, "Iz zhizni Petrogradskogo garnizona," *Krasnaia letopis',* No. 2 (17) (1926), pp. 36-37.

25. It is true that in early August, at the time of the Bolshevik Sixth Party Congress, Lenin abruptly abandoned the slogan, "All Power to the Soviets!" But the change had not been effectively implemented at the time of the Kornilov affair; after Kornilov's failure Lenin returned to the slogan once again.

26. *Pervyi legal'nyi Peterburgskii komitet,* p. 313.

27. V. I. Lenin, *Sochineniia,* 4th ed. (Moscow, 1941-57), 25, pp. 282-87.

28. Lenin, *Sochineniia,* 26, pp. 1-9.

29. I. V. Stalin, *Sochineniia,* 4 (Moscow, 1947), pp. 317-18.

30. Bukharin, *Proletarskaia revoliutsiia,* No. 10 (1922), p. 319.

31. Institut marksizma-leninizma pri TsK KPSS, *Protokoly Tsentral'nogo komiteta RSDRP(b): Avgust 1917-fevral' 1918* (Moscow, 1958), p. 55.

32. Ibid., pp. 85-86.

33. Lenin, *Sochineniia,* 26, pp. 47-50, 154-61. In this connection see the comments of V. I. Startsev in I. I. Mints, et al., *Lenin i Oktiabr'skoe vooruzhennoe vosstanie v Petrograde: Materialy Vsesoiuznoi nauchnoi sessii, sostoiavsheisia 13-16 noiabria 1962 g. v Leningrade* (Moscow, 1964), pp. 68-81.

34. *Protokoly Tsentral'nogo komiteta,* pp. 86-92.

35. Lenin, *Sochineniia,* 26, pp. 185-88, 192-96.

36. A detailed protocol of the Petersburg Committee meeting of October 15 is contained in V. I. Nevskii, "Istoricheskoe zasedanie Peterburgskogo komiteta RSDRP (bol'shevikov) nakanune Oktiabr'skogo vosstaniia," *Krasnaia letopis',* No. 2-3 (1922), pp. 316-32. (Reprinted in *Pervyi legal'nyi Peterburgskii komitet,* pp. 307-25.) A sum-

mary of the proceedings of the October 16 meeting of the Central Committee is contained in *Protokoly Tsentral'nogo komiteta,* pp. 93-105.

37. After the revolution Nevskii often acknowledged the impact of the July experience on the thinking of Military Organization leaders in October. See, for example, Nevskii, *Katorga i ssylka,* No. 11-12 (96-97) (1932), p. 36.

38. According to Trotsky, he and Military Organization leaders in the Soviet recognized the potential importance of troop transfer orders for the seizure of power as soon as they were announced. See Trotsky's comments in "Vospominaniia ob Oktiabr'skom perevorote," *Proletarskaia revoliutsiia,* No. 10 (1922), pp. 52-58.

39. K. Riabinskii, *Revoliutsiia 1917 goda: Khronika sobytii,* 5 (Moscow-Leningrad, 1926), p. 67.

40. Voitinskii, "Gody pobed i porazhenii: 1917," pp. 319-22.

41. Chaadaeva, *Istoricheskie zapiski,* No. 51 (1955), p. 14.

42. Riabinskii, *Khronika sobytii,* 5, pp. 57-73. In this connection see the resolutions published in Drezen, *Bol'shevizatsiia Petrogradskogo garnizona,* pp. 297-302.

43. "Kak oboroniat'sia," *Rabochii put',* October 11, 1917, p. 1.

44. On the origins, make-up, and activities of the Military Revolutionary Committee, see S. Piontkovskii, "Voenno-revoliutsionnyi komitet v Oktiabr'skie dni," *Proletarskaia revoliutsiia,* No. 10 (69) (1927), pp. 110-37; Iu. S. Tokarev, "K voprosu o sozdanii Petrogradskogo voenno-revoliutsionnogo komiteta," in Mints, *Lenin i Oktiabr'skoe vooruzhennoe vosstanie,* pp. 165-81. Pertinent documents are contained in D. A. Chugaev, et al., eds., *Petrogradskii voenno-revoliutsionnyi komitet: Dokumenty i materialy* (Moscow, 1966), Vol. 1.

45. K. Mekhonoshin, "Boevoi shtab Oktiabr'skoi revoliutsii," *Petrogradskaia pravda,* No. 5 (1922), p. 4, and "Vospominaniia ob Oktiabr'skom perevorote," *Proletarskaia revoliutsiia,* No. 10 (1922), pp. 72-83, 86-88.

46. Riabinskii, *Khronika sobytii,* 5, pp. 151-52.

47. In this connection see Dietrich Geyer, "The Bolshevik Insurrection in Petrograd," in Richard Pipes, ed., *Revolutionary Russia* (Cambridge, Mass., 1968), p. 178.

48. Robert V. Daniels, *Red October* (New York, 1967), pp. 217-18.

49. L. D. Trotskii, *Sochineniia,* 3 (Moscow, 1924), xlix-l.

In Praise of War Communism

1. *Ekonomika perekhodnogo perioda. Chast' I. Obshchaia teoriia transformatsionnogo protsessa* (Moscow, 1920). A German edition appeared two years later. N. Bucharin, *Ökonomik der Transformationsperiode* (Hamburg, 1922); and an English edition only recently (New York, 1971).

2. M. Pokrovskii, "Obshchestvennye nauki v SSSR za 10 let," *Vestnik kommunisticheskoi akademii,* Book 26 (1928), pp. 12-14. In Pokrovskii's opinion, the other two were Lenin's *State and Revolution* and L. Kritsman's *The Heroic Period of the Great Russian Revolution,* a study of the civil war period. For the influence of *The Economics* on Soviet thought, see Adam Kaufman, "The Origin of 'The Political Economy of Socialism': An Essay on Soviet Economic Thought," *Soviet Studies,* No. 3 (1953), pp. 244-45, 248.

3. For the origin and development of war communism, see E. H. Carr, *The Bolshevik Revolution,* 2 (New York, 1952), pp. 147-268; and Maurice Dobb, *Soviet Economic Development Since 1917,* rev. ed. (New York, 1966), chap. 5.

4. *Azbuka kommunizma: populiarnoe ob"iasnenie programmy rossiiskoi kommunisticheskoi partii bol'shevikov* (Moscow, 1919). For its status as a "party canon," see Bukharin's remarks in *Pravda,* January 25, 1923, p. 1.

5. This was already the impression of foreign communists in Russia. See, for example, M. N. Roy, *Memoirs* (Bombay, 1964), p. 386.

6. *Vos'moi s"ezd RKP(b). Mart 1919 goda: protokoly* (Moscow, 1959), p. 49.

7. I am aware that this statement is contrary to the commonplace assumption that Bukharin favored extreme economic policies from the outset. Suffice it to say that this mistaken impression apparently is based on his leadership of the dissident Left Communists in early 1918, an advocacy which in fact derived from his opposition to Lenin's decision to take Russia out of the war by making a separate peace with Germany. On economic matters, Bukharin was considerably less radical, and, in important respects, the policies he urged were distinctly unlike those of war communism. See, for example, his argument in May, 1918 for limiting nationalization to large, easily managed enterprises in his *Programma kommunistov (bol'shevikov)* (Petrograd, 1918), pp. 25-28.

8. Thus Lenin, to take the best example, despite his fabled pragmatism and subsequent deprecation of the follies of war communism, could say in 1919: "Now the organization of the proletariat's communist activities, and the entire policy of the Communists, has fully acquired a final, stable form; and I am convinced that we stand on the right road. . . ." V. I. Lenin, *Sochineniia,* 3rd ed., 24 (Moscow, 1932), p. 536.

9. N. Bukharin, *Ataka: sbornik teoreticheskikh statei,* 2nd ed. (Moscow, 1924), p. 104.

10. *Ekonomika perekhodnogo perioda,* pp. 5-6, 123, n.1. Piatakov co-authored chapter 10, one of the most controversial. He apparently agreed with the book's arguments, and later wrote jointly with Bukharin a defense of it. See "Kavaleriiskii reid i tiazhelaia artilleriia," *Krasnaia nov',* No. 1 (1921), pp. 256-74.

11. *Ekonomika perekhodnogo perioda,* p. 6.

12. Ibid., chaps. 1-3, 7, 11. Bukharin's original works on state capitalism, both completed before 1917, were *Mirovoe khoziaistvo i imperializm* (Petrograd, 1918) and "K teorii imperialisticheskogo gosudarstva," in *Revoliutsiia prava: sbornik pervyi* (Moscow, 1925), pp. 5-32. For an examination of these writings, see Stephen F. Cohen, "Bukharin, Lenin and the Theoretical Foundations of Bolshevism," *Soviet Studies,* April, 1970, pp. 436-57.

13. Carr, *The Bolshevik Revolution,* 2, pp. 191-96.

14. See, for example, Lenin's "The Proletarian Revolution and the Renegade Kautsky," in *Sochineniia,* 3rd ed., 23 (Moscow-Leningrad, 1931), pp. 331-412; and Leon Trotsky, *Terrorism and Communism: A Reply to Karl Kautsky* (Ann Arbor, 1961).

15. "Diktatura proletariata v Rossii i mirovaia revoliutsiia," *Kommunisticheskii internatsional,* No. 4 (1919), pp. 487-88. Also see *Ekonomika perekhodnogo perioda,* p. 95, n.1.

16. See, for example, *Kommunisticheskii internatsional,* No. 4 (1919), p. 487; and his *Historical Materialism: A System of Sociology* (New York, 1925), p. 266.

17. *Ekonomika perekhodnogo perioda,* chaps. 3, 6, and pp. 63-64.

18. Ibid., pp. 48, 97-98.

19. For Hilferding, see ibid., p. 47; and *Vestnik kommunisticheskoi akademii,* Book 26 (1928), p. 13. Bukharin described the prevailing social democratic view as follows: "the proletariat . . . removes the commanding 'heads,' whom it dismisses more or less gently, and then assumes control of the social apparatus of production, which has been developed to a splendid and uninjured maturity in the bowels of the capitalist Abraham. The proletariat installs its own 'heads' and the thing is done." *Historical Materialism,* pp. 259-60.

20. See the unnamed person mentioned in Ne-revizionist, "O knige tov. N. Bukharina (otvet tov. M. Ol'minskomu)," *Krasnaia nov',* No. 1 (1921), pp. 254-55.

21. Bukharin and Piatakov, ibid., pp. 257, 272.

22. See, for example, *Vestnik kommunisticheskoi akademii,* Book 26 (1928), pp. 13-14, where Pokrovskii calls it "a turning point" in political economy almost equal to

that of *State and Revolution* "in the area of law." Also see L. Kritsman, *Geroicheskii period velikoi russkoi revoliutsii (opyt analiza t.n. 'voennogo kommunizma'),* 2nd ed. (Moscow-Leningrad, 1926), pp. 19, n.2, 167, n.144; *Krasnaia nov',* No. 1 (1921), p. 254; and D. Maretskii, "Nikolai Ivanovich Bukharin," in *Bol'shaia sovetskaia entsiklopediia,* 8 (Moscow, 1926), pp. 280-82.

23. *Ekonomika perekhodnogo perioda,* pp. 52-56.

24. Ibid., p. 60; also, p. 58.

25. Rudol'f Gilferding, *Finansovyi kapital: novieshaia faza v razvitii kapitalizma,* 3rd ed. (Petersburg, 1918), chap. xvi (first published in 1910 in German).

26. *Ekonomika perekhodnogo perioda,* pp. 127-28; also see pp. 129-30, n.1.

27. Ibid., pp. 56, 113; for his discussion of the process of statization and militarization, see especially chaps. vi-viii.

28. Ibid., p. 108. This argument appears repeatedly. See pp. 63-64, 71-72, 83, 84.

29. Ibid., pp. 108-09.

30. Ibid., pp. 84, 138-39.

31. Ibid., pp. 7-8.

32. See Oskar Lange, *Political Economy,* 1 (New York, 1963), p. 84, n.46; and Kaufman, *Soviet Studies,* No. 3 (1953), p. 248. For confirmation that it was the majority Bolshevik view, see *Proletarskaia revoliutsiia,* No. 12 (1929), p. 178. Also see the debate of the question in 1925 in *Vestnik kommunisticheskoi akademii,* Book 11 (1925), pp. 257-346.

33. *Ekonomika perekhodnogo perioda,* pp. 124, 125, 134-35.

34. Both charges were levelled by M. S. Ol'minskii in *Krasnaia nov',* No. 1 (1921), pp. 247-51; and also in part by Lenin's sister A. I. Elizarova. See the discussion of an archive copy of her 1921 review, *Voprosy istorii,* No. 5 (1964), p. 24.

35. See, for example, *Ekonomika perekhodnogo perioda,* pp. 138-39, and his remark on the role of coercion in creating a communist man, p. 146.

36. Ibid., pp. 62-63, 101-103, 110, 132-33, and chap. viii *passim.*

37. Ibid., p. 87.

38. Ibid., pp. 132-33. Later, when Bukharin's thinking had changed, his critics would cite this passage as evidence that he once had understood that equilibrium did not apply to the transition period. See A. Leont'ev, *Ekonomicheskaia teoriia pravogo uklona* (Moscow-Leningrad, 1929), p. 41.

39. *Ekonomika perekhodnogo perioda,* p. 82 and chap. v.

40. Ibid., pp. 83-85, 146.

41. Ibid., pp. 85-87.

42. Ibid., p. 151.

43. L. Trotskii, *Sochineniia,* 12 (Moscow-Leningrad, 1925), p. 413, n.19. For evidence that parts of the book influenced non-Bolsheviks as well, see A. V. Chayanov, *The Theory of Peasant Economy* (Homewood, Ill., 1966), pp. xliii-xliv; and Chaianov quoted by Bukharin and Piatkov in *Krasnaia nov',* No. 1 (1921), pp. 272-73.

44. *Krasnaia nov',* No. 1 (1921), pp. 247-51. Ol'minskii apparently first planned to voice his objections in a letter to the Central Committee, but decided instead on a public review. It was dated April 1921, and written just after the introduction of NEP. He was especially incensed by Bukharin's statement that "proletarian coercion in all of its forms, beginning with shooting and ending with labor conscription, is . . . a method of creating communist mankind out of the human materials of the capitalist epoch. . . ." And, like other elder Bolsheviks, Ol'minskii was worried about the book's influence on the young. See *Voprosy istorii,* No. 5 (1964), p. 23, n.96, 24.

45. *Krasnaia nov',* No. 1 (1921), pp. 256-74. This same issue also contained a pseudonymous defense of Bukharin and *The Economics* (pp. 252-55).

46. *Leninskii sbornik,* 11 (Moscow-Leningrad 1929), pp. 347-403. Bukharin does not seem to have been embarrassed by the notes. Two years earlier his disciple-biog-

rapher had quoted from them at length. Maretskii, *Bol'shaia sovetskaia entsiklopediia,* 8, pp. 280-82.

47. See *Leninskii sbornik,* 11, pp. 355, 356, 359, 360, 361, 369, 371, 372, 385, 387, 400-401.

48. Early in his career, Lenin, too, had used "sociological" language. See, for example, his "Chto takoe 'druz'ia naroda' i kak oni voiuiut protiv sotsial-demokratov?," in *Sochineniia,* 3rd ed., 1 (Moscow-Leningrad, 1926), pp. 55-115. But his bitter philosophical dispute with Bogdanov in 1909 and after seems to have reinforced his natural distrust of Western social thought and particularly any effort to enrich Marxism with it. In this sense, his intellectual orientation was radically unlike Bukharin's and was to be the source of much friction between the two men. In September, 1920, for example, Bukharin protested a bad-tempered article on Bogdanov by V. Nevskii, which Lenin liked. Bukharin complained that the issue was not whether Bogdanov's ideas were correct, but rather to understand them, and "this minimum Nevskii does not have." *Leninskii sbornik,* 12 (Moscow-Leningrad, 1930), pp. 384-85.

49. *Leninskii sbornik,* 11, p. 396.

50. Ibid., p. 402.

51. "Professor s pikoi," *Pravda,* October 25, 1928, p. 3.

52. Eric Hoffer, *The True Believer* (New York, 1960), p. 20.

An Abortive Attempt at International Unity of the Workers' Movement

1. V. I. Lenin, *Collected Works,* 4 (Moscow, 1960), p. 354. This same idea had been developed earlier while Lenin was in Siberian exile in 1899. See ibid., p. 211.

2. A. V. Lunacharskii, *Vospominaniia o Lenine – O Vladimire Ilyiche. Sbornik statei i vospominanii* (Moscow, 1933), pp. 21-22.

3. Milorad M. Drachkovitch, ed., *Marxism in the Modern World* (Stanford, 1965), p. 49.

4. Lenin, *Collected Works,* 12 (Moscow, 1962), pp. 425-26; emphasis is Lenin's.

5. G. Zinoviev, *Sochineniia,* 15 (Leningrad, 1924), p. 256.

6. Lenin, *Sochineniia,* 42 (Moscow, 1963), p. 173.

7. Ibid., 43 (Moscow, 1963), pp. 234-35.

8. Ibid., pp. 245, 241-42.

9. Ibid., 44 (Moscow, 1964), pp. 30-31.

10. P. Renaudel, *L'Internationale à Berne, Faits et documents* (Paris, 1919), particularly pp. 125 ff.

11. Report and debates on the "Twenty-one Conditions" on July 27-30, 1920, in *Der zweite Kongress der Komm. Internationale. Protokoll der Verhandlungen* (Hamburg, 1921), pp. 240-400.

12. Independent Labour Party [ILP], *Report on the 27th Annual Conference,* Huddersfield, April, 1919 (London, 1919), p. 112.

13. MacDonald's article was quoted in full by Lenin in an article "On the Task of the Third International" in *The Communist International,* No. 4, 1919; see also Lenin, *Sochineniia,* 39 (Moscow, 1963), pp. 90-93.

14. Lenin, *Sochineniia,* 39, pp. 94-109; see also *Lenin on the I.L.P.,* Introduction by William Rust (London, 1933).

15. ILP, *Report on the 27th Annual Conference,* p. 52.

16. Philip Viscount Snowden, *An Autobiography* (London, 1934), 2, p. 536.

17. ILP, *Report on the 28th Annual Conference* (held at Glasgow, April, 1920), p. 86.

18. British Labour Delegation to Russia 1920, *Report* (London, n.d.), p. 5 (cited hereafter as *BLD Report 1920).*

19. Mrs. Philip Snowden, *Through Bolshevik Russia* (London, 1920), p. 30; on meeting with Trotsky, pp. 75-77.

20. *BLD Report 1920,* pp. 149-50, "Part List of Persons Interviewed."

21. Ibid., pp. 57, 73-79, 83-88.

22. Ibid., p. 64.

23. Ibid., pp. 63-64.

24. Ibid., p. 71.

25. R. Abramovich, unpublished manuscript, "The Mensheviks and the Socialist International," mimeographed copy at the Hoover Institution, p. 19.

26. *German Workmen in Russia, Report of Wilhelm Dittmann* (New York: The American-Russian Chamber of Commerce, n.d.), p. 8.

27. Segrew's telegram was published in Moscow in *Pravda,* September 12, 1920, and quoted in Lenin, *Sochineniia,* 3rd ed., 25, pp. 634-35.

28. Lenin, *Sochineniia,* 5th ed., 41, p. 277; Lenin's emphasis.

29. K. Radek, *Die Masken sind gefallen. Eine Antwort an Crispien, Dittmann und Hilferding* (Verlag der Komm. Intern., n.p., 1920), pp. 4, 12-13.

30. *Diktatur über das Proletariat oder: Diktatur des Proletariats.* Das Ergebnis von Moskau, von Tony Sender (Frankfurt, n.d.), p. 13.

31. USPD, *Protokoll über die Verhandlungen des ausserordentlichen Parteitages in Halle.* Von 12. bis 17. Oktober, 1920 (Berlin, n.d.), p. 261.

32. ILP, *Report of the 29th Annual Conference,* Southport, March 27-29, 1921 (London, 1921), p. 124.

33. ILP, *Report of the 28th Annual Conference,* Glasgow, April, 1920 (London, 1920), p. 67.

34. *Protokoll herausgegeben vom Sekretariat der Internationalen Arbeitsgemeinschaft Sozialistisher Parteien*—Internationale Sozialistiche Konferenz in Wien vom 22. bis 27. Februar 1921 (Vienna, 1921), pp. 3-4.

35. The text of the Geneva resolution is reported in BLP, *Report of the 21st Annual Conference,* Brighton, June, 1921 (London, 1921), p. 227.

36. Ibid., pp. 4-8.

37. Ibid., p. 8.

38. Ibid., pp. 147-48.

39. The report on this meeting was published in *Sotsialisticheskii vestnik,* No. 13 (August 5, 1921), pp. 10-12.

40. For the full text of this letter see ibid., p. 11. Soon afterwards the above mentioned "antagonism" was publicly exposed and discussed. In August, 1921, the Russian Menshevik leader L. Martov published an article on "The Reconstruction of the International" in *Sotsialisticheskii vestnik,* No. 13, developing the Vienna Union's point of view. K. Kautsky polemicized with Martov's argumentation in *Der Sozialist,* No. 35/36, and Martov replied to Kautsky in the same publication (Nos. 40, 41) with an article, "Zusammenarbeit der Klassen oder Klassenkampf." See *Sotsialisticheskii vestnik,* No. 19, pp. 3-6.

41. See *Sotsialisticheskii vestnik,* No. 20 (November 18, 1921), pp. 11-12 and BLP, *Report of the 22nd Conference in Edinburgh,* June 27-30, 1922, pp. 14-16, respectively.

42. BLP, *Report of the 22nd Conference,* p. 16.

43. *Deiatelnost' Ispolnitelnogo Komiteta i Prezidiuma I. K. Kommunisticheskogo Internatsionala ot 13 iiulia 1921 do 1 fevralia 1922* (Petrograd, 1922), pp. 72-73 (cited hereafter as *Deiatelnost' Ispolnitelnogo Komiteta*).

44. The following account of this session is based on ibid., pp. 339-55.

45. For the debates on December 18, 1921, see ibid., pp. 366-77; on December 25, see pp. 378-80.

46. Ibid., p. 407.

47. Ibid., pp. 396-97.

48. Ibid., pp. 413-16.

49. For the text of this appeal see *Sotsialisticheskii vestnik*, No. 2 (24), January 19, 1922, p. 9.

50. BLP, *Report of the 22nd Annual Conference,* pp. 17-18.

51. *Deiatelnost' Ispolnitelnogo Komiteta,* p. 420; there is an obvious printing mistake: February 1, instead of 21.

52. The meetings in Frankfurt are reported in BLP, *Report of the 22nd Annual Conference,* p. 18.

53. Ibid., pp. 18-19.

54. On January 16, 1922, in a note to the Politbureau members, Lenin mentioned that "perhaps special guarantees against the Fascists (for example an Italian man-of-war with radio facilities put at our disposal? the names of Italian army officers and policemen responsible for security, etc.?) should be requested"; in the same note he suggested that "personal (verbal) negotiations in Berlin and Moscow with the Germans on mutual *contact* in Genoa should be initiated *immediately*" (*Sochineniia,* 5th ed., 54, p. 117; Lenin's emphasis).

55. Lenin, *Sochineniia,* 45, pp. 2-3.

56. Ibid., 54, pp. 136-37, 601.

57. Ibid., pp. 130-31.

58. Ibid., p. 134; Lenin's emphasis.

59. Ibid., pp. 144, 149.

60. See E. H. Carr, *The Bolshevik Revolution 1917-1923,* 3 (London, 1953), p. 370.

61. Lenin, *Sochineniia,* 54, p. 140.

62. Ibid., pp. 148, 176-77.

63. Ibid., 44, pp. 377-78.

64. Ibid., 54, p. 609, n.260.

65. Ibid., 44, p. 379.

66. See ibid., 54, pp. 149, 608, n.254.

67. Ibid., 44, p. 405.

68. Ibid., 54, pp. 176-77.

69. Ibid., 44, pp. 362-63; 54, pp. 135-36, 139-40; compare Carr, *The Bolshevik Revolution,* 3, p. 372, n.2.

70. Lenin, *Sochineniia,* 44, pp. 374-76, 380, 382-84, 406-408; 54, pp. 133-35.

71. Ibid., 54, pp. 170-71, 614-15, n.385.

72. Not all of the participants had an equal right to vote: Germany, Russia, France, Czechoslovakia, Italy, and the Executives of the two Internationals and of youth and trade unions had been given four decisive votes each. The Ukraine, Poland, Bulgaria, Yugoslavia, Norway, England, the U.S., Spain, Finland, Holland, Sweden, Switzerland, Austria, Hungary, Latvia, Rumania, and Japan—two decisive votes each. Delegates from Canada, China, Lithuania, Persia, Estonia, India, South Africa, Iceland, Armenia, Georgia, Denmark, Australia, Java, and Argentina had only a consultative vote. *Bibliothèque Communiste, Compte-rendu de la Conférence de l'Éxecutif Élargi de l'Internationale Communiste, Moscou, 21 fevrier-4 mars 1922* (Paris, 1922), pp. 13-14.

73. Ibid., p. 59. On February 25, 1922, *Izvestiia* gave a more detailed report on Radek's communication than the official *Compte-rendu;* it was said in *Izvestiia* that Radek had had talks with Ledebour and Adler, that, in his opinion, a joint conference of the three Internationals would be a "natural counter-demonstration against a congress of world capitalism in Genoa," and that a unification of the Third and the Second-and-a-half Internationals alone, without the participation of the Second, would be unacceptable.

74. Despite the fact that since the beginning of February a positive decision on this question had been taken for granted, officially it was presented as a very controversial

matter, and on February 21 the editor-in-chief of *Izvestiia,* Iu. Steklov, published an editorial against any cooperation with the "social-traitors." The "new tactics" were debated in the course of six meetings, and the report on these debates fills about half of the *Compte-rendu* of the session, which had 21 points on its agenda. For Zinoviev's report of February 24, see *Compte-rendu,* pp. 62-80.

75. For Renault's speech see *Compte-rendu,* pp. 81-89; French declaration on p. 119; Treint's speech p. 140; Italian speeches pp. 90-102.

76. Ibid., pp. 103-33.

77. Ibid., pp. 220-24.

78. Ibid., pp. 224-25.

79. Ibid., pp. 225-27.

80. See Chicherin's plan in Lenin, *Sochineniia,* 45, pp. 35-40; for Lenin's reaction, see ibid., pp. 34-35.

81. Ibid., pp. 69-70.

82. Ibid., p. 41.

83. Ibid., p. 50.

84. On the Committee of Nine, the Comintern was represented by Radek, L. O. Frossard (a Frenchman who broke with the Comintern by the end of 1922), and Clara Zetkin; the Vienna Union by Adler, Bracke, and Crispien; the Second International by MacDonald, Vandervelde, and Wels. Frossard and Vandervelde were later replaced by Heckert (Germany) and Wauters (Belgium), respectively.

85. For proceedings of the conference see *Protokoll der internationalen Konferenz der drei internationalen Exekutivkomitees in Berlin vom 2 bis 5. April 1922,* Herausgegeben von Neunerkomitee der Konferenz (Vienna, 1922); Edition du Comité des Neuf, *Conférence des Trois Internationales, Tenue à Berlin, les 2, 4, et 5 avril 1922 (Compte-rendu sténographique) (Brussels, 1922)* cited hereafter as *Conférence des trois Internationales;* Izdanie Ispolnitelnogo Komiteta Kommunisticheskogo Internatsionala, *Mezhdunarodnaia Sotsialisticheskaia Konferentsiia (Ob"edinennoe zasednie Ispolkomov Trekh Internatsionalov), Stenograficheskii otchet* (Moscow, 1922); *The Second and Third Internationals and the Vienna Union, Official Report of the Conference between the Executives held at the Reichstag, Berlin, on the 2nd April, 1922 and following days* (London, 1922), cited hereinafter as *Official Report.* The English version seems to be the least accurate and it should be compared with the other editions; it is quoted when there is no doubt.

86. The following were present: from the Second International, delegates C. Huysmans, E. Vandervelde, Stauning (Denmark); O. Wels (Germany); H. Gosling, R. MacDonald, T. Shaw (Great Britain); Tsereteli (Georgia); W. N. Vliegen (Holland); and G. Moeller (Sweden); guests H. De Man (Belgium); A. Braun, Dr. Lûtkens, V. Schiff (Germany); E. Bevin, M. Cox, W. Gillies (Great Britain); from the Vienna Union, delegates A. Crispien (Germany); R. C. Wallhead (Great Britain); P. Faure, J. Longuet (France); B. Kalniņš (Latvia); F. Adler, O. Bauer (Austria); Iu. Martov (Russia); R. Grimm (Switzerland); K. Cermak (Czechoslovakia); guests W. Dittmann (Germany); A. Bracke, Compère-Morel (France); B. Locker, S. Kaplansky (Poale-Zion); R. Abramovich, A. Schreider (Russia, Menshevik and Left SR, respectively); from the Comintern, delegates C. Zetkin (Germany); L. O. Frossard, A. Rosmer (France); Katayama (Japan); Stoyanovitch (Yugoslavia); A. Warski (Poland); Bukharin, Radek (Russia); B. Smeral (Czechoslovakia); Bordiga (Italy); guests Buyanovitch and Vuyovitch (Yugoslavia); from the Italian Socialist Party, delegate Serrati; guests A. Baratono, D. Fioritto. Among the journalists sponsored by the Second International was the Russian SR leader, Victor Chernov.

For Adler's speech see *Official Report,* pp. 7-12.

87. Ibid., pp. 12-18.

88. For Vandervelde's speech, see ibid., pp. 20-28.

89. E. H. Carr, *The Bolshevik Revolution,* 3, p. 409.

90. For declaration of the Vienna Union see ibid., pp. 28-30.

91. *Conférence des Trois Internationales,* p. 46.

92. *Official Report,* pp. 31-33.

93. Ibid., p. 38.

94. Carr, *The Bolshevik Revolution,* 3, p. 410.

95. For MacDonald's speech see *Official Report,* pp. 39-47.

96. For Serrati's speech see ibid., pp. 48-56.

97. For O. Bauer's speech see ibid., pp. 57-65.

98. For Radek's speech see *Official Report,* pp. 65-78, with some inaccuracies corrected; Radek's emphasis.

99. Ibid., pp. 79-80.

100. Ibid., pp. 83-85.

101. *Conférence des Trois Internationales,* p. 149.

102. *Official Report,* pp. 88-89.

103. Ibid., p. 94.

104. BLP, *Report of the 22nd Annual Conference,* p. 21.

105. *Official Report,* pp. 90-92.

106. Ibid., p. 93.

107. See *Pravda,* No. 77 (April 5, 1922).

108. See G. W. F. Hallgarten, "General Hans von Seeckt and Russia, 1920-1922," *The Journal of Modern History,* 21 (1949), where it is said, among other things, that Chicherin "mentioned the fact that German officers had begun to work in Russia. Fearing some leak, Wirth immediately suggested to Seeckt that this German activity be kept in secret" (p. 32).

109. Lenin, *Sochineniia,* 45, p. 145.

110. Ibid., pp. 140-44.

111. Ibid., p. 534, n.95.

112. Ibid., pp. 149-51.

113. *Pravda,* No. 88 (April 22, 1922).

114. *Sotsialisticheskii vestnik,* No. 9 (31), May 2, 1922, p. 5.

115. Ibid., No. 10 (32), May 18, 1922, p. 13.

116. See ibid., No. 11 (33), June 3, 1922, pp. 3-4.

117. See Martov's article, "The Bloody Farce," in ibid., No. 12 (34), June 18, 1922.

118. Report on the meeting of May 23, 1922 see ibid., No. 11 (33), pp. 4-5, and BLP, *Report of the 22nd Annual Conference,* pp. 23-24.

119. *Sotsialisticheskii vestnik,* No. 11 (33), p. 6.

The Kaminsky Brigade

1. For other such groups, see Alexander Dallin and Ralph Mavrogordato, "Rodionov: A Case-Study of Wartime Redefection," *American Slavic and East European Review,* February, 1960; A. Dallin, "Portrait of a Collaborator: Oktan," *Survey,* No. 35 (1961); and A. Dallin, "From the Gallery of Wartime Disaffection: Lukin," *Russian Review,* 21, No. 1 (January, 1962).

2. Lokot' is located in Brasov *raion* of what was then Orel and is now Briansk *oblast'.*

3. The biography of Voskoboinikov and the account of Lokot' under his rule are based on author's interviews 321 and 359 (Harvard University Refugee Interview Project, series B6); and VAA (i.e., German Foreign Office representative) with AOK 2 Ic/AO (Anton Bossi-Fedrigotti), "Bericht Nr. 5," April 21, 1942, Himmler File 26 (hereinafter cited as Bossi-Fedrigotti). Glowing accounts eulogizing his performance appear in various Russian emigre publications. See, e.g. M. Bobrov (pseud.), "Strashnoe

bezmolvie Rossii," *Vozrozhdenie* (Paris), 7 (1949), pp. 130-32, and Vladimir Samarin, "Civilian Life under the German Occupation 1942-1944" (New York: Research Program on the USSR, 1954; Mimeographed Series no. 58) (hereinafter cited as RP-58); also two anonymous accounts, "Obshchestvennyi instinkt i popytka gosudarstvennogo stroitel'stva v usloviiakh nemetskoi okkupatsii," MS (M-11), and "Russkie voennye formirovaniia pri nemtsakh," MS (M-17).

According to one informant, Voskoboinikov had participated in an anti-Bolshevik rising along the Volga in 1921 but had managed to evade apprehension. A Soviet source identifies him as a *chaianovets,* i.e., a follower of Alexander Chaianov, the "neo-populist" leader implicated in the *Prompartiia* trial. (N. V. Tropkin, "Kommunisty orlovshchiny v partizanskom dvizhenii (1941-1943 gg.)," in *Sovetskie partizany* [Moscow, 1961], p. 202 n).

4. The Russian term was *Narodnaia Sotsialisticheskaia Partiia Rossii* (NSPR). The ambiguity of the term, *narodnaia,* made it possible for friend and foe alike later to refer to it as National-Socialist. See below, pp. 269 ff.

5. 321; Erkundungstrupp Lt. Glatz, PzAOK 2, Kdr.d.Eis.Pi., "Erkundungsbericht," January 26, 1942. See also *Orlovskaia oblast' v gody Velikoi Otechestvennoi Voiny (1941-1945 gg.)* (Orel, 1960), p. 150. A later German account erroneously places the size of the "self-defense" force at 500 men (Sven Steenberg [pseud.], *Wlassow: Verräter oder Patriot?* [Cologne, 1968], p. 83). See also Zakhar A. Bogatyr', *V tylu vraga* (Moscow, 1963), p. 33.

6. Bossi-Fedrigotti, p. 8.

7. 294; 321; 359.

8. Anatolii Shyian, *Partizanskyi krai* (Kiev, 1946), pp. 43-47. See also Bogatyr', pp. 43-47.

9. Alexander Saburov, *Za linieiu frontu,* 1 (L'viv, 1953), pp. 206-25; *Za liniei fronta* (Petrozavodsk, 1965), pp. 203-53. See also Tropkin, in *Sovetskie partizany,* p. 202n.

10. Two sources claim that it was common knowledge that Kaminsky had been a Communist Party member. There is nothing to support this assertion. (358; and Anton Dubovskii, "Gody bor'by i porazhenii," *Belaia Rus'* [Munich], 1 [1950].) A far from infallible Soviet source states that Kaminsky had been convicted "in the period of the Shakhty trial." (Vladimir Lobanok, *V boiakh za rodinu* [Minsk, 1964], p. 211.)

In addition to sources listed above, this section draws on the following: Friedrich Buchardt, "Die Behandlung des russischen Problems während der Zeit des n.-s. Regimes in Deutschland," MS; the only published wartime article on Kaminsky, Helmut von Kügelgen, "Der König von L.," *Armee-Zeitung,* No. 24 (1942), p. 3; "Die Aktion Kaminsky," MS (hereinafter cited as M-371), a manuscript by a German officer who for some time was close to Kaminsky; author's interviews with two German officials (G-3 and G-6) and two Russians, one a colonel in the brigade (317) and the other Kaminsky's representative in Minsk (650); and a detailed report, "Bericht des OKVR von Froreich über eine im Auftrage der Heeresgruppe Mitte/OQu/Abt VIII unternommene Besichtigung des Selbstverwaltungsbezirkes Lokot (25.-30.4.43.)," CDCJ, Paris (hereafter cited as 145a/45). See also Maximilian Preuss, "Kaminsky und seine Brigade," MS (Institut für Zeitgeschichte, ZS 415).

The earliest secondary account of the brigade was Boris Nicolaevsky, "Porazhencheskoe dvizhenie 1941-1945 godov," *Novyi zhurnal* (New York), 18 (1948), pp. 221-23. Other memoirs are largely uncritical eulogies, e.g., the Bobrov and Samarin pieces cited earlier; and A. Kazantsev, "Tret'ia sila," *Posev* (Limburg), No. 30 (217) (1950), pp. 13-14.

Various postwar sources erroneously assert that Kaminsky was born in Poznań in 1896, that he had moved to Russia after the First World War, or that he had been a Red Army captain taken prisoner by the Germans around Orel in 1942. See, e.g., [Erich von dem Bach-Zelewski, defendant], *Vor dem polnischen Staatsanwalt,* Jerzy Sawicki, ed. (Berlin, 1962), p. 32; and Jerzy Kirchmayer, *Powstanie Warszawskie* (Warsaw, 1959), p. 244.

11. M-371, p. 20; 650; 145a/45. A photograph of Kaminsky, taken in 1942, appears in Steenberg, facing p. 160.

12. Quoted in M-17.

13. 294; 359; 371. By 1944 Anna Veniaminovna Voskoboinikova bitterly rued her endorsement of Kaminsky's appointment.

14. Enclosure with Erkundungstrupp Lt. Glatz, op. cit.

15. Bossi-Fedrigotti, p. 9.

16. Gaupropagandaleiter der AO Felix Schmidt-Decker, "Russischer Selbstverwaltungsbezirk Lokotj," n.d. [December, 1942].

17. PzAOK 2, "Ermächtigung," and PzAOK 2, Ic/AO, memorandum, February 23, 1942.

18. (No author) "Bericht über den Bürgermeister von Lokotj Ing. Bronislaw W. Kaminski und die von ihm zur Partisanenbekämpfung geführte Miliz (derzeitiger Stand)," n.d. [July, 1942?] (hereafter cited as "Lokotj-Bericht"). The *raiony* in question were Navlia, Suzemka, Komarichi, Sevsk, Dmitrovsk, and Dmitriev. The maximum area under Kaminsky's jurisdiction had had a peacetime population of 1.7 million.

19. OB PzAOK 2 (Schmidt), "An den Bürgermeister von Lokot, Herrn Ing. Kaminski," July 19, 1942. German opinions of Kaminsky continued to differ sharply. A moderate view was expressed by a special investigator sent to Lokot' in mid-1942: ". . . Kaminsky is above all a practitioner who understands how to master a situation by cleverly taking advantage of all opportunities. . . . He is aware of his own limitations. . . . It seems doubtful whether Kaminsky, if torn loose from his area and men, would be able to establish a large organization from behind a desk." ("Lokotj-Bericht," p. 4.) Hostile comments came from German economic officers and from the staff of German and Hungarian units stationed near Lokot', who complained that Kaminsky failed to feed them and had adopted agrarian practices contrary to German directives. (E.g., Gebietslandwirt Ssewsk, "Bericht über die Besetzung des Kreises Lokot," July 9, 1942.) Some fellow Russians evidently denounced him to the *Sicherheitsdienst* (SD), for reasons unknown. But his German army protectors urged the SD to be circumspect in the matter, as Kaminsky "is rendering the army extraordinarily important services. Anything that he might interpret as suspicions on the part of German agencies must therefore be avoided." (PzAOK 2, Ic/AO, "An S.D. Kdo. 107B," September 2, 1942. See also WiStab Ost, Chefgr. La, "Betr. Verwaltungsmassnahmen beim PzAOK 2," November 5, 1942.) Whereas some German officers thought Kaminsky desirable because he had no political ambitions, he was objectionable to others precisely "because he seeks to promote political programs"; some found him appealing because he favored a Russian variant of Nazism. (See PzAOK 2, Ic/AO, to OKW/WPr/A P6 [Diercksen], September 30, 1942.)

20. OB PzAOK 2 (Schmidt), "Der Heeresgruppe Mitte," March 11, 1942.

21. Kaminsky to Hitler, n.d. [February, 1942], enclosure to OB PzAOK 2, *op. cit.*

22. OKH/GenStdH/GenQu/Abt. K-Verw., "Nr. II/7040/42 g.," October 9, 1942. Another document, much later, asserted that the Lokot' district was established with Hitler's explicit permission; see below, p. 260.

23. "Lokotj-Bericht," p. 1; PzAOK 2, Ia/OQu, "Befehl für die Neugliederung des Armeebereiches," July 11, 1942; Korück 532, Ia/Qu, "Korück-Befehl für die Neugliederung des Korückgebietes," August 14, 1942.

24. Korück 532, IIa, "Stabsbefehl Nr. 42," July 22, 1942. A subsequent order extended Veltheim's functions to include the coordination of anti-partisan operations outside the district's territory. (Korück 532, Ia, "Aufgabengebiet des Maj. v. Veltheim," September 11, 1942.) See also Peter Kleist, *Zwischen Hitler und Stalin* (Bonn, 1950), p. 200.

25. Korück 532, Qu/Ia, "Herrn Ingenieur Kaminski," October 11, 1942. An earlier German order instructed administrative personnel not to interfere in local government "directly." Kaminsky repeatedly complained about the conduct of the Hungarian troops in his area and reportedly threatened to resign unless they were made to respect his authority and the inhabitants' property. (Korück 532, Ic, "Betr. Ungarische Division," May 25, 1942; and "Betr. Front Kaminski," June 12, 1942.)

26. He was much mollified by the award of an honorary dagger by the Hungarian command. In November, 1942, General Bernhard awarded him the special medal for valor for "Easterners," second class, and an invitation to visit Field Marshal von Kluge. In his negotiations Kaminsky loved to observe all the formalities of his "co-equality" with the Germans. When German soldiers killed a peasant on "his" soil, Kaminsky condemned them to death, arranged for the Germans to send what he called a "diplomatic" mission to sign a "treaty of extradition," and turned the men over to their officers for summary shooting. (Kazantsev, in *Posev,* No. 30, p. 14, relates evidently the same episode in more dramatic version.) He enjoyed proving his authority by acts of generosity, such as donating several thousand geese as a present to the German civilian population. On Hitler's birthday, April 20, 1943, he issued an amnesty for prisoners jailed in his district. (Order No. 118, German trans. in 145a/45, Appendix; Preuss, p. 3.)

27. The RONA should not be confused with the ROA, the German-commanded Russian units nominally under General Vlasov.

28. "Lokotj-Bericht," p. 1. See also Eugen Hadamowsky and Eberhardt Taubert, "Bericht über die Propaganda-Lage im Osten," September 17, 1942, p. 16, Doc. Occ E 18-19, YIVO. An eyewitness (Steenberg, p. 84) claims that it had over 20,000 men.

29. See 321; 359; M-17; "Lokotj-Bericht." The brigade's symbol was a shield with the letters, RONA, over the black cross of St. George on a white background. With its reorganization and expansion, its men took an oath to Kaminsky, who assumed first the rank of colonel and then of *kombrig*—the equivalent of brigadier general in the Red Army prior to the reintroduction of generals' ranks. In the winter of 1942-43 a system of insignia and epaulettes was worked out which amounted to a mixture of Red Army and tsarist ranks and symbols. (M-371; Buchardt; Dubovskii.)

30. Korück 532, Ia, "Freiw. Btl. Lokot," October 8, 1942. The forces are reported to have included five infantry regiments, one armored brigade, one pioneer battalion, one guard battalion, and one anti-aircraft detachment (Steenberg, p. 84).

31. He did not hesitate to have men shot summarily, for instance, for cowardice. Four of his men were shot, after a partisan attack was repelled in bitter fighting in June, 1942, for retreating in the face of the enemy with their machine-guns at the ready. A hostile German officer reported in October 1942, that most of his troops were forcibly impressed villagers: "Only after the first who tried to run away were apprehended and shot did the rest remain together. . . ." (Korück 532, Ia, "Freiw. Btl. Lokot," October 8, 1942; and "Lokot-Bericht," p. 2.)

32. Stab Major von Veltheim, "Bericht über den Einsatz des Freiw. Btls. Lokot," September 5, 1942.

33. Korück 532, Ia, "Reisevermerk Rise 6.10.42," October 8, 1942; Korück 532 (Bernhard), "An PzAOK 2," November 14, 1942. See also *Partizany brianshchiny; sbornik dokumentov i materialov,* 2 (Briansk, 1962), pp. 66-67; and *Kurskaia oblast' v period Velikoi Otechestvennoi Voiny,* 1 (Kursk, 1960), p. 362.

34. Schmidt-Decker, p. 2. Italics in the original.

35. As a brigade member later recalled,

> when we would come into a village, we would ask who among the local residents was with the partisans. Then we would take the cow from these people's folks. We really tried to loot only the houses of partisans and communists. Usually their families would be killed. When the

> partisans came to the same village after we left, they did the reverse: they would rob the families of policemen and *kamintsy* [followers of Kaminsky]. In a village of 200, there might be forty with Kaminsky and fifty with the partisans. If the partisans raided it by night, the *starosta* would flee to us; normally he would keep his wife and children in the nearest *raion* center anyway if the village was on the border of partisan and Kaminsky-controlled territory.

See also Gen. August Winter, chief of staff, PzAOK 2, order, May 11, 1943, IMT, Doc. NOKW-472.

36. Kügelgen; 321; Dubovskii; Bossi-Fedrigotti.

37. A German report specified:

> While commander of the Royal Hungarian Division as well as the other German and Hungarian officers in Lokot' are on foot, it has been noted with displeasure that Kaminsky in the company of a woman (whom German officers are already addressing as "Gnädige Frau") uses a car to drive the short distance to the theater or movie, and that cars and trucks with huge signs, "In the service of the Wehrmacht," drive a lot in and out of Lokot'. Frequently the passengers (women) make it unmistakable that the trips are of no official nature, nor in the interest of presecuting the war.

(Korück 532, Ia, "Reisevermerk 6.10.42," October 8, 1942, and annexes.)

38. Korück 532 (Bernhard), "An PzAOK 2," November 14, 1942; 321; 358. For the Germans these "special supplies" represented something of a problem. In November, 1942, Gen. Bernhard requested the army once more to assign a special quota of wine, liquor, and cigarettes to Colonel Rübsam since "collaboration with Engineer Kaminsky imposes certain obligations." A year later the German liaison officer reminded his superiors that "until now Kaminsky has been receiving from the CG, PzAOK 2, a box of gifts on the average of once a month. This box contained: 100-200 cigars; 200-300 cigarettes; 8-10 bottles of cognac, vodka, or liqueur; 10-15 bottles of wine or champagne. Sometimes smaller consumer goods or items such as *eau de cologne* were added." (VSt PzAOK 3 zum SVB Lepel [Kraushaar], letter [to HGeb Mitte, OQu?].)

39. HGr Mitte, OQu/VII (Mil.-Verw.) [Günzel], "Bericht über den Selbstverwaltungsbezirk Lokot," May 25, 1943. There was also, one suspects, some carry-over from Soviet administration, which tends to provide for more personnel than equivalent Western organizations.

40. 145a/45; "Lokotj-Bericht"; Schmidt-Decker; 321.

41. 321; 358; PzAOK 2, OQu/VII, "Rechtspflege für die Landeseinwohner," January 1, 1943; "Lokotj-Bericht," p. 3; 145a/45. The following cases, reported in a random issue of the local newspaper, may give some idea of the nature of the cases and of standards applied. A resident, having insulted another peasant woman, was found guilty "under Art. 27, par. 6, and sentenced to a fine of 500 rubles to be paid to the state [i.e., Kaminsky] and is to be warned that the repetition of such instances would result in criminal charges against her." Another peasant woman, having stolen articles belonging to a German soldier, was sentenced to three months of forced labor. A local miller received a fine of 1,000 rubles for "beating up Policeman I. M. Senenkov."

42. G-2. Kügelgen states that in spite of the severe shortage of tractors and horses, actual acreage was reduced by only 8 percent.

43. The situation changed drastically in the first months of 1943. Whereas until then Kaminsky had been able to pay his troops from local receipts (3 to 4 million rubles a month), the Wehrmacht was obliged to assume the costs as of April 1, 1943, largely because most of the district was no longer effectively under Kaminsky's control.

44. Korück 532, Ia, "Kaminski Misstände," October 8, 1942. Ernst von Dohnanyi, "Combating Soviet Guerrillas," in T. N. Greene, ed., *The Guerrilla–And How to Fight*

Him (New York, 1962), pp. 206-209, gives far too positive an assessment of the Kaminsky forces.

45. For the only time in the record, Hitler referred to Kaminsky at his staff conference of July 26, 1943. As Hitler insists on a complete evacuation of civilians, cattle, and grain from the threatened area, Kluge worries about the difficulties this would cause.

> ...HITLER: What is going to be done with the harvested rye? Is it going to be burned?
> KLUGE: Certainly, we'll have to. Probably we will burn it, but I don't know whether we'll have time. We'll have to destroy it somehow. Especially the valuable cattle we have here. (Over a map of the central front) The famous Kaminsky is here, the one who played a great role that other time.
> HITLER: Where is he?
> KLUGE: Around here, near Lokot', in this area. That's his empire.

(Trans. in Felix Gilbert, ed., *Hitler Directs His War* [Oxford, 1950], pp. 64-65.) In speaking of "that other time," Kluge presumably referred to the strong partisan attacks in the Lokot' area early in 1943. For the original, see [Germany, OKW, FHQ], *Hitlers Lagebesprechungen* (Stuttgart, 1962), p. 378.

46. Wi In Mitte, Ib, "Aktenvermerk über Besprechung bei 286. Sich. Div. am 3.8.43." German wartime records and postwar accounts speak of a total of about 30,000. The figures given above are based on German records, such as HGr Mitte, OQu 2/VII, to OKG, GenQu, Abt. E (monthly report for September), October 12, 1943. The protocol of a conference on September 25 reported that 6,000 troops and 23,000 civilians had arrived at their destination, and some 3,800 more civilians were expected. PzAOK 3, OQu, Abt. VII, "Besprechung in Lepel am 24. u. 25. September, 1943" (hereafter cited as "Besprechung"). According to one account the brigade was thrown into frontline action near Dmitrovsk when the Soviet army broke through the German lines in mid-1943; and, to cover the retreat of the remainder, one of its regiments allegedly held the town of Sevsk, where it was cut off and decimated (Steenberg, p. 85).

47. HGr Mitte, Ia, to OKH/GenStdH/Op.-Abt., August 31, 1943.

48. "Besprechung."

49. Wi In Mitte, Ib, "Aktenvermerk"; "Besprechung."

50. 321; HGr Mitte, Ia, to OKH/GenStdH/Op.-Abt.

51. Einsatzgruppe B, to Chef der Bandenkampfverbände (von dem Bach), September 28, 1943; "Besprechung"; Wi In Mitte, Ib, "Aktenvermerk." See also below, pp. 264-65.

52. 321; and Gruppe Rübsam, Ic, "Bericht über die Mitte März aufgedeckte Verschwörergruppe in Lokot," March 24, 1943. See also John A. Armstrong, ed., *Soviet Partisans in World War II* (Madison, Wis., 1964), p. 237.

53. 321; 358; M-17; M-371; Buchardt; 038; "Besprechung." For the Soviet version of the Tarasov incident, see Vladimir Lobanok, *V boiakh za rodinu* (Minsk, 1964), pp. 211-12. See also PzAOK 3, OB, memorandum, April 12, 1944.

54. A few examples will illustrate Protsiuk's behavior and the terror he aroused.

> He was a confidant of Kaminsky [a former RONA man reports]. Like the NKVD, he thrashed anyone he could get his fingers on. He played ball with the Germans and personally killed a number of men.
>
> Protsiuk was both prosecutor and chief judge. He was a sadist. He personally beat women, hit them cruelly, tramped them with his feet [an eyewitness recalls].
>
> Protsiuk [a high-ranking officer testifies] regularly killed captured partisans or sentenced them to five to ten years of "prison."

55. A former member of the brigade described an operation near Lepel': "When we entered the village, I declared myself to be a partisan. The *starosta* could not tell whether I was really with Kaminsky or not. I would ask him to set up some moonshine vodka, which we would take from him. This made him suspicious. 'This is funny,' he said; 'usually the partisans don't take any liquor with them.' The people did not know who was raiding them. If some gang suddenly robbed his house, an old man would not know how to answer questions. There were cases of people . . . guessing wrong every time, so that they would be robbed and beaten in turn by the partisans, Kaminsky's men, again the partisans, and the German police."

56. The order stipulated that, with the complete transfer of the brigade, the authority of the German district commissars of Slonim and Nowogródek was to cease. The new "self-governing district," encompassing a smaller area than in its earlier locations, lay between the west-east railways from Central Poland to Minsk-Smolensk and to Polotsk-Velikie Luki. (Höherer SS- u. Polizeiführer Russland-Mitte und Weissruthenien [von Gottberg], "Befehl Nr. 1 zur Umsiedlung der Sturmbrigade RONA," February 23, 1944.)

57. HGr Mitte, OQu/VII, "Monatsbericht für März 1944," April 12, 1944; Generalkommissar Minsk (von Gottberg), "Selbstverwaltungsbezirk Kaminski," March 30, 1944.

58. M-371; M-17; Buchardt; SSFHA, "Generalstabsstellenbesetzung in der Waffen-SS: Stand vom 1.8.44." The German liaison staff was headed by *Obersturmführer* Loleit, who had been SS representative with Kaminsky. See also Hans von Krannhals, *Der Warschauer Aufstand 1944* (Frankfurt, 1962), p. 316; and George Stein, *The Waffen-SS* (Ithaca, 1966), pp. 264-65.

59. Reliable evidence is difficult to assemble. Former members of the brigade are reluctant to detail atrocities; few of the Soviet references can be taken as necessarily trustworthy; hostile Belorussian nationalist emigres have provided accounts many of which are evidently based on fact but defy confirmation.

One of the former brigade members admits that "when no supplies were at hand, Kaminsky would send a detachment into the nearest village, firing shots in the air and if necessary firing on the people, to exact from them 'contributions,' confiscating wantonly, sometimes accompanied by murders." (321) According to another account, his police meted out swift retribution for the slightest complaint. In many villages potatoes were looted for distilling. It was usually at night, after drinking, that Kaminsky's men got up the nerve to engage in terror raids, which often led the local peasants to flee and hide in the woods. (Dubovskii, 1, pp. 33-34.) According to a Belorussian informant, in Rozhna and Lipsk (near Lepel'), in a raid on a previously partisan-held area, they forced the inhabitants to take refuge in the churches and then burned them to the ground, with the result that after the fire "a few suffocating survivors were seen climbing over rows of corpses to the small windows up high." (870)

60. M-371; Krannhals, p. 126n.

61. Himmler pointed with pride to Kaminsky's unit as one of "his" formations which had successfully fought their way out of Soviet traps. ("Reichsführer-SS Himmler auf der Gauleitertagung am 3. August 1944 in Posen," *Vierteljahrshefte für Zeitgeschichte,* 1, No. 4 [October, 1953], p. 377.)

62. RMfdbO., Beauftragter beim OK HGr Nordukraine, z.Zt. bei HGr Mitte (O. W. Müller), "Bericht Nr. 2/44," July 16, 1944, NMT, Doc. NO-1869. As the brigade moved westward into the Bialystok area, which had been annexed *de facto* to East Prussia (whose Gauleiter, Erich Koch, was ruler of the Ukraine and the leading "Russian-hater") Koch initially refused to admit Kaminsky and his men; but Alfred Rosenberg, his perennial foe, promptly ordered Koch to let the brigade in and lodged a protest with State Secretary Lammers. In mid-July Kaminsky's men were allowed to proceed. (Koch to Rosenberg, July 7, 1944; Rosenberg to Koch, July 10, 1944;

Rosenberg to Lammers, July 10, 1944; and RMfdbO. [Labs], "Aktennotiz," July 24, 1944, NMT, Doc. NO-1827.)

63. It was not clear what plans the Germans had for the personnel. Reluctant to admit the unruly "Easterners" into the Reich, the Germans recommended Hungary as an asylum when the retreat across Poland continued. One source states, plausibly enough, that the Germans hoped to use the brigade in anti-partisan warfare. Indeed, a team of German and Kaminsky officers went to Budapest, only to learn that the SS had made the plans on its own and had not bothered to tell its Hungarian allies, who then raised serious objections: they had no use for a "horde of Russian savages." Kaminsky's officers demanded that a district near the border of Transcarpathian Munkachevo Province be turned over to them, on the same terms as Lokot', Lepel', and Diatlovo had been. This the Magyars flatly—and understandably—refused. Several officials of the Rosenberg ministry (von Mende, Knüpffer) argued, moreover, that the brigade would not perform adequately in anti-partisan warfare except on the Russian front. See also Krannhals, p. 126n.

64. M-17; Bobrov, p. 132; RP-58. Field Marshal Guderian (*Erinnerungen eines Soldaten* [Heidelberg, 1951], p. 322) and von dem Bach-Zelewski (cited in Krannhals, pp. 251-52) claim that Kaminsky was particularly "anti-Polish." There is nothing to support this assertion.

65. "Dziennik Iwana Waszenko," *Dzieje najnowsze* (Warsaw), 1, No. 2, pp. 324-25.

66. Krannhals, pp. 124, 126.

67. According to rumors, Colonel Belai, Kaminsky's eventual successor, refused to participate in the Warsaw operation.

68. Krannhals, pp. 131, 135, 139n. Von dem Bach had overall charge of the operation, including Frolov's regiment. However, operational responsibility lay initially with SS-*Gruppenführer* Reinefarth, later with Luftwaffe *Generalmajor* Rohr. See Krannhals, pp. 132, 135, 238, 241, 300; von dem Bach, affidavit, September 10, 1947, NMT, Doc. NO-5479; Heinz Reinefarth, "Kurze Schilderung des Kampfes um Warschau," NMT, Doc. NOKW-125; also von dem Bach's extensive account (in Polish), "Relacja von dem Bachu o powstaniu warszawskim," *Dzieje najnowsze,* 1, No. 2, pp. 295-323, and (in German) [von dem Bach, defendant], *Vor dem polnischen Staatsanwalt,* pp. 31-35, 39.

69. M-371; Buchardt.

70. The diary cited above (in note 65) seems to reflect an exceptional attitude—which may indeed account for its publication in the early years of postwar Poland. Its author's political perspicacity was clearly unusual when he wrote: "What are we fighting for? They tell us, for a new Russia, for a free Russia. This is only Kaminsky's fantasy, and we are fighting for the benefit of the Germans, who have abused millions of Soviet citizens. . . ." ("Dziennik Iwana Waszenko," pp. 329-30.)

71. After the war, von dem Bach, testifying against the SS chieftains, asserted that the Kaminsky brigade—"a real robber band"—"had received sanction from Himmler to plunder all of Warsaw." (NMT, Doc. NO-5479.) Von dem Bach's testimony is notoriously unreliable, and the question of German orders regarding looting is too complex to be examined here.

Various other eyewitnesses corroborate the general account. "In Warsaw," a former member of the division sums it up, "the *kamintsy* were savage and looted indiscriminately. They returned with gold watches, bracelets, even gold teeth." "They were loaded down with gold seized in Warsaw and drunk all the time," another soldier recalls; "the Germans and others bought their arms from them in exchange for vodka." Official German records, including the War Diary of Ninth Army, are full of entries reporting instances of looting, rape, and unprovoked shooting by Frolov's men, especially on August 7-10. Drunken brawls were endemic, and the fighting quality of the regiment was close to nil. See Krannhals, pp. 127n, 135, 138-39, 238, 246, 251, 317, 362, 368,

371, 381. See also T. Bór-Komarowski, *The Secret Army* (New York, 1951), pp. 235, 285; and Edward Serwański, ed., *Zbrodnia niemiecka w Warszawie, 1944 r.:* Documenta Occupationis Teutonicae, 2 (Poznań, 1946), p. 12. A difficulty in the use of memoirs and some secondary studies is the confusion of all Ex-Soviet elements. The population occasionally referred to the Kaminsky forces as "Vlasovites"; likewise, what appear to have been members of the Kaminsky regiment crop up as "Ukrainians"—in this context a generic term for hostile Eastern Slavs.

72. 105; 321; 358; 294; Preuss, p. 6.

73. IMT, Session of June 3, 1946, *Trial of the Major War Criminals* (Nuremberg, 1947-49), 15, p. 298; Guderian, pp. 322-24; Wilhelm Scheidt, affidavit, November 25, 1945, Doc. 3711-PS, *Trial,* 32, p. 477. See also Krannhals, pp. 319-20.

74. Buchardt, p. 143; M-371.

75. Ibid.; M-17; Kleist; 321; Krannhals, p. 320.

76. Perhaps unfairly, Guderian attributes this decision to von dem Bach's desire to rid himself of an inconvenient eyewitness of the Warsaw events (p. 324).

77. Von dem Bach-Zelewski, affidavit, February 21, 1946, Doc. Frank-8, *Trial,* 40, p. 116. There is no evidence that any other staff members were killed.

78. Buchardt, p. 144; G-3; 105; Krannhals, p. 319.

79. Von dem Bach later alleged, without foundation, that he had been afraid to arrest Kaminsky because of the latter's bodyguard and that Kaminsky's men had surrounded von dem Bach's headquarters, armed with machine guns, when they heard of Kaminsky's disappearance. He claims to have told them Kaminsky had been called to Cracow and would return the next day. (Krannhals, p. 320; [von dem Bach, defendant], p. 40.)

80. "Lokotj-Bericht," pp. 3-4.

81. Virtually all the officials of his party turned out to be former members of the Communist Party or the Komsomol.

82. M-371, p. 24.

83. 321; 358; 433; 294; M-17; *Golos naroda,* 1942, No. 17. In Lokot' two newspapers were published: *Golos naroda* for the civilian population, and *Boevoi put'* for the brigade. Later on, a large part of the "serious" literature disseminated by Kaminsky was printed in Minsk and Riga. One of the newspapers bore the slogan, "Everything for the people—everything through the people." The other used a quotation from Hitler: "The commonweal has precedence over the interests of the individual."

84. 145a/45. See also OKH-GenStdH. GenQu (Qu 4), "Nationalsozialistische Russische Arbeiterpartei," March 6, 1944.

85. OB HGr Mitte (Kluge), "An den Chef des Gen. Stabes des Heeres," May 22, 1943, and enclosure, "Plan für die Einsetzung eines National-Komitees im Bereich der Heeresgruppe Mitte," NMT, Doc. NOKW-3521.

86. OB PzAOK 2, "An den Herrn Oberbefehlshaber der Heeresgruppe Mitte," June 3, 1943, and enclosure, "Vorschlag für die Errichtung eines russischen Unterkomitees in Orel."

87. For the protocol of the Hitler conference, see George Fischer, ed., "Besprechung des Führers mit Generalfeldmarschall Keitel und General Zeitzler," IMT, Doc. 1384-PS, *Journal of Modern History,* 23 (1951), pp. 63-71.

88. M-27; 294; 433.

89. The foregoing account is based on Dubovskii; 382; 294; 433; M-27; Boris Bashilov, "Istoriia untermensha prevrativshegosia v morloka," *Znamia Rossii* (New York), No. 71 (September 30, 1952), and his "Taina smerti Kaminskogo," ibid., No. 77 (December 28, 1952), No. 78 (January 7, 1953).

90. The documents exist in variant versions. The two here cited appeared in *Novyi put'* (Vitebsk), No. 30 (275), April 13, 1944; and *Golos naroda* (Lokot'), No. 16 (April 5, 1943). See also Bashilov, "Pravda o brigade Kaminskogo," *Nasha strana* (Buenos

Aires), December 13, 1952; Boris Lewyckyj, "Ukraińcy a likwidacja powstania warszawskiego," *Kultura* (Paris), June, 1952, p. 76; and the leaflet, Tsentral'nyi komitet NSTPR, *Partizany i partizanki!* (April, 1944).

91. Some friction arose between the Central Committee, intent on building up Kaminsky, and some of the more remote sections, which demanded the calling of a Constituent Congress. "When finally the question reached the impasse of either a party congress or its dissolution, the Central Organizing Committee picked . . . Diatlovo as the locale of the conference." In the atmosphere of Kaminsky's dictatorship and full control by uniformed and secret police, any conference would have been no more than a demonstration, without any risk of effective criticism or dissent. But the Soviet breakthrough of 1944 forestalled the calling of even this Diatlovo conference. (Dubovskii, II, 9-10, and III, 19-21.)

92. 321; 650; M-17; 294; Dubovskii.

93. Mention should be made of the Kaminsky Brigade's attitude toward the Jews. On the one hand, his newspaper and printed propaganda systematically pilloried them as one of the major elements responsible for Bolshevism. His manifesto and leaflets repeatedly used them as scapegoats, usually without indicating their future fate and without indulging in Nazi-style fanaticism. On the other hand, people who knew him assert that Kaminsky looked upon Jews much as he did upon other people. If they worked with the partisans or with the hostile peasantry, he would kill them. Yet at least three sources insist that there were Jews even within the brigade.

"There were many Jews hiding with the partisans," a former Kaminsky colonel recalls. "When we captured them, they were usually treated like everybody else. Later on, in Diatlovo, we captured a group of Jews hiding in the woods and did not turn them over to the Germans. But when we continued our evacuation westward, we released them. Probably the Germans then caught and shot them." (321)

"No Jews were shot within the Kaminsky movement. When we moved west from the Briansk [Lokot'] area, Kaminsky took along two Jewish musicians and their mother. The mother died in Lepel' and was buried there in the presence of Kaminsky." (294)

"There were several Jews in the brigade, who hid the fact, but we knew it anyway. Our driver got drunk one night and told us that he was a Jew. All right, so what? The rich Jews got away, anyway, and the poor ones were killed by the Germans for no reason. There was no special anti-Semitism among the Kaminsky troops. They were not idea- or group-minded. They looted anyone, Jews and Gentiles alike." (358)

Both the public resort to anti-Semitism and the exceptions in actual practice would tend to reinforce the image of Kaminsky as not primarily "ideological" in motivation.

94. RMfdbO., P3 (von Knüpffer), "Aktenvermerk," March 8, 1944, with endorsements of other sections.

95. Eugen Hadamowsky and Eberhardt Taubert, "Bericht über die Propaganda-Lage im Osten," September 17, 1942, Doc. Occ E 18-19, YIVO.

96. 321; M-27.

97. It was characteristic, nonetheless, that the draft roster of guests to be invited to an International Anti-Jewish Congress to be held in Cracow, included among the five former Soviet citizens Kaminsky and the head of his party's Minsk branch, Soshal'skii. (RMfdbO., "225/44gr." July 14, 1944, Doc. G-PA-13, YIVO.) The congress never took place.

98. Taubert, final report, December 31, 1944, Doc. G-PA-14, YIVO, p. 33.

99. This section is based on M-17; 650; and D. Stepanov (pseud.), "Istoriia Rossiiskoi Natsional-Sotsialisticheskoi Partii v Minske, fevral'-mai 1944 g.," MS (Paris, 1951).

100. "Ansichten des Professors D. Soschalski über die deutsche Politik im Zusammenhang mit Russland und der sogenannten russischen Befreiungsbewegung," Doc.

Occ E-6, YIVO. Soshal'skii's personnel file from the archives of *Einsatzstab Reichsleiter Rosenberg* is to be found as Doc. Occ E-41, YIVO.

101. See his speech at the November 18, 1944, celebration of the launching of the so-called KONR ("Committee for the Liberation of the Peoples of Russia"), in W. Wladimirow, ed., *Dokumente und Materiale des Komitees zur Befreiung der Völker Russlands* (Berlin, 1944).

102. See Bobrov's personnel file, Einsatzstab Reichsleiter Rosenberg, Minsk, "Personalangaben," Doc. Occ E-41, YIVO; his article, "Strashnoe bezmolvie Rossii"; and his speech at the formation of the·Vlasov Committee, in Wladimirow, *Dokumente*.

103. M-371; Dubovskii, I, 32. The chief of Vlasov's chancellery and a colonel close to his headquarters state that in 1944 Khomutov and a delegation from Kaminsky came to see Vlasov, who refused to receive them. (321; 188). In 1944 the Polotsk branch of Kaminsky's party made a modest effort to reconcile the two groups, but in vain. Vlasov's representative in Riga states that a member of the Polotsk committee, A., came to see him to make contact with Vlasov. "I suggested that Kaminsky could perhaps go to Berlin. Soon A. returned with a new proposal that he [A.] would go to Berlin to negotiate. This time Vlasov replied: Let Kaminsky first publicly announce what he stands for and declare his willingness to recognize the command of the ROA." (433.) Bashilov (in *Znamia Rossii,* No. 78, p. 9) claims that in July, 1944 he sought to persuade the same man in Riga that RONA would accept Vlasov's command.

104. HGr Mitte, OQu/Abt. VII (Mil.-Verw.) [Günzel], "Bericht über den Selbstverwaltungsbezirk Lokot," May 23, 1943.

105. I. AK, Ic, "Nat.-soz. russ. Arbeiterpartei," May 7, 1944.

106. HGr Nord, OQu/VII, "Betr.: NSRAP," May 24, 1944.

107. In addition to the German "envoy" to Slovakia, Ludin, one who objected was Karl Albrecht, formerly a high Soviet official who later worked for the Goebbels Ministry in Berlin. Albrecht inspected the division after Kaminsky's death and (he later claimed) came away with a devastating impression of degradation and debauchery: they were nothing but a "horde of professional criminals." Berger, he asserts, thereupon refrained from using the division against the Slovak rebels. (Karl Albrecht, *Sie aber werden die Welt zerstören* [Munich, 1954], pp. 296-301.) Albrecht's account is rather unreliable. See also Krannhals, p. 319; and Jürgen Thorwald (pseud.), *Wen sie verderben wollen* (Stuttgart, 1952), p. 440 ff.

108. Buchardt; M-17; 294; 321; 358.

109. 55.

110. 55; 175; Preuss, p. 6.

111. 321; 650.

112. 358

The Presidium Meeting of February, 1961

1. *Pravda,* January 22, 1961; translation in *Current Digest of the Soviet Press,* 13, No. 8, p. 23 (hereinafter cited as *CDSP*).

2. *Pravda,* February 1, 1961; *CDSP,* 13, No. 5, p. 18.

3. *Pravda,* February 5, 1961; *CDSP,* 13, No. 6, p. 20.

4. *Pravda,* February 12, 1961; *CDSP,* 13, No. 6, p. 21.

5. *Pravda,* February 19, 1961; *CDSP,* 13, No. 7, p. 14.

6. *Pravda,* February 12, 1961; *CDSP,* 13, No. 6, p. 21.

7. *Pravda,* March 1, 1961; *CDSP,* 13, No. 9, pp. 11-12.

8. *Pravda,* March 7, 1961; *CDSP,* 13, No. 10, p. 16.

9. *Pravda,* March 12, 1961; *CDSP,* 13, No. 10, p. 21.

10. *Pravda,* March 26, 1961; *CDSP,* 13, No. 12, p. 18.

11. Ibid.

12. Harold W. Chase and Allen H. Lehrman, eds., *Kennedy and the Press: the News Conferences* (New York, 1965), pp. 19-20.

13. On Soviet use of alleged strategic superiority as a foreign policy tool, see Arnold L. Horelick and Myron Rush, *Strategic Power and Soviet Foreign Policy* (Chicago, 1965).

14. *Izvestiia,* February 8, 1961; *CDSP,* 13, No. 6, p. 33. Text in *Vneshniaia politika Sovetskogo Soiuza i mezhdunarodnye otnosheniia. Sbornik dokumentov, 1961 god* (Moscow, 1962), pp. 33-34.

15. F. J. Krieger, *Recent Soviet Advances in Aerospace Technology* (Santa Monica, 1962), p. 12.

16. Ibid., p. 15.

17. F. J. Krieger, *Soviet Astronautics: 1957-1962* (Santa Monica, 1963), p. 10; no source cited.

18. *Pravda,* March 4, 1961; *CDSP,* 13, No. 9, pp. 20-21.

19. *Pravda,* February 23, 1961; *CDSP,* 13, No. 8, p. 40.

20. Horelick and Rush, *Strategic Power,* p. 99, citing *Sovetskaia Rossiia* and *Ekonomicheskaia gazeta.*

21. James Reston, *New York Times,* January 4, 1961, p. 32; Marguerite Higgins, *New York Herald Tribune,* January 10, 1961, p. 1; *Survey of International Affairs, 1961* (London, 1965), p. 212.

22. *Documents on Disarmament, 1961* (Washington, D.C., 1962), p. 453.

23. *Pravda,* August 31, 1961; *CDSP,* 13, No. 35, pp. 3, 6-8.

24. Hans A. Bethe, "Disarmament and Strategy," *Bulletin of the Atomic Scientists,* 18, No. 7 (September, 1962), p. 18.

25. Arthur H. Dean, *Test Ban and Disarmament: The Path of Negotiation* (New York, 1966), p. 90.

26. William E. Griffith, *Albania and the Sino-Soviet Rift* (Cambridge, Mass., 1963), pp. 69-76.

27. Griffith, *Albania,* p. 76; Ivo Duchacek, "Czechoslovakia: the Past Reburied," *Problems of Communism,* 11, No. 3 (May-June, 1962), p. 24.

28. Griffith, *Albania,* pp. 74-75.

29. Ibid., p. 76, citing *Zëri i Popullit,* February 21, 1961.

30. *Pravda,* October 28, 1961; *CDSP,* 14, No. 5, p. 20.

The Rehabilitation of M. N. Pokrovskii

1. *Voprosy istorii,* No. 3 (1965), pp. 211-17.

2. For an appreciation of the state of Soviet historiography in 1961, see *Contemporary History in the Soviet Mirror,* John Keep and L. Brisby, eds. (London-New York, 1964). A more recent and highly perceptive evaluation is given by H. Rogger in *Soviet Studies,* 16, No. 3 (January, 1965), pp. 253-75.

3. On Pokrovskii's attitude during World War I, see O. Gankin and H. H. Fisher, *The Bolsheviks and the World War: the Origins of the Third International* (Stanford, 1940), pp. 162 ff.; L. D. Trotskii, *Permanentnaia revoliutsiia* (Berlin, 1930), p. 52.

4. ORF IIAN, f. Pokrovskii, d. 42, cited by E. A. Lutskii, "Razvitie istoricheskoi kontseptsii M. N. Pokrovskogo," *Istoriia i istoriki: istoriografiia istorii SSSR. Sbornik statei* (Moscow, 1965), p. 348.

5. *Russkaia istoriia v samom szhatom ocherke* (Moscow, 1920), p. 143.

6. M. N. Pokrovskii, *Istoricheskaia nauka i bor'ba klassov* (Moscow, 1933), 1, pp. 152-66.

7. *Vsesoiuznaia soveshchanie istorikov o merakh uluchsheniia podgotovki nauchno-pedagogicheskikh kadrov po istoricheskim naukam 18-21 dek. 1962 g.* (Moscow, 1964), p. 262. D. Dorotich, in his article, "The Disgrace and Rehabilitation of M. N.

Pokrovsky" (*Canadian Slavonic Papers,* 8 [1966], pp. 169-81), which appeared after this essay was submitted for publication, accepts this charge as valid. He does not ask himself whether the ultimate responsibility for this campaign should not rather be ascribed to Stalin.

8. See C. E. Black, ed., *Rewriting Russian History: Soviet Interpretations of Russia's Past* (New York, 1956), pp. 12-16; K. F. Shteppa, *Russian Historians and the Soviet State* (New Brunswick, 1962), pp. 94 ff.; A. G. Mazour, *Modern Russian Historiography* (Princeton, 1958), pp. 196 ff.; P. N. Miliukov, "Velichie i padenie M. N. Pokrovskogo," *Sovremennye zapiski* (Paris), 65 (1937), p. 379, for an interesting contemporary view.

9. K. F. Shteppa, *Russian Historians,* pp. 67-80.

10. TsPA IML, f. 147, op. 1, d. 42, 1. 35, cited by Lutskii, *Istoriia i istoriki,* p. 364.

11. P. H. Aron, "M. N. Pokrovskii and the Impact of the First Five-Year Plan on Soviet Historiography," *Essays in Russian and Soviet History in Honor of Geroid Tanquary Robinson* (Leiden, 1963), p. 301. Aron argues that Pokrovskii was saved by his eminence, but this had not prevented criticism before, and a personal decision by Stalin seems more plausible. For recent evidence on Stalin's attitude, see Sidorov's memoir quoted below, n.31.

12. Lutskii, *Istoriia i istoriki,* p. 337.

13. For a recent and valuable biography of Tarle, see E. Hösch, *Evgenij Viktorovic Tarle, 1875-1955 und seine Stellung in der sowjetischen Geschichtswissenschaft* (Wiesbaden, 1964).

14. *Protiv istoricheskikh kontseptsii M. N. Pokrovskogo* (Moscow, 1939), p. 9. (The second volume of this work, published in 1940, substituted the word "anti-Marxist" for "historical.") A. M. Pankratova, for example, alleged that in 1918 Pokrovskii had prepared the ground for treacherous anti-party activities by Bukharin and Trotsky, and hailed "our great security workers" for having "cleaned out this nest of counterrevolutionaries." The very fact that Pokrovskii had later recanted his errors enhanced his appeal for the unwary, and thus made him more dangerous.

15. Lutskii, *Istoriia i istoriki,* pp. 337-38.

16. Cited in ibid., p. 338.

17. *Voprosy istorii,* No. 1 (1956), p. 4.

18. Ibid., No. 10 (1957), p. 171.

19. Cited from the MS. by Lutskii, *Istoriia i istoriki,* p. 364.

20. V. I. Lenin, *Sochineniia,* 5th ed., 32, p. 348.

21. V. M. Nechkina, *Istoriia SSSR,* No. 1 (1960), pp. 83-85; she was supported by G. D. Alexeeva and E. N. Gorodetskii in ibid., pp. 92 ff., and ibid., No. 6 (1960), pp. 85 ff.; cf. also E. A. Lutskii's article in ibid., No. 2 (1961), pp. 102-115.

22. V. F. Inkin and A. G. Chernykh in ibid., No. 5 (1960), pp. 75-81.

23. Ibid., No. 1 (1961), pp. 81-97.

24. No. 9 (1961), p. 58.

25. *XXII s"ezd KPSS: stenograficheskii otchet* (Moscow, 1962), 2, p. 185.

26. *Voprosy istorii,* No. 3 (1962), p. 30 (text of report, pp. 3-31).

27. Ibid., p. 34. It is interesting that A. I. Gukovskii should have come to Pokrovskii's defense against Mints's charge that he did not know Lenin's works: cf. *Istoriia SSSR,* No. 6 (1965), p. 89.

28. Ibid., p. 40.

29. The proceedings were published under the title given in note 7. It is instructive to compare this record of the lively debates with the dry and abbreviated version initially given in *Voprosy istorii,* No. 2 (1963), pp. 3-75, which *inter alia* omitted the exchange discussed below.

30. *Vsesoiuznoe soveshchanie istorikov,* pp. 368-69.

31. *Istoriia SSSR,* No. 3 (1964), pp. 118-38.

32. Ibid., p. 136.

33. Ibid., p. 138.

34. Lutskii, *Istoriia i istoriki,* pp. 334-70; L. V. Danilova, "Stanovlenie marksistskogo napravleniia v sovetskoi istoriografii epokhi feodalizma," *Istoricheskie zapiski,* 76 (1965), pp. 62-119.

35. *Voprosy istorii,* No. 7 (1966), pp. 32-47.

36. *Izbrannye proizvedeniia M. N. Pokrovskogo* (Moscow, 1965-1967).

37. *Ocherki istorii russkoi istoriografii,* 4 (Moscow, 1966), p. 198.

38. Dorotich, in the article cited in n. 7, claims (p. 181) that "[Pokrovskii's] rehabilitation is certainly not forced from above. In the final analysis it is historical truth that is being rehabilitated, together with M. N. Pokrovskii." This judgment is perhaps a little too sweeping. Certainly a natural professional desire to tell more of the truth, if not all of it, is one of the motives behind the campaign; but Soviet historians are still far from able to present the truth as they see it. "Politics commands," as it always has done in the USSR.

39. This charge rested formally upon a remark of Pokrovskii's taken out of context: "History is the most political of all sciences, it is the politics of the past without which it is impossible to understand the politics of the present." Mazour, *Modern Russian Historiography,* p. 193, and Aron, *Essays,* p. 294, erroneously repeat this Stalinist allegation, which has been corrected by the revisionists. See *Voprosy istorii,* No. 8 (1963), p. 39, and R. Szporluk, "Pokrovsky and Russian History," *Survey,* 53 (October, 1964), pp. 107-18.

40. Stalin himself recognized the nature of his creed. He is said to have refused to allow the study of the history of Western philosophy in Soviet universities after World War II on the grounds that "we have to strengthen the faith before we can expose heresies" *(snachala nado ukrepit'sia v verouchenii a potom izoblichat' eresi).* M. T. Iovchuk of the Institute of Philosophy in *Istoriia i sotsiologiia* (Moscow, 1964), p. 203.

41. See, for example, N. E. Zatsenker, "Marks i Engel's ob istorii," *Voprosy istorii,* No. 6 (1964), p. 23.

42. Cf. H. Rogger, "Politics, Ideology and History in the USSR: the Search for Coexistence," *Soviet Studies,* 16, No. 3 (January, 1965), 267. When Rogger wrote he had at his disposal only the abbreviated report of the important conference on methodology held in January, 1964, the full proceedings of which have since been published (see note 39).

43. *Istoriia i sotsiologiia,* p. 83. Gulyga's views were sharply criticized by B. M. Kedrov, G. E. Glezerman, and other speakers, who accused him of empiricism (ibid., pp. 105, 130). For a favorable comment on Gulyga's views by a historian, see A. M. Sakharov, *Istoriia SSSR,* No. 4 (1965), p. 8.

44. *Voprosy istorii,* No. 8 (1965), p. 21.

45. M. N. Pokrovskii, *Leninizm i russkaia istoriia* (Moscow, 1930), p. 7.

46. M. N. Pokrovskii, *Vneshniaia politika Rossii v XX veke: populiarnyi ocherk* (Moscow, 1926).

47. One interesting example is the effort of I. S. Braginskii and others to rehabilitate some leaders of the pre-revolutionary Jadidist movement in Central Asia, which strove for national progress and cultural advance. See *Istoriia SSSR,* No. 6 (1965), pp. 26-38.

48. *Izbrannye proizvedeniia,* 1, p. 325.

49. *Istoriia i sotsiologiia* (Moscow, 1964), pp. 45-46.

50. This episode is fully discussed by V. Varlamov in C. E. Black, ed., *Rewriting Russian History,* pp. 318 ff. *Katorga i ssylka,* the organ of the Society of Former Political Prisoners and Exiles, most members of which were non-Bolshevik socialists, was suppressed in 1935.

51. M. N. Pokrovskii, *Ocherki russkogo revoliutsionnogo dvizheniia XIX-XX vv.* (Moscow, 1924), pp. 63-64.

52. *Obshchestvennoe dvizhenie v poreformennoi Rossii: sbornik statei k 80-letiiu so dnia rozhdeniia B. P. Koz'mina* (Moscow, 1965), pp. 78, 81.

53. Of more than thirty papers read between 1961 and 1965 to the Study Group on Social Movements in Post-Reform Russia, only one, by G. S. Ul'man of L'vov, treated such a theme: Tkachev's views on state and revolution. It has not been published. Ibid., p. 367.

54. *Voprosy istorii KPSS,* No. 4 (1963), p. 51n.

55. *Istoriia SSSR,* No. 3 (1962), pp. 72-78.

56. Pokrovskii, *Ocherki russkogo revoliutsionnogo dvizheniia,* pp. 150, 229.

57. *Ob osobennostiakh imperializma v Rossii* (Moscow, 1963), p. 7.

58. E. D. Chermenskii, *Istoriia SSSR: period imperializma (90-kh gg. XIX v.–mart 1917 g.): posobie dlia uchitelei i studentov pedvuzov* (Moscow, 1965), p. 10.

59. *Istoriia SSSR,* No. 5 (1964), pp. 74-91; No. 6 (1964), pp. 156-59.

Political Monism and Cultural Duality

1. An earlier version of this paper was presented at a Dartmouth College symposium in October, 1967, on the fiftieth anniversary of the Russian Revolution. The paper's first section, on political monism, draws on work supported generously by the Russian Institute of Columbia University in the late 1960s, including my book, *The Soviet System and Modern Society* (New York, 1968). The second section of this paper, on cultural dualism, goes back in part to two books on which B. I. Nicolaevsky helped me a great deal: *Soviet Opposition to Stalin* (Cambridge, Mass., 1952) and *Russian Liberalism* (Cambridge, Mass., 1958).

2. Historically, as I used it here, "modern" is no more than a shorthand term for *later* modernization. By contrast, "modernization" stands for the *earlier* stage of the same ongoing historical process.

At least implicitly, some leading American sociologists treat "modernity" as an end point of man's evolution. To them, present-day society in its Anglo-American form seems to serve the same role that the Prussian state did for Hegel and the full communist society of the future did for Marx: beyond that point, history no longer involves conflicting social forces as it had in the past. In each case, such a view points to an "end of politics," which in turn stands close to the "end of ideology" theme shared widely by the same group of American sociologists. In *The Soviet System and Modern Society,* I try to show how Talcott Parsons reflects this view (including on Russia) in his well-known works.

3. Barrington Moore, Jr., *Social Origins of Dictatorship and Democracy* (Boston, 1966); Jüergen Habermas, *Strukturwandel der Öffentlichkeit,* 2nd ed. (Neuwied, 1965).

4. On the concept of pluralism, see Helge Pross, "Zum Begriff der pluralistischen Gesellschaft," in *Zeugniss, Theodor W. Adorno zum sechzigsten Geburtstag,* edited by Max Horkheimer (Frankfurt, 1963), and Stanislas Ehrlich, "Le Problème du pluralisme," *L'Homme et la société,* No. 5 (July-August, 1967). Both of these authors note that it would be wrong to tie the pluralist model of society to the capitalist democracy of the West, as a number of writers now do. As yet no work has dealt at length with another form of this model, a socialist pluralism. This gap can be seen both in the realm of theory and on the empirical plane (we have no relevant study of Scandinavia, Israel, Yugoslavia).

5. Judging by biographic data on top Soviet party executives at the turn of the 1960s (in this author's *The Soviet System and Modern Society*), one such mechanism might turn out to be *dual leadership skills:* those facts point to a trend over the years toward leaders with "dual" skills, economic as well as political.

6. H. Gordon Skilling, "Interest Groups and Communist Politics," *World Politics,* 18, No. 3 (April, 1966), 449.

7. After the completion of the present paper, Bertram M. Gross put forth and applied to the United States a new model of totalitarianism: a *pluralistic* totalitarianism (*Social Policy,* 1, No. 4 [November-December, 1970]). His model refers to a "friendly" modern autocracy that makes no use of wholesale terror, of an officially enforced creed, or of most other forms of past totalitarian centralization. Similar prognoses on the United States can be found in George Fischer, ed., *The Revival of American Socialism* (New York, 1971).

In the terms used here, the Gross model spells out the possibility of a negative, anti-democratic convergence between the limited monism of a Soviet type and the limited pluralism of the West. Should such a convergence take place, it would mean the continuing rise of *tutelary* autonomy in both types of modern society.

8. Robert C. Tucker, "The Image of Dual Russia," and Henry V. Dicks, "Some Notes on the Russian National Character," both in *The Transformation of Russian Society,* edited by Cyril E. Black (Cambridge, Mass., 1960).

9. What marks aspiring "new men . . . of power and influence" in American society, according to E. Digby Baltzell's study of "the making of a national upper class," is "more than the ordinary desire to conform to upper class values and rituals" (*Philadelphia Gentlemen* [New York, 1958], p. 348).

10. In the words of Isaac Deutscher, "even though the peasantry is dwindling, the *muzhik* tradition still looms very large in Russian life, in custom and manners, in language, literature and the arts. . . . Even in his exit [the *muzhik*] casts a long melancholy shadow on the new Russia" (*The Unfinished Revolution* [New York, 1967], p. 53).

11. Murray Yanowitch and Norton Dodge, *Comparative Education Review,* 12, No. 3 (October, 1968).

12. With the new Soviet semi-affluence, what is apt to weigh the most is not the shift from coercion to the much-discussed material incentives. Still more important is whether these material incentives stress individual goals or collective ties. Thus far, the Soviet shift has stressed individual incentives much more than collective ones (Leo Huberman and Paul M. Sweezy, *Monthly Review,* 19, No. 6 [November, 1967], 11-17). While in the USSR semi-affluence or state policy seem to cut down collectivism as a norm, much more of it may live on in the "affluent society" of the West than we think. Raymond Williams and Thomas B. Bottomore stress that a good deal of collectivism will be found in the working class. See Williams, *Culture and Society* (New York, 1966), pp. 326-32, and Bottomore, *Classes in Modern Society* (New York, 1966), pp. 84-92.

The Contributors

ANNA M. BOURGUINA is Curator of the Boris I. Nicolaevsky Collection, The Hoover Institution, Stanford University. Formerly associated with the Inter-University Project on the History of the Menshevik Movement and for many years a close collaborator of B. I. Nicolaevsky and Iraklii Tsereteli, she is the author of *Russian Social Democracy, The Menshevik Movement: A Bibliography,* and the editor of I. Tsereteli, *Vospominaniia o fevral'skoi revoliutsii.*

STEPHEN F. COHEN is Assistant Professor of Politics, Princeton University. Co-editor (with Robert C. Tucker) of *The Great Purge Trial* and author of several scholarly articles, his major study of Bukharin and Russian Bolshevism, 1888-1938, is to be published in 1972.

ALEXANDER DALLIN is Professor of History and Political Science, Stanford University, and Senior Research Fellow, Hoover Institution. He is the author of *German Rule in Russia, 1941-1945, The Soviet Union at the United Nations, The Soviet Union and Disarmament,* and (with George W. Breslauer) *Political Terror in Communist Systems;* and the editor of *Diversity in International Communism* and *Soviet Politics since Khrushchev.*

GEORGE FISCHER is Professor of Social Science, Richmond College of the City University of New York, and a member of the Doctoral Program in Sociology at the City University's Graduate Center. He is the author of *Soviet Opposition to Stalin, Russian Liberalism,* and *The Soviet System and Modern Society,* as well as *The Revival of American Socialism* and *What's What on Staten Island.*

JONATHAN FRANKEL is a Senior Lecturer and Chairman of the Department of Russian Studies at the Hebrew University of Jerusalem. He is the editor of *Vladimir Akimov on the Dilemmas of Russian Marxism, 1895-1903* and is now at work on a study of the Jewish socialist parties in Tsarist Russia.

ISRAEL GETZLER is Professor of History, La Trobe University, Melbourne, and the author of *Martov: A Political Biography of a Russian Social Democrat* and *Neither Toleration nor Favour: The Australian Chapter of Jewish Emancipation.* He is presently working on a study of the Russian revolution, 1917.

BRUNO KALNIŅŠ, Doctor in Law, has been associated with Stockholm University since he fled his native Latvia in 1945. He was a prominent member of the Latvian Social Democratic Workers' Party and a one-time Secretary of its Central Committee. He is the author of *Fifty Years of the*

Latvian Social Democratic Party (published in Latvian in Sweden) and of numerous scholarly articles on the Latvian Social Democratic movement.

JOHN L. H. KEEP, Professor of History at the University of Toronto, is the author of *The Rise of Russian Social Democracy* and the editor of *Contemporary History in the Soviet Mirror.*

LADIS K. D. KRISTOF is Associate Professor of Political Science at Portland State University. Formerly Associate Director of the Inter-University Project on the History of the Menshevik Movement, he has written articles on political theory and geopolitics and is currently working on a study of the political system of Rumania.

PHILIP E. MOSELY (1905-1972) was, at the time of his death, Professor of International Relations and Director of the European Institute, Columbia University. His published works include *Russian Diplomacy and the Opening of the Eastern Question in 1838 and 1839* and *The Kremlin and World Politics.*

ALEXANDER RABINOWITCH is Associate Professor of History, Indiana University. He is currently finishing a two-part history of the Petrograd Bolsheviks in 1917. The first volume, *Prelude to Revolution: The Petrograd Bolsheviks and the July 1917 Uprising,* was published in 1968.

MARC RAEFF is professor of History, Columbia University. He is the author of *M. M. Speransky: Statesman of Imperial Russia, Siberia and the Reforms of 1822,* and *Origins of the Russian Intelligentsia.*

WALTER SABLINSKY, Assistant Professor of History, University of Virginia, is preparing a monograph on Father Gapon and Bloody Sunday.

ROBERT M. SLUSSER is Professor of History, Michigan State University. His published works include *The Soviet Secret Police* (with Simon Wolin), *A Calendar of Soviet Treaties, 1917-1957,* and *Theory, Law and Policy of Soviet Treaties* (both with Jan. F. Triska).

WIKTOR SUKIENNICKI received his doctorate in International Law at the University of Paris and prior to World War II was a professor at the University of Wilno. Associated with the Polish government-in-exile during the war, he later became affiliated with the Hoover Institution. His works include *La Souveraineté des états en droit international moderne* (Paris, 1927), *Evolution of the USSR Regime* (Wilno, 1938), and *Facts and Documents Concerning Polish Prisoners of War* (London, 1946).

ROBERT C. TUCKER is Professor of Politics and Director of the Program in Russian Studies, Princeton University. His published works include *Philosophy and Myth in Karl Marx, The Soviet Political Mind,* and *The Marxian Revolutionary Idea.* He is co-editor (with Stephen F. Cohen) of *The Great Purge Trial* and editor of *The Marx-Engels Reader.* At present he is completing a book on Stalin and Russian communism.

ALLAN K. WILDMAN is Associate Professor of History, State University of New York at Stony Brook. Author of *The Making of a Workers' Revolution: Russian Social Democracy, 1891-1903,* he is currently preparing a book on the Russian army and the 1917 revolution.

Index

Index